PRIESTHOOD AND CHURCH ORGANIZATION

BOARD OF EDITORS

PRIESTHOOD AND CHURCH ORGANIZATION

SELECTIONS FROM THE

ENCYCLOPEDIA OF MORMONISM

EDITED BY

DANIEL H. LUDLOW

DESERET BOOK COMPANY
SALT LAKE CITY, UTAH

Library of Congress Cataloging-in-Publication Data

Encyclopedia of Mormonism. Selections.
    Priesthood and church organization : selections from the
Encyclopedia of Mormonism / edited by Daniel H. Ludlow.
        p.   cm.
    Includes bibliographical references.
    ISBN 0-87579-926-4
    1. Aaronic priesthood (Mormon Church)—Encyclopedias.
2. Melchizedek priesthood (Mormon Church)—Encyclopedias. 3. Mormon
Church—Government—Encyclopedias. 4. Church of Jesus Christ of
Latter-day Saints—Government—Encyclopedias.   I. Ludlow, Daniel H.
BX8659.53   1995
262'.09332'03—dc20   95-7691
                                                                         CIP

Printed in the United States of America

10   9   8   7   6   5   4   3   2   1

CONTENTS

LIST OF ARTICLES

LIST OF CONTRIBUTORS

Harley K. Adamson
Weber State University, Ogden, UT
Teachers, Teacher Development

Stan L. Albrecht
Brigham Young University
Stake

Douglas D. Alder
Dixie College, St. George, UT
Ward

Ruel A. Allred
Brigham Young University
Instructor, The
Juvenile Instructor

J. Max Anderson
State of Utah, Salt Lake City
"Fundamentalists"

Paul L. Anderson
*Museum of Church History and Art, Salt
Lake City*
Building Program

Wendell J. Ashton
Deseret News, Salt Lake City
Deseret News

James H. Backman
Brigham Young University
Courts, Ecclesiastical, Nineteenth-
Century

J. Hugh Baird
Brigham Young University
Ballantyne, Richard
Bulletin

VerDon W. Ballantyne
Brigham Young University
Aaronic Priesthood: Powers and
Offices
Levitical Priesthood

Ariel S. Ballif
Brigham Young University
Patriarch: Stake Patriarch

Jae R. Ballif
Brigham Young University
Melchizedek Priesthood: Powers and
Offices in the Melchizedek
Priesthood
Melchizedek Priesthood: Restoration
of Melchizedek Priesthood

Ivan J. Barrett
Brigham Young University
Church of the Firstborn

Merrill J. Bateman
Brigham Young University
Conferences: Stake Conference

Jeffrey C. Bateson
*Church Finance and Records Dept., Salt
Lake City*
Clerk

Robert F. Bennett
Franklin Institute, Inc., Salt Lake City
Latter-day Saints (LDS)

LaMar C. Berrett
Brigham Young University
Endowment Houses

Susan Easton Black
Brigham Young University
  Name of the Church

Paul M. Bons
Church Personnel Dept., Salt Lake City
  Organization: Contemporary
  Organization

R. Wayne Boss
University of Colorado
  Home Teaching
  Priesthood Interview

Marian R. Boyer
*Former Counselor in General Presidency,
  Church Relief Society, Salt Lake City*
  Visiting Teaching

David C. Bradford
Church Correlation Dept., Salt Lake City
  Bishopric
  Priesthood Executive Committee,
  Stake and Ward

M. Gerald Bradford
University of California at Irvine
  Orthodoxy, Heterodoxy, Heresy

Ronald L. Bramble
Boy Scouts of America, Los Angeles
  Deacon, Aaronic Priesthood

Hoyt W. Brewster, Jr.
Church Curriculum Dept., Salt Lake City
  Ordination to the Priesthood

S. Kent Brown
Brigham Young University
  Apostle

Thomas E. Brown
Audio Visual Dept., Salt Lake City
  Membership Records

M. Dallas Burnett
Brigham Young University
  Conferences: General Conference

H. David Burton
*Church Presiding Bishopric's Office, Salt
  Lake City*
  Presiding Bishopric

J. LeRoy Caldwell
Brigham Young University
  Messenger and Advocate

Douglas L. Callister
Attorney, Glendale, CA
  Region, Regional Representative

J. Elliot Cameron
Church Temple President, Provo, UT
  Priesthood Blessings

Kim S. Cameron
Michigan State University
  Authority
  Stake President, Stake Presidency

Elaine Anderson Cannon
Author, St. George, UT
  Young Women

Janath Russell Cannon
*Church Temple Matron, Frankfurt,
  Germany*
  Relief Society

John K. Carmack
General Authority, Salt Lake City
  Organization of the Church, 1830

John Carr
*Former Director, Church Internal
  Communications, Salt Lake City*
  Distribution Centers

Linda A. Charney
Church Correlation Dept., Salt Lake City
  Joining the Church
  Membership

David J. Cherrington
Brigham Young University
  Societies and Organizations

Clayton Christensen
*Ceramics Process Systems Corp.,
  Belmont, MA*
  Testimony Bearing

Maribeth Christensen
Ricks College, Rexburg, ID
  Volunteerism

Jack R. Christianson
Church Educational System, Orem, UT
　Teacher, Aaronic Priesthood

Lewis R. Church
*Church Educational System, Pleasant
　Grove, UT*
　Prophet, Seer, and Revelator

C. Ross Clement
Church Social Services, Salt Lake City
　Social Services

Dean B. Cleverly
Church Missionary Dept., Salt Lake City
　Missions

Todd Compton
California State University, Northridge
　Apostasy

Spencer J. Condie
General Authority, Salt Lake City
　Missionary, Missionary Life

Richard O. Cowan
Brigham Young University
　Branch, Branch President
　Missionary Training Centers
　Temples: History of LDS Temples
　　from 1831 to 1990

John H. Cox
*Church Ecclesiastical Support System,
　Salt Lake City*
　Ward Welfare Committee

Soren F. Cox
Brigham Young University
　True and Living Church

Perry H. Cunningham
Church Correlation Dept., Salt Lake City
　Activity in the Church
　Area, Area Presidency

Gerald J. Day
Snow College, Ephraim, UT
　Mission President
　Region, Regional Representative

Ronald D. Dennis
Brigham Young University
　Evening and the Morning Star, The

Jill Mulvay Derr
Brigham Young University
　Relief Society

Roy W. Doxey [deceased]
Church Correlation Dept., Salt Lake City
　Presiding High Priest

Larry W. Draper
Church Historical Dept., Salt Lake City
　Publications

Reed C. Durham, Jr.
Church Educational System, Logan, UT
　Times and Seasons

William G. Dyer
Brigham Young University
　Leadership Training
　Meetings, Major Church

Wm. Gibb Dyer, Jr.
Brigham Young University
　Presiding Bishopric

Richard C. Edgley
*Church Finance and Records, Salt Lake
　City*
　Finances of the Church

Wilford G. Edling [deceased]
*Church Finance and Records, Salt Lake
　City*
　Finances of the Church

Richard G. Ellsworth
Brigham Young University
　Priesthood

J. Lynn England
Brigham Young University
　First Presidency
　President of the Church
　Stewardship

Irene Hewette Ericksen
Church Correlation Dept., Salt Lake City
　Auxiliary Organizations

William S. Evans
Church Public Communications, Salt Lake City
District, District President

William E. Evenson
Brigham Young University
Magnifying One's Calling

Larry C. Farmer
Brigham Young University
Interviews

Isaac C. Ferguson
Church Welfare Services, Salt Lake City
Fast Offerings

Donovan E. Fleming
Brigham Young University
High Council

Marvin K. Gardner
Ensign, Salt Lake City
General Authorities

R. Quinn Gardner
Business Consultant, Salt Lake City
Bishop's Storehouse

Arnold K. Garr
Brigham Young University
Liahona the Elders' Journal

H. Dean Garrett
Brigham Young University
Rebaptism

Crawford Gates
Beloit College, Beloit, WI
Sacrament Meeting

Georgia Gates
Writer, Beloit, WI
Sacrament Meeting

Bruce C. Hafen
Brigham Young University
Disciplinary Procedures

John Franklin Hall
Brigham Young University
April 6

C. Mark Hamilton
Brigham Young University
Meetinghouse

Bruce T. Harper
Church Missionary Dept., Salt Lake City
Priesthood Offices

William G. Hartley
Brigham Young University
Bishop, History of the Office
Organization: Organizational and Administrative History

Leon R. Hartshorn
Brigham Young University
Signs of the True Church

T. Glenn Haws
Church Educational System, Portland, OR
Welfare Farms
Welfare Square

D. Arthur Haycock
Former Church Temple President
Temples: LDS Temple Dedications

Darwin L. Hayes
Brigham Young University
Nauvoo Neighbor

"J" Malan Heslop
Deseret News, Salt Lake City
Church News

Martin B. Hickman [deceased]
Brigham Young University
Succession in the Presidency

W. Ladd Hollist
Brigham Young University
Priest, Aaronic Priesthood

Mark E. Hurst
Aaronic Priesthood Dept., Salt Lake City
Young Men

Paul V. Hyer
Brigham Young University
Sealing: Temple Sealings

Richard W. Jackson
Architect, Salt Lake City
Building Program

Peter N. Johnson
Brigham Young University
Man's Search for Happiness

Mary Jolley
Writer, Salt Lake City
Fast and Testimony Meeting

William N. Jones
*Intermountain Health Care, Inc., Salt
Lake City*
Hospitals

Ardeth Greene Kapp
*General President, Church Young
Women, Salt Lake City*
Youth

Brian K. Kelly
*Church International Magazines, Salt
Lake City*
International Magazines

Petrea Gillespie Kelly
Author, Highland, UT
Contributor
Young Woman's Journal

William Rolfe Kerr
*Utah Commission on Higher Education,
Salt Lake City*
Conferences: Conferences

Nephi K. Kezerian
Surgeon, Provo, UT
Sick, Blessing the

Dean L. Larsen
General Authority, Salt Lake City
Seventy: Quorums of Seventy

Victor L. Ludlow
Brigham Young University
Priesthood in Biblical Times

Immo Luschin
*Church Translation Dept., Frankfurt,
Germany*
Ordinances: Overview
Ordinances: Administration of
Ordinances
Temples: LDS Temple Worship and
Activity

Melvin J. Luthy
Brigham Young University
Priesthood

Carol Cornwall Madsen
Brigham Young University
Retrenchment Association

Garth L. Mangum
University of Utah
Welfare Services

Beth M. Marlow
Editor, Orem, UT
Meetinghouse Libraries

Robert J. Matthews
Brigham Young University
Proclamations of the First Presidency
and the Quorum of the Twelve
Apostles

Frank O. May, Jr.
*Church Curriculum Dept., Salt Lake
City*
Correlation of the Church,
Administration
General Handbook of Instructions
Policies, Practices, and Procedures

Mark L. McConkie
*University of Colorado at Colorado
Springs*
Following the Brethren

Lynn A. McKinlay
Brigham Young University
Patriarchal Order of the Priesthood

Byron R. Merrill
Brigham Young University
Assistants to the Twelve

Charles E. Mitchener
Church Sunday School, Salt Lake City
  Young Men

William James Mortimer
Deseret News, Salt Lake City
  Patriarchal Blessings

Stephen D. Nadauld
General Authority, Salt Lake City
  Financial Contributions

Jack A. Nelson
Brigham Young University
  Newspapers, LDS

William O. Nelson
Church Correlation Dept., Salt Lake City
  Quorum of the Twelve Apostles

Hugh W. Nibley
Brigham Young University
  Temples: Meanings and Functions of
  Temples

Beverly J. Norton
Brigham Young University
  Record Keeping

Alan K. Parrish
Brigham Young University
  Keys of the Priesthood
  Seventy: Overview

Ronald W. Patrick
*Church Educational System, Stirling,
Alberta, Canada*
  Firesides

Vivian Paulsen
Friend Magazine, Salt Lake City
  Children's Friend, The

Lynn Reed Payne
Church Correlation Dept., Salt Lake City
  Fellowshipping Members

Birger A. Pearson
University of California, Santa Barbara
  Melchizedek: Ancient Sources

Don M. Pearson
Attorney, Los Angeles
  Bishop

Lee Tom Perry
Brigham Young University
  Organization: Contemporary
  Organization

Stanley A. Peterson
*Church Educational System, Salt Lake
City*
  Millennial Star

R. Douglas Phillips
Brigham Young University
  Evangelists

Brian L. Pitcher
Utah State University, Logan, UT
  Callings

B. Lloyd Poelman
Attorney, Salt Lake City
  Sunday School

Ronald E. Poelman
General Authority, Salt Lake City
  Sealing: Cancellation of Sealings

Bruce Douglas Porter
*International Broadcasting, Springfield,
VA*
  Church of Jesus Christ of Latter-day
  Saints, The

Larry C. Porter
Brigham Young University
  Aaronic Priesthood: Restoration

Robert E. Quinn
University of Michigan
  Common Consent

A. LeGrand Richards
Businessman, Provo, UT
  High Priest

Stephen D. Ricks
Brigham Young University
  Temples: Temples Through the Ages

J. Bonner Ritchie
Brigham Young University
  Presidency, Concept of
  Priesthood Councils

Richard C. Roberts
Weber State University, Ogden, UT
  Seventy: First Council of the Seventy

Richard M. Romney
New Era Magazine, Salt Lake City
  New Era

Allen Claire Rozsa
Former Church Temple President, Los Angeles
  Temple Ordinances

Burns R. Sabey
Colorado State University, Ft. Collins, CO
  Head of the Church

Cecil O. Samuelson, Jr.
University of Utah Medical School
  Medical Practices

Bruce Satterfield
Church Educational System, Iona, ID
  Melchizedek: LDS Sources

Gilbert W. Scharffs
Church Educational System, Salt Lake City
  Apostate

Marianne Clark Sharp [deceased]
Former Counselor in General Presidency, Church Relief Society, Salt Lake City
  Relief Society Magazine

Naomi M. Shumway
Former General President, Church Primary, Salt Lake City
  Primary

Robert L. Simpson
General Authority, Salt Lake City
  Temples: Administration of Temples

Robert J. Smith
Brigham Young University
  Ward Budget

Calvin R. Stephens
Church College Curriculum, Salt Lake City
  Patriarch: Patriarch to the Church

Howard D. Swainston
Attorney, Los Angeles
  Tithing

Charles D. Tate, Jr.
Brigham Young University
  Conference Reports

George S. Tate
Brigham Young University
  Prayer Circle

Shirley W. Thomas
Former Counselor in General Presidency, Church Relief Society, Salt Lake City
  Woman's Exponent

Dennis L. Thompson
Brigham Young University
  Setting Apart
  Ward Council

Paul H. Thompson
Weber State University, Ogden, UT
  Lay Participation and Leadership

Richard Tice
Deseret Book Co., Salt Lake City
  Magazines

Sherman N. Tingey
Arizona State University, Tempe
  Priesthood Quorums

Jay M. Todd
Ensign, Salt Lake City
  Ensign
  Improvement Era

Robert A. Tucker
General Authority Office, Salt Lake City
  Temple Recommend

Richard E. Turley, Jr.
Church Historical Dept., Salt Lake City
  Confidential Records
  Solemn Assemblies

Dell Van Orden
Church News, Salt Lake City
  Almanacs

R. Richard Vetterli
Brigham Young University
  Elder, Melchizedek Priesthood

Elizabeth Wahlquist
Brigham Young University
  Friend, The

Steven C. Walker
Brigham Young University
  Seer

W. Keith Warner
Brigham Young University
  Council of the First Presidency and
    the Quorum of the Twelve Apostles
  First Presidency
  President of the Church

Christine Croft Waters
Salt Lake Community College
  Maternity and Child Health Care

Ronald G. Watt
Church Historical Dept., Salt Lake City
  Journal of Discourses

L. Robert Webb
Brigham Young University
  Ward Organization

Alan L. Wilkins
Brigham Young University
  Organization: Contemporary
    Organization

Barbara W. Winder
*Former General President, Church Relief
  Society, Salt Lake City*
  Relief Society in Nauvoo

Lael J. Woodbury
Brigham Young University
  Hosanna Shout
  Public Speaking

Raymond S. Wright III
Brigham Young University
  *Utah Genealogical and Historical
    Magazine*

David H. Yarn, Jr.
Brigham Young University
  Sealing: Sealing Power
  Temple President and Matron

Marilyn S. Yarn
Former Temple Matron, Atlanta, GA
  Temple President and Matron

Hulda P. Young
Author, Salt Lake City
  Compassionate Service

Lawrence A. Young
Brigham Young University
  Single Adults

Michael K. Young
Columbia University
  Oath and Covenant of the Priesthood

PREFACE

This preface appears in volume 1 of the Encyclopedia of Mormonism.
Its spirit applies to all the volumes containing selections from the
Encyclopedia.

According to a standard definition, an encyclopedia is to "treat
comprehensively all the various branches of knowledge" pertaining
to a particular subject. The subject of this *Encyclopedia* is The
Church of Jesus Christ of Latter-day Saints, widely known as the
Mormon church. This is the first major encyclopedia published
about the Mormons. It presents the work of hundreds of Latter-day
Saint (LDS) lay scholars and others from throughout the world and
provides a comprehensive reporting of Mormon history, scripture,
doctrines, life, and knowledge, intended for both the non-Mormon
and the LDS reader. Readers will find an article on almost any topic
conceivably related to the general topic of Mormonism, and yet no
article is exhaustive because of space limitations. Most articles
include bibliographic references; cross-references to other articles in
the *Encyclopedia* are indicated by small capital letters.

When Macmillan Publishing Company asked authorities at
Brigham Young University whether they would be interested in
developing an encyclopedia about The Church of Jesus Christ of
Latter-day Saints, President Jeffrey R. Holland took the query to his
Board of Trustees. They instructed him to proceed. Working closely
with Church authorities and Macmillan, President Holland chose an
editor in chief and a board of editors. Discussion of possible titles
concluded that the work should be called the *Encyclopedia of
Mormonism* since that is the term by which the Church is most widely known, though unofficially.

The contract called for a work of one million words in about
1,500 articles in four volumes including pictures, maps, charts,
appendices, indices, and a glossary. It soon became apparent that

references to what the Church calls the standard works—the Bible, the Book of Mormon, the Doctrine and Covenants, and the Pearl of Great Price—would be so frequent that readers who did not have ready access to those works would be at a serious disadvantage in using the *Encyclopedia.* A fifth volume was decided upon to include all the LDS standard works except the Bible, which is readily available everywhere.

The Church does not have a paid clergy or a battery of theologians to write the articles. It functions with a lay ministry, and all members are encouraged to become scholars of the gospel. Over 730 men and women were asked to write articles on topics assigned because of previous interest and study.

Six major articles unfold the history of the Church: (1) the background and founding period in New York; (2) the Ohio, Missouri, and Illinois period ending with the martyrdom of Joseph Smith; (3) the exodus west and the early pioneer period under Brigham Young; (4) the late pioneer Utah period ending at the turn of the century and statehood; (5) a transitional period during the early twentieth century; and (6) the post–World War II period of international growth. The history of the Church has been dramatic and moving, considering its brief span of just over 160 years. Compared to Catholicism, Judaism, ancient Far East religions, and many Protestant churches, the Church has a very short history. Nearly 250 articles explain the doctrines of the Church, with special emphasis on basic principles and ordinances of the gospel of Jesus Christ. Twenty-four articles are clustered under the title "Jesus Christ," and another sixteen include his name in the title or relate directly to his divine mission and atonement.

Over 150 articles relate the details on such topics as the First Vision, Zion's Camp, Handcart Companies, Plural Marriage, the Salt Lake Temple, Temple Square, and the Church throughout the world. Biographies cover men and women contemporary in the life of Joseph Smith, Presidents of the Church, and auxiliary founders and past presidents. The only biography of a person living at the time of publication is on the present prophet and President of the Church, Ezra Taft Benson. [Since the publication of the *Encyclopedia of Mormonism,* Howard W. Hunter was sustained as President of the Church.]

And finally, there are over a hundred articles primarily concerned with how Latter-day Saints relate to their families, the Church, and to society in general. It is said there is a "Mormon culture," and several articles explore Mormon lifestyle, folklore, folk art, artists, literature, and other facets that distinguish Latter-day Saints.

It may be that the growth of the Church in the last decades has mandated the encyclopedic account that is presented here. Yet, even as the most recent programs were set down and the latest figures listed, there is an acute awareness that the basic tenet of the Church is that its canon is open-ended. The contemporary President of the Church is sustained as a "prophet, seer, and revelator." While this makes some theological discussion moot, the basic beliefs of the Latter-day Saints, summarized in the Articles of Faith, do not change.

In several areas, the Church shares beliefs held by other Christians, and a number of scholars from other faiths were asked to present articles. However, the most distinctive tenets of the Church—those regarding the premortal and postmortal life, living prophets who receive continuous and current revelation from God, sacred ordinances for deceased ancestors, moral and health codes that provide increasingly well-documented benefits, and the potential within man for progression into an infinite future—are all treated primarily by writers selected from among Latter-day Saints.

Lest the role of the *Encyclopedia* be given more weight than it deserves, the editors make it clear that those who have written and edited have only tried to explain their understanding of Church history, doctrines, and procedures; their statements and opinions remain their own. The *Encyclopedia of Mormonism* is a joint product of Brigham Young University and Macmillan Publishing Company, and the contents do not necessarily represent the official position of The Church of Jesus Christ of Latter-day Saints. In no sense does the *Encyclopedia* have the force and authority of scripture.

ACKNOWLEDGMENTS*

The support and assistance of many persons and groups are necessary to produce a work as extensive as an encyclopedia. Special thanks are extended to the executives of Macmillan Publishing Company who introduced the idea of the the *Encyclopedia of Mormonism* to Brigham Young University. Charles E. Smith made initial contacts on the project, while Philip Friedman, President and Publisher of Macmillan Reference Division, and Elly Dickason, Editor in Chief of Macmillan Reference Division, have followed through on the multitudinous details, demonstrating skill and patience in working with us in the preparation of this five-volume work.

The editors also wish to thank the General Authorities of the Church for designating Brigham Young University as the contractual Author of the *Encyclopedia*. Two members of the Board of Trustees of the university, who are also members of the Quorum of the Twelve Apostles, were appointed by the First Presidency to serve as advisers to the project: Elder Neal A. Maxwell and Elder Dallin H. Oaks. Other General Authorities who accepted special assignments related to the project include four members of the Quorum of Seventy: Elders Dean L. Larsen, Carlos E. Asay, Marlin K. Jensen, and Jeffrey R. Holland.

Special support also came from the Administration of BYU. Jeffrey R. Holland, president of BYU at the time the project was initiated, was instrumental in appointing the Board of Editors and in developing early guidelines. Rex E. Lee, current president of BYU, has continued this support.

* The major parts of the acknowledgments appear in volume 1 of the *Encyclopedia of Mormonism.* The statement has been modified here by (1) deleting credits to individuals and institutions providing general help, illustrations, and photographs for the *Encyclopedia* and (2) adding the names of those giving special assistance to the preparation of this particular publication.

The efforts of the Board of Editors and the Project Coordinator, whose names are listed at the front of each volume, have shaped and fashioned every aspect of the project. We offer special thanks to them, and to companions and family members for graciously supporting our efforts over many months. Others who shared in final editing include Bruce B. Clark, Soren F. Cox, Marshall R. Craig, and Ellis T. Rasmussen.

Many others have provided assistance in specialized areas, including Larry E. Dahl, Michelle Eckersley, Gary R. Gillespie, Devan Jensen, Luene Ludlow, Jack M. Lyon, Robert J. Matthews, Frank O. May, Charlotte McDermott, Robert L. Millet, Don E. Norton, Monte S. Nyman, Patricia J. Parkinson, Charlotte A. Pollard, Larry C. Porter, Merle Romer, Evelyn E. Schiess, Judith Skousen, Charles D. Tate, Jr., Jay M. Todd, and John Sutton Welch. Special thanks also to Ronald Millett and Sheri Dew at Deseret Book Company for their help with this volume.

Finally, we express appreciation to the 738 authors who contributed their knowledge and insights. The hopes of all who were involved with this project will be realized if the *Encyclopedia* assists readers to come to a greater understanding and appreciation of the history, scriptures, doctrines, practices, and procedures of The Church of Jesus Christ of Latter-day Saints.

TOPICAL OUTLINE

The topical outline is designed to help the reader discover all the articles in this volume related to a particular subject. The title of every article in this volume is listed in the topical outline at least once.

The volume *Priesthood and Church Organization* contains the major articles from the *Encyclopedia of Mormonism* concerned with the priesthood offices and the organizational structure of the Church.

A. The restoration of priesthood authority, keys, and offices.

1. *Restoration of the Aaronic Priesthood, its authority, keys, and offices:* Aaronic Priesthood*; Keys of the Priesthood; Levitical Priesthood; Ordination to the Priesthood; Priesthood; Priesthood Offices; Priesthood Quorums.

2. *Restoration of the Melchizedek Priesthood, its authority, keys, and offices:* Keys of the Priesthood; Melchizedek*; Melchizedek Priesthood*; Oath and Covenant of the Priesthood; Ordination to the Priesthood; Priesthood; Priesthood Offices; Priesthood Quorums.

B. The organization of the Church on April 6, 1830.

1. *Date of the organization:* April 6.

2. *Circumstances of the organization:* Organization of the Church, 1830.

C. The development of the priesthood quorums and councils.

1. *The First Presidency:* Council of the First Presidency and the Quorum of the Twelve Apostles; First Presidency;

* Indicates additional related articles are clustered under that entry title.

Head of the Church; Presidency, Concept of; President of the Church; Presiding High Priest; Prophet, Seer, and Revelator; Succession in the Presidency.

2. *The Quorum of the Twelve Apostles:* Apostle; Council of the First Presidency and Quorum of the Twelve; Prophet, Seer, and Revelator; Quorum of the Twelve Apostles.

3. *The First Council of the Seventy, The First Quorum of the Seventy, and additional quorums of Seventy:* Area, Area Presidency; Assistants to the Twelve; Seventy*.

4. *The Presiding Bishopric:* Bishop; Bishop, History of the Office; Bishopric; Presiding Bishopric.

5. *The Patriarch to the Church and other patriarchs:* Evangelists; Patriarch*; Patriarchal Blessings.

6. *High Priests and High Priests Quorums and Groups:* High Priest; Priesthood Quorums.

7. *Elders and the Elders Quorum:* Elder, Melchizedek Priesthood; Priesthood Quorums.

8. *Bishops and the calling of a ward bishop:* Bishop; Bishop, History of the Office; Bishopric; Branch, Branch President.

9. *Priests and the Priests Quorum:* Priest, Aaronic Priesthood; Priesthood Quorums.

10. *Teachers and the Teachers Quorum:* Priesthood Quorums; Teacher, Aaronic Priesthood.

11. *Deacons and the Deacons Quorum:* Deacon, Aaronic Priesthood; Priesthood Quorums.

12. *Other topics associated with the restoration and development of priesthood quorums and groups:* Callings; Church of Jesus Christ of Latter-day Saints, The; Common Consent; Conferences*; Correlation of the Church, Administration; Following the Brethren; General Authorities; *General Handbook of Instructions;* Home Teaching; Keys of the Priesthood; Magnifying One's

Calling; Melchizedek Priesthood*; Oath and Covenant of the Priesthood; Ordinances*; Organization*; Patriarchal Order of the Priesthood; Priesthood; Priesthood Blessings; Priesthood Councils; Priesthood Executive Committee, Stake and Ward; Priesthood in Biblical Times; Priesthood Interview; Priesthood Offices; Setting Apart; True and Living Church.

D. **The development of Church units, and the leaders basic to those units.**

1. *Missions and Mission Presidents:* Mission President; Missionary, Missionary Life; Missionary Training Centers; Missions.

2. *Areas and Area Presidencies:* Area, Area Presidency.

3. *Regions and Regional Representatives:* Region, Regional Representative.

4. *Stakes and Stake Presidencies:* High Council; Stake; Stake President, Stake Presidency.

5. *Districts and District Presidencies:* District, District President.

6. *Wards and Ward Bishops:* Bishop; Ward; Ward Budget; Ward Council; Ward Organization; Ward Welfare Committee.

7. *Branches and Branch Presidents:* Branch, Branch President.

E. **The development of auxiliary organizations (auxiliary to the priesthood).**

1. *Relief Society:* Relief Society; Relief Society in Nauvoo.

2. *Sunday School:* Sunday School; Richard Ballantyne.

3. *Young Women Organization:* Retrenchment Association; *Young Woman's Journal;* Young Women.

4. *Young Men Organization:* Young Men.

5. *Primary:* Primary.

6. *Other Organizations and Groups Auxiliary to the Priesthood:* Auxiliary Organizations.

F. **Policies, procedures, and practices in administering the units and activities of the Church; other activities and concerns of the Church.**

1. *Lines of priesthood authority and direction:* Area, Area Presidency; Authority; Bishop; Bishopric; Branch, Branch President; Church of Jesus Christ of Latter-day Saints, The; Clerk; Council of the First Presidency and the Quorum of the Twelve Apostles; First Presidency; General Authorities; *General Handbook of Instructions;* Head of the Church; High Council; Keys of the Priesthood; Missions; Organization*; President of the Church; Presiding Bishopric; Presiding High Priest; Priesthood; Priesthood Councils; Priesthood Executive Committee, Stake and Ward; Prophet, Seer, and Revelator; Quorum of the Twelve Apostles; Region, Regional Representative; Seer; Seventy*; Stake; Stake President, Stake Presidency; Succession in the Presidency; Ward; Ward Council; Ward Organization; Ward Welfare Committee.

2. *Administration of Church units and activities:* Area, Area Presidency; Bishop; Bishopric; Branch, Branch President; Callings; Clerk; Common Consent; Conferences*; Correlation of the Church, Administration; Council of the First Presidency and the Quorum of the Twelve Apostles; First Presidency; Following the Brethren; *General Handbook of Instructions;* High Council; Home Teaching; Meetings, Major Church; Organization*; Policies, Practices, and Procedures; Presidency, Concept of; President of the Church; Priesthood Executive Committee, Stake and Ward; Priesthood Quorums; Quorum of Twelve Apostles; Region, Regional Representative; Sacrament Meeting; Setting Apart; Seventy*; Single Adults; Social Services; Societies and Organizations; Solemn Assemblies; Stake; Stake President, Stake Presidency; Stewardship;

Teachers, Teacher Development; Visiting Teaching; Ward; Ward Council; Ward Organization; Ward Welfare Committee; Youth.

3. *Means utilized to communicate with local units and with members of the Church through magazines and other media:* Almanacs; *Bulletin; Children's Friend, The; Church News; Conference Reports; Contributor; Deseret News; Ensign; Evening and the Morning Star, The; Friend, The; General Handbook of Instructions; Improvement Era; Instructor, The;* International Magazines; *Journal of Discourses; Juvenile Instructor; Liahona, the Elder's Journal;* Magazines; *Man's Search for Happiness; Messenger and Advocate; Millennial Star; Nauvoo Neighbor; New Era;* Newspapers, LDS; Press and Publications; Proclamations of the First Presidency and Quorum of the Twelve Apostles; Publications; *Relief Society Magazine; Times and Seasons; Utah Genealogical and Historical Magazine; Woman's Exponent; Young Woman's Journal.*

4. *Means utilized to train, develop, and strengthen Church units and members through priesthood and auxiliary procedures:* Activity in the Church; Compassionate Service; Fast and Testimony Meeting; Firesides; Interviews; Joining the Church; Latter-day Saints (LDS); Lay Participation and Leadership; Leadership Training; Meetinghouse; Meetinghouse Libraries; Testimony Bearing; Volunteerism.

5. *Means of financing the Church and helping to take care of the physical and material needs of the units and members of the Church:* Bishop's Storehouse; Building Program; Distribution Centers; Fast Offerings; Finances of the Church; Financial Contributions; Hospitals; Maternity and Child Health Care; Medical Practices; Tithing; Welfare; Welfare Farms; Welfare Services; Welfare Square.

6. *Church procedures for disciplining Church members, when necessary:* Confidential Records; Courts, Ecclesiastical, Nineteenth-Century; Disciplinary Procedures; Fellowshipping Members; Membership; Membership Records; Orthodoxy, Heterodoxy, Heresy; Rebaptism; Record Keeping.

7. *Temple work and worship:* Sealing: (Sealing Power; Temple Sealings; Cancellation of Sealing); Temple Ordinances; Temple President and Matron; Temple Recommend; Temples: (Latter-day Saint Temple Worship and Activity; History of LDS Temples from 1831 to 1990; LDS Temple Dedications; Administration of Temples; Meanings and Functions of Temples; Temples Through the Ages).

8. *Other articles related to the general topics of priesthood and Church organization, including activities and concerns of the Church:* Apostasy; Apostate; Church of the Firstborn; Endowment Houses; "Fundamentalists"; Hosanna Shout; Name of the Church; Prayer Circle; Public Speaking; Sick, Blessing the; Signs of the True Church.

KEY TO ABBREVIATIONS

AF	Talmage, James E. *Articles of Faith*. Salt Lake City, 1890. (All references are to pagination in printings before 1960.)
BOM	The Book of Mormon: Another Testament of Jesus Christ. Salt Lake City, 1981.
CHC	*Comprehensive History of the Church*, 6 vols., ed. B. H. Roberts. Salt Lake City, 1930.
CR	*Conference Reports*. Salt Lake City, 1898–.
CWHN	*Collected Works of Hugh Nibley*, ed. S. Ricks, J. Welch, et al. Salt Lake City, 1985–.
Dialogue	*Dialogue: A Journal of Mormon Thought*, 1965–.
D&C	The Doctrine and Covenants of The Church of Jesus Christ of Latter-day Saints. Salt Lake City, 1981.
DS	Smith, Joseph Fielding. *Doctrines of Salvation*, 3 vols. Salt Lake City, 1954–1956.
ER	*Encyclopedia of Religion*, 16 vols., ed. M. Eliade. New York, 1987.
F.A.R.M.S.	Foundation for Ancient Research and Mormon Studies. Provo, Utah.
HC	*History of the Church*, 7 vols., ed. B. H. Roberts. Salt Lake City, 1st ed., 1902; 2nd ed., 1950. (All references are to pagination in the 2nd edition.)
HDC	Historical Department of the Church, Salt Lake City.
IE	*Improvement Era*, 1897–1970.
JC	Talmage, James E. *Jesus the Christ*. Salt Lake City, 1915.
JD	*Journal of Discourses*, 26 vols., ed. J. Watt. Liverpool, 1854–1886.
JST	*Joseph Smith Translation of the Bible.*
MD	McConkie, Bruce R. *Mormon Doctrine*, 2nd ed. Salt Lake City, 1966.
MFP	*Messages of the First Presidency*, 6 vols., ed. J. Clark. Salt Lake City, 1965–1975.
PGP	The Pearl of Great Price. Salt Lake City, 1981.
PJS	*Papers of Joseph Smith*, ed. D. Jessee. Salt Lake City, 1989.
PWJS	*The Personal Writings of Joseph Smith*, ed. D. Jessee. Salt Lake City, 1984.
T&S	*Times and Seasons*, 1839–1846.
TPJS	*Teachings of the Prophet Joseph Smith*, comp. Joseph Fielding Smith. Salt Lake City, 1938.
WJS	*Words of Joseph Smith*, ed. A. Ehat and L. Cook. Provo, Utah, 1980.

A

AARONIC PRIESTHOOD

POWERS AND OFFICES

The two divisions of PRIESTHOOD in The Church of Jesus Christ of Latter-day Saints are the Aaronic and the Melchizedek. Young men twelve to eighteen years of age, and older men who are new converts, are ordained to offices in the Aaronic Priesthood, "which holds the keys [governing or delegating authority] of the ministering of angels, and of the gospel of repentance, and of baptism by immersion for the remission of sins" (D&C 13). It is the priesthood authority by which John the Baptist prepared the way for Jesus Christ, teaching faith, repentance, and baptism for the remission of sins (Matt. 3:1–17; Mark 1:1–11; Luke 1:5–80; John 1:15–34; Acts 8:14–17; D&C 84:25–28). The Aaronic Priesthood does not have the power to confer the Holy Ghost (Matt. 3:11; Mark 1:7–8; John 1:33–34; JS—H 1:70) or to administer totally the affairs of the kingdom of God. It is power and authority God has given to man to prepare him and those to whom he ministers to receive the greater power, authority, and blessings of the MELCHIZEDEK PRIESTHOOD.

Distinctive LDS insights into the origins of the Aaronic Priesthood stem from modern revelations indicating that when Moses led Israel out of Egypt, the Lord purposed to confer upon worthy men of all tribes the higher Melchizedek Priesthood. Disobedience and loss of faith and worthiness, however, caused the Israelites to harden

1

their hearts against the Lord and Moses. Therefore, the Lord eventually

> took Moses out of their midst, and the Holy Priesthood also; and the lesser priesthood continued, which priesthood holdeth the key of the ministering of angels and the preparatory gospel; which gospel is the gospel of repentance and of baptism, and the remission of sins, and the law of carnal commandments, which the Lord in his wrath caused to continue with the house of Aaron among the children of Israel until John [the Baptist], whom God raised up [D&C 84:25–27].

The Israelites, unwilling to abide by the higher law of the fulness of the gospel with its greater priesthood, were given the law of carnal commandments, as a portion of the law of Moses, with its emphasis on offering symbolic, redemptive sacrifices to prepare them to receive the divine Redeemer, and they were given the lesser priesthood to administer that law. The Lord called Aaron and his sons to be the priests and preside over this lesser priesthood (Num. 8). Only direct descendants of Aaron could be ordained priests. The firstborn among the sons of Aaron would preside over the other priests. To assist Aaron and his posterity, particularly with the tabernacle and the preparing and offering of sacrifices, the Lord also called other male members of the tribe of Levi (not of the family of Aaron) to receive and carry out assignments in the lesser priesthood (Num. 3:5–13). The Levites held lesser offices of the Aaronic Priesthood and functioned under the keys or directive authority of that priesthood conferred upon Aaron and his sons (Widtsoe, pp. 12–17). Hence, the lesser priesthood was called the Aaronic Priesthood, after Aaron, but a portion of that priesthood was also called the LEVITICAL PRIESTHOOD because all those to whom it was given belonged to the tribe of Levi. This type of priesthood organization and service continued in Israel until Jesus Christ came.

John the Baptist, a descendant of Aaron through both parents and thus a Levite, was the son of Zacharias, a righteous priest in Israel at the time of the birth of Christ. It was this John whom God chose to prepare the way for Christ's ministry on earth. From John's birth his mission was set and his priesthood functions anticipated (D&C 84:28; Luke 1:5–17).

After being baptized by John, Jesus called his apostles (some of them from among John's disciples) and ordained them (John 15:16); later he conferred upon Peter, James, and John the keys of the kingdom of God and a higher priesthood. Following his death, resurrection, and ascension, Christ continued to direct his Church by giving commandments to the apostles through the power of the Holy Ghost (Acts 1:2) and through the authority of the higher Melchizedek Priesthood that he had conferred upon them. After the death of the apostles there followed a general apostasy, during which many gospel principles were lost and all the powers of the priesthood were withdrawn from the earth (2 Thes. 2:1–4; 2 Tim. 3:1–5).

On May 15, 1829, John the Baptist appeared to Joseph Smith and Oliver Cowdery as a resurrected messenger from God and conferred the ancient "Priesthood of Aaron" upon them (D&C 13). As the organization of the Church proceeded through the following months and years, many male members received the Aaronic Priesthood and were organized into quorums of priests, teachers, and deacons. In the Restoration, the Aaronic Priesthood has not been restricted to those who are literal descendants of Aaron or of Levi, since those lineages are not at present identified and the priesthood authority that implemented the ordinances of the law of Moses has been replaced by the higher priesthood and laws and ordinances of the gospel of Jesus Christ. Beginning with the reorganization of the priesthood in 1877, the Church established the current practice of ordaining boys to the Aaronic Priesthood during their early teenage years, organizing them at the ward level into PRIESTHOOD QUORUMS by age group and PRIESTHOOD OFFICE, and advancing them periodically to higher offices and eventually to the higher priesthood. The BISHOP of each ward presides over the Aaronic Priesthood in the ward.

Over the Aaronic Priesthood, the "president is to be a bishop; for this is one of the duties of this priesthood" (D&C 107:88), but bishops are also ordained high priests of the Melchizedek Priesthood because they preside and are not literal descendants of Aaron. The other three offices of the Aaronic Priesthood are deacon, teacher, and priest. Under the direction of the bishop, someone with proper authority confers the Aaronic Priesthood upon a worthy young man when he is twelve years old, ordaining him to the office of deacon. If he remains faithful and worthy, he is ordained to the office of teacher when he is fourteen years old and is given additional responsibilities. If he continues to remain faithful and worthy, he is ordained to the office of priest in the Aaronic Priesthood when he is sixteen years old, again receiving increased responsibilities. As young men progress in the priesthood, they retain all the rights and duties of lower offices.

The Lord has instructed the Church that bearers of the priesthood be organized into quorums (D&C 107:85–88). Some reasons for this are to establish order, to facilitate effective instruction in gospel principles and priesthood duties, and to prepare them for greater service and leadership in the Church. In the Aaronic Priesthood, a president and two counselors, chosen from the quorum members, preside over each quorum of deacons and teachers. This presidency is set apart (given powers of presidency) to preside over, sit in council with, and teach the members of the quorum their duty. The bishop is president of the priests quorum. He selects one or more boys as leaders under his presiding leadership and trains them to direct the other members of the quorum. Though the bishop and his two counselors in the bishopric hold all of the keys of the Aaronic Priesthood for the ward, the bishop usually calls an adult adviser to help train the boy leaders and to help instruct quorum members. However, the adviser has no presiding authority.

Thus the Aaronic Priesthood continues in its role as a preparatory priesthood, training young men in gospel principles and priesthood powers as they mature in service related to the preparatory gospel: faith in the Lord Jesus Christ, repentance, baptism for the remission of sins, and love of God and fellow beings. These responsibilities are most evident as the young men prepare, bless, and pass the sacrament of the Lord's Supper each Sabbath day in the SACRAMENT MEETINGS of the Church and as they otherwise assist the bishop in serving the people of the ward.

Today the Aaronic Priesthood gives young men experience and prepares them to receive the Melchizedek Priesthood when they are eighteen years old, with the greater privileges and responsibilities of its oath and covenant (D&C 84:33–40). The Melchizedek Priesthood increases their capacity to serve, perform the saving ordinances of the gospel, and direct the Church when called to do so.

A major activity program for Aaronic Priesthood boys in many areas of the world is scouting. To effectively correlate priesthood and scouting activities, the bishop organizes the YOUNG MEN program in the ward. An adult man is called to serve as president of the Young Men under the bishop's direction. Where scouting is organized, he and his two counselors generally also serve as the scout leaders. In wards with many boys, additional adults may be called to assist in the scouting program.

The bishop also organizes the girls of the ward into a YOUNG WOMEN program, with adult women advisers, and in age groups that correspond with ages of boys in Aaronic Priesthood quorums. Joint activities are planned and carried out regularly with the young men of the Aaronic Priesthood.

[*For a more detailed history of the Aaronic Priesthood, see also* Bishop, History of the Office.]

BIBLIOGRAPHY
Hartley, William G. "The Priesthood Reorganization of 1877: Brigham Young's Last Achievement." *BYU Studies* 20 (Fall 1979):3–36.
McConkie, Oscar W. *Aaronic Priesthood.* Salt Lake City, 1977.
Palmer, Lee A. *Aaronic Priesthood Through the Centuries.* Salt Lake City, 1964.
Widtsoe, John A. *Priesthood and Church Government,* revised ed. Salt Lake City, 1954.

VERDON W. BALLANTYNE

RESTORATION

On May 15, 1829, John the Baptist appeared to Joseph Smith and Oliver Cowdery near Harmony, Pennsylvania, and bestowed the Aaronic Priesthood on them (*see* AARONIC PRIESTHOOD: POWERS AND OFFICES). This ordination gave the two men AUTHORITY to baptize, and they immediately performed that ORDINANCE for one another in the Susquehannah River. The Prophet Joseph Smith had received no previous revelations authorizing him to baptize; to perform that ordinance properly required specific authorization from God. The return of John to bestow the Aaronic Priesthood confirmed that divine authority had been lost from the earth and that a heavenly visitation was necessary to restore it.

Joseph Smith and Oliver Cowdery were engaged in translating the Book of Mormon at the Prophet's homestead on the Susquehannah River in Harmony when the question of baptism arose. A passage in 3 Nephi 11, in which the resurrected Savior instructed the

Nephites on the subject, led the two men to wonder about their own baptism. Determining to pray about it, they went to the woods, where, as Oliver later recounted, "on a sudden, as from the midst of eternity, the voice of the Redeemer spake peace to us, while the veil was parted and the angel of God came down clothed with glory, and delivered the anxiously looked for message, and the keys of the Gospel of repentance" (JS—H 1:71n). Joseph said that the angel placed his hands on them and ordained them, saying: "Upon you my fellow servants, in the name of Messiah, I confer the Priesthood of Aaron, which holds the keys of the ministering of angels, and of the gospel of repentance, and of baptism by immersion for the remission of sins; and this shall never be taken again from the earth until the sons of Levi do offer again an offering unto the Lord in righteousness" (JS—H 1:69; D&C 13).

The angel informed them that the Aaronic Priesthood did not have the power of laying on of hands for the gift of the Holy Ghost, but that that authority would be given to them later. He told Joseph to baptize Oliver, and Oliver to baptize Joseph, and each to ordain the other to the Aaronic Priesthood. The messenger said "that his name was John, the same that is called John the Baptist in the New Testament, and that he acted under the direction of Peter, James and John, who held the keys of the Priesthood of Melchizedek," which would be conferred later (JS—H 1:72; *see* MELCHIZEDEK PRIESTHOOD: RESTORATION).

In the time of Jesus, John the Baptist preached repentance to the Jews and baptized in the Jordan River. He baptized Jesus (Matt. 3:13–17; cf. 2 Ne. 31:4–13). John was a direct descendant of Aaron, through both his priestly father Zacharias and his mother Elisabeth, one of the "daughters of Aaron" (Luke 1:5). A later revelation to Joseph Smith said that an angel bestowed authority on John to perform his earthly mission when he was eight days old (D&C 84:28).

By ordination and calling, John the Baptist held the KEYS of the Aaronic Priesthood. These include the keys of the "ministering of angels," meaning that holders of the Aaronic Priesthood are eligible to have angels minister to them. This priesthood also has the keys of the preparatory gospel, which embraces the "gospel of repentance and of baptism, and the remission of sins, and the law of carnal commandments" (D&C 84:27).

As others were also to enjoy the blessings associated with baptism for the remission of sins administered under priesthood authority, a revelation was given in 1829 regarding the exact words and procedure that were to be followed in conducting the ordinance for those who repent and ask for baptism.

> Behold ye shall go down & stand in the water & in my name shall ye baptize them. And now behold these are the words which ye shall say calling them by name saying, Having authority given me of Jesus Christ I baptize you in the name of the Father & the Son & of the Holy Ghost Amen. And then shall ye immerse them in water [Cowdery, 1829 Ms.].

In the LDS Church today, only those having either the office of priest in the Aaronic Priesthood or the Melchizedek Priesthood may baptize people.

Monuments commemorating the restoration of the Aaronic Priesthood have been erected at Temple Square, Salt Lake City (1958), and in Harmony, Pennsylvania (1960).

BIBLIOGRAPHY

Cowdery, Oliver. "Written in the year of our Lord & Savior 1829—A True copy of the articles of the Church of Christ." Ms. in handwriting of Oliver Cowdery, LDS Church Archives.

McConkie, Oscar W. *Aaronic Priesthood*. Salt Lake City, 1977.

Palmer, Lee A. *The Aaronic Priesthood Through the Centuries*. Salt Lake City, 1964.

Porter, Larry C. "The Priesthood Restored." In *Studies in Scripture*, ed. R. Millet and K. Jackson, Vol. 2, pp. 389–409. Salt Lake City, 1985.

LARRY C. PORTER

ACTIVITY IN THE CHURCH

For Latter-day Saints, activity in the Church involves a broad range of public and private religious practices intended to enhance the spiritual well-being of the faithful and accomplish good works. When Latter-day Saints speak of being "active in the Church," they have reference to observing a full religious lifestyle of attendance, devotion, service, and learning. As one measure of their rate of activity, 48 percent of adult Latter-day Saints in the United States in 1989 reported that they attended church services weekly, compared to 38 percent of adult members in other denominations.

The religious practices of active Latter-day Saints include attendance at worship services and religious education classes on Sunday; donation of TITHING and other financial contributions; service in a variety of Church CALLINGS; performance of TEMPLE ORDINANCES on behalf of the deceased; personal and family prayer; scripture study; religious discussion with other family members; adherence to moral standards of personal honesty and integrity; genealogical research; service in the community; and development of habits of thrift and self-sufficiency. General surveys show that even though private religious practice is strongly encouraged by the Church, only 67 percent of active adult Latter-day Saints pray daily, compared to 83 percent in other denominations; and 41 percent reported reading the scriptures daily or several times a week, compared to 52 percent in other denominations (Research Division; cf. National Opinion Research Center; Princeton Religion Research Center).

Religious activity may fluctuate over the course of a person's lifetime, depending on a number of personal and situational variables. In general, the rates of public and private religious activity are somewhat higher among women than men. This gender difference in religious activity is found within every denomination. In addition, the religious activity of adult Latter-day Saints is influenced by (1) religious background, including parents' religious activity, home religious observance, and religious activity during childhood and adolescent years; and (2) current life situation, including marital status and educational or occupational status. Church members who are most likely to have lower levels of religious activity include adults married outside the faith, adults who are divorced or have never married, adults with less than a high school education working in blue-collar jobs, and adults without a religious background.

Age also has an important effect on religious activity. In the United States, 85 percent of Latter-day Saint children under age ten attend Church meetings three to four times a month, but the percentage of frequent attenders declines over the next fifteen years to 55 percent during their mid-twenties. It then rises to 60 percent at age forty, falls to a low of 50 percent during the mid-fifties, and rises again to 60 percent by age seventy.

The process by which people discontinue active participation in the religious life of their church for a period of time is called "disengagement." Disengaged Mormons are usually referred to as "inactive" or "less active" members. While they do not regularly attend church or participate in other public religious practices, inactive Latter-day Saints usually retain a strong identification with the Church and value that identity (Albrecht, Cornwall, and Cunningham). Research has shown that religious socialization in the family is an important predictor of the likelihood that a person will experience a period of inactivity during adolescence or young adulthood. This finding accurately describes the experience of Latter-day Saints. Church members from homes in which both parents are LDS and attend church frequently, pray, read the scriptures, and discuss religion with their children are much less likely to have a period of inactivity than those from homes in which one or neither parent attends church regularly nor practices religion in the home.

About 75 percent of lifelong Latter-day Saints experience a period of inactivity lasting a year or more. The process of disengagement most commonly begins sometime between the ages of fourteen and twenty. Of those who leave, 60 percent return to active participation between their mid-twenties and late thirties, when they marry and begin a family. Some Latter-day Saints who had stopped attending church were asked to list the reasons why they had left. Lifestyle issues and problems of social integration were mentioned most frequently. More than half said they had found other interests that led them to spend less and less time in Church-related activities; 42 percent reported that they felt their lifestyle was no longer compatible with participation in the Church; 40 percent said they did not feel as if they belonged or fit in; and 25 percent said they felt it did not matter to anyone whether they attended or not. Less frequently mentioned reasons included moving to a new community, work-schedule conflicts, poor health, marriage to an inactive member or marriage outside the Church, and conflicts with Church members, programs, or doctrines.

For those who convert to the Church as teenagers or adults, the period of greatest risk for inactivity is the first year or two after joining the Church. About 70 percent of the new Latter-day Saint converts in the United States who do become inactive stop attending within three to five years after joining the Church. Of those who drop out, 45 percent return to active participation in five to ten years. Activity among these converts is influenced by (1) the personal characteristics of the convert, such as religious background, age, and marital status; (2) how personally involved the convert was in the investigation process, such as experiencing the Spirit of God and attending Church worship services; and (3) the extent to which the convert developed social relationships with other Latter-day Saints both before and after baptism.

In any religious tradition, social relationships are critical in developing and maintaining religious activity. People's religious lives are acted out in the context of a network of social ties within the family, the congregation, and the community. In addition, social relationships are the means by which religious traditions are transmitted from one generation to the next and the medium through which religious practices are shared and expressed. LDS religious activity is centered in the family and in the congregation (*see* WARD). In these settings, children and new converts learn by instruction and example what it means to be an "active" Latter-day Saint.

BIBLIOGRAPHY

Albrecht, Stan L. "The Consequential Dimension of Mormon Religiosity." *BYU Studies* 29 (Spring 1989):57–108.

————, Marie Cornwall, and Perry H. Cunningham. "Religious Leave-Taking: Disengagement and Disaffiliation Among Mormons." In *Falling from the Faith*, ed. David G. Bromley, pp. 62–80. Newbury Park, Calif., 1988.

Center for Demography and Ecology, University of Wisconsin-Madison. *National Survey of Families and Households*. Madison, 1987.

Cornwall, Marie. "The Social Bases of Religion: A Study of Factors Influencing Religious Belief and Commitment." *Review of Religious Research* 29 (Sept. 1987):44–56.

————. "The Influence of Three Agents of Religious Socialization: Family, Church, Peers." In *The Religion and Family Connection: Social Science Perspectives*, ed. Darwin L. Thomas, pp. 207–231. Provo, Utah, 1988.

————. "The Determinants of Religious Behavior: A Theoretical Model and Empirical Test." *Social Forces* 68 (1989):283–99.

National Opinion Research Center. *General Social Survey*. Chicago, 1988.

Princeton Religion Research Center. *Religion in America*. Princeton, N.J., 1982.

Research Division, The Church of Jesus Christ of Latter-day Saints. Surveys of Church Members (1981–1984), unpublished.

PERRY H. CUNNINGHAM

ALMANACS

Early Mormon almanacs (1845–1866) first borrowed heavily from standard almanacs being published, but then came to focus on interests of members of The Church of Jesus Christ of Latter-day Saints. Since 1973 the *Church Almanac* has printed only information pertaining to the Church.

Orson Pratt, an apostle, published the first Mormon almanacs in New York City in 1845 and 1846. Basing his *Prophetic Almanac for 1845* on standard American almanacs, Elder Pratt added a few articles about doctrines of the Church. Then his 1846 issue broke from the standard mold and became a distinctively Mormon almanac.

Between 1851 and 1866, William Wines Phelps published fourteen known issues of *Deseret Almanac* (from 1859–1864 entitled *Almanac*) in Salt Lake City. Also borrowing from standard almanacs, he added religious and cultural articles and some notes pertaining to frontier-society needs.

The current *Deseret News Church Almanac* is prepared and edited by the staff of the CHURCH NEWS, in cooperation with the Historical Department of the Church. It was published annually from 1974 to 1983, but biennially thereafter. Presently it is a 352-page, soft-bound, ready-reference of facts and statistics of the Church. It is intended for use in libraries, schools, and other institutions, as well as private homes. The *Almanac* prints thousands of historical and contemporary items about the Church, such as brief biographical sketches of all past and present GENERAL AUTHORITIES; a year-by-year historical chronology of the Church since the 1820s; a month-by-month chronology of major events in the Church during the past two years; and past and current information about STAKES, MISSIONS, AREAS, and TEMPLES throughout the world, including histories, populations, and numbers of Church units.

Liberal use is made of photographs. In addition to photos of current events, users see photographs of all current and past General Authorities for whom there are pictures available, including an 1853 daguerreotype of the Prophet Joseph Smith's uncle, John Smith, who was an assistant counselor in the FIRST PRESIDENCY and later the PATRIARCH TO THE CHURCH.

Each biennial issue of the *Almanac* is updated and revised.

Copies may be purchased at Church DISTRIBUTION CENTERS or ordered by mail from the *Deseret News*, P.O. Box 1257, Salt Lake City, UT 84110.

BIBLIOGRAPHY
Deseret News Church Almanac. Salt Lake City, 1974–.
Whittaker, David J. "Almanacs in the New England Heritage of Mormonism." *BYU Studies* 29 (Fall 1989):89–113.

DELL VAN ORDEN

APOSTASY

Latter-day Saints believe that apostasy occurs whenever an individual or community rejects the revelations and ordinances of God, changes the gospel of Jesus Christ, or rebels against the commandments of God, thereby losing the blessings of the Holy Ghost and of divine AUTHORITY. The rise of revelatory communities, apostasies, and restorations has happened cyclically throughout the history of mankind, in a series of dispensations from the time of Adam and Enoch (Moses 7) to the present. Latter-day Saints see a historical "great apostasy" and subsequent loss of authority beginning in the New Testament era and spreading in the centuries immediately following that era. Though Latter-day Saints have not emphasized the great apostasy as much as they have the concept that the Church is a revelatory restoration, the need of a restoration implies that something important was lost after the departure of the primitive Christian church.

The English word "apostasy" derives from the Greek *apostasía* or *apóstasis* ("defection, revolt"; used in a political sense by Herodotus and Thucydides); it is mentioned in a religious context in the Septuagint and the New Testament (e.g., Josh. 22:22 and 2 Chr. 29:19; 2 Thes. 2:3 states that an *apostasía* must come before the second coming of Christ). It can mean the intransitive "to stand away from," or the active "to cause to stand away from." Thus an apostasy can be an active, collective rebellion or a "falling away."

Joseph Smith in his first vision (1820) was told by Christ that all existing churches had gone astray, both in their teachings and in their practice, although they had "a form of godliness" (JS—H 1:18–19). Thus it was necessary for a "restoration" of the gospel to take place.

In addition, in the Book of Mormon (1 Ne. 11–14; 2 Ne. 28; cf. Morm. 8), the prophet Nephi$_1$ had a vision of the early Christian church and its twelve apostles, against whom the "multitudes of the earth" and the house of Israel fought (1 Ne. 11:34–35). He foresaw a "great and abominable church" that persecuted true Christians and the poor, and whose members were motivated by such things as pride, clothing themselves in precious raiment, and indulging in sexual immorality. It altered the simplicity of the gospel insidiously, did away with covenants, excised important scriptures, and denied the existence of miracles. This apostasy can be linked, in the allegory of Zenos, with the scattering of Israel when all the trees in the Lord's vineyard had become corrupt (Jacob 5:39–48), and it was paralleled by the calamitous apostasy of the Nephites in the New World (1 Ne. 12:15–19; 4 Ne. 1:24–46).

However, this "great church" was not any one specific church, according to Nephi; in his apocalyptic vision there are only two churches, and "whoso belongeth not to the church of the Lamb of God belongeth to that great church" (1 Ne. 14:10). It is typological, symbolic of many historical and social movements (2 Ne. 27:1); even nominal adherents to Christ's church, if driven by pride, wealth, prestige, and their appurtenances, may find themselves members of that "great church" (cf. 1 Ne. 8:27–28).

All through their history, Latter-day Saints have written and theorized about historical events involved in the "great apostasy," a theme discussed in several Restorationist writings of the late eighteenth and early nineteenth centuries. In 1833, referring to Mark 16:17–18 and 1 Corinthians 12, Joseph Smith stated: "By the foregoing testimonies we may look at the Christian world and see [that] the apostasy there has been from the apostolic platform" (*TPJS*, p. 15). Oliver Cowdery wrote on the apostasy in the first issue of the MESSENGER AND ADVOCATE (1834). In 1840 Orson Pratt spoke of "a general and awful apostasy from the religion of the New Testament" (*Listen to the Voice of Truth*, 1.1). He particularly emphasized a lack of binding ordinances because of the absence of PRIESTHOOD authority; baptism was a key example. In Pratt's view all churches before the Restoration were wrong in some ways, doctrinally and ritually, even though they might be right in others. Benjamin Winchester, an early LDS pamphleteer, wrote an extensive treatise using New Testament sources to demonstrate that an apostasy had been prophesied (*A History of Priesthood*, Philadelphia, 1843, pp. 72–96). In the 1850s and 1860s many references were made to "the great apostasy" (O. Pratt, *JD* 12:247) and "the great falling away" (W. Woodruff, *JD* 8:262) in Latter-day Saint sermons.

This idea—breaking off from established religion because it seems out of tune with New Testament Christianity—has obvious Protestant overtones, but the LDS view differs from typical Protestant attitudes in its emphasis on the loss and restoration of exclusive, clear-cut priesthood authority, correct ordinances, and continuing revelation. In contrast, Protestants typically rely primarily on biblical reinterpretation.

In 1909 James E. Talmage wrote *The Great Apostasy*, in which he gathered New Testament passages that Latter-day Saints have cited to show that a great apostasy was predicted by Jesus Christ, Paul, and other apostles and prophets (esp. Matt. 24:4–13, 23–26; Acts 20:29–30; Gal. 1; 2 Thes. 2:7–8; 1 Tim. 4:1–3; 2 Tim. 3:1–6; 4:1–4; Jude 1:3–4; Rev. 13:4–9; 14:6–7; and in the Old Testament, Amos 8:11–12). Talmage also chronicled the persecution of early Christians that hastened the Apostasy and described the primitive Church as changing internally in several respects. He argued that the simple principles of the gospel were mixed with the pagan philosophical systems of the day (Trinitarianism, resulting in the Nicene Creed; false opposition of body and spirit, creating excessive asceticism); that rituals were changed and added to in unauthorized ways (simple early Christian rites were replaced by complex pagan-influenced ceremonies; baptism by immersion was lost; the baptism of infants was introduced [cf. Moro. 8]; communion was changed); and that church organization was altered (the apostles and prophets, the necessary foundation of the church of Christ, were martyred, leaving a void that could not be filled by bishops; thus the medieval church showed little similarity to the organization or practices of the New Testament church).

LDS teachings on the early Christian apostasy have received additional support in the twentieth century as some scholars have argued that the primitive Church began as a centralized Judaic organization, was faced with the challenge of a Hellenized/Oriental, ascetic Gnostic Christianity, and became like its enemy in order to compete. The very idea of a centralized Christianity has given way to a picture of diverse and fragmented early Christianity, where it is hard to determine what is orthodox and what is heretical, what is Gnostic and what is "mainstream." For instance, Peter Brown and William Phipps argue that Augustine's influential doctrine of original sin, with its concomitant ritual, infant baptism, was derived from his Gnostic background and was, in reality, heretical, while Pelagius' opposition to these ideas was orthodox. But Augustine's doctrines prevailed, and continue to influence Western theology and culture. Another early Christian doctrine that did not survive in Western Christianity was deification, though it remained central to Eastern Christianity.

A complex religious and cultural milieu both nurtured and transformed early Christianity. Many factors must be taken into consideration in analyzing this transformation of Christianity. For example, some have put the blame exclusively on Greek philosophy and the influence of philosophy on Gnosticism for the rise of the great apostasy. But asceticism (i.e., hatred of the body, of sexuality, of the physical world) played a major role in the apostasy of the early church, and extreme asceticism is characteristically Oriental. Moreover, much of Greek philosophy has been found to be consistent with the gospel; Elder Orson F. Whitney referred to Plato and Socrates as "servants of the Lord," although in a "lesser sense" than the prophets (*CR* [April 1921]:33).

The concept of a historical apostasy from early Christianity can present a barrier between Latter-day Saints and others concerned with interfaith relationships. But Latter-day Saints do not view these events judgmentally; much of spiritual value happened during the Middle Ages and in other Christian churches. Brigham Young emphasized that good men before the restoration had "the spirit of revelation" and stated that John Wesley was as good a man "as ever walked on this earth" (*JD* 7:5; 6:170; 11:126). President Young held that all churches and religions have "more or less truth" (*JD* 7:283), and he admonished the Saints to seek and accept truths wherever they might be found. In conference talks, General Authorities, including President Spencer W. Kimball and President Thomas S.

Monson, have quoted or praised such luminaries as Billy Graham and Mother Teresa.

BIBLIOGRAPHY

Bauer, Walter. *Orthodoxy and Heresy in Earliest Christianity.* Philadelphia, 1971.

Benson, Ezra T. "Apostasy from the Truth." *IE* 52 (Nov. 1949):713, 756–60.

Brown, Peter. *Augustine of Hippo*, pp. 395–400. Berkeley, Calif., 1967.

Brown, S. Kent. "Whither the Early Church?" *Ensign* 18 (Oct. 1988):7–10.

Bushman, Richard L. *Joseph Smith and the Beginnings of Mormonism*, p. 207. Urbana, Ill., 1984.

Dodds, Eric R. *Pagan and Christian in an Age of Anxiety.* Cambridge, 1965.

Nibley, Hugh. *The World and the Prophets.* In *CWHN* 3.

———. *Mormonism and Early Christianity*, in *CWHN* 4, treats the disappearance of Christian baptisms for the dead (1948, pp. 100–167); the reshaping of early Christian texts and histories in light of the failure of the infant church to survive (1955, pp. 168–322); the forgotten teachings of Jesus during his forty-day ministry after his resurrection (1966, pp. 10–44); and the loss of the early Christian prayer circle (1978, pp. 45–99); bibliography (p. xii, n.8).

Peterson, Daniel C., and Stephen D. Ricks. "Comparing LDS Beliefs with First Century Christianity." *Ensign* 18 (Mar. 1988):7–11.

Phipps, William. "The Heresiarch: Pelagius or Augustine?" *Anglican Theological Review* 62 (1980):130–31.

Roberts, B. H. *The "Falling Away."* Salt Lake City, 1931.

———. *Outlines of Ecclesiastical History.* Salt Lake City, 1893.

Robinson, Stephen E. "Early Christianity and 1 Nephi 13–14." In *First Nephi, The Doctrinal Foundation*, ed. M. Nyman and C. Tate, pp. 177–91. Provo, Utah, 1988.

Rudolph, Kurt. *Gnosis: The Nature and History of Gnosticism.* San Francisco, 1983.

Sperry, Sidney B. "New Light on the Great Apostasy." *IE* 53 (Sept. 1950):710–11, 744–51.

Talmage, James. *The Great Apostasy.* Salt Lake City, 1909.

Vogel, Dan. *Religious Seekers and the Advent of Mormonism*, pp. 49–66. Salt Lake City, 1988, contains valuable bibliography; reviewed by Grant Underwood, *BYU Studies* 30 (Winter 1990):120–26.

TODD COMPTON

APOSTATE

Members of the Church vary in their levels of participation or belief (*see* ACTIVITY IN THE CHURCH). Latter-day Saints who have seriously contravened or ignored cardinal Church teachings (publicly or privately) are considered apostates, whether or not they have officially left the Church or affiliated with another religion. By not participating in Church meetings one is not considered apostate. However, when individuals ask to have their names removed from Church records, policy requires such requests to be honored. A Church DISCIPLINARY PROCEDURE may be held for any member who violates important commandments and "will not repent" (Mosiah 26:32; D&C 42:28). Open repudiation of the Church, its leaders, and teachings is one ground for excommunication.

The steps to apostasy are usually gradual. All members are counseled to guard against all manifestations of personal apostasy (*DS* 3:293–312; Asay, pp. 67–68). The most frequent causes of apostasy are failure to maintain strict standards of morality, taking personal offense (real or perceived), marrying someone who is of another faith or who is irreligious, neglecting to pray and maintain spirituality, or misunderstanding of the teachings of the Church.

Apostasy may be accelerated by a faulty assumption that scripture or Church leaders are infallible. Joseph Smith taught that "a prophet was a prophet only when he was acting as such" (*HC* 5:265). He also declared he "was but a man, and [people] must not expect me to be perfect" (*HC* 5:181). Neither the Church nor its leaders and members claim infallibility.

Above all, the Church affirms that its members should seek personal revelation to know the truth and live in tune with the spirit of God. Those who have not done this may drop by the wayside when their faith is challenged or when difficulties arise.

Apostates sometimes become enemies of the Church. Leaving the Church, which claims to be God's official church, containing the fulness of the gospel, often results in feelings of guilt. While many return, others develop a need to defend their actions, "disprove" the Church, or become hostile enemies. The fruits of apostasy are generally bitter. The Book of Mormon warns of unfavorable conditions that result from transgression contrary to "light and knowledge" (Alma 9:23).

LDS scriptures establish a loving and hopeful attitude toward apostates. Latter-day Saints are strongly counseled to love those who have left the faith, and to encourage, plead, and work with those who have strayed, inviting "the lost sheep" back to the fold (Luke 15:3–7). Of the wayward, the resurrected Savior taught, "Ye shall not cast him out of your . . . places of worship, for unto such shall ye continue to minister; for ye know not but what they will return and repent, and come unto me with full purpose of heart, and I shall heal them; and ye shall be the means of bringing salvation unto them" (3

Ne. 18:32). The desire to return is motivated by the reality of repentance enabled by the atonement of Jesus Christ. "He who has repented of his sins, the same is forgiven, and I, the Lord, remember them no more. By this ye may know if a man repenteth of his sins— behold, he will confess them and forsake them" (D&C 58:42–43).

BIBLIOGRAPHY

Asay, Carlos E. "Opposition to the Work of God." *Ensign* 11 (Nov. 1981):67–68.

Foster, Lawrence. "Career Apostates: Reflections on the Works of Jerald and Sandra Tanner." *Dialogue* 17 (Summer 1984):35–60.

Howard, F. Burton. "Come Back to the Lord." *Ensign* 16 (Nov. 1986):76–78.

GILBERT W. SCHARFFS

APOSTLE

An "apostle" is an ordained leader in the MELCHIZEDEK PRIESTHOOD in The Church of Jesus Christ of Latter-day Saints. Apostles are chosen through inspiration by the PRESIDENT OF THE CHURCH, sustained by the general membership of the Church, and ordained by the FIRST PRESIDENCY and the QUORUM OF THE TWELVE APOSTLES by the laying on of hands. They serve as GENERAL AUTHORITIES—as distinguished from local and regional officers—holding their office as apostle for the duration of their lives. The senior apostle is the President of the Church.

In addition to serving as witnesses of Jesus Christ to all the world (D&C 107:23), as Jesus' apostles did, members of the current Quorum of the Twelve Apostles hold the KEYS OF THE PRIESTHOOD— that is, the rights of presidency (D&C 107:35; cf. 124:128). Of their priesthood authority, President Brigham Young said, "The keys of the eternal Priesthood, which is after the order of the Son of God, are comprehended by being an Apostle. All the Priesthood, all the keys, all the gifts, all the endowments, and everything preparatory to entering into the presence of the Father and of the Son, are in, composed of, circumscribed by, or I might say incorporated within the circumference of, the Apostleship" (*JD* 1:134–35). As a PRIESTHOOD QUORUM, the Quorum of the Twelve Apostles is next in authority to the Quorum of the First Presidency (D&C 107:24). Further, it directs the domestic and international ministry of the quorums of the SEVENTY (D&C 107:34; cf. 124:139–40), and except in the presence of a member of the First Presidency or a more senior member of the Twelve, an apostle presides wherever he may be in the Church.

In the New Testament, an apostle (from Greek *apostellein*, to send forth [as a representative or agent]) was a divinely chosen envoy (Mark 3:14; John 15:16; Acts 1:21–26) who was a witness to Christ's resurrection and carried a missionary obligation to testify to it.

Jesus himself was an apostle through whom God spoke (Heb. 1:2; 3:1). The Father sent Jesus, and whoever receives him receives the one who sent him (Mark 9:37; John 8:16–19). As the Father sent him, so Jesus sent his apostles (John 20:21). Initially, they were called from those who "companied with us [the Twelve] all the time that the Lord Jesus went in and out among us" (Acts 1:21). The number twelve, associated with the apostles, echoes the number of tribes of Israel whom the apostles are to judge (Matt. 19:28; Luke 22:30). In this connection, they stood as the foundation of the early Christian church (Eph. 2:19–21; 4:11–14).

At times, the term embraces more than the Twelve, as is implied both in the phrase "all the apostles" (1 Cor. 15:7)—which follows particular mention of "the twelve" by Paul (1 Cor. 15:5)—and in references to persons named as apostles who were known not to be among the Twelve (Acts 14:14; Rom. 16:7). It is probable that by A.D. 54 the Lord's brother James had become one of the Twelve (1 Cor. 15:7; Gal. 1:19). Even so, most New Testament references to apostles refer to members of Jesus' original Twelve or to Paul. They were the guarantors or prime witnesses of Jesus' resurrection, which itself constituted the assurance that he was the expected Messiah and Lord of glory (Acts 1:8–11). In the first century, apostles were traveling witnesses to Jesus' resurrection, sent by him into the world for this purpose (Acts 1:8; cf. Matt. 28:19–20). At the group's core—and the Church's foundation—stood Peter, James, and John, who had been with or near Jesus during critical experiences, including his transfiguration (Mark 9:2–9) and his agony in Gethsemane (Mark 14:32–34).

The significance of Jesus' twelve apostles is underscored in the Book of Mormon. First, about 600 B.C. both Lehi and his son Nephi$_1$ saw in vision the Twelve as followers of Jesus in Palestine and as victims of persecution (1 Ne. 1:10–11; 11:29, 34–36). Second, these Twelve are to judge the twelve tribes of Israel and the other twelve disciples whom the resurrected Jesus chose during his ministry in the Western Hemisphere about A.D. 34 (1 Ne. 12:9–10; Morm. 3:18–19; cf. D&C 29:12). Third, these latter twelve disciples—as distinguished from Jesus' twelve apostles in Palestine—are to judge their own people who are descended from the house of Israel (3 Ne. 27:27). Fourth, during his visit in the Western Hemisphere, the risen Jesus established the position of the Twelve in his church when he chose and instructed them carefully in his gospel (3 Ne. 11:18–12:1; cf. 13:25–34; 15:11–16:20; 18:36–37; 27:13–21). He conferred on them authority to teach the gospel and administer its ordinances— that is, to baptize both with water and the Spirit—thus making them the transmitters of the Church's doctrine and practices (3 Ne. 11:22; 18:36–37; 19:6–14; 26:17). Fifth, in harmony with the pattern in the New Testament, the Book of Mormon records that Jesus was sent by the Father (3 Ne. 18:27; cf. 16:3) and that he in turn commissioned those twelve disciples to "go forth unto this people, and declare the words which I have spoken" (3 Ne. 11:41).

Modern revelation adds further information. The apostolic office and authority were restored to the Prophet Joseph Smith and Oliver Cowdery by Peter, James, and John, thus underscoring the continuing significance of this office in the Church (D&C 27:12; *see also* MELCHIZEDEK PRIESTHOOD: RESTORATION OF). As early as June 1829, nearly a year before the Church was organized, Oliver Cowdery and David Whitmer, later joined by Martin Harris, were instructed concerning the kinds of men to be chosen as apostles and were commissioned to select the first Twelve in the modern era (D&C 18:26–38). This commission was carried out on February 14–15, 1835, when Cowdery, Whitmer, and Harris selected twelve men to be apostles and ordained the nine who were present (*HC* 2:186–98).

Modern scripture specifies that "every decision . . . must be by the unanimous voice" of the Quorum of the Twelve Apostles (D&C 107:27). Further, its members are empowered to baptize, declare the gospel, and ordain others to the priesthood (D&C 18:26–36). The Lord has instructed that the number of apostles in the Quorum of the Twelve must be maintained (D&C 118:1) and that their keys "have come down from the fathers, . . . being sent down from heaven" (D&C 112:32). Those who serve in this office are to "cleanse [their] hearts and [their] garments, lest the blood of this generation be required at [their] hands" (D&C 112:33).

BIBLIOGRAPHY

Kittel, Gerhard, ed., and Geoffrey W. Bromiley, ed. and transl. *Theological Dictionary of the New Testament*, Vol. 1, pp. 407–447. Grand Rapids, Mich., 1964–1976.

McConkie, Bruce R. *The Mortal Messiah*, Vol. 2, pp. 99–114, 303–326. Salt Lake City, 1980.

S. KENT BROWN

APRIL 6

April 6, 1830, is the date on which The Church of Jesus Christ of Latter-day Saints was organized. The Prophet Joseph Smith was divinely authorized to reestablish the Church of Christ on this day, and it may be the anniversary of the Lord's birth on earth (D&C 20:1). The Church commemorates the importance of April 6 by scheduling its annual general conference on or near this day.

Concerning the date of Christ's birth, one of the earliest known references to December 25 was in the third century A.D. (Hippolytus, *Commentarii in Danielem*, 4.23.3). Scholarly consensus recognizes that early Christians probably appropriated December 25 from pagan festivals such as the Dies Natalis Invicti, established by the Emperor Aurelian (cf. Hoehner, pp. 11–27). Controversy, ancient and modern, regarding that date has had little influence in the LDS community. Presidents of the Church, including Harold B. Lee (p. 2) and Spencer W. Kimball (p. 54), have reaffirmed that April 6 is the true anniversary of Christ's birth, but have encouraged Church members to join with other Christians in observing Christmas as a special day for remembering Jesus' birth and teachings.

Some discussion has centered on the actual year of Jesus' nativity. Some argue that the phrase "one thousand eight hundred and thirty years since the coming of our Lord and Savior Jesus Christ in the flesh" (D&C 20:1) should be interpreted to mean that Christ was born exactly 1,830 years before April 6, 1830 (Lefgren). This view has been both challenged (Brown et al., pp. 375–83) and supported (Pratt, pp. 252–54). Others assert that the phrase was not intended to fix the year of Christ's birth but was simply an oratorical mode of expressing the current year.

Attempts to determine the exact date of Christ's birth or death are complicated by a dearth of pertinent historical information and multiple dating systems. The present dating system derives from the determination that Christ was born in 753 A.U.C. (*ab urbe condita*— from the founding of the city [of Rome]), made by the Scythian monk Dionysius, commissioned by Pope John 1 in A.D. 525 (1278 A.U.C.). The accuracy of Dionysius' system stands at the center of all discussion concerning the date of Christ's birth (Hoehner, p. 11).

John the Baptist's ministry began in the fifteenth year of the reign of Tiberius Caesar (Luke 3:1), the only precise date in the New Testament. The fifteenth year would have begun in September A.D. 28 and ended in September A.D. 29. On this basis alone the dates of Christ's life can be reckoned from the New Testament.

The LDS Church has not taken an official position on the issue of the year of Christ's birth. Bruce R. McConkie, an apostle, offers what for the present appears to be the most definitive word on the question: "We do not believe it is possible with the present state of our knowledge—including that which is known both in and out of the Church—to state with finality when the natal day of the Lord Jesus actually occurred" (Vol. 1, p. 349, n. 2).

BIBLIOGRAPHY

Brown, S. Kent, et al. Book Review of Lefgren's *April 6. BYU Studies* 22 (Summer 1982):375–83.

Filmer, W. E. "The Chronology of the Reign of Herod the Great." *Journal of Theological Studies* 17 (1966):283–98.

Hoehner, H. W. *Chronological Aspects of the Life of Christ.* Grand Rapids, Mich., 1977.

Kimball, Spencer W. "Remarks and Dedication of the Fayette, New York, Buildings." *Ensign* 10 (May 1980):54.

Lee, Harold B. "Strengthening the Stakes of Zion." *Ensign* 3 (July 1973):2.

Lefgren, J. *April Sixth*, Salt Lake City, 1980.

McConkie, Bruce R. *Mortal Messiah*, Vol. 1, p. 349, n. 2. Salt Lake City, 1979.

Pratt, J. "Afterwords" (Letter to the Editor). *BYU Studies* 23 (Spring 1983):252–54.

JOHN FRANKLIN HALL

AREA, AREA PRESIDENCY

An area is the largest geographical administrative subdivision of the Church and is presided over by an area presidency, composed of three members of the quorums of the SEVENTY.

An area presidency consists of a president and two counselors who provide spiritual guidance and administrative direction to leaders and members of the Church in their area. As members of the quorums of the Seventy, area presidencies are also called to preach the gospel, to be special witnesses of Jesus Christ, and to build up and regulate the affairs of the Church as assigned under the direction of the FIRST PRESIDENCY and the QUORUM OF THE TWELVE APOSTLES.

The specific duties of an area presidency include implementing the policies and instructions of the General Authorities presiding over them; instructing area leaders and members in the principles of the gospel; selecting and training REGIONAL REPRESENTATIVES, stake presidencies, and mission leaders; counseling with local leaders, members, and missionaries about Church-related, personal, and spiritual problems; establishing priorities for a broad range of Church activities; supervising the work of area staff personnel; conferring with community and religious leaders on social and moral issues of common concern; and making regular reports to higher Church leaders on conditions and progress in their area.

Area presidencies in the United States and Canada live in Salt Lake City. On weekends they often travel to their assigned areas and meet with leaders and members in stake CONFERENCES and various regional and stake training meetings. They also spend several weeks a year touring MISSIONS and training missionaries and mission leaders. In addition, members of area presidencies in the United States have assignments at Church headquarters in Salt Lake City that occupy a large portion of their time during the week. Area presidencies in other parts of the world live in their assigned areas. They spend their full time directing the work of the Church in their area.

BIBLIOGRAPHY

"Area Presidencies Called as Church Modifies Geographical Administration." *Ensign* 14 (Aug. 1984):75.

Hinckley, Gordon B. "The Sustaining of Church Officers." *Ensign* 15 (May 1985):4–6.

PERRY H. CUNNINGHAM

ASSISTANTS TO THE TWELVE

In 1941 five men were called as Assistants to the Quorum of the Twelve Apostles. J. Reuben Clark, Jr., of the First Presidency explained at the conference that they had been called because of the rapid growth of the Church and the ever-expanding demands upon the Quorum of the Twelve. A total of thirty-eight men served the Church as Assistants to the Twelve before the office was merged with the SEVENTY in 1976.

As General Authorities, Assistants to the Twelve had the authority to minister throughout the Church and to fulfill assignments as directed by the Quorum of the Twelve. They presided over, and spoke at, stake conferences; helped organize stakes; toured missions; and directed missionary work in many parts of the world.

A number of men who first served as Assistants to the Twelve were later called to be members of the Quorum of the Twelve Apostles: George Q. Morris, Boyd K. Packer, Marvin J. Ashton, L. Tom Perry, David B. Haight, James E. Faust, Neal A. Maxwell, and Joseph B. Wirthlin. Several others who had served as Assistants to the Twelve also served in the Quorum of the Twelve and later as Counselors in the First Presidency, including Hugh B. Brown, N. Eldon Tanner, Marion G. Romney, and Gordon B. Hinckley.

An important 1835 revelation on priesthood describes the Seventy as the quorum standing next in authority to the Twelve, and under their direction, the Seventy share responsibility for the Church throughout the world (D&C 107:25–26, 33–34). According to President Spencer W. Kimball in 1976, the calling of the Assistants was "similar to that envisioned by the revelations for the First Quorum of Seventy," but "the scope and demands of the work at that time [1941]" did not yet justify the reconstitution of that quorum (p. 9). After accelerating growth in many parts of the world led to the organization of the First Quorum of Seventy in 1975, the nearly two dozen Assistants then serving became members of that quorum in 1976.

BIBLIOGRAPHY
Kimball, Spencer W. "The reconstitution of the First Quorum of the Seventy." *Ensign* (Nov. 1976):9.
Widtsoe, John A. "Assistants to the Twelve." *IE* 44 (May 1941):288.

BYRON R. MERRILL

AUTHORITY

The claim of The Church of Jesus Christ of Latter-day Saints to be the only TRUE AND LIVING CHURCH on the earth is centered on the concept of authority. The LDS belief has been well stated by President Joseph F. Smith: "As to the question of authority, nearly everything depends upon it. No ordinance can be performed to the acceptance of God without divine authority. No matter how fervently men may believe or pray, unless they are endowed with divine authority they can only act in their own name, and not legally nor acceptably in the name of Jesus Christ, in whose name all things must be done" (Smith, p. 102).

Because several different definitions are associated with authority in the scriptures, this doctrine has often been misunderstood:

1. Authority refers to formalized power associated with position, function, or legal designation as exemplified by the authority given Joseph in Egypt by Pharaoh (Gen. 41:40–41), by the man who gave his servants authority over his house when he departed (Mark 13:34), and by Church officers designated to have authority over members (Matt. 8:9; D&C 107:8). Authority in these cases presumes control by virtue of assigned position.

2. Authority is strength, might, or control of resources. This is exemplified by the power established by the Philistines over the Jews (Judg. 15) and by Rome's control of Judea at the time of Christ (Matt. 27:2). Authority in this sense connotes superiority or stature above another resulting from acquisitions, possessions, or physical strength.

3. Authority is expertise, as in the case of an expert on a subject. Examples include the authority ascribed to the twelve-year-old Jesus as a result of his teachings in the temple (Luke 2:42, 46–47), and the authority associated with the preaching of prophets such as Nephi$_1$, Lehi, Abinadi, and the sons of Mosiah$_2$ (Mosiah 13:6; Alma 17:3; Hel. 5:18).

4. Authority is a divine commission or calling from God. For example, Jesus gave his apostles specific authority to preach and to administer his gospel (Matt. 10:1; John 15:16; 3 Ne. 12:1), and certain individuals were empowered to baptize and perform

miracles by this authority (Acts 5:12–16; 8:5–17; Alma 5:3; Mosiah 18:13, 18; Moro. 2:1–3). As conveyed by Jesus Christ, this authority meant that ORDINANCES performed on earth would be honored in heaven and, conversely, to loose (dissolve an ordinance) on earth would mean it was loosed in heaven (Matt. 16:19). The name given to this kind of authority in the scriptures is PRIESTHOOD (Heb. 7:11–12, 14, 24; 1 Pet. 2:5, 9; D&C 84:107).

That these meanings have often been confused is exemplified by the scribes' query of Jesus regarding his own basis of authority: "By what authority doest thou these things?" (Matt. 21:23–27). Is your authority political (definition 1) or power from on high (definition 4)? they asked.

As Christ's authority was based on power from on high, so does the Church rest its claim as the only true and living church upon possessing the divine authority to act for God. This authority differentiates the Church from all others. Other systems and organizations may possess other types of authority, but the divine authority associated with Christ's church, the priesthood, resides only in this one.

An explanation of the characteristics of divine authority helps clarify the claims of the Church. First, "no man taketh this honour unto himself, but he that is called of God, as was Aaron" (Heb. 5:4). Divine authority cannot be obtained by study, graduation from school, or mere desire (Acts 19:13–16). It must be obtained in the divinely appointed way, as was the case with Aaron (Ex. 28:41).

Second, obtaining the authority to act in the name of God comes by the laying on of hands by one already holding this authority or priesthood (1 Tim. 4:14; 2 Tim. 1:6; Moro. 2:1–3; Deut. 34:9). Simon, for example, desired to purchase the apostles' authority, as he might have done with other types of authority. He was condemned by Peter for desiring to obtain the "gift of God" with money (Acts 8:14–20), and purchasing authority carries his name, simony.

Third, ordinances performed in the Church are spiritually binding only when performed under this divinely commissioned authority, received in the proper way (Mosiah 23:17; D&C 20:73; 132:13; 2 Sam. 6:6–7). For example, Paul rebaptized certain Ephesians who had been previously baptized by an unauthorized person (Acts 19:1–6). King Limhi and many of his followers were converted to Christ and were desirous of being baptized, but they waited to receive that ordinance because the one with authority did not feel worthy (Mosiah 21:33–35).

A fourth fact concerning divine authority is that it was lost from the earth sometime after the resurrection and ascension of Christ into heaven (*see* APOSTASY), so a restoration of divine authority was needed (2 Thes. 2:1–4; 1 Tim. 4:1–3; 2 Tim. 3:1–7). In 1829 heavenly messengers, previously endowed with divine authority by Christ himself, conferred authority upon Joseph Smith and Oliver Cowdery as part of the restoration of The Church of Jesus Christ of Latter-day Saints (*see* AARONIC PRIESTHOOD: RESTORATION OF; MELCHIZEDEK PRIESTHOOD: RESTORATION OF). Members of the Church ordained to this authority now record their personal "line of authority." This record indicates the path of ordinations connecting their priesthood authority to Jesus Christ himself.

Fifth, the authority to preside is efficacious for an individual only when it is accompanied by the COMMON CONSENT of the members of the Church over whom that person will preside (D&C 20:65; 26:2; 42:11).

Abuses of authority and authoritarianism are inherent in any organized system, and such abuses are especially associated with authority based solely on position, strength, or knowledge. Organizations such as the Church are sometimes perceived by outsiders as authoritarian, primarily because of confusion over the meanings of authority. If authority in the Church were based on politics, personal attributes, or expertise, then a charge of authoritarianism might have some validity. However, divine authority (definition 4) is inseparably connected to principles of righteousness, and when we "undertake to cover our sins, or to gratify our pride, our vain ambition, or to exercise control or dominion or compulsion upon the souls of the children of men, in any degree of unrighteousness, behold, the heavens withdraw themselves; the Spirit of the Lord is grieved; and when it is withdrawn, Amen to the priesthood or the authority of that man" (D&C 121:37).

Members of the Church understand that the exercise of divine authority includes the responsibility to bless people and minister to their well-being. Proper use of this authority is inconsistent with authoritarianism and the abuses of authority, so the negative connotations sometimes associated with authority are not generally present in the Church.

BIBLIOGRAPHY

Ehat, Andrew F., and Lyndon W. Cook, eds. *The Words of Joseph Smith*. Provo, Utah, 1980.
Richards, LeGrand. *A Marvelous Work and a Wonder*. Salt Lake City, 1968.
Smith, Joseph F. *Gospel Doctrine*. Salt Lake City, 1977.
Talmage, James E. *AF*. Salt Lake City, 1977.

KIM S. CAMERON

AUXILIARY ORGANIZATIONS

The LDS Church is characterized by two types of organizational entities: PRIESTHOOD QUORUMS and organizations auxiliary to the priesthood. Members of priesthood quorums, or groups of priesthood holders, along with those called to priesthood leadership positions, have the ecclesiastical responsibility and authority for carrying out the missions of the Church. The auxiliary organizations are complementary to priesthood line organization and exist primarily to assist the priesthood. The auxiliaries are the RELIEF SOCIETY (women, eighteen and older), SUNDAY SCHOOL (all members twelve and older), YOUNG WOMEN (twelve through eighteen), YOUNG MEN (twelve through eighteen), and PRIMARY (all children eighteen months through eleven years).

Auxiliary organizations seek to provide gospel instruction, wholesome activities, the sharing of resources, settings where supportive friendships can form, and formal and informal opportunities for the sharing of faith and values. Each organization tailors its program to a specific age group and gender and provides members with opportunities for Christian service. Each has a set of leaders functioning at the ward, stake, and general levels of the Church organization, and ward and stake auxiliary leaders receive training each year at an auxiliary training meeting.

Although the Relief Society (1842) had roots in the early years of the Church's development, the auxiliary organizations developed as formal parts of Church structure after it moved to Utah in 1847. The Relief Society and the Sunday School were established

Churchwide in the early 1860s by President Brigham Young, followed by the Cooperative Retrenchment Association in 1869 (forerunner of the Young Women organization), and the Young Men's Mutual Improvement Association in 1875 (forerunner to the Young Men organization). The Primary Association, emphasizing religious activities for children, began in 1878; weekday religion classes for children, emphasizing religious instruction, were instituted in 1890. These two entities were merged in 1929 to form the present-day Primary.

During the opening decades of the twentieth century, each auxiliary organization developed in its own way into a major facet of the Church programs for its members. Under the leadership of a presidency and board called at the general level of the Church to provide resources and direction to the local congregations, each auxiliary developed its own Churchwide curriculum, magazine, and set of regular meetings and activities. In addition, there was a general movement to structure classes and activities by age groupings. As each auxiliary expanded its program, it also developed a leadership structure staffed by the lay membership. Today, a presidency and board or staff are called at the ward level to implement the program and serve the members; at the stake level to provide leadership training and support and combine resources and activities; and at the general Church level to establish program guidelines and policies, develop materials and provide leadership.

In the early 1970s, an organization for SINGLE ADULTS was established at the general Church level under the direction of the Melchizedek Priesthood Committee. Its purpose was to develop programs and policies to address the needs and concerns of single adult members. Activities were instituted at the ward and stake level, and leaders were called to plan such activities. The general level was not continued beyond the 1970s, and local leaders and activities function under the direction of local priesthood and Relief Society leaders.

As the auxiliary programs expanded in the first half of the twentieth century, one of the challenges became coordinating and maintaining the relationship between the priesthood line of ultimate responsibility for the work of the Church and the auxiliaries as agents of the priesthood in accomplishing it. This challenge was recognized by President Joseph F. Smith as early as 1906. In the latter part of the twentieth century, the Church has made significant efforts to structure and define its work so that the principle of priesthood governance can be fully realized (*see* CORRELATION OF THE CHURCH, ADMINISTRATION). The thrust has been to link the efforts of priesthood leaders and auxiliary leaders more closely and to align them with the priesthood channel of decision making and action. Specifically, at each level of the Church organization, auxiliary leaders are accountable to priesthood leaders rather than to the auxiliary organization.

Priesthood correlation provides more direct representation of the needs of all Church members in Church government. When properly implemented, it is the process through which women participate in the governance of the Church. Female leaders express their views, represent their concerns, and share in the decision-making process in partnership with men holding priesthood offices.

BIBLIOGRAPHY
Cowan, Richard O. *The Church in the Twentieth Century*. Salt Lake City, 1985.
Jenson, Andrew. *Encyclopedic History of the Church of Jesus Christ of Latter-day Saints*. Salt Lake City, 1941.
Smith, Joseph Fielding. *Essentials in Church History*. Salt Lake City, 1950.

IRENE HEWETTE ERICKSEN

B

BALLANTYNE, RICHARD

Richard Ballantyne was born in Whitridgebog, Roxburgshire, Scotland, on August 26, 1817, to David Ballantyne and Ann Bannerman. He was strong-minded, and ever worked for justice for the oppressed and mercy for the sinner and the weak. In his early days, Richard was frugal, somewhat austere, and honest in his business; in later years, he displayed sympathy and affection. His concern for the moral and spiritual welfare of children led him to establish the first LDS SUNDAY SCHOOL, in 1849, in Salt Lake City.

Ballantyne was brought up in the Relief Presbyterian Church. As a youth he worked on his parents' farm. Between the ages of nine and fourteen he occasionally attended school during the winter. At fourteen he was apprenticed to a baker; subsequently, he bought the business and managed it until he left Scotland.

In December 1842, at age twenty-five, Ballantyne was baptized into the Church at Leith, in the waters of the Firth of Forth. The following year he, his mother, two sisters, and a brother immigrated to Nauvoo, where he managed several businesses and engaged in farming along the Mississippi River. In Nauvoo he suffered persecution along with many of the Saints. In the summer of 1846, he and four other men were kidnapped by a mob, held hostage, and threatened with death. After two weeks, the mob bargained with Church leaders and returned the men to Nauvoo to avoid being charged with the kidnapping.

That same year, Ballantyne was ordained a SEVENTY and, soon after, a HIGH PRIEST. At the exodus from Nauvoo in 1846, he remained behind to help settle the Saints' affairs. In September of that year, having completed his assignment, he moved to Winter Quarters. On February 17, 1847, he married Hulda Meriah Clark. They entered Utah in 1848, their first son having been born while they were crossing the plains.

Upon arriving in Salt Lake City, Ballantyne immediately considered the possibilities of schooling for the children. He asked for and received his bishop's permission to establish a Sunday School. Because no suitable meeting place was available, he added a room onto his home and held the first Sunday School in the Church on December 9, 1849. Approximately fifty students attended. Later this Sunday School was moved to the Fourteenth Ward meetinghouse. When asked why he had been so desirous of organizing a Sunday School, he replied:

> I was early called to this work by the voice of the spirit, and I have felt many times that I have been ordained to this work before I was born, for even before I joined the church I was moved upon to work for the young. Surely no more joyful nor profitable labor can be performed by an Elder [Jenson, Vol. 1, p. 705].

In the fall of 1852, Ballantyne was called on a mission to India, and arrived in Calcutta on July 24, 1853. Although the work was very discouraging, he worked hard until his release and return to Utah in September 1855.

He married Mary Pierce on November 27, 1855, as a plural wife, and about two years later married Caroline Sanderson. He and his three wives had twenty-two children and more than one hundred grandchildren.

During his life in Utah, Ballantyne managed several businesses, including two railroads, a newspaper, and several merchandising companies. He was a member of the Weber County Court for fourteen years. At the time of his death, November 8, 1898, he was a senior member of the HIGH COUNCIL of the Ogden Utah Stake.

BIBLIOGRAPHY

Ashton, Wendell J. *Theirs in the Kingdom,* 2nd ed., pp. 235–58. Salt Lake City, 1970.

Cannon, Donald Q., and David J. Whittaker, eds. *Supporting Saints: Life Stories of Nineteenth-Century Mormons.* Provo, Utah, 1985.

CHC, 3:6–9; 4:72–73; 5:478–80.

Jenson, Andrew, ed. *Latter-Day Saint Biographical Encyclopedia,* Vol. 1, pp. 703–706. Salt Lake City, 1971.

J. HUGH BAIRD

BISHOP

A bishop is the ecclesiastical leader of a Latter-day Saint congregation or WARD, and has comprehensive pastoral and administrative responsibility at that level. This differs from other Christian churches in which bishops administer large geographical areas involving a number of congregations.

The word "bishop" comes from the Greek word *episkopos,* meaning "overseer." He is the pastor or shepherd, and is charged with the care of his flock. In the apostolic period, Paul wrote to the bishops in Philippi (Phil. 1:1), and other letters speak of the bishop's duties and of his sacred role in caring for the Church of God (1 Tim. 3:1–7; Titus 1:7–9).

The bishop's office is a complex priesthood calling. The bishop is president of the ward's AARONIC PRIESTHOOD holders and is responsible for all their activities. He is also an ordained HIGH PRIEST in the MELCHIZEDEK PRIESTHOOD and is the presiding high priest in the ward, responsible for all ward activities and functions (D&C 107:15–17). As the common judge and the presiding high priest, he determines the worthiness of all members of his ward and directs the performance of sacred ordinances (D&C 107:68–76). He is assisted by two counselors, usually high priests, who with the bishop constitute the BISHOPRIC and share responsibility for all ward organizations. The bishop and his counselors extend calls to ward members as needed to fill the numerous assignments in the many programs of the ward, encompassing activities for ward members at all ages.

A bishop holds his official position for an indefinite time period. A new bishop is called when an existing bishop is replaced or when

a new ward is organized. After prayerful deliberation, the STAKE PRES-
IDENCY proposes a new bishop to the FIRST PRESIDENCY and QUORUM
OF THE TWELVE APOSTLES. The individual nominated must be a member of the priesthood body of the ward. He does not seek nor apply
for this position and no theological degree is necessary. A bishop is a
lay minister and receives no monetary compensation for his services.
Like other local Church officers, he must maintain himself and his
family through normal employment. In selecting a bishop, a stake
presidency ordinarily considers testimony, judgment, commitment,
and charity toward ward members, as well as the virtues of sobriety
and integrity and the administrative and teaching skills identified in
the New Testament description of bishops:

> A bishop then must be blameless, the husband of one wife, vigilant,
> sober, of good behavior, given to hospitality, apt to teach. Not given to
> wine, no striker, not greedy of filthy lucre; but patient, not a brawler, not
> covetous. One that ruleth well his own house, having his children in
> subjection with all gravity; (for if a man know not how to rule his own
> house, how shall he take care of the church of God?) Not a novice, lest
> being lifted up with pride he fall into the condemnation of the devil [1
> Tim. 3:2–6].

Receiving a call to be a bishop is often a powerfully spiritual
experience for a man as he realizes the awesome responsibility and
feels the spirit confirm the importance of the call.

The bishop is sustained by a vote of the congregation, after
which he is ordained and set apart to this holy office by the laying on
of hands generally by the stake president under assignment from the
First Presidency. After a bishop is released from active duty, he will
often be called "bishop" throughout his life because of the love and
respect that ward members have for him.

The bishop has overall responsibility for all functions of the
ward, which are designed to lead each individual member to Christ
and eternal life. He is to "watch over the Church" (D&C 46:27). With
other ward leaders, he is concerned for the daily physical needs of
each ward member, especially the sick, elderly, and handicapped.
He is like a father to the ward.

As the PRESIDING HIGH PRIEST of the ward, the bishop presides at
sacrament, priesthood, and ward council meetings, and at all other

ward services or activities. By these and other means he watches over both the spiritual and temporal affairs of the ward and its individual members and organizes the activities for preaching the gospel, serving in the temple, and helping ward members become more Christlike.

The bishop is the common judge of his ward. He spends much time visiting with or interviewing ward members. He determines their worthiness to participate in sacred ordinances, to receive the priesthood, to receive calls to serve in the ward and on missions, and to do temple work. He spends many hours interviewing and counseling youth as they become prospective missionaries.

Besides determining worthiness, the bishop must see that all Church ordinances are performed and recorded correctly. His direction or approval is necessary for baptism, confirmation, administration of the sacrament, blessing and naming of babies, priesthood ordinations, and all temple ordinances for members of his ward.

Where there is need, the bishop may be involved in counseling on a regular basis. He may help ward members establish goals for improvement, or he may impose appropriate discipline. In cases of serious transgression, he may initiate formal DISCIPLINARY PROCEDURES, which can affect membership, and may be necessary to bring some back to full fellowship.

As the president of the Aaronic Priesthood, a bishop has a specific responsibility to the YOUNG MEN and YOUNG WOMEN of the ward, ages twelve to eighteen. He is to see that all youth are instructed not only in scriptures and doctrine but also in the principles of charity and honesty, with special training of the young men in the duties of the priesthood, including administration of the sacrament, HOME TEACHING, baptizing, and missionary work. The bishop is automatically president of the quorum of priests in his ward, which generally consists of young men ages sixteen through eighteen. Bishops have similar responsibility for the young women of the ward. He meets monthly with a Bishop's Youth Committee, composed of adult and youth leaders for the young men and women.

Other duties of the bishop include receiving and accounting for the FINANCIAL CONTRIBUTIONS of ward members and caring of the needy through the BISHOP'S STOREHOUSE and the FAST OFFERING fund. He sees that all necessary supplies are at hand for ward functions.

He arranges for and conducts funeral services. When it is appropriate and civil laws permit, he may perform marriages.

The bishop, as a father in his own home, as a family provider with a normal occupation, and as a member of the community in which he lives, has many time demands beyond his ecclesiastical calling. He must organize well and delegate and supervise effectively to accomplish all his duties.

The bishop's Sunday schedule usually involves a twelve or more hour day, including attending and conducting organizational meetings, worship services, training sessions; counseling and interviewing ward members; extending invitations or calls to participate in Church service in the ward; visiting the sick in hospitals; and visiting ward members in their homes as needed. He spends many additional hours during the week in meeting ward needs. His counselors and priesthood and auxiliary leaders also spend many hours helping him with these ward responsibilities. However, the overall responsibility for ward members and certain specific duties, such as annual interviewing of individuals for temple recommends and tithing settlement, are not in ordinary circumstances delegated.

Ward members believe that a man called of God, as the bishop is, will be endowed with wisdom, understanding, and spiritual discernment (D&C 46:27). Thus they frequently seek and greatly appreciate his advice and assistance.

BIBLIOGRAPHY
Beecher, Dale. "The Office of Bishop." *Dialogue* 15 (Winter 1982):103–115.
Brandt, Edward J. "The Office of Bishop in The Church of Jesus Christ of Latter-day Saints—A Sesquicentennial Review." In *A Sesquicentennial Look at Church History*, pp. 57–70. Provo, Utah, 1980.

DON M. PEARSON

BISHOP, HISTORY OF THE OFFICE

The work of the office of bishop in The Church of Jesus Christ of Latter-day Saints has evolved over 160 years to accommodate changing Church needs. When the Church was small, bishops were concerned primarily with the temporal needs of the Church, and spiritual needs were left to the Prophet. At the 1846 exodus from Nauvoo, three kinds of bishops functioned: general bishops, WARD bishops, and traveling or regional bishops. In 1847 the first presiding bishop was called and was assigned Church-wide temporal and administrative duties. Ward bishops worked under the supervision of the presiding bishop, traveling or regional bishops, and STAKE PRESIDENTS. In the late 1800s ward bishops were assigned greater responsibility for ward members, seeing to their spiritual as well as temporal needs. Thus the need for traveling or regional bishops gradually diminished and the office soon ceased altogether. Contemporary Church organization includes ward bishops and a presiding bishop who is a General Authority (see PRESIDING BISHOPRIC).

BEFORE NAUVOO, 1830–1839.   Revelation to Joseph Smith restored the office of bishop in February 1831 (D&C 41:9; cf. 1 Tim. 3:1–7). Edward Partridge was called as the Church's first bishop and was made responsible for operating a storehouse to help the poor (D&C 42:30–39) and for administering property transactions connected with the law of consecration (D&C 42; 58:17). In December 1831 Newel K. Whitney was also called as a bishop (D&C 72). The two served as regional or traveling bishops (D&C 20:66), Whitney for Ohio and the eastern states and Partridge for Missouri (Latter-day Saint Biographical Encyclopedia 1:219–20, 224). The First Presidency ordained them and called two counselors to assist each one. In November 1831, the Lord had revealed the AARONIC PRIEST-HOOD organization, designating bishops as the presidents of the Aaronic Priesthood to preside over quorums of up to forty-eight PRIESTS (D&C 107:87–88). Bishops Partridge and Whitney helped organize these priesthood quorums and selected and set apart quorum presidents. After the organization of the first STAKES in 1834, bishops functioned much like stake officers.

In response to additional revelations (D&C 42:30–39; 51:1–20; 84:103–104), bishops Partridge and Whitney managed such Church temporal matters as paying bills, buying and selling lands and goods, helping with construction projects, printing, and assisting the poor. In Missouri, where members consecrated and pooled belongings, Bishop Partridge signed the consecration deeds, received donations into a BISHOP'S STOREHOUSE, and deeded back donated and purchased properties based on members' needs. He was remunerated for his full-time service.

NAUVOO PERIOD, 1839–1846.   In 1841, when the law of TITHING replaced deeding all of one's property to the Church, bishops helped receive and disburse tithes. However, the Prophet Joseph Smith as Church President and trustee-in-trust held title to Church properties and established Church financial policies.

The office of ward bishops began with the establishment of the first wards in Nauvoo. There, bishops Newel K. Whitney and George Miller, who replaced Bishop Partridge (who had died in 1840), had general jurisdictions and also served in an assigned municipal ward. By 1842 Nauvoo's thirteen wards each had a bishop with two counselors. Their main tasks were to process tithes and to assist newcomers and aid the poor, which they accomplished with donated FAST OFFERINGS. Bishops also carried a major responsibility for dealing with ward members in cases of wrongdoing. However, bishops rarely conducted Sunday worship meetings; such services were held outdoors on a citywide or stake basis or in individual homes. Nauvoo bishops collectively organized and directed the work of deacons, teachers, and priests quorums in the city.

By the time of the exodus from Nauvoo, the Church had three types of bishops: general bishops, who in 1845 became trustees for the Church; ward bishops; and traveling bishops sent beyond Nauvoo to receive Church funds.

EXODUS AND EARLY UTAH, 1846–1900.   During the exodus, ordained and acting bishops cared for the needy through tithes, offerings, and labor. Winter Quarters was divided into twenty-two wards, each with a bishop. By 1848 bishops in Kanesville, Iowa, exercised civil as well as ecclesiastical authority. On April 6, 1847, Bishop Newel K. Whitney became the first presiding bishop for the entire Church.

When Latter-day Saints first settled in Utah, the norm was for each settlement to have a president and at least one bishop (the nucleus of an embryonic stake). Salt Lake City, the largest settlement, was divided into nineteen wards in 1849, each with a bishop and two counselors. When Presiding Bishop Whitney died in 1850, he was replaced by Bishop Edward Hunter, who was given two counselors, thereby creating the first PRESIDING BISHOPRIC. They were responsible for Church temporal affairs, for local bishops, and for stake Aaronic Priesthood quorums. Bishop Hunter met every two weeks with northern Utah bishops to coordinate efforts regarding public works, tithes, resources, immigration and immigrants, and the needy. However, the First Presidency, not the Presiding Bishopric, made finance and resource policy and called and released bishops.

In each stake, bishops called men, and later, boys, to fill stake-level deacons' quorums, teachers' quorums, and priests' quorums, and gave them responsibilities in their wards. The basic ward officers for the pioneer Utah period were the BISHOPRIC and the teachers' quorum, then called block teachers or ward teachers (*see* HOME TEACHING). Under direction of the bishop, teachers visited members in their homes, settled disputes, and helped the needy. Teachers and bishoprics heard charges of wrongdoing and decided guilt or innocence. Bishops, as Church judges, conducted inquiries regarding sin and held bishops' courts, if necessary, to excommunicate, disfellowship, or exonerate (*see* DISCIPLINARY PROCEDURES). During the Reformation (LDS) of 1856–1857, bishops and teachers saw to the catechizations interviews, and rebaptism of members.

Bishops spent much of their time managing tithing. Most tithes were "in kind," necessitating the creation of bishop's storehouses, which included corrals for animals and bins for farm products. Tithing houses sometimes became commerce centers, serving as trading posts, banks issuing and receiving tithing scrip, wayside inns, and transportation and mail hubs. The Presiding Bishopric issued price valuations for donated and traded products, creating uniform prices for the territory. In the largely cashless pioneer economy, bishops used two-thirds of the local tithes to help the poor and to pay for public improvements. They forwarded one-third of the tithing commodities to Salt Lake City to pay laborers on the Salt Lake Temple and various public works projects. Bishops received a small percentage of the tithes to cover personal expenses incurred while managing the donations. By the mid-1850s, ward bishops had taken over the Presiding Bishopric's task of conducting annual tithing settlements with members.

During the consecration movement in the 1850s and the united order efforts in the 1870s, bishops received, recorded, and dispersed donated properties. Ward bishops recruited resources for use elsewhere, such as products in short supply, special funds, supplies for the militia, and teamsters and wagons to take immigrants west from staging points and supply depots in Nebraska, Iowa, and, later, Wyoming.

The First Presidency and the Presiding Bishopric supervised local bishops through visits to wards, two annual general conferences requiring the attendance of bishops, distribution of circular letters, and the reports of traveling and regional bishops. Stake presidents served as the bishops' ecclesiastical superior line officers. In the Salt Lake, Cache, and Utah valleys, stake presidents held regular bishops' quorum meetings.

During this period, bishops had both temporal and spiritual responsibility for their wards and communities. They called ward officers, conducted meetings and presided over funerals, supervised ORDINANCES, and gave blessings. They assisted the needy through the use of tithes, fast offerings, and volunteer labor. During the 1856 famine, bishops requisitioned foodstuffs to distribute within a ward and to share with other wards. In the mid-1850s some wards created RELIEF SOCIETIES to aid needy Indians. Ward Relief Societies became widespread in the 1870s, and the bishops relied on them to seek out and help the needy.

Elders, seventies, and high priests met in stake quorums and were not directly subject to the bishops. In the 1860s and 1870s bishops helped organize and supervise Relief Societies for women, and other ward AUXILIARY ORGANIZATIONS, such as Mutual Improvement Associations for youth and adults, Sunday Schools, and Primaries for children.

In 1877 bishops presided over wards varying in size from 171 members in Morgan Stake wards (northern Utah) to 808 members in Utah Stake wards (central Utah). Each stake contained an average of twelve wards. An average ward had 432 members, 81 families, 13 high priests, 19 seventies, 38 elders, 6 priests, 6 teachers, and 10 deacons. During a thorough reorganization of the priesthood in 1877, President Brigham Young added 140 wards to the existing 101, retaining 56 bishops and ordaining 185 new ones. Most bishopric counselors were newly called, too, and were required to be high priests. Thus in 1877 new personnel comprised about 80 percent of the Church's bishoprics.

New instructions directed bishops to account for their ward members; keep Aaronic Priesthood units staffed; attend weekly Aaronic Priesthood meetings and monthly stake priesthood meetings; operate an effective ward teaching program; conduct the sacrament during Sunday School; turn in monthly and quarterly reports of membership, finances, and ward activities; keep accurate records of disciplinary proceedings; support temple laborers; and hold proper Sabbath meetings, thus setting basic patterns for ward organization and procedures today. Bishops' agents replaced regional presiding bishops. In response to instructions to involve boys eleven to nineteen years old in an Aaronic Priesthood office, bishops called them to be deacons in their wards, beginning the shift of Aaronic Priesthood work to the youth. Bishops continued to call elders and high priests as acting priests and acting teachers to do the ward teaching.

Nineteenth-century Utah bishops were the civic leaders in their communities. They encouraged immigrants to become citizens and to vote. They discussed political matters at Church meetings; backed the development of the telegraph, railroad, mines, canals, and cooperative stores; and established and superintended local schools. The average length of service for all nineteenth-century Utah bishops was eleven years, but 15 percent served for more than twenty years. Bishops had above-average incomes. They entered into plural marriage more than other male members; at least 60 percent of bishops had one or more plural wives.

Because of federal antipolygamy efforts during the 1880s, many bishops were prosecuted or were forced into hiding, thus virtually halting their political involvement. Their wards were incorporated so that they, rather than the general Church, owned meetinghouses, saving them from confiscation by the federal government. The tithing system was disrupted and tithe paying declined. In 1889, stake tithing clerks replaced the bishops' agents.

1900–1930.   Beginning about 1900, after Utah had gained statehood (1896), the economic practices of the Church were modified. By the early 1900s tithing had changed from donations of commodities primarily to cash; tithing houses gradually disappeared and the collection task became simpler. Fast offerings also were most often donated in cash rather than food.

A priesthood reform movement from 1908 to 1922 designated the Aaronic Priesthood for boys, with ordination ages of twelve for deacons, fifteen for teachers, and seventeen for priests. Each age group received new duties and standardized lesson manuals. Bishops supervised the ward-level quorums and became presidents of the wards' Aaronic Priesthood.

Another change in 1908 required that all ward priesthood quorums cease meeting at separate times and instead meet together weekly in a ward priesthood meeting on Monday nights. For the first time bishops regularly met with and presided over all ward priesthood groups at once. In the 1930s ward priesthood meetings shifted from Monday nights to Sunday mornings.

1930–1960.   Stakes and wards continued to spread beyond the Rocky Mountain region. Bishops in outlying areas with LDS minorities faced new problems not found in the predominantly LDS state of Utah. Away from the Intermountain West, Church meetinghouses were few in number, and members often lived long distances from one another.

Changes during this period include the creation by the Presiding Bishopric of a central membership file so bishops could receive or send membership records more efficiently, a uniform WARD BUDGET system, achievement award programs for the youth, the regular publication of a bulletin from the Presiding Bishopric to be disseminated to all bishops, arrangement of funds for bishops to attend general conferences, and the improvement of the handbook for bishops. Since ward teachers were ward officers and personal representatives of the bishop, the bishopric personally selected and interviewed the ward teachers and conducted monthly report meetings with them.

With the introduction of the WELFARE SERVICES program in the late 1930s, bishops established and operated ward welfare projects and mobilized ward support for stake projects. They introduced more efficient methods of collecting and utilizing fast offerings and allocated food and clothing from the new bishop's storehouses to the needy.

DEVELOPMENTS SINCE 1960.   The postwar "baby boom" and rapid increases in convert baptisms produced sudden and steep growth in Church membership during the 1960s, which required more wards, bishops, and meetinghouses. The Church established stakes and wards internationally, producing a growing number of non-English-speaking bishops.

To help new bishops, the Church published a wide array of instruction manuals for the various organizations and activities of the Church. By the 1980s new bishops in the United States received several such manuals, a GENERAL HANDBOOK OF INSTRUCTIONS, and various priesthood guidebooks. Because the bishop's tasks became so numerous that many bishops in the 1950s and 1960s were spending most weeknights as well as all day Sunday attending to Church duties, the Church moved to ease and simplify the nature of the bishop's assignment.

In 1964, as part of a new Church emphasis on CORRELATION, "ward teaching," now known as home teaching, became a responsibility of Melchizedek Priesthood quorum leaders, thus removing a major supervisory assignment from the bishops, though bishops continued to visit members in their homes and conduct funerals, visit the sick, and bestow blessings. In the 1970s and 1980s the bishop's service tenure was generally shortened, although length of service was not set; and ward sizes were reduced. Computerization of membership and financial records simplified bishops' record-keeping tasks. LDS SOCIAL SERVICES became a counseling resource to which bishops could refer members with difficult problems. Monday nights were reserved for family home evenings, when no ward activities were to be held, thus giving both bishops and members more time for their families. By the 1980s the Church had consolidated all ward meetings, previously spread throughout the week, into one three-hour block on Sunday, saving bishops and members much travel and meeting time, particularly in wards that covered large areas. In 1990 Church headquarters began a quarterly allotment from the general tithing fund to cover ward expenses for wards in North America. This eliminated the bishop's need to solicit ward budget money through donations and fund-raising activities. The Church also simplified its disciplinary procedures.

[*See also* Bishop; Bishopric.]

BIBLIOGRAPHY

Arrington, Leonard J. *Great Basin Kingdom*. Lincoln, Neb., 1966.
Beecher, Dale F. "The Office of Bishop." *Dialogue* 15 (Winter 1982):103–15.
Hartley, William G. "The Priesthood Reform Movement, 1908–1922." *BYU Studies* 13 (Winter 1973):137–56.
Pace, Donald G. "Community Leadership on the Mormon Frontier: Mormon Bishops and the Political, Economic, and Social Development of Utah Before Statehood." Ph.D. diss., Ohio State University, 1983.
Widtsoe, John A. *Priesthood and Church Government*. Salt Lake City, 1939.

WILLIAM G. HARTLEY

BISHOPRIC

The bishopric, consisting of the BISHOP and two counselors, is the presiding or governing council in a WARD (congregation). These three men oversee all Church programs in the ward. They are assisted in the clerical, financial, and other administrative work by an executive secretary, a ward CLERK, and assistant clerks as needed. (*See also* PRESIDING BISHOPRIC.)

A bishop is called by the Lord to this office through the STAKE PRESIDENT, who presents the prospective bishop's name to the GENERAL AUTHORITIES for clearance and approval. The bishop selects two adult men to serve as his counselors and submits their names to the stake president for approval. Upon approval, the STAKE PRESIDENCY presents the names of the complete bishopric in a meeting of ward members for their sustaining vote. The stake president or a visiting General Authority ordains the bishop by the laying on of hands and sets him and his counselors apart in their positions.

The bishopric selects other men to serve as ward executive secretary, ward clerk, and assistant clerks; they are likewise approved by the stake president and priesthood executive committee, sustained by the members of the ward, and set apart by the stake president or his representative. The bishop and his counselors are ordained high priests (except in student wards, where elders may be called as counselors in the bishopric). All give voluntary, unpaid service.

The bishopric is charged to (1) promote the spiritual and temporal welfare of the members of the ward, with a primary focus on youth; (2) supervise the performance of priesthood ordinances and sacraments; (3) extend CALLINGS to members to staff ward organizations; (4) administer the programs of the Church in the ward, conduct meetings and maintain order in the Church organization and structure; (5) manage the financial affairs of the ward (including receiving local donations to the Church and transferring funds to Church headquarters, and supervising all expenditures of Church funds); (6) oversee the care and protection of the ward meetinghouse and other ward physical facilities that the Church owns or leases; (7) carry out Church DISCIPLINARY PROCEDURES for serious violations of moral law and Church standards; (8) foster a sense of community among ward members, with a special emphasis on fellowshipping new members;

and (9) encourage members to perform their religious responsibilities. Bishoprics are requested to do whatever is needed to encourage Church participation and religious activity among all ward members.

The bishopric is responsible for calling and conducting all of the executive meetings of the ward, including a weekly bishopric meeting, a weekly priesthood executive committee meeting, and various meetings to plan and coordinate youth activities and train youth leaders. Bishopric members also divide responsibility and attend the leadership and training meetings of each AUXILIARY ORGANIZATION they supervise (*see* PRIMARY; RELIEF SOCIETY; SUNDAY SCHOOL; YOUNG MEN; YOUNG WOMEN).

After prayerfully considering recommendations from ward organization leaders who request members to serve in teaching, leadership, and other service callings, the bishopric decides whom to call and issues the invitation to serve. The bishop delegates supervisory responsibility for the various auxiliary organizations, maintenance of membership records, receipting of financial contributions to the Church, and certain matters pertaining to Church education. The bishop cannot delegate such duties as counseling members involved in serious transgressions, convening disciplinary councils, presiding over the PRIEST quorum in the ward, performing civil marriages for members of the ward, and conducting TITHING settlement (an annual, personal report by ward members concerning the donations they have made).

The bishopric has the primary responsibility for developmental programs involving the youth in the ward. This entails promoting and attending activities for the youth, interviewing young men and women regularly, and overseeing the work of adults called to assist in teaching or planning activities. Activities are designed to provide youth with opportunities for recreation, service, and the application of religious principles to everyday life. The bishop focuses his efforts on the young men and women aged sixteen through eighteen, and assigns his counselors to work with youth aged twelve through thirteen and fourteen through fifteen. The bishop is to interview all young persons in the ward individually at least once each year (usually near their birthdays), and the counselors are to interview those twelve through sixteen years old at least annually. The bishop is the only member of the bishopric who discusses individual matters of personal worthiness with the youth.

Those who serve in a bishopric are expected to live with honesty, integrity, and devotion to their spiritual commitment. Their example of Christian service is essential to the quality of their influence among all ward members.

BIBLIOGRAPHY

Hinckley, Gordon B. "To the Bishops of the Church." *Ensign* 18 (Nov. 1988):48–51.
———. "In . . . Counsellors There Is Safety." *Ensign* 20 (Nov. 1990):48–51.

DAVID C. BRADFORD

BISHOP'S STOREHOUSE

The bishop's storehouse system is a network of Church-owned and -operated commodity resource centers that function much like retail stores, with the major difference that goods cannot be purchased but are given to needy individuals whom local LDS bishops judge to be worthy and deserving of Church assistance. Recipients are invited to work or render service in various ways in exchange for goods to avoid allowing the goods given to be a form of dole.

The storehouse stocks basic food and essential household items, produced largely from Church agricultural properties, canneries, and light manufacturing operations. The entire system, where practical, is vertically integrated, from farming and harvesting through processing and distributing. All work is performed by Church volunteers and recipients and is largely independent of the commercial economy. The contribution of time, talents, and resources of the membership of the Church in various areas sustains the storehouse.

The concept of the storehouse and the Church WELFARE SERVICES emerged from scriptural principles, elucidated by a series of revelations given to the Prophet Joseph Smith beginning in 1831, a year after the Church was organized. In one revelation, Church members were directed to "remember the poor, and consecrate [their] properties for [the poor's] support" (D&C 42:30). The goods and money thus contributed were to be "kept in [the Lord's] storehouse, to administer to the poor and the needy" under the direction of the local presiding leader, the bishop (verse 34). Bishops were charged to seek donations as well (D&C 104:15–16; *Welfare Services Resource Handbook*, p. 9).

As defined by Church doctrine, the concept of the bishop's storehouse is founded on the belief that members of the Church should care for themselves and for each other. This is done, first, in families and, second, through the Church. Members are discouraged from seeking assistance from governmental or other social agencies.

The implementation of the mutual help program has varied considerably according to the economic conditions of the members and the organizational structure of the Church. At various times, distribution of goods has occurred through bishops, tithing offices, or bishop's storehouses. Utilization of the storehouse concept received intense emphasis during the united order effort of the 1870s. From that time forward, most WARDS maintained their own storehouse until the introduction of regional storehouses (1934–1936). Storehouses figured prominently in the Church's effort to care for its people during the economic depression of the 1930s and formed the basis for a more systematic approach to shared assistance.

After World War II, the Church welfare system, centered in the storehouse, evolved into an integrated and complex Church-wide production and distribution system. A higher level of coordination between welfare farms, dairies, and canneries was established, and a wider range of goods became available. The Church established central storehouses to supply regional storehouses. In the 1970s, with the maturing of the storehouse system, the Church selectively introduced local production and storehouses in areas outside the United States where need and resources warranted. The storehouse system is also available for assistance in cases of disaster.

Presently, the entire Bishop's Storehouse Resource System operates with efficiency and quality equal to commercial commodity activities, but maintains its spirit of volunteer service and local administration. While the bishop's storehouse system effectively assists thousands of people every year with material necessities, its additional value lies in the character development and spiritual growth of both givers and receivers.

BIBLIOGRAPHY

Arrington, Leonard J. *Great Basin Kingdom.* Cambridge, Mass., 1958.

————; Feramorz Y. Fox; and Dean L. May. *Building the City of God,* pp. 337–58. Salt Lake City, 1976.

Cook, Lyndon W. *Joseph Smith and the Law of Consecration.* Provo, Utah, 1985.

Stewart, George; Dilworth Walker; and E. Cecil McGavin. *Priesthood and Church Welfare*, 2nd ed. pp. 49–61. Salt Lake City, 1939.
Welfare Services Resource Handbook. Salt Lake City, 1980.

R. QUINN GARDNER

BRANCH, BRANCH PRESIDENT

A branch is generally the smallest organized congregation of the Church (normally fewer than two hundred members). At first, local Latter-day Saint congregations were known as "churches" (D&C 24:3; 26:1). Soon these units were more commonly called "branches" (D&C 72:23; 107:39), reflecting the manner in which they were formed—members sharing the gospel and creating new congregations in neighboring communities.

As the Church has grown, STAKES, composed of several large congregations known as WARDS, are formed in centers of strength. In MISSION areas, DISTRICTS are composed of smaller congregations known as branches. Branches may also be found in stakes, typically in outlying communities where a smaller number of Church members can support only a less complete organization. In recent years a new kind of branch has emerged. In large urban centers an increasing number of ethnic minorities, isolated from the majority because of language and too small as a group to form a ward, have been organized as a branch. Furthermore, the Church has outlined programs that may be followed by isolated families or groups that are too small to form even a branch.

A branch is headed by a branch president, whereas a ward is presided over by a BISHOP. Unlike the bishop, who must hold the office of HIGH PRIEST, the branch president need not be a high priest, but must be an ELDER in the MELCHIZEDEK PRIESTHOOD. The branch president and his two counselors have responsibilities similar to, and function like, a BISHOPRIC.

In the United States in 1990 there were 72 missions, 1,112 stakes, 7,750 wards, and 1,286 branches. Elsewhere there were 156 missions, 627 stakes, 2,786 wards, and 4,483 branches (*Ensign* 20 [May 1990]:22; *Deseret News 1991–1992 Church Almanac*, p. 94).

RICHARD O. COWAN

BUILDING PROGRAM

Throughout its history the Church has faced the challenge of providing adequate buildings to serve its growing membership for worship and for cultural, educational, and recreational activities. The "building program" is the term given to the Church's system of central direction, design, and financing for the construction of meetinghouses and temples throughout the world. Under the direction of the First Presidency and Presiding Bishopric, a professional staff headquartered in Salt Lake City creates standard building plans and specifications and establishes procedures for construction and expenditures. Although this program has been extensively developed in the years since World War II, some central direction and planning have existed from the Church's beginnings.

The Church's first two important buildings, the temples at Kirtland, Ohio, and Nauvoo, Illinois, were both projects initiated, financed, and supervised by general Church leaders. Members throughout the Church contributed money, and many local Saints contributed every tenth day's labor. Some young men were called for full-time work, and more experienced craftsmen were employed at subsistence wages paid from contributed funds. Similar procedures were followed for the never-completed Nauvoo House and, after the move west, the Salt Lake Temple and Tabernacle.

As Church membership grew and dispersed throughout hundreds of settlements in the West, design and construction of meetinghouses, stake tabernacles, Church schools, and other buildings became a local responsibility. In many cases, Church Presidents or other general leaders encouraged such projects, and occasionally provided designs and financial assistance, but usually the responsibility for raising funds and supervising construction remained with local ecclesiastical officers.

In 1923 the Church Architectural Department in Salt Lake City began furnishing plans for meetinghouses and seminary buildings throughout the Church. Over the next decade, about 350 meetinghouses and 35 seminary buildings were constructed from these plans, most of them red-brick buildings in an adaptation of colonial style. Willard Young, a son of Brigham Young, directed the department, with architect Joseph Don Carlos Young, another son, providing most of the plans. Non-Mormon architects also provided plans for more than 185 buildings during this period, mostly outside of Utah. Funding and construction remained a local responsibility, except for about 50 buildings that received some Church support. This department ceased providing plans around 1933, and local congregations again became responsible for the design of their own buildings, with only general direction from the department.

The decades following the Great Depression and World War II left the Church with pressing needs for many new meetinghouses, because of unprecedented growth, particularly outside the Great Basin. The Church Building Committee, led by Howard J. McKean, was organized in 1946 to fill these needs. The program began with a ratio of 40 percent general Church financing and 60 percent raised locally, but within a few years this ratio changed in most cases to 50–50. Under this program, the Church Building Department supervised the preparation of building plans by independent architects. The local bishop or branch president became the contractor for each project, working with an experienced construction foreman, usually a local member. Local congregations contributed as much labor and skill as possible. The value of their work was credited toward their share of the building cost, usually not more than 10 percent of the total. The local branch or ward was required to raise half of its share of the cost before construction could begin, and all of it before completion. If the cash flow stopped, construction stopped. More than 630 meetinghouses were built between 1945 and 1955 following this procedure, with few delays because of funding. In Utah and most other areas of the United States, these red-brick colonial buildings with white steeples became prominent features of the landscape. After 1950, various standard architectural plans were also provided for seminary and institute buildings.

By the early 1950s the growth of the Church in the South Pacific created need for meetinghouses and schools in areas where money and skilled labor were in short supply. In 1954, Church leaders, including the new Building Committee chairman, Wendell Mendenhall, responded with a building missionary program. Members with construction skills were called to oversee projects in Polynesia. Supervisors took their families with them and received living allowances. They were to train and supervise young building missionaries and other local volunteers while they built the buildings. This program began with the construction of the Church college and temple in New Zealand. In 1956 it expanded to provide meeting-houses and schools throughout the South Pacific and Australia, using plans sent from Salt Lake City. In 1960–1961 the program extended to meetinghouses in the British Isles and continental Europe, with offices in England, Holland, and Germany. Because of differences in language and building procedures in these countries, local architects prepared plans based on standard guidelines. In 1962 the building missionary program was extended to the Far East, Latin America, the United States, and Canada. Difficulties in supervision and financial management caused the discontinuance of this program in 1965. More than 2,000 buildings were constructed under this system.

In the late 1950s, increased construction in the United States and Canada led to the creation of four area offices within the Building Department in Salt Lake City, each supervising property acquisitions, plan refinement, construction, and financial management of projects within a geographical area. These area offices have been divided and extended through the years to include other countries as well. During the late 1950s and early 1960s, building plans evolved toward more diversified styles.

In 1965 a new Church Building Committee, under the chair-manship of Mark B. Garff, instituted more centralized control of the building program. The headquarters office continued to prepare detailed standardized plans and specifications, including color schemes and landscape designs, for virtually all new buildings. Local architects were retained for each project to help in preparing site plans, obtaining competitive bids and building permits, and over-seeing construction. In 1978 the Real Estate, Building, and Operations and Maintenance divisions were combined into the Department of Physical Facilities, with Fred A. Baker as managing director. Area offices were expanded, increased in number, extended worldwide, and placed under the direction of General Authorities assigned as area presidencies in 1984, with many offices moved to the regions they served. Plans for meetinghouses were still produced in the headquarters office in Salt Lake City and distributed through these offices. The ratio of Church to local financial participation in building projects changed over these years, to 70–30 in 1960, to

96–4 in 1982, and to 100–0 in 1990. In the United States, nearly all construction is performed by contractors, while in some other countries local members still contribute some labor. Where practical, meetinghouses are shared by two or more wards or branches.

The building of temples throughout the world has remained under the close supervision of the First Presidency. The Temples and Special Projects Division of the Building Department (later the Department of Physical Facilities) in Salt Lake City began supervising the preparation of plans and construction of temples throughout the world in 1965. In 1983 the design of temple standard plans was transferred to the Architectural and Engineering Division. In most cases, local architects have been retained to adapt these standard designs to local conditions and styles and to aid in supervising bidding and construction.

The centrally directed building program has been one of the largest and most costly programs of the Church. While the high degree of central control and standardization may have discouraged architectural innovation and flexibility in meeting local circumstances, the system has provided consistent guidelines and orderly procedures for an enormous undertaking. Between 1948 and 1990, it directed the construction of more than 8,500 buildings, supporting and aiding the growth and development of the Church around the world.

BIBLIOGRAPHY

Allen, James B., and Glen M. Leonard. *The Story of the Latter-day Saints*. Salt Lake City, 1976.

Cowan, Richard O. *The Church in the Twentieth Century*. Salt Lake City, 1985.

Cummings, David W. *Mighty Missionary of the Pacific*. Salt Lake City, 1961.

PAUL L. ANDERSON
RICHARD H. JACKSON

BULLETIN

The *Bulletin* (1980–) constitutes official correspondence from Church headquarters to all general and local-unit Church leaders. It was formerly called the *Messenger* (1956–1964), the *Priesthood Bulletin* (1965–1974), and the *Messages* (1975–1980). Issued as needed by the Correlation Department of the Church under the direction of the FIRST PRESIDENCY and the QUORUM OF THE TWELVE, it communicates or reaffirms current Church policies, practices, procedures, and programs. All previous *Bulletins* are periodically superseded by the issuance of a revised GENERAL HANDBOOK OF INSTRUCTIONS and by policy letters from the First Presidency.

J. HUGH BAIRD

C

CALLINGS

The Church of Jesus Christ of Latter-day Saints is organized to benefit all who participate, and all are expected to assist in its labors (*see* ACTIVITY IN THE CHURCH; LAY PARTICIPATION AND LEADERSHIP; WARD ORGANIZATION). The Church is administered according to the principles of individual involvement, service, and self-government. There is no paid ministry in local WARDS or STAKES, and the work of the Church is carried out through volunteer service by the members, who are called by priesthood leaders to contribute in various capacities. Callings may be general requests or assignments to follow some particular instruction for the benefit of the Church, assignments to serve in the PRIESTHOOD, or requests to fill specific administrative, teaching, or service-oriented positions. They are usually for indefinite periods of time. Committed Latter-day Saints accept and fulfill one or more callings at any given time. Called by Church leaders whom Latter-day Saints support as inspired representatives of the Lord, members serve until they are released, often because they are called to other positions that need their talents, and as the inspiration of the Holy Ghost indicates.

The most frequent callings are charges to Church members to take certain actions or to perform specific functions. Early examples of this are seen in the revelations from God—recorded from 1830 on in the Doctrine and Covenants—that call for the gathering of his people (D&C 29:7–8; 57:1–2). These calls initiated the dynamic missionary effort of the Church, the migration and gathering of Saints to form a new society of those striving to be pure in heart (D&C 97:21), and the development of support organizations to encourage and finance these activities.

Calls to action can be issued by leaders to the members overall, to a congregation, or to an individual. These calls may be permanent or temporary, depending upon the needs of the Church and the members. Another type of calling is the selection of a member to receive the priesthood. Every worthy male member of the Church age twelve or older may be called to receive the Aaronic, and later the Melchizedek Priesthood and is sequentially ordained to an office in each priesthood (D&C 20:60; *see also* PRIESTHOOD OFFICES). One who holds the priesthood has a permanent calling and obligation to remain worthy to help build the kingdom of God on earth, with family responsibilities being central to that call. In a message "To the Home Teachers of the Church" in the May 1989 *Ensign,* President Ezra Taft Benson wrote that an essential priesthood calling, equal in importance to any other in the church, is to assist Church families through a HOME TEACHING assignment. All offices and callings in the church derive their "rights, powers, and prerogatives" from the priesthood (McConkie, p. 353).

A third type of calling, and the most typical, involves positions in local congregations in either the priesthood or auxiliary programs of the Church. Latter-day Saints believe that a calling as an officer or teacher is a stewardship, where they are to bless those they have been called to serve (Matt. 20:26–28).

The majority of callings are unpaid and temporary. But callings in certain governing quorums of the Church require full-time service and in some cases are permanent, with financial support if needed (*see* GENERAL AUTHORITIES). Any worthy member can receive a full-time unpaid call to serve as a missionary, MISSION PRESIDENT, or as a TEMPLE PRESIDENT AND MATRON, but these callings are for a limited number of months or years. As of 1990, for example, every worthy unmarried young man (eligible at age nineteen) is expected to serve a period as a full-time missionary, without reimbursement from the Church. Worthy young women who so choose may receive mission calls at age twenty-one.

One purpose of Church callings is to benefit individual members by letting them do the work of the Church. Responsibility and authority are distributed locally. Leaders delegate to officers and teachers the responsibility of conceiving, planning, preparing, and executing the activities pertinent to their callings (D&C 107:99). This decentralized organization encourages initiative and personal growth among members of local wards and stakes. Through service, members learn their responsibility and their capacity, enlarge their understanding, and increase their commitment to the gospel (D&C 58:26–28; Matt. 10:39).

Calls are issued through an orderly process. The first step involves the selection of those to be called. For example, the presiding authority (the STAKE PRESIDENT or BISHOP) is to thoughtfully and prayerfully evaluate possible candidates for each office or teaching responsibility. Other leaders who eventually will be working closely with the person may be asked to suggest the names of a few candidates they think could serve ably. Newly called presidents of quorums or auxiliaries are given the right and responsibility of submitting the names of those they wish to be their counselors, and unless there are problems of availability or worthiness, such candidates are given priority. Personal worthiness, ability, willingness to serve, individual and family circumstances, whether the calling would benefit those being served, and the possible impact on the lives of the member and the member's family are to be considered carefully. The prime consideration for a leader in selecting a person for a calling is confirmation by the Holy Ghost of the correctness of the final selection. When leaders select members to fulfill callings in this manner, members understand that callings have divine approval.

The second step involved in extending a call requires the authorized leader to hold a private interview with the member to issue and explain the calling. When a wife, husband, or child is to receive a call, it is recommended that the husband, wife, or parents of the candidate be consulted regarding the calling. Support by family members of the one who is receiving a call is an important consideration.

All calls respect individual agency with the decision to accept or decline resting with the member being called. It is considered an opportunity and honor to be asked to serve; however, calls require sacrifice, and they may come at inconvenient times. Therefore, the persons called are counseled to make the decision by examining their circumstances and taking the matter to the Lord in prayer. To accept a calling requires humility, invites personal prayer, and inspires increased commitment. Many of the blessings associated with callings result from the voluntary nature of the service. When the calling is viewed as a sacred stewardship, the dedication to the calling is of high quality. If a member decides, because of an unwillingness to serve, not to accept a call from God, the decision is viewed with regret by those issuing the call (Widtsoe, p. 199).

The third step in the process is the presentation of the name of the person called to a constituent body of members for a sustaining vote. According to the principle of COMMON CONSENT in the Church, no person is to serve in an official calling without the consent of the membership (D&C 20:65). The sustaining vote is not an election, but signifies that members know of no reason why the individual should be disqualified from service and that they are willing to offer cooperation and support (Arrington and Bitton, p. 208). Members are instructed to have faith and be supportive of those called to serve. At least once a year, members have the opportunity in a ward or branch conference to formally sustain their entire general and local Church leadership.

After receiving the consent of the Church, the call is completed by the laying on of hands by authorized priesthood holders. This act of ordination, or SETTING APART, confers the authority of the office or position and testifies "visibly and without question, that the powers or keys or prerogatives are vested in the recipient" (McConkie, p. 326). A priesthood blessing is given to the one called, the fulfillment of which is conditional upon faithful service. Generally, members anticipate receiving the ordinance of being set apart and are spiritually uplifted.

Once sustained and set apart in a calling, members receive training in their new responsibilities through their leaders and Church-produced manuals, as well as during in-service meetings and special conferences (see LEADERSHIP TRAINING). It is understood that individuals will serve in particular callings for a time then be released, giving them the opportunity to support others in the position who once supported them. Ordinarily, members do not resign from their callings; they are released by the presiding authority.

However, a member may go to the presiding authority to ask that new circumstances be considered and a release extended, if necessary. Releases are announced to the congregation and a vote of appreciation is offered to recognize the member's service.

Duration of service in a calling depends on the member's circumstances, the needs and resources of the Church, and the whisperings of the Spirit to the presiding authority. It is not the practice of the Church to "promote" persons from one position to another. All positions are considered equally necessary (1 Cor. 12:12–31), and positions of high visibility often involve increased responsibility and commitment of time. Similarly, members do not volunteer, campaign, or call themselves to positions. President J. Reuben Clark, Jr., explained that "in the service of the Lord, it is not where you serve but how" (*IE* 54 [June 1951]:412). The collective strength of the Church is enhanced through every member receiving broad experience in a variety of callings.

BIBLIOGRAPHY

Arrington, Leonard R., and Davis Bitton. *The Mormon Experience*, pp. 207–208. New York City, 1979.

McConkie, Bruce R. *A New Witness for the Articles of Faith*, pp. 305–354. Salt Lake City, 1985.

Widtsoe, John A. *Priesthood and Church Government*, pp. 193–205, 233–45. Salt Lake City, 1939.

BRIAN L. PITCHER

CHILDREN'S FRIEND, THE

Published by the PRIMARY, the *Children's Friend* was the children's magazine of the Church from 1902 through 1970. Reflecting its pioneer heritage, the January 1902 first issue (2,000 copies) was mailed out hand-wrapped in used but ironed wrapping paper and tied with string collected from nearby homes. May Anderson, editor of the magazine from 1902 until 1940, wrote in the first issue, "The basis of all our work will be to make the children want to live better lives." The first attempt to accomplish this was made by printing materials for the leaders and teachers of children: lesson guides, stories from the lives of outstanding men and women, stories about children, songs, memory work, handiwork projects, and specific instructions to Primary workers. Later a section for parents was added, and in 1909 a more direct approach was attempted by including materials for the children themselves in girls' and boys' departments. Later, pictures, riddles, continued stories, and a "Just for Fun" page were added (1913). In 1923 the size of the pages was doubled and the contents were directed more toward the children. Some of its stories were dramatized on "The Children's Friend of the Air" program over a local radio station in Salt Lake City.

Sister Anderson was succeeded as editor by May Green Hinckley (1940–1943), Adele Cannon Howells (1943–1951), and LaVern W. Parmley (1951–1970). In January 1971, as the Church consolidated its magazines, the *Children's Friend* was replaced by the FRIEND magazine, the current publication designed expressly for the children of the Church.

BIBLIOGRAPHY
Kerr, Marion Belnap. *"The Children's Friend* for Fifty Years." *Children's Friend* 51 (Jan.–Feb. 1952):29, 76.

VIVIAN PAULSEN

CHURCH OF THE FIRSTBORN

The church of the Firstborn is Christ's heavenly church, and its members are exalted beings who gain an inheritance in the highest heaven of the celestial world and for whom the family continues in eternity.

In the scriptures Jesus Christ is called the Firstborn. He was the first spirit child born of God the Father in the premortal existence and was in the beginning with God (John 1:1–5, 14). Christ also became the Firstborn from the dead, the first person resurrected, "that in all things he might have the preeminence" (Col. 1:18; Acts 26:23; 1 Cor. 15:23; Rev. 1:5). Even as the first principles and ORDI-NANCES, including baptism in water and the reception of the Holy Ghost, constitute the gate into the earthly Church of Jesus Christ, so higher ordinances of the priesthood constitute the gate into the church of the Firstborn. To secure the blessings that pertain to the church of the Firstborn, one must obey the gospel from the heart, receive all of the ordinances that pertain to the house of the Lord, and be sealed by the Holy Spirit of promise in the celestial kingdom of God (D&C 76:67, 71, 94; 77:11; 78:21; 88:1–5; *TPJS*, p. 237).

Revelations to the Prophet Joseph Smith supplement those of the New Testament to indicate that the church of the Firstborn consists of those who have the inheritance of the Firstborn and become joint-heirs with Christ in receiving all that the Father has (Rom. 8:14–17; D&C 84:33–38). The Lord said, "If you keep my commandments you shall receive of his fulness, and be glorified in me as I am in the Father; . . . I . . . am the Firstborn; . . . And all those who are begotten through me are partakers of the glory of the same, and are the church of the Firstborn" (D&C 93:20–22). The church of the Firstborn is the divine patriarchal order in its eternal form. Building the priesthood family order on this earth by receiving sealings in the temple is a preparation and foundation for this blessing in eternity.

When persons have proved themselves faithful in all things required by the Lord, it is their privilege to receive covenants and obligations that will enable them to be heirs of God as members of the church of the Firstborn. They are "sealed by the Holy Spirit of promise" and are those "into whose hands the Father has given all things" (D&C 76:51–55). They will be priests and priestesses, kings and queens, receiving the Father's glory, having the fulness of knowledge, wisdom, power, and dominion (D&C 76:56–62; cf. 107:19). At the second coming of Jesus Christ, the "general assembly of the church of the Firstborn" will descend with him (Heb. 12:22–23; JST Gen. 9:23; D&C 76:54, 63).

BIBLIOGRAPHY

Smith, Joseph Fielding. *DS*, Vol. 2, pp. 8–9, 41–49. Salt Lake City, 1973.

IVAN J. BARRETT

CHURCH OF JESUS CHRIST OF LATTER-DAY SAINTS, THE

The Church of Jesus Christ of Latter-day Saints is the official name of the Church established on April 6, 1830, at Fayette, New York, under the direction of the Prophet Joseph Smith. It is commonly referred to as the Mormon Church because of its belief in the Book of Mormon, and members are often called Mormons or Latter-day Saints. Originally chartered with six members, the Church has grown into an international organization encompassing millions of members in many countries in the world.

From 1830 until 1838, members of the Church referred to it as "The Church of the Latter-day Saints" or "The Church of Christ." On April 26, 1838, the official title of the Church was given by revelation: "For thus shall my church be called in the last days, even The Church of Jesus Christ of Latter-day Saints" (D&C 115:4).

Each phrase in this name is significant. "The Church of Jesus Christ" indicates that Jesus Christ stands at the head of the Church, and that his gospel, teachings, and divine AUTHORITY constitute the fundamental basis of the Church. The term "Saints" is in accord with New Testament usage connoting a member of the covenant group (Acts 9:13, 32, 41; Rom. 1:7; Phil. 1:1; *see* LATTER-DAY SAINTS). It has no direct relationship to the connotation of "saints" as used in Roman Catholic or Orthodox traditions. The term "Latter-day" indicates that the Church was restored in the last era of human history prior to the second coming of Christ and also distinguishes today's Church from the "Former-day" organization established by Christ during his mortal ministry in Palestine. The Church of Jesus Christ of Latter-day Saints is a divinely restored embodiment of the original Church of Jesus Christ, and the appointed guardian of its doctrine, authority, and divine mission (*see* ORGANIZATION: CONTEMPORARY).

The Church is the kingdom of God on the earth, a divinely established institution through which God accomplishes his purposes pertaining to the salvation of his children. President Spencer W. Kimball suggested that the Church has three primary objectives to help people come unto Christ, sometimes identified as its three principal missions. The first is to *proclaim the gospel* to all mankind. The Church does this through a large missionary force, as well as through the efforts of individual Church members. The second mission is to *perfect the Saints*, which includes teaching them the gospel of Christ, administering the essential ordinances of salvation, and assisting them in a lifelong process of repentance, discipleship, and preparation for eternal life. The third mission of the Church is to *redeem the dead*, making it possible for generations of the deceased, who had no opportunity to accept the gospel in mortality, to receive the truths and ordinances of salvation. This work is accomplished by proxy ordinances performed in the temples of the Church. It leads to Church encouragement of family history research. Later, Church Presidents may alter or add to these missions as directed or inspired by the Lord.

The Church is also a society of believers to provide a framework for cooperative effort, mutual support, and temporal assistance as needed. The bonds of love among the Saints are a vital prerequisite to the accomplishment of the Church's purposes and are identified in the scriptures as one sign of the true church of God (John 13:35; *see* SIGNS OF THE TRUE CHURCH). Latter-day Saints regard themselves as the "covenant people" of the Lord, heirs to the ancient covenant between God and Abraham, and, by birth or adoption, members of the house of Israel. The Church is the instrument through which God is gathering the dispersed tribes of Israel in the latter days in accordance with his promises to Abraham and other biblical prophets.

The Church of Jesus Christ of Latter-day Saints is distinguished from other Christian churches in several fundamental ways. Most of these differences stem from the Church's essential belief in continuing revelation. Thus, Latter-day Saints accept the Holy Bible as the word of God, and also accept the Book of Mormon, Doctrine and Covenants, and Pearl of Great Price as scripture and as standard works. They accept the calling of modern prophets and APOSTLES, beginning with Joseph Smith, and continuing to the present. LDS doctrines regarding the nature of the Godhead, the plan of salvation, vitality of priesthood authority, and the interpretation of scriptural prophecies also differ in various ways from those of the Roman Catholic, Orthodox, or Protestant branches of Christianity. Latter-day Saints emphasize religious freedom and tolerance. The Church does not typically participate in formal ecumenical activities; however, it is committed to cooperate with other religious, civic, and educational organizations in advancing common moral and social purposes.

The Church is governed by priesthood authority. The term "priesthood" among Latter-day Saints refers not only to the body of men who hold ecclesiastical offices in the Church, but also to the actual authority or power given them by ordination to the priesthood. There are two divisions within the priesthood, a lesser or Aaronic

Priesthood, and a higher priesthood or Melchizedek Priesthood. All worthy male members of the Church from age twelve onward are ordained to the priesthood, normally holding offices within the Aaronic Priesthood from ages 12 to 18, and offices in the Melchizedek Priesthood thereafter. Offices in the Aaronic Priesthood include: DEACON, TEACHER, PRIEST, and BISHOP. The Melchizedek Priesthood offices are ELDER, HIGH PRIEST, PATRIARCH, SEVENTY, and apostle.

The Church sees itself as organized after the basic pattern of the first century Church of Christ and in accordance with a series of revelations to Joseph Smith (D&C 20 and 107; A of F 6). Successive Presidents of the Church have refined the organization to meet changing needs and demands of an expanding international organization but have not altered the fundamental structure of the Church as it was first organized. The Church is presided over by a president, who generally has two counselors; together with him, they constitute the First Presidency of the Church.

A second governing body, the QUORUM OF THE TWELVE APOSTLES, consists of twelve men called to be "special witnesses of the name of Christ in all the world" (D&C 107:23). The Quorum of the Twelve collectively holds in latent form the same priesthood authority as the President of the Church, and in the event of his death is the body that governs the Church and installs a new president. Members of the First Presidency and the Quorum of the Twelve Apostles are regarded and sustained by vote of Latter-day Saints as PROPHETS, SEERS, AND REVELATORS, receiving direct revelation from Jesus Christ. These brethren are assisted by members of the quorums of the Seventy and the Presiding Bishopric.

The quorums of the Seventy, each consisting of up to seventy men, have special responsibility for missionary work and also supervise Church activities in geographic areas under the direction of the Twelve. The Presiding Bishopric is responsible for the temporal affairs of the Church, including finances, records, buildings, and administration of the Church welfare services program. All these men are designated by Latter-day Saints as General Authorities because their authority extends over the entire Church. The headquarters and central administrative offices of the Church are located in Salt Lake City, Utah.

The President of the Church receives revelation from God that relates to the whole Church, but all leaders and members are entitled to divine inspiration within the scope of their responsibilities and regarding their personal lives. Such revelation helps bring unity and common purpose to the Church, making it like a living organism, the "body of Christ" (1 Cor. 12:12–28; Col. 1:18).

General Authorities preside over the Church throughout the world, overseeing those who administer geographical units known as wards, stakes, regions, and areas. A stake is a cluster of wards, a region is a group of stakes, and an area is a group of regions. A ward is a congregation of Saints, usually numbering between 200 and 600 members. Wards are usually organized according to geographical boundaries, and all members living within those boundaries belong to the same ward. A ward is led by a bishop who serves usually about five years and is called from among the membership of the congregation; under the direction of the bishop, the ward is usually staffed entirely by its own members. Several wards together, usually no more than ten, constitute a stake, led by a stake president, also called from among the members of the stake. The term "stake" was given by revelation (D&C 101:21) and is linked to Old Testament imagery of Zion as a great tent upheld by lengthened cords and stakes (Isa. 33:20; 54:2). In areas where Church population is too small for wards and stakes to be formed, it is administered through missions, districts, and branches. While the main function of missions is to proclaim the gospel, in some areas of the world they also administer smaller units of the Church known as districts, which are made up of branches, usually consisting of fewer than 200 members. Branches can also exist under stakes if the units are too small to constitute a ward.

Within the wards and branches of the Church, there are specialized auxiliary organizations intended to meet specific needs of groups within the Church. They provide important support to the quorums of the priesthood. The largest of these is the Relief Society, the women's organization established in 1842 under the direction of the Prophet Joseph Smith. It provides cultural, social, and spiritual enrichment to the women of the Church and also renders compassionate service to families in need, hence the name Relief Society.

Other auxiliaries of the Church are the Primary, responsible for the instruction of children under the age of twelve; the Young Men organization, for young men between the ages of twelve and eighteen; the Young Women organization, for young women of the same age group; and the Sunday School organization, which administers Sunday instruction in gospel doctrine to youth and adults.

Local officers and teachers throughout the Church receive no financial compensation. Formal training is not required for holding positions in the Church, nor is there a ministerial career track of any kind (*see* LAY PARTICIPATION AND LEADERSHIP). An individual receives a calling, like a formal invitation, to serve in a specific position by Church authorities responsible for that unit of the Church; such callings are believed to be made under divine inspiration.

Regular worship services in the Church are conducted in individual wards. Members of the ward meet together each Sunday for a general worship service known as SACRAMENT MEETING. The sacrament, or the Lord's Supper, is administered, ward business is conducted, hymns are sung, and members of the congregation give inspirational talks on gospel subjects. Members also meet each Sunday in smaller priesthood or auxiliary groups. In all, formal Sunday meetings may last up to three hours. Latter-day Saint communities are involved in an entire way of life, and a typical family is likely to spend many hours each week in Church-related activities, meetings, and service (*see* MEETINGS, MAJOR CHURCH). Regular CONFERENCES—ward, stake, regional, area, and general—provide continuity and association with the larger community of the Church.

Latter-day Saints regard the family as the basic unit of the Church, and of society, and emphasize the sanctity of marriage and the importance of family ties. Mormons believe that marriage and family relationships can continue beyond this life into the eternities, that men and women are equal in the sight of God, and that the blessings of the gospel revolve around the family.

Observers in the past may have regarded the Church as largely a western U.S. phenomenon, or at least as an American church. However, as of 1990, nearly 40 percent of the members lived outside the United States. Church growth internationally has been rapid since the end of World War II, especially in Latin America, the South

Pacific, Australia, and parts of Asia and Africa. This growth has been perhaps the greatest challenge facing the Church in recent decades. By the end of 1990, nearly 50,000 members were serving as missionaries for one to three years, the majority outside the United States. This missionary corps, becoming skilled in many languages, imparts a cosmopolitan dimension to the contemporary Church.

To the Prophet Joseph Smith, the Lord described The Church of Jesus Christ of Latter-day Saints as "the only true and living church upon the face of the whole earth, with which I, the Lord, am well pleased" (D&C 1:30).

BRUCE DOUGLAS PORTER

CHURCH NEWS

The *Church News* is a weekly supplement to the daily *Deseret News* of Salt Lake City, Utah. It reports the worldwide happenings of The Church of Jesus Christ of Latter-day Saints.

Coverage includes official Church announcements, appointments, conferences, and activities. Regular features are: Messages of Inspiration, Church News Viewpoint, LDS Calendar, current gospel study information, Mormon Forum on timely topics, and This Week in Church History. A staff of reporter-photographers travels worldwide to report on Church events and people. They are aided by an international corps of *Church News* correspondents.

The aim of the *Church News* is to inform readers of happenings in the Church by publishing well-edited stories, colorful graphics and photographs, and attractive displays in a readable format.

News of the Church had been covered previously in the regular issues of the *Deseret News* from 1850 to April 1931, when a separate Saturday "Church Section" appeared. It proved popular and the name was changed to *Church News* in 1943. The *Church News* is circulated as part of the *Deseret News* in home delivery areas and mailed separately to subscribers elsewhere.

"J" MALAN HESLOP

CLERK

Almost since the Church was organized in 1830, clerks have been divinely charged with the sacred responsibility of RECORD KEEPING. Although STAKE PRESIDENTS and BISHOPS have overall responsibility for the records kept in their STAKES and WARDS, clerks are charged with the stewardship of creating and maintaining membership, historical, and financial records. Clerks are lay members of the Church called by stake presidents to serve on a volunteer basis between three and ten hours a week in a stake or ward. Most serve for two to three years, but some have served for as many as thirty years in different clerk roles.

LDS scriptures speak of the calling of clerks and the importance of making a record of ordinances and other significant events in the Church and in the lives of members:

> It is the duty of the Lord's clerk, whom he has appointed, to keep a history, and a general church record of all things that transpire in Zion, and of all those who consecrate properties, and receive inheritances legally from the bishop; and also their manner of life, their faith, and works [D&C 85:1–2].

Clerks record ordinances performed for both the living and the dead, tithes and offerings given, minutes of Church meetings, and historical events. They are encouraged to be accurate and thorough in gathering information and reporting details. They must keep strict confidence and guard the privacy rights of Church members because they keep personal and sensitive information about them.

The stake clerk and assistant stake clerks perform record-keeping activities at the stake level and often are invited to supervise the training and work of ward clerks. The ward clerk and his assistant clerks have responsibility for gathering most statistical data about members that enable the Church to function properly.

To ensure accurate and complete Church records, clerks coordinate the gathering of information, train assistant clerks, supervise record keeping, and make certain that proper financial controls and procedures are followed. They also ensure compliance with audit findings and oversee the use and support of computer information systems. Clerks keep the financial records, recording the expenditure of funds to support Church programs and making it possible for bishops to provide members with information regarding their personal tithes and offerings.

Clerks maintain MEMBERSHIP RECORDS that include demographic information and ordinance information for each member. They record the participation of members in some Church services. Stake and ward priesthood leaders use this information to help members prepare to receive the ordinances and covenants of the gospel. Modern technology has simplified record keeping in the Church. Most stake and ward clerks in the United States and Canada use computer systems that enable them to produce information quickly for stake presidents and bishops and to send information to Church headquarters.

JEFFREY C. BATESON

COMMON CONSENT

Common consent is a fundamental principle of decision making at all levels in The Church of Jesus Christ of Latter-day Saints. In selecting new officers and making administrative decisions, Church leaders are instructed to seek the will of God. Once the Lord makes his will known and a decision is reached, the matter is brought before the appropriate quorum or body of Church members, who are asked to sustain or oppose the action. This process provides for direction of the Church by revelation, while protecting the agency of the members to verify in their own minds whether decisions have been proper and made according to the will of God.

The principle of common consent has functioned in the Church since its inception, though the actual practices incorporating this principle have evolved significantly. The revelation on LDS Church government, received when it was organized in April 1830, states: "No person is to be ordained to any office in this church, where there is a regularly organized branch of the same, without the vote of that church" (D&C 20:65). This instruction was reemphasized three months later: "All things shall be done by common consent in the church" (D&C 26:2). LDS practices may have been influenced in these earliest years by the Book of Mormon model of theocratic government that conducted its "business by the voice of the people"

(Mosiah 29:25–26), and by biblical example (e.g., Ex. 24:3; Num. 27:19).

Evidence from accounts of some early meetings and conferences indicates that many of the New England leaders of the Church felt that the membership should be directly involved in decision-making meetings, including making motions on policy issues, following standard parliamentary procedure for public meetings, and voting to finalize decisions. Individual members sometimes exercised the prerogative to call a meeting, and once it was in session, anyone had the right to address the group. The conduct of their meetings followed the congregational model that was familiar to them. However, before long early Latter-day Saints began to realize that having a prophet as their leader was a reality that must be recognized in decision making, and that they could not follow the traditional congregational model without denying the authority and revelations that God had bestowed on Joseph Smith, these being the essential features of the Restoration that brought them together in the Church.

An incident in September 1830, wherein Hiram Page claimed to have received revelations for the direction of the Church, brought the issue into focus. The confusion of Oliver Cowdery and other Church members that was caused by Page's claim to be a second revelator provided the occasion for a revelation through Joseph Smith clarifying the distinctive role of Joseph as the prophet. This revelation also indicated that "all things must be done in order, and by common consent in the church" (D&C 28:13). As the authority of Joseph Smith and his successors in the office of President of the Church was clarified over the following years by subsequent revelations (D&C 107:65–67, 91–92), the principle that the sustaining voice of the members of the Church should be sought was also repeatedly reaffirmed (D&C 38:34; 42:11; 102:9; 124:144). As priesthood councils and priesthood quorums were introduced into the Church organization, general discussion of policy issues and decision making became more their responsibility in council meetings, and less an agenda item for conferences, which in turn focused more on preaching the gospel.

Today the Church continues to operate by divine revelation and common consent. CALLINGS to positions of Church service at all levels of the organization and ordination to the priesthood are made by the inspiration of authorized leaders and are then brought before the appropriate body of members to be sustained or opposed. Members do not nominate persons to office, but are asked to give their sustaining vote to decisions of presiding councils by raising their right hand, and anyone may give an opposing vote in the same way. This procedure is also followed in accepting important revelations and scriptural additions.

In a much less visible but equally important practice, decision makers at all levels present policy decisions and callings to priesthood councils for their comment and approval. At the local level a BISHOP will ordinarily discuss decisions with his counselors in the bishopric before presenting a matter to the ward membership for a sustaining vote. On many policy and program decisions the bishopric will consult with the ward council and work for consensus in that group before taking action. Following the same pattern, the stake president consults with his counselors in the stake presidency and then with the high council. The First Presidency consults in this same way on matters of general Church policy and action in regular meetings with the Quorum of the Twelve Apostles.

Unanimity is the ideal for all these decision processes because of the importance of unity in the Church: "If ye are not one ye are not mine" (D&C 38:27). The three presiding quorums over the whole Church are of equal authority within their own spheres (D&C 107:22–26), but their decisions are of "the same power or validity" only when made "by the unanimous voice" of the quorum (D&C 107:27). Many important decisions take shape over what seem like long periods because achieving unanimity is highly valued by the quorums.

Because of the emphasis on divine and prophetic leadership and because of well-established norms and values in decision-making procedures, public dissent on a proposed calling or policy is unusual. There are, however, mechanisms for accommodating dissent. Normally, if one or more members find the proposed action objectionable, the dissenting member or members are asked to meet with the presiding officer privately to make known the reason for the question or objection. After considering the objections, presiding officers are free to pursue whatever decision they believe to be right.

BIBLIOGRAPHY

Cannon, Donald Q., and Lyndon W. Cook, eds. *Far West Record: Minutes of The Church of Jesus Christ of Latter-day Saints, 1830-1844.* Salt Lake City, 1983.

Quinn, D. Michael. "The Evolution of the Presiding Quorums of the LDS Church." *Journal of Mormon History* 1 (1974):21–38.

Widtsoe, John A. *Evidences and Reconciliations*, pp. 269–75. Salt Lake City, 1960.

Zuckerman, Michael. *Peaceable Kingdoms.* New York, 1970.

ROBERT E. QUINN

COMPASSIONATE SERVICE

The term "compassionate service" is used in the Church to refer to love-inspired assistance willingly given to meet physical, spiritual, and emotional needs. It requires a sensitivity that perceives human distress beyond spoken words (Luke 10:30–37; cf. 8:43–48), an eye that recognizes the good in people (Mosiah 4:16–18), and an understanding heart attuned to the Holy Spirit to discern what is appropriate to say and do (3 Ne. 17:5–8; John 19:25–27). A call to Christlike service undergirded the Prophet Joseph Smith's formal charge to the Female RELIEF SOCIETY organized in 1842. Aware of the dire needs of the Saints, he said that "the object of the society [is to search] after objects of charity and [administer] to their wants" (Minutes of the Female Relief Society of Nauvoo, p. 7). A Necessity Committee of sixteen sisters was appointed "to search out the poor and suffering, to call upon the rich for aid, and thus, as far as possible, relieve the wants of all" (*History of Relief Society*, p. 68). Since that time, not only Relief Society members but also other Church members have been involved in formal and informal acts of compassionate service.

Present-day Relief Society visiting teachers continue to carry out Joseph Smith's commission with regular visits to each LDS family, discerning needs and providing caring support. Ezra Taft Benson stated, "We urge you, particularly priesthood brethren and Relief Society sisters, to be sensitive to the needs of the poor, the sick, and the needy . . . [and] see that the widows and fatherless are assisted" (p. 7). Through appropriate channels of the PRIESTHOOD and Relief Society, assistance is to be given to the poor, sick, bereaved, homeless, and members with special personal problems and burdens (Mosiah 18:8–9; D&C 52:40).

When compassionate service is clothed in the true spirit of charity—which the Book of Mormon defines as the pure love of Christ—it becomes an all-encompassing and rewarding experience for the giver as well as the receiver (1 Cor. 13:4–8; Moro. 7:6–8, 45–47).

[*See also* Visiting Teaching.]

BIBLIOGRAPHY

A Centenary of Relief Society, 1842–1942. Salt Lake City, 1942.
Benson, Ezra Taft. "Council to the Saints." *Ensign* 14 (May 1984):6–8.
History of Relief Society, 1842–1966. Salt Lake City, 1966.
Minutes of the Female Relief Society of Nauvoo, March 17, 1842, p. 7.

HULDA P. YOUNG

CONFERENCE REPORTS

Since 1899, the Church has published official reports of its annual (April) and semiannual (October) general conferences, commonly called Conference Reports. These reports are distributed in booklet form only to Church leaders (bishoprics and higher), Church employees, and libraries, but because other members of the Church wanted to study the conference addresses, the IMPROVEMENT ERA began in 1942 to devote two issues a year to conference reports. The *Ensign* has followed that pattern since replacing the *Era* in 1971. Those issues have made reports of conference addresses available to the world by subscription or single issue bookstore or newsstand purchase. The talks as printed in the Conference Report volumes (see below) and in the Church magazines have mostly been identical. Those publications are significant resources for the study of the theology, progress, and development of the Church.

When the Church first began holding conferences, many attending the meetings recorded in their private journals what was said and done. These personal records now constitute the primary sources available on the various conference addresses in the early years because no official Church publication printed much more than a list of conference events. It appears that the first full report of any Church conference address was published in the *Deseret News* in 1850, even though several partial reports were published in *Times and Seasons* from November 1839 to February 1846, in Nauvoo. The *Deseret News* was able to print word-for-word transcriptions because a young reporter, George D. Watt, had learned shorthand and transcribed the talks for publication. Watt and others thereafter transcribed a great many conference addresses and other talks for publication in the *Deseret News* and also in the *Journal of Discourses* (Liverpool and London, 1854–1886).

The Conference Report for the Church's fiftieth jubilee year (1880) was the first to be published as a separate booklet (110 pages) exclusively of general conference addresses. The next volume in that series contained the talks given at the October 1897 Semiannual General Conference (78 pages). Since 1899, the Church has published a Conference Report volume for each general conference.

CHARLES D. TATE, JR.

CONFERENCES

[*This entry is composed of three articles:*

    Conferences
    General Conference
    Stake Conference

The first article explains the doctrinal concepts of holding conferences and the various types of conferences held by members of the Church. The second article focuses on the history of holding general conferences. The third article gives the background of holding stake conferences and their usual format.]

CONFERENCES

Latter-day Saints are counseled, as were the New Testament saints, to "meet together oft." Conferences are among the most frequent types of meeting. Because The Church of Jesus Christ of Latter-day Saints is administered by a constantly changing core of lay leaders, teachers, and officers, there is perpetual need for instruction, inspiration, and renewal. The scriptures state: "And now, behold, I give unto you a commandment, that when ye are assembled together ye shall instruct and edify each other, that ye may know how to act and direct

my church, how to act upon the points of my law and commandments, which I have given" (D&C 43:8). The word "edify" means to
enlighten, lift, or elevate spiritually. By "union of feeling," the
Prophet Joseph Smith taught the sisters of the RELIEF SOCIETY, "we
obtain power with the heavens." Conferences contribute to building
that union. In practice, Latter-day Saints often say to each other, "If
you cannot come to receive, come to give." In conferences, as in
other types of Church meetings, the "strong in the Spirit" may "take
with him him that is weak" (D&C 84:106).

There are only general guidelines for conferences. For "it always
has been given to the elders of my church from the beginning, and
ever shall be, to conduct all meetings as they are directed and guided
by the Holy Spirit" (D&C 46:2).

Specific objectives, scheduling, and activities of conferences
vary according to the group being served and may vary from one conference to another of the same group. WARD conferences are held
annually to bring the STAKE leaders, ward leaders, and ward members
together in local congregations to "review the status of individuals
and organizations and to plan for improvement" (*General Handbook
of Instructions* 2–4). Stake conferences are held twice annually, and
are administered by stake, regional, and GENERAL AUTHORITIES.
YOUTH, young adult, and singles conferences are held annually; typically these conferences focus on inspirational experiences and social
interchange. Women's conferences and Church women's FIRESIDES are
also held each year.

The growth of the Church has led to area and regional conferences, which may involve thousands of participants in designated
geographic areas. These conferences are planned, organized, conducted, and addressed by General Authorities.

Two general conferences are held each year, one in April (designated the "annual" conference) and the other in October (designated as a "semiannual" conference). These are the most far-
reaching conferences of the Church and for many years have been
held in the Salt Lake Tabernacle. They provide opportunities to
share the common bonds of fellowship in an environment charged
with spirituality and in a setting different from the local meeting
places of the Church. Prayers, music, addresses by General
Authorities and others, shared expressions of faith, meeting new

acquaintances, and renewal of self and commitments combine to enrich the lives of all who attend or who experience the conferences on radio or television.

The Savior petitioned: "I pray not that thou shouldest take them out of the world, but that thou shouldest keep them from the evil" (John 17:15). Conferences of the Church serve an important purpose in aiding the members to be shielded from the evils of worldly influence and nurtured in discipleship.

BIBLIOGRAPHY

General Handbook of Instructions. Salt Lake City, 1989.

WILLIAM ROLFE KERR

GENERAL CONFERENCE

About two months after being organized on April 6, 1830, The Church of Jesus Christ of Latter-day Saints held its first general conference at the Peter Whitmer home in Fayette, Seneca County, New York. At that June 9 meeting about thirty members were in attendance and other people who were anxious to learn. This commenced a vital and enduring tradition. Each April and October, members of the Church throughout the world assemble in Salt Lake City, Utah, for two days of meetings called general conference. For more than a century these meetings have been held in the 7,500-seat Salt Lake Tabernacle located on Temple Square. Temple Square is virtually inseparable from the tradition of general conference and has been the site of nearly every one of them.

The April conferences of the Church are called annual conferences; those in October, semiannual conferences. Current practice includes four two-hour general sessions on Saturday and Sunday, with a special priesthood session Saturday night carried by satellite to thousands of priesthood bearers throughout the world. Prior to 1977, the conferences met for three days.

Through the years general conference has accommodated the needs of the Church in a variety of ways. In 1954 David O. McKay, President of the Church from 1951 to 1970, listed the following twentieth-century objectives:

(1) to inform the membership of general conditions of the Church— including whether it is progressing or retrogressing, and of its eco-

nomic, ecclesiastic, and spiritual status; (2) to commend true merit; (3) to express gratitude for divine guidance; (4) to give instruction in principles, in doctrine, in the law of the gospel; (5) to proclaim the restoration, with divine authority to administer in all the ordinances of the gospel of Jesus Christ, and to declare, quoting the Apostle Peter, that there is none other name under heaven given among men than Jesus Christ whereby we may be saved (Acts 4:12); (6) to admonish and inspire to continue in greater activity [*IE* (Dec. 1954), p. 872].

From a historical perspective, the conferences from 1830 to 1837 were called as needed by the Prophet Joseph Smith, the first President of the Church. Those attending early conferences conducted the Church's business, heard announcements of new revelations, and exercised the principle of COMMON CONSENT in approving leaders and doctrine.

From 1838 to 1844 the concept of a regular general conference for the Church was set firmly in place and the precedents were established for the annual and semiannual conferences in April and October. Although the business of the Church was still transacted, emphasis was placed on expounding and teaching the doctrines of the Church. A significant body of doctrine was reviewed and revealed during this period.

One researcher has identified six major issues addressed in the conferences prior to 1845 that demonstrate flexibility and sensitivity to timely issues: (1) emergence and development of common consent; (2) initial experiment with a Zion concept and its temporary suspension; (3) teaching and expounding the doctrines of the Church, including new revelations; (4) institutionalizing of the conference system itself; (5) development of a temple-oriented worship, including covenants and principles associated with the preparing of a people worthy to inherit Zion; and (6) exodus of the Church from organized society into the wilderness (Lowe, p. 398).

Clashes with tradition, tensions with neighbors of other faiths, and preparations for the westward movement all imposed adaptation on the general conferences of the Church just prior to the exodus to the Great Basin in 1847.

Conferences continued during the exodus and into the permanent settlement in Utah, although there was no general conference in

October 1846, which occurred during the transition period after the Latter-day Saints had been driven from Nauvoo, Illinois, and before the first company of settlers arrived in the Salt Lake Valley in July 1847.

The conferences from 1848 to 1877 considered pressing needs such as emigration from the east and foreign countries, colonization, and missionary work. Assignments to colonize and calls to serve missions were frequently announced from the conference pulpit without prior notice. Leonard J. Arrington has characterized these conferences as "the cement which held together the Mormon Commonwealth. . . . It was through the instrumentality of the conference that church leaders were able to effect the central planning and direction of the manifold temporal and spiritual interests of their followers. It was in the conference that Latter-day Saints experienced most keenly the sense of belonging to a whole—a worshipping, building, expanding Kingdom" (p. 32).

The last two decades of the nineteenth century were troubled times for the Church because federal legislation against plural marriage brought a financial and societal crisis. General conferences reflected those concerns. From 1885 to 1887, five conferences were held outside of Salt Lake City, and many of the GENERAL AUTHORITIES were in exile.

In the twentieth century because of technology and the Church's improving image, conference sessions began reaching beyond the Tabernacle and to peoples other than Latter-day Saints. In October 1924, KSL Radio began broadcasting conferences. Coverage was extended in 1938 to other radio stations that wished to carry all or part of the sessions. In 1949 the conference was televised by KSL Television. Satellite transmission to interested television stations and cable systems in other parts of the United States was initiated in 1975, and in 1980 the conference sessions were first carried by satellite to Church centers outside of Utah. More than 2,600 Church satellite dishes in North America now receive general conference twice each year.

Conference sessions were first translated simultaneously into other languages in 1962, and by 1990 they were being translated into twenty-nine languages. Conferences can now be heard in multiple languages on Temple Square. As a result of the worldwide broadcasting and translation of conferences, the sessions are more structured and planned than they were in earlier years. Most of the speakers are presiding authorities of the Church, although on occasion other men and women are asked to participate.

General conference of The Church of Jesus Christ of Latter-day Saints continues today as a vital doctrinal and social institution. It touches the lives of hundreds of thousands of Latter-day Saints worldwide. The conference sermons are printed in the Church magazines and are recorded on video tapes.

BIBLIOGRAPHY

Arrington, Leonard J. *Great Basin Kingdom.* Cambridge, Mass., 1958.

Godfrey, Kenneth W. "150 Years of General Conference." *Ensign* 11 (Feb. 1981):66.

Lowe, Jay R. "A Study of the General Conferences of the Church of Jesus Christ of Latter-day Saints, 1830–1901." Ph.D. diss., Brigham Young University, 1972.

McKay, David O. "Seek Ye First the Kingdom of God." *IE* (Dec. 1954):872–74.

M. DALLAS BURNETT

STAKE CONFERENCE

In the revelation on Church organization and government received by the Prophet Joseph Smith in April 1830, Church members were instructed to "meet in conference once in three months, or from time to time as said conferences shall direct or appoint; and said conferences are to do whatever church business is necessary to be done at the time" (D&C 20:61–62).

Once STAKES were organized, the Saints began meeting in stake conferences every three months. The practice of quarterly stake conferences continued from the mid-1800s until 1979, when the frequency was reduced to two per year. GENERAL AUTHORITIES of the Church presided at most stake conferences until the mid-1980s, when the growth in Church membership and the number of stakes made it impossible for an authority to attend each conference. In 1986, General Authorities were assigned to preside at one of the stake conferences, and the STAKE PRESIDENT was authorized to preside at the other. In 1990 General Authorities were assigned to visit each stake for a conference only once every other year.

Stake conferences bring together members and friends who reside within the geographical boundaries of a stake. At least four sessions are held during a two-day period: (1) the first meeting is with the stake presidency and the visiting authorities, if any, to review the activity and progress of the stake during the last six months; (2) a priesthood leadership meeting to train stake and WARD priesthood leaders in Church doctrine and principles; (3) a general assembly of all adults (eighteen years of age and over) where the presiding authority and invited stake members speak; and (4) a Sabbath general session for all stake members, including children and interested friends of the Church. The Sabbath general session features congregational hymns, specially arranged choir selections, stake business, and sermons from the presiding authority, stake leaders, and other invited speakers.

The major purposes of stake conference are: (1) sustaining general and stake officers; (2) releasing stake officers; and (3) approving ordinations to the MELCHIZEDEK PRIESTHOOD, and also enhancing the faith and testimony of the members through leadership training, music, sermons, and the fellowship of the Saints. The meetings are often considered a spiritual feast. The General Authority and stake leaders are well versed in the scriptures, are excellent teachers, and present strong witness to the divinity of Jesus Christ.

MERRILL J. BATEMAN

CONFIDENTIAL RECORDS

Latter-day Saints have developed a long tradition of keeping detailed records about Church activities and their own lives (see RECORD KEEPING). As is true for the working files of most private institutions, the current records of the Church are not generally available to outside researchers. Undeterred public access to everyday work files would disrupt the organization's work flow and impinge on the privacy of individual Church members. The current membership records of the Church maintained by the Finance and Records Department are kept confidential, as are records of voluntary FINANCIAL CONTRIBUTIONS. The Missionary Department keeps the applications it receives from prospective missionaries confidential because they contain private information about the applicants' health and personal life. Similarly, the Personnel Department does not make employee files available.

Despite the general restriction of access to these current records, the Church allows exceptions in extraordinary cases that promise substantial benefits to mankind. For instance, Church officials have provided extensive membership data to cancer researchers and others who have established a legitimate need for such information (Lyon, pp. 129–33).

Most of the noncurrent records of the Church are stored in the Historical Department, one of the world's largest religious archival institutions. Besides housing institutional records, the department also accepts donations of personal historical materials, such as the diaries and papers of individual Church members.

The majority of the thousands of collections in the Historical Department are open and available to most members of the public. Like other major archival institutions, however, the Historical Department restricts access to some of its collections for several legal and ethical reasons. Some other materials are restricted by the terms of their donation. Some of these donor-imposed restrictions eventually expire, making the donated materials more accessible to the public.

The Historical Department restricts some materials to protect the privacy of persons mentioned in them. Experts on archival law have written that "privacy is by far the most pervasive consideration in restricting materials in archives" (Peterson and Peterson, p. 39). The Church's view of privacy embraces more than the legal principle that recognizes persons' privacy until death. "In addition," Dallin H. Oaks explained, "our belief in life after death causes us to extend this principle to respect the privacy of persons who have left mortality but live beyond the veil" (p. 65). Examples of materials restricted for privacy reasons include the records of Church disciplinary proceedings, confidential minutes of Church councils, and journals of Church officials who record confidential information disclosed to them by Church members.

The Historical Department restricts other records because they are sacred. Examples of such records include transcripts of PATRIARCHAL BLESSINGS. Generally, researchers are given access only to their own blessing transcripts, those of their spouses, and their direct-line descendants and deceased ancestors.

BIBLIOGRAPHY

Clark, James R. *MFP* 2:315–20.

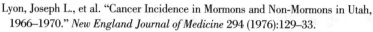

Lyon, Joseph L., et al. "Cancer Incidence in Mormons and Non-Mormons in Utah, 1966–1970." *New England Journal of Medicine* 294 (1976):129–33.

Oaks, Dallin H. "Recent Events Involving Church History and Forged Documents." *Ensign* 17 (Oct. 1987):63–69.

Peterson, Gary M., and Trudy Huskamp Peterson. *Archives & Manuscripts: Law.* Chicago, 1985.

RICHARD E. TURLEY, JR.

CONTRIBUTOR

Edited and published independently by Junius F. Wells, the founder of the Young Men's Mutual Improvement Association (YMMIA; renamed YOUNG MEN in 1977), the *Contributor* (1879–1896) proposed "to represent the Mutual Improvement Associations, and to furnish a publication of peculiar interest to their members and to the mature youth of our people" ("Salutation," p. 12). One of its purposes was to encourage and foster the development of literary talents among the young men and young women in the Church. It contained articles on such subjects as travel, philosophy, history, biography, and gospel topics. There were also letters from the General Authorities, conference reports, lesson outlines for the youth weekly meetings, hymns, fiction, and a little poetry.

The Contributor Company was formed on January 11, 1886, and Wells continued as editor, publisher, and business manager. But when it was purchased by the Cannon Publishing Company in 1892, Abraham H. Cannon became the editor and publisher. Cannon died suddenly in July 1896, and the *Contributor* ceased publication with the October issue.

In November 1897 the general board of the YMMIA launched an official magazine, the IMPROVEMENT ERA (1897–1970).

BIBLIOGRAPHY

Anderson, Edward H. "The Past of Mutual Improvement." *IE* 1 (Dec. 1897):85–93.

Wells, Junius F. "Salutation." *Contributor* 1 (Oct. 1879):12.

PETREA GILLESPIE KELLY

CORRELATION OF THE CHURCH, ADMINISTRATION

Correlation is the process of identifying the role of each part of the Church, placing each in its proper relationship to the others, and ensuring that each functions properly. The parts include doctrines and ordinances, organizations and agencies, programs and activities, meetings, and printed and audiovisual materials. All of these parts should be "fitly framed together" (Eph. 2:21). They function properly when they are connected systematically and operate in harmony and unity. Like the parts of a human body, each has its function, none is sufficient of itself, and none can usurp the tasks of others (cf. 1 Cor. 12:12–28; D&C 84:108–110).

Correlation is a unifying process in which each organization of the Church subordinates limited views to the good of the whole Church. It is not censorship in the sense of inhibiting or channeling free expression and creativity. Rather, it is the way the Church ensures suitable and effective use of its resources.

Correlation serves under the direction of the First Presidency and the Twelve. It provides order to the many parts of the Church (cf. 1 Cor. 14:40; D&C 28:13; 107:84; 132:8) and systematic reviews of proposed action (cf. Matt. 18:16; D&C 6:28). It helps organizations avoid unnecessary duplication. Correlation ensures that Church programs, materials, and activities

- Support and strengthen families in learning and living the gospel.
- Are directed by the PRIESTHOOD.
- Use the scriptures and the words of the prophets as the basis for teaching.
- Comply with policies and meet standards approved by the COUNCIL OF THE FIRST PRESIDENCY and QUORUM OF THE TWELVE APOSTLES.
- Are simple to comprehend and use.
- Conserve demands in effort, time, or money on Church members.
- Encourage people to use local resources whenever appropriate and authorized, rather than to make them totally dependent on Church headquarters.

When the Church was organized in 1830, its structure and operation were relatively simple. However, as the restoration of the gospel unfolded, the Church grew rapidly in numbers and organizational complexity. Various Church Presidents created or adopted the following auxiliary organizations: RELIEF SOCIETY in 1842 (for women), SUNDAY SCHOOL in 1849, Young Ladies' RETRENCHMENT ASSOCIATION in 1869 (which developed into the Young Women's Mutual Improvement Association for teaching YOUNG WOMEN), Young Men's Mutual Improvement Association in 1875 (for teaching YOUNG MEN), and PRIMARY in 1878 (for children). (*See also* AUXILIARY ORGANIZATIONS.) Church leaders also organized priesthood quorums, expanded missionary work into many countries, acquired family records to identify ancestors, constructed temples and meetinghouses, held religion classes, established schools, and implemented a program for assisting needy people.

As the programs and activities of Church organizations expanded in number and complexity, they came to have their own general and local officers, curricula, reporting systems, meetings, magazines, funding, and lines of communication.

Part of the role of correlation was to maintain order among these organizations. In 1907, the First Presidency appointed the Committee of Correlation and Adjustments; in 1908, the Correlation Committee and the General Priesthood Committee on Outlines; in 1916, the Social Advisory Committee (combined with the Correlation Committee in 1920); in 1939, the Committee of Correlation and Coordination; and in 1940, the Union Board of the Auxiliaries. Relying on the mandates found in latter-day scripture, these groups were to correlate Church organizations in their structures, curricula, activities, and meetings.

In 1960, the First Presidency directed a committee of General Authorities to review the purposes and courses of study of the priesthood and auxiliaries. The work of this committee laid the foundation for present-day correlation efforts. The committee identified the purposes of each organization from its inception, traced its expansions and changes, and reviewed its courses of study and activities. On the basis of the committee's recommendations, the First Presidency established three coordinating committees in 1961—one for children, one for youth, and one for adults—and a coordinating council that directed the activities of the three committees. The council and committees, each headed by a member of the Quorum of the Twelve

Apostles, were to correlate the instructional and activity programs of priesthood quorums, auxiliaries, and other Church agencies.

By 1962, the Church had organized its curricula and activities around three groups: children, youth, and adults. In 1965, it introduced a family home evening program with a study manual for families to learn gospel principles and values in their homes. By 1971, the Church had reformatted its magazines by age group rather than by organization—*Ensign* for adults, *New Era* for youth, and *Friend* for children.

In 1972, the First Presidency created the Department of Internal Communications to plan, correlate, prepare, translate, print, and distribute instructional materials and periodicals. As part of this reorganization, the First Presidency created the Correlation Department and placed all organizations, curricula, and periodicals under the direction of the priesthood.

In 1979 the Church published its own edition of the Bible in English, using the text of the King James Version. New editions of the Book of Mormon, the Doctrine and Covenants, and the Pearl of Great Price were published in 1981.

The Church instituted a consolidated meeting schedule in 1980 to decrease the time required for meetings and allow more time for family instruction and activities, placing most local Sabbath meetings within a three-hour period.

Strengthening priesthood direction, the First Presidency organized the First Quorum of the SEVENTY in 1975 and, in 1980, assigned its Presidents to be executive directors of departments at Church headquarters. In 1984, the First Presidency appointed AREA PRESIDENCIES from the Quorums of the Seventy to supervise the affairs of the Church in assigned areas of the world.

In 1987, the First Presidency restated the role of correlation: All proposed official Churchwide materials, programs, and activities must be submitted for evaluation by the Correlation Department. Moreover, no proposed item could be developed under Church auspices or placed in formally authorized use without written direction to do so from the Council of the First Presidency and Quorum of the Twelve.

During the 1990s, the focus of Church correlation shifted from maintaining order among Church entities to simplifying and reducing programs and materials, and to limiting volume, complexity, and cost.

Church leaders have determined that excessively complex and

expensive programs and materials can impede taking the gospel to "all nations, kindreds, tongues and people" (D&C 42:58). As the Church grows in developing areas of the world, it will include many members who have limited education and resources.

The present (1990) correlation process at Church headquarters permits representatives of departments and auxiliaries to propose annually the materials, programs, and activities they want to have considered. An originator proceeds with a proposed item only after it has appropriate concept and final production approval.

From Church headquarters, all communications are transmitted through a single priesthood line from the First Presidency and Council of the Twelve to STAKES and WARDS and thereby to families and individuals.

In local stakes and wards (congregations), leaders correlate programs and activities through councils whose members represent everyone within stake or ward boundaries. These councils ensure that Church programs and resources are available to the people to help them learn and live the principles of the gospel.

BIBLIOGRAPHY

Church News. Oct. 21, 1961, p. 3; Jan. 20, 1962, pp. 6, 14; Dec. 5, 1970, p. 3; Jan. 8, 1972, p. 3.

Cowan, Richard O. *Priesthood Programs of the Twentieth Century.* Salt Lake City, 1974.

First Presidency letters. June 7, 1922; Mar. 24, 1960; Apr. 10, 1973; Jan. 15, 1976; June 7, 1978; Apr. 15, 1981; June 30, 1987; June 15, 1989.

Lee, Harold B. "The Plan of Coordination Explained." *IE* 65 (Jan. 1962):34–37.

———. "Report from the Correlation Committee." *IE* 65 (Dec. 1962):936–41.

FRANK O. MAY, JR.

COUNCIL OF THE FIRST PRESIDENCY AND THE QUORUM OF THE TWELVE APOSTLES

Each week the two presiding quorums of The Church of Jesus Christ of Latter-day Saints meet jointly as the Council of the First Presidency and the Quorum of the Twelve Apostles. Meeting in a room in the Salt Lake Temple, this council discusses and decides all major Church appointments and policy matters.

The presiding members in this council are the FIRST PRESIDENCY, consisting of the PRESIDENT OF THE CHURCH, who has ultimate authority for all matters in the Church, and his counselors, who assist him in directing the affairs of the Church. The Council also includes the QUORUM OF THE TWELVE APOSTLES. The members of these two quorums are the only men on earth who hold all the KEYS, or authorization, of the priesthood, and only they are sustained as prophets, seers, and revelators for the Church.

N. Eldon Tanner, counselor to four Church Presidents, said, "It is in this body [the Council] that any change in administration or policy is considered and approved, and it then becomes the official policy of the Church" (Tanner, 1979, p. 47). Responsibilities of the Council include such matters as approval of new bishops; changes in ward, stake, mission, and temple boundaries and organizations; and approval of general officers and central administration of the auxiliary organizations of the Church, such as the Primary, Sunday School, and Relief Society.

The order and procedure of the Council are rarely discussed in public, but can be inferred from published accounts of the process by which a revelation was announced in 1978. After a considerable period of prayer and discussion among the General Authorities, President Spencer W. Kimball felt inspired to extend eligibility for the priesthood to all worthy male members of the Church. He first presented it to his counselors, who accepted and approved it, and then to the Quorum of the Twelve Apostles in the Council of the First Presidency and the Quorum of the Twelve Apostles. The same inspiration came to the members of the Council, who then approved it unanimously (McConkie, p. 128). After the Council had sustained the President in this action, the revelation was subsequently presented to all other GENERAL AUTHORITIES and to the general membership of the Church, who approved it unanimously (Tanner, 1978).

BIBLIOGRAPHY

McConkie, Bruce R. "The New Revelation on Priesthood." In *Priesthood*. Salt Lake City, 1981.

Tanner, N. Eldon. "Revelation on Priesthood Accepted, Church Officers Sustained." *Ensign* 8 (Nov. 1978):16–17.

———. "The Administration of the Church." *Ensign* 9 (Nov. 1979):42–48.

W. KEITH WARNER

COURTS, ECCLESIASTICAL, NINETEENTH-CENTURY

In the nineteenth century, the LDS court system functioned in adjudicating virtually all kinds of legal disputes among Church members. Since the late 1800s, however, the Church courts, now entitled disciplinary councils, have not been used for the arbitration of private disputes.

The scriptural basis for Church courts originated in the early 1830s. At first, elders conducted trials for determining membership status. In 1831, a bishop, designated as a "judge in Israel" (D&C 58:17), and his counselors were authorized to function as a bishop's court. In 1834, Doctrine and Covenants 102 established the HIGH COUNCIL court and its procedures for hearing original cases and appeals from bishop's courts. The high council court consists of a STAKE PRESIDENT, his two counselors, and the twelve members of the stake high council. The FIRST PRESIDENCY court is the highest available for considering appeals from high council courts (D&C 102:27).

The roles of these courts have varied. In the 1830s, years marked by rapid expansion in Church membership and extensive migration to escape persecution in Ohio and Missouri, Church courts usually provided members an easy, appropriate, and friendly forum for settling non-Church related disputes. Then for several years prior to the Nauvoo Charter, and again in the westward migration until 1850, Church courts pronounced, enforced, and adjudicated a full range of civil and criminal ordinances. Thereafter, until the passage of the Poland Act (1874), Church courts continued to handle civil disputes even though alternative courts were available through the federal territorial government (judges appointed by the president of the United States) and through the county probate judges (appointed by the territorial legislature). Probate judges were almost always Mormon PRIESTHOOD leaders, including local stake presidents and bishops, and the probate courts had broad powers over all criminal and civil court matters in addition to normal probate functions. During this period, however, Church courts handled most disputes between members of the Church. Latter-day Saints turned to the county probate courts mostly in criminal actions, in actions against non-Mormons, and when it was important to obtain a formal court decree.

With passage in 1874 of the Poland Act and with the Supreme Court decision in *Reynolds v. United States* (1879), the federal assault on Mormon polygamy intensified, and the Church courts provided the only forum to assist wives and children in settling disputes with their polygamous husbands and fathers. Government courts could offer little assistance because polygamous marriages were outside the law.

In the nineteenth century members used Church courts in private disputes largely because of the principle of exclusive jurisdiction widely enforced by the Church. Applying this principle, leaders used sermons and scripture to encourage members to avoid the civil courts; they also imposed disfellowshipment or excommunication on members who sued another member in the civil courts. Thus non-Mormons initiated most of the cases in the civil courts of the Utah Territory even though the population was overwhelmingly Mormon.

After Utah acquired statehood in 1896, a regular state court system was instituted. Thereafter the Church court system ceased to consider temporal disputes.

Historically, at all times, many Church court cases have involved sexual offenses. In the early Utah decades land disputes were adjudicated by Church courts because the bishops had allocated land holdings to members according to their needs and abilities to put the land into productive use. In deciding contract matters, the main objective was reconciliation of brothers and sisters in the gospel. In such cases, Church courts gave weight to the likely outcome of a similar dispute in civil court. However, they never felt strictly bound by common law precedents; they used inspiration, custom, scripture, and ecclesiastical instructions to reach equitable solutions with reconciliation and benefit to the entire community as the guiding objectives.

BIBLIOGRAPHY

Firmage, Edwin B., and Richard C. Mangrum. *Zion in the Courts: A Legal History of The Church of Jesus Christ of Latter-day Saints, 1830–1900.* Chicago, 1988.

Leone, Mark P. "Ecclesiastical Courts: Inventing Labels and Enforcing Definitions." *Roots of Modern Mormonism.* Cambridge, Mass., 1979.

Swenson, Raymond T. "Resolution of Civil Disputes by Mormon Ecclesiastical Courts." *Utah Law Review* (1978):573–95.

JAMES H. BACKMAN

D

DEACON, AARONIC PRIESTHOOD

Twelve-year-old LDS males usually receive the AARONIC PRIESTHOOD and are ordained deacons, continuing in that PRIESTHOOD OFFICE until age fourteen. Deacons receive assignments from their BISHOPS that may include distributing the sacrament to the congregation, serving as messengers, collecting FAST OFFERINGS, providing assistance to the elderly or disabled, and caring for the meetinghouse and grounds.

Although the exact role of deacons (from the Greek *diakonos*, or "servant") in the Christian church of the New Testament is not known, tradition indicates that they were ordained to their positions and were ranked below bishops and elders. Their duties apparently involved collecting and distributing alms and waiting on tables. Also, relatively early in the Catholic tradition, deacons may have assisted in the administration of communion and taken the sacrament to the homes of those who could not attend church. They also maintained church properties and read the gospel lection in Eucharist assembly. While closely associated with bishops in their service at the sacrament table, deacons were younger and were understood to be in schooling for greater service upon reaching maturity (Shepherd, Vol. 1, pp. 785–86).

The office of deacon was introduced by Joseph Smith at least as early as the Church conference held on June 9, 1830 (D&C 20:39). Some deacons may have been ordained at the organizational meeting on April 6, 1830 (*HC* 1:79), but the records are not specific.

Latter-day scriptures provide that teachers and deacons are "to warn, expound, exhort, and teach, and invite all to come unto Christ" (D&C 20:59) and are to edify one another (D&C 20:85). Deacons may be ordained by any elder or priest at the direction of the local bishop, contingent on a worthiness interview and the sustaining vote of the congregation (D&C 20:39, 48).

Deacons are organized into quorums of twelve or fewer members, with one called as president, two as counselors, and another as secretary (*see* PRIESTHOOD QUORUMS). The BISHOPRIC assigns an adult adviser to teach and help train the quorum members to emulate the example of Jesus Christ in word and deed and helps prepare them for ordination to the Melchizedek Priesthood and for missionary service.

Church-sponsored Boy Scout troops provide the major activity program for deacons in the United States and Canada, and give them important learning and leadership experiences.

BIBLIOGRAPHY

Lowrie, Walter. *The Church and its Organization in Primitive and Catholic Times: An Interpretation of Rudolph Sohm's KIRCHENRECHT*. New York, 1904.

Palmer, Lee A. *The Aaronic Priesthood Through the Centuries*. Salt Lake City, 1964.

Shepherd, M. "Deacon." In *Interpreter's Dictionary of the Bible*, Vol. 1. Nashville, Tenn., 1962.

RONALD L. BRAMBLE

DESERET NEWS

The *Deseret News* began as a weekly newspaper in Salt Lake City on June 15, 1850, just three years after the Mormon pioneers founded the city. Established by the Church under the direction of Brigham Young, the *News* has had uninterrupted publication to the present. It became a daily on November 21, 1867. From the beginning, the *Deseret News* has championed the U.S. Constitution and "truth and liberty." Editorially it has promoted free enterprise, the work ethic, and high moral values.

The early pioneers launched a newspaper against great odds. Because paper had to be brought in from California or Missouri by oxcart, they tried to make their own locally from rags in 1854. The result was a thick, gray paper that was often streaked with colors from the old shirts, pants, and dresses from which it was made.

The first editor of the *Deseret News* was Willard Richards (1850–1854), who was also a counselor in the FIRST PRESIDENCY of the Church. George Q. Cannon was the editor from 1867 to 1873 and from 1877 to 1879. As a youth, he had worked in the *Times and Seasons* printing office in Nauvoo, Illinois, and had edited the *Millennial Star* in Great Britain. He was mentioned by Charles Dickens in *The Uncommercial Traveler* in connection with his work in Church emigration.

As editor from 1880 to 1892 and again from 1899 to 1907, Charles W. Penrose was a tireless editorial defender of the Church. He fought over many topics, particularly polygamy, and was fond of referring to an opposing editor as "my friend, the enemy." Horace G. (Bud) Whitney, as business manager of the *Deseret News* from 1899 to 1920, increased circulation nearly 500 percent, doubled the number of pages, and left the *News* a substantial financial surplus.

Mark E. Petersen became editor of the *Deseret News* in 1946 after working as a reporter, news editor, and manager. Called to be an apostle in the Church in 1944, he handled both full-time jobs for several years. He wrote editorials for the *Church News*, a weekly supplement, until his death in January 1984.

In 1952 Elder Petersen brought the *Deseret News* into a newspaper agency arrangement with its competitor paper, the *Salt Lake Tribune*. Under the Federal Newspaper Preservation Act, the two newspapers combined their printing, circulation, and advertising departments but remained independent in editorial and news areas. The *Tribune* was the morning newspaper, and the *News* the evening one. Since the partial merger, both papers have shown an annual profit, and circulation at the *News* was increasing as it entered the 1990s.

BIBLIOGRAPHY

Alter, J. Cecil. *Early Utah Journalism*. Salt Lake City, 1938.

Ashton, Wendell J. *Voice in the West: Biography of a Pioneer Newspaper*. New York, 1950.

WENDELL J. ASHTON

DISCIPLINARY PROCEDURES

To aid the spiritual development of its members, The Church of Jesus Christ of Latter-day Saints has developed a system of counseling, rehabilitation, and, where needed, disciplinary action.

Members are accountable to the Lord for the way they conduct their lives, and personal worthiness is requisite for enjoying the full blessings of Church MEMBERSHIP. The judge of such worthiness is in most cases the BISHOP of the WARD, who is appointed "to be a judge in Israel" (D&C 107:72) and is "to judge his people by the testimony of the just, and by the assistance of his counselors, according to the laws of the kingdom which are given by the prophets of God" (D&C 58:18). General Authorities and stake, mission, district, and branch presidents may, in some circumstances, also exercise judicial responsibilities. The term "bishop" in this article usually refers to any Church officer acting in such a judicial role.

Bishops function as judges and also as counselors when they hear voluntary, private confessions from members. They must also determine a member's worthiness before signing the temple recommend that permits a member to participate in temple ordinances. Moreover, bishops judge worthiness before recommending persons to serve as full-time missionaries, before calling officers or teachers to serve in Church organizations, or before a member enrolls at a Church-owned college or university. Although required standards of worthiness vary somewhat in these different situations, most worthiness interviews focus on conduct-oriented questions concerning personal morality and chastity, payment of tithes, observance of the Word of Wisdom, sustaining local and general Church leadership, obedience to gospel commandments, and general activity in the Church.

Because bishops are primarily concerned with the spiritual development of each member, they have wide discretion to make judgments and to give the counsel most likely to assist the member's spiritual progress and, where needed, the member's repentance. A bishop may simply accept a confession from a repentant person without imposing a penalty, may decide not to extend a proposed call for Church service, or may temporarily withhold other privileges of membership. In the most serious cases, bishops may impose disciplinary sanctions ranging from informal, probationary restrictions to formal proceedings that can result in disfellowshipment or excommunication from the Church.

Church discipline may proceed from any or all of three purposes:

1. To aid the transgressors' repentance, thereby helping them receive the Savior's atonement for personal sins. The Lord has said,

"Whosoever transgresseth against me, him shall ye judge according to the sins which he has committed; and if he confess his sins before thee and me, and repenteth in the sincerity of his heart, him shall ye forgive, and I will forgive him also. . . . And whosoever will not repent of his sins the same shall not be numbered among my people" (Mosiah 26:29, 32; see also D&C 64:12–13). Toward this end, bishops often encourage repentance without the necessity of formal disciplinary proceedings. However, in certain cases, unless a bishop invokes formal discipline, a transgressor may be unable to experience the change of heart and behavior necessary to achieve complete repentance.

2. To identify unrepentant predators and hostile apostates and thereby protect innocent persons from harm they might inflict. "But if he repent not he shall not be numbered among my people, that he may not destroy my people" (3 Ne. 18:31).

3. To safeguard the integrity of the Church.

Standard guidelines for conducting disciplinary proceedings are provided to Church officers in the GENERAL HANDBOOK OF INSTRUCTIONS. Disciplinary councils are not normally convened to resolve civil disputes among members (see D&C 134:10), nor are they convened simply because a member does not attend Church meetings or is similarly neglectful. Furthermore, members who request to have their names removed from Church membership records for reasons of personal choice unrelated to serious misconduct need not appear before a disciplinary council to have their request honored.

When there has been transgression, bishops must decide each case according to its unique circumstances, including the extent of the member's repentance. Therefore, the Church does not impose rigid requirements on bishops; rather, they are instructed to weigh all relevant factors and to seek spiritual guidance to accomplish the purposes of Church discipline as the individual case requires. When a bishop imposes discipline informally, the proceedings are strictly confidential and no official Church record is made.

Formal proceedings may involve a three-member ward BISHOPRIC or a fifteen-member STAKE PRESIDENCY and high council. Formal disciplinary councils are typically convened only for such extraordinary behavior as murder or other serious crimes, incest, open and harmful APOSTASY, and flagrant or highly visible transgressions against the law of chastity. Members for whom a formal disciplinary council is convened are given advance notice of the reasons for the council and an opportunity for a hearing. Although legal procedures do not govern the proceedings, the Church observes basic standards of fairness. The proceedings are officially recorded by written minutes. Both the hearing and the formal record are treated as confidential information, and disciplinary penalties are announced only to those Church officers who have a need to know, except when the offender poses serious risks to uninformed Church members. Those subjected to disciplinary sanctions have a right of appeal.

A formal disciplinary council can result in four possible outcomes: (1) no action; (2) a formal probation involving restricted privileges; (3) disfellowshipment; or (4) excommunication. Disfellowshipment is a temporary suspension of membership privileges. A disfellowshipped person remains a Church member but may not enter Church temples, hold Church callings, exercise the priesthood, partake of the sacrament, or participate openly in public meetings. An excommunicated person is no longer a member of the Church, and all priesthood ordinances and temple blessings previously received are suspended. Excommunicants may not pay tithing and, if previously endowed in a temple, may not wear temple garments. They may attend Church meetings. Excommunicants may later qualify for REBAPTISM after lengthy and full repentance and still later may apply for a formal restoration of their original priesthood and temple blessings.

Authorization to reinstate disfellowshipped persons or to rebaptize excommunicated persons must be given by a disciplinary council in the area where the applicant resides. In some cases, clearance by the FIRST PRESIDENCY is required. The ordinance of restoration of temple blessings may be authorized only by the First Presidency.

The isolation of the Latter-day Saints during the settlement era in the Great Basin gave a broader jurisdiction to Church judicial courts than is presently the case, in part because of the absence of a developed state court system. In addition, Church policy has in recent years given greater protection to the confidentiality of disciplinary decisions. For example, until the 1970s, decisions of excommunication and disfellowshipment were announced openly in ward Melchizedek Priesthood meetings, although the nature of the transgression was usually not announced.

Because the fundamental purpose of Church discipline has

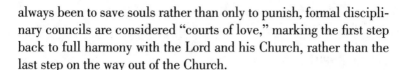

always been to save souls rather than only to punish, formal disciplinary councils are considered "courts of love," marking the first step back to full harmony with the Lord and his Church, rather than the last step on the way out of the Church.

BIBLIOGRAPHY

Ballard, M. Russell. "A Chance to Start Over: Church Disciplinary Councils and the Restoration of Blessings." *Ensign* 20 (Sept. 1990):12–19.

"The Church Judicial System." In *Seek to Obtain My Word: Melchizedek Priesthood Personal Study Guide 1989*, pp. 29–36. Salt Lake City, 1988.

Firmage, Edwin Brown, and Richard Collin Mangrum. *Zion in the Courts: A Legal History of the Church of Jesus Christ of Latter-day Saints, 1830-1900*. Urbana, Ill., 1988.

Kimball, Spencer W. "The Church Will Forgive." *The Miracle of Forgiveness*, pp. 323–37. Salt Lake City, 1969.

Moss, James R. "The Historical Development of the Church Court System." Church History Symposium Paper, 1977. Abstract published in *First Annual Church Educational System Religious Educators Symposium*, pp. 75–77. Salt Lake City, 1977.

Preston, James J. "Expulsion." *ER* 5:233–36.

Simpson, Robert L. "Courts of Love." *Ensign* 2 (July 1972):48–49.

BRUCE C. HAFEN

DISTRIBUTION CENTERS

In order to make standardized administrative and teaching materials available to its members, The Church of Jesus Christ of Latter-day Saints has developed a system of distribution centers around the world. These distribute authorized Church literature and curriculum materials to Church units, members, and officers in approximately one hundred languages. Such materials include scriptures, lesson manuals, teaching aids, handbooks, forms, reports, supplies, and video and cassette tapes.

The item in greatest demand is the Book of Mormon, with over four million copies distributed annually. Since 1989 the majority of these copies are in languages other than English. Some centers also coordinate local printing and distribution of Church magazines in their areas. Each center offers services geared to the particular proselytizing, teaching, and administrative needs of Church programs in its area. Some centers are equipped to print many of the materials they distribute, thus reducing the expense of shipping from Salt Lake City. Materials required in large quantities and hardbound books are often produced by commercial vendors. Wherever printed and regardless of language, all materials are uniform in their content.

BIBLIOGRAPHY

"A Conversation about the Church's Distribution Centers." *Ensign* 16 (Oct. 1986):78–79.

"Family Resources from the Church's Distribution Center." *Ensign* 15 (Mar. 1985): unnumbered insert opposite p. 40.

JOHN CARR

DISTRICT, DISTRICT PRESIDENT

A "district" is an ecclesiastical unit similar in function to a STAKE. Districts are found within missions in developing areas of the Church mostly outside the United States and Canada. Districts are meant to be transitional. Once membership in a district has grown to an average of 250–300 members per BRANCH, with 10 percent or more of these members holding the MELCHIZEDEK PRIESTHOOD, the district will normally be made into a stake and the qualifying branches within the district made into WARDS. Insofar as possible and practical, all Church programs are made available to members living within districts.

Until recent years, there were more districts in the Church than stakes. But Church growth from 1965 to 1990 has changed that ratio. As of January 1, 1991, there were 1,784 stakes and 482 districts in the Church (457 of these districts were outside the United States and Canada).

A district is presided over by a district president, who must hold the Melchizedek Priesthood (either elder or high priest). The district president is nominated by the mission president, approved by the AREA PRESIDENCY, called and set apart by the mission president, and sustained by a vote at district conference or district general priesthood meeting. He serves with two counselors and generally serves with a district council of twelve Melchizedek Priesthood holders.

The word "district" is also used to describe certain other Church geographical divisions. For example, a temple district is made up of a number of stakes and/or missions whose members are encouraged to perform their TEMPLE ORDINANCES in a designated temple.

WILLIAM S. EVANS

E

ELDER, MELCHIZEDEK PRIESTHOOD

"Elder" is an office in the MELCHIZEDEK PRIESTHOOD of The Church of Jesus Christ of Latter-day Saints to which worthy male members may be ordained at the age of eighteen or older. The name "elder" is also used as a general title for all bearers of that priesthood, regardless of the specific PRIESTHOOD OFFICE they hold (D&C 20:38; cf. 1 Pet. 5:1; 2 Jn. 1:1; 3 Jn. 1:1).

In May 1829 Joseph Smith and Oliver Cowdery were promised by John the Baptist, who had conferred the Aaronic Priesthood on them, that they would "in due time" become the first and second elders of the Church (JS—H 1:72; *HC* 1:40–41). Soon thereafter, they prayed for further information:

> We had not long been engaged in solemn and fervent prayer, when the word of the Lord came unto us in the chamber, commanding us that I should ordain Oliver Cowdery to be an Elder in the Church of Jesus Christ; and that he also should ordain me to the same office; and then to ordain others, as it should be made known unto us from time to time. We were, however, commanded to defer this our ordination until such time as it should be practicable to have our brethren, who had been and who should be baptized, assembled together [*HC* 1:60–61; cf. JS—H 1:72].

These particular ordinations were performed at the ORGANIZATION OF THE CHURCH, April 6, 1830 (D&C 20:1–4).

The duties of elders are to be "standing ministers" (D&C 124:137) to watch over the Church, help administer its affairs, teach, and counsel. They have the AUTHORITY to confer the gift of the Holy Ghost by the laying on of hands and to give blessings, including healing the sick. Elders may perform all functions of the Aaronic Priesthood, including baptizing and administering the sacrament. They have authority under the direction of ward BISHOPS or STAKE PRESIDENTS to confer either the Aaronic or the Melchizedek Priesthood upon worthy recipients, and to ordain them to be DEACONS, TEACHERS, PRIESTS, and other elders. Elders may serve as MISSIONARIES (see D&C 20:38–50, 70; 42:12, 44) and may be called to various other positions of leadership or service. In the October 1904 general conference, President Joseph F. Smith said that the elders are to be "standing ministers at home; to be ready at the call of the presiding officers of the Church and the stakes, to labor in the ministry at home, and to officiate in any calling that may be required of them, whether it be to work in the temples, or to labor in the ministry at home, or whether it be to go out into the world, along with the Seventies, to preach the Gospel" (*CR* [Oct. 1904]:4). In areas where the Church is not fully organized, members meet together in BRANCHES under the jurisdiction of a presiding elder, called a branch president (*see* ORGANIZATION: CONTEMPORARY).

All elders residing in any ward are organized into a quorum of up to ninety-six members (D&C 107:89). They are led by a president, two counselors, and a secretary, called from the quorum members by the stake president. The elders' quorum presidency reports to the stake president, but for all, local activity and service remain under the operating jurisdiction of the bishop of the ward. The elders meet as a quorum at least each Sunday. They are responsible to fellowship one another and to assist in administering the programs and activities of the quorum, ward, and stake, with the intent to lift and improve the condition of humankind (*see* WELFARE SERVICES). Elders are directed by revelation to function in a spirit of love, gentleness, patient persuasion, and righteousness (D&C 121:41–46).

The LDS use of "elder" differs from the use of the term in those societies where it refers to the older people who exert influence and authority in the community because of their age, status, wisdom, experience, and character, or by appointment of the group. The term was common to ancient societies such as those in Egypt, Midian, and Moab (Gen. 50:7; Num. 22:7). Elders (i.e., the *zeqenim*, the "old ones") were prominent leaders of the Israelite tribes during the Exodus (Ex. 4:29). They apparently assisted Moses in administering justice (Lev. 4:13–21; 9:1; Num. 16:25), and some were evidently authorized to participate in sacred religious ceremonies (Ex. 24:9–11; Num. 11:16–26). After the conquest of Canaan, the civic authority of elders increased, and they assisted in the government of the tribal communities. They served in accepting a king (2 Sam. 3:17–21; 5:3) and in other community and religious functions (1 Kgs. 8:1–3; 20:7–8). Scores of such functions are mentioned throughout the historical books of the Old Testament. With the prophet Ezekiel, these elders provided the primary leadership during the captivity in Babylon (605 B.C.; e.g., Ezek. 8:1; 14:1–5). Many years after the return from exile, the chief priests, scribes, and elders composed the Sanhedrin, the governing council of Judah. A local council of twenty-three elders governed each community. In New Testament times, elders were appointed as ecclesiastical leaders for each of the local Christian congregations (Acts 14:23; 15:6; 20:17–28; Titus 1:5; James 5:14; 1 Pet. 5:1–4). They associated with the apostles in the councils and governance of the Church, and functioned among their Christian brethren in ways similar to the Jewish Sanhedrin (Acts 11:30; 15:2; 16:4; 21:18). From among the elders of good repute, "overseers" or "bishops" may have been chosen (Acts 20:17–28; Titus 1:5–9; cf. 1 Tim. 3:1–7).

BIBLIOGRAPHY

Davies, G. Henton. "Elder in the Old Testament." *Interpreter's Dictionary of the Bible*, Vol. 2, pp. 72–73. Nashville, Tenn., 1962.

McConkie, Bruce R. *Only an Elder*. Salt Lake City, 1978.

Shepherd, M. H., Jr. "Elder in the New Testament." *Interpreter's Dictionary of the Bible*, Vol. 2, pp. 73–75. Nashville, Tenn., 1962.

Widtsoe, John A. *Priesthood and Church Government*, rev. ed. Salt Lake City, 1954.

R. RICHARD VETTERLI

ENDOWMENT HOUSES

An endowment house is a building or place where certain temple ordinances may be administered, outside of the temple itself. Moses erected a tabernacle in the wilderness as a "temporary temple"; by analogy, so did the Prophet Joseph Smith. Before the Nauvoo Temple was completed, the large upper room of Joseph Smith's red-brick store building in Nauvoo, Illinois, was used to confer the first TEMPLE ORDINANCES on a few leaders of the Church on May 4, 1842, and then on their wives. These ordinances, called endowments, consisted of a course of instruction and rites that included prayers, washings, anointings, and the making of covenants with the Lord Jesus Christ.

The Latter-day Saints occasionally used a mountaintop as their temporary temple, and President Brigham Young dedicated Ensign Peak, a hill just north of Salt Lake City, Utah, as a "natural temple." Though Brigham Young designated a temple site in Salt Lake Valley on July 28, 1847, just four days after his arrival, the temple took forty years to build. In the meantime, the upper floor of the Council House, Salt Lake City's first public building, served 2,222 members of the Church as their endowment house between February 21, 1851, and May 5, 1855.

A more permanent endowment house, designed by Truman O. Angell, Church architect, was soon built on the northwest corner of Temple Square. Brigham Young named it "The House of the Lord." It was dedicated on May 5, 1855, by Heber C. Kimball. The main structure was a two-story building 34 feet by 44 feet, with small one-story extensions on both ends. The first floor had a room for washing and anointing, and also "garden," "world," and "terrestrial" rooms. The upper floor was the "celestial room," with an adjacent SEALING room.

On the average, 25 to 30 endowments were given daily, for a total of 54,170 in the thirty-four years it was used. And an average of 2,500 marriages were also performed annually. In addition, the endowment house served as a place for special PRAYER CIRCLES and the SETTING APART and instruction of newly called MISSIONARIES.

As the Salt Lake Temple neared completion, the Endowment House was torn down in November 1889. The Salt Lake Temple was dedicated April 6, 1893. A long-anticipated holy place for temple ordinances was then permanently established in Salt Lake City.

BIBLIOGRAPHY

Cowan, Richard O. *Temples to Dot the Earth.* Salt Lake City, 1989.
Lund, A. William. "History of the Salt Lake Endowment House." *IE* 39 (Apr. 1936):213.

LAMAR C. BERRETT

ENSIGN

Since 1971 the full title of the official monthly magazine for the English-speaking adult members of the Church is the *Ensign of The Church of Jesus Christ of Latter-day Saints.* Printed in ten regular issues and two general conference issues (May and November), the *Ensign* is the publication link between Church headquarters and its adult members and friends, serving as a general-interest magazine, house organ, and instructional guide. It replaced the *Improvement Era, Instructor,* and the *Relief Society Magazine* in serving members of the Church eighteen years and older.

The word "ensign" is rich in meaning. The King James Bible translators used it to mean a signal, sign, identifying symbol, standard, or banner. Hence, we read the biblical prophecy that in the last days the Lord would "set up an ensign for the nations" (Isa. 11:12), a standard to which Israel and the righteous of all nations might gather in preparation for the Millennium (Isa. 5:26; 18:3; 31:6–9; 49:22; 62:10; Zech. 9:16). In latter-day scriptures, "ensign" symbolizes such "standards" as the new and everlasting covenant (D&C 45:9), the gospel of salvation (D&C 49:8–9; 2 Ne. 29:2), the latter-day Zion (D&C 64:41–43), and The Church of Jesus Christ of Latter-day Saints (D&C 115:4–6).

The *Ensign* magazine proposes to strengthen the faith of members of the Church, to promulgate gospel truths, and to keep members abreast of Church policies, programs, and happenings. In addition to publishing the conference issues, it provides a monthly First Presidency message, used also in HOME TEACHING; a monthly Relief Society VISITING TEACHING message; articles on scripture, doctrine, and member experiences and testimonies; and support articles for individuals, couples, parents, and local Church leaders and teachers.

Circulation in 1971 was 300,000; in 1990 it was 615,000, nearly a 4 percent annual gain, reflecting Church growth trends. All its editors since Doyle L. Green (1971–1976) have been General Authorities: Dean L. Larsen (1976–1978), James E. Faust (1978–1979), M. Russell Ballard (1979–1984), Carlos E. Asay (1984–1986), Joseph B. Wirthlin (1986), Hugh W. Pinnock (1987–1989), and Rex D. Pinegar (1989–). Jay M. Todd has been the managing editor since 1972.

BIBLIOGRAPHY

Editorial. *Ensign* 1 (Jan. 1971):97.

Green, Doyle L. "The Church and Its Magazines." *Ensign* 1 (Jan. 1971):12–15.

JAY M. TODD

EVANGELISTS

The sixth Article of Faith names evangelists together with APOSTLES, PROPHETS, and TEACHERS among the essential offices in the organization of the Church (cf. Eph. 4:11; Acts 21:8).

In an address on June 27, 1839, the Prophet Joseph Smith identified the office of evangelist as a PATRIARCH, who as "the oldest man of the blood of Joseph or of the seed of Abraham" was to bless "the posterity of the Saints" as Jacob blessed his sons (*TPJS*, p. 151). This was the office of Patriarch to the Church. Evangelists, as patriarchs, had been ordained beginning in 1833, although not mentioned in revelation until 1835 (D&C 107:39–40).

Scholars have been unable to define precisely the role or office of the evangelist (Greek, *euaggelistēs*, "one bringing good tidings") in the New Testament. Apparently it was an office or activity that could be combined with the calling of BISHOP (2 Tim. 4:5). The sense of evangelist as an author of one of the canonical Gospels is late. The earliest known pagan and pre-Christian use of the term refers to a person who pronounced oracular statements (Kittel, 2:736).

Whatever the exact nature of the office, the early Christian evangelist was closely linked with apostles and prophets. He was viewed as one who carried on the work of the apostles, but always in a charismatic or prophetic office. One New Testament reference hints that Philip was an evangelist, and mentions his four daughters, who "did prophesy" (Acts 21:8–9).

BIBLIOGRAPHY

Kittel, R. *Theological Dictionary of The New Testament*. Grand Rapids, Mich., 1964.

R. DOUGLAS PHILLIPS

EVENING AND THE MORNING STAR, THE

The *Evening and the Morning Star* was the first newspaper of The Church of Jesus Christ of Latter-day Saints. It was published in fourteen eight-paged, double-columned monthly issues in Independence, Missouri, from June 1832 to July 1833. When the press in Missouri was destroyed by a mob, publication was resumed several months later in Kirtland, Ohio, with ten issues published from December 1833 to September 1834. W. W. (William Wines) Phelps, its editor in Missouri, printed in it a brief history of the Church, a number of LDS hymns, instructions to members of the Church, letters reporting its progress throughout the country, and many of the revelations received by the Prophet Joseph Smith. Oliver Cowdery, its editor in Ohio, printed reports and commentaries about the Saints' difficulties in Missouri and some of the doctrinal writings of Sidney Rigdon, a counselor in the First Presidency.

Because the circulation of the Missouri-printed *Star* was small and localized, Cowdery reprinted all the original twenty-four issues in Kirtland between January 1835 and October 1836, in a new sixteen-page format, with numerous grammatical improvements, and a few articles deleted. The *Evening and the Morning Star* was succeeded by the *Latter Day Saints' Messenger and Advocate* in October 1834 (*HC* 2:167).

[*See also* Messenger and Advocate.]

RONALD D. DENNIS

F

FAST OFFERINGS

The first Sunday of each month is designated as a Fast Sunday, and Latter-day Saints are asked to fast for twenty-four hours and donate at least the value of the meals not eaten as fast offerings. Fast offerings are cash or in-kind donations given to the BISHOP to help the needy following a short period of fasting.

The concept of fast offerings appears as early as the time of Isaiah, who encouraged people to fast and "deal thy bread to the hungry" and to "bring the poor that are cast out to thy house" when fasting (Isa. 58:7). Fasting was also practiced in the postapostolic Church, in which several early Christian fathers advised that "to help the poor with the food saved, fasting is a good work" (Kittel, Vol. 4, p. 934). By the mid-second century some churches held twice-weekly voluntary fasts, and leaders collected funds for the poor following weekly worship services (Swenson, pp. 373–78).

The Prophet Joseph Smith, instituted the practice of collecting fast offerings for the poor in Kirtland, Ohio (*JD* 12:115), where Church members had begun gathering in the early 1830s. Later, on May 17, 1845, in Nauvoo, Illinois, the QUORUM OF THE TWELVE APOSTLES sent a general letter to the Church defining "the principles of fasts," stating:

> Let this be an example to all saints, and there will never be any lack for bread: When the poor are starving, let those who have, fast one day and

give what they otherwise would have eaten to the bishops for the poor, and everyone will abound for a long time; and this is one great and important principle of fasts approved of the Lord. And so long as the saints will all live to this principle with glad hearts and cheerful countenances they will always have an abundance [*HC* 7:413].

During the exodus from Nauvoo the pioneers seldom observed a common fast day but often were asked to give to the poor. It appears that the giving of regular fast day donations was reinstituted in the Salt Lake Valley during the drought of 1855–1856. Of that period George A. Smith wrote:

In all these times of scarcity . . . measures were taken to supply those who were unable to furnish themselves. A fast day was proclaimed for the church on the first Thursday of each month, and the food saved in that way distributed among the poor; and thousands of persons, who had abundance of bread put their families on rations, in order to save the same for those who could not otherwise obtain it [*CHC* 4:109–110].

Since that time, the observation of a monthly fast of two meals on the first Sunday of each month and the donation of fast offerings have become regular practices in the Church. In the pioneer economy most donations—both tithing and fast offerings—were of food or livestock, and members took donations to the local tithing office or BISHOP'S STOREHOUSE. The goods were then distributed to the needy. Today, fast offerings usually consist of cash. Aaronic Priesthood DEACONS often serve as agents of the bishop in collecting fast donations.

WARDS and STAKES are encouraged to be self-reliant in caring for their poor. Bishops are instructed to seek out those in need and to provide them with life's essentials. Surplus fast offering funds in stakes are forwarded to Church headquarters, where they are redistributed to areas of greatest need.

Special fasts are occasionally proclaimed by the FIRST PRESIDENCY when urgent needs arise. Such was the case on May 15, 1845, when "enough was contributed to supply the wants of the poor until harvest" (*HC* 7:411). In 1985, Church members observed two special fast days and donated $10,465,000 to hunger relief and community development projects in Africa, South America, and elsewhere.

Historically, fast offerings have seldom been sufficient to provide for all the welfare needs of the Church, and shortages have been met from general Church funds. The counsel of Church President Spencer W. Kimball remains in effect: "I think that when we are affluent, as many of us are, that we ought to be very, very generous. . . . I think we should . . . give, instead of the amount we saved by our two meals of fasting, perhaps much, much more—ten times more where we are in a position to do it" (*CR* [Apr. 1974], p. 184).

BIBLIOGRAPHY
Kittel, Gerhard, ed. *Theological Dictionary of the New Testament*, Vol. 4, pp. 924–35. Grand Rapids, Mich., 1964.
Swenson, Russel B. "Welfare Work in the Early Christian Church." *Instructor* 82 (Aug. 1947):373–78.

ISAAC C. FERGUSON

FAST AND TESTIMONY MEETING

An LDS fast and testimony meeting is normally held on the first Sunday of each month, where faithful members of the Church are invited to bear a verbal witness of their feelings of the gospel of Jesus Christ. The meeting usually follows a fast by the members, usually from at least two consecutive meals and from liquids also. The fast is officially broken by partaking of the sacrament of the Lord's Supper. In modern scripture, fasting is described as "rejoicing and prayer" (D&C 59:14), which implies that it is more than just abstaining from food. That tone of devotion is also the feeling associated with contributing fast offerings, giving the equivalent cost of the meals, or more, to be used for the poor. The fast and testimony meeting becomes the locus of spiritual sensitivity and contrition, of concentration on the things of God.

A member of the BISHOPRIC or branch presidency conducts the fast and testimony meeting. Usually it begins with an opening hymn and an invocation or prayer, which may be followed by the naming and blessing of newborn children and the confirming of recently baptized members of the Church.

After the sacrament has been administered, the person conducting the meeting expresses his testimony, then invites the members of the congregation of all ages to do likewise. Sometimes they stand in place to speak; at other times they come forward to the pulpit. Each one arises, as prompted by the Spirit, and addresses the congregation extemporaneously. In this setting feelings of profoundest concern are often expressed: appreciation of good family relationships, thanksgiving for the blessings of the gospel, recognition of significant changes in lives, and the fruits of obedience. A faith-promoting experience may be shared or a witness given regarding a point of doctrine or attesting divine inspiration. Such expressions are usually concluded by a prayer or petition in the name of the Lord. The experience is at once enlightening, sobering, and moving. Tears are not uncommon amid acknowledgment of weaknesses and efforts to improve, along with gratitude for divine goodness.

Rarely are such individual expressions longer than five or six minutes. Thus a number of children and adults generally participate in a meeting, which usually lasts a little more than an hour, but may be extended or shortened at the discretion of the presiding officer. In any given year a majority of the membership of the Church, young and old, will have participated in this earnest form of witness on fast Sunday.

One precedent for formal testimony bearing was set at the dedication of the Kirtland Temple. On that occasion several stood and, under the outpouring of the Spirit, spoke of things they had seen and felt. In Kirtland it was customary to hold fast meetings on Thursday afternoons. Since 1896 these meetings have usually been held on Sunday.

MARY JOLLEY

FELLOWSHIPPING MEMBERS

Latter-day Saints consider themselves brothers and sisters responsible to help one another. Their informal acts of friendship and kindness foster congeniality within the Church and assist new members as they move into its social context. In addition, the Church has developed some practices specifically intended to help integrate new members.

After baptism, the full-time and stake missionaries present to new members a series of lessons entitled *Discussions for New*

Members. Home teachers also teach them and help them become part of the local Church unit. The BISHOPRIC, priesthood quorum, and auxiliary leaders also help converts feel welcome. New members are encouraged to attend Church meetings and participate in other scheduled ward activities. Converts are also invited to accept Church CALLINGS (such as teaching a class or serving in an administrative capacity). Women are welcomed into RELIEF SOCIETY activities, and girls into YOUNG WOMEN; male adults and teenagers receive the PRIESTHOOD and begin functioning in their priesthood responsibilities. Newly baptized members grow in love for the gospel as they serve others. After one year of membership, worthy adult members are encouraged to attend the TEMPLE, where they receive TEMPLE ORDINANCES that bind families together as eternal units.

[*See also* Joining the Church; Membership.]

BIBLIOGRAPHY
Discussions for New Members. Salt Lake City, 1987.

LYNN REED PAYNE

FINANCES OF THE CHURCH

The financial strength of The Church of Jesus Christ of Latter-day Saints derives primarily from the commitment of its members to the scriptural principle of TITHING and other forms of voluntary contributions and service. The collection and disbursement of all funds are carefully managed according to standard procedures worldwide and under the direct supervision of the FIRST PRESIDENCY. The Church also maintains limited business investments and financial reserves as part of its larger strategy for supporting expanding ecclesiastical programs. The handling of all funds is regularly audited in accordance with sound financial practices.

Latter-day Saints take seriously the commandment to pay tithing and the Lord's promises as given in the Old Testament:

Will a man rob God? Yet ye have robbed me. But ye say, Wherein have we robbed thee? In tithes and offerings. Ye are cursed with a curse: for ye have robbed me, even this whole nation. Bring ye all the tithes into the storehouse, that there may be meat in mine house, and prove me now herewith, saith the Lord of hosts, if I will not open you the windows of heaven, and pour you out a blessing, that there shall not be room enough to receive it [Mal. 3:8–10].

This law of finance for God's Church has been reiterated in latter-day scripture. In 1838 the Lord emphasized this important law in a revelation to the Prophet Joseph Smith and defined tithing as "one-tenth of all their interest [income] annually" (D&C 119:4).

The years preceding the turn of the century were financially difficult for the young, struggling Church because of the 1890s depression and the escheat of Church funds during the long antipolygamy campaign of the federal government. In May 1899 the aged Lorenzo Snow, President of the Church, traveled from Salt Lake City to St. George, Utah, to comfort members whose lands had been plagued with severe drought. Streams and wells had dried up, and they faced starvation. During this visit President Snow was inspired to invoke the words of Malachi and promise the Saints in their dire and destitute circumstances that if they would pay an honest tithing, the "windows of heaven would be opened." The Saints responded, the rains came, and the people were blessed (Cowan, pp. 15–18).

From this event, the principle of tithing received renewed emphasis throughout the Church. Members responded with increased commitment and faith, and within a few years, the Church was financially sound, and has remained so since. Through the faith and sacrifices of its members, the Church has been able to sustain steady worldwide growth. Latter-day Saints regard the payment of tithing as a privilege and often tell of spiritual and financial blessings that have come through obedience to this law.

In addition to paying tithing, members may contribute to several specially designated funds (see FINANCIAL CONTRIBUTIONS). On the first Sunday of each month, members fast for two meals and contribute, at a minimum, the cash equivalent of two meals to a FAST OFFERING fund, used exclusively to provide assistance to the poor and needy. MISSIONARY support is primarily a family responsibility. Since January 1, 1991, the monthly cost to missionaries and their families has been standardized to the average monthly expense of missionaries worldwide. However, members are also encouraged to contribute to assist those missionaries who have insufficient finances.

FINANCIAL ADMINISTRATION.   Sound cash management procedures are used in the collection and disbursement of funds. Tithing is contributed at the local WARD or BRANCH and is remitted to designated Church headquarters. AREA or regional offices around the world collect and disburse funds as directed by the presiding officers at Church headquarters.

Fast offering funds are collected in the wards, where they are first used to care for the needy in the ward. Surplus fast offerings not required for use in the local areas are sent to Church headquarters or area offices. Any deficits from the care of the poor in the local unit are supplemented from general surplus fast offerings. Thus, a local BISHOP has the means to take care of his ward's welfare needs.

On July 8, 1838, a revelation was received by the Prophet Joseph Smith making known the method for the disbursement of tithing received by the Church: "Verily, thus saith the Lord, the time is now come, that it [tithing] shall be disposed of by a council, composed of the First Presidency of my Church, and of the bishop and his council, and by my high council" (D&C 120:1).

Subsequently, the Council on the Disposition of Tithes, consisting of the First Presidency of the Church, the QUORUM OF TWELVE APOSTLES, and the PRESIDING BISHOPRIC, was established. This council meets regularly and oversees the expenditures of all Church funds worldwide. It approves budgets and financial strategy and establishes financial policy.

Two subcommittees of the Council on the Disposition of Tithes are the Budget Committee and the Appropriations Committee. Both committees consist of the First Presidency, selected members of the Quorum of the Twelve Apostles, and members of the Presiding Bishopric.

The Church Budget Office provides staff support to the First Presidency and gives overall administrative direction to the preparation of the annual Church budget. At the beginning of each annual budgeting cycle, budget guidelines are given to Church administrative department heads, international offices, missions, temples, and other units. Within these guidelines, budgets are constructed at the lowest levels of accountability and scrupulously reviewed through various levels of management and councils. The Budget Committee meets periodically to provide in-depth budget review and to formulate budget recommendations to the Council on the Disposition of Tithes.

The Appropriations Committee meets each week. All expenditure requests throughout the world, except those few which have been delegated to a lower level of administration by the Council on the Disposition of Tithes, are reviewed, checked to make certain the request is within budget, and appropriated. Expenditures that have been delegated are reported to the committee.

FINANCIAL CONTROLS.   Financial controls are administered through the use of financial policy, budgeting, organization structure, and regular, comprehensive audits. Key financial policy comes from the Council on the Disposition of Tithes. Additional financial policy and procedure directives are issued by the Finance and Records Department, which, under the direction of the First Presidency and the Presiding Bishopric, is responsible for the administration of treasury accounting/controllership, taxation, and risk-management functions.

The Church has an Audit Committee composed of experienced businessmen who are not associated with the Church as employees or General Authorities. This committee reports directly to the First Presidency of the Church and works closely with the Finance and Records Department and the Auditing Department to ensure strict adherence to ethical principles and rigid financial policies and procedures. The Auditing Department also reports directly to the First Presidency of the Church and thus maintains its independence from all other departments. Its staff of certified public accountants performs ongoing audits of finance, operation, and computer systems for Church departments and other Church-controlled organizations. Responses to all audits are required and are monitored.

PARTICIPATION AND INVESTMENTS IN BUSINESS.   The First Presidency has established other boards and committees to oversee the management of the Church's investments and reserves. Each of these key committees is chaired either by a member of the First Presidency or by another appointed General Authority.

The Investment Policy Committee is chaired by the First Presidency and includes the president of the Council of the Twelve, other members of the Twelve as appointed, and the Presiding

Bishopric. Its purpose is to establish investment policy and strategy and to review key investment decisions.

The Deseret Management Corporation (DMC) is a corporation with its own board of directors. DMC functions as a holding company for most of the commercial businesses owned by the Church. These companies pay all taxes that are paid by commercial corporations. Some properties are also held for reasons other than investment. In addition to protecting the surroundings of sacred properties, such investments may be maintained to support the ecclesiastical efforts of the Church.

The Church still holds a few properties that were originally established to support commerce in LDS communities. However, as a result of an evaluation of these holdings and their contributions to its mission, the Church has divested many such holdings.

BIBLIOGRAPHY
Cowan, Richard O. *The Church in the Twentieth Century*. Salt Lake City, 1985.
Doxey, Roy W. *Tithing: The Lord's Law*. Salt Lake City, 1976.

RICHARD C. EDGLEY
WILFORD G. EDLING

FINANCIAL CONTRIBUTIONS

Members of the Church may make financial contributions in several ways, including payment of TITHING, donation of FAST OFFERINGS, and contributions to missionary work. Each kind of contribution is directed to a specific purpose and is based on admonitions in both ancient and modern scriptures (Mal. 3:8; D&C 119:4; cf. 2 Chr. 3:5–12; Rom. 15:26).

The payment of tithing is expected of each member regardless of age, income level, or circumstance. Faithful Latter-day Saints contribute one-tenth of their income annually to the Church. Members consider these tithing funds to be sacred monies, and leaders carefully administer their expenditures at each level of Church organization. Tithing is used to pay most of the operating expenses of the Church and also now funds the construction of buildings, including meetinghouses and temples.

Fast offerings are a second kind of financial contribution

expected of all Church members. Once each month Church members are to abstain from food for at least two meals and contribute the cash equivalent of the savings as a "fast offering" to assist the poor and needy. These contributions are dispersed on both a local and Churchwide basis; they are shared as needed throughout the Church and are available to local bishops for the aid of needy persons in their wards. In extraordinary circumstances, as in the case of the 1985 Ethiopian famine, the Church has called a special fast to raise relief funds for a specific disaster. For many years, the value of the two meals foregone during the fast determined the amount of the monthly fast offering contribution. Today Church leaders suggest that the amount of the voluntary offering be associated less with the value of the two meals and more with ability to respond generously to need.

A third kind of contribution made by Church members supports missionary work, a major activity of the Church that is financed largely by individual families. Young men and women can be "called" on missions, usually at the ages of nineteen and twenty-one, respectively, and are responsible for most of their own financial support, including food, rent, clothes, and local transportation. Major travel expenses and medical care are provided from Church funds. Parents and Church leaders urge young people to begin earning and saving money for their missions at an early age. Contributions from parents, family members, and friends supplement the missionaries' own funds to make up the total financial support required. Beginning in 1991, support for missionaries called from North American stakes is donated directly to the Church at uniform rates, but redistributed by the Church to missionaries according to varying costs of living in different areas of missionary service. Married couples may also be called to serve missions, and they, too, are responsible for their own financial support.

Members confidentially submit tithing and other donations to their local BISHOPS. Each ward bishop receives tithing and then remits it to central Church offices. Assisted by financial clerks, bishops provide contribution slips to donors and maintain complete records. They also review contribution summaries confidentially with each member once a year. Contribution records are forwarded to Church headquarters in accordance with uniform practices. Stake officers conduct regular audits of these records and practices.

Bishops, assisted by other ward leaders, prepare and submit annual ward budgets to be approved by stake presidents (*see* WARD BUDGET). Funding levels are determined by the membership and activity level of the ward. One outcome of this procedure is that local expenditures are determined by local need and not by the resources of members in a particular ward.

Until 1990, ward operating budgets were mostly dependent on contributions from local members made in addition to regular tithes, fast offerings, and missionary fund contributions. Youth and adult activities, instructional manuals and equipment, and building maintenance were funded locally. Since 1990, in North American stakes tithing paid by Church members is used to fund all local programs, activities, and maintenance of physical facilities. Members perform some maintenance functions as a voluntary service.

The method of funding construction of Church buildings has also varied considerably over time. For many years, the building of meetinghouses was financed largely through contributions from the local members who would use the building. These building fund contributions were made in addition to the tithes, fast offerings, and missionary funds contributed by Church members. Building fund monies could be raised through request (assessment of members), through a variety of fund-raising projects (dinners, socials, etc.), and sometimes through donations of labor and materials (*see* BUILDING PROGRAM). Temples, which are buildings for special religious ceremonies, were financed for many years in much the same manner as local meetinghouses. Now meetinghouses and temples are constructed largely out of tithing funds.

Because the Church has no professional clergy, it is administered at every level through LAY PARTICIPATION AND LEADERSHIP, and officials other than the General Authorities contribute their time and talents without remuneration. Thus, events such as weddings, funerals, and baptisms are conducted by the lay ministry in Church-owned buildings at no charge to the member for services or facilities. Because the General Authorities are obliged to leave their regular employment for full-time Church service, they receive a modest living allowance provided from income on Church investments.

STEPHEN D. NADAULD

FIRESIDES

Firesides are informal gatherings of Church members and friends, often in homes or other congenial surroundings, as if around a fire. The premises are that the home is sacred ground and that all members are to "teach one another" and share experiences and training, that "all may be edified of all and that every man may have an equal privilege" (cf. D&C 88:122). Typically, firesides feature a single speaker reporting new developments, insights, or interesting experiences.

Religious firesides exhibit ties to the ancient fascination of the warmth and protection of a fire. In LDS life, firesides may be traceable to the exodus across the plains. After an arduous day of travel, the pioneers in the evening would arrange their wagons in a circle, and gather around the campfire to pray, sing, share their spiritual experiences, and rejoice in the progress and blessings of the day. Eliza R. Snow wrote a typical song of this exodus:

> The camp, the camp—its numbers swell
> Shout! Shout! O camp of Israel!
> The king, the Lord of hosts is near,
> His armies guard our front and rear [Journal of Eliza R. Snow].

In this spirit, one journal records, "It verily seemed that the glory of God rested down on the wagons and overspread the prairie."

Holding firesides has become a common Sunday evening practice for socializing, fellowshipping, and learning. WARDS, STAKES, or REGIONS commonly sponsor firesides. They are frequently a forum for returned MISSIONARIES presenting cultural insights from their mission experiences, often with the use of slides, tapes, photos, and so forth.

By extension of the term, there are "morningsides" for high-school seminary students who attend religious classes before school, and "noonsides" for some who want to add meaningful religious moments to their lunch hour. Multistake firesides with large audiences are regularly held at Brigham Young University. Some satellite broadcasts beamed throughout the world from the Salt Lake Tabernacle and featuring presentations from the general Church leaders are also called firesides.

In all firesides, essential elements prevail: prayer, music, the spoken word, and sometimes special activities or workshops. All in all, they encourage lay participation, sharing, and free expression, and lead to deeper comprehension of one's heritage, both religious and cultural, and a "knowledge of history and of countries and of kingdoms" (D&C 93:53; 88:79).

BIBLIOGRAPHY

Journal of Eliza R. Snow. Bancroft Library, UC Berkeley.

RONALD W. PATRICK

FIRST PRESIDENCY

The First Presidency is the governing body of and highest ranking quorum in The Church of Jesus Christ of Latter-day Saints. Its AUTHORITY, duties, and responsibilities extend over every person and all matters in the Church. This quorum usually consists of three persons—the PRESIDENT OF THE CHURCH and two counselors selected by the President. Joseph Smith, the first President, called more than two men to assist him. Other Presidents have occasionally also used this practice of additional counselors as needed. Most recently, Spencer W. Kimball was assisted at times by three counselors.

The First Presidency was established in March 1832, two years after the founding of the Church. Jesse Gause and Sidney Rigdon were called to be counselors to Joseph Smith. Gause served in this position only until that December, when he proved unfaithful and was excommunicated. The calling was subsequently given to Frederick G. Williams, who was ordained on March 18, 1833 (D&C 81, 90). Further direction pertaining to the organization of the First Presidency was given in a revelation on priesthood in 1835. Three men were to be chosen and appointed, and ordained to that office by the QUORUM OF THE TWELVE APOSTLES, "and upheld by the confidence, faith, and prayer of the church" (D&C 107:22).

Latter-day Saints believe that the New Testament APOSTLES— Peter, James, and John—comprised a First Presidency with Peter as the presiding officer, and with James and John as counselors. As an ancient First Presidency, they functioned in a manner similar to the

First Presidency today. For instance, the Bible describes occasions when Jesus dealt with Peter alone (Matt. 18:19; Luke 24:34), and others when the three apostles were involved (Matt. 17:1–3; 26:37–39; Mark 5:37–42). These passages suggest that the roles of these three men were different from the roles of the other apostles. As a First Presidency, Peter, James, and John possessed the special authority to give Joseph Smith and Oliver Cowdery the KEYS of ministry in the dispensation of the fulness of times. It is these keys that control the exercise of the priesthood by all others in the vital functions of the Church in modern times.

Members of the First Presidency are not coequal. The authority rests solely with the President, the counselors having a subordinate role, with the first counselor having precedence over the second counselor. In the absence of the President, the counselors preside in meetings with the Council or Quorum of the Twelve Apostles and other GENERAL AUTHORITIES, and in the conferences of the Church. If the President is ill and unable to carry out all his functions, the counselors may conduct the affairs of the Church under his direction. In such a case, the counselors operate in close consultation with the President of the Council of the Twelve. However, the President of the Church remains the final authority.

The selection of the counselors is the prerogative of the President. A new President may or may not choose to retain the counselors of his predecessor. The counselors are usually apostles, but in a few cases men have been called who were not ordained apostles, the first such being Sidney Rigdon (1832) and Frederick G. Williams (1833). More recently, Thorpe B. Isaacson was called in 1965 to serve in the First Presidency under David O. McKay. In some cases, the counselors have been apostles but not members of the Twelve, such as Alvin R. Dyer, another counselor to President McKay.

The general membership of the Church votes to sustain the First Presidency but does not elect them. Because members of the Church believe that the calling and authority of the First Presidency come from God, their vote is one of COMMON CONSENT, to ratify or oppose a selection that has already been made.

Doctrine and Covenants 107:9 states, "The Presidency of the High Priesthood, after the order of Melchizedek, have a right to officiate in all the offices in the church." As the highest level of authority, the Quorum of the First Presidency has the ultimate power of appointment, presidency, interpretation of doctrine, and all other matters pertaining to the Church. Thus, all other quorums, councils, and organizations of the Church operate under the authority of this quorum.

Affairs administered directly by the First Presidency have included planning general and area conferences and solemn assemblies; budgeting, auditing, educational, historical, personnel, and other general Church departments; and temples. All other matters are administered by the Council of the Twelve, the PRESIDING BISHOPRIC, or the SEVENTY, under the direction of the First Presidency.

In the First Presidency, the decision making is to be unanimous. Close and careful consultation between the President and his counselors helps to assure a consensus (Hinckley, p. 50).

The First Presidency normally meets at least weekly as a unit, then in joint session with the Quorum of the Twelve Apostles to consider matters needing their attention. It is in this COUNCIL OF THE FIRST PRESIDENCY AND THE QUORUM OF THE TWELVE APOSTLES that any changes in administration or policy for the Church are considered and approved.

The First Presidency also meets weekly with the Presiding Bishopric. Meetings are held each month with all the General Authorities, where they are informed about any changes in programs or procedures. In addition, the First Presidency meets as needed with other councils, boards, and groups to which various responsibilities have been delegated.

Upon the death of the President, the Quorum of the First Presidency is automatically dissolved and the ultimate authority of the Church passes immediately to the Twelve, with the presiding officer being the President of the Quorum of the Twelve Apostles. The counselors, if they are apostles, return to their respective positions in that quorum according to seniority of appointment. The First Presidency is reconstituted at the calling of a new President, who in every instance has been the President of the Quorum of the Twelve Apostles, and then he selects his own counselors. Once this is accomplished, supreme authority returns to the First Presidency.

BIBLIOGRAPHY

Hinckley, Gordon B. "In . . . Counsellors There Is Safety." *Ensign* 20 (Nov. 1990):48–51.

Tanner, N. Eldon. "The Administration of the Church." *Ensign* 9 (Nov. 1979):42–48.

J. LYNN ENGLAND
W. KEITH WARNER

FOLLOWING THE BRETHREN

Latter-day Saints believe that God gives revelations to living PROPHETS and that their words, when so inspired, are to be received as his (D&C 1:38). It has therefore become common in the Church to say that Christ and his prophets are as one because they represent him (cf. John 17:21–23). This means that prophets, as agents of Christ, announce his gospel, and are one with him in teaching, testimony, and purpose. Thus, the scriptural injunction to follow Jesus and the baptismal covenant to obey his commandments also require following his prophets.

Among Latter-day Saints the injunction to "follow the Brethren" derives from this requirement of obedience to Jesus and to prophetic instruction. In this context, "the Brethren" are the GENERAL AUTHORITIES, particularly the FIRST PRESIDENCY and the QUORUM OF THE TWELVE APOSTLES, who are formally sustained as prophets, seers, and revelators. The principle involved can be extended to include local priesthood leaders such as PRIESTHOOD QUORUM presidencies, BISHOPS and STAKE PRESIDENTS, and the presidencies of the women's auxiliary organizations—RELIEF SOCIETY, YOUNG WOMEN, and PRIMARY—within their respective jurisdictions. This extension of the principle to all Church leaders at every level is based on the recognition that all officers in the Church are entitled to revelation in their CALLINGS and on the assumption that they are in harmony with the Brethren. Referring specifically to the prophet who is currently President of the Church, the Lord has instructed members to "give heed unto all his words and commandments which he shall give unto you as he receiveth them, walking in all holiness before me; For his word ye shall receive, as if from mine own mouth, in all patience and faith" (D&C 21:4–5).

Latter-day Saints claim a variety of blessings from following prophetic instruction. Not only does following the Brethren unite the Saints, enabling them to advance the purposes of the restoration more effectively, but it also allows them to receive the rewards of such obedience, which include the gifts of the Spirit.

Following the Brethren, however, does not imply blind obedience, for every member of the Church is entitled to an individual witness of the Holy Spirit that the leadership of the Church is inspired by God. For this reason, following the living prophet obliges members to live worthy to receive personal inspiration and revelation. It gives contemporary meaning to Moses' desire that "all the Lord's people" be prophets and thus recipients of inspiration (Num. 11:29), and to the Savior's saying that all should "live by every word that proceedeth forth from the mouth of God" (D&C 84:44; Deut. 8:3; Matt. 4:4).

Because Church members are entitled to divine confirmation of prophetic declarations, there is no teaching among Latter-day Saints of "prophetic infallibility." As Joseph Smith taught, "a prophet was a prophet only when . . . acting as such" (*TPJS*, p. 278). Prophets have personal and private opinions, and they are "subject to like passions," as all people are (see James 5:17; Mosiah 2:10–11). However, when acting under the influence of the Holy Spirit in the prophetic role, "whatsoever they shall speak . . . shall be the will of the Lord" (D&C 68:3–4). As the Savior told Joseph Smith, "He that receiveth my servants receiveth me; and he that receiveth me receiveth my Father" (D&C 84:36–37; see also Matt. 10:40; 3 Ne. 28:34).

BIBLIOGRAPHY

Christiansen, ElRay L. "Sustaining the Authorities of the Church." *Relief Society Magazine* 44 (Feb. 1957):76–79.

Packer, Boyd K. "Follow the Brethren." *Speeches of the Year*, pp. 1–10. Provo, Utah, 1965.

Stapley, Delbert L. "Respect for Authority." *IE* 60 (Dec. 1957):914–15, 938.

MARK L. MCCONKIE

FRIEND, THE

Published monthly since January 1971 for children to age twelve, the *Friend* replaced the CHILDREN'S FRIEND, which was published from

1902 through 1970. The goal of the *Friend* is to reach the children of the Church directly, even those not involved with the PRIMARY, by presenting the gospel "while reinforcing the values of the stable homes" (Anderson, p. 13). It attempts to fulfill this goal by printing contemporary, historical, scriptural, and imaginative stories, often with pictures; recipes and crafts; games and pencil activities such as hidden pictures, scriptural matching, and connect-the-dots drawings; a calendar for the month; stories of Church leaders and other inspiring people; suggestions for reading; specials for the holidays; "Friend to Friend" discussions with Church leaders; and "Messages from the First Presidency" or from other GENERAL AUTHORITIES.

Keenly aware of the challenges facing children in the 1990s, the *Friend* tries to fill their needs and help parents as they raise their children in the very difficult modern world. The *Friend* attempts to meet President Spencer W. Kimball's challenge "to support the parents in teaching their children to pray and walk uprightly before the Lord" (Oman and Madsen, p. 39).

The editors of the *Friend* have been Lucile Reading (1971–1982) and Vivian Paulsen (1982–).

BIBLIOGRAPHY

Anderson, Lavina Fielding. "The Church and Children." *Ensign* 8 (Apr. 1978):6–13.
Hinckley, Gordon B. "A Friend for Every Child." *IE* 73 (Dec. 1970):97–98.
Oman, Susan, and Carol Madsen. "100 Years of Primary." *Ensign* 8 (Apr. 1978):32–39.

ELIZABETH WAHLQUIST

"FUNDAMENTALISTS"

"Mormon Fundamentalism" denotes the beliefs and practices of contemporary schismatic groups that claim to follow all the teachings of the Prophet Joseph Smith. They often style themselves believers in the "fulness of the gospel," which they assert must include plural marriage and sometimes the United Order.

The Fundamentalist movement began after the issuance of the Manifesto of 1890, which publicly declared an official end to plural marriage in The Church of Jesus Christ of Latter-day Saints. The period from 1890 to 1904 was one of confusion for some over the application and extent of the ban on new plural marriages in the Church. For example, since the Manifesto referred to "marriages violative of the law of the land," some felt the prohibition did not apply outside the United States. In 1904 the Manifesto was therefore officially and publicly proclaimed to be worldwide in jurisdiction and overall scope.

Following this second pronouncement, unyielding Fundamentalists continued to hold that God requires all "true" believers to abide by the principle of polygamy, irrespective of Church mandate. This insistence has separated Fundamentalists from mainstream Mormonism. In the 1920s, Lorin C. Woolley of Centerville, Utah, claimed God had authorized him to perpetuate plural marriage, saying he received this commission while a young man in 1886 through the ministration of Jesus Christ, John Taylor, and Joseph Smith. His assertion further polarized the Fundamentalists and the Church.

Some Fundamentalists of the 1920s rejected Woolley's claims to authority and went their separate ways. Charles Kingston settled in Bountiful, Utah, and set up a type of United Order community that persists as a relatively closed society. Alma Dayer LeBaron moved to Mesa, Arizona, and eventually to Juarez, Mexico, laying the groundwork for the Church of the Firstborn of the Fulness of Times and offshoots such as the Church of the Lamb of God. Other Fundamentalists have broken away through the years, making various religious claims.

Despite these defections, the majority of Fundamentalists remained an organized group, showing small but steady gains in adherents. In the mid-1930s, a United Order colony was established in an isolated community near the Utah-Arizona border called Short Creek, now Colorado City, Arizona. Property was held in a trust called the United Effort. This colony has become a haven for many Fundamentalists, although a majority of their followers still reside in the Salt Lake City area.

In the mid-1940s, Utah and Arizona law officials raided the Short Creek community and broke up polygamous families, putting husbands in jail and children in foster homes. Fundamentalist leaders remained in state prison until September 24, 1945 (the fifty-fifth anniversary of the Woodruff Manifesto), when they issued a public statement indicating their intention to cease ignoring the law of the land. They returned to their families and refrained from violating the law for a time.

A few years later, a major schism in the Colorado City group occurred over the question of priesthood authority and the right to rule. Joseph Musser (the ostensible leader of the group), Rulon Allred, his brothers, and a few others broke away and started their own group, which has grown to about 2,000 members through conversion and births and is now known as the United Apostolic Brethren. In 1976, Rulon Allred, then leader of the group, was murdered, evidently by a plural wife of Ervil LeBaron, of the Church of the Lamb of God. Owen Allred replaced his brother as leader. The Colorado City group reorganized, with Leroy Johnson assuming leadership, and in 1990 was one of the largest fundamentalist groups, numbering in the thousands. Upon Johnson's death (Nov. 25, 1986, at Hilldale, Utah) a power struggle ensued; schisms continue in the Colorado City group over authority and legal title to property.

Fundamentalists claim to believe in the four LDS standard works, the early History of the Church, and the prophets of the restoration up to, and including, John Taylor. Fundamentalist doctrines of priesthood presidency are derived from a unique interpretation of Doctrine and Covenants section 84, which they claim refers to a priesthood council or hierarchy of seven men designated as "high priest" apostles. Various claims to succession have led to the current schisms in these groups. Many independent Fundamentalists believe the claims to authority of the two main groups are flawed; they thus live and believe apart from those groups.

The thread that binds all Fundamentalists together is their belief that the LDS Church has improperly changed doctrines and practices. One independent Fundamentalist published a book listing ninety-five purported changes, thus mimicking Martin Luther's ninety-five theses. Prominent among these criticisms are the abrogation of plural marriage, cessation of living the United Order, alleged loss of revelation to the Church since 1890, purported forfeiture of keys of the priesthood due to termination of the practice of plural marriage, supposed repudiation of "true" knowledge of the Godhead, changes in the method of missionary work (failure to preach without purse or scrip), asserted corruption of temple garments and ordinances, cessation of the gathering of Israel to Utah, changing the method of priesthood conferral, and allowing all worthy male members of the Church to hold the priesthood, regardless of race.

BIBLIOGRAPHY
Anderson, J. Max. *The Polygamy Story: Fiction and Fact*. Salt Lake City, 1977.
Kraut, Ogden. *Ninety-five Theses*. Dugway, Utah, n.d.
Truth Magazine. Salt Lake City, 1935–1956.

J. MAX ANDERSON

G

GENERAL AUTHORITIES

General Authorities are men called to serve at the highest levels of leadership in The Church of Jesus Christ of Latter-day Saints. As general PRIESTHOOD officers of the Church, they have Churchwide rather than local stewardship and may receive assignments anywhere in the world. In order of precedence, the General Authorities include the FIRST PRESIDENCY, QUORUM OF THE TWELVE APOSTLES, quorums of the SEVENTY, and PRESIDING BISHOPRIC (*see* ORGANIZATION). First Presidency members and the senior member of the Quorum of the Twelve are addressed as "President." The Twelve Apostles and members of the quorums of the Seventy are addressed as "Elder." Members of the Presiding Bishopric are addressed as "Bishop." As a group, they are often referred to as "the Brethren."

Like all who serve in the Church, these men are lay leaders and do not solicit their assignments. They are "called of God, by prophecy, and by the laying on of hands by those who are in authority" (A of F 5; *see* LAY PARTICIPATION AND LEADERSHIP). They are called by a member of the First Presidency; subsequently, their names are presented to the Church MEMBERSHIP for a sustaining vote each year during general conference and in WARD and STAKE conferences.

Members of the First Presidency and Quorum of the Twelve are sustained as PROPHETS, SEERS, AND REVELATORS. They are commissioned to be special witnesses of Jesus Christ and his Church, and together with the Seventy they are to bear witness of him and "to build up the church, and regulate all the affairs of the same in all nations" (D&C 107:21–26, 33–35).

As assigned, General Authorities may travel throughout the world to preach the gospel, train and instruct local leaders and members, preside at stake conferences, organize new stakes, call and set apart new STAKE PRESIDENCIES, and generally look after the interests of the Church. They may also be called upon to address the Church membership at general conference.

In addition, General Authorities fulfill administrative responsibilities at Church headquarters, directly overseeing the Church's efforts in such areas as MISSIONARY work, Church history, family history (genealogy), TEMPLE WORSHIP, priesthood, FINANCES and RECORD KEEPING, curriculum, public communications, and the BUILDING PROGRAM. Some serve on the Church Board of Education, overseeing the Church Educational System and sitting on boards of trustees for Church-owned colleges and Brigham Young University.

General Authorities, particularly members of the quorums of the Seventy, may be assigned to live away from Church headquarters for a time and serve in AREA PRESIDENCIES, presiding over regions and stakes in those areas. Occasionally some are called as MISSION PRESIDENTS or TEMPLE PRESIDENTS, although non-General Authorities most often serve in these positions.

Wives and children of General Authorities may be called to serve in regular Church assignments in their home wards and stakes. Wives of General Authorities who are serving in area presidencies may be called to assist with AUXILIARY ORGANIZATIONS such as the PRIMARY, YOUNG WOMEN, and RELIEF SOCIETY in the countries where their husbands are serving. General Authorities themselves are not called to serve in the local organizations.

The general presidencies and boards of the Church's auxiliary organizations are sustained as general officers of the Church, but they are not General Authorities. They are set apart for a time as general officers for their specific auxiliary organization.

Unlike local leaders, who maintain their normal vocations while serving in Church assignments, General Authorities set aside their careers to devote their full time to the ministry of their office. The living allowance given General Authorities rarely if ever equals the earnings they sacrifice to serve full-time in the Church.

Members of the First Presidency and Quorum of the Twelve serve for life. Other General Authorities serve either until limited by age or health or for temporary periods. They may be released or receive emeritus status. After their service they return to ward and stake responsibilities.

Calls from one group to another are possible. For example, any General Authority may be called to serve in the First Presidency or Quorum of the Twelve, although previous service as a General Authority is not a prerequisite for these positions. Men from many nations have been called to serve as General Authorities.

Life as a General Authority demands great sacrifices of time and energy. It requires heavy involvement in decision making and continual travel away from home and family. But the work is rewarding. "I have witnessed the miracles that come with faith," said President Gordon B. Hinckley when serving as Second Counselor in the First Presidency. "I have seen the evidences of true goodness and greatness in men and women living under a great variety of circumstances. I have observed in a very intimate and wonderful way the workings of the power of the Almighty among his children" (p. 7).

There is striking unity among the General Authorities, which is at least partly due to decision making by COMMON CONSENT. "The General Authorities are all individuals, each with his own personality," said President Hinckley. "Each brings to his responsibilities a wide variety of experience and background. When matters come up for discussion in the leading councils of the Church, each is free to express his views. As one observes that interesting process at work, it is fascinating to witness the power of the Holy Spirit influence these men. Initial differences, never sharp but nonetheless perceptible, soften and meld into an expression of unity" (p. 6).

Although they have general administrative authority and are entitled to inspiration regarding the governing of Church affairs, General Authorities respect the right each member of the Church has to receive personal revelation. The Lord told Joseph Smith that the gospel was restored so "that every man [and woman] might speak in the name of God" (D&C 1:20).

General Authorities are men who, through years of experience in Church service, have proven to be faithful, effective, and devoted leaders and servants. As witnesses of the Lord and as general officers of the Church, they are trusted, loved, and respected throughout the Church.

[*See also* Following the Brethren.]

BIBLIOGRAPHY

Arrington, Leonard J., ed. *The Presidents of the Church: Biographical Essays.* Salt Lake City, 1986.

Flake, Lawrence R. *Mighty Men of Zion: General Authorities of the Last Dispensation.* Salt Lake City, 1974.

Hinckley, Gordon B. "He Slumbers Not, nor Sleeps." *Ensign* 13 (May 1983):5–8.

Presidents of the Church: "They That Move the Cause of Zion." Salt Lake City, 1979.

Tanner, N. Eldon. "The Administration of the Church." *Ensign* 9 (Nov. 1979):42–48.

Updated information on newly called General Authorities is available in the *Deseret News Church Almanac*, published biennially.

MARVIN K. GARDNER

GENERAL HANDBOOK OF INSTRUCTIONS

The *General Handbook of Instructions* is the official book of instruction for Church leaders, mainly STAKE PRESIDENTS and BISHOPS. Church leaders who receive the handbook include GENERAL AUTHORITIES, Church department heads, general auxiliary presidencies, temple presidents, and officers in STAKES, WARDS, MISSIONS, DISTRICTS, and BRANCHES. It is a handbook of Church policy and practices, not doctrine. The FIRST PRESIDENCY and QUORUM OF THE TWELVE APOSTLES prepare the handbook to provide uniform procedures and methods for local leaders as they minister to the members and direct Church affairs in their areas throughout the world. Other Church handbooks, such as those for PRIESTHOOD and AUXILIARY ORGANIZATIONS, are based on the *General Handbook of Instructions*.

Handbooks have included such things as instruction on (1) Church administration and meetings; (2) calling members to Church positions and releasing them from such calls; (3) ordaining members to priesthood offices; (4) performing ORDINANCES and giving blessings; (5) doing sacred temple work, and family history; (6) responding to calls for missionary service; (7) keeping records, reports, and accounting for finances; (8) applying Church discipline; and (9) implementing Church policies on such matters as buildings and property, moral issues, and medical and health issues.

The first edition of the handbook was a fourteen-page booklet of shirt-pocket size published in 1899. It instructed stake and ward leaders in how to receive, process, and account for members' tithing, most of which was farm produce and livestock rather than money. The Church revised the handbook annually until 1910 and, thereafter, about every five years. The most significant and constant change that has prompted the revisions has been the growth of the Church from 271,681 members in 1899 to more than 7 million in 1990. Other factors that have prompted revisions include the shift in North American members from an agrarian to an urban society, the immigration of converts, the Depression of the 1930s, the wars in the twentieth century, the increase of sensitive social issues, and the transitions from a membership centered in Utah to a membership in North America, and ultimately, to an international Church. Between revisions, letters from the First Presidency to local leaders and items in the priesthood *Bulletin* update instructions in the handbook.

The handbook is written in terms of principles, as far as possible, rather than explicit directions. Local leaders apply the principles in their stakes, wards, and branches as they are directed by spiritual inspiration.

The *General Handbook of Instructions* is preeminent among Church publications in both its preparation and its use as an authoritative guide for local Church leaders.

FRANK O. MAY, JR.

H

HEAD OF THE CHURCH

Members of The Church of Jesus Christ of Latter-day Saints believe that Jesus Christ is personally the Head of the Church, leading and guiding it by revelation (D&C 10:69; 3 Ne. 21:22).

According to the New Testament, God gave Jesus authority to be "the head over all things to the church" (Eph. 1:22; cf. 2:20; Col. 1:18). For Latter-day Saints, the restoration of the Church was similarly initiated in 1820 when God the Father, following an ancient pattern, appeared in vision with his Son Jesus Christ, who instructed Joseph Smith (JS—H 1:17; see Matt. 3:17; 2 Pet. 1:17–18; 3 Ne. 11:7). The Savior gave information and counsel to Joseph on that and later occasions.

Latter-day Saints affirm that subsequent revelations to his prophets have verified that Christ was and is both the Head of the Church and the author of its restoration and development (JS—H 1:30–42; D&C 1:1; 20:1, 37). No mortal, including the PRESIDENT OF THE CHURCH, considers himself to be the head. In fact, the President and all Church leaders consider themselves servants called by Christ or his authorized agents to represent him by teaching, training, and edifying members of the Church and by taking the gospel message to those not in the Church.

BIBLIOGRAPHY
Faust, James E. "Continuous Revelation." *Ensign* 19 (Nov. 1989):8–10.

BURNS R. SABEY

HIGH COUNCIL

A high council is a body of twelve HIGH PRIESTS who are called and set apart in each STAKE to assist and advise the STAKE PRESIDENCY under whom they serve.

Following the organization of the Church, in 1830, the Prophet Joseph Smith served as the spiritual leader for the growing body of members. However, with the rapid growth in membership and a commitment to LAY PARTICIPATION AND LEADERSHIP, it soon became evident that a more extensive governing structure would be required. The FIRST PRESIDENCY was organized in 1832.

At a conference held in Kirtland, Ohio, on February 17, 1834, Joseph Smith established a standing stake high council composed of twelve high priests, with himself, Sidney Rigdon, and Frederick G. Williams comprising the First Presidency and also as the presidency of the Kirtland Stake. Later that year, a separate stake presidency and high council were organized in Missouri. They operated independent of the Kirtland council, except for cases that went from Missouri to Kirtland on appeal. These initial standing high councils became the prototype for future stake organizations as the Church continued to grow and expand. Following the organization in 1835 of the "traveling high council," or QUORUM OF THE TWELVE APOSTLES (D&C 107:33–36), stake high councils concerned themselves only with stake matters.

With continued Church growth, additional areas were organized into stakes under the direction of the First Presidency to provide a means of coordinating the spiritual activities of the local WARDS and BRANCHES. In each case, a three-member stake presidency, assisted by a twelve-member high council, was called to preside over the stake. Their authority was limited to the stake in which they functioned.

As in the Quorum (or Council) of the Twelve Apostles, a seniority system exists within a stake high council; as vacancies occur in the council, the stake presidency calls new members, and the oldest in term of service is recognized as the senior member.

Under the direction of the stake presidency, the high council has important executive, legislative, and judicial powers (see D&C 102). Members of the stake high council serve as advisers to the stake presidency on any matter about which the presidency might seek counsel, and they carry out specific assignments. For example, a high councilor may have an assignment to represent the stake presidency, to assist in the training of a new ward BISHOPRIC, to attend a ward's priesthood executive committee meetings and ward council meetings, or to train and advise ward MELCHIZEDEK PRIESTHOOD quorum leaders. He may be asked to report regularly to the stake presidency concerning the status of a particular ward. In addition, he may serve as a member of the stake Melchizedek Priesthood committee, which assists the stake presidency in installing, training, and advising Melchizedek Priesthood leaders. Other assignments that are generally given to a member of a high council include membership on the AARONIC PRIESTHOOD/Boy Scouting Committee; adviser to the stake YOUNG WOMEN organization; stake mission president; coordinator of stake WELFARE programs; coordinator for temple service and family history programs; stake emergency preparedness director, or other such administrative roles. A high councilor will usually also be assigned to speak periodically in ward SACRAMENT MEETINGS under the direction of the stake presidency.

At regular meetings of the stake high council, the presidency presents matters of business to the council for its approval. Such matters may include endorsing an individual's name for an assignment in the stake organization, recommending a person as a potential ward bishop or counselor in a bishopric, or considering an individual for ordination to an office in the Melchizedek Priesthood. The stake president may also ask for discussion of particular issues, and high councilors may be asked to report on the status of their assignments.

As part of its judicial function, the high council serves as a disciplinary council when convened by the stake president to consider cases of serious transgression that affect the standing or fellowship of a Church member. Following the presentation of the facts of the case and due deliberation and prayer, a decision is rendered by the stake president and ratified by the stake high council (*see* DISCIPLINARY PROCEDURES).

DONOVAN E. FLEMING

HIGH PRIEST

The term "high priest" refers to an office in the MELCHIZEDEK PRIEST-HOOD. Men must be ordained high priests to serve as BISHOPS, on high councils, or in STAKE PRESIDENCIES, or as GENERAL AUTHORITIES (see HIGH COUNCIL; PRIESTHOOD). Stake presidents may ordain high priests for other reasons as well. When released from any of these callings, a high priest continues to be a member of the high priests quorum in his resident stake and to participate in the activities of his ward's high priests group (see PRIESTHOOD QUORUMS).

The PRESIDENT OF THE CHURCH is the PRESIDING HIGH PRIEST in the Church (D&C 107:65–66), the president of the stake is the presiding high priest in the stake, and the bishop is the presiding high priest in the ward. Since 1956, stake presidencies have been serving as the presidencies of their respective stake high priests quorums. Each ward in a stake has a high priests group with a group leader and one or more assistants, as needed. Ward groups of high priests meet weekly to be instructed in their duties and in the principles of the gospel (D&C 124:134; J. Taylor in *JD* 23:219). During group meetings they also receive and report on assignments such as HOME TEACHING and volunteer service projects.

To be ordained a high priest, an ELDER must be recommended by the ward bishopric to the stake presidency. After approval by the stake presidency and high council, his name is presented to the general body of stake priesthood bearers for a sustaining vote after which he is ordained by or under the direction of the stake president.

The first ordinations to the office of high priest in The Church of Jesus Christ of Latter-day Saints were done at the fourth conference of the Church, held in June 1831 in Kirtland, Ohio. Twenty-three men were ordained at that time, including the Prophet Joseph Smith, who was ordained a high priest under the hands of Lyman Wight, who had been ordained to that office by the Prophet. Joseph Smith had received this authority earlier at the hands of Peter, James, and John (see MELCHIZEDEK PRIESTHOOD: RESTORATION OF). Current records do not specify when high priests were first organized as a quorum, but it apparently was before January 1836. For a period of time, high priests quorums were organized in each ward with their own presidencies, but in 1877 Brigham Young indicated that stake presidents had responsibility over these quorums. In December 1975 the First Presidency clarified details of the current arrangement under which ward high priests groups function as units of the stake high priests quorum, with the stake president as the president of the quorum and ward high priest group leaders functioning under his direction. As of 1989, there were approximately 246,000 high priests in the Church.

From Adam to Moses, righteous men holding the holy priesthood were ordained high priests. Adam, Enoch, Noah, Melchizedek, Abraham, Moses, and many others were all ordained high priests (D&C 107:53; Alma 13). After the time of Moses the Melchizedek Priesthood was generally withdrawn from the earth, except among the prophets, and the law functioned under the Aaronic Priesthood. Thus, under the law of Moses a high priest was the chief priest in the AARONIC PRIESTHOOD. He presided over all other priests in their functions and ordinances, particularly those of the temple. Only a direct descendant of the firstborn son of Aaron anointed to be the spiritual head of the people could become the high priest.

In the Book of Mormon, there were apparently no Levites or descendants of Aaron among the people. High priests were the presiding spiritual authorities and held the Melchizedek Priesthood (e.g., Alma 8:23; 30:20, 23).

In the epistle to the Hebrews, Paul declares Christ to be the promised high priest "after the order of Melchisedec," an order higher in authority than the Aaronic Priesthood and not dependent upon the Aaronic lineage (Heb. 5:4–6, 10; 7:3, 11, 14–15; Ps. 110:4). As the great high priest, Christ made an eternal sacrifice, once for all time and all people (Heb. 9:11–12), and he continues to preside over all the ordinances and the organization of the Church, which bears his name (*see* HEAD OF THE CHURCH).

BIBLIOGRAPHY

Cotton, J. Harry, and Alexander C. Purdy. *The Interpreter's Bible*, Vol. 11, pp. 637–708. New York, 1955.

Schrenk, Gottlob. "Priest, High Priest." *Theological Dictionary of the New Testament*, ed. G. Kittel, Vol. 3, pp. 257–83. Grand Rapids, Mich., 1965.

Widtsoe, John A. *Priesthood and Church Government*, rev. ed. Salt Lake City, 1954.

A. LEGRAND RICHARDS

HOME TEACHING

Each ward of The Church of Jesus Christ of Latter-day Saints assigns priesthood holders as home teachers to visit the homes of members every month. They go in pairs; often a youth holding the AARONIC PRIESTHOOD accompanies an adult holding the MELCHIZEDEK PRIEST-HOOD. Home teachers are called by their local priesthood quorum leaders and are typically assigned to visit between three and five families. They report on the needs and welfare of their assigned families in regularly scheduled interviews with their priesthood leaders. The home teaching program is a response to modern revelation commissioning those ordained to the priesthood to

> teach, expound, exhort, baptize, and watch over the church . . . and visit the house of each member, and exhort them to pray vocally and in secret and attend to all family duties, . . . to watch over the church always, and be with and strengthen them; and see that there is no iniquity in the church, neither hardness with each other, neither lying, backbiting, nor evil speaking [D&C 20:42–54].

At one time called "acting teachers" (1909), the name was formally changed to "ward teachers" in 1912. However, for years before that time the effort was informally called "block teaching" because of the geographic way in which families were assigned (Hartley, pp. 375–98). In April 1963, the ward teaching program was expanded and renamed "home teaching," with emphasis "on the responsibilities of the entire priesthood to 'watch over the Church' as commanded in the early revelations—to be concerned with the whole family as a group and as individuals" (*IE* 66 [June 1963]:504).

In a Home Teachers Meeting during general conference in 1966, Marion G. Romney, then an apostle, instructed home teachers to live so that they could always enjoy the companionship of the Holy Ghost and act under his inspiration in their home teaching responsibilities and to encourage and inspire every family to make and keep the home a truly Latter-day Saint home.

In 1987 Church President Ezra Taft Benson gave three basic guidelines to be followed by home teachers:

First, Church leaders are to encourage home teachers to know as well as possible the people they are called to teach. Home teachers need to be aware of individual attitudes, interests, and general welfare, working closely with the head of each family to meet the family's temporal and spiritual needs.

Second, the Church expects home teachers to deliver a short monthly message. When possible, messages are to come from the scriptures, particularly the Book of Mormon. Leaders are to instruct home teachers to prepare intellectually and spiritually, giving prayerful consideration to both the temporal and spiritual needs of each family as they prepare lessons. The companionship of the Holy Ghost is essential for successful home teaching, for "if ye receive not the Spirit ye shall not teach" (D&C 42:14). The Church instructs home teachers, therefore, to pray together before each visit, invoking the blessings of the Lord upon the family, and, where possible, to pray with family members at the conclusion of the visit.

Third, home teachers are to magnify their callings (Jacob 1:19) by rendering devoted service. This includes visiting each family early in the month, by appointment, and making additional visits as needed.

Organizationally, home teaching provides a system for effective Churchwide communication. Through stakes, wards, and home teachers, Church leaders have a direct line to every member and have the potential, if necessary, to communicate quickly with the total Church membership, via the local priesthood leaders.

Effective home teaching makes significant contributions to members' lives. Alert, insightful home teachers find various ways of rendering service, such as providing recognition for achievements; informing families of Church activities; assisting during family emergencies, including illness or death; strengthening and encouraging less active members; and arranging transportation. They serve as resources and share the burden of support that would otherwise be carried by the bishop.

As home teachers are called to work directly with families, they are often in a better position to help these family members than are other Church officers or teachers. As a result, home teaching is one of the most effective ways the Latter-day Saints manifest their commitment to "bear one another's burdens, that they may be light; . . . mourn with those that mourn; yea, and comfort those that stand in need of comfort, and stand as witnesses of God" (Mosiah 18:8–9).

BIBLIOGRAPHY

Benson, Ezra Taft. "To the Home Teachers of the Church." *Ensign* 17 (May 1987):48–51.

Cullimore, James A. "Home Teachers—Watchmen over the Church." *Ensign* 3 (Jan. 1973):124–26.

Hartley, William. "Ordained and Acting Teachers in the Lesser Priesthood, 1851–1883." *BYU Studies* 16 (Spring 1976):375–98.

Packer, Boyd K. "The Saints Securely Dwell." *Ensign* 3 (Jan. 1973):88–90.

R. WAYNE BOSS

HOSANNA SHOUT

Among Latter-day Saints, the sacred ceremony of the Hosanna Shout is usually reserved for TEMPLE DEDICATIONS. It is given in the spirit of thanksgiving and petition, fulfilling the instruction to bless the name of the Lord with loud voices and "with a sound of rejoicing," with "hosannas to him that sitteth upon the throne forever" (D&C 19:37; 36:3; 39:19; 124:101).

When the ordinance of the washing of feet was introduced at Kirtland, shouts of hosanna were viewed as a sealing benediction on both private and quorum prayer and then on the dedicatory prayer. At prayer meetings in the Kirtland Temple, the Saints sometimes used related phrases such as "Blessed is the name of the Most High God" and "Glory to God in the highest" (*HC* 2:386).

The Hosanna Shout is whole-souled, given to the full limit of one's strength. The congregation stands and in unison shouts the words "Hosanna, Hosanna, Hosanna to God and the Lamb. Amen, Amen, and Amen," repeating them three times. This is usually accompanied by the rhythmic waving of white handkerchiefs with uplifted hands. The epithet "Lamb" relates to the condescension and atonement of Jesus Christ.

The Hosanna Shout memorializes the pre-earthly Council in Heaven, as "when . . . all the sons of God shouted for joy" (Job 38:7). It also recalls the hosannas and the waving of palm branches accorded the Messiah as he entered Jerusalem. And hosannas welcomed him as he appeared to the Nephites. President Lorenzo Snow taught that this shout will herald the Messiah when he comes in the glory of the Father (cf. 1 Thes. 4:16).

BIBLIOGRAPHY

Woodbury, Lael J. "The Origin and Uses of the Sacred Hosanna Shout." In *Sperry Lecture Series*. Provo, Utah, 1975.

LAEL J. WOODBURY

HOSPITALS

Members of The Church of Jesus Christ of Latter-day Saints have historically felt a responsibility to care for the physical well-being of fellow Church members and their neighbors. This early commitment was typified by the establishment of a board of health for the city of Nauvoo, Illinois, and a formal council of health in Salt Lake City in 1849. The Church has continued to sponsor health services through the operation of several hospitals and a welfare program.

In 1874, because of the high infant and maternity mortality rate, RELIEF SOCIETY president Eliza R. Snow, with the support of Church President Brigham Young, urged a number of women to obtain medical degrees at Eastern medical colleges. In 1882, under her direction, the Deseret Hospital was established in Salt Lake City and staffed and administered primarily by Latter-day Saint women doctors. While it was highly regarded by the community and supported in part by the Relief Society and the retrenchment society, it closed only eight years later because of inadequate funding.

Though the Deseret Hospital was short-lived, interest in having a hospital sponsored by the Church continued. In January 1905, the Dr. W. H. Groves LDS Hospital opened, also in Salt Lake City, becoming one of several denominational hospitals in the area. It was largely funded through a bequest of W. H. Groves, an LDS dentist who had come to Utah from Nottingham, England. The hospital, a five-story complex with eighty beds, was equipped with up-to-date medical equipment and innovations, including an elevator and a nurse-calling system. In 1924 the Cottonwood Maternity Hospital, a major facility in childbirth care, was established and was maintained thereafter for several years by the Cottonwood Stake Relief Society in Salt Lake County.

LDS Hospital, the 571-bed successor to the Groves LDS Hospital, is regarded as one of the West's premier tertiary care cen-

ters. The hospital supports continuous physician and nursing education and is a leader in medical research, including the treatment of
heart disease, organ transplants, respiratory disorders, and obstetri-
cal care, and in its pioneering use of computers in health care, both
clinically and administratively.

In 1911 May Anderson of the Primary Association recognized
the need for a medical center to meet the unique needs of children.
Her efforts, with support of general Primary president Louie B. Felt,
led to the establishment of the children's ward at the LDS Hospital
in 1913. In 1922 the Primary proposed that a separate facility be
established, emphasizing the need for children to be treated by pediatric professionals. Consequently, the Church purchased and remodeled an old home in downtown Salt Lake City for use as the LDS
Children's Convalescent Hospital, under the supervision of the
Primary Association.

During the next twenty-five years, nearly 6,000 children were
treated, and the hospital attracted pediatric specialists of national
and international reputation. By 1937 this facility became inadequate, but not until after World War II were sufficient funds gathered
to build a new one.

In 1922, to help support charity cases, Primary board member
Nelle Talmage suggested an annual "Penny Day" when Church
members would contribute pennies equaling their age. Children
would contribute pennies on their birthdays. The program continues
presently as the Pennies by the Inch campaign (a penny donated for
each inch of the donor's height), which furthers the idea of children
helping other children in need.

A new Primary Children's Hospital facility was completed in
1953, and its size was doubled in 1966. The LDS Hospital shortly
thereafter closed its pediatric unit, shifting its care for infants and
children to the Primary Children's Medical Center. In 1990 the
Center moved to a larger facility at the University of Utah Medical
Complex and has become one of the finest children's hospitals in the
United States.

In 1963 the Church owned or administered fifteen hospitals in
the intermountain area under the direction of the PRESIDING BISH-
OPRIC. In 1970 the Health Services Corporation of the Church was
organized and a commissioner of health was appointed to oversee the

rapidly expanding health needs of the Church and to unite the fifteen hospitals into a coordinated health care system. This system demanded increasing amounts of administrative time and financial commitment by the Church.

In 1974 the First Presidency announced that the Church's fifteen hospitals would be donated and turned over to a new nonprofit organization so that the Church could devote "the full effort of [its] Health Services . . . to the health needs of the worldwide Church." While noting that the hospitals were "a vigorous and financially viable enterprise," the First Presidency emphasized that "the operation of hospitals is not central to the mission of the Church." The First Presidency further indicated that with the expansion of the Church in many nations it was "difficult to justify the provision of curative services in a single, affluent, geographical locality" (news release, Sept. 6, 1974).

On April 1, 1975, the Presiding Bishopric signed the final divestiture agreement transferring ownership and management of LDS Hospital, Primary Children's Hospital, and thirteen other facilities to the new philanthropic organization. This nonprofit organization was named Intermountain Health Care. It is directed by a geographically and religiously diverse board of trustees. With the divestiture of the hospitals, the Church rapidly expanded its medical missionary program—a program more compatible with its worldwide religious mission.

BIBLIOGRAPHY
Bush, Lester E., Jr. "The Mormon Tradition." In *Caring and Curing*, ed. R. Numbers and D. Amundsen, pp. 397–420. New York, 1986.
DeWitt, Robert J. *Medicine and the Mormons*. Bountiful, Utah, 1981.
Josephson, Marba. "The Primary Children's Hospital." *IE* 55 (Oct. 1952):714–17, 734, 736, 738, 740, 742, 744–45.

WILLIAM N. JONES

I

IMPROVEMENT ERA

One of six publications begun as Church auxiliary magazines between 1866 and 1902, the *Improvement Era* (1897–1970) was the official arm of the Young Men's Mutual Improvement Association (YMMIA, which became the YOUNG MEN in 1977). It followed the demise of the CONTRIBUTOR magazine (1879–1896), an independent journal associated with the YMMIA. Joined officially to the YMMIA, the *Era* immediately became the premier adult periodical of the Church through its General Authority sponsorship and its focus on theology, history, contemporary affairs, and life in the Church. Its name reflected its sponsor's goal to be for the intellectual, moral, and spiritual mutual *improvement* of its readers in a new Church *era* just one year after Utah achieved statehood. The *Era*'s preeminence from 1901 onward for more than half a century was in part due to the participation of the President of the Church as its principal editor; thus, its pages were often used to voice concerns important to Church leadership and to respond to queries concerning Church doctrine and LDS lifestyle. Its circulation of 2,000 in 1897 reached 275,000 when it was succeeded by the ENSIGN in January 1971.

The *Era* soon served more than the YMMIA. It was the publication arm of the Seventies in 1908, of other PRIESTHOOD QUORUMS in 1909, and of Church schools in 1913. It merged with YOUNG WOMAN'S JOURNAL, the publication of the Young Women's Mutual

Improvement Association (YWMIA, which became YOUNG WOMEN in 1977) in 1929. By 1936 it had become the arm of the music committee, ward teaching, and other agencies of the Church. Beginning in 1942, the *Era* printed all General Conference addresses (it had previously printed selected addresses).

In 1897 the *Era* had a 5¾-by-8⅜-inch format. Thereafter, it usually contained eighty pages, with photographs printed on stitched-in leaves. In 1908 the paper was upgraded, and the number of photographs was increased. At its 1929 merger, the *Era* changed to an 8-by-10⅞-inch magazine format, printed its covers in color, and began forty-one years of advertisements for its readers. It also added more general-interest articles. In 1957 the *Era* began publishing anniversary issues with four-color sections, but it did not use four-color printing regularly until 1969. In 1960 it began the section "The Era of Youth," a prelude to the NEW ERA.

The list of editors of the *Era* includes five Presidents of the Church: Joseph F. Smith, Heber J. Grant, George Albert Smith, David O. McKay, and Joseph Fielding Smith; two members of the QUORUM OF THE TWELVE APOSTLES: John A. Widtsoe and Richard L. Evans; and two members of the First Council of the SEVENTY: B. H. Roberts and Richard L. Evans. Other editors or managing editors were Edward H. Anderson, Hugh J. Cannon, Harrison R. Merrill, and Doyle L. Green. "The Era of Youth" section was edited by Elder Marion D. Hanks of the Seventy, and Elaine A. Cannon, who later became president of the Young Women (1978–1984).

BIBLIOGRAPHY
Green, Doyle L. "*The Improvement Era*—The Voice of the Church (1897–1970)." *IE* 73 (Nov. 1970):12–20.

JAY M. TODD

INSTRUCTOR, THE

The *Instructor* was originally published as JUVENILE INSTRUCTOR, from 1866 to 1929. At first a children's magazine, it became the official publication of the SUNDAY SCHOOL of the Church in January 1901. As its pages gradually filled with articles on teaching methods and gospel subjects to be used by the several Church AUXILIARY ORGANI-ZATIONS, especially the Sunday School, its name was changed to the *Instructor* in November 1929, better to reflect its content.

The Presidents of the Church were identified as editors of the magazine from 1901 through 1970, but coeditors were often largely responsible for its contents.

The *Instructor* ceased publication in December 1970, when the Church consolidated its English language magazines into three: ENSIGN, for adults; NEW ERA, for youth; FRIEND, for children. Some of the instructional materials for teachers previously published in the *Instructor* are now published in the lesson manuals of the Church.

BIBLIOGRAPHY

McKay, David L. "Goodbye, the Instructor." *Ensign* 1 (Dec. 1970):444–48.

RUEL A. ALLRED

INTERNATIONAL MAGAZINES

In 1967 The Church of Jesus Christ of Latter-day Saints began uni-fying the foreign language magazines that were being independently published to serve its Danish, Dutch, Finnish, French, German, Norwegian, Spanish, and Swedish-speaking missions to give its mag-azines similar editorial content and a general format. This unifica-tion of content greatly reduced redundant staff efforts in the various mission offices and provided Church-approved materials for all issues. The resulting *Unified Magazine* was renamed *International Magazines* in 1974, an umbrella title that in 1990 covered twenty dif-ferent magazines, each with its own language-specific title. An edi-torial staff in Salt Lake City chooses materials from the Church's three English publications, *Friend, New Era,* and *Ensign,* that will appeal to international readers of all ages and prepares those and other original articles for international publication.

An English version, *Tambuli,* is prepared in Salt Lake City, and film of the completed layouts, containing both text and art is shipped for local printing in the Philippines. Similar print-ready film is pre-pared in Salt Lake City for other language editions and is then sent to various printing sites around the world. Some of the translations are prepared in Salt Lake City, but most in the local areas. The various editions contain from eight to sixteen pages of local Church news that is gathered, edited, and printed in the language areas.

The idea of publishing local, foreign-language magazines for Church members started in Wales in 1846, a year before the Mormon Pioneers moved into the Salt Lake Valley. Dan Jones edited and published thirty-two issues of *Prophwyd y Jubili, Neu Seren y Saints* (Prophet of Jubilee, New Star of Saints), filled with doctrinal and historical articles, messages from Church leaders, and replies to attacks from antagonists of the Church. Other magazines followed. The first issues of *Skandinaviens Stjerne* (Scandinavian Star) in Denmark, *l'Etoile du Deseret* (The Star of Deseret) in France, and *Zions Panier* (Zion's Banner) in Germany were all published in 1851. In subsequent years the Church has published magazines in other languages, with the larger number beginning in the twentieth century. In 1990 the Church is increasing the number of its foreign language periodicals.

For a fuller list of Church magazines and newspapers, *see* Church Periodicals chart in Appendix 2.

BIBLIOGRAPHY
Flake, Chad J. *A Mormon Bibliography, 1830–1930.* Salt Lake City, Utah, 1978.

BRIAN K. KELLY

INTERVIEWS

Church leaders conduct a variety of interviews essential to the administration of the Church and the nurturance of members. Interviews of Church members are conducted to determine personal worthiness, approve participation in religious ceremonies and ORDINANCES, assess needs, issue calls to service, listen to members' concerns, receive an accounting of performance in a Church assignment, and record a member's status regarding the payment of TITHING.

Worthiness is required of those who are to serve in Church CALLINGS, represent the Church as missionaries, and attend the temple (*see* TEMPLE RECOMMEND). An interview is used in each of these situations to determine the member's willingness to serve and worthiness to participate. For example, when a person prepares for baptism or an engaged couple seek permission to be married by priesthood authority in the temple, they first answer questions of a Church leader (usually a bishop or stake president) in a confidential worthiness interview regarding their honesty, integrity, moral cleanliness, and overall obedience to the gospel of Jesus Christ.

Church leaders are expected to seek inspiration as they determine worthiness, extend callings, and give counsel to members who are having difficulties. Members may seek an interview for counsel regarding matters of personal anguish, spiritual concerns, moral transgression, marital disharmony, financial welfare, and family functioning. They may come feeling anxious and bearing burdens of guilt. Although Church leaders are not given specific training in the techniques of interviewing, they are encouraged to be supportive and nonthreatening and to create an atmosphere in which the Spirit of the Lord can be present to provide guidance, comfort, and discernment. N. Eldon Tanner, counselor in the First Presidency of the Church, offered the following advice to Church interviewers: "It is important that those we interview realize that they are spirit children of God and that we love them . . . and are interested in their welfare and in helping them succeed in life" (p. 41).

Interviews are also used to issue callings and report service rendered. For example, most adult men and women accept calls to visit specific members of the congregation monthly (*see* HOME TEACHING; VISITING TEACHING) and then discuss these visits in an interview with their supervisor. Members in any calling report on their performance and provide their supervisors with nonconfidential information concerning those they are called to serve (*see* STEWARDSHIP). They report any confidential matters directly to the bishop.

Interviews are regularly scheduled to maintain lines of communication between Church leaders and members. Bishops and their counselors are asked to interview youth twelve to eighteen years of age frequently to encourage obedience to the gospel, the development of talents, the pursuit of education, and preparation for service in the Church and community. These interviews should support family goals and commitments and supplement parental guidance (which often includes appropriate father's and mother's interviews and counsel with their children).

Successful interviews invite unity and build faith. Leaders who conduct worthiness interviews are to remember that they are "representatives of the Lord and [therefore they] must conduct the interviews as the Lord himself would conduct them" (Tanner, p. 42).

BIBLIOGRAPHY

Dyer, Alvin R. "How Oral Evaluation Can Help Home Teachers Keep Close to the Families They Visit." *IE* 72 (Dec. 1969):18–19.

Tanner, N. Eldon. "The Blessing of Church Interviews." *Ensign* 8 (Nov. 1978):41–42.

LARRY C. FARMER

J

JOINING THE CHURCH

Converts to The Church of Jesus Christ of Latter-day Saints have various motivations for their initial interest in the Church, and many factors influence them in the conversion process. However, they generally share three common experiences as they seek baptism and membership in the Church. First, most of those interested in joining the Church meet with missionaries for a series of brief lessons on basic LDS beliefs and religious practices. Second, all prospective converts must demonstrate in a prebaptism interview with a Church representative that they are making an informed decision of their own free will and that they willingly fulfill the baptismal requirements. Third, every convert must receive the ORDINANCES of baptism and confirmation as performed by authorized representatives of the Church and be accepted as a member of the local WARD or BRANCH by the common consent of the members.

LDS converts come from a wide age range and from all socioeconomic groups. Often they have friends or acquaintances who are already members, but sometimes they are located by missionary contacting. They typically have a desire to improve their lives by learning correct gospel principles and by uniting themselves with others having similar needs and attitudes. Thus, the common essential in most conversions to the Church is obtaining a personal conviction that the Church today is authorized by God to teach and administer the gospel of Jesus Christ.

All who are interested in joining the Church must know and understand the responsibilities that Church membership will bring. To this end, they receive a series of lessons from LDS missionaries or from members of the Church. At this stage, prospective converts are called "investigators," because they are investigating or studying the Church. The lessons are called the missionary "discussions," because although they cover standardized topics, missionaries are encouraged to present them in an informal, conversational manner. For example, missionaries typically share their personal experiences and feelings about the topics discussed, and encourage investigators to do likewise, asking questions and giving reactions to LDS teachings. These lessons are usually taught in a home setting, to individuals or to a small group.

The lessons teach the gospel of Jesus Christ, including the nature of the Godhead, the plan of salvation, keeping the commandments, and living a Christlike life. They also discuss the life and mission of the Prophet Joseph Smith, the coming-forth of the Book of Mormon, the restoration of the PRIESTHOOD, and the importance of following the PROPHETS living today.

Investigators are asked to make various commitments during their course of study, which may last a few weeks or several months, depending on their individual rate of preparation toward baptism. For example, they are challenged and encouraged to engage in daily prayer and scripture study, especially prayerful study of the Book of Mormon. Those who wish to join the Church are urged to begin living an LDS lifestyle. This includes striving for Christlike attitudes and behavior in all circumstances; attending Church meetings; abstaining from harmful substances, including tobacco, alcoholic beverages, coffee, tea, and drugs; beginning to tithe; living a moral and chaste life; and laboring to serve those in need.

In the interview customarily conducted by an authorized Church representative prior to baptism, the interviewer determines the candidate's willingness and worthiness to enter into the baptismal covenant. During this interview, baptismal candidates are asked whether they have a heartfelt testimony of the fundamental doctrine of the Church. All baptismal candidates also must declare whether they currently keep, and will continue to keep, God's commandments through their lives.

Baptism is required for Church membership. It represents a covenant with God whereby the candidate agrees to follow Christ and live his commandments. The requirements for baptism are described in the Doctrine and Covenants as follows: "All those who humble themselves before God, and desire to be baptized, and come forth with broken hearts and contrite spirits, and witness before the church that they have truly repented of all their sins, and are willing to take upon them the name of Jesus Christ, having a determination to serve him to the end, and truly manifest by their works that they have received of the Spirit of Christ unto the remission of their sins, shall be received by baptism into his church" (D&C 20:37). Baptism symbolizes the washing away of sins as well as a rebirth and the beginning of a new life on earth leading to eternal life with God.

Baptism is followed by confirmation into the Church by the laying on of hands of one holding the MELCHIZEDEK PRIESTHOOD. During this ordinance, the new convert is confirmed a member of the Church and receives the gift of the Holy Ghost. This is typically a momentous and joyous occasion for all involved. Following his confirmation the convert is presented for acceptance by the local membership as a member in full fellowship and embarks on a life of spiritual growth through obedience to the laws of God and activity and service in the Church.

BIBLIOGRAPHY

Rector, Hartman, and Connie Rector. *No More Strangers*, 4 vols. Salt Lake City, 1971–1990.

LINDA A. CHARNEY

JOURNAL OF DISCOURSES

The *Journal of Discourses* was a sixteen-page semimonthly subscription publication privately printed in Liverpool, England, in 1854–1886. It served as the printed word of The Church of Jesus Christ of Latter-Day Saints, particularly for members who had no access to the Salt Lake City *Deseret News*. While the *Journal* most often published sermons of Church leaders, these speeches were not always considered to be official statements of doctrine. Many different kinds of speeches were printed, including the prayer given at the laying of a cornerstone of the Salt Lake Temple, a report of a HIGH COUNCIL court decision, a funeral sermon, and a plea for the defendant and the charge to the jury in a murder trial. In all, the collected *Journal of Discourses* contains 1,438 speeches given by fifty-five people, including Presidents of the Church, members of the QUORUM OF THE TWELVE APOSTLES, members of the SEVENTY, and sixteen other speakers. Brigham Young gave 390; John Taylor, 162; Orson Pratt, 127; Heber C. Kimball, 113; and George Q. Cannon, 111. Twenty-one people gave a single speech, and the rest gave from 2 to 66 speeches. The semimonthly issues have been bound into twenty-six annual volumes and are currently available in a lithograph reprinting "of the original edition."

The origin of the *Journal of Discourses* is tied to George D. Watt, an English convert baptized in 1837 by Heber C. Kimball. Before immigrating to the United States in 1842, Watt learned Pitman shorthand. He used this new skill in his adopted land to record the proceedings of conferences of the Church. He also recorded the trial of the accused murderers of the Prophet Joseph Smith.

After 1852 Watt transcribed Church conference addresses for the *Deseret News*. But because the *News* was not generally available outside central Utah and because Watt received little pay for his work, he proposed to publish privately and sell sixteen-page semiweekly issues of the *Journal of Discourses* containing selected sermons of the GENERAL AUTHORITIES. The sale of these to the Saints at large would enable Watt to earn a living with his shorthand skill. He was supported in this proposal by Brigham Young, who authorized him to print his sermons.

David W. Evans, also an English convert, an associate editor of the *Deseret News*, and the first violinist in the Salt Lake Theatre Orchestra, succeeded Watt as the main reporter to the *Journal* from 1867 to 1876. Another major reporter was George F. Gibbs, who was born in Wales and was the secretary to the FIRST PRESIDENCY of the Church for fifty-six years. In all, twelve people reported sermons for the *Journal of Discourses*, including one of Brigham Young's daughters, "Miss Julia Young," who reported one of his speeches.

BIBLIOGRAPHY
McConkie, Joseph Fielding, ed. *Journal of Discourses Digest*. Salt Lake City, 1975.
Watt, Ronald G. "Sailing the Old Ship Zion: The Life of George D. Watt." *BYU Studies* 18 (Fall 1977):48–65.

RONALD G. WATT

JUVENILE INSTRUCTOR

The *Juvenile Instructor* began publication in January 1866 and was the first children's magazine published between the Mississippi River and the West Coast of the United States. Its first issue identified its primary audience as the children of The Church of Jesus Christ of Latter-day Saints, and its purpose was to help prepare them for future responsibilities. It was originally published as a 10½-by-15½-inch four-page, three-column, semimonthly publication.

The magazine was initiated, owned, edited, and published by Elder George Q. Cannon until shortly before his death in 1901. During his lifetime he was the general superintendent of the Church's Sunday School, a member of the QUORUM OF THE TWELVE APOSTLES, a Counselor in the First Presidency of the Church, and also a territorial delegate from Utah to the U.S. Congress. The *Juvenile Instructor* published editorials, poetry (some by Eliza R. Snow), and a monthly column, "Voices from Nature," by Karl G. Maeser (president of Brigham Young Academy, later Brigham Young University). It also printed essays, stories, and biographical sketches that often focused on moral issues or the history of other cultures.

Officially owned and published by the Sunday School from 1901 to 1929, the *Juvenile Instructor* contained important organization and business matters of the Sunday School as well as adult and youth stories and essays. As its interests turned more toward filling the needs of teachers, it became the teachers' magazine of the Church and was renamed the *Instructor* in 1929.

[*See also* Instructor, The.]

BIBLIOGRAPHY
Green, Doyle L. "The Church and Its Magazines." *Ensign* 1 (Jan. 1971):12–15.

RUEL A. ALLRED

K

KEYS OF THE PRIESTHOOD

The keys of the priesthood refer to the right to exercise power in the name of Jesus Christ or to preside over a priesthood function, quorum, or organizational division of the Church. Keys are necessary to maintain order and to see that the functions of the Church are performed in the proper time, place, and manner. They are given by the laying on of hands in an ordination or setting apart by a person who presides and who holds the appropriate keys at a higher level. Many keys were restored to men on earth by heavenly messengers to the Prophet Joseph Smith and Oliver Cowdery.

The keys of the kingdom of God on earth are held by the APOSTLES. The PRESIDENT OF THE CHURCH, who is the senior apostle, holds all the keys presently on earth and presides over all the organizational and ordinance work of the Church (D&C 107:8–9, 91–92). He delegates authority by giving the keys of specific offices to others (D&C 124:123). Only presiding priesthood officers (including General Authorities, stake presidents, mission presidents, temple presidents, bishops, branch presidents, and quorum presidents) hold keys pertaining to their respective offices. Latter-day Saints distinguish between holding the priesthood and holding keys to direct the work of the priesthood: one does not receive additional priesthood when one is given keys (Joseph F. Smith, *IE* 4 [Jan. 1901]:230).

The Prophet Joseph Smith taught that "the fundamental principles, government, and doctrine of the Church are vested in the keys of the kingdom" (*TPJS*, p. 21). "The keys have to be brought from heaven whenever the Gospel is sent"; they are revealed to man under the authority of Adam, for he was the first to be given them when he was given dominion over all things. They have come down through the dispensations of the gospel to prophets, including Noah, Abraham, Moses, Elijah; to Peter, James, and John; and to Joseph Smith and the designated prophets of the latter days (*HC* 3:385–87). Keys to perform or preside over various priesthood functions were bestowed upon Joseph Smith and Oliver Cowdery by John the Baptist (*see* AARONIC PRIESTHOOD: RESTORATION OF AARONIC PRIESTHOOD), by Peter, James, and John (*see* MELCHIZEDEK PRIESTHOOD: RESTORATION OF MELCHIZEDEK PRIESTHOOD), and by Moses, Elias, and Elijah in the Kirtland Temple.

Many types of keys are mentioned in the scriptures of the Church (see *MD*, pp. 409–13). Jesus Christ holds all the keys. Joseph Smith received the keys pertaining to the restoration of the gospel of Jesus Christ (D&C 6:25–28; 28:7; 35:18), and through him the FIRST PRESIDENCY holds the "keys of the kingdom," including the SEALING ordinances (D&C 81:1–2; 90:1–6; 110:16; 128:20; 132:19). Specific mention of certain keys and those who hold them include the following: The QUORUM OF THE TWELVE APOSTLES exercises the keys "to open the door by the proclamation of the gospel of Jesus Christ" in all the world (D&C 107:35; 112:16; 124:128). Adam holds "the keys of salvation under the counsel and direction of the Holy One," and "the keys of the universe" (D&C 78:16; *TPJS*, p. 157); Moses, "the keys of the gathering of Israel" (D&C 110:11); Elias, the keys to bring to pass "the restoration of all things" (D&C 27:6); and Elijah, "the keys of the power of turning the hearts of the fathers to the children, and the hearts of the children to the fathers" (D&C 27:9). Holders of the Melchizedek Priesthood are said to have "the keys of the Church," "the key of knowledge," and "the keys of all the spiritual blessings of the church" (D&C 42:69; 84:19; 107:18), while belonging to the Aaronic Priesthood are "the keys of the ministering of angels, and of the gospel of repentance, and of baptism by immersion for the remission of sins" (D&C 13:1; 84:26). All these stewardships will eventually be delivered back into the hands of Jesus Christ (*TPJS*, p. 157).

BIBLIOGRAPHY

Durham, G. Homer. "The Keys of the Priesthood." In *Priesthood*, ed. S. Kimball et al. Salt Lake City, 1981.

Nelson, Russell M. "Keys of the Priesthood." *Ensign* 17 (Nov. 1987):36–39.

ALAN K. PARRISH

L

LATTER-DAY SAINTS (LDS)

The Church of Jesus Christ of Latter-day Saints (D&C 115:4) sees itself as a restoration of the original Church of Jesus Christ "of Former-day Saints." Members of the Church in the time of Christ are often referred to as "saints." Actually, the word "saint" predates Christ, and it is used thirty-six times in the Old Testament. It appears sixty-two times in the New Testament. The term "Christian" appears only three times in the New Testament, used by others to identify the followers of Christ. At the time of Christ and the Apostles, the term "saint" was accepted as a proper name for anyone who was a member of the Church, and was not used as a term of special sanctity as in earlier and later traditions. The phrase "latter days" designates the period leading to the last days and the series of events that will culminate in the reappearance of Christ to all the world. By referring to themselves as Latter-day Saints, members of the Church reaffirm their historical tie to original Christians (the Former-day Saints of the New Testament) but differentiate the two time periods. Also, they are striving to become sanctified through obedience to the laws and ordinances of the gospel.

The name unites three themes: (1) the *restoration* theme, since the term has a New Testament origin; (2) the *preparation* theme, since the Saints in the latter days anticipate the coming of Christ; and (3) the *revelation* theme, since the name was received by revelation and recorded in Doctrine and Covenants, section 115.

It is interesting to some that the people of the Dead Sea Scrolls also called themselves Latter-day Saints. These individuals believed themselves tied to the PROPHETS and the covenant (hence the name Saint) and anticipated the imminent coming of the Messiah (hence the term Latter-day).

BIBLIOGRAPHY
Nelson, Russell M. "Thus Shall My Church Be Called." *Ensign* 5 (May 1990):16–18.
Cross, Frank M., Jr. *The Ancient Library of Qumran.* New York, 1961.

ROBERT F. BENNETT

LAY PARTICIPATION AND LEADERSHIP

One of the important defining characteristics of The Church of Jesus Christ of Latter-day Saints is lay participation and leadership. The scope of volunteer service in the Church is extensive, both in the number of people involved and in the amount of their service.

In practice, the building up of the kingdom of God on earth is accomplished by individuals serving in numerous lay assignments, or CALLINGS. They speak in Church meetings and serve as athletic directors, teachers, family history specialists, financial secretaries, children's music directors, and women's and men's organization presidents. The goal of many leaders is to make sure that each member has a calling, reflecting the belief that personal growth comes through service. Millions of people serve in the Church, and that service represents a significant time commitment. In one study, researchers found that on average a BISHOP, the leader of a local WARD (congregation), spends approximately twenty-seven hours weekly in his duties; the president of the RELIEF SOCIETY, or women's organization, thirteen hours; the ward CLERK, eight hours; and so on. As of 1990, there were nearly 50,000 full-time MISSIONARIES contributing one and a half to two years of service. Lay members and leaders are organized and assisted through an extensive Church organization, including a substantial staff of employees located primarily at Church headquarters in Salt Lake City, Utah.

The scriptures indicate that to serve in a priesthood office, a man must be called of God (Heb. 5:4; A of F 5). Likewise, men and women are called, by prophecy and by the laying on of hands, to serve one another in a variety of settings. No Church calling requires extensive formal training. The Lord outlined the requirements of service when speaking about missionary work: "Faith, hope, charity and love, with an eye single to the glory of God, qualify [members] for the work" (D&C 4:5).

Though not formal in nature, training for leadership is provided in a variety of ways. First, and very important, members are given early and repeated opportunities to serve, thereby learning from experience. Beginning at age twelve, young men and women can serve as teachers for children or as members of class presidencies or of youth activities committees. In addition, teacher development courses and in-service lessons assist teachers, and LEADERSHIP TRAINING meetings instruct leaders of various organizations. Manuals and handbooks outline the responsibilities of individuals serving in different organizations at both ward and STAKE levels.

Lay participation and leadership have several implications for the Church and its members. Part of the mission of the Church is to perfect the Saints (Eph. 4:12), to sponsor growth in individual members. Utilizing volunteer members at all levels of the organization may not ensure peak efficiency, but it does provide the experiences and interactions that will help members progress. Volunteer staffing also means that in most of the callings members work part-time and that this service is in addition to regular employment and other responsibilities. This provides the opportunity for learning to sacrifice and to balance commitments. In general, members who serve maintain a high level of commitment to the Church, in part because of their awareness that they are responsible for making a contribution and because they take satisfaction from doing so. Because professional training is not required, lay leadership lessens the sense of hierarchy and increases feelings of unity. The children's music leader may have more formal education than the bishop. After being released in a few years, that bishop may serve as children's music leader. Opportunities to serve in a variety of callings and to be served by people in different capacities can increase the sense of brotherhood and sisterhood shared by Church members.

Many callings require men and women to serve as administrators, doing practical tasks to enable the organization to run smoothly. While the role of administrator is a necessary one, it is not the most vital aspect of leadership, which is to minister. Christ's admonition "Feed my sheep" (John 21:15–17) applies to latter-day discipleship. The characteristics of effective spiritual leadership are those that enable individuals to minister to their brothers and sisters in the gospel, including a willingness to seek and follow the counsel of the Lord as manifested through the Holy Ghost, on one's own behalf and on behalf of those in need of direction. In addition, leaders are to understand the nature of their STEWARDSHIPS and seek to fulfill their responsibilities in meekness and humility. Good leaders understand their roles as servants to others (Matt. 20:27). Thus, doubly benefited, persons gain from leadership experiences through unselfishly serving in a Christlike way and, through such service, come to know the Lord (Mosiah 5:13).

The gospel teaches that this life is a preparatory state for the life to come and that all people are on a course of eternal progression. Lay participation plays an important role in that progression by providing opportunities for service and learning. Church callings offer many opportunities to develop practical skills and spiritual qualities that contribute to continued service and fulfillment throughout life. Individuals may hold many different callings over a period of time and sometimes those callings increase in complexity or scope of influence. However, Latter-day Saints are encouraged not to view such changes as promotions. Callings of greater visibility or apparent influence are of no greater importance than humble and unseen service. The progression that is important, to the individual and to the Lord, is not evidenced by the different callings held by a person, but by the increase in Christlike characteristics developed through years of prayerful and thoughtful service. The potential for personal growth and righteous influence is as great for a nursery leader as for a STAKE PRESIDENT.

Latter-day scriptures encourage widespread participation, declaring that men and women "should be anxiously engaged in a good cause, [doing] many things of their own free will" (D&C 58:27). King Benjamin in the Book of Mormon taught that "when ye are in the service of your fellow beings ye are only in the service of your

God" (Mosiah 2:17). Though he was the Master in all things, Christ stressed his role as servant, setting an example for others to follow (John 13:15). The emphasis on service as a mode of worship, as a requirement for becoming like Christ, and as a means of establishing the unity that distinguishes the people of God is a major reason for the commitment of the Church and its members to lay participation and leadership.

PAUL H. THOMPSON

LEADERSHIP TRAINING

The local and general leaders of The Church of Jesus Christ of Latter-day Saints are lay members; they have not received professional training for the ministry (*see* LAY PARTICIPATION AND LEADERSHIP). Instead, Church members prepare to fulfill their callings by personal scripture study, prayer, inspiration, and righteous living; observing other leaders; assuming informal apprenticeships; studying Church-produced handbooks and manuals; participating in leadership training ("in-service") lessons; and accepting counsel and guidance from their presiding officers and from the General Authorities.

The expectation is that all faithful Latter-day Saints are entitled to the inspiration of the Holy Ghost and personal revelation to aid them in meeting the needs of those they teach, counsel, and serve. Reliance on divine guidance makes personal worthiness and Christlike attributes the most important qualifications for all callings in the Church. Attributes qualifying one for the work are "faith, hope, charity and love, with an eye single to the glory of God, . . . virtue, knowledge, temperance, patience, brotherly kindness, godliness, charity, humility, diligence" (D&C 4:5–6).

There are Church handbooks that outline the duties and activities of every leadership position and state the general principles that should apply. These handbooks are prepared by and revised periodically by appointed committees and reviewed by the Correlation Committee.

All Church officers are responsible for training those who serve under them. Leadership training or instructional meetings are held regularly for every group of leaders. For example, members of the

First Presidency and the Quorum of the Twelve meet weekly in the Salt Lake Temple for counsel and instruction. These leaders hold training sessions for other General Authorities, who in turn instruct the STAKE PRESIDENTS and other stake leaders under their jurisdiction. Stake officers periodically conduct training sessions for WARD leaders, who in turn instruct other ward officers under their supervision.

Leaders are given virtual autonomy in the performance of their duties and responsibilities. At the same time, they are charged to follow the principles of the gospel and policies of the Church, and they are enjoined to be mindful of service, gentleness, and humility: "Whosoever will be chief among you, let him be your servant" (Matt. 20:27). They are also charged to avoid unrighteous dominion: "No power or influence can or ought to be maintained . . . [except] by persuasion, by long-suffering, by gentleness and meekness, and by love unfeigned" (D&C 121:39–42).

Emphasis is placed on the need for leaders to learn their duties: "Wherefore, now let every man learn his duty, and to act in the office in which he is appointed, in all diligence. . . . He that learns not his duty and shows himself not approved shall not be counted worthy to stand" (D&C 107:99–100).

Leadership training of LDS boys and girls begins at a young age. As children, they observe their parents and other adults serving in a variety of callings. As youth they are called to serve in presidencies in their Aaronic Priesthood, Young Men, Young Women, and seminary organizations. The attempt is made to have all boys and girls hold some kind of leadership position during their teens. Serving missions places many young men and women into a wide variety of leadership positions (e.g., as senior companions, district leaders, zone leaders, and assistants to the mission president). Virtually all Latter-day Saints are asked to serve in the Church in one way or another. In general, the guidelines for leadership are the same for men and women.

For many callings, an unofficial apprenticeship system is followed. Often, a counselor in a PRESIDENCY or another officer in the respective organization will be called as its next president; similarly, a man trained as an assistant clerk may be called as the next clerk. Sometimes, however, one is appointed to a position to which he has had no training, as the BISHOP or stake president follows the impressions of the Spirit in extending calls to service.

Bishops, Relief Society presidents, and other leaders concerned with the welfare of individuals employ many leadership and organizational skills, such as evaluating alternatives, scheduling, delegating, and motivating others. However, all Church leaders are encouraged to focus principally on people, to feed the sheep in the Lord's flock, to know and love the members, to listen, love, and help with personal needs. "It is the leader's duty . . . to teach the member to love—not the leader or teacher, but the truth of the gospel" (D. McKay, *IE* 71 [Dec. 1968]:108). To do this, leaders are frequently counseled to seek the spiritual gifts of discernment and wisdom (cf. Luke 12:12; D&C 84:85).

In addition to inspiration, leaders may look to others for training or assistance. A leader may confer with his or her own priesthood leader about a problem or need, especially in one's "stewardship review" a one-on-one session with one's organizational leader. These personal interviews are customarily held four times a year, "for it is required of the Lord, at the hand of every steward, to render an account of his stewardship, both in time and in eternity" (D&C 72:3).

BIBLIOGRAPHY

Barker, Shade R. *Youth Leading Youth*. Salt Lake City, 1987.

Bennion, Lowell L. *Fundamentals of Leadership*. Salt Lake City, 1965.

Lythgoe, Dennis L. *The Sensitive Leader*. Salt Lake City, 1986.

Maxwell, Neal A. *A More Excellent Way*. Salt Lake City, 1967.

Price, Kendall O., and Kent Lloyd. "New Approaches to Church Executive Leadership: Behavioral Science Perspectives." *Dialogue* 2 (Winter 1967):41–49.

WILLIAM G. DYER

LEVITICAL PRIESTHOOD

Levitical Priesthood is a rarely used term today, and it is sometimes applied to the AARONIC PRIESTHOOD (Heb. 7:11; D&C 107:1, 6, 10). Moses and his brother Aaron belonged to the tribe of Levi. Latter-day revelation indicates that before Moses died, the Melchizedek Priesthood and the higher law of the gospel were withdrawn from the Israelites because of their disobedience. Aaron and his sons were then given a lesser PRIESTHOOD to administer the lesser law of Moses as priests in Israel (D&C 84:18–28; Ex. 28:1). To assist Aaron and his sons, other worthy male members of the tribe of Levi were also given authority in the lesser priesthood, although they could not be priests. The keys of that priesthood remained with Aaron and his direct posterity (*MD*, pp. 9–10; Widtsoe, pp. 12–17). Hence, the lesser priesthood was called the Aaronic Priesthood, after Aaron, but is sometimes referred to as the Levitical Priesthood because all those who possessed it in ancient times belonged to the tribe of Levi (Num. 3:12–13). In the strict sense the Levitical Priesthood is a lesser part of the Aaronic Priesthood, held among those who were Levites, but not of the family of Aaron. The Doctrine and Covenants states that "there are, in the church, two priesthoods, namely, the Melchizedek and Aaronic, including the Levitical Priesthood" (D&C 107:1). It is anticipated that in the restoration of all things, the sons of Levi will once again function in the Levitical Priesthood on the earth (Mal. 3:2–3).

BIBLIOGRAPHY

Palmer, Lee A. *Aaronic Priesthood Through the Centuries*. Salt Lake City, 1964.
Widtsoe, John A. *Priesthood and Church Government*, rev. ed. Salt Lake City, 1954.

VERDON W. BALLANTYNE

LIAHONA THE ELDERS' JOURNAL

The official publication for all the North American missions of the Church from 1907 to 1945 was *Liahona the Elders' Journal*, published in Independence, Missouri. It arose from the merger of the *Elders' Journal*, published by the Southern States Mission from 1903 to 1907, and the *Liahona*, a multimission publication begun by the Central States Mission in Independence on April 6, 1907. Publishing articles of interest to missionaries, people considering membership in the Church, and general members, it helped build a feeling of community among the Saints scattered throughout the North American missions. Thomas C. Romney's *World Religions in the Light of Mormonism* (1946) grew out of articles he first published in the *Liahona*. In its prime, the journal had nearly 20,000 subscribers.

With several missions publishing their own bulletins after World War I and the *Deseret News* introducing the weekly "Church Section" in 1931, *Liahona* subscriptions continually decreased until it ceased publication in 1945.

BIBLIOGRAPHY

Garr, Arnold K. "A History of *Liahona the Elders' Journal*, A Magazine Published for the Mormon Missions of America, 1903–1945." Ph.D. diss., Brigham Young University, 1986.

ARNOLD K. GARR

M

MAGAZINES

From the earliest years of the Church, it has sought to build and strengthen the LDS community through a wide variety of periodical publications. Although the early LDS periodicals looked like newspapers (some were called "papers" and carried some news), they mostly printed religious and general interest articles, multipart serials, editorials, sermons, revelations, Christian and Church history, hymns, poems, advertisements, and letters from missionaries. Church magazines have always endeavored "to strengthen the faith of Church members, . . . promulgate the truths of the restored gospel, [and] keep members abreast of current and vital Church policies, programs, and happenings" (*IE* 73 [July 1970]:8). Many LDS missions started their own publications to communicate with and teach their people (*see* INTERNATIONAL MAGAZINES).

Other periodicals were financed, edited, and published independently by members of the Church, and thus technically were not official Church publications. However, some of these journals were brought under the umbrella of the Church AUXILIARIES, and then of the Church. After 1866, many LDS English-language periodicals printed lesson materials and fiction. In 1971, the Church consolidated its English-language periodicals into three new magazines assigned to serve different groups: ENSIGN (adults), NEW ERA (youth, ages twelve to eighteen), and FRIEND (children, to age twelve). *BYU Studies* (1959–)

was retained to be published by Brigham Young University for LDS scholars. The chart in Appendix 3 lists the major Church periodicals.

BIBLIOGRAPHY

"Church Publications." *Deseret News 1989-1990 Church Almanac*, pp. 187–91. Salt Lake City, 1989.

Green, Doyle L. "The Church and Its Magazines." *Ensign* 1 (Jan. 1971):12–15.

RICHARD TICE

MAGNIFYING ONE'S CALLING

Magnifying one's calling is a common exhortation among Latter-day Saints. In the OATH AND COVENANT of the priesthood the promise that "all that [the] Father hath" is given to those who are faithful in obtaining both the Aaronic and Melchizedek priesthoods and "magnifying their calling" (D&C 84:33–39). Paul told the Romans that he magnified his office by teaching the gentiles (Rom. 11:13). Jacob taught his Book of Mormon people to magnify their CALLINGS (Jacob 1:19; 2:2). And the Lord has given modern admonitions to Latter-day Saints to "magnify" or prepare to "magnify" their callings (D&C 24:3, 9; 66:11; 88:80).

Magnifying one's calling means taking callings seriously, following through responsibly, and realizing the importance of one's efforts. Magnifying one's calling does not mean to enlarge it beyond one's STEW-ARDSHIP or to make it appear great in the eyes of others, although there is a need to give one's own calling appropriate personal importance.

In Paul's declaration to the Romans that he magnified his office, the Greek verb *doxazo* is used, meaning to make honorable or glorious, the same verb used by New Testament authors to exhort their readers to glorify God (cf. Matt. 5:16; Rom. 15:6). Thus, to magnify a calling means to make it honorable and glorious, even to glorify God through service. Jacob explained that magnifying callings meant that he and his brother Joseph took upon themselves "the responsibility [of] answering the sins of the people upon our own heads if we did not teach them the word of God with all diligence" (Jacob 1:19). The Lord told William E. McLellin that if he, McLellin, would carry out his assignment fully as explained to him, including obeying the injunction to personal worthiness, he would thereby magnify his office (D&C 66:10–11).

Those who seek to respond to the Lord's admonition to magnify their callings take even the simplest calling seriously as an opportunity to glorify God and serve his children.

BIBLIOGRAPHY
Millet, Robert L. *Magnifying Priesthood Power*. Bountiful, Utah, 1989.

WILLIAM E. EVENSON

MAN'S SEARCH FOR HAPPINESS

"Man's Search for Happiness" (1964) is a motion picture noted for its skillful blending of aesthetic and spiritual qualities. The film was produced by the Brigham Young University Motion Picture Studio. It is less than fifteen minutes long, yet explores everyone's search for meaning in life: the whence, the why, and the whither.

Narrated by Elder Richard L. Evans, longtime announcer of the Mormon Tabernacle Choir broadcasts, the film stresses the gifts of life, freedom, and time, and the blessings of the atonement of Jesus Christ. It is climaxed by a poignant family reunion scene in the life to come.

Over 5 million people saw the film at the Mormon Pavilion in the 1964 New York's World Fair, and over 6.5 million at the Japan World Exposition in 1970. It has since been shown daily at the Temple Square Visitors Center in Salt Lake City and has had special screenings elsewhere. In 1986 the Church commissioned an updated version of the film for worldwide use. The remake retains the original narration by Elder Richard L. Evans.

BIBLIOGRAPHY
Top, Brent L. "Legacy of the Mormon Pavilion." *Ensign* 19 (Oct. 1989):22–28.

PETER N. JOHNSON

MATERNITY AND CHILD HEALTH CARE

Before professional doctors and nurses assumed primary responsibility for delivering health care, LDS women played a major role in providing maternity and child health care in their communities. Their efforts continued into the twentieth century with the establishment of maternity and children's hospitals and clinics under the sponsorship of the RELIEF SOCIETY and PRIMARY and with some women still serving as midwives in rural areas. The Relief Society also sponsored educational programs to prepare mothers for the delivery and care of infants and children. Concern for the health of mothers and children continues in Relief Society lessons today, and members are advised to seek the best medical care available. Specially trained Church missionaries also assist in programs to improve health care in developing countries.

At the time the Church was established (1830), the methods of many doctors were experimental and often harsh, and women usually did not call upon men for maternity care because it was thought unseemly. When available, midwives often assisted during childbirth. As the Church grew, leaders called and set apart women to serve as midwives. In Nauvoo in the 1840s, the Prophet Joseph Smith set apart three midwives. After the main body of the Church moved to the Salt Lake Valley, other women were called to serve as midwives both in Salt Lake City and in the outlying settlements. Because midwives were called by priesthood authority, they were accorded trust and respect similar to that given ecclesiastical leaders. They often dispensed herb treatments, passed on by experimentation and word of mouth, and sometimes administered health blessings.

Ward Relief Societies began coordinated health programs in the late 1860s after President Brigham Young assigned two of his plural wives, Eliza R. Snow and Zina D. H. Young, to promote health-care education among the Saints and to train midwives. In 1873 he asked each ward Relief Society to appoint three women to study nursing and midwifery, and a nursing school was opened for their training.

In the same year, President Young said that the time had come for women to study at medical schools in the East. At least six women responded, earning medical degrees in the 1870s. Most influential among these early doctors were Romania Pratt, Ellis Shipp, and Ellen Ferguson, who set up Utah's earliest professional training programs. Dr. Pratt wrote many articles on health. Dr. Shipp opened the School of Obstetrics and Nursing in Salt Lake City in 1878 and taught two six-month long courses each year, from which more than five hundred students eventually graduated. In 1888 she helped found Utah's first medical journal, the *Salt Lake Sanitarian*. Dr. Ferguson helped initiate plans for the Church-sponsored Deseret hospital, which opened in 1882 and shortly thereafter became the center for the School of Obstetrics and Nursing.

In 1899 the Salt Lake Stake organized the Relief Society Nursing School to provide nursing training especially for women who lived in rural communities and came to Salt Lake City for instruction. The school continued successfully until 1920.

By 1900 there were at least 34 female and 236 male doctors practicing medicine in Utah (Waters, pp. 108–111). The role of midwives began to diminish, but the Church's concern for maternity and child health care continued.

In 1911 the general presidency and general board of the Primary undertook the establishment of a hospital fund and the endowment of two rooms for children in the LDS Hospital. Primary-sponsored hospital care for children continued, culminating in 1952 in the establishment of the Primary Children's Hospital, which was operated by the Church until 1975, when it was transferred to private ownership (*see* HOSPITALS).

In 1912, following the publication of a Utah State Board of Health report linking many infant deaths to inadequate prenatal and postnatal care (Morrell, p. 197), the Relief Society began an intensive program for educating mothers in health care for infants and children. Local Relief Societies sponsored day-long clinics. Stake Relief Societies in Cottonwood, Utah, and Snowflake, Arizona, established their own maternity hospitals. Clinics and health care for children remained high-priority items for Relief Societies until the mid-1930s, when the federal Social Security Act was passed, subsidizing educational programs, prenatal clinics, and immunization programs.

Today, Relief Society women are encouraged to seek appropriate professional medical care and to participate in nursing and first-aid classes. Relief Society manuals include chapters on health care and nursing. Among the full-time missionaries of the Church are a great many young women (approximately 270 in 1990) with health and teaching backgrounds who, in addition to fulfilling proselytizing responsibilities, are assigned to teach disease prevention, nutrition, and home health care to Church members in developing countries.

Like the midwives of the early Church, they devote their time and talents to improving health care in the various communities where they have been called to serve.

BIBLIOGRAPHY

Divett, Robert T. *Medicine and the Mormons.* Bountiful, Utah, 1981.

Morrell, Joseph R. *Utah's Health and You: A History of Utah's Public Health.* Salt Lake City, 1956.

Waters, Christine Croft. "Pioneering Physicians in Utah, 1847–1900." Master's thesis, University of Utah, 1977.

CHRISTINE CROFT WATERS

MEDICAL PRACTICES

At the time the Church was established (1830), medical science was in its infancy. Fundamental mechanisms of disease were just beginning to be understood, and modern diagnostic approaches and notions about infection were only embryonic. Medical treatment for most conditions was ineffective and sometimes harmful. Early Church leaders, including the Prophet Joseph Smith and President Brigham Young, urged reliance on faith and priesthood blessings and treatment with herbs and mild food. Consistent with advances in medical science and education, Church leaders, including Brigham Young, began about 1870 to rely more on professionally trained physicians than in earlier years. Since that time, Latter-day Saints have been urged by their leaders to take advantage of the best possible medical care along with availing themselves of appropriate priesthood blessings.

In the early nineteenth century, practitioners trained in orthodox medicine relied heavily on bleeding and calomel (mercurous chloride) purges, treatments that were sometimes fatal. Joseph Smith lost his brother Alvin in 1823 when calomel, prescribed for what may have been appendicitis, lodged in his intestines, causing gangrene. This was one of several unfortunate experiences that supported a family inclination against these methods (sometimes called "heroic medicine").

Other practitioners, including Willard Richards, an early member of the Quorum of the Twelve, were trained (most often self-trained) in the Thomsonian system, which used various botanical products, water, and massage. Neither allopathic nor homeopathic in orientation, Thomsonian medicine was perhaps closest to today's naturopathy. While not aggressively dangerous, as were many of the then common practitioners of quackery or some of the orthodox practitioners, most often the Thomsonians could do little more than offer kindness.

In 1831 Joseph Smith received the following revelation regarding health care: "And whosoever among you are sick, and have not faith to be healed, but believe, shall be nourished with all tenderness, with herbs and mild food, and that not by the hand of an enemy. . . . And again, it shall come to pass that he that hath faith in me to be healed, and is not appointed unto death, shall be healed" (D&C 42:43, 48). Many Latter-day Saints from that era recorded remarkable healing experiences following priesthood blessings.

Against this background, Brigham Young, who succeeded Joseph Smith, cautioned Church members against heroic medical care and emphasized reliance on common sense, safe and conservative treatments, and blessings by the priesthood. While critical of both the medical profession and individual practitioners on occasion, he acknowledged their value with fractures and some other conditions.

Medical science advanced rapidly in the latter half of the nineteenth century, and Brigham Young began to rely on physicians for more of his own medical care. During the decade beginning in 1867, he was responsible for sending several of the most gifted young men and women in the Church, among them his nephew Seymour Young, to medical schools in the East. Brigham Young died in 1877 of what his nephew later concluded must have been appendicitis.

Today, many LDS women and men are involved in health care practice and research. Church members, who are advised to seek medical assistance from competent licensed physicians, generally believe that advances in medical science and health care have come though the inspiration of the Lord. They also continue to seek priesthood blessings together with appropriate medical care.

[*See also* Hospitals; Maternity and Child Health Care.]

BIBLIOGRAPHY

Bush, Lester E. "The Mormon Tradition." In *Caring and Curing: Health and Medicine in Western Religious Traditions*, ed. R. Numbers and E. Amundsen, pp. 397–420. New York, 1986.

Divett, Robert T. *Medicine and Mormons: An Introduction to the History of Latter-day Saint Health Care*. Bountiful, Utah, 1981.

CECIL O. SAMUELSON, JR.

MEETINGHOUSE

Meetinghouses for members of The Church of Jesus Christ of Latter-day Saints are often called chapels, but technically the chapel is a special part of the meetinghouse in which worship services are held. In the tradition of the New England meetinghouse, LDS meetinghouses are multipurpose facilities. They developed from a single-room, multiuse building to multiroom complexes.

THE MEETINGHOUSE, 1847–1869.   Before 1847 there were few LDS meetinghouses. Soon after the Saints arrived in the Great Basin region in 1847, single-room structures were constructed of indigenous materials in all established communities. Where it was deemed prudent to build forts for the protection of the settlers, such meetinghouses were included within the overall design of the protective enclosure. They had earthen or plank floors, small paned windows, open ceilings, and a roof that could be made from a variety of natural materials. Each served as a chapel, a general meeting facility, and often also a school, making it the focus for the activities of the community or settlement.

Later meetinghouses in this period exhibited a greater sense of style than their earlier counterparts. Classical pediments, bracket motifs, pilasters, small steeples, and inside columns became more frequent. Yet one may not classify these meetinghouses stylistically as Federal, Greek, or Gothic Revival, or as New England variations on English architect Christopher Wren. Rather, the majority remained either eclectic or of a vernacular "high style."

THE MEETINGHOUSE, 1869–1890.   More sophisticated designs were developed to accommodate the rapid growth of the Church following the completion of the transcontinental railroad in 1869. Ward needs were met by the construction of halls or chapels of appropriate size with seating benches that faced a raised pulpit area. In some meetinghouses, the floor of the hall was sloped downward toward the pulpit area, and there was a backwall gallery, reached by staircases located at either corner of the hall or by an outside entrance. At times, the gallery extended from the back along the side walls of the meetinghouse. The ceilings were either flat or elliptical depending on the abilities of the artisans. Often, instructional and meeting rooms were placed behind the pulpit area to augment those in the undercroft or basement.

THE MEETINGHOUSE, 1890–1920.   Important changes were made in the general design of LDS meetinghouses in the early twentieth century. At first separate halls were built adjacent to many meetinghouses for use in needed cultural and recreational activities of the AUXILIARY ORGANIZATIONS of the Church and for the service activities of the RELIEF SOCIETY. Later modified designs incorporated the separate structures into the overall design of the meetinghouse. The combination of prospering LDS communities, growing numbers of qualified artisans, and a broader knowledge of architectural design led to a greater level of architectural sophistication. Wrenish entrance fronts with associated towers and spires became more frequent. The overall architectural styles of meetinghouses in this period can best be described as Classical, Romanesque/Gothic, and Victorian.

The period between 1890 and 1920 is usually regarded as the most individualistic period in Church architecture. Some of the Church's gifted artisans were sent to study at distinguished educational institutions and brought their knowledge and skills back to Utah. For instance, Joseph Don Carlos Young, a son of Brigham Young, went to Rennselaer Polytechnical Institute in New York and earned a degree in architecture. Shortly after his return, he was appointed Church architect. One of his responsibilities was to complete the Salt Lake Temple, which he did in 1893. His virtuosity in architecture soon led him and others to employ distinctive and sometimes exotic variations in style.

The most unique aspect late in this period was the introduction of the "Wrightian style." Derived from the cubic forms of the American modernist Frank Lloyd Wright, it was adapted to LDS meetinghouse architecture by Utah architects Hyrum Pope, Harold W. Burton, and Taylor Woolley (the latter having served as the head of Wright's Detroit office). It became known as the "Mormon style."

THE MEETINGHOUSE AND STANDARD PLANNING, 1920–1990. Standard planning has characterized LDS architecture since 1920, beginning with Joseph Don Carlos Young in the late years of his work as Church architect. The transformation came in response to Church growth and the need for a more cost effective use of limited Church funds. In the process, attempts were made to arrive at what might be considered an authentic form of LDS architecture. Young devised a plan that structurally joined the previously separate chapel and classrooms with the recreational or cultural hall through a connecting foyer / office / classroom complex. The joining of the two building types created a diversity in ground plans reminiscent of sixteenth- and seventeenth-century English domestic architecture. They became known as "Young's Twins" or the "Colonel's Twins." Most often they were designed in the Colonial style, and soon they became the prominent building type within the Church in the western United States.

During the Depression and war years of the 1930s and 1940s, the Colonial style of the 1920s gave way to a pragmatic or "plain style."

Then in the administration of President David O. McKay (1951–1970), a new plan was introduced to replace what had become an impoverished form born of economic necessity. Devised by architect Theodore Pope, the new plan connected the cultural hall to the back of the chapel. A modification of the plan connected two chapels on the opposite ends of a single cultural hall, creating a double-ender or double-chapel design. The latter configuration was intended to reduce land and construction costs where there were larger concentrations of Church members in a small geographic area. Both arrangements allowed for the potential overflow from the chapel to expand into the cultural hall, making both areas more functional and increasing the frequency of use. Classrooms and other meeting areas were attached to or extended around the chapel and cultural hall areas. This concept remains in effect today, though there are differences in outward appearances, interior spatial flow, and room arrangements.

Another concept developed in recent years allows for structural expansion by building additions in regulated phases, to accommodate a small but growing congregation. These later changes stem from events associated with the energy crisis in the 1970s, the rapid growth of the Church, and rising construction costs.

Colonial or classical exterior styles continue to be popular both in America and internationally. Whatever historical or modern motifs are now used, they remain subordinate to the overall standard design concept based on pragmatic functionalism. However, some individualistic plans have been used to conform to special geographic or cultural requirements. Regardless of the resulting style or plan, a Latter-day Saint meetinghouse still serves the same function as the New England meetinghouse—as a multipurpose center for worship and cultural activities.

C. MARK HAMILTON

MEETINGHOUSE LIBRARIES

Meetinghouse libraries in the wards and branches of the Church are provided to assist Latter-day Saints in both learning and teaching the gospel, whether in Church meetings or at home. Instructional materials are indexed to correlate with the Churchwide curriculum and are designed to enrich lives, helping people develop spiritually, emotionally, and intellectually.

An integral part of each meetinghouse, the library ideally contains selected books, pictures, flannel board stories and flannel boards, audiocassettes and players, videocassettes and players, a photocopier, a typewriter, screens, and projectors for the available videocassette tapes, filmstrips, and slides. Additional teaching resources include supplies such as easels, maps, charts, indexes, paper, and chalk. Ward members are allowed access to virtually all library materials for both teaching and home use.

Printed materials in the library typically consist of the standard works, doctrinal works by Church authorities, copies of the current hymnal and children's songbook, current and back issues of Church magazines, copies of current and past lesson manuals for all courses of study, general conference reports, and guide books for self-instruction in genealogical or family history work.

Learning and teaching aids are available for the Bible, Book of Mormon, Doctrine and Covenants, Pearl of Great Price, Church history, Church leaders, family life, and other resources used in the Church organizations. Many of these materials are prepared under the Church's CORRELATION guidelines.

The librarian and one or more assistants, who are called to the work by the ward BISHOP, instruct members about available items and how to use them. The librarian is normally trained by both the previous librarian and the stake or regional librarian. The librarian orders needed supplies normally from a Church DISTRIBUTION CENTER, planning the order in coordination with ward organization leaders, and subject to an established budget.

Teachers in Church organizations use the library most heavily on worship days. During the week, ward members may draw on library resources for family activities, family home evenings, FIRESIDES, and other occasions.

BETH M. MARLOW

MEETINGS, MAJOR CHURCH

Members of The Church of Jesus Christ of Latter-day Saints are a meeting-going people. When the Church was organized, the instruction was given, "It is expedient that the church meet together often" (D&C 20:75). The pattern for meeting every Sunday to pray, speak, and partake of the sacrament or "Lord's Supper" was established immediately, following the Book of Mormon norm (Moro. 6:5–6). The pattern of holding a Church CONFERENCE every three months also began in 1830 (D&C 20:61–62). Since that time other meetings have been added to the Church agenda. The main meetings on Sunday are (1) SACRAMENT MEETING; (2) SUNDAY SCHOOL; and (3) concurrent PRIESTHOOD quorum meetings for men and RELIEF SOCIETY for women, with children under twelve years of age simultaneously attending PRIMARY. Young women meet in their own sessions, while young men of equivalent age are in priesthood meeting.

In addition, families are expected, usually on Monday evening, to meet in their own homes in a family home evening, which can include instruction from a Church-prepared manual, an activity, and refreshments. Most families also use this evening as a time to discuss family concerns and make plans for the week. Single Latter-day Saints are encouraged to participate with nearby family groups or in groups of their peers.

Besides the meetings for all members, there are special meetings related to Church CALLINGS. For example, a presidency of three plus a secretary or clerk meet regularly to oversee the many functions of a stake and its wards. Then within each ward are the bishopric, priesthood quorums, Sunday School, Relief Society, Primary, Young Women, and so forth. Each of these presidencies typically also holds a planning meeting each week. Even though there are many meetings, leaders are encouraged to spend less time in meetings and more time in service.

Most Church meetings are formally organized with hymns, prayers, sermons, lessons, and/or instructions. To involve teenagers and children, many meetings use participative methods such as discussion groups, panels, case studies, and role playing.

In all conferences—ward, stake, regional, and general— Church leaders give presentations of counsel and inspiration. Special meetings are held during the year for the priesthood (e.g., stake and general priesthood meetings), and for the women of the Church (general meeting). There are likewise seminary meetings for participating teenagers attending high school, missionary meetings for those on MISSIONS, and meetings for temple workers, scout leaders, activity directors, nursery teachers, and Sunday School workers. The Latter-day Saint culture flourishes on the principle of meeting together often in order to "be prepared in all things" (D&C 88:80).

In business and planning meetings, there is an attempt to have everyone contribute, but those with official status usually conduct the proceedings and have the most decisive influence. These meeting patterns extend worldwide and are a major part of the cohesiveness that keeps Mormons in touch, involved, acquainted, and united in the common cause of building the kingdom of God on earth.

BIBLIOGRAPHY

Allen, James B., and Glen M. Leonard. *The Story of the Latter-day Saints*. Salt Lake City, 1976.

Arrington, Leonard. *Great Basin Kingdom*. Lincoln, Neb., 1966, pp. 28–33.

McKay, David O. *Gospel Ideals*, chap. 11. Salt Lake City, 1975.

WILLIAM G. DYER

MELCHIZEDEK

[*This entry consists of two articles:* LDS Sources, *a discussion of what is known of Melchizedek from Church scripture and revelation, and* Ancient Sources, *a historical view of Melchizedek from ancient writings and traditions.*]

LDS SOURCES

As a king and HIGH PRIEST of the Most High God (Gen. 14:18), Melchizedek holds a place of great honor and respect among Latter-day Saints. An example of righteousness and the namesake of the higher PRIESTHOOD, he represents the scriptural ideal of one who obtains the power of God through faith, repentance, and sacred ORDINANCES, for the purpose of inspiring and blessing his fellow beings.

Melchizedek was evidently a prince by birth, for he became king of Salem (later Jerusalem—Gen. 14:18; Ps. 76:2), where he reigned "under his father" (Alma 13:18). "Melchizedek was a man of faith, who wrought righteousness; and when a child he feared God, and stopped the mouths of lions, and quenched the violence of fire" (JST Gen. 14:26). Yet the people among whom he lived "waxed strong in iniquity and abomination; yea, they had all gone astray; they were full of all manner of wickedness" (Alma 13:17).

Though living among a wicked people, Melchizedek "exercised mighty faith, and received the office of the high priesthood according to the holy order of God" (Alma 13:18). This priesthood was after the order of the covenant that God had made with Enoch (JST Gen. 14:27), and Melchizedek ruled both as king and priest over his people.

As high priest, some of his functions were keeping "the storehouse of God" where the "tithes for the poor" were held (JST Gen. 14:37–38), giving blessings to individuals such as Abraham (JST

Gen. 14:18, 25, 37), preaching repentance (Alma 13:18; cf. 5:49), and administering ordinances "after this manner, that thereby the people might look forward on the Son of God . . . for a remission of their sins, that they might enter into the rest of the Lord" (Alma 13:16; JST Gen. 14:17). With extraordinary goodness and power, Melchizedek diligently administered in the office of high priest and "did preach repentance unto his people. And behold, they did repent; and Melchizedek did establish peace in the land in his days" (Alma 13:18). Consequently, Melchizedek became known as "the prince of peace" (JST Gen. 14:33; Heb. 7:1–2; Alma 13:18). "His people wrought righteousness, and obtained heaven" (JST Gen. 14:34). His Hebrew name means "King of Righteousness."

For Alma$_2$ and several biblical authors, the order of the priesthood to which Melchizedek was ordained was of prime importance. It was this "order," coupled with faith, that gave Melchizedek the power and knowledge that influenced his people to repent and become worthy to be with God. This order was "after the order of the Son of God; which order came, not by man, nor the will of man; neither by father nor mother; neither by beginning of days nor end of years; but of God" (JST Gen. 14:28; JST Heb. 7:3; Ps. 110:4). It was given to Melchizedek "through the lineage of his fathers, even till Noah," and from Melchizedek to Abraham (D&C 84:14). Those ordained to this order were to "have power, by faith," and, according to "the will of the Son of God," to work miracles. Ultimately, those in this order were "to stand in the presence of God" (JST Gen. 14:30–31). This was accomplished by participating in the ordinances of this order (Alma 13:16; D&C 84:20–22). The result was that "men having this faith, coming up unto this order of God, were translated and taken up into heaven" (JST Gen. 14:32). Accordingly, the Prophet Joseph Smith taught that the priesthood held by Melchizedek had "the power of 'endless lives'" (*TPJS*, p. 322).

So righteous and faithful was Melchizedek in the execution of his high priestly duties that he became a prototype of Jesus Christ (Heb. 7:15). The Book of Mormon prophet Alma said of him, "Now, there were many [high priests] before him, and also there were many afterwards, but none were greater" (Alma 13:19). The Doctrine and Covenants states that Melchizedek was "such a great high priest" that the higher priesthood was called after his name. "Before his day it was called *the Holy Priesthood, after the Order of the Son of God.* But out of respect or reverence to the name of the Supreme Being, to avoid the too-frequent repetition of his name, they, the church, in the ancient days, called that priesthood after Melchizedek, or the Melchizedek Priesthood" (D&C 107:2–4; italics in original).

It was asserted by some early LDS leaders that Melchizedek was Shem, son of Noah (see, e.g., *T&S* 5:746). Though Shem is also identified as a great high priest (D&C 138:41), it would appear from the Doctrine and Covenants 84:14 that the two might not be the same individual (*MD*, p. 475), and Jewish sources equating Melchizedek and Shem are late and tendentious.

BIBLIOGRAPHY

Madsen, Ann N. "Melchizedek, the Man and the Tradition." Master's thesis, Brigham Young University, 1975.

Welch, John W. "The Melchizedek Material in Alma 13:13–19." In *By Study and Also by Faith*, ed. J. Lundquist and S. Ricks, Vol. 2, pp. 238–72. Salt Lake City, 1990.

Widtsoe, John A. "Who Was Melchizedek?" *Evidences and Reconciliations*, pp. 231–33. Salt Lake City, 1960.

BRUCE SATTERFIELD

ANCIENT SOURCES

Genesis 14:17–24 reports that Abram ("the Hebrew," 14:3), upon his victorious return from a battle, was met by the king of Sodom ("Bera," 14:2), who was eager to reward Abram for coming to his and his allies' aid. The narrative is interrupted by an enigmatic insertion (14:18–20) featuring "Melchizedek king of Salem," "priest of God Most High" (RSV). Melchizedek "brought out bread and wine" and blessed Abram in the name of God Most High (Hebrew *'el 'elyôn*). Abram then gave Melchizedek a tithe of his booty. This priest-king of Salem has enjoyed a wide range of interpretation among Jewish, Christian, and Gnostic writings, some that brought him up to the heights of heaven, and others—of developing Christian and Jewish orthodoxy—that brought him down to earth again.

The story of Genesis 14 has raised numerous questions. Most modern scholars entertain a possible connection of this Melchizedek with a pre-Israelite kingship and/or priesthood in the Jebusite city of Jerusalem ("Salem") before its conquest by King David (2 Sam.

5:6–10). The incorporation of the story into Judean traditions reflects the interests of the Jerusalem royal ideology.

The only other Old Testament occurrence of the name Melchizedek is found in a royal Jerusalemite psalm, Psalm 110:4. There God ("the Lord") addresses the king thus: "You are a priest for ever after the order of Melchizedek."

Melchizedek occurs in the New Testament only in the Epistle to the Hebrews (5:6–10; 6:20; 7:1–17), where the Old Testament figure is interpreted as a type of the "high priest" of the New Covenant, Jesus Christ. The key passage is Hebrews 7:3, where it is said that Melchizedek "resembles the Son of God." Melchizedek's priesthood, superior to that of the "descendants of Levi" (Heb. 7:5), is a fore-shadowing of the priesthood of the Son of God. Hebrews 7:3 becomes the basis for most Christian interpretation of the figure of Melchizedek (Horton, pp. 111, 152, 161–64).

An important witness to pre-Christian Jewish speculation on Melchizedek has surfaced among the Dead Sea Scrolls: 11QMelch. The fragmentary Hebrew text, usually dated to the first century B.C., features Melchizedek as a heavenly end-time redeemer, with attrib-utes of the archangel Michael. He appears in the tenth and final jubilee of world history to rescue the elect, the "men of the lot of Melchizedek" (ii.8), doing battle with Belial and his fellow evil spir-its. Melchizedek's triumph is described as a high-priestly act of "expiation" (ii.8; cf. Kobelski, pp. 5–23).

Melchizedek is mentioned by Philo, a first-century Jewish philosopher of Alexandria, in three writings (*Legum Allegoriae* 3.79–82; *De Congressu* 89; *De Abrahamo* 235). Philo interprets the text of Genesis in a Platonic-allegorical fashion, seeing in Melchizedek a reference to the divine Logos, the thought of God in which the pattern of all existing things is conceived and the "image" of God according to which man was created.

Another important text, 2 Enoch, attests to early Jewish interest in the figure of Melchizedek. The date and place of this document are controversial, but recent scholarship places its original Greek version in the first century A.D. in Alexandria (cf. F. I. Andersen's introduction and translation in Charlesworth, Vol. 1, pp. 91–213). In this text (chaps. 71–72), a child is born miraculously to Noah's recently deceased sister-in-law, and the child, marked on his chest with a priestly seal, speaks and praises God. The boy is named Melchizedek by Noah and his brother Nir, whose wife had been posthumously delivered. In a night vision Nir is told of the impending flood; he is also informed that the archangel Michael will bring Melchizedek to paradise, thus enabling him to escape the flood waters. Melchizedek will eventually become the chief of priests among the people, and in the end of days he will be revealed yet another time as the chief priest. In this text, Melchizedek has three different earthly manifestations: born before the Flood, serving in the postdiluvian age as a great priest, and functioning in the end-time as a messianic priest (cf. Gruenewald, pp. 90–92; Delcor, pp. 127–30).

Some of these Jewish interpretations were taken over by Gnostics and are now reflected in some Christian Gnostic texts preserved in Coptic manuscripts of the fourth and fifth centuries (Pearson, 1990). In one fragmentary manuscript, the disciple John asks Jesus to explain what is said about Melchizedek in Hebrews 7:3. Unfortunately, the text breaks off before Jesus' interpretation is given.

A fragmentary text from Nag Hammadi (IX.1: *Melchizedek*; cf. Pearson, 1981, pp. 19–85) contains an apocalypse given by angels to Melchizedek, "priest of God Most High." It is revealed to Melchizedek that he will ultimately reappear as Jesus Christ, Son of God, to do battle with the cosmic forces of darkness. Here one can see influence not only from the Epistle to the Hebrews but also from non-Christian lore.

In the *Second Book of Jeu*, "Zorokothora Melchizedek" is a heavenly priest who presides over a heavenly baptism. No trace of influence from Hebrews is found in this text.

The most developed levels of speculation on Melchizedek, also lacking any influence from Hebrews, are found in *Pistis Sophia*, Book 4, in which Melchizedek plays a key role in the process of purifying human souls for entry into the "Treasury of Light" and transferring them from the domain of the archons, or earthly rulers, to that heavenly region. The younger material in books 1–3 of *Pistis Sophia* develops these ideas further: Melchizedek is a heavenly being who seals the saved souls upon their entry into the realm of light.

The church fathers attest to several heterodox ideas associated with Melchizedek. Hippolytus of Rome (*Refutatio* 7.35–36) and Epiphanius of Salamis (*Panarion* 55) are the most important witnesses to a group of heretics called Melchizedekians. They had a low Christology and exalted Melchizedek as a heavenly power superior to Christ. Others equated Melchizedek with the Holy Spirit (*Panarion* 67), and some "even in the true church" (i.e., not "heretics") naively regarded Melchizedek as the Son of God (*Panarion* 55.7.3). The later view seems also to have been present among the monasteries of Egypt (*Apophthegmata Patrum*, in *Patrologia Graeca* 65.160) and was even defended in a treatise on Melchizedek by a fifth-century resident of the Judean desert, Mark the Hermit (*PG* 65.1117–40). Such views were eventually overcome by teacher-bishops such as Cyril of Alexandria (*PG* 65.160).

On the Jewish side, while early rabbis continued to speculate on Melchizedek's role in scripture (e.g., equating him with Shem, son of Noah; cf. *b. Nedarim* 32b; *Midrash Gen. R.* 44.7; *Targum Ps.-J.* Gen. 14:18), a major stream of rabbinic tradition viewed Melchizedek negatively, a fact that indicates some Jewish sensitivity to the use of Melchizedek traditions by Christians (Gianotto, pp. 172–85).

BIBLIOGRAPHY

Charlesworth, James H. *Old Testament Pseudepigrapha.* Garden City, N.Y., 1983.
Delcor, M. "Melchizedek from Genesis to the Qumran Texts and the Epistle to the Hebrews." *Journal of Jewish Studies* 2 (1971):115–35.
Gianotto, Claudio. *Melchisedek e la sua tipologia.* Supplementi alla Rivista Biblica 12. Brescia, 1984.
Gruenewald, Ithamar. "The Messianic Image of Melchizedek" (in Hebrew). *Mahanayim* 124 (1970):88–98.
Horton, Fred L., Jr. *The Melchizedek Tradition.* Society for New Testament Studies Monograph Series 30. Cambridge, 1976.
Kobelski, Paul J. *Melchizedek and Melchireša'.* Catholic Biblical Quarterly Monograph Series 10. Washington, D.C., 1981.
Pearson, Birger A. "The Figure of Melchizedek in Gnostic Literature." In Pearson, *Gnosticism, Judaism, and Egyptian Christianity.* Studies in Antiquity and Christianity 5. Minneapolis, 1990.
———, ed. *Nag Hammadi Codices IX and X.* Leiden, 1981.

BIRGER A. PEARSON

MELCHIZEDEK PRIESTHOOD

[*This entry consists of two articles:* Powers and Offices in the Melchizedek Priesthood *is a general discussion of the Melchizedek*

Priesthood, and Restoration *is a historical treatment of the restoring of this priesthood in this dispensation.]*

POWERS AND OFFICES IN THE MELCHIZEDEK PRIESTHOOD

The Melchizedek Priesthood is the AUTHORITY, responsibility, and power to act in the name of Jesus Christ and to organize and direct part of his work. Through the opportunities of this PRIESTHOOD, men and women in partnership with God can conduct the work of the family and the Church. "It is the duty of this vast body of men holding the holy Priesthood . . . to exert their influence and exercise their power for good among the people of Israel and the people of the world . . . to preach and to work righteousness, both at home and abroad" (Smith, p. 157).

In the words of the Prophet Joseph Smith, "All Priesthood is Melchizedek, but there are different portions or degrees of it" (*TPJS*, p. 180). Most often, however, the name Melchizedek Priesthood is used in the Church to describe the higher priesthood and its offices. "There are, in the church, two priesthoods, namely, the Melchizedek and Aaronic. . . . The Melchizedek Priesthood holds the right of presidency, and has power and authority over all the offices in the church in all ages of the world, to administer in spiritual things" (D&C 107:1, 8). The Melchizedek Priesthood holds the keys to the kingdom, and "in the ordinances thereof, the power of godliness is manifest" (D&C 84:20).

ORDINATION TO THE MELCHIZEDEK PRIESTHOOD.   Every faithful, worthy man in the Church may receive the Melchizedek Priesthood. As with the AARONIC PRIESTHOOD, the Melchizedek Priesthood is conferred on those who have qualified themselves and have been called by those in authority.

Specific standards of worthiness to receive the Melchizedek Priesthood include personal integrity, chastity, obedience to the divine laws of health, and faithful contribution of tithes to the Church. Beyond these traits, it is expected that men will progress in developing attributes of godliness. Like all followers of Christ, they should be faithful, diligent, and amenable to righteous change, learning, and loving: "We can make advancement only upon the principles of eternal truth. In proportion as we become established upon the foundation of these principles which have been revealed from the heavens in the latter days, and determine to accomplish the purposes of the Lord, will we progress, and the Lord will all the more exalt and magnify us" (Smith, p. 141).

The PROPHET and PRESIDENT OF THE CHURCH holds and exercises all of the authority and KEYS of the Melchizedek Priesthood. He delegates to STAKE PRESIDENTS and BISHOPS and others the authority to ordain others to priesthood offices. Conferral of the Melchizedek Priesthood by the laying on of hands must also be approved by the COMMON CONSENT of the priesthood bearers or general membership of the candidate's STAKE or DISTRICT.

After the Melchizedek Priesthood is conferred upon them, all priesthood holders are ordained to an office within the priesthood, usually ELDER. They may later be ordained to the office of HIGH PRIEST or PATRIARCH as their Church CALLINGS require. Those called to be GENERAL AUTHORITIES for the whole Church will be ordained SEVENTIES or APOSTLES. Ordination to an office within the priesthood gives specific responsibilities within the Church.

Finally, a man may be SET APART to carry out an assignment, such as to be president of a quorum of elders, a stake president, or a member of the QUORUM OF THE TWELVE APOSTLES. As appropriate, he will be given the keys of authority necessary to carry out that assignment. This procedure makes it possible for every act performed under priesthood authority to be done at the proper time and place and in the proper way. The authority to direct those specific activities constitutes the keys of the priesthood.

An individual accepts his ordination to the Melchizedek Priesthood by making a covenant in his mind and heart with God (*TPJS*, p. 323; *see also* OATH AND COVENANT OF THE PRIESTHOOD). He covenants to honor, dignify, and learn the duties of his priesthood, to keep the commandments of God, to live by God's counsel, and to walk uprightly and virtuously as he carries out his responsibilities. God promises that if the man keeps his commitments, he will be given eternal life and be exalted in a godly state, inheriting all that the Father has, and will participate with God and the Savior in their continued work (D&C 84:39).

FUNCTIONING OF THE MELCHIZEDEK PRIESTHOOD.   All who hold the priesthood can use it to benefit others, regardless of their particular Church assignment or priesthood office. For example, in working with their families, men are authorized to carry out their patriarchal responsibilities, including blessing family members. In addition, they are authorized to heal the sick, seek personal knowledge, and give general help and comfort to those whom they contact.

To supervise and carry out priesthood ordinances within the Church, it is necessary to have both the Melchizedek Priesthood and the appropriate keys. For example, to confirm baptized members and bestow the gift of the Holy Ghost upon them, it is necessary to have the power of the Melchizedek Priesthood and to be authorized to use it. In this way, there is order, and the work done on earth is acceptable to the Savior in mortality and in the hereafter (*see* SEALING).

In addition to providing the authority to represent Christ on earth, the Melchizedek Priesthood provides a revelatory channel through which instructions and doctrine from Christ can be made known. Every individual has access to God and the right to receive personal revelation pertaining to his or her life and callings, but when revelation concerning principles or the implementation of principles is required for the Church or a priesthood unit of it, God gives this revelation only through appropriate priesthood leaders. The prophet and President of the Church receives revelation for the entire Church. A bishop receives the revelation necessary for leading the WARD. This way of making truth known underscores the right and responsibility of each individual to seek and obtain revelation and at the same time preserves order and harmony by working through the priesthood structure that Christ has set in place.

"The rights of the priesthood are inseparably connected with the powers of heaven; . . . [this power] cannot be controlled nor handled [except] upon the principles of righteousness" (D&C 121:36). One can officiate for God only when administering the work in wisdom and love, in a way consistent with the ways of God. Assignments must be pursued with long-suffering, gentleness, meekness, kindness, love unfeigned, pure knowledge, and charity toward all. In this way, God promises that the "doctrine of the priesthood shall distil upon thy soul as the dews from heaven" (D&C 121:41–45).

Priesthood can be lost as a result of a DISCIPLINARY PROCEDURE for serious sin. When a man is excommunicated, he loses his priesthood. Disfellowshipment or probation may restrict a man from using his priesthood until the repentance process is complete. In addition, "when we undertake to cover our sins, or gratify our pride, our vain ambition, or to exercise control or dominion or compulsion upon the souls of the children of men, in any degree of unrighteousness . . . Amen to the priesthood or the authority of that man" (D&C 121:37).

ANCIENT HISTORY OF THE MELCHIZEDEK PRIESTHOOD. The Melchizedek Priesthood is an eternal priesthood. Before mortality, God delegated authority and responsibility to worthy individuals. This holy priesthood was the means by which that action was taken. After this life, those who have been valiant and have honored their priesthood will continue to bear it and to have the responsibility to use it in serving others.

Adam, the first of the spirit children of God to live on earth, received the holy priesthood, with all its power, authority, and keys. "And thus all things were confirmed unto Adam, by an holy ordinance" (Moses 5:59). This authority was delegated to others in an unbroken chain from one prophet to another. "All the prophets had the Melchizedek Priesthood" (*TPJS*, p. 181).

Abraham sought the blessings of his fathers and the right to be ordained to the priesthood. Because he had qualified himself for the priesthood, even though his own father had not, Abraham obtained the priesthood from MELCHIZEDEK, the king of Salem and a priest of God (Abr. 1:2–5). Melchizedek met Abraham and blessed him, and Abraham gave him a tenth part of all he had (Heb. 7:1–3). Melchizedek exercised mighty faith and used his priesthood to bring a people practicing iniquity to repentance. None was greater than he (Alma 13:17–19). Originally, the priesthood was known as the "Holy Priesthood, after the Order of the Son of God" (D&C 107:3). To avoid too frequent use of God's name, the Church in ancient days called the priesthood by the name of this noted priesthood leader, Melchizedek (D&C 107:2–4).

Moses received the Melchizedek Priesthood from his father-in-law, Jethro (D&C 84:6). Moses held the Melchizedek Priesthood until he was translated, at which time the keys of the greater priesthood went with him, and what remained with the people was an appendage to the Melchizedek Priesthood called the Aaronic Priesthood, a priesthood with limited authority. After the time of Moses, individual prophets were given the holy priesthood at various times by God, but it was restricted from the general populace.

The Book of Mormon reports that Nephite prophets held the priesthood called after the order of the Son of God, the Melchizedek Priesthood (Alma 13:10). Those who had the authority directed the work of God among the people (Alma 29:13).

The apostles were given the Melchizedek Priesthood by Jesus Christ while he ministered on earth. He gave them authority and responsibility to direct his Church. After Christ left, the apostles continued to officiate for him and conferred the Melchizedek Priesthood on others when it was appropriate (Eph. 4:11–13; Acts 1:22–26). Over time, both the principles and the priesthood authority and keys were lost through APOSTASY.

MODERN HISTORY OF THE MELCHIZEDEK PRIESTHOOD. The Melchizedek Priesthood was given to Joseph Smith and Oliver Cowdery (*see below*). As directed, they ordained one another first and second elders of the Church on April 6, 1830 (*see* ELDER). In turn, they conferred the priesthood upon, ordained, and set apart others to offices and callings in the priesthood (*see* ORGANIZATION OF THE CHURCH, 1830). The first bishop was ordained in 1831 to care for the poor and needy and to govern the temporal affairs of the Church. On June 3, 1831, Joseph Smith directed more than twenty men to be ordained to the "high priesthood," as the president of this high priesthood. High priest councils governed the Church until 1834.

In 1835 the Church structure was adjusted to accommodate the additional revelation and increased numbers; PRIESTHOOD QUORUMS made up of men ordained to particular offices were in operation. Three PRESIDING HIGH PRIESTS were established as the quorum of the FIRST PRESIDENCY. The Quorum of the Twelve Apostles was a traveling high council directed by the First Presidency. The Seventy were to travel internationally to preach. Stake high councils were established to govern within their stakes, and bishops cared for the temporal concerns of the Church.

It was necessary for additional Melchizedek Priesthood keys to be restored to carry out the higher temple ordinances. Messengers from God brought these keys and instructions on April 3, 1836 (see D&C 110).

On July 12, 1843, Joseph Smith recorded the revelation concerning eternal marriage relationships, wherein Christ said he would "give unto thee the law of my Holy Priesthood, as was ordained by me and my Father before the world was" (D&C 132:28). He conferred upon Joseph "the keys and power of the priesthood" (D&C 132:45; *see also* PATRIARCHAL ORDER OF THE PRIESTHOOD).

The First Presidency presides over the Melchizedek Priesthood and directs the work of the Church. The Quorum of the Twelve Apostles shares this responsibility according to the keys given to the apostles. In turn, stake presidents supervise the wards and branches of the Church by the authority of the Melchizedek Priesthood and the specific keys given them.

All men who have the Melchizedek Priesthood are members of a priesthood quorum. These quorums are established within geographic boundaries and are made up of a group of men who hold the same office in the priesthood or who are of the same age group and may come to hold that office. Quorums administer the work of the Church assigned to them, train members in their priesthood responsibility, and provide opportunities for service and brotherhood for those working toward common goals.

In each stake there is one high priests quorum. The stake president and his counselors serve as the quorum presidency. A high priests group functions in each ward, presided over by a group leader, one or more assistants, and a secretary. An elders quorum, presided over by a president, two counselors, and a secretary, is organized in every ward and independent branch. The stake presidency and high councilors oversee all Melchizedek Priesthood quorum activities in the stake.

BIBLIOGRAPHY
Backman, Milton V., Jr. *The Heavens Resound: A History of the Latter-day Saints in Ohio 1830–1838*, pp. 237–56. Salt Lake City, 1983.
Critchlow, William J., Jr. "Priesthood—Asset or Liability?" *IE* 66 (Dec. 1963):1067–69.
Hartley, William G. "The Priesthood Reform Movement, 1908–1922." *BYU Studies* 13 (Winter 1973):137–56.
Kimball, Spencer W., et al. *Priesthood*. Salt Lake City, 1981.
Smith, Joseph F. *GD*, pp. 136–200.
Widtsoe, John A. *Priesthood and Church Government*, rev. ed. Salt Lake City, 1954.

JAE R. BALLIF

RESTORATION OF MELCHIZEDEK PRIESTHOOD

To act for God in organizing his Church and administering all the ordinances, Joseph Smith received the Melchizedek Priesthood in the divinely established way. Authority and responsibility for specific assignments are essential (D&C 18:9, 27–32, 35–37; 27:12; *see* KEYS). In addition, Joseph Smith and others received and taught the significance of each ordinance and key. Since no one on earth possessed that authority at the time, the Prophet Joseph Smith and his associate Oliver Cowdery received both instruction and ordination from God and from his messengers.

The Prophet and Oliver Cowdery received the Aaronic Priesthood on May 15, 1829, under the hands of John the Baptist. He informed them that he acted under the direction of Peter, James, and John, who held the keys of the Melchizedek Priesthood, and that that priesthood would be given to them (JS—H 1:72). Although the precise date of this restoration is not known, it is certain that it occurred after May 15, 1829, and before August 1830 (D&C 27:12). The documents available and the date of the formal organization of the Church give support to a time of restoration before April 6, 1830. Many students have concluded that late May or early June 1829 is the most probable time frame (*HC* 1:40n-42n; Porter, pp. 5–10).

Sometime before June 14, 1829, the Lord instructed Joseph Smith and Oliver Cowdery concerning their ordination as ELDERS, which is a Melchizedek Priesthood office (*HC* 1:60–61). Furthermore, when Peter, James, and John appeared to Joseph and Oliver, they ordained them also as apostles (D&C 27:12) and committed to them "the keys of the kingdom, and of the dispensation of the fulness of times" (D&C 128:20; cf. 27:13).

Several records document the occurrence and significance of this visitation. An early confirmation of the receipt of apostolic powers is evidenced in an 1829 revelation recorded in the hand of Oliver Cowdery in which the Lord stated, "I command all men every where to repent & I speak unto you even as unto Paul mine apostle for ye are called even with that same calling with which he was called" (Cowdery, 1829; cf. D&C 18:9). In his 1832 History of the Church the Prophet Joseph Smith declared that he had received "the holy Priesthood by the ministering Angels to administer the letter of the Gospel" and that he had been given "a confirmation and reception of the high Priesthood after the holy order of the son of the living God power and ordinance from on high to preach the Gospel in the administration and demonstration of the spirit the Keys of the Kingdom of God conferred upon him and the continuation of the blessings of God to him" (Jessee, p. 3).

Oliver Cowdery on many occasions bore witness that he "was present with Joseph when an holy angel from God came down from heaven and conferred, or restored, the Aaronic Priesthood and . . . was also present with Joseph when the Melchizedek Priesthood was conferred on each other, by the will and commandment of God" (Anderson, p. 22).

Joseph Smith said that Peter, James, and John made their visit "in the wilderness between Harmony, Susquehanna county, and Colesville, Broome county, on the Susquehanna river" (D&C 128:20).

On April 3, 1836, Joseph Smith and Oliver Cowdery knelt in prayer in the Kirtland Temple and received another profoundly important vision in which certain Melchizedek Priesthood keys were restored. Moses appeared and committed the keys of the gathering of Israel. Elias gave to them keys of the dispensation of the gospel of Abraham. Finally, Elijah stood before them as promised by Malachi and Moroni and bestowed the keys of SEALING families together (D&C 110:11–16; 2:1–3).

BIBLIOGRAPHY

Anderson, Richard L. "The Second Witness of Priesthood Restoration." *IE* 71 (Sept. 1968):15–24.

Barney, Ronald O. "Priesthood Restoration Narratives in the Early LDS Church." Planned for *BYU Studies* 31 (Summer 1991).

Bushman, Richard L. *Joseph Smith and the Beginnings of Mormonism*. Urbana, Ill., 1984.

Cowdery, Oliver. "Written in the year of our Lord & Savior 1829—A true copy of the articles of the Church of Christ." Ms. 1829. LDS Church Archives. Ms. in handwriting of Oliver Cowdery.

Hartley, William G. "Upon You My Fellow Servants: Restoration of the Priesthood." In *The Prophet Joseph: Essays on the Life and Mission of Joseph Smith*, ed. Larry C. Porter and Susan Easton Black, pp. 49–72. Salt Lake City, 1988.

Jessee, Dean C., ed. *The Papers of Joseph Smith*, Vol. 1. Salt Lake City, 1989.

Porter, Larry C. "Dating the Restoration of the Melchizedek Priesthood." *Ensign* 9 (June 1979):5–10.

JAE R. BALLIF

MEMBERSHIP

Membership in The Church of Jesus Christ of Latter-day Saints is a fulfilling, lifelong undertaking. It begins with the ordinance of baptism, which represents a covenant made between the convert and God. By this act, the convert promises to follow Jesus Christ and keep all his commandments in love and righteousness. God, in return, promises the gift of the Holy Ghost and the opportunity for eternal life. A newly baptized individual is confirmed a member of the Church by the laying on of hands by a MELCHIZEDEK PRIESTHOOD holder, who also blesses the new member with the gift of the Holy Ghost. This is a gift of spiritual discernment to help and sustain members as they attempt to live Christlike lives.

Figuratively, membership means becoming a member of the body of Christ: Each member is an essential part of the whole, just as the foot, the hand, or the eye is an integral part of the body. Each member serves different purposes and has individual gifts, but each is necessary, and if one suffers, "all the members suffer with it"; they are "many members, yet but one body" (1 Cor. 12:20).

The purpose of such membership is to facilitate fulfillment of one's baptismal covenant and to promote personal and spiritual growth unto the "perfecting of the saints, . . . for the edifying of the body of Christ" (Eph. 4:12). To this end, members participate in many religious activities. These include personal activities (such as prayer, fasting, scripture study, payment of tithing and other offerings; observing wholesome behavioral standards regarding sexual and moral conduct; observing the health principles of the Word of Wisdom); family endeavors (such as family prayer and family home evening); congregational and community functions (such as attending Sunday meetings, especially SACRAMENT MEETING, where members may partake of the Sacrament); and serving faithfully in various CALLINGS (such as acting as a teacher, a clerk, or a musician). Members are encouraged to participate in various welfare projects designed to provide goods and services to needy people. Activity in the Church is considered both a privilege and a duty of membership.

Another important characteristic of membership is proclaiming the gospel (McKay, p. 479). Members fulfill this responsibility in several ways: by serving full-time missions and financially supporting missionaries; by donating several hours per week proselytizing in their own locale as stake or ward missionaries; and by sharing their religion both by word and way of life as opportunities arise during informal daily interactions with others.

Members are also responsible for gathering the names of their ancestors and performing ordinances in the TEMPLE on behalf of those who did not receive them while alive. Once converts have been members for at least a year and have met certain standards of worthiness, they can enter the temple and receive these ordinances personally and thereafter can receive them as proxies for deceased persons.

Membership in the Church is highly valued by Latter-day Saints. It figures prominently in the self-image of faithful members who willingly consecrate and donate as needed of their time, talents, and blessings from God to the building up of the Church of Jesus Christ on this earth.

BIBLIOGRAPHY
McKay, David O. "Closing Address." *IE* 62 (June 1959):479.

LINDA A. CHARNEY

MEMBERSHIP RECORDS

When the Church was organized in 1830, Joseph Smith was instructed "that a regular list of all the names of the whole church . . . be kept" (D&C 20:82). This revelation was in harmony with other scriptures (cf. Ex. 28:9–12; Num. 1:2; Phil. 4:3; Mosiah 6:1; 26:36; Alma 5:58). Accordingly, each congregation (WARD and BRANCH) kept records thereafter containing the names of all members in the congregation and all blessings, baptisms, confirmations, ordinations, marriages, excommunications, and deaths. Through the years, the Church used several successive ways to keep track of membership information prior to the present electronic automated system. Many improvements have been made in the automated records system, and with rapid growth, reaching more than 7 million members by 1990, the Church is studying ways to reduce and simplify the amount of information being kept. Information concerning Church ordinances (baptism, confirmation, priesthood ordination, etc.) is so important that if the record is lost, the ordinances must be performed again.

In the 1800s, the presiding officer of a congregation would give members who were moving a letter to take to the presiding officer in the new congregation who would then enter that information in his own record book of members. In 1906 the Church formalized the procedure for transferring membership records as members moved from one congregation to another by having the presiding officer send a certificate of membership to the new congregation via the office of the Presiding Bishopric, even though at that time no duplicate or "master" record was kept at central Church offices. There were, however, member censuses taken approximately every five years to update records between 1914 and 1950.

In 1941, membership books were replaced by individual membership record cards, and duplicate records were created for each member. One copy was retained by the congregation, and the other was sent to the Church's master file in Salt Lake City. (Church membership at the time was approximately 890,000.) Each time a baptism, ordination, endowment, or marriage took place, it was recorded on the membership record in the local congregation. All changes were sent to Salt Lake City once a year. When members moved, their membership records were routed through the office of the Presiding Bishopric, and the new address was added to the master record.

The Church conducted a worldwide audit of membership records during 1969 as a forerunner to converting to an automated membership system, which was completed in the United States and Canada in 1975. The Church began decentralization of records that year. The records of all members living outside of the United States and Canada were sent to one of six area offices in which automation began in 1985. All international areas, except Samoa, were using automated systems in 1990. Master records are housed in thirty-five regional offices around the world.

BIBLIOGRAPHY

Membership Records Handbook. Salt Lake City, 1990.

Widtsoe, John A. *Priesthood and Church Government.* Salt Lake City, 1939; rev. ed., 1980.

THOMAS E. BROWN

MESSENGER AND ADVOCATE

The *Latter Day Saints' Messenger and Advocate* was published in Kirtland, Ohio, from October 1834 to September 1837—thirty-six sixteen-page, double-column issues. It succeeded the EVENING AND THE MORNING STAR. The name *Messenger and Advocate* described its purpose: to be the messenger and advocate of The Church of Jesus Christ of Latter-day Saints, thus to help the Saints better understand its doctrines and principles. Main doctrinal contributions came from Joseph Smith, Sidney Rigdon, Oliver Cowdery, W. W. Phelps, and John Whitmer. Other entries continued articles from the *Star*, a history of the Christian church, letters from missionaries, hymns, news of current Church events such as the building of the Kirtland Temple and its dedicatory services, editorials, minutes of conferences, summaries of news of the day, marriages, notices, and obituaries. The last issue of each annual volume contained an index of all twelve issues.

Oliver Cowdery edited the *Messenger and Advocate* from October 1834 to May 1835. He was succeeded by John Whitmer from June 1835 to March 1836, but returned as editor from April 1836 to January 1837. Thereafter, his brother Warren A. Cowdery served from February to September 1837, when publication ceased. Joseph Smith and Sidney Rigdon were listed as publisher for the 1837 February and March issues. In April 1837 the printing office and contents were transferred to William Marks, who was then listed as the publisher.

When Warren A. Cowdery declined further publishing, the *Messenger and Advocate* noted that "a large body of the elders of the church of Latter Day Saints have united and rented the printing establishment" (3:571–72) to publish the *Elders' Journal of The Church of Latter Day Saints*, which ceased publication in Far West, Missouri, in 1838.

BIBLIOGRAPHY

Backman, Milton V., Jr. *The Heavens Resound: A History of the Latter-day Saints in Ohio, 1830–1838*. Salt Lake City, 1983.

J. LEROY CALDWELL

MILLENNIAL STAR

The *Latter-day Saints' Millennial Star* was the official publication of the Church in the British Isles from 1840 to 1970. Filled with editorials often written by GENERAL AUTHORITIES and with expositions of the history, doctrine, and organization of the Church, the *Millennial Star* became a literary landmark in the Church. Parley P. Pratt, an APOSTLE of the Church and the first editor of the periodical, outlined its purpose in its first issue, May, 1840, "The *Millennial Star* will stand aloof from the common political and commercial news of the day. Its columns will be devoted to the spread of the fulness of the gospel—the restoration of the ancient principles of Christianity—the gathering of Israel—the rolling forth of the kingdom of God among the nations—the signs of the times—. . . in short, whatever is shown forth indicative of the coming of the 'Son of Man,' and the ushering in of his universal reign on the earth."

That first issue also contained an editorial; extracts of revelations given to the Prophet Joseph Smith and published in the United States in the Doctrine and Covenants; challenges to circulars against the Church from other churches; articles on what other religions believe; a report of the CONFERENCE on the Church in Preston, England; current History of the Church in the United States; letters from MISSIONARIES; poetry; and two hymns. Subsequent issues of the *Star* (as it was popularly known) followed a similar pattern throughout the years. Some of its poems became the lyrics for Church hymns, such as "Israel, Israel, God Is Calling."

The presidents of the British Mission were always listed as the editors, among whom were five future PRESIDENTS OF THE CHURCH: Wilford Woodruff, Joseph F. Smith, Heber J. Grant, George Albert Smith, and David O. McKay.

The *Star* was nearly discontinued three times: in 1841 and in 1843 due to lack of subscribers, and a century later during World War II, when all the American missionaries were withdrawn from England. Its pages are an excellent source for the history and development of the Church. Its serial "History of Joseph" was a foundation document for the multivolume *History of the Church*.

The *Millennial Star* was officially retired in 1970, when it was subsumed into the *Ensign*, the current English-language magazine for adults in the Church.

BIBLIOGRAPHY
Hill, James P. "Story of the Star." *Millennial Star* 130:12 (1970):10–13.

STANLEY A. PETERSON

MISSIONARY, MISSIONARY LIFE

Members of The Church of Jesus Christ of Latter-day Saints accept Jesus' injunction to his ordained disciples, "Go ye therefore, and teach all nations, baptizing them in the name of the Father, and of the Son, and of the Holy Ghost" (Matt. 28:19). They accept, indeed, a reiteration of it in modern times: "Go ye into all the world, preach the gospel to every creature, acting in the authority which I have given you, baptizing in the name of the Father, and of the Son, and of the Holy Ghost" (D&C 68:8). Missionaries consider themselves emissaries of the Lord in proclaiming his message.

WHO ARE CALLED.   In the first generation of the Church, married men frequently were called to be missionaries, and they left wives and families for an indeterminate length of time. In recent decades, the majority of missionaries have been young men and women who serve about two years.

Currently, the Church calls as missionaries, on a voluntary, temporary basis, single men from the ages of nineteen to twenty-six, single women twenty-one years and older, and older married couples with no dependent children. Missionary service is coordinated with military service as required.

Missionaries or their families generally cover the major costs of serving a mission. Missionaries called from developing nations may receive needed financial assistance from the general missionary fund of the Church. This assistance covers only basic living costs, as the Church has no paid ministry. No one is paid for missionary service.

As the Church has expanded, more and more missionaries have been called. Approximately 76 percent currently are young men, 18 percent are women, and 7 percent are couples. The number of retired couples accepting calls to serve missions is increasing, with many couples serving more than one mission.

CALLING AND TRAINING. The official missionary call is preceded by an interview, often requested by the prospective missionary, with the ward BISHOP, who assesses the person's worthiness and spiritual preparation. Prolonged formal study to preach the gospel is not required, but LDS parents are expected to prepare their children for missionary service through family scripture study and participation in Church classes and programs. Parents are also encouraged to teach children basic nutrition, health care, and homemaking skills that are essential for missionary service.

When a bishop has approved a missionary candidate, he sends the recommendation to the STAKE PRESIDENT, who also interviews the prospective missionary. When this process is complete, the stake president sends the recommendation to the Missionary Department of the Church. Designated members of the QUORUM OF THE TWELVE APOSTLES suggest a preliminary assignment for each missionary or couple. These assignments are then sent to the FIRST PRESIDENCY of the Church, who confirms or modifies them on the basis of inspiration. These procedures are in keeping with the scriptural admonition that "no man taketh this honour [of ministering in the Church or preaching the gospel in the world] unto himself, but he that is called of God, as was Aaron" (Heb. 5:4). Missionaries may be called to serve in nearby states or countries or anywhere in the world where there is an established mission of the Church. A letter calling the missionary or couple to a specific mission, bearing the signature of the President of the Church, is sent requesting a reply of acceptance or rejection of the call.

The prospective missionary generally is allowed several weeks to prepare before reporting at an appointed date to the nearest Church MISSIONARY TRAINING CENTER (MTC). Often the newly called missionary receives a letter from his assigned MISSION PRESIDENT with specific recommendations for the climate and mission service rules. Missionaries who already are fluent in the language of their assigned mission typically stay in an MTC for three weeks. Otherwise, they receive several weeks of intensive language and cultural training included with their courses in scripture study and methods of teaching the gospel.

Missionaries in an MTC also attend regular inspirational meetings and study classes. One day a week, they may attend a nearby TEMPLE and also write letters and take care of other personal needs. Sundays are devoted to attending regular Church services and studying the gospel.

At an MTC and in the mission field, missionaries are divided into administrative units called zones and districts. Single missionaries are assigned companions of the same gender who are studying the same language or going to the same mission. Married couples, of course, serve as companions to each another. Companionship is one of the most pervasive aspects of missionary life: a missionary never labors alone. The need for harmonious relationships between companions is urgent, and, although it can sometimes be a challenge, it usually leads to lifelong friendships. For missionary couples, it typically leads to an enhanced marriage relationship.

While in an MTC, missionaries begin to experience the meaning and rewards of full-time service to the Lord. The training is intensive. They do not watch television, listen to the radio, or go to places of entertainment. Letters, phone calls home, and nonmission business are limited. Their clothing is conservative business wear with distinctive name tags, except on preparation days or for service projects, physical-fitness activities, or special circumstances. The missionary's time is accounted for on reports submitted to the MTC or mission president; the principle is that one's time as a missionary is dedicated to the Lord.

ENTERING THE MISSION FIELD.   When missionaries arrive in their assigned geographic areas, they are welcomed by their mission president and are given a brief orientation in the mission home or headquarters office. Each new single missionary is assigned to be trained by an experienced missionary companion. Missionary couples may be trained by another couple for a short time before they go to their assigned area within the mission.

All single missionaries are asked to follow a daily schedule somewhat as listed below, with variations as suggested by the mission president or as needed according to the customs of the country:

6:30 A.M.	Arise
7:00 A.M.	Study with companion
8:00 A.M.	Breakfast
8:30 A.M.	Personal study
9:30 A.M.	Teaching and contacting
12:00 P.M.	Lunch
1:00 P.M.	Teaching and contacting
5:00 P.M.	Dinner
6:00 P.M.	Teaching and contacting
9:30 P.M.	Plan next day's activities
10:30 P.M.	Retire

Missionary couples may be given considerable latitude with their schedules because they often fill several different assignments, such as helping new converts gain experience in administering a Church unit, serving as guides at visitors centers and historic sites, or serving as nonproselytizing representatives of the Church in communities that do not allow proselytizing.

If missionaries are serving where they are learning another language, they spend time each day in language study. They also are encouraged to keep journals and exercise regularly. Missionaries spend most of their time finding receptive people and teaching them the restored gospel of Jesus Christ. Frequently they meet with people who have expressed an interest in knowing more about the way of life of their LDS friends and neighbors. Other people develop an interest in the Church and its teachings from media programs, street displays, pamphlets, or from simply seeing missionaries and inquiring about their background and purpose. When missionaries have time between teaching appointments, they often go door to door through a neighborhood asking those at home if they would be interested in learning more about the Church.

Missionaries work closely with local Church members, teaching people in their homes, speaking in ward or branch meetings about the importance of missionary work and on other gospel themes, and participating in social and athletic functions when their duties allow. Ward or branch members are encouraged to invite the missionaries to their homes for a meal as often as they can, to ease the financial burdens and to free their time for missionary work. Church members are often grateful to have the missionaries in their homes as role models for their children, while missionaries appreciate an hour of relaxation, home cooking, and LDS family life. Missionaries also often depend on local members for transportation, repairs on bicycles or other equipment, and advice and encouragement. Often, members of the elders quorum or Relief Society volunteer to serve as companions to male or female missionaries, respectively, so that the two full-time missionaries can split up for an evening and double their effectiveness.

Missionary apartments, while far from luxurious, must meet certain standards for health and safety, minimal space, and furniture. Apartments are rented and often become "missionary apartments" as a succession of missionaries transfer in and out of an area. In some places, Church members have apartments attached to their homes in which they invite missionaries to live. Missionaries travel on foot, by public transportation, by bicycle, or in mission cars, assigned at the mission president's discretion based on the distances missionaries must travel and other circumstances.

Almost every missionary experiences a test of faith and courage. The experience of telling people that one represents Jesus Christ and has a message that will change their lives forever leads to solemn introspection, earnest prayer, and continual study. While some missionaries have already moved through this process, others find that they must spend many hours in prayer and scripture study before they receive a testimony.

After several months of service, missionaries become proficient in teaching the gospel, and more effective in bearing testimony of its truth. If they are speaking a foreign language, they accommodate to its dialects. As they grow and mature in experience, they may be transferred to different areas in the mission and placed with different companions, or assigned to meet new challenges and work with new people. They may in time become trainers for newly arrived missionaries. One missionary may be called to organize and preside over a branch of the Church. Another may not do formal missionary work but be called to serve the needs of underprivileged people as a welfare worker or to teach English and cultural information to refugees awaiting resettlement. Other missionaries may be placed in charge of the finances or other business of the mission and do direct missionary work only in the evenings. Older missionaries are sometimes called to serve in temples as ordinance workers.

The tasks of a missionary often are traumatic. Missionaries may experience cultural shock, language barriers, health problems, personality adjustments, hostility, and sometimes severe persecution. Yet missionaries are, for the most part, dedicated, enthusiastic, and faithful, and later may describe their service as "the best two years" of their lives to that time. Companions encourage one another, and the missionaries gain a new perspective of themselves, of people, of the place where they serve, and of the gospel. Often missionaries continue their association with a foreign country or language through their choice of a college major or profession.

GOAL OF MISSIONARY WORK. The ultimate goal of missionary work in the Church is to invite all the inhabitants of the earth to come unto Christ, through personal testimony, "by gentleness and meekness, and by love unfeigned" (D&C 121:41). People throughout the world respond differently to the gospel message. Some quickly accept the message and within a few days or weeks request baptism into the Church. For others, it may be more difficult to leave past traditions, overcome social pressure, or break personal habits to conform to gospel standards. Occasionally, political and economic pressures countermand the inclination to conversion. Others simply feel no need for religion. All newly baptized members are accepted into The Church of Jesus Christ of Latter-day Saints as "no more strangers and foreigners, but fellow citizens with the saints, and of the household of God" (Eph. 2:19). Missionaries develop Christlike love for those they teach about the Church and for the people in the area where they serve. They are grateful for those who "hear [the Lord's] voice and harden not their hearts" (D&C 28:7).

BIBLIOGRAPHY
Bishop, Joseph. *The Making of a Missionary*. Salt Lake City, 1982.

SPENCER J. CONDIE

MISSIONARY TRAINING CENTERS

In 1832 a revelation given through the Prophet Joseph Smith in Kirtland, Ohio, directed the elders to tarry and conduct a SOLEMN ASSEMBLY to study the "doctrines of the kingdom," as well as a variety of secular subjects, so that they might "be prepared in all things" to go out and preach to the people (D&C 88:70–81). This initial assembly became the basis for the School of the Prophets with similar purposes, which opened on January 24, 1833. When Church schools were founded in Utah during the latter part of the nineteenth century, they created programs for MISSIONARY training. In 1883 "missionary meetings" were added to the offerings of the Theological Department at Brigham Young Academy, the predecessor to Brigham Young University in Provo, Utah. Similar programs were inaugurated at Ricks College in Idaho and at the Latter-day Saints University in Salt Lake City.

As missionary training progressed, the FIRST PRESIDENCY approved a Church Missionary Home and Preparatory Training School. A Salt Lake City home was purchased, remodeled, and furnished to accommodate up to ninety-nine missionaries. Inaugurated in 1925, the week-long program for departing missionaries emphasized gospel topics, Church procedures, personal health, and proper manners. This home accommodated the outgoing missionaries until the 1960s, but as the number of missionaries increased, other facilities were needed.

PROGRAM AT BRIGHAM YOUNG UNIVERSITY (BYU). For several years prior to 1960, Church and BYU officials considered the advisability of offering language instruction to missionaries. The occasion to launch this program came when missionaries assigned to Mexico and Argentina experienced lengthy delays in obtaining visas. On December 4, 1961, the Missionary Language Institute (MLI) opened with a class of twenty-nine elders in temporary quarters in a Provo hotel and various BYU buildings. Through classes, leadership meetings, and conferences, missionaries attending the MLI were able to develop facility in Spanish as well as in self-discipline and missionary spirit.

To enhance this program, in 1963 Church leaders gave its director the authority and stature of a MISSION PRESIDENT, and the MLI became known as the Language Training Mission (LTM). Portuguese and German were soon added to its curriculum.

In 1968 Church leaders decided to offer language instruction in all sixteen languages then being used by missionaries. To meet this major challenge, separate LTMs were established at Ricks College to teach Dutch and the Scandinavian languages and at the Church College of Hawaii to teach Polynesian and Oriental languages.

SCOPE BROADENED. The need for missionary training increased with the expansion of the Church. In 1971 over 2,500 missionaries received training at Brigham Young University in classrooms and housing that became increasingly inadequate. In 1973 the Church Missionary Committee approved plans to build a complex in Provo large enough to meet the needs of all language training for missionaries and decided to combine the three existing programs there. By 1976 the first phase was established. This multimillion-dollar complex demonstrated the Church's resolute commitment to missionary work.

Prior to 1978, while foreign-language missionaries were trained at the LTM in Provo, the Missionary Home in Salt Lake City continued to train the English-speaking missionaries. Beginning in 1978, however, all elders, sisters, and couples called from the United States or Canada reported directly to Provo for training, and the name of the facility was changed to Missionary Training Center (MTC) to reflect its more comprehensive program.

ORGANIZATION AND ADMINISTRATION. In the 1980s, the GENERAL AUTHORITIES became more involved in personal direction of missionary training. Although past MTC leaders had customarily handled policies and procedures through BYU, from 1980 on they increasingly reported directly to the Missionary Committee in Salt Lake City.

The internal organization was also at this time restructured to separate ecclesiastical from professional responsibilities. Missionaries were organized into branches whose presidents, called as lay leaders from among Church members in the Provo area, provided needed ecclesiastical authority and service in counseling missionaries and in conducting Sunday meetings. In addition, full-time staff members supervised professional activities such as training and business affairs.

MTC REGIMEN. The MTC is regarded as a mission field. All costs are paid by the missionaries, including board and room, books, and study materials. Every missionary is assigned another new missionary as a companion, and they are together twenty-four hours a day.

The schedule is rigorous. Classes have ten to twelve students who meet in three-hour sessions, morning, afternoon, and evening. Studies include the scriptures, languages, and missionary methodology. Academic responsibilities are balanced by spiritual development and recreational opportunities. Temple attendance and weekly devotional addresses given by visiting General Authorities aid spiritual well-being. Exercise programs promote physical fitness.

The intensive methodology used in foreign-language instruction is based in part on a program developed by the U.S. Army: Trainees learn by listening and repeating. Classroom instructors are usually experienced former missionaries and foreign students from nearby campuses. Linguistic drills are related to the culture, customs, and characteristics of the assigned mission field. In one week basic grammar is learned, and after two weeks a missionary begins to converse, pray, and sing in a new language. In eight weeks, missionaries are reasonably adept in conversation and can teach gospel lessons in a foreign language.

INTERNATIONAL EXPANSION.　The Church now operates Area Missionary Training Centers beyond Provo. Previously, missionaries called from outside the United States and Canada typically went directly to the mission field without orientation. Area centers have now been developed to give missionaries from other lands advantages similar to those provided in Provo. The first of these centers was established at São Paulo, Brazil, in 1977. By 1990, thirteen Area MTCs functioned in Latin America, Europe, Asia, and the Pacific. All are adjacent to Latter-day Saint temples.

The goal of the Missionary Training Centers is to provide initial training for full-time missionaries, preparing them to teach more efficiently the restored gospel of Jesus Christ. All programs are continuously evaluated in terms of this objective.

RICHARD O. COWAN

MISSION PRESIDENT

In 1990, some 257 mission presidents, along with their wives, and sometimes families, served in geographical mission areas in more than a hundred nations. The period of service for a mission president is usually three years. In the Church being a mission president is regarded as a challenging and exhilarating spiritual assignment, a link of fellowship with the Master. Calls are issued by the FIRST PRESIDENCY. Both husband and wife are set apart as missionaries by the laying on of hands by an assigned General Authority, often a member of the First Presidency or QUORUM OF THE TWELVE APOSTLES, and receive blessings and counsel appropriate to their assignment.

The calling is not a regular remunerative position, but interrupts professional employment; whatever financial losses accrue are part of the expected sacrifice. The family involved gives of its time and energies without salary, though there is a modest allowance for living expenses. Men and women from all walks of life and all nationalities and backgrounds serve, called, as it were, "from everywhere to everywhere." Typically, the president is a high priest with extensive prior service in the Church. His wife is likewise experienced in Church leadership and teaching. Their competence in the language and culture of their designated country is enhanced by mission presidents' seminars and training sessions.

A strong legacy of mission presidents permeates Church autobiography and biography, oral tradition, fiction, and folklore. Narratives range from some of flagrant and even life-threatening opposition and martyrdom to sublime accounts of conversions to Christ. It is a common feeling that the Spirit attends missionary work as it does no other.

An important concern of the mission president and his wife is naturally the continued nurture and care of their own children who have come with them. A second concern is the nurture and care of the missionaries, the majority of whom are young, uprooted, often struggling with a new language, and facing new stresses. The mission president trains, counsels, assigns, and gives spiritual support to each missionary, and his wife plays a vital role in training programs and the health, welfare, and safety of each missionary.

A mission is generally assigned from 120 to 250 full-time missionaries, with young men serving two years and young women serving eighteen months. In addition, there are some part-time missionaries and older couples. Older couples generally serve from one year to eighteen months. Single missionaries always labor in same-gender pairs; married couples labor together. Leadership roles are assigned to senior companions, district leaders, and zone leaders. Each mission has a rotating central missionary staff: typically a secretary, recorder-historian, supplies manager, and travel coordinator. Since new missionaries arrive and seasoned missionaries are released each month, training, retraining, and making new assignments and transfers are perpetual tasks.

The mission president, under supervision from Church headquarters, establishes mission rules, study patterns, goals, and discipline. His assignment requires constant travel to zone conferences, which are also testimony meetings, at least every six to eight weeks. The president and his wife have direct contact with the missionaries by phone, mail, and personal visits. They continually foster programs of goodwill, service, and understanding.

At the end of three years, the mission president and his family return home to resume their vocational and regular family lives.

GERALD J. DAY

MISSIONS

The mission of The Church of Jesus Christ of Latter-day Saints is to invite everyone to come to Christ. This includes a mandate to proclaim the gospel of Jesus Christ to every nation, kindred, tongue, and people (cf. Matt. 28:19; Mark 16:15; D&C 42:58). "Therefore, go ye into all the world; and unto whatsoever place ye cannot go ye shall send, that the testimony may go from you into all the world unto every creature" (D&C 84:62). From the earliest days of the Church, missionaries have been called to the nations of the earth to preach that message.

The ultimate destiny of missionary work was envisioned by the Prophet Joseph Smith in 1842:

> Our missionaries are going forth to different nations. . . . The Standard of Truth has been erected; no unhallowed hand can stop the work from progressing; persecutions may rage, mobs may combine, armies may assemble, calumny may defame, but the truth of God will go forth boldly, nobly, and independent, till it has penetrated every continent,

visited every clime, swept every country, and sounded in every ear, till the purposes of God shall be accomplished, and the Great Jehovah shall say the work is done [*HC* 4:540].

Two basic types of missions are organized to carry forward the missionary effort: full-time missions and stake missions.

FULL-TIME MISSION.   A full-time mission is an ecclesiastical unit of the Church in a designated geographical area. A MISSION PRESIDENT and his wife are called to preside over the mission and supervise from 120 to 250 full-time missionaries. Small missions in newly opened areas begin with fewer missionaries. In areas where STAKES have not yet been established, the mission president also bears ecclesiastical responsibility for all Church members who live within the boundaries of his mission. In areas where stakes have been established, the mission president does not carry this responsibility but is available as a resource to help members advance missionary work. Full-time missions have been organized in nations wherever the Church has official recognition.

STAKE MISSION.   A stake mission is organized in each stake of the Church to supplement or extend the resources of the full-time mission in that area. A stake mission president and two counselors preside over the stake mission. Unlike full-time missionaries, stake missionaries serve part-time, mostly in the evenings, and continue to live in their own homes and to fulfill their normal family and occupational responsibilities. They are generally expected to spend ten or more hours a week doing missionary work.

President Spencer W. Kimball described missionary work as the lifeblood of the Church. He wrote,

If there were no converts, the Church would shrivel and die. But perhaps the greatest reason for missionary work is to give the world its chance to hear and accept the gospel. The scriptures are replete with *commands* and *promises* and *calls* and *rewards* for teaching the gospel. I use the word *command* advisedly, for it seems to be an insistent directive from which we, singly and collectively, cannot escape. Furthermore, the command is clear that not only must all members of His church give missionary service, but we must take the gospel to all the children of our Heavenly Father on this earth [p. 4].

HISTORY OF MISSIONARY WORK.   In April 1830, immediately after the Church was organized, the first formal missionary activity began. Samuel H. Smith, a brother of the Prophet Joseph, filled his knapsack with copies of the Book of Mormon and traveled through neighboring towns in upstate New York to acquaint people with the newly published book of scripture. He sold a copy to Phinehas H. Young, who read the book and later joined the Church. The same book came into the hands of Brigham Young and, in conjunction with additional contacts, led to his conversion.

In the fall of 1830, four brethren, Oliver Cowdery, Peter Whitmer, Jr., Parley P. Pratt, and Ziba Peterson, were called to undertake a mission to the western frontier to preach to the Lamanites. They met with several Indian tribes, but their work was hampered by government Indian agents, and their principal success was among the white settlers in Ohio. By the end of December 1830, several hundred people had joined the infant Church, including such leaders as Sidney Rigdon and Frederick G. Williams, later named as counselors to Joseph Smith, and Edward Partridge, its first Presiding Bishop.

Through the efforts of several beginning in 1830, missionary work extended into Canada. John Taylor, who later became the third President of the Church, was an early convert there in the spring of 1836.

In 1837 Heber C. Kimball was called to open the first mission abroad. He and Orson Hyde were set apart to begin the work in the British Isles. In that same year, Parley P. Pratt issued his pamphlet *Voice of Warning*, the first tract published for missionary use in the Church. In April 1839, in response to revelation (D&C 118), the Quorum of the Twelve Apostles and others departed for a mission to Great Britain. Thousands of converts joined the Church, and great numbers of them emigrated to America during the 1840s and strengthened the Church as it endured dissension within and persecution from without.

By the 1850s, missions had been opened in Chile, France, Germany, Gibraltar, Hawaii, India, Italy, Malta, Scandinavia, South Africa, the South Pacific, and Switzerland. Many of these were discontinued after only a few years; but in the final decades of the nineteenth century, a time when the Church was facing severe persecution and extreme financial difficulties, additional missions were founded in Mexico, Samoa, Tahiti, and Turkey.

In 1901, President Lorenzo Snow renewed the emphasis on taking the gospel into all the world. Heber J. Grant of the Quorum of the Twelve Apostles dedicated Japan for the preaching of the gospel. Over the next two years, Francis M. Lyman, also of the Twelve, dedicated the lands of Africa, Finland, France, Greece, Italy, Palestine, Poland, and Russia for missionary work.

In 1920–1921, David O. McKay of the Twelve traveled some 56,000 miles in a world survey of Church missions for the FIRST PRESIDENCY. He made stops in the Pacific islands, New Zealand, Australia, Asia, India, Egypt, Palestine, and Europe. While in Asia, he dedicated China for the preaching of the gospel.

In December 1925, Melvin J. Ballard of the Twelve established a mission in South America, with headquarters in Buenos Aires, Argentina, predicting, "The work of the Lord will grow slowly for a time here just as an oak grows slowly from an acorn. It will not shoot up in a day as does the sunflower that grows quickly and then dies. But thousands will join the Church here. It will be divided into more than one mission and will be one of the strongest in the Church. The work here is the smallest that it will ever be. The day will come when the Lamanites in this land will be given a chance. The South American Mission will be a power in the Church" (quoted in *Melvin J. Ballard: . . . Crusader for Righteousness* [Salt Lake City, 1977], p. 84). By 1990, Central and South American converts had emerged as one of the largest segments of the Church.

During President McKay's administration as President of the Church, he instituted a vigorous missionary effort that increased the number of full-time missionaries from 5,000 to 13,000 and soon transformed the Church from an American institution into an international one. Preparation and training for missionaries were formalized and intensified. The first seminar for mission presidents was held in June 1961. A new teaching plan of six lessons was introduced and his "every member a missionary" program coordinated missionary efforts of Church members. In November 1961 a language training institute was established at Brigham Young University in Provo for missionaries called to Spanish-speaking missions. This institute became the Language Training Mission in 1963 and the MISSIONARY

TRAINING CENTER in 1978. During the 1960s and the 1970s, the Church built visitors centers at many temple sites and other locations, including major pavilions for the New York World's Fair in 1964–1965 and the expositions in San Antonio, Texas, in 1968; Japan in 1970; and Spokane, Washington, in 1974. A large visitors center was opened on Temple Square in August 1966.

In April 1974, in his first major address as President of the Church, Spencer W. Kimball emphasized that every able, worthy young man should serve a mission. Under his leadership, the missionary force more than doubled in twelve years, and new missions were established in many parts of the world. The June 1978 revelation extending the priesthood to all worthy male members of the Church opened up additional missionary opportunities.

Ezra Taft Benson, who became the thirteenth President of the Church in November 1985, continued to emphasize proclaiming the gospel as an important and basic part of the mission of the Church, emphasizing the role of the Book of Mormon as a necessary and powerful tool.

Changing political conditions throughout the world in the final decades of the twentieth century opened nations previously inaccessible to missionaries—principally in Africa, Asia, and Central and Eastern Europe.

MISSIONARY ORGANIZATION. Under the direction of the First Presidency, the Quorum of the Twelve Apostles is the Missionary Committee of the Church. The members of the Twelve "are called to be the Twelve Apostles, or special witnesses of the name of Christ in all the world, . . . being sent out, holding the keys, to open the door by the proclamation of the gospel of Jesus Christ" (D&C 107:23, 35). The Twelve are assisted in their ministry by the SEVENTY, who "are also called to preach the gospel, and to be especial witnesses unto the Gentiles and in all the world" (D&C 107:25).

The Missionary Department is the staff organization at Church headquarters that assists the Missionary Committee of the Church in providing direction, training, programs, resources, and administrative support to the missions of the Church. Calls to full-time missionaries are processed through the Missionary Department.

A mission president is called by the First Presidency to preside over each mission of the Church, normally for three years (*see*

MISSION PRESIDENT). He calls two full-time missionaries as his assistants, and they help him in training and supervising other missionaries. In his stewardship of Church units, the mission president is generally assisted by two local counselors. These counselors help the mission president in training and coordinating with local priesthood leaders and members who live within the stakes and WARDS within the mission area.

CALLS TO MISSIONARY SERVICE. In 1842, Joseph Smith summarized the procedure for calling a person to serve in the Church: "We believe that a man must be called of God, by prophecy, and by the laying on of hands by those who are in authority, to preach the Gospel and administer in the ordinances thereof" (A of F 5).

In the early days of the Church, missionaries were called individually during Church conferences. After the Saints moved to the Salt Lake Valley, the First Presidency announced mission calls at general conferences—often to the surprise of those called. Later, written calls were sent from the office of the President of the Church. The return address on these letters was simply Box B, Salt Lake City, Utah, and for generations of Latter-day Saints, "Box B" became a symbol of the call to serve a mission.

At first, mission calls were issued to anyone, and married men often left their wives and children to serve for an unspecified period of time, ranging from a few weeks to several years. During the latter half of the nineteenth century and the first quarter of the twentieth, wives occasionally accompanied their husbands on missions. The first calls to single women were issued near the end of the nineteenth century.

The ages and terms of service of full-time missionaries have varied over the years, and exceptions are made according to circumstance. In 1990, unmarried men ages nineteen through twenty-five, or occasionally older, were called to serve for twenty-four months. Unmarried women ages twenty-one through thirty-nine were called to serve for eighteen months, and those age forty through sixty-nine were called to serve for twelve months. Married couples normally served for either twelve or eighteen months.

In addition to the traditional tasks of missionaries, couples and sister missionaries may also be given assignments in such areas as leadership training, mission office staff, visitors center staff, public communications, temple work, family history research, health welfare services, education, and other full-time Church service.

MISSIONARY PREPARATION AND TRAINING.   Informal missionary training often begins in the homes of Latter-day Saints and continues in the various Church priesthood and AUXILIARY ORGANIZATIONS at the local level. A specific purpose of bearing the AARONIC PRIESTHOOD, designated in the scriptures as the preparatory priesthood (D&C 84:26), is to prepare young men for the responsibilities of the MELCHIZEDEK PRIESTHOOD, including missionary service. Some stakes sponsor missionary-preparation seminars or classes to assist young men and women and older couples in preparing for full-time missions. Brief formal missionary training for those already called is given at local Missionary Training Centers located around the world. Missionaries assigned to missions where they will speak their native language remain at a training center for approximately three weeks. Missionaries who must learn a new language remain for approximately two months (see MISSIONARY TRAINING CENTERS).

On arrival in an assigned field of labor, each missionary receives on-the-job training from a senior companion and other mission leaders. Each missionary pair or married couple spends a portion of each day studying the scriptures, practicing the missionary discussions, and strengthening other missionary skills and attributes. Language study also continues for those who are learning a new language. District meetings held every week and zone conferences held every four to six weeks provide opportunities for missionaries to be instructed, motivated, and further trained by the mission leaders.

MISSIONARY APPROACHES.   Historically, missionaries have endeavored to find those who are interested in listening to their message so they can teach them the gospel, baptize those who desire to join the Church, and fellowship new converts as they begin their membership in the Church.

During the first 150 years of the Church, missionary work centered on public meetings and contacting people in their homes: tracting (see below); street meetings; debates; exhibits at fairs, expositions, or shopping malls; FIRESIDES held in public buildings or Church meetinghouses; and "cottage meetings" held in private homes.

Door-to-door contacting is commonly called "tracting" because missionaries in the past often left printed tracts with people as they called on them. As the number and influence of Church members have grown, missionaries have come increasingly to rely on referrals from members to find people to teach. In the latter half of the twentieth century, missionaries have had the benefit of standardized lessons, usually referred to as missionary discussions, to assist them in teaching the gospel.

People who are being taught are invited to become actively involved by reading and studying on their own, praying about the message they are receiving, attending Church meetings, coming to know Church members, and living the principles of the gospel as they learn them. Full-time and stake missionaries are often assigned specific duties in shepherding new members and helping them become "fellowcitizens with the saints, and of the household of God" (Eph. 2:19).

BIBLIOGRAPHY
Kimball, Spencer W. "It Becometh Every Man." *Ensign* 7 (Oct. 1977):3–7.

DEAN B. CLEVERLY

N

NAME OF THE CHURCH

The name The Church of Jesus Christ of Latter-day Saints was given by the Lord in revelation to Joseph Smith on April 26, 1838 (D&C 115:4). The Church had been known as The Church of Christ from 1830 to 1834 (D&C 20:1); The Church of the Latter Day Saints in 1834; and The Church of Christ of Latter Day Saints from 1836 to 1838. The Church is commonly, but unofficially, referred to today as the Mormon Church and its members as Mormons because of their belief in the Book of Mormon. But the use of the term "Mormon" to refer to the Church is unsatisfactory from the point of view of Church members because it does not convey the conviction that Jesus Christ is the head of the Church and that members strive to live Christian lives. In the Book of Mormon, Christ's disciples asked him, "Tell us the name whereby we shall call this church" (3 Ne. 27:3). He answered, "How be it my church save it be called in my name? For if a church be called in Moses' name then it be Moses' church, or if it be called in the name of a man then it be the church of a man; but if it be called in my name then it is my church, if it so be that they are built upon my gospel" (3 Ne. 27:8). By implication, calling the Church by the name Mormon would make it Mormon's church. While most Church members are not offended by the title Mormon, they prefer the name that properly underscores their relationship to Christ.

Members of the Church are often referred to as saints, meaning men and women who are committed to live in accordance with the gospel. The New Testament similarly refers to followers of Christ as saints. The term "Latter-day" comes from the belief that the world is passing through the last days prior to the second coming of Christ.

BIBLIOGRAPHY
Anderson, Richard Lloyd. "I Have a Question." *Ensign* 9 (Jan. 1979):13–14.
Nelson, Russell M. "'Thus Shall My Church Be Called.'" *Ensign* 20 (May 1990):16–18.

SUSAN EASTON BLACK

NAUVOO NEIGHBOR

The *Nauvoo Neighbor* was a weekly newspaper published and edited by John Taylor in Nauvoo, Illinois, from May 3, 1843, through October 29, 1845. It replaced the *Wasp* (begun April 16, 1842, with William Smith as editor). Funded by subscriptions and advertising, the *Neighbor* regularly featured literature, science, religion, agriculture, manufacturing, commerce, and local, national, and international news. It reported actions of the state legislature, the Nauvoo City Council, and local courts.

As an advocate of truth, the *Neighbor* detailed conflicts involving the members of the Church, their neighbors, their enemies, and state and federal governments. It also carried correspondence between the Prophet Joseph Smith and Henry Clay (both U.S. presidential candidates) as well as the letters between Emma Smith and Governor Thomas Carlin concerning Joseph Smith's harassment by Missouri officials. It detailed the *Nauvoo Expositor* case and the events of the assassinations of Joseph and Hyrum Smith in Carthage Jail, including other newspaper accounts and correspondence. The *Nauvoo Neighbor* is a valuable record of the events and attitudes in and around Nauvoo from 1843 to 1845.

BIBLIOGRAPHY
Nauvoo Neighbor. Microfilm, Lee Library, Brigham Young University.

DARWIN L. HAYES

NEW ERA

The *New Era* is the official English language publication of The Church of Jesus Christ of Latter-day Saints for YOUTH (ages 12–18), their parents, and their Church leaders and teachers. Established in 1971 during a period of consolidation of all Church MAGAZINES, the *New Era* is published monthly. In its earliest days, it was addressed to readers twelve to twenty-six years old (to include single college students), but after four years its scope was reduced to twelve- to eighteen-year-olds to coincide with the age levels of the AARONIC PRIESTHOOD and YOUNG WOMEN programs. Its features include inspirational messages from GENERAL AUTHORITIES; stories about young Latter-day Saints throughout the world; first-person accounts of family life, MISSIONARY experiences, conversion stories, and spiritual insights; personality profiles; a question-and-answer section; a news and information section; Church history; poetry; photography; and humor. Another special feature is *Mormonads*, which appear as one-page "advertisements" of gospel ideals. Some of these ads are made into posters and sold through Church DISTRIBUTION CENTERS and LDS book outlets.

Special issues of the *New Era* have covered such topics as Christlike service, courtship and marriage, sharing the gospel, the Aaronic Priesthood, the Young Women program, career preparation, leadership, its own tenth anniversary, and a guide to "surviving and thriving in the 1990s." Special insertions have included a recording of speeches by PRESIDENTS OF THE CHURCH, a leadership game, and an advent calendar based on the life of Christ.

The *New Era* is a significant source of LDS fiction and music. It sponsors an annual creative talent contest for the youth of the Church with categories in writing, art, photography, and music. The winning entries are published in subsequent issues of the magazine. Consequently, the *New Era* is known for its policy of encouraging promising young LDS authors, artists, and composers, which includes an internship program in writing and editing for LDS college students who show promise.

The *New Era* has a reputation for being positive and idealistic, and it does not hesitate to combat problems like drug abuse, depression, alcoholism, immorality, suicide, exploitation of "nannies," and eating disorders. It has also won awards for design and typographical excellence.

The magazine's charter statement reflects its editorial philosophy: "As an official line of communication to the youth of the Church, the *New Era* is to provide a positive, uplifting voice for young people to hear. Therefore, each issue must be an example of editorial, photographic, and artistic excellence. The *New Era* shows every twelve- through eighteen-year-old Latter-day Saint what blessings can come from living the restored gospel. Readers learn from the examples and testimonies of others that being spiritually committed, wholesome, and LDS is the most desirable way to be, that righteous living is the only source of peace and happiness in life." Its managing editors have been Brian K. Kelly (1972–1989) and Richard M. Romney since 1989.

BIBLIOGRAPHY

Gostick, Adrian. "So You Want to Write for the *New Era?*" *New Era* 21 (Aug. 1991).

Todd, Jay M. "The New Era." *New Era* 1 (1971):3.

Wilkins, Richard G. "How to Write for the *New Era* Without Developing Ulcers." *New Era* 7 (Feb. 1977):16–19.

RICHARD M. ROMNEY

NEWSPAPERS, LDS

The Latter-day Saints have seldom been without a Church-sponsored or -oriented newspaper from the days of the *Evening and the Morning Star* (Independence, Missouri, 1832–1833, and Kirtland, Ohio, 1833–1834) to the current *Deseret News* (Salt Lake City, 1850–) and *Church News* (1931–). Even during their exodus to the West, the Saints could read their *Frontier Guardian* (Kanesville, Iowa, 1849–1852). For a time they supported both a religious Church paper and a single-sheet local newspaper. Such paired papers were the *Upper Missouri Advertiser* (Independence, 1832–1833) and the *Evening and the Morning Star*; the *Northern Times* (Kirtland, c. 1835–1836) and the *Latter Day Saints' Messenger and Advocate* (1834–1837); and the *Wasp* (Nauvoo, 1842–1843) replaced by the *Nauvoo Neighbor* (1843–1845) and the *Times and Seasons* (1839–1846).

When Latter-day Saints settle in an area, they often start an unofficial Church-oriented paper to share local news and to keep posted on the international Church. Some of the best-known unofficial twentieth-century local LDS newspapers are *California Intermountain News* (Los Angeles, 1935–1985, which became *Latter-day Sentinel* 1985–1989), the *Latter-day Sentinel* (Phoenix, Arizona 1979–1989), and the *Hawaii Record Bulletin* (Honolulu, 1977–), currently *Hawaii LDS News*.

[See the chart of Church periodicals in Appendix 2.]

BIBLIOGRAPHY
McLaws, Monte Burr. *Spokesman for the Kingdom: Early Mormon Journalism and the Deseret News, 1830-1898*. Provo, Utah, 1977.

JACK A. NELSON

O

OATH AND COVENANT OF THE PRIESTHOOD

Among the most important covenants is the oath and covenant of the priesthood, a set of mutual promises between God and those who receive the Melchizedek Priesthood. Doctrine and Covenants 84:33–42 states the obligations involved, affirming the rewards that will be given to those who faithfully discharge their oath, and confirming the consequences of breaking this covenant.

The priesthood holder's first responsibility is to receive in good faith and with honest intent both the Aaronic and the Melchizedek priesthoods. The covenant then obligates that priesthood holder to magnify his callings by fulfilling all the responsibilities associated with the office, teaching the word of God, and laboring with all his might to advance the purposes of the Lord (*see* MAGNIFYING ONE'S CALLING; cf. Jacob 1:19). The priesthood holder is required to "obtain a knowledge of the gospel . . . [and] to render service—service in carrying the restored gospel, with all the blessings of the priesthood, to the peoples of the earth; and service in comforting, strengthening, and perfecting the lives of one another and all the Saints of God" (Romney, p. 43).

God then promises that those who fulfill their part of the agreement will be "sanctified by the Spirit unto the renewing of their bodies," will become "the sons of Moses and of Aaron and the seed of Abraham" and members of "the church and kingdom, and the elect of God," and will receive the Father's kingdom, and, thus, "all" that the "Father hath shall be given unto" them (D&C 84:33–38). Latter-day Saints see in the first of these promises a change that purifies not only the minds of worthy priesthood holders, but also their bodies, until they are enlivened and strengthened to minister among the nations of the earth. Those who keep this covenant are then counted among those in the celestial kingdom, "into whose hand the Father has given all things—they are they who are priests and kings, who have received of his fulness, and of his glory; . . . they are gods, even the sons of God" (D&C 76:55–58).

This oath and covenant of the priesthood also carries a severe warning. The Lord has stated that anyone who breaks this covenant and "altogether turneth therefrom, shall not have forgiveness of sins in this world nor in the world to come" (D&C 84:41).

Ancient prophets received the priesthood by oath and covenant. Latter-day Saints understand several Old and New Testament covenantal texts to refer to the oath and covenant by which the priesthood has been received through all generations (e.g., Num. 25:13; 1 Chr. 16:15–17; Ps. 110:4; Heb. 7:20–21, 28). Enoch, Melchizedek, Abraham, and all others who received the fulness of the gospel of Jesus Christ have obtained the priesthood after the order of the Son of God in a covenant-based relationship with the Lord (e.g., JST Gen. 13:13; 14:27–30). In this way, the priesthood has been transmitted to man since the beginning of time with an eternal obligation and unfailing promise, both of which the Lord communicates through the sacred medium of an oath and a covenant.

BIBLIOGRAPHY

Asay, Carlos E. "The Oath and Covenant of the Priesthood." *Ensign* 15 (Nov. 1985):43–45.

Brown, Hugh B. "Participation: The Way to Salvation." *IE* 66 (June 1963):506–507.

Kimball, Spencer W. "Becoming Pure in Heart." *Ensign* 15 (Mar. 1985):2–5.

Monson, Thomas S. *First British Area General Conference Report*, pp. 142–46. Salt Lake City, 1972.

Romney, Marion G. "The Oath and Covenant Which Belongeth to the Priesthood." *Ensign* 2 (July 1972):43–45.

MICHAEL K. YOUNG

ORDINANCES

[*This entry consists of two articles:* Overview, *a general discussion of the nature of ordinances in the broadest sense, and* Administration of Ordinances, *the actual ecclesiastical procedures involved in the authorization and performance of ordinances in the Church.*]

OVERVIEW

The word "ordinance" is derived from the Latin *ordinare*, which means to put in order or sequence; or to act by authorization or command. Members of The Church of Jesus Christ of Latter-day Saints regard religious ordinances not as arbitrarily established but as purposefully instituted by God and eternal in scope.

The power to perform ordinances whose validity is recognized by God is inseparably connected with the divine AUTHORITY conferred on mortal man, that is, the PRIESTHOOD of God: "Which priesthood continueth in the church of God in all generations. . . . Therefore, in the ordinances thereof, the power of godliness is manifest. And without the ordinances thereof, and the authority of the priesthood, the power of godliness is not manifest unto men in the flesh" (D&C 84:17, 20–21).

Ordinances in the Church contain instructions and rich symbolism. Anointing with consecrated oil (e.g., as in the temple) is reminiscent of the use of sacred oil in the coronation of kings and the calling of prophets in ancient days. Laying hands on the head of the sick symbolically suggests the invocation and transmission of power from on high. The "waters of baptism" richly symbolize the actuality of new birth.

Latter-day scriptures give ample evidence that God has established unchangeable, eternal ordinances as essential elements of the plan of salvation and redemption (Isa. 24:5; Mal. 3:7; Alma 13:16; D&C 124:38). The Prophet Joseph Smith taught that "the ordinances of the Gospel . . . were laid out before the foundations of the world" and "are not to be altered or changed. All must be saved on the same principles" (*TPJS*, pp. 367, 308).

A biblical example of the necessity of ordinances can be found in the Lord's statement to Nicodemus that one must "be born again" (John 3:3). The Prophet Joseph Smith taught that "being born again comes by the spirit of God through ordinances" (*TPJS*, p. 162). The process of salvation is experienced as a "mighty change in your hearts" (Alma 5:14) under the guidance and assistance of the Spirit of God through keeping the divine ordinances. The test of obedience is reiterated in modern times, a pattern that is said to apply "in all cases under the whole heavens." One is fully accepted of God and is "of God" if, and only if, she or "he obey mine ordinances" (D&C 52:14–19). Some ordinances are universal in nature (cf. Lev. 18:4; Rom. 13:2; Alma 30:3; D&C 136:4), while others are rites and ceremonies decreed for special purposes within the Lord's work (e.g., Num. 18:8; Heb. 9:10; Alma 13:8; D&C 128:12).

Ordinances, in the sense of rituals and ceremonies, embrace the entire mortal life of God's sons and daughters and are performed by the Lord's authorized representatives, the bearers of his priesthood. Indeed, ordinances are the visible aspect of priesthood efficacy, the operation of proper divine authority conferred upon mortal man.

Some ordinances are prerequisite for entering celestial glory (baptism, gift of the Holy Ghost) and for exaltation (priesthood ordination, temple endowment, celestial marriage). Each human who lives, who has ever lived, or who will yet live upon the earth has need of these ordinances. Therefore, ordinances are to be performed vicariously in behalf of those who had no opportunity to receive them during their mortal lives.

Other ordinances enhance the physical, emotional, and spiritual welfare of their recipients though they may not be prerequisites for celestial glory or entering into the actual presence of God the Father. Such additional ordinances include the naming of children, confirmation, consecration of oil, dedication of buildings, and dedication of graves. Administering to the sick contributes to health and well-being and to emotional relief and comfort. Spiritual guidance is provided by the bestowal on children of patriarchal and paternal blessings. Vital covenant renewal occurs in partaking of the sacrament, when one makes a solemn commitment to conduct one's self appropriately as a bearer of the name of Christ, to always remember him, and to keep the commandments that he has given. Such obedience increases susceptibility to the guidance and sanctification of the Spirit.

Ordinances reflect the truth that the Lord's Church is a house of order. They also remind members of their standing in God's kingdom on earth.

Not only should the one performing an ordinance qualify to do so, but those receiving the ordinance should prepare themselves for the occasion. The fourth Article of Faith says, "We believe that the first principles and ordinances of the Gospel are: first, Faith in the Lord Jesus Christ; second, Repentance; third, Baptism by immersion for the remission of sins; fourth, Laying on of hands for the gift of the Holy Ghost." These initiatory steps are in precise and divinely appointed sequence, and by following them one moves "from grace to grace" as did the Son of God himself (D&C 93:13; cf. Luke 2:52). Indeed, modern revelation teaches, "If a man gets the fulness of the priesthood of God, he has to get it in the same way that Jesus Christ obtained it, and that was by keeping all the commandments and obeying all the ordinances of the House of the Lord" (*TPJS*, p. 308).

When ordinances are performed with authority and power, they are followed by divine blessings. They have "efficacy, virtue, [and] force" (D&C 132:7). They are enlightening to the mind and enlivening to the whole soul (JS—H 1:74). The first man, after he entered the process of baptism, was "quickened in the inner man" (Moses 6:65). Ordinances unify man with God, and man with man: "Behold, thou art one in me, a son of God; and thus may all become my sons" (Moses 6:68).

BIBLIOGRAPHY
Smith, Joseph F. *GD.*

IMMO LUSCHIN

ADMINISTRATION OF ORDINANCES

Ordinances performed in The Church of Jesus Christ of Latter-day Saints are to "be done in order" (D&C 20:68) by one who is ordained. The common linguistic root of the words "ordinance," "order," and "ordain" implies fixed succession, privilege, right, and solemn responsibility.

The administration of all ordinances presupposes worthiness of the administrator and the recipient. Most are performed by the laying on of hands of one properly ordained. It must be "known to the church that he [the officiator] has authority" (D&C 42:11), which can be traced in a documented line to the source of all AUTHORITY, Jesus

Christ. All ordinances are performed in the name of the Son, Jesus Christ, and in the authority of the AARONIC PRIESTHOOD or MELCHIZEDEK PRIESTHOOD. For some ordinances, such as baptism and administration of the sacrament, the scriptures prescribe exact words. For others, such as administration to the sick, the pronouncement of the recipient's name and a statement of the authority of the officiator are followed by a spontaneous blessing as inspiration directs.

Ordinances that are essential to salvation must be performed under the direction of those who hold the KEYS to assign the administration (see Heb. 5:4; cf. D&C 132:7). The validity of ordinances performed and their divine ratification or SEALING require this approval.

In harmony with biblical precedent and latter-day commandment, all saving and exalting ordinances, from baptism to temple marriage, are performed in the presence of witnesses, and a proper and faithful record is made and kept in the archives of the Church (2 Cor. 13:1; cf. D&C 128:2–5). Thus, ordinances become "a law on earth and in heaven" and, unless the covenants are violated, they cannot be annulled, "according to the decrees of the great Jehovah" (D&C 128:6–10).

BIBLIOGRAPHY
Melchizedek Priesthood Handbook. Salt Lake City, 1989.

IMMO LUSCHIN

ORDINATION TO THE PRIESTHOOD

Ordination to the priesthood is required in The Church of Jesus Christ of Latter-day Saints of all who administer the ORDINANCES of the gospel of Jesus Christ.

The pattern of ordaining men to PRIESTHOOD OFFICES and CALLINGS is found in the Bible as well as in sacred history. Joshua was ordained by Moses (Num. 27:18–23), and Christ chose and ordained his APOSTLES (John 15:16). Latter-day Saints believe these ordinations involved the laying on of hands. The sequence of ordaining ancient prophets and thereby transmitting authority from Adam to Noah is outlined in modern revelation (D&C 84:6–16; 107:40–52).

LDS officers trace their "line of authority" in steps back to the Lord Jesus Christ. Modern conferrals of priesthood authority are based on the specific historical claim of ordinations under the hands of ancient worthies (*see* AARONIC PRIESTHOOD: RESTORATION; MELCHIZEDEK PRIESTHOOD: RESTORATION). Priesthood authority and power from on high can be transmitted by the laying on of hands to all men who qualify for it in a spirit of humility. They who are ordained by an authorized agent of God look upon their ordinations as coming from the Lord himself (cf. Alma 13:1). An 1830 revelation declared in the voice of the Lord, "I will lay my hand upon you by the hand of my servant" (D&C 36:2).

Efficacy of ordination depends not simply upon the formula or words, but upon worthiness and the sanction of the Spirit. One may forfeit his priesthood authority by abusing it. The priesthood is not a domineering power. "No power or influence can or ought to be maintained by virtue of the priesthood, only by persuasion, by long-suffering, by gentleness and meekness, and by love unfeigned" (D&C 121:41).

In LDS understanding, those who are ordained to the priesthood are not an elite or professional priestly class distinct from laymen. They are all laymen. It is taught that "a man must be called of God by prophecy and the laying on of hands" by those who are in authority (A of F 5; cf. 1 Tim. 4:14). "By prophecy" means the right to receive and the power to interpret manifestations of the divine will.

At the age of twelve, all worthy LDS men may receive the Aaronic Priesthood and be ordained to the office of DEACON. At later ages they may be ordained TEACHERS and PRIESTS. Adult male converts are generally ordained priests shortly after baptism. An ordained BISHOP is set apart to preside over the Aaronic Priesthood and to serve as the PRESIDING HIGH PRIEST of his WARD. He authorizes all ordinations in the Aaronic Priesthood in his ward, which are performed either by a priest or a member of the Melchizedek Priesthood, often the father. Other priesthood holders usually join in the ordination standing in a circle around the seated person and laying their hands on his head. The one serving as voice invokes the authority of the priesthood and the name of Jesus Christ and pronounces the specific ordination, with accompanying words of counsel and promise.

Worthy men eighteen years of age and older may receive the

Melchizedek Priesthood and be ordained ELDERS. Men called to presiding positions in the Church such as BISHOPRICS, HIGH COUNCILS, and STAKE PRESIDENCIES, as well as PATRIARCHS and apostles, are ordained high priests.

At the present time only those called to serve as GENERAL AUTHORITIES in a quorum of SEVENTY are ordained to the office of seventy. Members of the QUORUM OF THE TWELVE APOSTLES are ordained apostles. Counselors in the First Presidency generally, but not always, also hold the office of apostle. The prophet of the Church is the Senior Apostle. When he becomes the presiding officer, he is ordained and set apart as the PRESIDENT OF THE CHURCH by the Quorum of the Twelve Apostles.

HOYT W. BREWSTER, JR.

ORGANIZATION

[*This entry is divided into two parts:*

Organizational and Administrative History
Contemporary Organization

The first article summarizes 160 years of Church organization and programs, and Contemporary Organization *examines the organization of the Church in 1990. There are separate entries for most major officers and units. See* Auxiliary Organizations *for an overview of subsidiary units that support the work of* Priesthood. *For details of local organization, consult* District, Ward, *and* Stake *entries; see also those associated with* Mission. Correlation of the Church, Administration *reviews more recent efforts to streamline and coordinate all Church curricula and administration.*]

ORGANIZATIONAL AND ADMINISTRATIVE HISTORY
Church organization and administration since 1830 have been the result of the restoration of ancient PRIESTHOOD authority and offices, of decisions made by living prophets receptive to divine revelation, and of practical responses to changing world and Church circumstances. From its inception the Church has been hierarchical, with authority flowing from the PRESIDENT OF THE CHURCH. Most positions

are filled by lay members called to serve without remuneration, and members are entitled to sustain or not sustain decisions and officers proposed by their leaders (*see* COMMON CONSENT; LAY PARTICIPATION AND LEADERSHIP).

THE FOUNDATION.   Joseph Smith and Oliver Cowdery received priesthood ordination and baptism under the direction of heavenly messengers in 1829. They then baptized others. This cluster of believers gathered on April 6, 1830, for the formal ORGANIZATION OF THE CHURCH, with Joseph Smith as First Elder and Oliver as Second Elder. Two months later the Church held its first conference and soon established a tradition of semiannual general conferences. From the beginning, Church officers were sustained by conference vote, and members and officials received certificates of membership or ordination from conferences.

During the first two years of the Church, DEACONS, TEACHERS, PRIESTS, and ELDERS constituted the local ministry. "The Articles and Covenants" served as a handbook explaining the duties of these officers (see D&C 20).

A revelation in 1831 instituted the office of BISHOP, initially one for Missouri and another for Ohio. Temporal affairs were their primary stewardship at first; they received consecrations of property in the 1830s, tithes afterward, and cared for the poor. Soon bishops also received responsibility for disciplinary procedures and for the AARONIC PRIESTHOOD. Not until 1839, in Nauvoo, Illinois, did the Church have bishops assigned to local geographical subdivisions called WARDS, under the jurisdiction of the bishop responsible for the larger region.

The office of HIGH PRIEST was instituted in 1831, with Joseph Smith as the PRESIDING HIGH PRIEST over the Church. In 1832 he chose counselors to assist him, initiating what became the FIRST PRESIDENCY. Revelation in March 1833 (D&C 90) gave the presidency supreme authority over all affairs of the Church; their roles at the head of the hierarchy remain essentially unchanged. Late in 1833 a second general officer, the PATRIARCH TO THE CHURCH, was called and ordained.

In 1834 two STAKES—geographic entities—were formed (one in Ohio and the second in Missouri) to direct the operation of BRANCHES (congregations) and local officers. Stakes were led by a three-man

STAKE PRESIDENCY and a twelve-member HIGH COUNCIL (D&C 102). High councils arbitrated disputes, investigated and tried charges of misconduct, and generally oversaw local ecclesiastical operations. Outside stake boundaries, members clustered into isolated branches led by elders or priests.

In 1835 the QUORUM OF THE TWELVE APOSTLES and the quorum of the SEVENTY were organized. The Twelve, subordinate to the First Presidency, were assigned by revelation to preside outside organized stakes as a traveling high council. This included ordaining and supervising other officers of the Church outside stakes, including patriarchs. They were also to direct proselytizing in all lands, assisted by the Seventy. The Seventy's presidency of seven, called the First Council of the Seventy, were sustained with other GENERAL AUTHORITIES in August 1835.

By 1835 revelations defined two orders of priesthood: the higher, or MELCHIZEDEK PRIESTHOOD, including the offices of high priest, seventy, and elder; and the lesser, or Aaronic Priesthood, comprising priests, teachers, and deacons. PRIESTHOOD QUORUMS in the stakes consisted of up to ninety-six elders, forty-eight priests, twenty-four teachers, and twelve deacons, each with its own presidency except the priests, whose president is a bishop.

In the fall of 1835 the Church published the first edition of the Doctrine and Covenants. The three revelations placed first (now sections 20, 107, and 84) described priesthood and its organization.

Visitations by Moses, Elias, and Elijah in 1836 restored the KEYS OF THE PRIESTHOOD and responsibility to gather scattered Israel and the SEALING powers by which families could be linked for eternity in temples (see D&C 109–110). These keys are still the basis for LDS missionary, family history/genealogy, and temple work.

After a mission to Great Britain, in 1839–1841, the Twelve received broadened responsibility, under the First Presidency, for Church government within the stakes as well as outside them, a responsibility they have carried since. In Nauvoo they received temple ordinances and the keys necessary to govern the Church if there were no First Presidency.

To complete Church organization and prepare the women, along with the men, for the temple, in 1842 Joseph Smith organized the women's RELIEF SOCIETY IN NAUVOO. A counterpart of priesthood organization for men, the RELIEF SOCIETY was seen as a more integral part of Church organization than were later AUXILIARY ORGANIZATIONS.

In 1841 Joseph Smith established the office of Trustee-in-Trust to manage Church properties at the general level. The role of bishops in temporal affairs thus became subordinate to that of the Trustee-in-Trust, generally the PRESIDENT OF THE CHURCH. In Nauvoo, and for the next decade after, a Council of Fifty assisted as political and temporal administrators.

The last body in the governing hierarchy to emerge was the PRESIDING BISHOPRIC. Until 1847 the Church had two general bishops, but that year Bishop Newel K. Whitney became Presiding Bishop. When his successor (1851), Bishop Edward Hunter, received two regular counselors in 1856, the three constituted the first full Presiding Bishopric. Initially, the Presiding Bishopric's primary responsibility was the overall management of temporal affairs, including the supervision of ward bishops in their temporal duties. Beginning in the 1850s, the Presiding Bishopric also oversaw Aaronic Priesthood matters.

The First Presidency, Twelve, Seventy, and Presiding Bishopric—all dating from this first generation—continue to be the main administrative officers of the Church. These General Authority offices are generally life-tenured callings except in cases of calls to a higher position or removal for cause or health problems, though emeritus status has recently been introduced. The Second Quorum of the Seventy is comprised of men called to serve a five-year period. Between 1941 and 1976 additional General Authorities known as ASSISTANTS TO THE TWELVE also served. The office of Patriarch to the Church, which earlier had administrative functions, was eventually limited to giving PATRIARCHAL BLESSINGS to Church members outside stakes, and in 1979 was discontinued.

After Joseph Smith's death in 1844, the Twelve Apostles led the Church under the direction of senior apostle and quorum president Brigham Young. In 1847 he was sustained as President in a new First Presidency. SUCCESSION IN THE PRESIDENCY continues to adhere to that basic pattern.

THE PIONEER ORGANIZATION.   After migration to the West in the late 1840s, Church organization adapted to facilitate colonization of the undeveloped Great Basin. Church officers directed the establishment of hundreds of colonies and helped provide settlements with economic, political, judicial, social, and spiritual programs. Often, one of the Twelve presided in larger settlements. Mormon villages combined private enterprise and economic cooperation, with bishops or stake presidents supervising the dispensing of land, building of roads, digging of ditches and canals, and conducting of business ventures. Although civil government gradually assumed an increasing role, the Church remained a significant influence in local and regional affairs throughout the pioneer period.

In a largely cashless economy with little investment capital, Church leaders promoted colonization and industrial enterprises by calling individuals on special missions and by using Church resources to foster community enterprises. A Church public works program, directed by the First Presidency and managed by the Presiding Bishopric, provided employment and helped build the Salt Lake Temple and Tabernacle and create other community improvements. In the 1870s Brigham Young directed the organization of united orders, economic endeavors managed by stake presidents and bishops. Since tithing donations were usually in "kind" rather than cash, local bishops and the Presiding Bishopric directed a gigantic barter and transfer system that paid for needed services, fed public works employees, and assisted the needy.

Much Church effort went toward assisting with immigration to the Great Basin. The Perpetual Emigrating Fund, a revolving loan fund, helped poorer immigrants, including handcart immigrants, make the trek. In the 1860s Church wagon trains were sent from Utah to convey immigrants from the railroad terminus. After they arrived in Utah, the First Presidency and Presiding Bishopric directed immigrants to settlements where they were needed.

In the 1850s and thereafter, the ward became the primary Church organization in the lives of the Saints. In the pioneer era, bishops selected by the First Presidency and priesthood "block teachers" called by bishops were the main ward officers. General Authorities maintained contact through semiannual general conferences in Salt Lake City, visits to the settlements, *Deseret News* articles, and epistles.

Missionary work, most of it outside the Great Basin, also had to be organized. In 1850 several of the Twelve opened new missions in

Europe. Usually an apostle residing in Britain supervised all European missionary work. Missions were divided into conferences, districts, and branches, each with a president selected by the line officer above him.

During the 1860s and 1870s auxiliary organizations started locally and then became general Church organizations under the supervision or presidency of General Authorities. These included SUNDAY SCHOOLS; the RETRENCHMENT ASSOCIATION, predecessor to the Young Ladies' Mutual Improvement Association (YLMIA; *see* YOUNG WOMEN); the Young Men's Mutual Improvement Association (YMMIA; *see* YOUNG MEN); and the PRIMARY for children. Relief Society for women was revived in Utah and established throughout the Church beginning in 1867.

In 1877 President Brigham Young implemented a massive reordering of wards, stakes, and priesthood quorums. This reform removed the Twelve from local leadership assignments, created new quorums for elders and Aaronic Priesthood, expanded the role of bishops as ward leaders, gave stakes increased responsibility, and, for the first time, involved most young men in Aaronic Priesthood offices. These and other changes at that time, such as quarterly stake conferences and reporting procedures, remained standard for nearly a century.

During the changes of 1877, Elder Orson Pratt explained the Church's organizational flexibility in terms that also foreshadowed future developments:

> To say that there will be a stated time, in the history of this church, during its imperfections and weaknesses, when the organization will be perfect, and that there will be no further extension or addition to the organization, would be a mistake. Organization is to go on, step after step, . . . just as the people increase and grow in the knowledge of the principles and laws of the kingdom of God [*Deseret News Weekly*, July 18, 1877].

Led by PROPHETS, SEERS, AND REVELATORS, the Church has exhibited its flexibility in adapting to changing needs and circumstances.

ELABORATION AND CONTINUITY.   The Church faced the 1880s with a well-developed and well-functioning organization; in addition, it was beginning to create auxiliary organizations for children and youth.

Over decades these would mature and be fine-tuned to function more effectively in an increasingly complex world.

Church pioneering institutions also remained. During the 1880s and 1890s, the Church continued to direct colonization and economic development. Building on the cooperative movement of the 1860s and the united orders of the 1870s, by the 1880s the First Presidency was coordinating development and regulated economic competition through a central Board of Trade and similar stake boards. During this period as well, revelations to President John Taylor initiated a revitalization of quorums of Seventy and moved these quorums toward becoming stake rather than general Church entities.

Federal prosecutions of polygamists during the 1880s disrupted Church administration as General Authorities, stake presidents, and bishops went into hiding or left Utah. Franklin D. Richards, an apostle whose plural wife had died, carried on many of the public functions of general Church leadership under the direction of the First Presidency, who were in hiding. With general Church ownership of property severely restricted, stakes, wards, and individuals formed nonprofit associations to hold Church property, including temples, meetinghouses, tithing houses, and livestock. After the Manifesto of 1890 and the granting of amnesty, Church leaders resumed their full administrative duties.

During the 1880s stake boards or committees were created for YMMIA, YLMIA, Relief Society, Primary, and Sunday School to promote and supervise auxiliary work locally. In 1889 the Relief Society began holding conferences in connection with the Church's general conferences, as did the Primary. By 1902 each of the auxiliaries was publishing its own magazine.

Though an extensive bureaucracy was not necessary until rapid international growth began in the 1960s, between 1900 and 1930 the Church modernized management and constructed important new facilities. The Church acquired historical sites, supported HOSPITALS, established recreation centers in local meetinghouses, and erected new offices in Salt Lake City, including a Bishop's Building (1910) for the Presiding Bishopric and auxiliary organizations, and the Administration Building (1917), in which the First Presidency and Quorum of the Twelve still have their offices. Zions Securities

Corporation was created to manage taxable Church properties, and the Corporation of the President was established to oversee ecclesiastical properties.

Church leaders also attended to programs for youth. Early COR-RELATION efforts saw the autonomy of Church auxiliaries decline as the Church assumed greater control over auxiliary magazines; the YMMIA's IMPROVEMENT ERA became a magazine for priesthood and Church readership. In 1911 the Church adopted the Boy Scout program as part of the YMMIA. In response to the secularization of Utah schools during the late nineteenth century, the Church had created stake academies and conducted religion classes after school for elementary-school children. By 1910 a General Board of Education supervised thirty-four stake academies; Brigham Young College in Logan, Utah; Latter-day Saints University in Salt Lake City; and Brigham Young University in Provo, Utah. By the 1920s the Church had closed most of its academies or transferred them to the state. Starting in 1912 released-time seminaries provided religious instruction for high school students. In 1926 the first institute of religion for college students opened adjacent to the University of Idaho.

Correlation efforts also extended to the work of priesthood, including missionary work, and to auxiliaries. A Priesthood Committee on Outlines began publishing lesson materials for each priesthood quorum during a priesthood revitalization movement (1908–1922). Church leaders also grouped deacons, teachers, and priests by age and defined their duties more fully; instituted weekly ward priesthood meetings, conducted by the bishops; and improved ward (formerly "block") teaching. After 1923 members of the Quorum of the Twelve directly supervised Melchizedek Priesthood work while the Presiding Bishopric supervised the Aaronic Priesthood, and in 1928 the Church published its first Melchizedek Priesthood handbook. A Priesthood-Auxiliary Movement, in 1928–1937, made Sunday School the instructional arm and YMMIA the activity arm of priesthood. This plan defined auxiliaries as aids to the priesthood and made the adult Gospel Doctrine class in Sunday School an integral part of adults' Sunday activity. Junior Sunday School for children became part of the Sunday School program Churchwide in 1934.

The Presiding Bishopric began providing aggressive leadership to Aaronic Priesthood work and to the YMMIA in 1938, and shortly thereafter they were given supervision of the young women. They provided counsel to bishops and stake presidents on Aaronic Priesthood, buildings, records and reports, and ward teaching through a weekly bulletin, *Progress of the Church.*

Beginning in 1925 a mission home in Salt Lake City provided training for new full-time missionaries. During the 1920s radio and motion pictures first helped missionaries convey the LDS message. Stake missionary work (part-time proselytizing by local members), started locally by 1915, was supervised by the First Council of Seventy after 1936. In 1937 the first missionary handbook was published, and in 1952 missionaries began using *A Systematic Program for Teaching the Gospel,* the Church's first official proselytizing outline. In 1954 a Missionary Committee, under General Authorities, began overseeing missionary appointments, the mission home in Salt Lake City, and publicity and literature. A Language Training Mission for full-time missionaries called to foreign lands opened in 1961 at Provo, Utah, and in 1978 it was expanded to become a MISSIONARY TRAINING CENTER for most new missionaries. Eventually Mission Training Centers were established in other countries; collectively these provide intensive training in dozens of languages.

In 1936, to ease hardships caused by the Great Depression, the First Presidency introduced the Church Security Program. Renamed the Welfare Program in 1938, it established through existing priesthood channels a network of farms, canneries, and factories that sent food, clothing, furniture, and household goods to BISHOP'S STOREHOUSES to assist the needy and, later, disaster victims. Soon after World War I, the Relief Society developed a SOCIAL SERVICES department to help families. This was gradually expanded to provide professional assistance, available through priesthood leaders, in such matters as counseling, therapy, and adoptive services. Eventually Social Services joined health services, employment bureaus, and other guidance programs as part of WELFARE SERVICES.

To meet the needs of LDS servicemen far from home wards and stakes, the Church responded with servicemen's groups on military bases, LDS chaplains, servicemen's coordinators, a Military Relations Committee, servicemen's conferences, seminars to prepare young men for the service, and an English-speaking servicemen's stake in West Germany. Native Americans also received renewed administrative attention. An Indian mission was formed in 1936 in the American Southwest, a general-level Indian Committee in the late 1940s, and the Indian Student Placement Services beginning in 1947.

CHALLENGES OF GROWTH AND INTERNATIONALIZATION.   Between 1960 and 1990, Church membership more than quadrupled, with especially rapid growth outside the United States. Many organizational developments during these decades were designed to streamline operations, enhance communication and leadership training, and focus resources on the needs of Church members far from headquarters.

By the 1960s three kinds of organizations were operating within the Church: (1) an ecclesiastical system under a priesthood chain of command; (2) auxiliaries, each with its own general officers, manuals, conferences, and publication; and (3) professional services and departments for education, social work, legal affairs, building, communications, accounting, etc. Early in the 1960s, efforts began to correlate these organizations. A Correlation Committee consolidated and simplified Church curriculum, publications, meetings, and activities. Further elements of the correlation program, implemented in 1964, grouped priesthood responsibilities into four categories: missionary, genealogy, welfare, and home teaching. Ward teaching became HOME TEACHING, giving the priesthood quorums new responsibility for carrying Church programs to LDS families. Wards developed PRIESTHOOD EXECUTIVE COMMITTEES and WARD COUNCILS to coordinate functions and reach out to individuals. In 1965 family home evening was established Churchwide and, in 1970, Monday nights were set aside for families; special manuals provided suggestions for gospel-oriented family activities.

Beginning in 1965 all messages from general Church agencies to wards and stakes were funneled into the priesthood BULLETIN. Regional publications merged in 1967 into a unified INTERNATIONAL MAGAZINE, published in several languages. In 1971 Church magazines in the United States and Great Britain were restructured with the publication of the ENSIGN for adults, the NEW ERA for teens, and the FRIEND for children. By 1970 the Church had implemented a worldwide translation and distribution organization with publishing and DISTRIBUTION CENTERS in European countries, the Americas, and the Pacific Rim.

Members of the First Council of the Seventy were ordained high priests in 1961 in order to better assist the Twelve in overseeing the growing number of wards and stakes. REGIONAL REPRESENTATIVES and Mission Representatives of the Twelve were called in 1967 and 1972, respectively (and merged in 1974). These officers played a key role in training and advising local leaders, an increasing number of whom were relatively recent converts with little administrative experience.

Spencer W. Kimball's presidency (1973–1985) saw important administrative changes, often in the direction of regionalizing responsibilities. Several functions previously reserved for General Authorities were delegated to stake presidents. In 1975 the First Quorum of the Seventy was reinstated as a body of General Authorities; a decade later the office of Seventy became exclusively a General Authority position. Regional Representatives received limited line authority to supervise stake work (1976). In 1978 the Twelve became more directly involved in such ecclesiastical matters as curriculum, activity programs, and Scouting; the Presiding Bishopric retained responsibility for temporal programs but no longer for the youth. To enhance general Church supervision of local operations throughout the world and at the same time facilitate regionalization, in 1984 an AREA PRESIDENCY (a president and two counselors, all of the Seventy) was organized for each of several major geographic areas. As the Church expands, boundaries are redrawn, and the number and importance of area presidencies increase.

Church programs have also been redesigned to meet the needs of an increasingly international membership. During the 1960s a labor missionary program (modeled after one that earlier constructed a college and a temple in New Zealand, and numerous chapels, especially in the South Pacific) helped the Church build meetinghouses in all parts of the world (see BUILDING PROGRAM). In the mid-1970s the Church divested itself of hospitals that benefited primarily residents of the Intermountain West and focused increased attention on the construction of chapels and temples worldwide—this time not by labor missionaries but by professional builders. A consolidated Sunday three-hour meeting schedule for priesthood, SACRAMENT MEETING, and auxiliary meetings was introduced in the United States and Canada in 1980 and later worldwide. By the 1980s a satellite communications network linked headquarters with many local stakes; that, and the widespread use of videotapes, made general conferences and communications from Church headquarters much more accessible. By 1990 much of the training of local leaders had been assumed by area presidencies and regional representatives.

In the 1980s Church financing became increasingly centralized, relieving local units of a major burden. Beginning in 1982 ward and stake buildings were funded fully from general Church funds (from tithes). In 1990 general funds also became the source for financing all local operations in the United States and Canada (*see* FINANCES OF THE CHURCH).

Though the basic administrative officers date from the founding generation, the challenges faced and the way the Church organizes itself to meet those challenges have changed dramatically. Such changes will continue. As President John Taylor said in 1886, the priesthood must not be fettered by "cast iron rules," for it is "a living, intelligent principle, and must necessarily have freedom to act" as circumstances require (First Council of the Seventy, Minutes, Dec. 15, 1886, Church Archives).

BIBLIOGRAPHY

Allen, James B., and Glen M. Leonard. *The Story of the Latter-day Saints*. Salt Lake City, 1976.

Cowan, Richard O. *The Church in the Twentieth Century*. Salt Lake City, 1985.

Hartley, William G. "The Priesthood Reform Movement, 1908–1922." *BYU Studies* 13 (Winter 1973):137–56.

———. "The Priesthood Reorganization of 1877: Brigham Young's Last Achievement." *BYU Studies* 20 (Fall 1979):3–36.

Quinn, D. Michael. "The Evolution of the Presiding Quorums of the LDS Church." *Journal of Mormon History* 1 (1974):21–38.

Widtsoe, John A. *Priesthood and Church Government*. Salt Lake City, 1954.

WILLIAM G. HARTLEY

CONTEMPORARY ORGANIZATION

Members of The Church of Jesus Christ of Latter-day Saints believe that certain organizational principles, laws, and arrangements are divinely inspired. As evidence of this they point to callings and offices in the contemporary organization of the Church (e.g., prophet, apostle, the seventy, and evangelist or patriarch) that were also present in the early Christian church. Several early revelations, including the original articles of Church organization and government (D&C 20) and the revelation on PRIESTHOOD (D&C 107), are seen by members of the Church as sources of a divinely inspired organizational pattern. All offices and callings are filled by lay leaders, as the Church has no professional clergy. Even full-time missionaries and GENERAL AUTHORITIES are drawn from the laity (see LAY PARTICIPATION AND LEADERSHIP).

PRINCIPLES OF ORGANIZATION.   Six basic principles that can be inferred from the revelations have shaped the historical and contemporary organization of the Church.

First is the guiding principle that the Church functions in the context of God's eternal plan. Latter-day Saints believe that God's work and glory is to "bring to pass the immortality and eternal life" of mankind (Moses 1:39). To further this plan, the Church pursues a complex mission that can be described as threefold: (1) proclaiming the gospel of Jesus Christ to every nation, kindred, tongue, and people; (2) perfecting the Saints by preparing them to receive the ordinances of the gospel and, by instruction and discipline, to gain exaltation; and, (3) redeeming the dead by performing vicarious ordinances in the temple for those who have lived on the earth (Kimball, p. 5). The structures, programs, and processes of the contemporary organization of the Church are designed to fulfill one or more dimensions of the Church mission.

The second principle establishes the priesthood of God as the organizing authority of the Church. Structurally, the Church follows a strict hierarchical form, and authority is exercised through priesthood KEYS, which determine who presides over the Church and who directs its affairs at each organizational level. The PRESIDENT OF THE CHURCH is the only person on earth authorized to exercise all priesthood keys. But through his authority different keys are delegated to individuals when they are called and "set apart" to specific positions of priesthood leadership and responsibility.

Third is the principle of presidencies and councils (see PRESIDENCY, CONCEPT OF; PRIESTHOOD COUNCILS). Presidents, because they hold priesthood keys and are entitled to the powers of presidency, possess the ultimate decision-making authority for their assigned stewardships. Nevertheless, all presidents are instructed to meet in presidencies and councils to hear various points of view. For example, it is the responsibility of counselors to presidents to give counsel; in Church disciplinary councils, council members may even be assigned to represent competing points of view. The same patterns are observed in the presidencies of the AUXILIARY ORGANIZATIONS, even though no priesthood keys may be involved.

Fourth is the law of COMMON CONSENT. Church leaders are selected through revelation by those in authority. Before new leaders may serve, they must receive a formal sustaining vote from the members whom they will serve or over whom they will preside. When members of the Church sustain leaders, they commit themselves to support these leaders in fulfilling their various stewardships.

Fifth is the principle of orderly administration. The organization of the Church follows prescribed policies and procedures that in the contemporary Church are defined in the GENERAL HANDBOOK OF INSTRUCTIONS, the *Melchizedek Priesthood Handbook*, and other handbooks and manuals for specific programs. An order or pattern is indicated for such procedures as ordinations, ordinances, and blessings; conducting meetings; extending callings and releases to members in various callings in the Church; keeping records and reports; controlling finances; and exercising Church discipline (*see* DISCIPLINARY PROCEDURES).

Sixth, the contemporary organization of the Church continues to change in response to the demands of rapid international growth. New auxiliary organizations and new levels of geographic representation (e.g., REGION and AREA) have been added since the original revelations were received. Nevertheless, the influence of the first five organizing principles can still be seen at every organizational level, in both the ecclesiastical order and the administrative support system of the Church. In this respect, the contemporary organization of the Church is a product of both constancy and change.

Most people experience the organization of the LDS Church principally at the local level, where congregations are organized into WARDS. Although the local ward organization meets most of the religious needs of the members within its boundaries, many specialized services are provided at a higher level. In addition, ward officers are in continuing contact with a hierarchy of priesthood leaders linking them directly to the central authorities in Salt Lake City. Wards are organized into STAKES, stakes into regions, and regions into areas, which constitute the major international divisions of the Church organization. The present article will describe the organization beginning with the most general level and ending with the local wards.

A body of priesthood leaders called the General Authorities heads the organization of the Church. They are full-time ecclesiastical leaders drawn from the laity, and they receive modest living allowances from returns on investments made by the Church, not from the tithes and offerings paid by members of the Church. The General Authorities consist of the FIRST PRESIDENCY of the Church, the QUORUM OF THE TWELVE APOSTLES or Council of the Twelve, the quorums of the SEVENTY, and the PRESIDING BISHOPRIC.

These General Authorities preside over the entire ecclesiastical organization of the Church, from the central headquarters in Salt Lake City, and its area offices in major cities in different parts of the world. They also manage the departments of the central office, which are composed largely of full-time employees who serve the administrative needs of the Church from offices in Salt Lake City and other locations as needed. This administrative support system functions in cooperation with the normal ecclesiastical channels, maintaining clear and direct lines of authority and responsibility between local and general officers of the Church.

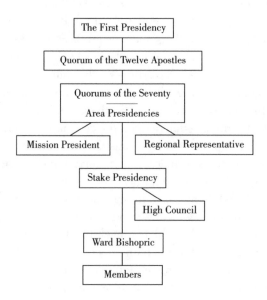

THE FIRST PRESIDENCY.   The First Presidency is the highest council of the Church, and is composed of the President of the Church and usually two counselors. The First Presidency performs the central and authoritative role of receiving revelation and establishing policies and procedures for the Church. When the President dies, the senior apostle (i.e., the member of the Quorum of the Twelve Apostles with the longest tenure) becomes President of the Church, and he chooses his counselors usually from among the other apostles, without regard to seniority. A new apostle is then chosen to fill the complement of twelve.

Since the First Presidency is a policymaking body, relatively few organizations and departments of the Church administrative support system report directly to it. For example, the various units of the Church Educational System (CES), including institutes and seminaries, report through a Board of Education. Brigham Young University, BYU—Hawaii, Ricks College, the LDS Business College, and several small colleges and schools located outside the United States also report through their boards of trustees.

The Church Auditing Department, the Budget Office, and the Personnel Department report directly to the First Presidency or its committees, as do the advisers to the Mormon Tabernacle Choir and the Mormon Youth Symphony and Chorus. Although not a part of the Church administrative system, TEMPLE PRESIDENTS likewise report directly to the First Presidency.

THE COUNCIL OF THE TWELVE.   The Council, or Quorum, of the Twelve Apostles is a quorum "equal in authority and power" to the First Presidency, meaning that when the First Presidency is dissolved (which occurs upon the death of the President of the Church) the Council of the Twelve exercises all of the power and authority previously reserved to the First Presidency until a new First Presidency is organized (D&C 107:23–24). The Council of the Twelve is presently organized into four executive groups—the Correlation Executive Committee composed of the Council of the Twelve's three most senior apostles; the Missionary Executive Council; the Priesthood Executive Council; and the Temple and Family History Executive Council.

The Correlation Executive Council reviews the work of the three other councils. It also directs the Correlation Department, which

evaluates manuals and other materials disseminated to the membership of the Church and conducts research for the General Authorities
(*see* CORRELATION). The Evaluation Division of the Correlation
Department includes lay-member committees responsible for review-
ing all Church materials, research, and the translation of materials.

The Missionary Executive Council directs the work of the
Missionary Department of the Church, which provides support to a
worldwide proselytizing effort. It is made up of several major
sections, including the Proselyting Resource Division; several
Missionary Training Centers; the Missionary Operations Division, for
handling day-to-day missionary activities; and the Media Division.

The Priesthood Executive Council directs the Priesthood
Department and the Curriculum Department of the Church. The
Priesthood Department supervises the activities of the MELCHIZEDEK
PRIESTHOOD and the auxiliaries of the Church. Among these auxiliary
organizations are the PRIMARY (for young children), the YOUNG MEN
and YOUNG WOMEN (for youth ages twelve to eighteen), the RELIEF
SOCIETY (for adult women), and the SUNDAY SCHOOL. The members of
the general presidencies of the Relief Society, Young Women, and
Primary are women who are called to serve on a part-time basis,
while members of the general presidencies of the Young Men and
Sunday School are members of the quorums of the Seventy. The principal role of the general presidencies of the auxiliaries is to train and
serve the leaders and members of their respective organizations in
the stakes and wards of the Church. The Curriculum Department is
responsible for planning, developing, and producing printed, audio,
and audiovisual materials for the Church. It includes the Curriculum
Planning and Development Division, the Audiovisual Planning and
Development Division, the Publications Coordination Division, the
Scriptures Coordination Division, and the Church Magazines
Division.

The Temple and Family History Executive Council directs the
Temple Department, the Family History Department, and the
Historical Department of the Church. The Temple Department super-
vises the operation of the Church's temples throughout the world. The
major divisions of the Temple Department are the Recording and
Ordinance Procedures Division, the Ordinance Recording Systems
Division, and the Audiovisual Services Division. The Family History

Department manages the genealogical research done by members of the Church all over the world and assists members in researching their ancestors. It engages in the acquisition and storage of genealogical records, manages the worldwide system of genealogical libraries, and supervises the preparation of individual names for temple ordinance work. The Historical Department acquires, organizes, preserves, and oversees the use of materials of enduring value to the Church. The department includes the Archives Division, the Library Division (for historical research), and the Museum Division.

Members of the Missionary, Priesthood, and Temple and Family History executive councils also have "first contact" assignments in various areas of the Church. This means that these members of the Council of the Twelve work with specific area presidencies and are ultimately responsible for all the work of the Church in their assigned areas.

THE QUORUMS OF THE SEVENTY. Members of the First Quorum of the Seventy are called to serve usually until they reach seventy years of age, while members of the Second Quorum of the Seventy are normally called to serve for five years. Members of the quorums of the Seventy serve under the direction of the Presidency of the Seventy. The seven presidents of the Seventy presently serve as Executive Directors of, respectively, the Correlation, Missionary, Priesthood (two Executive Directors assigned), Curriculum, Temple, and Family History departments of the Church. Members of the quorums of the Seventy are assigned to serve in area presidencies throughout the world. Area presidencies oversee both the local units and the missions of the Church. Each mission is presided over by a MISSION PRESIDENT, who oversees the proselytizing activities of approximately two hundred missionaries.

Those members of the quorums of the Seventy assigned to the areas of North America work at the general headquarters of the Church in Salt Lake City. They also receive assignments as assistant executive directors over the departments of the Church or as members of general presidencies of the Young Men and Sunday School organizations of the Church.

THE PRESIDING BISHOPRIC. The Presiding Bishopric is made up of three General Authorities—the Presiding Bishop and two counselors—responsible for many of the temporal affairs of the Church. They report directly to the First Presidency of the Church and oversee the WELFARE SERVICES, Physical Facilities, Materials Management, Information Systems, Finance and Records, Investments, LDS Foundation, and Security departments of the Church. The members of the Presiding Bishopric also support directors for temporal affairs assigned to each of the areas of the Church, who oversee all the temporal affairs of the Church in their assigned areas.

The Welfare Services Department is charged with helping members of the Church to care for themselves and for the poor and needy. The department consists of the Employment Services Division, Deseret Industries (organized for the employment and rehabilitation of disadvantaged members of the Church), and the Production/Distribution Division (responsible for the production, processing, and distribution of sustenance to temporarily disadvantaged Church members).

The Physical Facilities Department provides, maintains, and manages Church buildings and sites in the United States and Canada, and provides functional support for Church-owned physical facilities throughout the world. The department is divided into the Architecture and Engineering Division, the Headquarters Facilities Division, the Real Estate Division, and the Temple and Special Projects Division.

The Materials Management Department provides Church members and the local units of the Church with equipment, functional services, supplies, sacred clothing, and published materials. The divisions of this department include Printing Services, Beehive Clothing (a production facility for articles of sacred clothing), the Purchasing Division, the Translation Division, the Vehicle Fleet Division, and the Food Services Division.

The Information Systems Department provides information services to the administrative departments and the areas, regions, stakes, and wards of the Church. The department is composed of the Client Services Division, the Operations Services Division (Data Center), and the Applications Services Division.

The Finance and Records Department protects the assets and vital administrative records of the Church. It is organized into the

Treasury Services, Controller, Tax Administration, Risk Management, and Membership and Statistical Records divisions.

The Investments Department is responsible to the Presiding Bishopric for investment securities and investment properties of the Church and is organized into separate divisions to perform these responsibilities.

The purpose of the LDS Foundation is to encourage and facilitate charitable giving to the Church and its programs. The LDS Foundation consists of the Donor Services, Donor Services Support, and Administrative Services divisions.

Finally, the Security Department is charged with providing security for properties at Church headquarters and other locations and personal protection as determined by the First Presidency. The department is organized into divisions responsible for each activity.

THE LOCAL UNITS OF THE CHURCH.   The General Authorities oversee the geographical areas of the Church and normally become involved in local Church affairs through regional representatives. Regional representatives, like stake and ward leaders, serve on a part-time basis. All are lay members, and receive no financial compensation from the Church for their services. Regional representatives perform an advisory and training role. Their principal responsibility is to train local Church leaders in their assigned regions, as directed by the Council of the Twelve through the area presidencies.

The local units of the Church are stakes and wards. Stakes are centers of Church activity. The size of a stake may range from 2,000 to 7,000 members, and each stake provides its members with the full range of programs and services of the Church. Each stake is presided over by a STAKE PRESIDENT and two counselors, assisted by a HIGH COUNCIL of twelve or more men. The stake presidency and high council form the Stake Priesthood Executive Committee, which directs all stake activities. The Stake Priesthood Executive Committee is usually divided into the Stake Melchizedek Priesthood Committee and the Stake Aaronic Priesthood Committee. The Stake Melchizedek Priesthood Committee, under the direction of the stake president (chairman) and a counselor in the stake presidency (vice-chairman), supervises Melchizedek Priesthood quorums and trains quorum and group leaders. The Stake Aaronic Priesthood Committee, chaired by the other counselor in the stake presidency, meets to correlate and supervise stake and multiward Aaronic Priesthood programs. Finally, the Stake Council, formed of the members of the Stake Priesthood Executive Committee and the presidents of the stake auxiliaries, meets regularly to coordinate the planning of stake programs and activities.

Wards are the basic ecclesiastical unit of the Church. They normally have between 200 and 800 members and are presided over by a BISHOP and two counselors. The operation of substantially all the programs of the Church takes place in wards. Moreover, all Aaronic Priesthood quorums are ward quorums, in contrast to Melchizedek Priesthood quorums, which are primarily supervised by stakes. The organization of wards resembles the organization of stakes, with the BISHOPRIC serving as the presidency of the ward and the Ward Priesthood Executive Committee and the ward council serving as the major councils. Ward members meet together frequently for spiritual and social purposes. According to President Harold B. Lee, "Perhaps the most important of all the work done in the Church is done in the wards." In areas where there is a smaller Church membership, members are organized into local BRANCHES and DISTRICTS under the direction of missions, until there is sufficient membership strength to organize them as self-operating wards and stakes.

The contemporary organization of the Church is unique in its complexity and its use of lay members, though experience indicates that many details of that organization are necessarily subject to change. It is the intent of the Church to provide multiple opportunities for its members to serve in formal organizational roles and to perform Christian service, such as visiting the sick, caring for the poor, and serving as missionaries. Accordingly, a ward of 400 members may involve as many as 250 of those members in a variety of ward and stake positions. Members view their positions in the Church as "callings." Those who are in positions of Church authority seek inspiration from God in determining which member should receive a particular calling and then extend the call accordingly. Soon thereafter, the member is sustained by the body of membership that he or she serves, and is then set apart to the position by the presiding authority. Members of the Church expect to serve in a variety of positions throughout their lives. Although some positions are seen to carry greater status—roughly correlated with the ecclesiastical hierarchy—there is no prescribed sequence of Church positions. For example, a man might serve as a stake president and, upon his release, be called as a Sunday School teacher. Members accept such changes as inspired and as new opportunities to serve.

BIBLIOGRAPHY

The Church of Jesus Christ of Latter-day Saints. "Instructions to Bishops." Salt Lake City, Dec. 13, 1967.

Coleman, Neil K. "A Study of the Church of Jesus Christ of Latter-day Saints as an Administrative System, Its Structure and Maintenance." Ph.D. diss., New York University, 1967.

Kimball, Spencer W. "A Report of My Stewardship." *Ensign* 11 (May 1981):5–7.

LEE TOM PERRY
PAUL M. BONS
ALAN L. WILKINS

ORGANIZATION OF THE CHURCH, 1830

On Tuesday, April 6, 1830, under the direction of the Prophet Joseph Smith, a group of friends assembled in Peter Whitmer, Sr.'s log farmhouse to organize the Church, later named The Church of Jesus Christ of Latter-day Saints (*see* NAME OF THE CHURCH). Whitmer, a German immigrant from Pennsylvania, had come to Fayette, New York, in the Seneca Lake region in 1809. Joseph and Emma Smith and Oliver Cowdery had lived and worked in the Whitmer farmhouse in 1829 while they completed the translation of the Book of Mormon.

Prior to this date, Joseph Smith and his small but growing group of believers had held meetings regularly in Fayette, Manchester, and Colesville, New York, but April 6 was the day given them by revelation to organize formally as a church, in compliance with laws regulating the creation of new churches in New York State. It appears that the legal requirements were checked and steps taken to comply with New York law prior to the organization. The law required notice on two successive sabbaths, nomination and election of three to nine trustees, and nomination of two members to preside at the election (Carmack, p. 16). These steps assured formal status to the fledgling Church, validating property and ecclesiastical actions in the eyes of the state. Joseph Smith's official history reports his conclusion that the organizers held the meeting agreeable to the laws of the country. There is no record of any challenge to the action, and thereafter the Church conducted both religious rites and business transactions on a regular basis.

The organizational meeting commenced with prayer. The small congregation, made up of about fifty men and women, unanimously voted approval to organize a new church and elected Joseph Smith, Oliver Cowdery, Hyrum Smith, Peter Whitmer, Jr., Samuel H. Smith, and David Whitmer as trustees. They also unanimously elected Joseph Smith and Oliver Cowdery as teachers and first and second elders of the newly organized Church of Christ. Smith ordained Cowdery as an elder of the Church, and in turn Cowdery ordained Smith, even though they had previously ordained each other to the priesthood office of ELDER (*see* MELCHIZEDEK PRIESTHOOD: RESTORATION). The second ordination signified that the two elders were empowered to act in the new Church. They blessed and shared the bread and wine of the Lord's Supper with those present in honor of the special occasion, bestowed the gift of the Holy Ghost on each individual member present by the laying on of hands, and confirmed each of those previously baptized as members. Smith and Cowdery called and ordained men to different offices of the PRIESTHOOD. Those present at the meeting enjoyed an unusual outpouring of the Spirit of the Lord. After the spiritual feast, they dismissed the formal meeting. Having authority bestowed upon them, the newly appointed Church officers baptized several persons, including Joseph Smith, Sr., Martin Harris, and Orrin Porter Rockwell. On this day the Prophet Joseph Smith also received revelations to guide the Church (cf. D&C 21).

Important events such as the restoration of priesthood AUTHORITY and the translation and publishing of the Book of Mormon preceded this date, and subsequent revelations and administrative changes defined and expanded Church organization, but Latter-day Saints consider April 6, 1830, as the birthday of the Church.

BIBLIOGRAPHY
Anderson, Richard L. "The House Where the Church Was Organized." *IE* 73 (Apr. 1970):16–19, 21–25.
Carmack, John K. "Fayette, the Place the Church Was Organized." *Ensign* 19 (Feb. 1989):15–19.
Porter, Larry C. "A Study of the Origins of The Church of Jesus Christ of Latter-day Saints in the States of New York and Pennsylvania, 1816–1831." Ph.D. diss., Brigham Young University, 1971.

JOHN K. CARMACK

ORTHODOXY, HETERODOXY, HERESY

Concepts of orthodoxy, heterodoxy, and heresy are found in virtually all religious traditions. This is also the case among Latter-day Saints, but with important distinctions that arise from the emphasis placed on individual agency, accountability, behavior, and growth.

The traditional terms "orthodoxy," "heterodoxy," and "heresy" are used rarely by Latter-day Saints. Moreover, in words like "orthodoxy" and "heresy" the stress is on religious belief rather than on religious practice. In the determination of an individual's standing within the LDS tradition, emphasis is placed more on what a member says or does than on what he or she believes. Thus, the terms "orthodoxy," "heterodoxy," and "heresy," in a traditional sense, are less significant to Latter-day Saints.

In general, the word "orthodoxy," which derives from the Greek *orthos*, "straight" or "right," and *doxa*, "opinion" or "belief," means adhering to what is commonly accepted, customary, or traditional. The term "heterodoxy" means not being in agreement with accepted teachings or holding beliefs that go contrary to established norms. The word "heresy," from the Greek *hairesis*, initially was a value-free term based on the word meaning "to choose" or "to act with purposive effort." This term came to mean any school, movement, or religious system of belief that was freely chosen. By the second century A.D., however, "heresy" was used in a strictly negative sense, referring to the doctrine of those who publicly dissented from or denied any of the established teachings of the tradition to which they belonged. The dissenter was thus a "heretic."

The traditional Christian concept of "church" (*ekklēsia*) excluded the concept of private "choice" (*hairesis*). Religious groups characteristically identify certain beliefs and practices that they view as being primary or foundational. On that basis they establish criteria for determining what is deemed acceptable belief and behavior for their adherents, often appealing to an established canon of scripture, to recognized sources of authority, and to the requirements of an organized ecclesiastical structure. How these criteria are interpreted and implemented determines the extent to which deviant belief or practice is allowed or tolerated.

Instead, the Church admonishes its members to use their agency to do all they can to accept and live all the teachings and principles of the gospel of Jesus Christ (Moro. 10:32–33), knowing that they will eventually be held accountable for their choices and, for those who have lived worthily, lay claim to the promises made to them when they entered into covenants with God. Each member, at any given time, may be at any stage in this process. Each is encouraged to grow closer to the Heavenly Father and to emulate the Savior in thought and action. Members are urged to expand their knowledge of truth, grace upon grace, line upon line, and precept upon precept. Provided one continues in this effort, relying on the means of repentance that lead from baptism to eternal life, no rigid conceptual checkpoints or belief requirements are imposed to challenge a person's membership in the Church.

Distinctions arise, however, when worthiness to teach, to preach, to hold office, or to participate in temple worship comes into question. The more a person may influence others by virtue of his or her Church assignments or activities, the greater is the concern about worthiness to serve. In these instances, members are asked if they follow certain basic Church tenets (*see* INTERVIEWS; TEMPLE RECOMMEND). These include, among others, having faith in God the Father and in his Son Jesus Christ, believing in the fundamental concepts set forth in the Articles of Faith, acknowledging Joseph Smith as a prophet of God, and sustaining the current PRESIDENT OF THE CHURCH, the GENERAL AUTHORITIES, and local Church leaders. They also are asked if they abide by certain prescribed patterns of conduct. The goal is that each Latter-day Saint will obtain a personal testimony of all gospel truths and will increasingly understand and live in accordance with those truths.

All members who live the gospel are promised the companionship of the Holy Ghost and personal revelation to help them grow in their knowledge of the Lord and to bring their lives into greater conformity with his will while they work out their "own salvation with fear and trembling" (Philip. 2:12). Thus, there will always be individual diversity within the overall unity of the Church, as each member grows in his or her chosen way in harmony with fundamental principles. Such choice and individuality are looked upon as sources of strength within the tradition so long as individuals remain within the confines of the doctrine of Jesus Christ (3 Ne. 11:31–35), the consistent teachings of the scriptures, and the clear words of the living prophets on what is required of each member to gain his or her salvation and exaltation.

Those who break their covenants or whose conduct brings discredit upon the Church may be dealt with in a DISCIPLINARY PROCEDURE. Occasionally such action may arise when a member publicly disavows certain basic tenets of the faith, actively teaches against Church doctrines, or tries to subvert the work of the Church. However, most disciplinary action is taken because a member's dealings with others are deemed to be morally improper. Virtually every disciplinary action has as its ultimate purpose to assist a member in the difficult process of repentance, which can in time result in his or her being restored to full fellowship in the Church.

BIBLIOGRAPHY
Barlow, Philip L., ed. *A Thoughtful Faith*. Centerville, Utah, 1986.
Bradford, M. Gerald. "On Doing Theology." *BYU Studies* 14 (Spring 1974):345–58.
Widtsoe, John A. "What Is Orthodoxy." In *Evidences and Reconciliations*, pp. 276–78. Salt Lake City, 1960.

M. GERALD BRADFORD

P

PATRIARCH

[*This entry consists of two articles:* Stake Patriarch *and* Patriarch to the Church. *A patriarch is a Church priesthood calling. Each stake has one or more patriarchs and their duties are given in the first article. The second article gives the history of the Church office patriarch to the Church.*]

STAKE PATRIARCH

Each STAKE in the Church has at least one patriarch ordained, as the Prophet Joseph Smith wrote, "for the benefit of the posterity of the Saints as it was with Jacob in giving his patriarchal blessing unto his sons" (*WJS*, p. 6). Age is not a factor, and the call, which is for voluntary service in giving patriarchal blessings to stake members, may come to any worthy, spiritually mature high priest.

The fathers from Adam to Jacob are seen as patriarchs of this order. The word "patriarch" is often used in the Bible as a title of honor for the early leaders of the Israelites. It is perhaps in this sense that Peter spoke of "the patriarch David" (Acts 2:29). Stephen spoke of the sons of Jacob as "the twelve patriarchs" (Acts 7:8–9). These men may have been natural patriarchs, being fathers, and some of them may also have been ordained to the patriarchal priesthood. By right of this priesthood and under inspiration, they could confer upon their sons and daughters promises, privileges, and duties like unto those of the family of Abraham.

252

The Doctrine and Covenants speaks of "evangelical ministers," which is understood to refer to patriarchs. The Council of the Twelve Apostles has the responsibility of calling and ordaining stake patriarchs "as they shall be designated unto them by revelation" (D&C 107:39). This responsibility is now generally delegated to stake presidents. A stake patriarch may also give patriarchal blessings outside his stake to members of his own family. If he moves to another stake, his jurisdiction there requires approval through the Council of the Twelve.

The training and preparation of patriarchs includes spiritual enhancement through prayer and righteous living, constant study of the scriptural and historical heritage of the calling, and occasional meetings where they are instructed by their leaders.

Members of the Church receive a blessing from a stake patriarch only on a bishop's recommendation following an interview. Approval is based on a desire and readiness to receive the blessing, and on personal worthiness as shown by faithfulness in the gospel and Church service. The blessing is given in a quiet setting, usually a room in the stake center or the home of the patriarch. Parents, a spouse, or other immediate family members may be invited to witness the blessing. The recipient is seated. The patriarch lays his hands on the head of the person and invokes the inspiration of the Holy Ghost. In the spirit of fasting and prayer all present are united in faith to seek inspired insight into the birthright blessings and destinies of the recipient. The patriarch also seeks inspiration to specify the dominant family line that leads back to Abraham. Then, as manifested by the Spirit, the patriarch gives admonitions, promises, and assurances.

The stake patriarch always records and transcribes the blessings he gives. The original copy is sent to the patriarchal division of the Church Historical Department. A copy given to the individual becomes a permanent record that is held sacred. It is usually available only to the recipient, or later to his family and descendants.

The appointment of stake patriarchs does not preempt the calling and right of every father in the Church who holds the MELCHIZEDEK PRIESTHOOD also to give each of his children father's blessings. Both ordained patriarchs and priesthood-bearing fathers have the power, through spiritual inspiration, to give a priesthood blessing that will look down the corridor of time and expand the vision, strengthen the faith, and clarify the life mission of the one receiving the blessing.

BIBLIOGRAPHY

Widtsoe, John A. *Evidences and Reconciliations*, chap. 16, pp. 321–25. Salt Lake City, 1967.

ARIEL S. BALLIF

PATRIARCH TO THE CHURCH

Before 1979, Patriarch to the Church was a Church officer whose chief duty was to confer patriarchal blessings on Church members who generally did not have the service of stake patriarchs readily available to them. The Prophet Joseph Smith explained that an "evangelist" (as in Ephesians 4:11) is a "patriarch" (*TPJS*, p. 151); that is, he confers the blessings of a patriarch upon members of the Church. Patriarchs are currently ordained in individual stakes of the Church, but for many years there was a patriarch to the entire Church. He was considered one of the GENERAL AUTHORITIES.

On December 18, 1833, in Kirtland, Ohio, Joseph Smith, Sr., was ordained the first Patriarch to the Church (D&C 107:39–56), with jurisdiction throughout the Church. Upon his death, he was succeeded by his oldest living son, Hyrum Smith, who served until he was martyred on June 27, 1844. William Smith, a younger brother, was ordained Patriarch to the Church on May 24, 1845, by the Quorum of the Twelve Apostles, but William was rejected by the Church on October 6, 1845, for misconduct. The office was vacant until January 1, 1849, when John Smith, brother of Joseph Smith, Sr., was called. He served until his death on May 23, 1854.

A second John Smith, son of Hyrum Smith, was Patriarch to the Church from February 18, 1855, until November 6, 1911. Hyrum Gibbs Smith, grandson of the second John Smith, then served from May 9, 1912, until February 4, 1932. For ten years Acting Patriarchs were called who were not in the direct hereditary line. They included Nicholas G. Smith (October 1932 to October 1934), Frank B. Woodbury (June 1935 to October 1937), and George F. Richards (October 1937 to October 1942).

The call returned to the hereditary line on October 3, 1942, with the call of Elder Joseph Fielding Smith (1899–1964), a great-grandson of Hyrum Smith. He was released at his own request on October 7, 1946, because of poor health. Eldred G. Smith, eldest son of Hyrum Gibbs Smith, was called in April 1947.

In 1979 the office of Patriarch to the Church was retired

"because of the large increase in the number of stake patriarchs and the availability of patriarchal service throughout the world." Eldred G. Smith was designated "a Patriarch Emeritus, which means that he is honorably relieved of all duties and responsibilities pertaining to the office of Patriarch to the Church" (*CR* [Oct. 1979]:25).

BIBLIOGRAPHY

Smith, Joseph Fielding. In *Doctrines of Salvation*, comp. Bruce R. McConkie, Vol. 3, pp. 104–108, 162–72. Salt Lake City, 1956.

CALVIN R. STEPHENS

PATRIARCHAL BLESSINGS

The practice of a father blessing his sons and daughters can be traced from earliest times. Adam, as the first patriarch and father of the human race, blessed his son Seth, promising that "his posterity should be the chosen of the Lord, and that they should be preserved unto the end of the earth" (D&C 107:42). Abraham, Isaac, and Jacob blessed their children, opening up a vision of their inheritance and their destinies (e.g., Gen. 28:4; 49:3–27).

Each family in the Church, and the larger family that is the Church, perpetuates this heritage. Members have the right to go to the stake patriarch for a Church blessing. Stake patriarchs are ordained wherever the Church is organized that all may have this privilege.

Patriarchal blessings are given by the authority of the MELCHIZEDEK PRIESTHOOD which "is to hold the keys of all the spiritual blessings of the Church" (D&C 107:18).

When God covenanted with Abraham that through his posterity all the families of the earth would be blessed, he promised "the blessings of the Gospel, which are the blessings of salvation, even of life eternal" (Abr. 2:11). The scope of these promises, both here and hereafter, is outlined in modern day scripture:

> Abraham received promises concerning his seed, and of the fruit of his loins . . . which were to continue so long as they were in the world; and as touching Abraham and his seed, out of the world they should continue. . . . This promise is yours also, because ye are of Abraham, and the promise was made unto Abraham [D&C 132:30–31].

An essential part of a patriarchal blessing is a declaration of lineage. The patriarch seeks inspiration to specify the dominant family line that leads back to Abraham. The majority of modern blessings have designated Ephraim or Manasseh as the main link in this tracing, but others of every tribe of Israel have also been named. Whether this is a pronouncement of blood inheritance or of adoption does not matter (see Abr. 2:10). It is seen as the line and legacy through which one's blessings are transmitted. Thus the blessings "of Abraham, Isaac and Jacob" are conferred.

In addition, as the patriarch seeks the Spirit he may be moved to give admonitions, promises, and assurances. Individual traits of personality and strengths and weaknesses may be mentioned. Against the backdrop of the prophetic anticipation of world events, individual roles and CALLINGS may be named. One's spiritual gifts, talents, skills, and potentials may be specified with their associated obligations of gratitude and dedication. Karl G. Maeser described these blessings as "paragraphs from the book of one's possibilities" (Alma P. Burton, *Karl G. Maeser: Mormon Educator*, p. 82 [Salt Lake City, 1953]).

It is continually taught in the Church that the fulfillment of patriarchal blessings, as of all divine promises, is conditioned on the faith and works of the individual. Typically, blessings close with such a statement as, "I pronounce these blessings upon your head according to your faith and your diligence in keeping the commandments of the Lord."

The practice of giving patriarchal blessings is a constant reminder of the honor and glory of family: that one is not alone and that every person stands on the shoulders of those who have gone before. They prompt those who receive blessings to "look unto Abraham, your father," (2 Ne. 8:2) to "do the works of Abraham" (D&C 132:32; cf. John 8:39), to be willing to be "chastened and tried even as Abraham" (D&C 101:4), and to recognize that Abraham's willingness in offering up his son was "a similitude of God and his Only Begotten Son" (Jacob 4:5). In short, the command to honor one's father and mother does not end with death, nor with the unfolding growth of the human family.

All patriarchal blessings are recorded and transcribed; copies are preserved in official Church archives and by the recipient. They are held sacred by those receiving them.

In the history of Israel, as of the Latter-day Saints, the moving appeal of these blessings is incalculable. They open many doors to self-awareness. They have inspired men and women of renown, as well as those in the most obscure and remote places, to lose themselves in a realization of mission; to serve and give in the spirit of consecration. They have been a strength amidst the tests and temptations of life, a comfort in the darkness of bereavement and loss, and an anchor in stormy days, a "daily help in all the affairs of life" (Widtsoe, p. 74).

BIBLIOGRAPHY

Widtsoe, John A. *Evidences and Reconciliations*. Salt Lake City, pp. 72–77.

WILLIAM JAMES MORTIMER

PATRIARCHAL ORDER OF THE PRIESTHOOD

To Latter-day Saints, the patriarchal order of the priesthood is the organizing power and principle of celestial family life. It is the ultimate and ideal form of government. It answers the query of Elder Parley P. Pratt: "Who can endure to be forever banished and separated from father, mother, wife, children and every kindred affection and from every family tie?" (Pratt, *Utah Genealogical and Historical Magazine* 23 [Apr. 1932]:59).

In The Church of Jesus Christ of Latter-day Saints there are two priesthood divisions: the Aaronic and the Melchizedek. The highest order of the MELCHIZEDEK PRIESTHOOD is patriarchal authority. The order was divinely established with father Adam and mother Eve. They are the fount and progenitors of all living, and they will appear at the culmination of earth's history at the head of the whole sealed family of the redeemed. The promises given to Abraham and Sarah pertain to this same order.

Three principles underlie the patriarchal order. First, the primal parents of the race were in their paradisiacal state in Eden united in eternal bonds before death entered their lives. Second, the fall of man and the continual source of degeneration in this world have resulted in the estrangement of parents from God, from each other, and from their children. Third, the healing of this broken harmony is the essence of eternal life, as is the perpetuation of powers of creation and procreation—eternal increase.

The patriarchal order is, in the words of Elder James E. Talmage, a condition where "woman shares with man the blessings of the Priesthood," where husband and wife minister, "seeing and understanding alike, and cooperating to the full in the government of their family kingdom" (*Young Woman's Journal* 25 [Oct. 1914]:602–603). A man cannot hold this priesthood without a wife, and a woman cannot share the blessings of this priesthood without a husband, sealed in the TEMPLE.

Concerning patriarchal authority, the Prophet Joseph Smith admonished the Saints: "Go to and finish the [Nauvoo] temple, and God will fill it with power, and you will then receive more knowledge concerning this priesthood" (*TPJS*, p. 323, cf. D&C 107:18, 20). This priesthood and its associated powers were introduced in Nauvoo, Illinois, in 1843. It was first conferred upon the FIRST PRESIDENCY, the APOSTLES, and their wives (*WJS*, pp. 244–45).

Today dedicated husbands and wives enter this order in the temple in a covenant with God. The blessings of this priesthood are given only to husbands and wives together. Their covenants extend beyond this life (D&C 76:59, 60), beyond death (D&C 132:20–24), and into the resurrection, to eternal lives, the eternal giving and receiving of life.

Thus united, they work in love, faith, and harmony for the glorification of their family. If they are not united in obedient love, if they are not one, they are not of the Lord. Eventually, through this order, families will be linked in indissoluble bonds all the way back to the first parents, and all the way forward to the last child born into this world. This priesthood order will be both the means and the end of reconciliation, redemption, peace, joy, and eternal life.

LYNN A. MCKINLAY

POLICIES, PRACTICES, AND PROCEDURES

The FIRST PRESIDENCY and the QUORUM OF THE TWELVE APOSTLES have developed policies, practices, and procedures to give order and continuity throughout the units of the Church and to provide guidelines for its leaders. These guidelines, policies, and procedures have been formalized in the GENERAL HANDBOOK OF INSTRUCTIONS, which is distributed to priesthood leaders of the Church. The handbook is revised and brought up to date from time to time to keep instructions current. The following statements have been selected as samples from the latest edition of that handbook (1989), and references are to section and page numbers in that edition.

MORAL ISSUES

Abortion. "Abortion is one of the most revolting and sinful practices of this day. Members must not submit to, be a party to, or perform an abortion. The only exceptions are when—

1. Pregnancy has resulted from incest or rape;
2. The life or health of the woman is in jeopardy, in the opinion of competent medical authority; or
3. The fetus is known, by competent medical authority, to have severe defects that will not allow the baby to survive beyond birth" (11-4).

As far as has been revealed, a person may repent and be forgiven for the sin of abortion.

Abuse and Cruelty. "Members who abuse or are cruel to their spouses, children, or other family members violate the laws of God and man" (11-4).

Artificial Insemination. "Artificial insemination with semen from anyone but the husband is discouraged. . . . Artificial insemination of single sisters is not approved" (11-4).

Chastity and Fidelity. "God's standard for sexual morality has always been clear: 'Thou shalt not commit adultery' (Ex. 20:14). In modern and . . . ancient times God has commanded all of his children to lead strictly [chaste] lives before and after marriage— intimate relations being permissible only between a man and a woman legally and lawfully married. Accordingly, intimate relations outside of marriage are out of harmony with God's eternal plan for his children. To be morally clean, a person must refrain from adultery and fornication, from homosexual or lesbian relations, and from every other unholy, unnatural, or impure practice" (11-4).

Donation of Sperm. "The donation of sperm is discouraged" (11-4).

In Vitro Fertilization. "In vitro fertilization using semen other than that of the husband or an egg [from anyone] other than the wife is discouraged. However, this is a personal matter that ultimately must be left to the judgment of the husband and wife" (11-4).

Rape or Sexual Abuse Victims. "Victims of the evil acts of others are not guilty of sin." Church officers should help victims of rape and other sexual abuse "regain their sense of innocence and overcome any feelings of guilt" (11-5).

Sex Education. "Parents have primary responsibility for the sex education of their children. Teaching this subject honestly and plainly in the home greatly improves the chance that young people will avoid serious problems. . . . Where schools have undertaken sex education, it is appropriate for parents to seek to ensure that the instructions given their children are consistent with sound moral and ethical values" (11-5).

Suicide. People who take their own lives "may not be responsible for [their] acts. Only God can judge such a matter" (11-5).

Surgical Sterilization (Including Vasectomy). "Surgical sterilization should only be considered (1) where medical conditions seriously jeopardize life or health, or (2) where birth defects or serious trauma have rendered a person mentally incompetent and not responsible for his or her actions. Such conditions must be determined by competent medical judgment and in accordance with law. Even then, the person or persons responsible for this decision should consult with each other and with their bishop (or branch president) and receive divine confirmation through prayer" (11-5).

Surrogate Motherhood. The Church discourages surrogate motherhood (11-5).

MEDICAL AND HEALTH ISSUES

Acquired Immune Deficiency Syndrome (AIDS). "Local leaders should encourage members with AIDS to consult competent medical authority. Leaders and members should treat a member who has AIDS with dignity and compassion. Though AIDS can afflict innocent victims, the principal guides to safety are chastity before marriage, total fidelity in marriage, abstinence from any homosexual relations, avoidance of illegal drugs, and reverence and care for the body" (11-5).

Euthanasia. "A person who participates in euthanasia—deliberately putting to death a person suffering from incurable conditions or diseases—violates the commandments of God" (11-5).

Organ Transplants. The decision of whether to will one's personal body organs or authorize "the transplant of organs from a deceased family member [rests with] the individual or the deceased person's family. The decision to receive a donated organ should be made with competent medical counsel and confirmation through prayer" (11-6).

Prolonging Life. "When severe illness strikes, Church members should exercise faith in the Lord and seek competent medical assistance. However, when dying becomes inevitable, it should be looked upon as a blessing and a purposeful part of eternal existence. Members should not feel obligated to extend mortal life by means that are unreasonable" (11-6).

Stillborn Children. "Although temple ordinances are not performed for stillborn children, no loss of eternal blessings or family unity is implied. The family may record the name of a stillborn child on the family group record followed by the word *stillborn* in parentheses. Memorial or graveside services may or may not be held as determined by the parents" (11-6).

Word of Wisdom. In addition to avoiding the use of tea, coffee, and alcoholic beverages, members should not misuse legal drugs and "should not use any substance that contains illegal drugs or other harmful or habit-forming ingredients" (11-6).

ADMINISTRATIVE ISSUES

Church Discipline. "The purposes of Church discipline are to (1) save the souls of transgressors; (2) protect the innocent; and (3) safeguard the purity, integrity, and good name of the Church. [It] includes giving cautions in private interviews, imposing restrictions in probations, and withdrawing fellowship or membership" (10-1). Church discipline is administered by leaders of local congregations; it can affect only a person's standing in the Church. "A person who is disfellowshipped is still a member of the Church, but is no longer in good standing. . . . A person who is excommunicated is no longer a member of the Church and cannot enjoy any membership privileges" (10-5). "All persons who are excommunicated, disfellowshipped, or placed on formal probation by a disciplinary council have a right to appeal the decision" (10-8).

The bishop, or another appropriate priesthood leader, should continue to help a disciplined person return to full fellowship in the Church (*see* DISCIPLINARY PROCEDURES).

Funerals. "When a funeral service is held in a Church building or conducted by a Church officer, it is a Church meeting. A member of the bishopric conducts the service. . . . Bishops may offer the use of Church meetinghouses for the funeral services of nonmembers. Such services may be held in the manner prescribed by the deceased person's church and, if the family desires, may be conducted by a clergyman of that church, provided the service is dignified and appropriate" (2-7).

Income Taxes. Church members in any nation are to obey applicable tax laws. "If a member disapproves of tax laws, he may attempt to have them changed by legislation or constitutional amendment, or, if he has a well-founded legal objection, he may attempt to challenge them in the courts. A member who refuses to file a tax return, to pay required income taxes, or to comply with a final judgment in a tax case is in direct conflict with the law and with the teachings of the Church" (11-2).

Political Action. "The Church does not endorse political parties or candidates. Branch, ward, or stake meetinghouses and other Church facilities, and Church directories or mailing lists must not be used in any way for political purposes." (11-2).

Prayers. "Both men and women may offer prayers in Church meetings" (11-3; *see* MEETINGS, MAJOR CHURCH).

BIBLIOGRAPHY
General Handbook of Instructions. Salt Lake City, 1989.

FRANK O. MAY, JR.

PRAYER CIRCLE

The prayer circle is a part of Latter-day Saint TEMPLE WORSHIP, usually associated with the endowment ceremony. Participants, an equal number of men and women dressed in temple clothing, surround an altar in a circle formation to participate unitedly in prayer.

The circle is an ancient and universal symbol of perfection. In a public discourse, Joseph Smith once used a ring as an image of eternity, "one eternal round," without beginning or end (*TPJS*, p. 354). The formation of the prayer circle suggests wholeness and eternity, and the participants, having affirmed that they bear no negative feelings toward other members of the circle (cf. Matt. 5:23–24), evoke communal harmony in collective prayer—a harmony underscored by the linked formation, uniformity of dress, and the unison repetition of the words of the leader. The prayer has no set text, but is, among other things, an occasion for seeking the Lord's blessing upon those with particular needs whose names have been submitted for collective entreaty.

Prayer in circle formation can be traced to many early Christian sources. In the apocryphal Acts of John, for example, participants are bidden to "make as it were a ring, holding one another's hands, and [Jesus] standing in the midst" led the prayer (James, p. 253). Other texts require the participants to prepare by washing or reconciling themselves, or to receive secret words and signs, or to dress in special clothing; some suggest a ritual ring dance.

"Prayer rings" were also common in nineteenth-century Protestant revivals, and Freemasons of the period arranged themselves in circular formation around an altar, repeating in unison the received Masonic signs.

Despite these analogues, the LDS prayer circle is a distinctive ceremony, integrally connected with temple worship. The ceremony may have been introduced in May 1842, when Joseph Smith taught the endowment to several of his closest associates; and a prayer circle group was formed on May 26, 1843, with Joseph Smith as its leader. This prayer circle, referred to in many early records as the "Quorum of the Anointed," to which others (including women) were gradually initiated, met and prayed together regularly during the last year of Joseph Smith's life and continued after his martyrdom in June 1844 until endowments began to be performed in the Nauvoo Temple in December 1845.

Although deriving in all instances from temple worship, some prayer circles were formally organized apart from the endowment ceremony. Membership in these special prayer circles, which began in 1851 and continued until 1929, did not depend upon Church position. Other prayer circles were formed for priesthood groups: stake presidencies and high councils, priesthood quorums, ward bishoprics—all of them formed under the authority of the First Presidency and generally in response to specific requests. On May 3, 1978, the First Presidency announced that all prayer circles outside the temple were to be discontinued. Apart from the endowment ceremony, the only prayer circles still held are part of the weekly meeting of the First Presidency and Quorum of the Twelve and the monthly meeting of all General Authorities in the Salt Lake Temple.

BIBLIOGRAPHY

James, M. R. *Apocryphal New Testament.* Oxford, 1924.

Nibley, Hugh. "The Early Christian Prayer Circle." *BYU Studies* 19 (Fall 1978):41–78; reprinted in *CWHN* 4:45–99.

Quinn, D. Michael. "Latter-day Saint Prayer Circles." *BYU Studies* 19 (Fall 1978):79–105.

GEORGE S. TATE

PRESIDENCY, CONCEPT OF

The administrative/leadership CALLING of presidency is part of the presiding structure at all levels in virtually every unit of The Church of Jesus Christ of Latter-day Saints. A presidency generally consists of the president (or BISHOP) and two counselors, with assistance from secretaries and/or CLERKS. Presidencies are responsible for all members and programs within their organizational jurisdiction and range from the FIRST PRESIDENCY of the Church to a presidency of a small priesthood quorum or class.

Presidents are usually called by the next higher level in the ORGANIZATION, and their calling is "sustained" by COMMON CONSENT of the group over which they will preside. Counselors are then nominated by the president, but are likewise approved and called by the higher level. They are designated first and second counselors to establish relative AUTHORITY and areas of responsibility. The president makes specific assignments to counselors, but in general they assist and support the president in gathering information, analyzing problems, making decisions, and implementing programs.

Decision making in a presidency is not a democratic voting process. The counselors sit in council with the president and give counsel, but the president is responsible to make decisions and to work for unanimity if it has not already been reached. Counselors are similar to a vice-president or assistant administrator except that they do not have independent decision-making power for organizational subunits. The two most common presidencies in the Church, the STAKE PRESIDENCY and the ward BISHOPRIC, call or release all individuals in positions under their jurisdiction, usually in consultation with the appropriate PRIESTHOOD QUORUM or AUXILIARY presidency. When a president is released, the counselors are automatically also released.

A statement representative of the responsibilities of a president contained in the Doctrine and Covenants includes sitting in council with members, teaching them, edifying them, and presiding over the organization (D&C 107:79–95). The LDS presidency model ensures that no one administrator is responsible alone but always has others who share the burden and perspective of the office and in most matters can act in the president's absence. The authority of the president is clear, but the shared responsibility adds strength and assistance and provides an opportunity for individual development, which is helpful for future leadership.

J. BONNER RITCHIE

PRESIDENT OF THE CHURCH

The President of the Church is the PROPHET, SEER, AND REVELATOR who is authorized to direct the affairs of the Church throughout the earth. He speaks and acts under divine guidance from Jesus Christ, who is the HEAD OF THE CHURCH. Presidents of the Church to 1991 have been Joseph Smith, Brigham Young, John Taylor, Wilford Woodruff, Lorenzo Snow, Joseph F. Smith, Heber J. Grant, George Albert Smith, David O. McKay, Joseph Fielding Smith, Harold B. Lee, Spencer W. Kimball, and Ezra Taft Benson.

In principle and in practice, no other office or calling elicits the same love and respect from Church members as the President of the Church. The President is the prophet and, as such, is revered by the members of the Church. He is the only person in the Church who may direct and authorize all uses of the KEYS OF THE PRIESTHOOD. He is the chief administrative officer in the Church, assisted by his counselors in the FIRST PRESIDENCY and the members of the QUORUM OF THE TWELVE APOSTLES. They direct the work of other GENERAL AUTHORITIES and the lay leaders of the Church serving in hundreds of callings.

The Doctrine and Covenants specifies that the President's duty is "to be like unto Moses" (D&C 107:91–92; 28:2), relaying the will of God to his people and teaching them the gospel. His work is somewhat analogous to that of Peter, who presided over the APOSTLES and the early Christian Church. In response to Peter's affirmation that Jesus was the son of God, Jesus pointed out that the testimony had been divinely revealed to Peter, saying, "Thou art Peter, and upon this rock I will build my church" (Matt. 16:13–20). Latter-day Saints understand the "rock" to be the divine revelation through which ancient and modern prophets have directed the membership of Christ's Church (*TPJS*, p. 274).

Latter-day Saints believe that there is need for revealed knowledge from God to direct the affairs of the Church and provide insight into God's will today just as there was anciently. Revelations to the President of the Church may include declaration or clarification of doctrines or direction concerning theological issues, organizational matters, moral conduct, and practical administration. The unity of the Church worldwide is enhanced by the prophet of the Church as God's spokesperson. As such, the President may speak authoritatively on such matters as scriptural interpretation, spiritual concerns, and temporal issues. His official statements in his time may take precedence over revelations in scripture pertinent to other times or over statements by previous presidents of the Church, though in fact these rarely are in conflict (cf. Benson, pp. 27–28).

The President possesses the inspired capacity to discern between truth and error for the Church. Consequently, he may recognize and denounce mistaken beliefs and movements within the Church and in the world. While it is understood that he may at times speak or act as a private person outside his calling as prophet (*TPJS*, p. 278), the general view is that the counsel of the President of the Church is always to be taken seriously.

Whenever new doctrines are to be introduced, they are first presented by the President to his counselors and then to the Quorum of the Twelve Apostles in a meeting of the COUNCIL OF THE FIRST PRESIDENCY AND THE QUORUM OF THE TWELVE APOSTLES. If unanimously approved, they are then presented to the membership of the Church at a general conference for a sustaining vote.

Latter-day Saints are counseled that following the prophet is wise, even in personal matters (*see* FOLLOWING THE BRETHREN). The President of the Church, as prophet, will never be allowed by the

Lord to lead members of the Church into apostasy or error (D&C, Official Declaration—1).

The President of the Church is the only person on earth who directs the use of all the keys of the priesthood, though these keys are held also by the ordained apostles and are directed by their quorum upon the death of the President and until a new First Presidency is organized. This means that the President holds the power and authority to govern and direct all of the Lord's affairs on earth in the Church. All worthy males in the Church who are twelve years of age or older may also be given privileges and powers appropriate to various offices of the priesthood, but every act performed under this AUTHORITY must be exercised in the proper way. The power to direct these acts at any level is called the keys of the priesthood. Although all the keys are exercised by the President alone, he delegates the use of some of them to other leaders under his direction. The authority to perform ordinances and teach the gospel comes from the Lord, but the orderly use thereof is regulated by those holding keys given to Joseph Smith and passed on to his successors (D&C 1:38; 28:2; *see also* MELCHIZEDEK PRIESTHOOD: RESTORATION OF).

Instituted through revelation, the position or calling of President of the Church has developed together with the ORGANIZATION of the Church as a whole. Prior to the official ORGANIZATION OF THE CHURCH in 1830, Joseph Smith held the central leadership role as prophet of the Restoration. In a revelation given on May 15, 1829, Joseph Smith was instructed that he and Oliver Cowdery should be ordained the first and second ELDERS when the Church was formally organized (JS—H 1:72). This took place on April 6, 1830.

During the organizational meeting, Joseph Smith received a revelation in which he was given the titles of seer, translator, prophet, apostle of Jesus Christ, and elder of the Church of Jesus Christ. He was also told how to lay the foundation of the Church (D&C 21:1–2). Those present at the first meeting voted unanimously to accept Joseph Smith as first elder and prophet. At this meeting the fundamental precedent for Church government was established: Callings, including that of prophet, require that the mind and will of God be made manifest and that the will and consent of the people to abide by it be indicated through a sustaining vote (*see* COMMON CONSENT).

While the Church was in its early years, Joseph Smith, Oliver

Cowdery, and a small group of elders met quarterly and made basic policy decisions for the Church. In September 1830 the uniqueness of Joseph Smith's position in the Church was affirmed when Hiram Page, a member of the Church, claimed to have received revelations for the Church. Joseph Smith inquired of the Lord and received a clarifying revelation that he alone was to receive commandments and revelations for the entire Church (D&C 28:2, 11–14).

In January 1832, at a small conference of elders in Amherst, Ohio, Joseph Smith was sustained as President of the High Priesthood and ordained to that office by Sidney Rigdon. In March of that same year, the office of President of the Church was further elaborated by the announcement of the organization of a Presidency to consist of a President and counselors (D&C 81:1–3). On April 26, 1832, a general conference of the Church was held in Jackson County, Missouri, where Joseph Smith was sustained and acknowledged as President of the High Priesthood.

Presidents of the Church serve for life and are not released because of age or health. The authority to designate a successor after receiving revelation from the Lord, rests in the hands of the Twelve, who meet for that purpose after the death of the President. Once a new president has been designated and approved by the unanimous vote of the apostles, he selects his counselors, who are also sustained by the Twelve. These actions are then sustained by the Church membership at the next general conference.

The procedures of SUCCESSION IN THE PRESIDENCY have developed gradually since the organization of the Church. After the Prophet Joseph Smith was assassinated, some members thought his counselor, or even his son, should be his successor; but the Twelve knew that they held the keys and that the senior apostle should preside. Accordingly, Brigham Young, the president of the Quorum of the Twelve Apostles, led the Church from that position for three and a half years until he was installed and sustained with counselors as a First Presidency. The next two Presidents were also ordained after about the same lapse of time; but since 1898 the succession process has been invoked without delay after the death of a President.

BIBLIOGRAPHY

Allen, James B., and Glen M. Leonard. *The Story of the Latter-day Saints*. Salt Lake City, 1976.

Benson, Ezra Taft. "Fourteen Fundamentals in Following the Prophet." In *1980 Devotional Speeches of the Year*. Provo, Utah, 1981.

Esplin, Ronald K. "Joseph, Brigham and the Twelve: A Succession of Continuity." *BYU Studies* 21 (Summer 1981):301–341.

Kimball, Spencer W. "We Thank Thee, O God, for a Prophet: The Privilege of Sustaining the Leaders of the Church." *Ensign* 3 (Jan. 1973):33–35.

Petersen, Mark E. "Follow the Prophets." *Ensign* 11 (Nov. 1981):64–66.

Tanner, N. Eldon. "The Administration of the Church." *Ensign* 9 (Nov. 1979):42–48.

J. LYNN ENGLAND
W. KEITH WARNER

PRESIDING BISHOPRIC

The Presiding Bishopric consists of three men, the Presiding Bishop and his two counselors, who comprise one of the presiding councils of The Church of Jesus Christ of Latter-day Saints. These GENERAL AUTHORITIES, who each hold the office of BISHOP, serve in their positions under the direct supervision of the FIRST PRESIDENCY. Since its formation, the Presiding Bishopric has been responsible for many of the temporal affairs of the Church. These have included involvement in receiving, distributing, and accounting for member tithes, offerings, and contributions; administration of programs to assist the poor and needy; design, construction, and maintenance of places of worship; and auditing and transferring records of membership (*see* BISHOP, HISTORY OF THE OFFICE; FINANCIAL CONTRIBUTIONS; RECORD KEEPING; WELFARE). Men chosen to be Presiding Bishops have been recognized for their business and management skills as well as their religious commitment. Historically, the Presiding Bishopric has presided over the AARONIC PRIESTHOOD. As General Authorities, members of the Presiding Bishopric regularly speak at general conferences, often specifically addressing the young men of the Church.

The Presiding Bishop is selected by the First Presidency and then approved by the QUORUM OF THE TWELVE APOSTLES. He chooses two men to serve as his counselors, who are also approved by the First Presidency and the Quorum of the Twelve, and they are all then sustained by the Church membership. The Presiding Bishop and his counselors are set apart and empowered by the First Presidency and given the priesthood keys and authority to act in their respective offices. At first, Presiding Bishops held office for life, but in the twentieth century they have been released and replaced as circumstances and Church needs have dictated.

On February 4, 1831, the Prophet Joseph Smith called Edward Partridge to serve as the first bishop of the Church. Bishop Partridge was to spend the majority of his time managing the receipt, control, and disposition of the consecrated properties and of donations received by the Church (*see* FAST OFFERINGS; TITHING). He was to care for the poor and needy and to store surplus items for the future needs of the Church. After Bishop Partridge was called, it was revealed to Joseph Smith that other bishops would be chosen. On December 4, 1831, Newel K. Whitney was also called, by revelation (D&C 72:8), to serve as a bishop. The two bishops had different jurisdictions, Whitney in Ohio and Partridge in Missouri. In Nauvoo they both had a general jurisdiction but also supervised donations and the caring for the poor in a particular city WARD. In 1847, Newel K. Whitney was designated the first Presiding Bishop.

Throughout the history of the Church, the First Presidency has assigned Presiding Bishoprics extensive but varying responsibilities with the Aaronic Priesthood and the youth of the Church. In 1873 President Brigham Young assigned the Presiding Bishopric to organize full Aaronic PRIESTHOOD QUORUMS of priests, teachers, and deacons throughout the Church. In 1876 he clarified the Presiding Bishop's position as general president of the Aaronic Priesthood. In 1937 the Presiding Bishopric was assigned responsibility for the Young Men's Mutual Improvement Association, and in 1946 for the Young Women's Mutual Improvement Association. These programs were designed to provide a balance of religious study, social skills, community awareness, and physical development for LDS youth (*see* YOUNG MEN; YOUNG WOMEN). Since 1977 the First Presidency has administered the Aaronic Priesthood programs directly through a Young Men's presidency called from the Quorums of the Seventy.

Prior to 1847, Bishops Partridge, Whitney, and Partridge's replacement, George Miller, served as general bishops to the Church. Presiding Bishops and their terms of service after 1847 have been Newel K. Whitney (1847–1851), Edward Hunter (1851–1883), William B. Preston (1884–1907), Charles W. Nibley (1907–1925), Sylvester Q. Cannon (1925–1938), LeGrand Richards (1938–1952),

Joseph B. Wirthlin (1952–1961), John H. Vandenberg (1961–1972), Victor L. Brown (1972–1985), and Robert D. Hales (from 1985).

Until recent times, these men visited wards and stakes, conducted training sessions for bishops at general conferences, and published bulletins and training materials for bishops and local priesthood quorums. At the present time the Presiding Bishopric does not directly supervise other bishops or preside over local wards of the Church.

By scriptural designation the Presiding Bishopric, the First Presidency, and the Quorum of the Twelve Apostles constitute the Council on the Disposition of Tithes (D&C 120). This council monitors receipt of tithes and controls expenditure of funds. It meets periodically to consider matters of financial importance and to authorize budgets for Church organizations and departments (*see* FINANCES OF THE CHURCH). Members of the Presiding Bishopric, as appointed by the First Presidency, additionally serve on various other administrative, executive, and policy-determining committees and councils, such as the Appropriations Committee, General Welfare Services Committee, Priesthood Executive Council, Temple and Family History Executive Council, and the Missionary Executive Council (*see* ORGANIZATION: CONTEMPORARY).

In 1977 a major organizational restructuring took place within the Church under the direction of the First Presidency. With the significant growth in Church membership the Presiding Bishopric was assigned much broader responsibilities for temporal administration throughout the world. Under the direction of the Presiding Bishopric, directors for temporal affairs were sent to a number of international locations to supervise the administration of the construction of meetinghouses and temples, the maintenance of membership records, and the preparation and distribution of scriptures and other curriculum materials. Departments at Church headquarters responsible for temporal operations were also assigned to the Presiding Bishopric for their direction. Since that time, the Presiding Bishopric has appointed managing directors for the various departments that support activities of the directors of temporal affairs, which include finance and records, LDS Foundation, printing services, distribution of curriculum materials, purchasing, scripture and curriculum translation, temple clothing production, transportation, information systems and communications, security, investments, temples and special project construction and remodeling, real estate acquisitions and sales, meetinghouse construction, welfare production and processing, LDS SOCIAL SERVICES, and property management.

In 1986 the First Presidency called AREA PRESIDENCIES to give supervision to ecclesiastical activities within defined geographical areas of the world. These area presidencies presently give direct supervision to directors for temporal affairs in international areas and to welfare and physical facilities activities in the United States and Canada. The Presiding Bishopric, along with headquarters departments, provides training, evaluation, manpower planning, technical support, and program design to assist area presidencies in their roles.

BIBLIOGRAPHY

Cowan, Richard O. *The Church in the Twentieth Century*, pp. 140, 270, 297, 406–407, 420. Salt Lake City, 1985.

Palmer, Lee A. *Aaronic Priesthood through the Ages*, pp. 321–31. Salt Lake City, 1964.

Widtsoe, John A. *Priesthood and Church Government*, rev. ed., pp. 277–79. Salt Lake City, 1954.

H. DAVID BURTON
WM. GIBB DYER, JR.

PRESIDING HIGH PRIEST

"Presiding high priest" is a phrase sometimes used in The Church of Jesus Christ of Latter-day Saints to refer to the priesthood officer in charge of a particular unit of Church organization (e.g., D&C 106:1). When used without qualification, it ordinarily refers to the PRESIDENT OF THE CHURCH.

Local congregations or WARDS are presided over by a BISHOP, who may also be spoken of as the presiding high priest in his ward. Similarly, a STAKE PRESIDENT presides over a STAKE, and an AREA president presides over the stakes of a major geographical area. All of these preside as ordained high priests, even though the bishop and area president function on the basis of an additional ordination as a bishop or seventy, respectively.

Only the President of the Church, by right of his ordination to this office, is designated the presiding high priest of the whole Church (D&C

107:91). His calling includes being "President of the High Priesthood of the Church; or, in other words, the Presiding High Priest over the High Priesthood of the Church" (D&C 107:65–66). In 1832 the Prophet Joseph Smith was sustained as President of the High Priesthood and ordained to that office by Sidney Rigdon. An 1835 revelation further directed that a FIRST PRESIDENCY of three men be chosen, "appointed and ordained to that office, and upheld by the confidence, faith, and prayer of the church" (D&C 107:22). The President's counselors may preside in his absence, and are also called presiding high priests (D&C 107:22), but do not function independently in this role.

ROY W. DOXEY

PRESS AND PUBLICATIONS

[*From its beginning, The Church of Jesus Christ of Latter-day Saints was frequently attacked and abused by the press. At the same time, the Church has used the printed word to convey its message to the world. For a fuller study of the Church's use of the printed word to produce books, pamphlets, broadsides, newspapers, and magazines, see* Publications. *For a listing of the periodicals and newspapers published by the Church, see* Magazines *and* Newspapers, LDS. *For separate articles on several different publications see* Almanacs; Bulletin; Conference Reports; Journal of Discourses; Juvenile Instructor; Liahona the Elders' Journal; Messenger and Advocate; Millennial Star; Nauvoo Neighbor; New Era; Relief Society Magazine; Times and Seasons; Utah Genealogical and Historical Magazine; Woman's Exponent; *and* Young Woman's Journal.]

PRIEST, AARONIC PRIESTHOOD

Priest is the highest office of the AARONIC PRIESTHOOD to which young male members of the Church may be ordained. To receive this office the candidate must be sixteen or older; most priests are between the ages of sixteen and nineteen.

Priests in the restored Church are empowered to "preach, teach,

[and] expound" the doctrines and the covenants of the Church and to "visit the house of each member, and exhort them to pray . . . and attend to all family duties" (D&C 20:46–47). Priests fulfill these duties in Church meetings and in visits to members as HOME TEACH-ERS. They also have AUTHORITY to baptize, to administer the sacra-ment, to ordain other priests, TEACHERS, and DEACONS under the direction of their BISHOP, to preside at meetings when no ELDER is pre-sent, and to perform all duties of deacons and teachers.

Historically the term "priest" has been used to describe a variety of offices and functions. From the time of Aaron until the ministry of John the Baptist, priests in the Aaronic order taught the law of Moses, offered sacrifices, officiated or performed in numerous temple functions and priesthood ordinances, and thereby mediated between the people and God. Only the lineal descendants of Aaron could be priests. Christ's sacrifice and atonement fulfilled the "law of carnal commandments," thereby ending for Christians the priests' role as officiators in Mosaic ordinances.

In the New Testament, Jesus Christ is named the great "high priest" and as such is seen as the everlasting mediator by whom all men may come unto God (Heb. 5:1–10; 9:24–26). For Latter-day Saints, HIGH PRIEST is an office in the MELCHIZEDEK PRIESTHOOD. While most English-speaking Christian traditions use the word priest to refer both to the ancient Levitical roles and to the presbyters (elders) of the early Christian churches who had responsibilities to preside over and instruct congregations, the two offices are separated in the LDS Church in that priests are of the Aaronic Priesthood and perform basic ordinances and otherwise assist the elders and high priests of the Melchizedek Priesthood.

Because there were no descendants of Aaron among the Nephites or Lamanites, priests in the Book of Mormon held the Melchizedek Priesthood and thus engaged both in the sacrificial functions and in broader presiding and teaching functions (Alma 18:24; 45:22).

Joseph Smith and Oliver Cowdery received the Aaronic Priesthood from John the Baptist on May 15, 1829 (see D&C 13; *see* AARONIC PRIESTHOOD: RESTORATION). They subsequently ordained the first priests in this dispensation on June 9, 1830.

Today, priests in each ward are organized into quorums of forty-eight or fewer members. The ward bishop presides over this quorum, with two priests called to assist him, and another as secretary. An adult adviser is also assigned by the bishopric to teach and assist quorum members. As in all of the offices of the Aaronic Priesthood, members of this PRIESTHOOD QUORUM receive instruction to prepare them for ordination as elders in the Melchizedek Priesthood and for missionary service. Each priest is expected to emulate the example of Jesus Christ.

In addition to performing their priesthood duties, priests participate together in a variety of educational, recreational, and social activities (*see* YOUNG MEN). For example, the priests in a ward in the United States participate as a group in the Explorer program of the Boy Scouts of America. In social and service activities they often join with the Laurels, who are sixteen- to eighteen-year-old members of the YOUNG WOMEN organization of the Church.

BIBLIOGRAPHY

Abba, R. "Priests and Levites." In *The Interpreter's Dictionary of the Bible*, Vol. 3, pp. 876–89. Nashville, Tenn., 1962.

Palmer, Lee A. *The Aaronic Priesthood Through the Centuries*. Salt Lake City, 1964.

Shepherd, M. H., Jr. "Priests in the New Testament." In *The Interpreter's Dictionary of the Bible*, Vol. 3, pp. 889–91. Nashville, Tenn., 1962.

W. LADD HOLLIST

PRIESTHOOD

[*Other articles dealing with various aspects of the priesthood are* Aaronic Priesthood; Authority; Keys of the Priesthood; Lay Participation and Leadership; Levitical Priesthood; Magnifying One's Calling; Melchizedek Priesthood; Oath and Covenant of the Priesthood; Presidency, Concept of; Presiding High Priest; Priesthood Councils; *and* Priesthood Quorums.

On the specific offices of the priesthood, see Apostle; Bishop; Deacon, Aaronic Priesthood; Elder; High Priest; Patriarch; Priest, Aaronic Priesthood; Priesthood Offices; Seventy; Teacher, Aaronic Priesthood.

For discussions of various priesthood ordinances, see Ordinances; Ordination to the Priesthood; Patriarchal Blessing; Priesthood Blessings; Rebaptism; Sealing; Setting Apart; Sick, Blessing the; Temple Ordinances.]

THE SOURCE OF PRIESTHOOD POWER.   Jesus Christ is the great High
Priest of God; Christ is therefore the source of all true priesthood
authority and power on this earth (Heb. 5–10). Man does not take
such priesthood power unto himself; it must be conferred by God
through his servants (Heb. 5:4; D&C 1:38).

Before the world was created, Jesus Christ, the great Jehovah
and firstborn of God the Father in the spirit world, covenanted to use
the power he had obtained from the Father to implement God's program for the eternal happiness of all God's children (cf. *TPJS*,
p. 190). The actual name of the priesthood is "the Holy Priesthood
after the Order of the Son of God"; but to avoid the too-frequent repetition of the name of deity, it is called by other names, particularly
the Melchizedek Priesthood; i.e., it is the same authority held by that
righteous king and high priest (Gen. 14:18; Heb. 5:6; Alma 13:6,
17–19; D&C 107:1–4; 124:123).

As the divine Savior, Mediator, and Redeemer, Jesus sets the
example for all priesthood performance. "Therefore, what manner of
men ought ye to be?" Jesus asked his Nephite disciples whom he had
ordained: "Verily I say unto you, even as I am" (3 Ne. 27:27).

DEFINITIONS.   Joseph Smith defined priesthood as "an everlasting
principle, [which has] existed with God from eternity, and will to eternity, without beginning of days or end of years, . . . holding the keys
of power and blessings. In fact, [the Melchizedek] Priesthood is a
perfect law of theocracy" (*TPJS*, pp. 157, 322). It is the power and
AUTHORITY by which The Church of Jesus Christ of Latter-day Saints
is organized and directed.

The word "priesthood" has several meanings for Latter-day Saints:

1. Priesthood is *power*, the power of God, a vital source of eternal
   strength and energy delegated to men to act in all things for the
   well-being of mankind, both in the world and out of it (*DS* 3:80;
   Romney, p. 43).

2. Priesthood is *authority*, the exclusive right to act in the name of
   God as his authorized agents and to perform ORDINANCES for the
   purpose of opening certain spiritual blessings to all individuals.

3. Priesthood is the right and responsibility to *preside* within the organizational structure of the Church, but only in a manner consistent
   with the agency of others.

4. Sometimes the word priesthood is used to refer to the men of the Church in general (as in "the priesthood will meet in the chapel").

Priesthood power may be exercised only under the direction of the one holding the right, or KEYS, to authorize its use. Priesthood power functions in accord with the characteristics and attributes of God himself, namely persuasion, long-suffering, gentleness, meekness, love unfeigned, righteousness, virtue, knowledge, justice, judgment, mercy, and truth (D&C 121:41; *Lectures on Faith* 4). It ceases to exist in a man who uses it to obtain the honors of the world, or to gratify pride, or to cover sin or evil, or to exercise unrighteous dominion (D&C 121:33–37).

Priesthood embraces all forms of God's power. It is the power by which the cosmos was ordered, universes and worlds were organized, and the elements in all their varied structures and relationships were put into place. Through the priesthood, God governs all things. By this power, the gospel is preached and understood, and the ordinances of exaltation for both the living and the dead are performed. Priesthood is the channel for obtaining revelation, the channel through which God reveals himself and his glory, his intents and his purposes, to mankind: The priesthood holds "the key of the mysteries of the kingdom, even the key of the knowledge of God" (D&C 84:19–20; cf. *TPJS*, pp. 166–67). It conveys the mind and will of God; and, when employed by his servants on his errand, it functions as if by the Lord's own mouth and hand (D&C 1:38).

Thus, the LDS doctrine of priesthood differs from all other views. Priesthood is not vocational or professional. It is not hereditary, passed by inheritance from father to son (even the LEVITICAL PRIEST-HOOD was conferred by ordination). It is not offered for money. It is not held by a group of specialists who are separated from the community (all worthy Latter-day Saint men are eligible to be ordained to the priesthood). And yet it is not a "priesthood of all believers," as in the Protestant conception (*ER* 11:529).

HISTORY, ORDERS, AND OFFICES OF THE PRIESTHOOD. Whenever the government of God has existed on the earth, it has functioned through this priesthood power, held by righteous men chosen of God, as were Aaron (Heb. 5:4) and Joshua (Num. 27:18–19). In times of APOSTASY and wickedness, God has not permitted his servants to confer the priesthood on the unworthy, and it has been lost from the earth. When necessary, the priesthood has been restored with each new dispensation of the gospel.

Following the ascension of Jesus Christ and the death of his apostles, apostasy occurred in the Christian church and priesthood authority was taken from the earth. However, after preparation by God through the lives of earnest and sincere reformers and seekers, mankind again received priesthood authority from angelic ministers who held the keys to this power. Beginning on May 15, 1829, heavenly messengers conferred priesthood authority upon Joseph Smith and Oliver Cowdery in a series of visitations (*see* AARONIC PRIESTHOOD: RESTORATION; MELCHIZEDEK PRIESTHOOD: RESTORATION). These restorations included the Aaronic Priesthood (D&C 13), the Melchizedek Priesthood (D&C 27), the keys of the gathering of Israel (D&C 110:11), the keys of the fulfillment of the Abrahamic covenant (D&C 110:12), the keys of the binding and sealing power (D&C 110:13–16), and the keys of all dispensations of the gospel "from Michael or Adam down to the present time" (D&C 128:21). These keys of presiding authority have been in turn conferred upon each succeeding prophet and PRESIDENT OF THE CHURCH. All priesthood power and authority function today under the direction of the President of the Church, who holds all priesthood keys and powers (*see* FIRST PRESIDENCY; QUORUM OF THE TWELVE APOSTLES; SUCCESSION IN THE PRESIDENCY).

"There are three grand orders of priesthood referred to [in the Epistle to the Hebrews]" (*TPJS*, p. 322–23; *HC* 5:554–55)—the Melchizedek, the Patriarchal, and the Aaronic:

1. The Melchizedek Priesthood is the "higher priesthood" that incorporates all priesthoods within itself (*TPJS*, p. 180). It holds "the right of presidency, and has power and authority over all the offices in the church in all ages of the world, to administer in spiritual things" (D&C 107:8). This order of ordination is an unchanging order that has been present in all dispensations (cf. Matt. 10:1; 16:19; John 20:23; Eph. 4:11; Heb. 7:24). From Adam to Moses, all major prophets held the Melchizedek Priesthood; Joseph Smith taught that the prophets after the death of Moses and before the time of Christ held this same priesthood and were "ordained by God himself" (*TPJS*, p. 181). This authority is superior to the

lesser or Aaronic Priesthood that functioned under the law of Moses. The Nephites held the Melchizedek Priesthood and observed the law of Moses under that authority (cf. Alma 13:6–18).

2. The PATRIARCHAL ORDER OF THE PRIESTHOOD is the right of worthy priesthood-holding fathers to preside over their descendants through all ages; it includes the ordinances and blessings of the fulness of the priesthood shared by husbands and wives who are sealed in the temple (*see* SEALING: TEMPLE SEALINGS).

3. The Aaronic Priesthood, including the Levitical Priesthood, was instituted under the law of Moses at the time when Israel rejected the greater powers, blessings, and responsibilities of the Melchizedek Priesthood. God gave them a "lesser priesthood" comprising specific areas of authority dealing with sacrifices and temporal concerns of salvation (Ex. 20:19; JST Ex. 34:1–2). This authority was granted as a right to Aaron and his lineal descendants forever. Levitical Priesthood refers to certain duties within the Aaronic Priesthood that were delegated to worthy male members of the tribe of Levi (*see* PRIESTHOOD IN BIBLICAL TIMES).

Within the Melchizedek and Aaronic Priesthoods, men may be ordained to various offices. Those who hold certain offices may then be called and set apart to particular positions of Church service. Beginning at age twelve, young men, if they are worthy and desire it, may have the Aaronic Priesthood conferred upon them and be ordained to the office of deacon; they may be ordained a teacher at age fourteen, and a priest at age sixteen. At the age of eighteen, they may have the Melchizedek Priesthood conferred upon them and be ordained to the office of elder. Later, as need and calling dictate, they may be ordained to other offices in the Melchizedek Priesthood. The office of BISHOP is an appendage to the Melchizedek Priesthood (D&C 84:29), but its function is to preside over the Aaronic Priesthood (D&C 107:87–88). The office of PATRIARCH is an office in the Melchizedek Priesthood.

All faithful and worthy Latter-day Saint men may be ordained to the priesthood and be authorized to act and participate in any of the offices, powers, blessings, and authorities of priesthood (*see* ORDINATION TO THE PRIESTHOOD). Ordination to each different priesthood office is by the authority and under the direction of the presiding priesthood officer in the ward, branch, stake, or mission of the

Church where the person resides, by the laying on of hands by one holding appropriate priesthood office and designated to so act.

For all holders of the Melchizedek or Aaronic Priesthood, activity, training, service, and fellowship occur in PRIESTHOOD QUORUMS, organized according to priesthood office with appropriate presiding officers (see D&C 20; 107).

PRIESTHOOD AND THE FAMILY.   The priesthood achieves its highest function in the family. In the family, the husband and father presides in righteousness and uses his priesthood to bless the lives of his family members, teaching by example and by counsel, giving righteous advice and decisions, openly expressing love and concern, and bestowing priesthood blessings by the laying on of hands when appropriate for the direction, healing, and comfort of his family. As the presiding priesthood bearer in his home, he is accountable to the Lord: Both the husband and wife are accountable to God for their respective responsibilities over the spiritual and temporal well-being of their family.

Exaltation and eternal life in the highest degree of the celestial kingdom are achieved only as the fulness of the priesthood is attained through building and achieving an eternal marriage. The highest intellectual and spiritual development of both male and female is to become as God is. Both male and female are in the image of God (Gen. 1:27); godhood cannot be achieved by male or female alone. Everyone in the premortal life was begotten as a spirit child of Heavenly Parents before being born into mortality by earthly parents, and life on earth is part of the progression of men and women toward becoming like their Heavenly Parents. Only through the sealing ordinances of the holy priesthood, performed in the temples of the Lord, and through faithful, righteous living can male and female join in an eternal marriage unit wherein they may attain a fulness of the priesthood and exaltation together.

Fulness of the priesthood, which is the highest order of priesthood, is attained only through an eternal union of male and female, sanctified by the sealing ordinances in a temple of the Lord and ratified by the Holy Spirit of Promise (D&C 132:18–19). Those so united, who honor their covenants with each other and the Lord, will in the Resurrection inherit exaltation and eternal life, consisting of an eternal union together and an eternal family, including eternal increase, spirit children, and the creation and possession of worlds and universes.

Thus, all blessings, benefits, and inheritances of the priesthood are equally shared and achieved by husband and wife alike if they carry out their respective responsibilities in faith, love, harmony, and cooperation in the Lord. The apostle Paul stated, "Neither is the man without the woman, neither the woman without the man, in the Lord" (1 Cor. 11:11).

In the temples of the Lord, sacred priesthood ordinances (e.g., washings, anointings, clothings) are administered to men by men and to women by women who have received the endowments of the priesthood in the temple (*TPJS*, p. 337) and have been given that specific priesthood responsibility. Women thus may act in priesthood power when called, set apart, and authorized by those who hold the keys; however, women officiators are not ordained to the priesthood or to an office in the priesthood to do this work.

THE POWER OF GOD UNTO EXALTATION. Joseph Smith said: "I advise all to go on to perfection. . . . A man can do nothing for himself unless God direct him in the right way; and the Priesthood is for that purpose" (*TPJS*, p. 364). Perfection is attained by obedience to the principles and ordinances of the gospel. Without priesthood authority, no ordinances—no matter how, when, where, or by whom performed— are valid, ratified by the Holy Ghost, or recorded in heaven (D&C 132:7). The sealing power, the power to bind on earth and in heaven (Matt. 16:19; 18:18; D&C 132:46), belongs solely to the priesthood of God; and proper baptism, the gift of the Holy Ghost, the holy endowment, eternal marriage, and family sealings come only through the authorized servants of the Lord. Through these powers and authorities of the holy priesthood, the work of salvation proceeds as it was planned in the grand councils of heaven before the world was.

Under the direction and authority of the priesthood in this last dispensation, the Dispensation of the Fulness of Times, the work of the priesthood includes proclaiming the gospel, perfecting the Saints, and performing ordinances for the redemption of the dead. Priesthood bearers are charged to teach the gospel to all nations and peoples, to proclaim the knowledge of salvation. Doing this missionary work is a responsibility of all members of the Church, and a particular obligation for bearers of the priesthood. They are also charged to watch over the Saints everywhere, to labor to increase faith, understanding, and testimony, and to improve the spiritual welfare and physical comfort of all who will receive them. Priesthood bearers are further charged to "redeem the dead" through the sealing power of the priesthood (D&C 128:14–18). Latter-day Saints are taught and encouraged to seek out the names and records of their dead progenitors, to actively engage in genealogical research, to turn their hearts to their ancestors, that every individual may be sealed by sacred temple ordinances in eternal families and ultimately in the family of Adam, which becomes the family of Jesus Christ (D&C 39:4–6; 42:52).

Essentially and eternally, the work of the priesthood is the work of Christ delegated to righteous servants. "This is my work and my glory," the Lord said to Moses, "to bring to pass the immortality and eternal life of man" (Moses 1:39). The work of priesthood is to assist in bringing souls to Christ and thereby to exaltation in the kingdom of the Father.

Achieving the fulness of the priesthood of the Son of God is the great goal of all faithful Latter-day Saints, because it is the power of God unto salvation and eternal lives. It is the power by which mortal bodies will be resurrected immortal, to be possessed forever by the spirits who dwelt in them, glorified by God according to their works while in mortality. It is the power by which eternal joy may be attained, but always and only through obedience to the laws and principles of righteousness as exemplified and taught by the Savior.

BIBLIOGRAPHY

Kimball, Spencer W., et al. *Priesthood.* Salt Lake City, 1981.

McConkie, Bruce R. "The Doctrine of the Priesthood." *Ensign* 12 (May 1982):32–34.

Romney, Marion G. "Priesthood." *Ensign* 12 (May 1982):43.

Smith, Joseph F. *GD.* Salt Lake City, 1919.

Taylor, John. *The Gospel Kingdom.* Salt Lake City, 1964.

Widtsoe, John A. *Priesthood and Church Government.* Salt Lake City, 1939.

Young, Brigham. *Discourses of Brigham Young,* ed. John A. Widtsoe, pp. 130–51. Salt Lake City, 1954.

RICHARD G. ELLSWORTH
MELVIN J. LUTHY

PRIESTHOOD IN BIBLICAL TIMES

Throughout the biblical period, God called prophets and other servants to direct his work and to be his authorized representatives by sharing his power or PRIESTHOOD with them. Through that priesthood, God administered his spiritual and temporal kingdom on earth, taught redeeming gospel truths, and provided saving ORDINANCES in all generations (D&C 84:17–21). An understanding of the priesthood in biblical times facilitates an appreciation of the contemporary LDS priesthood, since it represents a restoration of priesthood authority in the latter days.

The priesthood or authority to act for God is governed by KEYS, which open God's greatest blessings, including the "privilege of receiving the mysteries of the kingdom of heaven, . . . [and] the communion and presence of God the Father, and Jesus" (D&C 107:19). These divinely bestowed powers came down in an unbroken line from Adam to Moses (D&C 84:6–17; 107:14–52), but the titles of priesthood officers changed periodically along with the type of social and religious structures that they administered.

PATRIARCHAL PRIESTHOOD AND MELCHIZEDEK. From Adam to Jacob, the main office of God's priesthood was that of patriarch. Adam, Enoch, Noah, and Abraham administered the Lord's work, established covenants between God and the faithful, recorded their teachings and prophecies, and gave special PRIESTHOOD BLESSINGS. A patriarch could bless his offspring by calling upon the powers of heaven. As he gave the birthright blessing to one of his sons, for instance, the keys and powers of the priesthood were extended to the next generation. In the patriarchal order, under the law of primogeniture, these priesthood rights normally were to be given to the eldest son; from Abraham to Ephraim the birthright blessing went to younger sons because of their righteousness (Gen. 21, 27–28, 48–49).

MELCHIZEDEK, one of the most important biblical priesthood bearers, remains something of a mystery in the Bible because the precise lineage of his priesthood is not noted. He is simply identified as "priest of the most high God" (Gen. 14:18); a revelation to Joseph Smith adds that Melchizedek received the priesthood "through the lineage of his fathers, even till Noah" (D&C 84:14). Melchizedek not only blessed Abraham and gave him the priesthood after the order of the Son of God, but he was such a righteous high priest that the "greater" priesthood was named the MELCHIZEDEK PRIESTHOOD after him (D&C 84:19; 107:1–4; Alma 13:1–19). Jesus also was identified as a priest "after the order of Melchisedec" (Heb. 5:6). The Prophet Joseph Smith observed, "All priesthood is Melchizedek, but there are different portions or degrees of it. That portion which brought Moses to speak with God face to face was taken away; but that which brought the ministry of angels remained. All the prophets had the Melchizedek Priesthood and were ordained by God himself" (*TPJS*, pp. 180–81).

Although little is known from the Bible about these patriarchs, their righteousness set a pattern referred to in later generations (e.g., Ps. 110:4; 1 Kgs. 18:36). The books of Abraham and Moses in the Pearl of Great Price reveal more of the visions, revelations, ordinations, and divine experiences of many of these ancient priesthood holders than the Bible does.

AARON AND THE LEVITICAL PRIESTHOOD. With Moses, a new social and religious order with special priesthood offices was established among the Israelites. The priesthood emphasis shifted from patriarchs presiding over extended families to a designated tribe of Levitical priesthood holders, who served Israel for centuries. Under the Lord's direction, Moses ordained his older brother, Aaron, to preside over the tribe of Levi, which served all the people (Lev. 8:1–13; Num. 8:13–22; Heb. 5:4). Over time, Aaron became exemplary in his priesthood service and the "lesser" priesthood was named the AARONIC PRIESTHOOD after him (Heb. 7:11; D&C 84:18, 26; 107:13–16). The major priesthood offices were the priests, including a "high" (Hebrew "great") priest, and the Levites.

Priests were worthy male descendants of Aaron. The high priest was designated from among the first-born descendants of Aaron. His office was responsible for the annual Day of Atonement rituals (Lev. 16) and for all the tithes and offerings of the Israelites (*see* TITHING). The priests supervised the system of worship and sacrifices at the holy sanctuary and helped regulate the religious affairs and holy days of Israel.

The Levites included all male descendants of Levi. They assisted the priests in collecting and distributing the tithes and offerings, in the elaborate system of animal and food sacrifices, in teaching the law, in singing, and in building and maintaining places of worship, especially the tabernacle and the temple.

Prophets in Old Testament times held the Melchizedek

Priesthood, as noted above (*TPJS*, p. 181); and some of them held special priesthood keys for the gathering of Israel and the SEALING powers of eternal ordinances (D&C 132:38–39). In an extension of their mortal ministries, Moses and Elijah delivered these keys to Jesus' apostles on the Mount of Transfiguration (Matt. 17:1–8) and, along with Elias, delivered them also to Joseph Smith in the Kirtland Temple in 1836 (D&C 110). In general, however, the various PRIEST-HOOD OFFICES of the Aaronic and Melchizedek priesthoods were not held by Israelite men from the time of Moses to the New Testament period.

Although the Melchizedek Priesthood was limited to those prophets specially called and commissioned, the Aaronic Priesthood continued "with the house of Aaron among the children of Israel" from Aaron to John the Baptist (D&C 84:26–27; *TPJS*, p. 319). However, after Malachi (c. 400 B.C.), political corruption occurred involving the office of high priest. Persian, Greek, and Roman rulers sought to control the Jewish priesthood office by making the high priest a political appointee of the state rather than a true and righteous descendant of Aaron. This political manipulation led to rival claimants to priesthood offices and authority, with particular opposition between the Sadducees of Jerusalem and the Essenes of Qumran.

CHRIST'S MINISTERS.   John the Baptist was a priesthood bridge between the Old and New Testament periods. Being of priestly descent through both parents, he was a legal administrator of the law of Moses, yet he received additional blessings and keys to usher in Christ's ministry, being set apart to this power by an angel of God when he was eight days old (D&C 84:28).

As Jesus organized his Church, he established a religious order with new priesthood leaders. While he retained features of the earlier structures such as the Twelve (cf. Num. 1:4, 44; Ezra 8:24–30) and the SEVENTY (cf. Ex. 24:1–11), he gave new titles and ordained new offices, especially the apostles, who served as special witnesses of his ministry and resurrection. Upon the foundation of apostles and prophets, Christ's Church was administered by EVANGELISTS, seventies, ELDERS, BISHOPS, priests, TEACHERS, and DEACONS (Eph. 4:11–16; 1 Cor. 12:12–28).

As part of the restoration of all things (Acts 3:21; cf. Moses 6:7),

The Church of Jesus Christ of Latter-day Saints received elements from all the biblical priesthood periods, with the greater part coming from the pattern and offices of Christ's New Testament Church. Under the direction of modern prophets, priesthood holders of both the Melchizedek and Aaronic orders officiate today in a variety of offices and callings, continuing God's pattern of administering to his children's needs.

BIBLIOGRAPHY

De Vaux, Roland. *Ancient Israel*, Vol. 2. New York, 1965.

Palmer, Lee A. *Aaronic Priesthood Through the Centuries*. Salt Lake City, 1964.

Smith, Joseph Fielding. *DS* 3:80–90.

Sperry, Sidney B. *Doctrine and Covenants Compendium*, pp. 388–93, 567–70. Salt Lake City, 1960.

Tvedtnes, John A. *The Church of the Old Testament*, pp. 30–44. Salt Lake City, 1980.

Widtsoe, John A. *Priesthood and Church Government*, pp. 1–25. Salt Lake City, 1939.

VICTOR L. LUDLOW

PRIESTHOOD BLESSINGS

Priesthood blessings are pronounced in connection with most of the essential ORDINANCES of the gospel: blessing and naming children; confirmation; ORDINATION TO THE PRIESTHOOD; SETTING APART; and other occasions. In addition, any person may request a blessing at the hands of a worthy Melchizedek Priesthood bearer at any time. The person who does so is usually seeking inspired counsel and asking for official prayer and blessing under the hands of one who is authorized and discerning.

In The Church of Jesus Christ of Latter-day Saints, the PRIESTHOOD is not a centralized elite. Ideally, the priesthood is held by every husband and father. The home is viewed as his constant and most important ministry, regardless of the offices he may hold in the Church. One who seeks a priesthood blessing is encouraged to approach father or brother, BISHOP or HOME TEACHERS rather than prominent Church authorities. In principle and in practice, this recognizes the diversity of spiritual gifts, the individual heritage of faith, and the shared sanctity of priesthood service.

Priesthood blessings are usually conferred by laying on of hands, which is seen as the New Testament pattern. Exceptions are found in administering the sacrament and in apostolic blessings given to a congregation (see *HC* 2:120; 5:473).

All priesthood blessings are given in the name of Jesus Christ and by authority of the MELCHIZEDEK PRIESTHOOD (so named to avoid the too frequent repetition of its sacred title [D&C 107:4]). The blessing process may vary according to circumstance and individual need: e.g., the extent of preparation, the use of consecrated oil, involvement of other persons as participants or witnesses, recording or writing the blessing (often the counsel is to "write it in your heart"), and whether and when further blessings may be appropriate. Blessings given by a man to his wife are known as husband's blessings, to his children as father's blessings; those given by a PATRIARCH, as PATRIARCHAL BLESSINGS; when related to a personal crisis or need, as comfort blessings; those given in response to illness or injury, as administration to the sick.

Priesthood blessings are to be "spoken with care, and by constraint of the Spirit" (D&C 63:64). To refuse to give a blessing when one is called or to attempt to give a blessing when one is unworthy is to "trifle with [sacred] things" (D&C 8:10).

In giving blessings, priesthood bearers are constantly admonished to seek the Spirit. The Prophet Joseph Smith taught, "The Holy Ghost is God's messenger to administer in all those priesthoods" (*TPJS*, p. 323). The officiator strives for the promptings and impressions of the Holy Ghost, and these may not be what he anticipated or planned. By fasting and prayer, by experience in the things of God, and by patience, he learns to distinguish authentic inspiration from subjective factors that distort or mislead. He strives during the blessing to use appropriate language to express the ideas that impress his mind by the Spirit. The process is often strenuous: Jesus felt virtue go out of him at the touch of the woman of faith (Mark 5:25–34). Similarly, one who seeks to serve in blessing others "is liable to become weakened" (*TPJS*, p. 281).

Recipients are charged to unite their faith in God and Christ with the faith of others present, and to bring contrite and teachable hearts. Concentration and communion are required for both receiving and understanding blessings. As blessings are pronounced, the recipients are to take to heart the counsel offered, and adjust their lives accordingly. In cases where the recipients are unconscious, infirm, or out of touch, the main burden of faith is upon the person pronouncing the blessing, and other concerned persons present.

The efficacy of priesthood blessings is not presumed to be automatic or formulaic, or simply a matter of saying the right words. Priesthood authority does not entitle one to act independently of God, but rather bestows the right to seek the mind and will of God and then to transmit it through the priesthood blessing. Neither can a blessing be given with intent to infringe on the recipient's own agency but "only by persuasion, by long-suffering, by gentleness and meekness, and by love unfeigned" (D&C 121:41). These are called "the principles of righteousness" (D&C 121:36). Unless they are complied with, the blessing "is of no use, but withdraws" (*TPJS*, p. 148).

Latter-day Saints cherish priesthood blessings as a vital source of grace in facing the crossroads, crises, setbacks, anxieties, and decisions of life. Those who give and receive blessings at the hands of the priesthood in this spirit are lifted up and sustained, and healed in mind, body, and spirit.

BIBLIOGRAPHY

"Performing Priesthood Blessings and Ordinances." *Melchizedek Priesthood Personal Study Guide*, 1988, pp. 151–55.

J. ELLIOT CAMERON

PRIESTHOOD COUNCILS

The concept of a council in The Church of Jesus Christ of Latter-day Saints embodies both a philosophy of administrative behavior and an organizational body or unit. There are formally constituted councils, such as the Council of Twelve Apostles (*see* QUORUM OF THE TWELVE APOSTLES), stake HIGH COUNCILS, and councils consisting of PRIESTHOOD QUORUM and AUXILIARY officers who work together as WARD COUNCILS or stake councils. To these latter councils concerned representatives (athletic, single adult, etc.) are sometimes added. Church councils coordinate and schedule activities, gather information, plan future programs or events, and make decisions and resolve problems for their units.

At the most basic level of organization—the family—a family council ideally exemplifies both the spirit and function of the whole concept of Church councils. In a family council, family members meet regularly to discuss plans, decisions, and problems that affect them individually and as a whole. Family councils reinforce shared commitment to the well-being of each individual and effective management of group activities.

The philosophy of a council is what sociologist Thomas O'Dea called a "democracy of participation" in Mormon culture (*The Mormons* [Chicago, 1964], p. 165). At periodic council meetings both individual and organizational needs are considered. Recognizing the unique circumstances surrounding a particular unit, geographical area, or set of individuals, the council identifies the programs and activities that need to be planned and correlated. (The council does not have final decision-making power; this resides with the unit leader, such as the STAKE PRESIDENT or BISHOP.)

Councils are more than operational coordinating mechanisms. They also serve as vehicles for family, WARD, STAKE, REGION, AREA, or general Church teaching and development. As members participate in councils, they learn about larger organizational issues. They see leadership in action—learning how to plan, analyze problems, make decisions, and coordinate across subunit boundaries. Participation in councils helps prepare members for future leadership responsibilities.

Church councils are also convened for DISCIPLINARY PROCEDURES. Such councils, which may be held at the ward, stake, or general Church level, consider serious infractions where individuals may need institutional help in the repentance process beyond the personal counseling of a leader or where excommunication or other disciplinary action may be necessary. Individual circumstances are considered by the council and the final decision is made by the bishop or president, with council ratification. Disciplinary councils are set up to protect both the individual and the Church by assigning council members to represent the interests of both parties (D&C 102:15).

J. BONNER RITCHIE

PRIESTHOOD EXECUTIVE COMMITTEE, STAKE AND WARD

The WARD priesthood executive committee (PEC) consists of the leaders of key ward organizations. The PEC generally meets weekly under the direction of the BISHOP and his counselors to direct and coordinate ward PRIESTHOOD programs that have been designed to promote the spiritual and temporal welfare of each individual and family in the ward. This committee includes leaders of MELCHIZEDEK PRIESTHOOD quorums, who administer welfare (physical and material well-being), temple, missionary, and family history (genealogy) activities, and leaders responsible for youth priesthood programs. A ward executive secretary prepares each meeting's agenda, and the ward clerk records its minutes. The PEC also coordinates ward efforts to activate its members not regularly participating in the Church.

The PEC thus provides a forum for ward priesthood officers to foster the well-being of ward members; discuss applications of Church policy; participate in and sponsor leadership training; and report their stewardship concerns to the bishop, including problems discovered through monthly home teaching visits to congregation members.

The STAKE PRESIDENCY and HIGH COUNCIL compose the Stake Priesthood Executive Committee. They oversee the administration of all Church programs in the stake; consider issues that affect all wards in the stake; and approve nominations of members to be called for service in ward BISHOPRICS, stake priesthood quorums, and stake AUXILIARY ORGANIZATIONS. The stake PEC usually meets twice a month. The stake president presides and conducts. The stake executive secretary and stake clerk assist the stake presidency with the agenda and minutes of the meeting. Both the ward and stake priesthood executive committees are augmented periodically by leaders of the PRIMARY, YOUNG WOMEN, and RELIEF SOCIETY organizations to form two additional councils.

[*See also* Home Teaching; Ward Council.]

DAVID C. BRADFORD

PRIESTHOOD INTERVIEW

The Church has developed a system of regularly scheduled priesthood interviews for effective overseeing of delegated responsibilities. Commonly used in HOME TEACHING accountability (referred to as Home Teaching Interviews) and in other Church programs, these private meetings between a priesthood leader and a member who reports to him are designed to increase communication, resolve concerns, maintain accountability, build spirituality, and empower members to fulfill their responsibilities.

The interview typically begins with a prayer about the issues at hand, and the first few minutes are spent following up on assignments generated during the previous session. When assignments have not been completed, plans are made to ensure completion before the next meeting. Although the format for the remainder of the interview varies to fit the needs and circumstances, it might include the following: discussion and resolution of administrative or organizational problems; training in administrative and management skills; resolution of interpersonal problems; sharing information on what is happening in the organization, including success experiences; identification of individual and organizational needs; and discussion of personal problems as appropriate. The last matter on the agenda of a priesthood interview is often a review of new assignments generated during the meeting, ensuring mutual understanding and verifying the accuracy of the notes recorded.

The priesthood interview is widely used as an administrative procedure between levels of Church organization and assists Church leaders to "organize [themselves] and appoint every man his stewardship; that every man may give an account . . . of the stewardship which is appointed unto him" (D&C 104:11–12). Interviews are often scheduled on a monthly or quarterly basis at the initiative of the priesthood leader.

Research shows that applying the principles of interviews to secular organizations in the private and public sectors can produce a number of benefits. Employed by either religious or nonreligious organizations, such interviews can increase the quantity and quality of communication, build higher levels of trust, improve the organizational climate and group effectiveness, and prevent regression that normally follows team-building meetings. Managers also report that regular interviews consistently save them time by reducing unscheduled interruptions.

BIBLIOGRAPHY

Boss, R. Wayne. "Team Building and the Problem of Regression: The Personal Management Interview as an Intervention." *Journal of Applied Behavioral Science* 19 (1983):67–83.

———. "Just Between You and the Boss." *Training and Development Journal* 39 (Nov. 1985):68–71.

Faust, James E. "These I Will Make My Leaders." *Ensign* 10 (Nov. 1980):34–37.

R. WAYNE BOSS

PRIESTHOOD OFFICES

Priesthood offices are appointments or CALLINGS in The Church of Jesus Christ of Latter-day Saints to serve in specified areas of PRIEST-HOOD responsibility. Each priesthood office includes a specific set of rights and duties, in addition to responsibilities shared by all bearers of the priesthood. These offices provide needed service to the Church and its members and give priesthood bearers opportunities to learn and serve. Both are important in a church operated by LAY PARTICIPATION AND LEADERSHIP.

All priesthood offices derive their AUTHORITY from the priesthood itself, which is greater than any of those offices. Hence, ORDINATION to an office does not increase an individual's authority or power, but rather focuses the individual's service in particular functions. When a person receives the priesthood by the laying on of hands, he first has the priesthood *conferred* upon him, after which he is *ordained* to a specific office in the priesthood.

The four offices in the AARONIC PRIESTHOOD are DEACON, TEACHER, PRIEST, and BISHOP. The offices in the MELCHIZEDEK PRIESTHOOD include ELDER, HIGH PRIEST, PATRIARCH, SEVENTY, and APOSTLE. The general title "elder" is applied to all bearers of the Melchizedek Priesthood.

Hierarchy of priesthood authority is associated more with presiding PRIESTHOOD QUORUMS and presidencies and less with the offices of the Melchizedek Priesthood themselves. For example, although an elder and an apostle have different rights and responsibilities, they both hold the same priesthood (cf. 1 Pet. 5:1, in which the apostle Peter refers to himself as an elder).

Scriptural records show that priesthood offices were established in ancient as well as modern times, although it is not known in some cases what duties these officers had in earlier dispensations. MELCHIZEDEK was ordained to the office of high priest (JST Gen. 14:26–27; JST Heb. 7:3; Alma 13:14–18; D&C 84:14). Moses consecrated Aaron and his sons to minister "in the priest's office" (Ex. 28:1, 41). Elders and seventies officiated in ancient Israel (Ex. 24:9–11; Num. 11:16). The Book of Mormon indicates that teachers, priests, and elders were ordained among the Nephites, and that a high priest presided over the Church (Mosiah 23:16–18; Alma 4:7; 5:3). The New Testament records that Church organization included priesthood offices such as apostles, teachers, seventies, bishops, deacons, priests, and high priests (Luke 10:1, 17; Eph. 4:11–16; 1 Tim. 3:1–13).

Following the restoration of priesthood authority in modern times, Joseph Smith and Oliver Cowdery were ordained elders on April 6, 1830 (*HC* 1:60–61, 75–78). Other ordained offices were instituted as the growth and needs of the Church required. The first ordinations to the offices of bishop and high priest took place in 1831 (D&C 41:9; *HC* 1:176). The first apostles and seventies were called in 1835 (*HC* 2:187, 201–2). In the Aaronic Priesthood, the first priests and teachers were ordained in 1830, and the first deacons in 1831 (*see* ORGANIZATION: ORGANIZATIONAL AND ADMINISTRATIVE HISTORY).

All priesthood bearers belong to a quorum corresponding to their priesthood office, either within local WARDS and STAKES (deacons quorum, high priests quorum, etc.) or in the general Church ORGANIZATION (the QUORUM OF THE TWELVE APOSTLES, etc.).

In addition to ordained priesthood offices, administrative positions in the priesthood, such as the presidency of a quorum, are sometimes referred to as offices. In this sense, the members of the FIRST PRESIDENCY, who preside over the entire Church, are sometimes spoken of as PRESIDING HIGH PRIESTS. Individuals are installed in these offices by SETTING APART rather than by ordination. Such a setting apart bestows upon the individual the rights and blessings pertaining to the leadership of that quorum.

BIBLIOGRAPHY

Lowrie, Walter. *The Church and Its Organization in Primitive and Catholic Times: An Interpretation of Rudolph Sohm's Kirchenrecht.* New York, 1904.

Palmer, Lee A. *The Aaronic Priesthood Through the Centuries.* Salt Lake City, 1964.

Widtsoe, John A. *Priesthood and Church Government.* Salt Lake City, 1939.

BRUCE T. HARPER

PRIESTHOOD QUORUMS

All bearers of any given priesthood office in The Church of Jesus Christ of Latter-day Saints are organized into priesthood quorums. A male member is ordained to a specific priesthood office when he receives the priesthood and may subsequently be ordained to other offices as he grows older and receives new Church callings.

STRUCTURE AND PURPOSE. In WARDS and BRANCHES where there are sufficient AARONIC PRIESTHOOD bearers, the young men twelve to eighteen are organized into three quorums: DEACONS (ages twelve to fourteen), TEACHERS (ages fourteen to sixteen), and PRIESTS (ages sixteen to eighteen). All MELCHIZEDEK PRIESTHOOD bearers residing in a ward or branch who hold the office of ELDER are organized into an elders quorum. The maximum number of members for each of these quorums is set by revelation: twelve deacons, twenty-four teachers, forty-eight priests, and ninety-six elders (D&C 107:85–89). All Melchizedek Priesthood bearers living within a stake who hold the office of HIGH PRIEST are members of the high priests' quorum of that stake, which is presided over by the stake presidency. The high priests' quorum is divided into high priests' groups at the ward level. In most parts of the world, priesthood quorums and groups meet every Sunday.

The BISHOP is president of the Aaronic Priesthood in his ward. He also is president of the priests' quorum; two priests serve as assistants and one as a secretary. The bishop's first and second counselors in the BISHOPRIC oversee the activities of the teachers and deacons quorums, respectively. Each of these quorums has a president, two counselors, and a secretary, who are members of the quorum. Adult men, called to serve as quorum advisers, guide and help the Aaronic Priesthood quorum presidencies and members. Advisers do not preside over the quorums; they assist the presidencies in building a properly functioning priesthood quorum. In addition, advisers are expected to watch over and teach quorum members, build quorum leadership, and fellowship young men of quorum age.

Melchizedek Priesthood quorums and groups are responsible to assist quorum members, their families, and single women members in their temporal and spiritual needs. The purposes of priesthood quorum and group meetings at the local level are to conduct priesthood business, teach members their duties, study the gospel, and encourage members to use their priesthood to serve and bless others. They also provide opportunities for personal growth and leadership experiences; most members are called to serve in quorum or group leadership positions from time to time. Quorum presidencies are responsible for planning and conducting quorum meetings and activities, teaching quorum members their duties, and extending fellowship and support to each quorum member (*see* LAY PARTICIPATION AND LEADERSHIP).

Three other priesthood quorums preside over the entire Church. The highest is the Quorum of the FIRST PRESIDENCY, composed of the PRESIDENT OF THE CHURCH and his counselors. The second is the QUORUM OF THE TWELVE APOSTLES, composed of twelve APOSTLES, or special witnesses, who form a quorum "equal in authority and power" to the Presidency (D&C 107:23–24); however, that power is exercised fully only with the dissolution of the First Presidency, which occurs upon the death of the President. The third quorum of priesthood bearers who have Churchwide responsibilities and authority is the SEVENTY. Seventies are organized into quorums that do not exceed seventy members each.

ORIGINS OF QUORUM ORGANIZATION. Shortly after being chosen and ordained, the Twelve Apostles gathered in Kirtland, Ohio, on March 28, 1835, before departing to the eastern states on missions. They asked the Prophet Joseph Smith to inquire of the Lord concerning their duties. In response, the Lord gave an important revelation on the priesthood and the relationship of the respective quorums to each other and to the Church (see D&C 107).

As years passed and circumstances changed, the need arose for a reorganization of the priesthood. In 1877, Brigham Young effected such a reorganization (Hartley, 1979). Some of the main results of this historic action included (1) moving members of the Quorum of the Twelve Apostles out of stake presidencies into full-time service as General Authorities; (2) making stakes independent of one another and placing them under their own locally supervised priesthood quorums; (3) modifying the role of then-existing seventies quorums; (4) filling up elders quorums; and (5) filling Aaronic Priesthood quorums with youth. Later (1908–1922), under the direction of presidents Joseph F. Smith and Heber J. Grant, a specially appointed General Priesthood Committee instituted Churchwide priesthood changes and reorganization that eventually led to the present system (Hartley, 1973).

BIBLIOGRAPHY
Backman, Milton V., Jr. "Church Policies, Programs, and Administration." In *The Heavens Resound: A History of the Latter-day Saints in Ohio, 1830–1838,* pp. 237–61. Salt Lake City, 1983.
Hartley, William. "The Priesthood Reform Movement, 1908–1922." *BYU Studies* 13 (Winter 1973):137–56.
———. "The Priesthood Reorganization of 1877: Brigham Young's Last Achievement." *BYU Studies* 20 (Fall 1979):3–36.
Roberts, B. H. *CHC* 1:371–86.

SHERMAN N. TINGEY

PRIMARY

The Primary is an organized program of religious instruction and activity in The Church of Jesus Christ of Latter-day Saints for children from eighteen months of age until their twelfth birthdays. Its purpose is to teach children the gospel of Jesus Christ and help them learn to live it.

ORIGINS.   In the summer of 1878, Aurelia Spencer Rogers, a Farmington, Utah, mother, who felt the need for a united effort to help parents teach their children the gospel, voiced her concerns to Eliza R. Snow, president of the RELIEF SOCIETY of the Church: "Could there not be an organization for little boys, and have them trained to make better men?" (Rogers, p. 208). Sister Snow presented the matter to President John Taylor, and he authorized establishment of the organization.

Under the direction of local Church leaders, the first Primary was organized on August 11, 1878, with Aurelia Rogers as president. On August 25, the first Primary meeting was held in Farmington, where 224 boys and girls met to be taught obedience, faith in God, prayer, punctuality, and good manners. The girls were included to make the singing "sound as well as it should" (Rogers, p. 209).

EARLY PRIMARIES.   Within a short time, more Primaries were organized throughout the territory. By the mid-1880s, a Primary group had been organized in nearly every LDS settlement. The women of the Church were given the responsibility to organize and administer the Primary program. The bulk of the weekly program was devoted to songs, poems, and activities presented by children. Primary general officers did not take a controlling leadership role until the 1890s, and curricular materials were few, although most Primaries used a hymnbook, a tune book, and a catechism of Old and New Testament questions and answers prepared by Eliza R. Snow in 1881. In many localities, children remained in Primary through their early teens and often served as Primary secretaries.

1890–1939.   During this period, Primary general officers assumed the leading role in Primary development. Louie B. Felt (1880–1925), the first Primary general president, and her counselor and successor, May Anderson (1925–1939), sought professional training in education. Exposed to the ideas of progressive education, they initiated curriculum development and teacher training. General officers encouraged local Primaries to establish age-graded classes with lessons appropriate to the children's development. They began publication of the CHILDREN'S FRIEND (1902), at first with lessons and instructions for leaders and, within a few years, with stories, handiwork, and music for children. In 1913 the Primary established a children's ward in the Grove's Latter-day Saint Hospital in Salt Lake City, the first in a series of Primary efforts to provide pediatric hospital care. When religion classes, instituted in 1890 for weekday religious instruction for children, were discontinued in 1929, the Primary assumed greater responsibility for children's spiritual education. Lessons were scheduled three weeks each month, and activities were reduced to one per month, except during the summer program. Stake boards held monthly training meetings for ward leaders; general board members visited regularly.

1940–1974.   Spiritual education remained the focus of Primary programs under presidents May Green Hinckley (1940–1943) and Adele Cannon Howells (1943–1951). Mission lessons were written for the growing number of Primaries in Church missions throughout the world and, during World War II, for the hundreds of home and neighborhood Primaries developed because of wartime travel restrictions. Under President LaVern Watts Parmley (1951–1974), the Primary lessons were made applicable to all units in the growing Church, including mission Primaries. When a comprehensive Church correlation program was begun in the 1960s, responsibility for Primary lesson materials was transferred to priesthood leaders and professional departments.

The Primary Children's Hospital, authorized by Church leaders in 1949, was completed in 1952, and President Parmley became the first chair of the hospital's board of trustees (*see* HOSPITALS). While the majority of patients were from the intermountain region, others came from many areas of the world. Children of all races and creeds were welcomed. Patients' families usually paid for their medical costs, but charitable funds assisted many. The hospital, transferred to private ownership in 1975, made possible some of the most important contributions that the Primary has made to the lives of individual children.

In 1952 the Primary was given responsibility for Cub Scouting for LDS boys eight, nine, and ten years of age and Boy Scouting for eleven-year-old boys. Since that time, a close working relationship has existed between the Primary and the Boy Scouts of America. Primary is also involved with Scouts in Canada, throughout the United Kingdom, and in New Zealand.

Until 1952, women could serve only as den mothers in Cub Scouting. That year the Primary obtained permission from the National Scout Committee for women to serve as leaders of the eleven-year-old Scouts. Since then, women have become registered Scouters and serve on local and national boards.

1974–1990.   With the growth of a more geographically widespread Church, annual general conferences of Church auxiliaries were discontinued in 1975. Under presidents Naomi M. Shumway (1974–1980), Dwan J. Young (1980–1988), and Michaelene P. Grassli (1988–), communication with local leaders continued through materials prepared for regional conferences, a *Primary Handbook*, information published in the BULLETIN, and periodic visits to regional training sessions. Responsibility for planning lesson concepts for Primary manuals was returned to the Primary General Board in 1977.

In the consolidated Sunday meeting schedule (1980), Primary meetings were moved from midweek to Sunday, junior Sunday Schools were discontinued, and Primary was given responsibility for all formal religious classroom instruction of children in the Church. With that change, callings to teach in the Primary began to be extended to men as well as women, although only women serve in Primary presidencies. Weekday activities involving all Primary children were reduced to four per year, and spiritual education was further emphasized. Children were encouraged to read the scriptures regularly, and Primary lessons taught gospel principles from their scriptural foundations. Music and activities culminating in the yearly children's sacrament meeting presentation (e.g., "The Book of Mormon—A Witness of Jesus Christ," 1988; "I Am a Child of God," 1989; and "I Belong to The Church of Jesus Christ of Latter-day Saints," 1990) focused on scriptures and gospel principles.

CURRENT STRUCTURE. As of 1990, Primaries serve over a million and a half children with lessons taught in many languages. Primary meetings are held each Sunday for approximately an hour and a half. A nursery program is provided for children between eighteen months and three years of age. Children between the ages of three and eleven meet as a group under the direction of the ward Primary presidency. The children offer prayers, read from the scriptures, and give short gospel-related talks. They learn gospel principles through role playing, readers' theaters, choral readings, buzz sessions, panel discussions, and other activities. They also learn and sing music selected from a children's songbook.

The children divide according to age for small group classroom sessions. Age-appropriate lesson materials are selected to help children grow in understanding gospel principles; learn that the Heavenly Father and Jesus love them; and prepare to be baptized, receive the Holy Ghost, and keep their baptismal covenants.

Classroom presentations and discussions help girls prepare to fulfill their roles as righteous young women and to live lives of service. Classes help boys prepare to receive the PRIESTHOOD and be worthy to use this power to bless the lives of others.

In addition to Sunday Primary meetings, twice-a-month weekday activities are held for ten- and eleven-year-old boys and girls. In some countries, eleven-year-old boys use Scouting activities for their weekday activities. A quarterly activity is held for all Primary children. The weekday and quarterly activities encourage children to interact with each other and have wholesome fun involving them in physical, creative, cultural, and service activities.

Children with disabilities are nurtured in Primary and are given opportunity to participate in the full program. Leaders assess their needs individually and tailor programs to meet specific needs. They are integrated into the regular program whenever possible by giving additional support and training to their teachers, leaders, and peers.

Church leaders call and set apart lay officers and teachers to oversee the Primary; and Primary general officers and Church curriculum committees prepare handbooks, teaching guides, visual aids, lesson manuals, and a variety of training videos for their use. Monthly in-service lessons help teachers improve their teaching skills and relate appropriately to children. Periodically, the Primary general presidency and board members conduct multistake or regional training sessions. Leaders and teachers seek and receive inspiration in their Primary service.

The Primary's mission, the impetus for its historical development, and the purpose for its current structure are summarized in the scripture that has become the Primary's theme: "All thy children shall be taught of the Lord; and great shall be the peace of thy children" (3 Ne. 22:13).

[*See also* Auxiliary Organizations.]

BIBLIOGRAPHY

Madsen, Carol Cornwall, and Susan Staker Oman. *Sisters and Little Saints*. Salt Lake City, 1979.

Primary Handbook. Salt Lake City, 1985.

Rogers, Aurelia A. *Life Sketches*. Salt Lake City, 1898.

NAOMI M. SHUMWAY

PROCLAMATIONS OF THE FIRST PRESIDENCY AND THE QUORUM OF THE TWELVE APOSTLES

In performance of their calling as apostles, prophets, seers, revelators, and spokesmen for The Church of Jesus Christ of Latter-day Saints, the First Presidency and the Quorum of the Twelve Apostles have from time to time issued formal written proclamations, declarations, letters, and various public announcements. These have been addressed sometimes to the members of the Church (as a type of general epistle) and sometimes to the public at large. All such declarations have been solemn and sacred in nature and were issued with the intent to bring forth, build up, and regulate the affairs of the Church as the kingdom of God on the earth. Subject matter has included instruction on doctrine, faith, and history; warnings of judgments to come; invitations to assist in the work; and statements of Church growth and progress.

Only a few of the many formal declarations have been labeled "Proclamations." Others have been characterized "Official Declarations," "Doctrinal Expositions," or "Epistles." Some have the signature of the First Presidency, some of the First Presidency and the Twelve, and some of the Twelve only. This article considers four documents: (1) Proclamation of the First Presidency on January 15, 1841, at Nauvoo, Illinois; (2) Proclamation of the Twelve Apostles on April 6, 1845, in New York City, and on October 22, 1845, in Liverpool, England; (3) Proclamation of the First Presidency and the Twelve Apostles on October 21, 1865, in Salt Lake City, Utah; and (4) Proclamation from the First Presidency and the Quorum of the Twelve Apostles, April 6, 1980, issued from Fayette, New York.

1. A Proclamation of the First Presidency of the Church to the Saints Scattered Abroad (January 15, 1841, Nauvoo, Illinois)

[*This document, signed by Joseph Smith, Sidney Rigdon, and Hyrum Smith, reviews the progress of the Church in spite of hardships and persecution, and speaks at length on the prospects of the settlement of Nauvoo, as the following excerpts illustrate.*]

BELOVED BRETHREN:—The relationship which we sustain to The Church of Jesus Christ of Latter-day Saints, renders it necessary that we should make known from time to time, the circumstances, situation, and prospects of the Church, and give such instructions as may be necessary for the well being of the Saints, and for the promotion of those objects calculated to further their present and everlasting happiness.

We have to congratulate the Saints on the progress of the great work of the "last days," for not only has it spread through the length and breadth of this vast continent, but on the continent of Europe, and on the islands of the sea, it is spreading in a manner entirely unprecedented in the annals of time. This appears the more pleasing when we consider, that but a short time has elapsed since we were unmercifully driven from the state of Missouri, after suffering cruelties and persecutions in various and horrid forms. . . .

It would be impossible to enumerate all those who, in our time of deep distress, nobly came forward to our relief, and, like the good Samaritan, poured oil into our wounds, and contributed liberally to our necessities, and the citizens of Quincy *en masse*, and the people of Illinois, generally, seemed to emulate each other in this labor of love. . . .

We would likewise make mention of the legislators of this state, who, without respect to parties, without reluctance, freely, openly, boldly, and nobly, have come forth to our assistance, owned us as citizens and friends, and took us by the hand, and extended to us all the blessings of civil, political, and religious liberty, by granting us, under date of December 16, 1840, one of the most liberal charters, with the most plenary powers ever conferred by a legislative assembly on free citizens, "The City of Nauvoo," the "Nauvoo Legion," and the "University of the City of Nauvoo." . . .

The name of our city (Nauvoo) is of Hebrew origin, and signifies a beautiful situation, or place, carrying with it, also, the idea of rest; and is truly descriptive of the most delightful location. It is situated on the east back of the Mississippi river, at the head of the Des Moines rapids, in Hancock county, bounded on the east by an extensive prairie of surpassing beauty, and on the north, west, and south, by the Mississippi. . . .

Having been instrumental, in the hands of our heavenly Father, in laying a foundation for the gathering of Zion, we would say, let all those who appreciate the blessings of the Gospel, and realize the importance of obeying the commandments of heaven, who have been blessed with the possession of this world's goods, first prepare for the general gathering; let them dispose of their effects as fast as circumstances will possibly admit, without making too great sacrifices, and remove to our city and county; establish and build up manufactures in the city, purchase and cultivate farms in the county. This will secure our permanent inheritance, and prepare the way for the gathering of the poor. This is agreeable to the order of heaven, and the only principle on which the gathering can be effected. Let the rich, then, and all who can assist in establishing this place, make every preparation to come on without delay, and strengthen our hands, and assist in promoting the happiness of the Saints. . . .

The Temple of the Lord is in process of erection here, where the Saints will come to worship the God of their fathers, according to the order of His house and the power of the Holy Priesthood, and will be so constructed as to enable all the functions of the Priesthood to be duly exercised, and where instructions from the Most High will be received, and from this place go forth to distant lands. Let us then concentrate all our powers, under the provisions of our *magna charta* granted by the Illinois legislature, at the "City of Nauvoo" and surrounding country, and strive to emulate the action of the ancient covenant fathers and patriarchs, in those things which are of such vast importance to this and every succeeding generation. . . .

The greatest temporal and spiritual blessings which always flow from faithfulness and concerted effort, never attended individual exertion or enterprise. The history of all past ages abundantly attests this fact. In addition to all temporal blessings, there is no other way for the Saints to be saved in these last days [than by the gathering], as the concurrent testimony of all the holy Prophets clearly proves, for it is written—"They shall come from the east, and be gathered from the west; the north shall give up, and the south shall keep not back." "The sons of God shall be gathered from far, and His daughters from the ends of the earth."

It is also the concurrent testimony of all the Prophets, that this gathering together of all the Saints, must take place before the Lord comes to "take vengeance upon the ungodly," and to be glorified and admired by all those who obey the Gospel." The fiftieth Psalm, from the first to the fifth verse inclusive, describes the glory and majesty of that event.

The mighty God, and even the Lord hath spoken, and called the earth from the rising of the sun unto the going down thereof. Out of Zion, the perfection of beauty, God hath shined. Our God shall come and shall not keep silence; a fire shall devour before Him, and it shall be very tempestuous round about Him. He shall call to the heavens from above, and to the earth (that He may judge the people). Gather my Saints together unto me; those that have made covenant with me by sacrifice.

We might offer many other quotations from the Scriptures, but believing them to be familiar to the Saints, we forbear.

We would wish the Saints to understand that, when they come here, they must not expect perfection, or that all will be harmony, peace, and love; if they indulge these ideas, they will undoubtedly be deceived, for here there are persons, not only from different states, but from different nations, who, although they feel a great attachment to the cause of truth, have their prejudices of education, and, consequently, it requires some time before these things can be overcome. . . . Therefore, let those who come up to this place be determined to keep the commandments of God, and not be discouraged by those things we have enumerated, and then they will be prospered—the intelligence of heaven will be communicated to them, and they will eventually, see eye to eye, and rejoice in the full fruition of that glory which is reserved for the righteous.

In order to erect the Temple of the Lord, great exertions will be required on the part of the Saints, so that they may build a house which shall be accepted by the Almighty, in which His power and glory shall be manifested. Therefore let those who can freely make a sacrifice of their time, their talents, and their property, for the prosperity of the kingdom, and for the love they have to the cause of truth, bid adieu to their homes and pleasant places of abode, and unite with us in the great work of the last days, and share in the tribulation, that they may ultimately share in the glory and triumph.

We wish it likewise to be distinctly understood, that we claim no privilege but what we feel cheerfully disposed to share with our fellow citizens of every denomination, and every sentiment of religion; and therefore say, that so far from being restricted to our own faith, let all those who desire to locate themselves in this place, or the vicinity, come, and we will hail them as citizens and friends, and shall feel it not only a duty, but a privilege, to reciprocate the kindness we have received from the benevolent and kind-hearted citizens of the state of Illinois.

> Joseph Smith,
> Sidney Rigdon,
> Hyrum Smith,
> Presidents of the Church
> [*HC* 4:267–73].

2. Proclamation of the Twelve Apostles of The Church of Jesus Christ of Latter-day Saints (April 6 and October 22, 1845)

[*The Proclamation of 1845 was issued by the Twelve only, because at that time there was no First Presidency due to the martyrdom of the Prophet Joseph Smith on June 27, 1844, and a new First Presidency was not organized until December 1847. The Proclamation was apparently made in response to a revelation given January 19, 1841 (D&C 124:1–11). It was first printed in a sixteen-page pamphlet in New York City on April 6, 1845, and again in Liverpool, England, October 22, 1845. It was addressed to the rulers and people of all nations. This document was an announcement that God had spoken from the heavens and had restored the gospel of Jesus Christ to the earth. It spoke of blessings and of punishments to come, issued a warning voice, and invited all who were interested to assist in the building of the kingdom of God on the earth in preparation for the Savior's second coming. On October 3, 1975, President Ezra Taft Benson, president of the Quorum of the Twelve Apostles, spoke of this Proclamation and quoted portions of it in his general conference address (Ensign 15 [Oct. 1975]:32–34).*

Extracts from the 1845 Proclamation follow.]

TO ALL THE KINGS OF THE WORLD, TO THE PRESIDENT OF THE UNITED STATES OF AMERICA; TO THE GOVERNORS OF THE SEVERAL STATES, AND TO THE RULERS AND PEOPLE OF ALL NATIONS.

Greeting.

Know ye that the kingdom of God has come, as has been predicted by ancient prophets, and prayed for in all ages; even that kingdom which shall fill the whole earth, and shall stand for ever. . . .

Therefore we send unto you, with authority from on high, and command you all to repent and humble yourselves as little children before the majesty of the Holy One; and come unto Jesus with a broken heart and a contrite spirit, and be baptized in his name for the remission of sins (that is, be buried in the water, in the likeness of his burial, and rise again to newness of life in the likeness of his resurrection), and you shall receive the gift of the Holy Spirit, through the laying on of the hands of the apostles and elders, of this great and last dispensation of mercy to man.

This Spirit shall bear witness to you of the truth of our testimony, and shall enlighten your minds, and be in you as the spirit of prophecy and revelation; it shall bring things past to your understanding and remembrance, and shall show you things to come. . . .

By the light of this Spirit, received through the ministration of the ordinances—by the power and authority of the Holy Apostleship and Priesthood, you will be enabled to understand, and to be the children of light; and thus be prepared to escape all the things that are coming on the earth, and so stand before the Son of Man.

We testify that the foregoing doctrine is the doctrine or gospel of Jesus Christ in its fulness; and that it is the only true, everlasting, and unchangeable gospel; and the only plan revealed on earth whereby man can be saved. . . .

And we further testify that the Lord has appointed a holy city and temple to be built on this continent, for the endowment and ordinances pertaining to the priesthood; and for the Gentiles, and the remnant of Israel to resort unto, in order to worship the Lord, and to be taught in his ways and walk in his paths; in short, to finish their preparations for the coming of the Lord. . . .

The Latter-day Saints, since their first organization in the year 1830, have been a poor, persecuted, abused, and afflicted people. They have sacrificed their time and property freely, for the sake of laying the foundation of the kingdom of God, and enlarging its dominion by the ministry of the gospel. They have suffered privation, hunger, imprisonment, and the loss of houses, lands, home, and political rights for their testimony.

And this is not all. Their first founder, Mr. Joseph Smith, whom God raised up as a prophet and apostle, mighty in word and in deed, and his brother Hyrum, who was also a prophet, together with many others, have suffered a cruel martyrdom in the cause of truth, and have sealed their testimony with their blood; and still the work has, as it were, but just begun.

A great, a glorious, and a mighty work is yet to be achieved, in spreading the truth and kingdom among the Gentiles—in restoring, organizing, instructing, and establishing the Jews—in gathering, instructing, relieving, civilizing, educating, and administering salvation to the remnant of Israel on this continent—in building Jerusalem in Palestine, and the cities, stakes, temples, and sanctuaries of Zion in America; and in gathering the Gentiles into the same covenant and organization—instructing them in all things for their sanctification and preparation, that the whole Church of the Saints, both Gentile, Jew and Israel, may be prepared as a bride for the coming of the Lord. . . .

Again, we say, by the word of the Lord, to the people as well as to the rulers, your aid and your assistance is required in this great work; and you are hereby invited, in the name of Jesus, to take an active part in it from this day forward.

Open your churches, doors, and hearts for the truth; hear the apostles and elders of the Church of the Saints when they come into your cities and neighbourhoods; read and search the scriptures carefully, and see whether these things are so; read the publications of the Saints, and help to publish them to others; seek for the witness of the Spirit, and come and obey the glorious fulness of the gospel, and help us to build the cities and sanctuaries of our God. . . .

To this city [Zion or New Jerusalem], and to its several branches or stakes, shall the Gentiles seek, as to a standard of light and knowledge; yea, the nations, and their kings and nobles shall say—Come, and let us go up to the Mount Zion, and to the temple of the Lord, where his holy priesthood stand to minister continually before the Lord; and where we may be instructed more fully, and receive the ordinances of remission, and of sanctification, and redemption, and thus be adopted into the family of Israel, and identified in the same covenants of promise. . . .

The city of Zion, with its sanctuary and priesthood, and the glorious fulness of the gospel, will constitute a *standard* which will put an end to jarring creeds and political wranglings, by uniting the republics, states, provinces, territories, nations, tribes, kindred, tongues, people, and sects of North and South America in one great and common bond of brotherhood; while truth and knowledge shall make them free, and love cement their union.

The Lord also shall be their king and their lawgiver; while wars shall cease and peace prevail for a thousand years. . . .

We say, then, in life or in death, in bonds or free, that the great God has spoken in this age.—*And we know it.*

He has given us the holy priesthood and apostleship, and the keys of the kingdom of God, to bring about the restoration of all things as promised by the holy prophets of old.—*And we know it.*

He has revealed the origin and the records of the aboriginal tribes of America, and their future destiny.—*And we know it.*

He has revealed the fulness of the gospel, with its gifts, blessings, and ordinances.—*And we know it.* . . .

He has commanded us to gather together his Saints, on this continent, and build up holy cities and sanctuaries.—*And we know it.*

He has said, that the Gentiles should come into the same gospel and covenant, and be numbered with the house of Israel, and be a blessed people upon this good land for ever, if they would repent and embrace it.—*And we know it.* . . .

He has said, that the time is at hand for the Jews to be gathered to Jerusalem.—*And we know it.*

He has said, that the ten tribes of Israel should also be revealed in the north country, together with their oracles and records, preparatory to their return, and to their union with Judah, no more to be separated.—*And we know it.*

He has said, that when these preparations were made, both in this country and in Jerusalem, and the gospel in all its fulness preached to all nations for a witness and testimony, he will come, and all the Saints with him, to reign on the earth one thousand years.—*And we know it.*

He has said, that he will not come in his glory and destroy the wicked, till these warnings were given, and these preparations were made for his reception.—*And we know it.* . . .

Therefore, again we say to all people, repent, and be baptized in the name of Jesus Christ, for remission of sins, and you shall receive the Holy Spirit, and shall know the truth, and be numbered with the house of Israel. . . .

New York, April 6th, 1845

TO THE ENGLISH READER.

It will be borne in mind that the foregoing was written in the United States of America, therefore the language, which we have not altered, will be understood as emanating from thence. . . .

W. WOODRUFF.

Liverpool, October 22nd, 1845 [Liverpool pamphlet, BYU Library, Provo, Utah: see also *MFP* 1:252–66].

3. Proclamation of the First Presidency and the Twelve Apostles (October 21, 1865)

[*This document was issued to members of the Church to correct certain theories about the nature of God that had been published by one of the Twelve in official Church literature, without having those statements cleared and verified by the First Presidency and the Twelve.*

An apparent major purpose of this Proclamation was to emphasize the established order of the Church, that new doctrine is to be announced only by the First Presidency. A paragraph near the end of the Proclamation states:]

It ought to have been known, years ago, by every person in the Church—for ample teachings have been given on the point—that no member of the Church has the right to publish any doctrines, as the doctrines of the Church of Jesus Christ of Latter-day Saints, without first submitting them for examination and approval to the First Presidency and the Twelve. There is but one man upon the earth, at one time, who holds the keys to receive commandments and revelations for the Church, and who has the authority to write doctrines by way of commandment unto the Church. And any man who so far forgets the order instituted by the Lord as to write and publish what may be termed new doctrines, without consulting with the First Presidency of the Church respecting them, places himself in a false position, and exposes himself to the power of darkness by violating his Priesthood (*MFP* 2:239).

[*The Proclamation is signed by Brigham Young, Heber C. Kimball, Orson Hyde, John Taylor, Wilford Woodruff, George A. Smith, Amasa M. Lyman, Ezra T. Benson, Charles C. Rich, Lorenzo Snow, Erastus Snow, Franklin D. Richards, George Q. Cannon (MFP 2:235–40).*]

4. Proclamation of the First Presidency and the Quorum of the Twelve Apostles of The Church of Jesus Christ of Latter-day Saints (April 6, 1980)

[*This document was put forth in commemoration of the 150th anniversary of the organization of the Church. On Sunday, April 6, 1980, a portion of the Sunday morning session of general conference was broadcast from the newly reconstructed Peter Whitmer, Sr., home in Fayette, New York. President Spencer W. Kimball spoke briefly of the organization of the Church that had occurred on that very spot of ground. He then announced that the Church had a proclamation to declare. President Kimball's concluding words were:*

> *Now, my brothers and sisters, with the future before us, and sensing deeply the responsibilities and divine mission of the restored Church on this sacred occasion, the First Presidency and the Quorum of the Twelve Apostles declare to the world a proclamation. We have felt it appropriate to issue this statement from here, where the Church began. Accordingly, I shall ask Elder Gordon B. Hinckley of the Quorum of the Twelve Apostles, to speak in my behalf and in behalf of my brethren, to read this proclamation to you and to the world (CR, Apr. 1980, p. 74).*

Elder Gordon B. Hinckley then read the Proclamation from the Whitmer home in Fayette, New York, which was broadcast by satellite to the Tabernacle in Salt Lake City, and published in the April 12, 1980 Church News, in the May 1980 Ensign, and in the April 1980 Conference Report. The full text of the proclamation follows.]

The Church of Jesus Christ of Latter-day Saints was organized 150 years ago today. On this sesquicentennial anniversary we issue to the world a proclamation concerning its progress, its doctrine, its mission, and its message.

On April 6, 1830, a small group assembled in the farmhouse of Peter Whitmer in Fayette Township in the State of New York. Six men participated in the formal organization procedures, with Joseph Smith as their leader. From that modest beginning in a rural area, this work has grown consistently and broadly, as men and women in many lands have embraced the doctrine and entered the waters of baptism. There are now almost four and a half million living members, and the Church is stronger and growing more rapidly than at any time in its history. Congregations of Latter-day Saints are found throughout North, Central, and South America; in the nations of Europe; in Asia; in Africa; in Australia and the islands of the South Pacific; and in other areas of the world. The gospel restored through the instrumentality of Joseph Smith is presently taught in forty-six languages and in eighty-one nations. From that small meeting held in a farmhouse a century and a half ago, the Church has grown until today it includes nearly 12,000 organized congregations.

We testify that this restored gospel was introduced into the world by the marvelous appearance of God the Eternal Father and His Son, the resurrected Lord Jesus Christ. That most glorious manifestation marked the beginning of the fulfillment of the promise of Peter, who prophesied of "the times of restitution of all things, which God hath spoken by the mouth of all his holy prophets since the world began," this in preparation for the coming of the Lord to reign personally upon the earth (Acts 3:21).

We solemnly affirm that The Church of Jesus Christ of Latter-day Saints is in fact a restoration of the Church established by the Son of God, when in mortality he organized his work upon the earth; that it carries his sacred name, even the name of Jesus Christ; that it is built upon a foundation of Apostles and prophets, he being the chief cornerstone; that its priesthood, in both the Aaronic and Melchizedek orders, was restored under the hands of those who held it anciently: John the Baptist, in the case of the Aaronic; and Peter, James, and John in the case of the Melchizedek.

We declare that the Book of Mormon was brought forth by the gift and power of God and that it stands beside the Bible as another witness of Jesus the Christ, the Savior and Redeemer of mankind. Together they testify of his divine sonship.

We give our witness that the doctrines and practices of the Church encompass salvation and exaltation not only for those who are living, but also for the dead, and that in sacred temples built for this purpose a great vicarious work is going forward in behalf of those who have died, so that all men and women of all generations may become the beneficiaries of the saving ordinances of the gospel of the Master. This great, selfless labor is one of the distinguishing features of this restored Church of Jesus Christ.

We affirm the sanctity of the family as a divine creation and declare that God our Eternal Father will hold parents accountable to rear their children in light and truth, teaching them "to pray, and to walk uprightly before the Lord" (D&C 68:28). We teach that the most sacred of all relationships, those family associations of husbands and wives and parents and children, may be continued eternally when marriage is solemnized under the authority of the holy priesthood exercised in temples dedicated for these divinely authorized purposes.

We bear witness that all men and women are sons and daughters of God, each accountable to him; that our lives here on earth are part of an eternal plan; that death is not the end, but rather a transition from this to another sphere of purposeful activity made possible through the Atonement of the Redeemer of the world; and that we shall there have the opportunity of working and growing toward perfection.

We testify that the spirit of prophecy and revelation is among us. "We believe all that God has revealed, all that He does now reveal; and we believe that He will yet reveal many great and important things pertaining to the Kingdom of God" (Articles of Faith 1:9). The heavens are not sealed; God continues to speak to his children through a prophet empowered to declare his word, now as he did anciently.

The mission of the Church today, as it has been from the beginning, is to teach the gospel of Christ to all the world in obedience to the commandment given by the Savior prior to his ascension and repeated in modern revelation: "Go ye into all the world, preach the gospel to every creature, acting in the authority which I have given you, baptizing in the name of the Father, and of the Son, and of the Holy Ghost" (D&C 68:8).

Through the Prophet Joseph Smith the Lord revealed these words of solemn warning:

> Hearken ye people from afar; and ye that are upon the islands of the sea, listen together. For verily, the voice of the Lord is unto all men, and there is none to escape; and there is no eye that shall not see, neither ear that shall not hear, neither heart that shall not be penetrated. And the rebellious shall be pierced with much sorrow; for their iniquities shall be spoken upon the housetops, and their secret acts shall be revealed. And the voice of warning shall be unto all people, by the mouths of my disciples, whom I have chosen in these last days [D&C 1:1–4].

It is our obligation, therefore, to teach faith in the Lord Jesus Christ, to plead with the people of the earth for individual repentance, to administer the sacred ordinances of baptism by immersion for the remission of sins and the laying on of hands for the gift of the Holy Ghost—all of this under the authority of the priesthood of God.

It is our responsibility to espouse and follow an inspired program of instruction and activity, and to build and maintain appropriate facilities for the accomplishment of this, that all who will hear and accept may grow in understanding of doctrine and develop in principles of Christian service to their fellowmen.

As we stand today on the summit of 150 years of progress, we contemplate humbly and gratefully the sacrifices of those who have gone before us, many of whom gave their lives in testimony of this truth. We are thankful for their faith, for their example, for their mighty labors and willing consecrations for this cause which they considered more precious than life itself. They have passed to us a remarkable heritage. We are resolved to build on that heritage for the blessing and benefit of those who follow, who will constitute ever enlarging numbers of faithful men and women throughout the earth.

This is God's work. It is his kingdom we are building. Anciently the prophet Daniel spoke of it as a stone cut out of the mountain without hands, which was to roll forth to fill the whole earth (see Dan. 2:31–45). We invite the honest in heart everywhere to listen to the teachings of our missionaries who are sent forth as messengers of eternal truth, to study and learn, and to ask God, our Eternal Father, in the name of his Son, the Lord Jesus Christ, if these things are true.

> And if ye shall ask with a sincere heart, with real intent, having faith in Christ, he will manifest the truth of it unto you, by the power of the Holy Ghost. And by the power of the Holy Ghost ye may know the truth of all things [Moro. 10:4–5].

We call upon all men and women to forsake evil and turn to God; to work together to build that brotherhood which must be recognized when we truly come to know that God is our Father and we are his children; and to worship him and his Son, the Lord Jesus Christ, the Savior of mankind. In the authority of the Holy Priesthood in us vested, we bless the seekers of truth wherever they may be and invoke the favor of the Almighty upon all men and nations whose

God is the Lord, in the name of Jesus Christ, amen [*CR*, Apr. 1980, pp. 75–77; see also *Ensign* 10 (May 1980):51–53].

BIBLIOGRAPHY
Messages of the First Presidency, James R. Clark, comp., 5 vols. Salt Lake City, 1965–1975.

ROBERT J. MATTHEWS

PROPHET, SEER, AND REVELATOR

"Prophet, seer, and revelator" is the threefold title applied to all who have received the fulness of the KEYS of the MELCHIZEDEK PRIESTHOOD associated with the apostleship. Ordinarily, those to whom this title applies are members of the FIRST PRESIDENCY or the QUORUM OF THE TWELVE APOSTLES. All members of these two governing bodies are sustained as prophets, seers, and revelators by the Latter-day Saints in a public congregational vote (*see* COMMON CONSENT).

Though there are technical distinctions between the functions of a prophet, a SEER, and a revelator (cf. Mosiah 8:12–18), this threefold term is applied in its entirety to describe all these leaders. It was applied to Hyrum Smith when he was made Assistant President of the Church and Patriarch to the Church, and to Joseph Smith in his role as President of the Church (D&C 124:94). Also, at the dedication of the Kirtland Temple in 1836, Joseph Smith invited the members of the Church to acknowledge the Twelve Apostles as prophets, seers, and revelators (*TPJS*, p. 109).

LEWIS R. CHURCH

PUBLICATIONS

From its inception in 1830, The Church of Jesus Christ of Latter-day Saints has been a diverse and prolific publisher of the printed word. The varied publications have included scriptures, doctrinal treatises, missionary tracts, newspapers, magazines, histories, accounts of persecutions and petitions for redress, proclamations and warnings to the world, hymnals and books of poetry, and replies to anti-Mormon attacks. While the history of the Mormon press is unique, it does fit into the context of American religious printing in general. The period from 1800 to 1865 saw the printing of religious literature in America reach a high point—the result of the Second Great Awakening and the activities of various interdenominational Bible and tract societies. It was in this environment of vigorous printing activity that the Church emerged and grew.

Church publishing in the years 1830–1844 is best described as informal and quasi-official because the Prophet Joseph Smith was occupied with more pressing concerns and left much of the business of printing and disseminating literature to others. After 1844, President Brigham Young and the QUORUM OF THE TWELVE APOSTLES assumed more control over Church publishing. As the main body of Saints made their permanent move to the Great Basin (1846–1852), the responsibility for publishing Church literature moved to Great Britain until the late 1870s because of the unavailability of suitable presses and inexpensive paper in the intermountain area.

SCRIPTURES. To Latter-day Saints, the most important publications are the four standard works of scripture: the Bible, Book of Mormon, Doctrine and Covenants, and Pearl of Great Price. As Christians, Latter-day Saints accept the Holy Bible as sacred scripture from God (the Church endorses the King James Version for English-speaking members). However, they get their popular nickname, Mormons, from their acceptance of the Book of Mormon as additional scripture from God. Since its first printing (Palmyra, New York, 1830), the Book of Mormon has had scores of editions published in many languages. Subsequent English-language editions of significance include those printed in Kirtland, Ohio, 1837; Nauvoo, Illinois, 1840; Liverpool, England, 1841, and 1879; and Salt Lake City, Utah, 1871, 1920, and 1981.

The Doctrine and Covenants contains most of the important recorded revelations received by Joseph Smith. Many of these first appeared in the Church's early newspapers, the EVENING AND THE MORNING STAR (Independence, Missouri, 1832–1833) and *Latter Day Saints'* MESSENGER AND ADVOCATE (Kirtland, 1834–1838). The first collection of the revelations was to be published as the Book of Commandments (Independence, 1833). But the press was destroyed by a mob before the printing was completed, and a fuller collection was published in Kirtland, as the Doctrine and Covenants, in 1835 by the Kirtland Literary Firm (cf. D&C 72:20–21), the publications committee apparently then in charge of Church publications in Kirtland. Later editions of the Doctrine and Covenants were published in Nauvoo, 1844; Liverpool, 1845, 1879; and Salt Lake City, 1876, 1908, 1918, 1921, and 1981.

The fourth volume of LDS scripture is a compilation entitled the Pearl of Great Price, published first in Liverpool in 1851, with other editions printed in Liverpool in 1879 and in Salt Lake City in 1878, 1902, 1921, 1976, and 1981.

PERIODICALS.   Periodical literature has been used extensively by Church leaders to disseminate information to members. Early on, it was the pattern to publish two papers, one religious and the other secular. The first of these pairs, the *Evening and the Morning Star* and the *Upper Missouri Advertiser*, commenced publication in Independence, Missouri, in June 1832. The *Star* was printed monthly to provide members of the Church with appropriate reading material and included the text of many revelations given to the Prophet Joseph Smith. The *Advertiser* was a weekly single-sheet paper intended for the community. Both were printed from June 1832 to July 1833, when the press at Independence was destroyed. Other early periodicals include *Latter-day Saints' Messenger and Advocate* (Kirtland, Ohio, 1834–1837); *Northern Times* (Kirtland, c. 1835–1836); *Elders' Journal of the Church of Latter Day Saints* (Kirtland, Ohio, and Far West, Missouri, 1837–1838); *Times and Seasons* (Nauvoo, 1839–1846); and the *Wasp* (1842–1843), which was replaced by *Nauvoo Neighbor* (1843–1846).

The longest-published periodical was the MILLENNIAL STAR (full name, *Latter Day Saints' Millennial Star*, Manchester, Liverpool, and London, England, 1840–1970). First issued for the fast-growing British membership, it later served American Saints as the most substantial Church periodical between their Nauvoo exodus in 1846 and the commencement of the weekly newspaper DESERET NEWS (Salt Lake City, 1850–); from 1850 to 1971, it continued as a substantial missionary periodical read worldwide. Another important periodical printed in England, JOURNAL OF DISCOURSES (Liverpool, 1854–1886), provided Latter-day Saints on both sides of the Atlantic with reports of sermons given at several places, including the Church's semiannual general conferences. After the Church formally announced the practice of plural marriage in 1852, President Brigham Young assigned different brethren to establish periodicals in the large cities to counter the increased attacks on the Church that resulted from that announcement. The following journals were responses to his request: the *Seer* (Orson Pratt, ed., Washington, D.C., 1853–1854); *St. Louis Luminary* (Erastus Snow, ed., 1854–1855); the *Mormon* (John Taylor, ed., New York, 1855–1857); and the *Western Standard* (George Q. Cannon, ed., San Francisco, 1856–1857). Much of what would eventually be published in book or pamphlet form was first issued in one of these journals.

After the Church became established in Utah Territory, other periodicals (issued from Salt Lake City unless otherwise noted) included: *Juvenile Instructor* (1866–1929), which became the *Instructor* (1929–1970); *Contributor* (1879–1896); *Young Woman's Journal* (1889–1929); *Improvement Era* (1897–1970); the *Elders' Journal* (Chattanooga, Tennessee, 1903–1907), which became *Liahona the Elders' Journal* (Independence, 1907–1945); *Children's Friend* (1902–1970); *Utah Genealogical and Historical Magazine* (1910–1940); and *Relief Society Magazine* (1915–1970).

As the Church expanded into other lands, its missions often established periodicals in their respective languages. The earliest was the Welsh *Prophwyd y Jubili* (1846–1848), and the longest running was the Danish *Skandinaviens Stjerne* (1851–1956). Other early journals were *Der Stern* (German, 1869–), *Nordstjärnan* (Swedish, 1877–), and *De Ster* (Dutch, 1896–).

Current English language periodicals include three monthly magazines (published since 1971): *Ensign*, for adults (over 18); *New Era*, for young adults and youth (ages 12 to 18); and *Friend*, for children (to 12). Selected articles from these periodicals are gathered into *International Magazines*, which in 1990 was printed with local additions in some twenty non-English languages. *BYU Studies* (1959–), a scholarly quarterly, is produced at Brigham Young University. (*For a fuller list of most of the major LDS periodicals, see Appendix 2.*)

DOCTRINAL WORKS. Following the formal organization of the Church on April 6, 1830, a rigorous missionary effort began that ultimately became the impetus for much early publishing in the Church. The successes of a number of Protestant tract societies in early nineteenth-century England and America provided LDS writers an effective model for disseminating the restored gospel through the printed word. A sizable portion of early LDS printing took the form of doctrinal and missionary tracts and pamphlets.

Early influential tracts of a doctrinal nature included Orson Hyde's *A Prophetic Warning to All the Churches, of Every Sect and Denomination*, published in Canada in 1836. Although only a short treatise, this broadside was the first tract to be used for proselytizing purposes. Elder Hyde, a member of the Quorum of the Twelve Apostles, suggested that the Christian world must prepare for the second coming of the Savior. He asserted the LDS claim that the New Testament prophecy of future apostasy from primitive Christianity had already occurred and that men and women need baptism performed by someone with proper authority from Jesus Christ.

Other early doctrinal works were written by several LDS writers. The Church's most notable early author was Parley P. Pratt, also an apostle, whose *A Voice of Warning* (New York, 1837) was arguably the most influential nineteenth-century nonscriptural book of LDS literature. Its descriptions of the unique doctrines of the Church would be repeated and imitated by others in many publications that followed. He also produced *Mormonism Unveiled* (New York, 1838), the first LDS tract responding to anti-Mormon criticisms; *The Millennium and Other Poems* (New York, 1840), a book of poetry expressing LDS ideas; and *Key to the Science of Theology* (Liverpool, 1855), the first comprehensive treatment of the doctrines of the Church.

Another writer who made significant doctrinal contributions in print was Orson Pratt, Parley's younger brother, also an apostle, whose important tracts include *A[n] Interesting Account of Several Remarkable Visions* (Edinburgh, Scotland, 1840); *A Series of Sixteen Pamphlets* (Liverpool, 1851) containing sixteen doctrinal tracts which formed a book later published under the title *Orson Pratt's Works* (1945); and a second series of tracts, *Eight Pamphlets on the First Principles of the Gospel* (Liverpool, 1856–1857).

Yet other important early doctrinal works include Lorenzo Snow's *The Only Way To Be Saved* (London, 1841); Orson Spencer's *Correspondence Between the Rev. W. Crowel, A.M., and O. Spencer, B.A.* (Liverpool, 1847), later known as *Spencer's Letters*; and Franklin

D. Richards's *A Compendium of the Faith and Doctrines of the Church of Jesus Christ of Latter-day Saints* (London, 1857).

Examples of influential doctrinal works from the twentieth century include James E. Talmage's *Articles of Faith* (1899) and *Jesus the Christ* (1915), B. H. Roberts's *Seventy's Course in Theology* (5 volumes, 1907–1912), Joseph Fielding Smith's compilation *Teachings of the Prophet Joseph Smith* (1938) and *Doctrines of Salvation* (3 volumes, 1954–1956), Bruce R. McConkie's *Mormon Doctrine* (1958), and Spencer W. Kimball's *Miracle of Forgiveness* (1969).

HISTORICAL WORKS. During the Church's early years, Latter-day Saints experienced intense and extensive religious persecutions, which resulted in forced moves for the entire Church on several occasions. Important published histories that document the Saints' difficulties in Missouri include John P. Greene's *Facts Relative to the Expulsion of the Mormons or Latter Day Saints, from the State of Missouri* (Cincinnati, 1839); Parley P. Pratt's *Late Persecution of the Church of Jesus Christ of Latter Day Saints* (Detroit, 1839; enlarged ed., New York, 1840); and Sidney Rigdon's *An Appeal to the American People* (Cincinnati, 1840). In Illinois the persecutions continued, culminating in the martyrdom of the Prophet Joseph Smith and his brother Hyrum. An important history of that dark day is William M. Daniels's *A Correct Account of the Murder of Generals Joseph and Hyrum Smith, at Carthage* (Nauvoo, 1845). Other nineteenth-century histories of note include *Biographical Sketches of Joseph Smith the Prophet* (Liverpool, 1853), by Joseph's mother, Lucy Mack Smith, and *The Autobiography of Parley Parker Pratt* (New York, 1874).

Significant historical works published in the twentieth century include the seven-volume *History of the Church* (1901–1932, formerly referred to as the Documentary History of the Church), edited by B. H. Roberts, and his six-volume *A Comprehensive History of the Church of Jesus Christ of Latter-day Saints* (1930); Joseph Fielding Smith's *Essentials in Church History* (1922); John Henry Evans's *Joseph Smith, an American Prophet* (1933); Leonard J. Arrington's *Great Basin Kingdom* (1958); and James B. Allen and Glen M. Leonard's *The Story of the Latter-day Saints* (1976). The years 1960 1990 saw a virtual explosion of monographs and professional journal articles documenting the history of the Church. This same period saw the publication of several independent, non-Church periodicals, including *Dialogue* (1966–), *Journal of Mormon History* (1974–), *Sunstone* (1975–), and *This People* (1979–).

HYMNALS. Music and hymns have always been an important part of Latter-day Saint worship services. As early as July 1830, Emma Smith was instructed to select a group of hymns for publication. The first LDS hymnal, though dated 1835, was not published until March 1836 in Kirtland. Entitled *A Collection of Sacred Hymns, for the Church of the Latter Day Saints*, this first hymnal, that printed the texts of the hymns without music, served as a model for several subsequent editions compiled by Church members. Another early hymnal was the first British edition, *A Collection of Sacred Hymns, for the Church of Jesus Christ of Latter-day Saints, in Europe, Selected by Brigham Young, Parley P. Pratt, and John Taylor* (Manchester, 1840). This hymnal was the basis for more than a dozen subsequent editions. Other significant hymnals include the first Salt Lake City edition (1871), the first edition to add music to the texts (Salt Lake City, 1889), and revised editions in 1927 and 1948. The current 1985 edition was a major revision of the Church's hymnal.

OTHER PUBLICATIONS. The Church has also issued ALMANACS printed independently from 1845–1866, and by the Church since 1974. The Church also printed emigrant guidebooks, a multivolume biographical encyclopedia, and many historical works.

CURRENT PUBLICATIONS. In addition to official publications such as scriptures, hymnals, and monthly periodicals, the Church produces a large body of educational curriculum material, including instructional manuals for the study of the scriptures, doctrine, and Church history for all organizations within the Church—the priesthood, Relief Society, Sunday School, Young Men, Young Women, and Primary. The Church Educational System produces materials for use in the secondary school seminaries and college and university institutes of religion.

In addition, numerous independent publishers serve the LDS market.

BIBLIOGRAPHY
For a comprehensive bibliographic listing of pre-1930 publications relating to the Church, see Chad J. Flake, *A Mormon Bibliography, 1830–1930* (Salt Lake City, 1978), and its companion volume, *Ten-Year Supplement* (Salt Lake City, 1989),

compiled by Flake and Larry W. Draper. These two publications list approximately 12,000 books, pamphlets, and broadsides that contain discussions of LDS doctrine, history, and culture during the Church's first century. Lengthier discussions of specific early LDS publications include Peter Crawley, "A Bibliography of The Church of Jesus Christ of Latter-day Saints in New York, Ohio, and Missouri" (*BYU Studies* 12 [Summer 1972]:465–537); David J. Whittaker, "Early Mormon Pamphleteering" (Ph.D. diss., Brigham Young University, 1982); Crawley and Flake, *A Mormon Fifty* (Provo, Utah, 1984); and Crawley and Whittaker, *Mormon Imprints in Great Britain and the Empire, 1836–1857* (Provo, Utah, 1987). For a bibliography listing more recent publications on LDS subjects, see "Mormon Bibliography," a serial article appearing in one issue annually of *BYU Studies* since 1960.

LARRY W. DRAPER

PUBLIC SPEAKING

The Church of Jesus Christ of Latter-day Saints encourages its members at all ages to express publicly not only their faith and testimony but also their wisdom, humor, and gratitude. Anyone may be invited to speak in an LDS meeting, whether man, woman, or child. Children begin their public speaking experience by sharing two or three sentences learned at home; later, talks of original construction and longer duration are given. Subject matter may be assigned or left to the selection of the speaker. Although some Latter-day Saints write out and read their speeches aloud, that practice is less common as members mature in their gospel experience and become more confident in their speaking ability. Experienced speakers, such as Church officers, often "take no thought" beforehand (Matt. 10:19) as to precisely what they will say, but "study the word of the Lord" and then speak "as they [are] directed by the Spirit" (D&C 42:12–14). Thousands of young people who serve on MISSIONS for the Church become adept at public speaking.

Typically, an LDS speaker addresses the congregation as "brothers and sisters" and may introduce the topic by using a story, humorous event, or personal experience. The speaker then presents the substance of the speech, sometimes in traditional rhetorical form, giving general thesis statements with supporting data for each, and sometimes very informally. The information is usually based on observation, logic, authority of the scriptures, personal experience, writings of Church leaders, and sometimes comparative social or religious approaches (e.g., why Mormons may live longer than others). In summary, the speaker often declares faith in the principles discussed and testifies to their truthfulness, generally concluding the talk invoking the name of Jesus Christ and saying amen. The audience affirms agreement by uttering an audible "Amen."

Latter-day Saints believe that admission to the Kingdom of Heaven is achieved through obedience to ORDINANCES and the development of personal perfection. Such spiritual growth comes in part from individual enlightenment, which is reason to receive the spoken or written word. Inspiration often derives from hearing the oral testimony of others, for if people do not nourish the word, they "can never pluck of the fruit of the tree of life" (Alma 32:40).

Thus, public speaking is a basic LDS exercise, for "how shall they believe in him of whom they have not heard? and how shall they hear without a preacher?" (Rom. 10:14–17). As opportunity allows, a speaker introduces the restored gospel to others and, significantly, preaches the gospel in the Church's meetings. Speaking in church carries the responsibility of teaching and inspiring others. The speaker becomes a voice for God and is expected to prepare so that the word of God can effectively be expressed. The speaker is therefore admonished to use "great plainness of speech" (2 Cor. 3:12) and to speak as "moved upon by the Holy Ghost" (D&C 68:3).

Public speaking is periodically encouraged on a local level through speech festivals and contests. These events focus on the art of speaking, involve members in refining their speaking abilities in a Church context, and provide an appropriate arena for the enjoyment and appreciation of public speaking.

LAEL J. WOODBURY

Q

QUORUM OF THE TWELVE APOSTLES

Twelve men ordained to the MELCHIZEDEK PRIESTHOOD office of APOSTLE constitute the Quorum of the Twelve Apostles, the second-highest presiding quorum in the government of The Church of Jesus Christ of Latter-day Saints. The highest presiding quorum is the FIRST PRESIDENCY, three HIGH PRIESTS who have generally been apostles, who hold all keys (AUTHORITY) pertaining to the spiritual and temporal affairs of the Church. The Twelve serve under the direction of the First Presidency. Latter-day Saints sustain these fifteen men as PROPHETS, SEERS, AND REVELATORS for the Church, who receive "a special spiritual endowment in connection with their teaching of the people. . . . Others of the General Authorities are not given this special spiritual endowment and authority covering their teaching" (J. Reuben Clark, Jr., *Church News* [July 31, 1954]:9).

Several titles refer to the body of the twelve apostles: the Quorum of the Twelve, the Council of the Twelve, or simply the Twelve. The designation Quorum of the Twelve is the scriptural title and the formal name used by the First Presidency in presenting the Twelve to Church members for their sustaining vote. The designation Council of the Twelve is used commonly in Church publications and in communicating with persons of other faiths.

HISTORY.   The first members of the Quorum of the Twelve in modern times were ordained on February 14, 1835. This type of quorum has its roots in New Testament precedent (Matt. 10:1) and in modern revelation (D&C 18:26–39). After the Zion's Camp expedition of 1834, the Prophet Joseph Smith called together in 1835 those who had participated and revealed that "it was the will of God that those who went to Zion, with a determination to lay down their lives, . . . should be ordained to the ministry" (HC 2:182). He then directed the three witnesses of the Book of Mormon (Oliver Cowdery, David Whitmer, and Martin Harris) to prayerfully choose the Twelve in harmony with an earlier revelation (D&C 18:37). The Presidency then laid hands on the Three Witnesses, empowering them to make the selection (HC 2:186–87). Those chosen were Thomas B. Marsh, David W. Patten, Brigham Young, Heber C. Kimball, Orson Hyde, William E. McLellin, Parley P. Pratt, Luke S. Johnson, William B. Smith, Orson Pratt, John F. Boynton, and Lyman E. Johnson. These twelve men were then ordained apostles by the Three Witnesses and given the keys pertaining to their holy calling. The First Presidency also laid their hands on them and confirmed these blessings and ordinations (T&S 2 [Apr. 15, 1845]:868). Oliver Cowdery then gave to the Twelve a charge to "preach the Gospel to every nation" (HC 2:195).

A month later, the Twelve requested further divine guidance as they prepared to preach. The response was a revelation that defined their duties and the duties of the newly formed Quorum of the Seventy (see D&C 107:21–39). Primary duties of the Quorum of the Twelve are to be "special witnesses of the name of Christ in all the world," "to officiate in the name of the Lord, under the direction of the Presidency of the Church," "to build up the Church, and regulate all the affairs of the same," and "to open the door [of all nations] by the proclamation of the gospel of Jesus Christ" (D&C 107:23, 33, 35; cf. 112:16–21; 124:128).

Joseph Smith assigned the members of the Quorum of the Twelve to regulate the scattered branches of the Church. Later, he sent them on proselytizing missions to foreign lands. In 1840–1841 nine of the Twelve served special missions to the British Isles. When they left Great Britain after twelve months, more than 4,000 new members had joined the Church. These nine brethren also established procedures for a continuing program of immigration of the British convert Saints to America.

Missionary success in Britain bonded members of the Twelve into a united quorum under the leadership of the quorum president, Brigham Young, who was appointed January 19, 1841. When they returned to Church headquarters at Nauvoo, Illinois, Joseph Smith expanded their duties to include regulating the affairs of the STAKE there.

In late March 1844, Joseph Smith conferred on the Quorum of the Twelve all of the ORDINANCES, keys, and authority that he possessed. Describing this event, Wilford Woodruff said Joseph Smith "lived until every key, power and principle of the holy Priesthood was sealed on the Twelve and on President Young, as their President." He further quoted the Prophet's explanation and injunction to the Twelve: "I have lived until I have seen this burden, which has rested on my shoulders, rolled on to the shoulders of other men; . . . the keys of the kingdom are planted on the earth to be taken away no more for ever. . . . You have to round up your shoulders to bear up the kingdom. No matter what becomes of me" (*JD* 13:164).

After a mob assassinated Joseph Smith on June 27, 1844, and the First Presidency was dissolved, the Church faced the question of SUCCESSION IN THE PRESIDENCY for the first time. The resulting confusion was resolved when the Quorum of the Twelve, as the next highest presiding quorum, stepped forward and was sustained to succeed the First Presidency. From June 1844 to December 1847, the Twelve governed the Church under their president, Brigham Young. In their presiding capacity, they published an 1845 proclamation to the kings of the world and the President of the United States of America (*see* PROCLAMATIONS OF THE FIRST PRESIDENCY AND THE QUORUM OF THE TWELVE APOSTLES). President Young was sustained as PRESIDENT OF THE CHURCH on December 5, 1847, by the Twelve and by the Saints in conference on December 27, 1847.

This transition of leadership established the precedent and order that have been followed in all subsequent reorganizations of the First Presidency. Upon the death of a Church President, the First Presidency is dissolved and the Quorum of the Twelve becomes the presiding council of the Church. The President of the Twelve who is the senior apostle on the earth becomes the presiding officer of the Church and remains in that capacity until a new First Presidency is organized.

An event that was highly significant to the Twelve occurred at the close of the administration of President Lorenzo Snow in 1901. For more than five decades preceding this time, the Twelve had spent less time taking the gospel to other nations because of the need to preside over the Saints at home. Also, U.S. government prosecution of polygamists had driven some of them into exile. Shortly before the October 1901 general conference, President Snow reminded the Twelve that they had a scriptural duty to preach the gospel to all the world; presiding over the STAKES was not sufficient (*Juvenile Instructor* 36 [Nov. 1901]:689–90.)

At the final session of that conference, President Snow defined the duties of the apostles, seventies, high priests, and ELDERS. The Twelve were "to look after the interests of the world" (*CR* [Oct. 1901]:61). President Snow died four days after the conference, but the Twelve recognized the importance of his instruction. The Quorum president, Joseph F. Smith, wrote that "we accept what [President Snow said] on the duties of the Twelve . . . as the word of the Lord to us all" (*Juvenile Instructor* 36 [Nov. 1901]:690). Consequently, the Twelve renewed their international missionary effort. Since that time, by direction of the First Presidency, the Twelve have dedicated many nations for preaching the gospel and continue to supervise missionary work throughout the Church.

APPOINTMENT. A member of the Quorum of the Twelve is selected by the First Presidency, which may consider several candidates. The Presidency then chooses one person by revelation and calls him to the position. This involves essentially the same principles as the selection of Matthias to fill the vacancy that resulted from the death of Judas Iscariot (Acts 1:15–26).

When a new appointment to the Quorum is to be announced (usually at a general conference), a member of the First Presidency presents the names of GENERAL AUTHORITIES, including the new apostle, and other general Church officers to be sustained by Church members. The sustaining complies with the principle of COMMON CONSENT (D&C 26:2).

After Church members sustain the newly called person, the First Presidency and Quorum of the Twelve ordain him to the office of apostle and give him all the keys of the holy apostleship. These are the same keys Jesus Christ conferred on the Twelve he called in New Testament times, and also the same keys restored by Peter, James, and John to Joseph Smith and Oliver Cowdery in this dispensation. The keys given to the new apostle include the authority to preach the gospel in all the world and to seal ordinances on earth that will be sealed eternally (Matt. 16:19; 28:19–20; John 20:22–23).

Callings to the Quorum of the Twelve are for life. The date on which a person becomes a member of the Quorum (usually the date he is sustained as an apostle) establishes his position of seniority in the Quorum relative to other quorum members. Seniority within the Quorum determines who will be the next President of the Church, for that office passes to the senior apostle. This divinely revealed order identifies the most experienced apostle as the future president and prevents any striving for office or vying for power or position (*see* SUCCESSION IN THE PRESIDENCY).

DUTIES.   Consistent with earlier revelations, the Twelve today are commissioned to open the nations of the world to the preaching of the gospel (D&C 107:35). By assignment from the First Presidency, members of the Twelve meet with heads of state to obtain official permission for the Church to teach the gospel consistent with the laws of those countries.

When the Twelve act under direction of the First Presidency, they have authority to receive revelation for their assignments, which include supervising the Seventy, overseeing the stakes, and training leaders (D&C 107:33). Only the President of the Church, however, has the right and authority to receive revelation for the whole Church (D&C 28:2–3).

Members of the Twelve serve on committees established by the First Presidency and those within the Quorum. Committee assignments are rotated periodically.

The Quorum of the Twelve directs the work of the Seventy. The Twelve are to "call upon the Seventy, when they need assistance . . . instead of any others" (D&C 107:38). The presidents of the Quorums of the Seventy report to the Twelve.

The Twelve meet in the Salt Lake Temple, usually weekly, to transact all business that requires decisions by the Quorum. The Quorum normally brings the decisions it reaches to its meetings with the First Presidency. These two bodies together constitute the

Council of the First Presidency and the Quorum of the Twelve Apostles. This council takes final action on all matters that affect the Church, including new Church leadership callings; establishment of policies, procedures, and programs; creation, division, and reorganization of missions and stakes. Church PRIESTHOOD QUORUMS strive for unanimity in their decisions, in accordance with revelation (D&C 107:27). Until agreement is reached, the Quorum of the Twelve takes no action. Instead, the President of the Twelve usually defers the matter for reconsideration. Unanimity among the presiding quorums of the Church provides Church members with an assurance that "the united voice of the First Presidency and the Twelve" will never "lead the Saints astray or send forth counsel to the world that is contrary to the mind and will of the Lord" (Joseph Fielding Smith, *Ensign* 2 [July 1972]:88).

The First Presidency assigns members of the Twelve and other General Authorities to speak at semiannual general conferences of the Church, but normally does not assign a topic. Members of the First Presidency and the Twelve speak at every general conference; other General Authorities speak periodically as assigned. Church members regard messages of the First Presidency and the Twelve as inspired (D&C 68:4).

Each stake has semiannual stake conferences. A General Authority or a Regional Representative usually presides at one of these conferences each year, as assigned by the President of the Quorum of the Twelve. Because of the large and increasing number of stakes, members of the Twelve are generally assigned to attend stake conferences only to organize new stakes, divide existing stakes, or reorganize STAKE PRESIDENCIES.

The President of the Quorum also assigns Quorum members to attend conferences where several stakes meet together. These multiregional conferences give Church members a more frequent opportunity to see and hear members of the First Presidency and the Twelve.

Members of the Twelve are "special witnesses" of the name of Jesus Christ in all the world; they possess a knowledge, by revelation, of the literal resurrection of Christ and a knowledge that he directs the affairs of his Church today. That shared conviction unites the Twelve in a bond of unity and love.

BIBLIOGRAPHY

Allen, James B., and Malcolm R. Thorp. "The Mission of the Twelve to England, 1840–41: Mormon Apostles and the Working Classes." *BYU Studies* 15 (Summer 1975):499–526.

Esplin, Ronald K. "The Emergence of Brigham Young and the Twelve to Mormon Leadership, 1830–1841," pp. 427–512. Ph.D. diss., Brigham Young University, 1981.

Larsen, Dean L. "Apostle and Prophet: Divine Priesthood Callings." *Priesthood*, pp. 38–47. Salt Lake City, 1981.

McConkie, Bruce R. "Succession in Presidency." *Church News* (Mar. 23, 1974):7–9.

Smith, Joseph Fielding. "The Holy Apostleship." *DS*, Vol. 3, pp. 144–59.

———. "The Twelve Apostles." *IE* 59 (Nov. 1956):786–88.

———. "The First Presidency and the Council of the Twelve." *IE* 69 (Nov. 1966):977–79.

Talbot, Wilburn D. "The Duties and Responsibilities of the Apostles of The Church of Jesus Christ of Latter-day Saints, 1835–1945." Ph.D. diss., Brigham Young University, 1978.

WILLIAM O. NELSON

R

REBAPTISM

Once a person joins The Church of Jesus Christ of Latter-day Saints, circumstances requiring rebaptism are unusual. In current policy and practice, a person would be rebaptized only in two cases: (1) if membership records were irretrievably lost and no other proof of membership could be established; or (2) if an excommunicated person qualified for reentry into the Church. As members partake of the sacrament weekly, repenting of sin, their baptismal covenants are renewed and rebaptism is unnecessary.

One enters into membership in the Church only through baptism by immersion for the remission of sins by one holding the appropriate priesthood, regardless of any prior baptism or initiation ordinance. Latter-day scriptures refer to baptism as a new and everlasting covenant. It is the ordinance received by one who accepts the gospel of Jesus Christ, with the promise that proper baptism opens onto the path that leads to eternal life. But baptisms performed outside the framework of the restored priesthood are of no avail for one who wishes to enter in at the strait gate and onto that path (D&C 22:1–2).

Rebaptism is rare among Latter-day Saints in modern times. Historically, however, many members were rebaptized as an act of rededication. This was first practiced in Nauvoo and was continued in the Utah Territory. Rebaptism served as a ritual of recommitment but was not viewed as essential to salvation. Members often sought rebaptism when called to assist in colonization or to participate in one of the united orders. On some occasions, the Saints were rebaptized as they prepared for marriage or entrance into the temple. Early members also rebaptized some of the sick among them as an act of healing. Because of misuse by some Church members, all such practices of rebaptism were discontinued in 1897.

H. DEAN GARRETT

RECORD KEEPING

The keeping of records is done in response to a direct commandment from the Lord and is considered a sacred trust and obligation. "The matter of record keeping is one of the most important duties devolving on the Church," said Elder Joseph Fielding Smith (p. 96). Indeed, the very day the LDS Church was organized, the Prophet Joseph Smith received a revelation: "Behold, there shall be a record kept among you" (D&C 21:1). This requirement apparently has been the same in every dispensation. The Pearl of Great Price states that a book of remembrance was first kept in the Adamic language, and Adam's children were taught to read and write, "having a language that was pure and undefiled"; therefore, it was given unto many "to write by the spirit of inspiration" (Moses 6:5–6). Enoch, seventh in descent from Adam and the father of Methuselah, also kept a record and commented upon the divine prototype of it: "For a book of remembrance we have written among us, according to the pattern given by the finger of God" (Moses 6:46). Abraham continued the practice, affirming that "records of the fathers" had come into his hands and stating, "I shall endeavor to write some of these things upon this record, for the benefit of my posterity that shall come after me" (Abr. 1:31). Such records are of three types: (1) accounts of God's dealings with his children (the scriptures, for example); (2) records of religious ORDINANCES; and (3) histories of nations and peoples, including personal histories.

SCRIPTURES. Prophets have been commanded to write scripture. For example, Moses in his time received a great revelation concerning the creation of heaven and earth with the divine imperative, "Write the words which I speak" (Moses 2:1). Those words are largely preserved in Genesis in the Bible. During Jeremiah's difficult mission a king desecrated a scroll containing some of God's revelations and the word of the Lord came to Jeremiah saying, "Take thee again another roll, and write in it all the former words that were in the first roll" (Jer. 36:27–32). Jeremiah and his scribe did so, and those words are in the book of Jeremiah.

Near the time of Jeremiah's vicissitudes, the Book of Mormon prophet Lehi took his family and fled from Jerusalem into the wilderness in 600 B.C. He was commanded by the Lord to send his sons back to Jerusalem to obtain certain plates of brass that had been kept by his forebears. The plates were engraved with the genealogy of Lehi's family, the five books of Moses, and writings of the prophets down to Jeremiah (1 Ne. 5:11–14). Laman and Nephi$_1$, two of the sons of Lehi, tried to get Laban, the keeper of the plates, to give them the plates or to exchange them for certain other treasures, but Laban refused and sought to kill Lehi's sons. Eventually Laban himself was condemned of the Lord and slain, for "it is better that one man should perish than that a nation should dwindle and perish in unbelief" (1 Ne. 4:12–13). Thus the plates were procured and preserved, and they provided the cultural and spiritual foundation of the Nephite civilization in their promised land in the Western world (Mosiah 1:3–5; *DS* 2:198).

After his resurrection at Jerusalem, Jesus Christ appeared to the Nephites and personally emphasized the importance of record keeping. He provided them some of the revelations given to Malachi. The Lord then commanded Nephi$_3$ (the record keeper at the time of Jesus' advent and a descendent of the first Nephi) to bring out the records kept by the Nephites. He examined them and reminded Nephi that Samuel, a Lamanite prophet, had testified that he (Christ) should arise from the dead and prophesied that at Christ's resurrection others would also arise and appear to many. Jesus then inquired, "How be it that ye have not written this thing . . . ? And it came to pass that Jesus commanded that it should be written; therefore it was written according as he commanded" (3 Ne. 23:11, 13).

RELIGIOUS ORDINANCES.   Just as the doctrines and commandments from God must be recorded, so also must the responses and actions of the children of God be written. Prophetic scriptures warn that God's children will be judged out of sacred records kept both on earth and in heaven. Those responsible for keeping the records on earth are charged to make them as accurate as possible. Ordinances such as baptisms, confirmations, ordinations to the priesthood, patriarchal blessings, endowments, and sealings—all should be precisely recorded. Financial records of donations are especially carefully preserved, such as the TITHING record. Earthly and spiritual conduct is to be measured by the things written (Mal. 3:16–18; Rev. 20:12). The Prophet Joseph Smith affirmed, "Our acts are recorded, and at a future day they will be laid before us, and if we should fail to judge right and injure our fellow-beings, they may there, perhaps, condemn us; there they are of great consequence, and to me the consequence appears to be of force, beyond anything which I am able to express" (*TPJS*, p. 69).

To qualify for eternal blessings, each person must come unto God through Christ, make commitments and covenants through certain ordinances, and have them properly recorded. Those who have died without hearing the gospel of Jesus Christ must have the ordinances of salvation and exaltation performed in their behalf, and record keeping is vital for all such ordinances performed in the Church. Vicarious ordinances can be performed only for individuals properly identified through dependable records. The Church sponsors programs to locate and microfilm family records worldwide and make them available to members and others in their genealogical research and family history work. Many members are involved in such research and in vicarious service in the TEMPLES of the Church in behalf of the dead. It is all done in the faith that whatsoever is done by proper authority, in the name of the Lord, truly and faithfully, and with accurate records kept, is established on earth and in heaven, and cannot be annulled, according to the decrees of the great Jehovah (cf. D&C 128:9).

HISTORIES. Church members are counseled to include personal histories among the records they keep. All such records are valuable in the preservation and transmission of culture within each family, and they often have an impact broader than anticipated by those who write them. Nephi₁, who wrote a history of his people as commanded by God, did anticipate its benefit to others, saying, "I write the things of my soul. . . . For my soul delighteth in the scriptures, and my heart pondereth them, and writeth them for the learning and the profit of my children" (2 Ne. 4:15).

President Spencer W. Kimball offered this challenge: "Get a notebook . . . a journal that will last through all time, and maybe the angels may quote from it for eternity. Begin today and write in it your goings and comings, your deepest thoughts, your achievements and your failures, your associations and your triumphs, your impressions and your testimonies" (1975, p. 5). Parents may not see, in the present moment, the potential value of what they write in a personal journal, nor can they predict the response of their descendants to it, but anyone who holds the journal of an ancestor can testify of the joy in possessing it. Minimally, parents should record accurately special events such as dates of birth, marriages, ordinations, and deaths. While it is not necessary to write everything that occurs each day, things of a spiritual nature and other happenings that arouse poignant feelings should be recorded. One parent recounted with regret, "I remembered [a] . . . spiritual experience I had had years earlier, just before my baptism. I hadn't written that in my journal, . . . and now I couldn't remember enough details of the story to retell it. I wanted to share that event with my son—and because I hadn't recorded it, I could not" (Espinosa, p. 24). President Kimball promised: "As our posterity read of our life's experiences, they, too, will come to know and love us. And in the glorious day when our families are together in the eternities, we will already be acquainted" (1980, p. 61).

Record keeping has resulted in the creation of sacred scriptures of incalculable value; records of ordinances done and covenants made will have eternal significance; and the histories of nations and individuals have helped throughout the ages in the developments of civilization.

BIBLIOGRAPHY

Espinosa, Luis V. "The Voice Spoke Spanish." *Ensign* 7 (Jan. 1977):24.

"Eternal Implications of the Gospel: Life Everlasting, Family Records, Temple Blessings." *Ensign* 7 (Jan. 1977):2–75.

Kimball, Spencer W. "The Angels May Quote from It." *New Era* 5 (Oct. 1975):4–5.

———. "President Kimball Speaks Out on Personal Journals." *Ensign* 10 (Dec. 1980):61.

Smith, Joseph Fielding. *Church History and Modern Revelation*, pp. 96–97, 99. Salt Lake City, 1946.

BEVERLY J. NORTON

REGION, REGIONAL REPRESENTATIVE

Regions are intermediate geographic units positioned between the STAKE and the general AREA levels of administration in The Church of Jesus Christ of Latter-day Saints. In 1990, 447 regions around the world consisted of two to six stakes per region in close geographical proximity, each stake being comprised of between four and ten local WARDS of 200 to 700 members each. Groups of ten to forty regions are organized into areas determined by geographic and administrative convenience. Each area is presided over by three seventies who constitute the area presidency.

Regional Representatives are part-time lay officers of the Church that are called by the First Presidency, receive general instructions from the Quorum of the Twelve Apostles, and serve under the direction of the area presidency. Because Regional Representatives do not preside as line officers, they serve without counselors, and stake presidencies report directly to area presidencies. A Regional Representative may preside at a stake conference when assigned.

The principal responsibility of a Regional Representative is to train stake leaders. This training may take place through personal visits, regional council meetings consisting of the stake presidencies in the region, stake CONFERENCES, or other leadership meetings. A Regional Representative has no authority to call local leaders or to counsel individual members in connection with personal matters, but serves as an organizational link providing information and feedback between local Church officers and the General Authorities at area or Church headquarters.

A Regional Representative serves for a period determined by the First Presidency, typically five years. The first Regional Representatives were called in October 1967, and with the growth of the Church, the number has increased steadily.

With the approval of the area presidency, the regional council may organize occasional conferences, special training, athletic competitions, or other events. For members who might otherwise be somewhat isolated or limited by circumstance, such occasions provide perspective, motivation, and exposure to other members and to Church leaders.

[*See also* Organization: Contemporary.]

DOUGLAS L. CALLISTER
GERALD J. DAY

RELIEF SOCIETY

The Relief Society is the official adult women's organization of The Church of Jesus Christ of Latter-day Saints and is an essential part of the structure of the Church at general, STAKE, and WARD levels. The organization provides opportunities for association, leadership, COMPASSIONATE SERVICE, and education. Through the Relief Society, "women of the Church are given some measure of divine authority particularly in the direction of government and instruction in behalf of the women of the church" (J. F. Smith, p. 5).

The motto "Charity Never Faileth" expresses the commitment of Relief Society members to love and nurture one another and to minister graciously to the needs of Church members and others. The binding sense of sisterhood that characterizes the Relief Society is founded upon the women's common faith and enhanced by the lessons, activities, and interpersonal involvements that constitute the Relief Society program. Current lesson materials for a weekly Sunday class focus twice a month on spiritual themes; the other two weeks have lessons on compassionate service and on home and family education. Lessons on cultural refinement and varied interests provide an optional midweek activity for interested sisters. Once a month, a midweek homemaking meeting features instructions for visiting teachers, a short home management lesson, and miniclasses emphasizing homemaking arts, WELFARE SERVICES projects, and individual and family development. Members especially appointed as "visiting teachers" are expected to make regular contacts with each woman once a month in her home, or more often if needed.

When the Prophet Joseph Smith organized the Female Relief Society of Nauvoo in 1842, he stated that the restored Church of Jesus Christ could not be perfect or complete without it. Elder Joseph Fielding Smith later confirmed that "the Relief Society was revealed to the Prophet Joseph Smith as a fundamental part of the gospel" (J. F. Smith, p. 4). As an integral part of the Church organization, the Relief Society functions in close connection with, rather than independent of, the ecclesiastical priesthood structure. Ward Relief Society presidents work with BISHOPS, stake Relief Society presidents, with stake presidents, and the general Relief Society presidency, with designated GENERAL AUTHORITIES in what has been described as "a companionship relationship—not inferior or subordinate, but companion, side-by-side" (B. B. Smith, p. 11). Final decision-making responsibility rests with priesthood leaders.

ORIGINS 1842–1844.   In 1842 a small group of women met at the home of Sarah M. Kimball in Nauvoo to organize a sewing society to aid Nauvoo Temple workmen. When they sought the Prophet's endorsement for their proposed constitution, he praised their efforts but proffered an alternative: he would "organize the sisters under the priesthood after a pattern of the priesthood" ("Story of the Organization of the Relief Society," p. 129). Meeting with twenty women on March 17, 1842, he organized the Female Relief Society of Nauvoo. The women elected Emma Smith president, and like presidents of priesthood quorums, she selected two counselors. The three presiding officers were SET APART for their callings by the laying on of hands by priesthood leaders. Joseph Smith explained that the decisions of this presidency, together with minutes of society proceedings, would serve as the group's constitution. A secretary and treasurer were appointed, and the presidency could appoint other officers as necessary. New members were admitted individually when standing members voted to give them full fellowship. By 1844, there were 1,341 members.

The Female Relief Society of Nauvoo brought women into the formal structure of the Church and gave them significant responsibility and authority. They contributed to the Nauvoo Temple, supported moral reform, and petitioned the governor of Illinois on behalf of Joseph Smith. Primarily occupied with "looking to the wants of the poor," society members donated cash, commodities, housing, and labor. In July 1843 a visiting committee of four was appointed in each ward to assess needs, solicit contributions from Church members, and distribute necessities. Visiting teachers have remained part of the Relief Society's basic organizational structure ever since (*see* VISITING TEACHING).

Joseph Smith further charged members with the responsibility to "save souls." He personally instructed them in the same gospel principles he taught the men, with particular emphasis on humility, charity, and unity. He also introduced them to sacred doctrines related to TEMPLE WORSHIP. This instruction set the precedent for meetings in which women could discuss religious principles and testify of their faith in the restored gospel, a continuing aspect of the Relief Society.

1844–1866.   The Nauvoo society held its last recorded meeting on March 16, 1844, apparently unable to maintain unity of purpose during the factious events preceding the June 1844 martyrdom of Joseph Smith. Brigham Young, the next President of the Church, did not initially encourage women to resume formal meetings, nor did the organization function during the Saints' westward trek and early settlement of Utah, though women continued their charitable works and gathered as friends to support and minister to one another through prayer, testimony, and the exercise of the gifts of the spirit. The Female Council of Health, organized in Salt Lake City in 1851 for midwives and others interested in healing by faith and herbs, preceded the 1854–1857 renewal of collective effort.

In early February 1854, sixteen women in Salt Lake City responded to President Young's exhortation to befriend and aid the Indians by organizing "a society of females for the purpose of making clothing for Indian women and children." This charitable Indian Relief Society elected its own officers and met weekly until June 1854, when President Young explicitly encouraged women to "form themselves into societies" and meet "in their own wards" to make clothing for the Lamanites (the Indians). Members of the initial group later disbanded to join their respective ward organizations. During 1854, some twenty-two Indian Relief Societies were organized in Salt Lake City and outlying LDS settlements, and their members contributed enough bedding and clothing to meet the demand for such goods. Many of these societies remained organized for the long-range goal of assisting the poor within their wards, as well as for short-range projects such as meetinghouse carpets and clothing and bedding for destitute handcart companies.

The 1857 Utah expedition resulted in a widespread disorganization of wards that greatly diminished Relief Society operations for several years. There had been strong local leadership in a number of the wards, but the guiding central organization that would become a permanent and stabilizing feature of Relief Society was lacking.

1866–1887.   In 1866 President Young initiated Churchwide reorganization of the Relief Society, appointing Eliza R. Snow to assist bishops in establishing the organization in each ward. The minutes that she had recorded in Nauvoo became the common "constitution" for all local units, providing continuity of name, purpose, and organizational pattern. Though not formally called and set apart as general president until 1880, Eliza R. Snow directed Relief Society work from 1867 until her death in 1887. She was aided by her counselors Zina D. H. Young and Elizabeth Ann Whitney and by the RETRENCHMENT SOCIETY, which served informally as a central board.

By 1880, the Relief Society had 300 local units, and each one cared for the suffering and needy within its ward boundaries, using an expanded corps of visiting teachers to collect and distribute donations. Ward Relief Societies managed their own financial resources, and many of them built their own meeting halls.

The Relief Society engaged in a number of bold and innovative economic activities spurred by the Church's movement for economic self-sufficiency. Ward societies initiated cooperative enterprises for making and marketing homemade goods, raised silk, established a grain storage program with local granaries, and helped finance the medical training of midwives and female doctors. With the support of ward units, the central board established the Deseret Hospital (1882–1895). Assuming a new political role, the Relief Society sponsored a series of "indignation meetings" to voice women's opposition to proposed antipolygamy legislation. After Utah women were enfranchised in 1870, the Relief Society encouraged women to vote. Then they actively campaigned for woman suffrage after they were disfranchised by the federal government in 1887.

The Relief Society helped to organize and nurture the Young Ladies' Retrenchment Association (later YOUNG WOMEN) and the PRIMARY. Though separate general presidencies were appointed for these groups in 1880, President Eliza R. Snow served as their general head, and she and her board visited local congregations in Utah and Idaho to instruct all three groups. Local visits and conferences, the appointment of stake Relief Society presidents and boards (beginning in 1877), and publication of the semimonthly *Woman's Exponent* (1872–1914) strengthened women's sense of sisterhood. In assuming new responsibilities at ward, stake, and general levels, hundreds of

LDS women entered the public sphere, simultaneously strengthening the community and developing their individual talents.

1888–1921.   Economic and political activity continued during the administration of Zina D. H. Young (1888–1901). During the 1895 debate over the proposed constitution for the new state of Utah, Relief Society members successfully campaigned for a provision assuring women's right to vote and hold public office. Committed to cooperating with non-Mormons for the advance of women and later for international peace, the Relief Society affiliated with the National Woman Suffrage Association and the International Council of Women (1888). It was a charter member of the National Council of Women (1891) and, as such, became incorporated in October 1892 as the National Woman's Relief Society, establishing a twenty-three-member board of directors or general board composed of its general presidency and stake Relief Society presidents. Many ward units were also incorporated to facilitate management of property.

The Relief Society's political and economic involvement in the western United States did not displace its primary concern of spiritually nurturing its members and caring for the poor. These purposes united women across cultures, as members attested at their 1892 Relief Society Jubilee celebration. "Whether the language spoken is the English, French, German, Hawaiian or whatever tongue . . . they are all partakers of the same Spirit" ("The Jubilee Celebration," p. 133).

The increase in Relief Society membership and geographical spread that accompanied Church growth prompted greater centralization to assure continuity and unity. Annual dues for members, introduced in 1898, helped to defray the general board's traveling and operating expenses. Under the direction of President Bathsheba W. Smith (1901–1910), the general presidency and board published its initial handbook (1902) and established its first official headquarters in the newly constructed Bishop's Building in Salt Lake City (1909).

The physical housing of the Relief Society and Church AUXILIARIES with the PRESIDING BISHOPRIC was one manifestation of emerging efforts to correlate a larger and more complex Church. The building of separate stake and ward Relief Society halls was likewise discouraged, though some local units maintained their own halls into the 1940s. Effective correlation required greater communication and interdependence between priesthood and Relief Society leaders, and they began meeting together more regularly to discuss common concerns such as charity and community work.

The nineteenth-century format for local Relief Society meetings—based on charity work, sewing, testimony bearing, and scripture study—made way in the twentieth century for a more varied and extensive educational program. As the society's membership aged, leaders attempted to meet the needs of these older women as well as of the younger ones of a new generation. Mothers classes, introduced in 1902, featured a widely varied curriculum prepared by each stake. During the administration of President Emmeline B. Wells (1910–1921), the general board introduced new standardized lessons in the *Relief Society Bulletin* (1914) and the next year commenced publication of the RELIEF SOCIETY MAGAZINE through which it regularly issued standardized monthly lesson plans on theological, cultural, and homemaking topics, designating a week each month for each topic, while still reserving time for "work" (charity projects) and testimonies. This monthly format of rotating topics has been maintained, though subject matter has varied with changing interests and needs.

The most long-lived of the society's economic enterprises was the grain storage program directed initially by Sister Wells in 1876 and continued until the close of World War I (1918), when the Relief Society sold 205,518 bushels of their storage wheat to the U.S. government at its request. The sale capped the Relief Society's intensive involvement in the war effort. A "Wheat Trust Fund" was then established that made possible the purchase and storage of more wheat in 1941. Responsibility for the wheat continued until 1978, when the Relief Society transferred 266,291 bushels of wheat and nearly 2 million dollars in assets to the First Presidency for use in the welfare program. In 1920 the general board terminated another longstanding enterprise, and closed its Nurse School as adequate professional schools were then in place.

1921–1945.   Relief efforts and community involvement reached a high point during these years. Under the innovative and businesslike administration of President Clarissa S. Williams (1921–1928), the Relief Society enlarged the professional component of its traditional charity work and increased cooperation with public and private welfare agencies. The Relief Society Social Services Department, established in 1919 by general secretary-treasurer Amy Brown Lyman, served as the Church's professional link with other welfare agencies and trained Relief Society workers in modern methods of family casework. Between 1920 and 1942, more than 4,000 women participated in its intensive two- and six-week "institutes," returning to their wards and stakes to aid Relief Society and priesthood leaders in welfare work. The department also provided an employment bureau for women and girls and served as the Church's licensed agency for child placement until 1963.

Beginning in 1921, at a time of national concern over high rates of maternal and infant mortality, stake and ward societies used interest from the Wheat Trust Fund to sponsor hundreds of health clinics for expectant mothers, babies, and preschool children. Two stake Relief Societies established and operated maternity hospitals, the Cottonwood (Utah) Maternity Hospital (1924–1951) and the Snowflake (Arizona) Maternity Hospital (1939–1960). Branches attached to the European missions prepared "maternity chests" for needy mothers and home deliveries.

The worldwide depression of the 1930s at first intensified the direct-aid efforts of Relief Society officers, particularly in the United States, where they cooperated with county and later with federal agencies in dispensing temporary relief to the unemployed and needy. As a new system of permanent federal aid was established, Church leaders developed their own comprehensive Church Welfare Plan (1936), in which the Relief Society had a supportive role. Priesthood leaders directed the new program, but the society was represented on the governing committees and took the main responsibility for preserving food, providing clothing and bedding, and teaching welfare principles to the sisters.

The Relief Society's own traditional relief efforts through the visiting teachers gradually phased out and finally terminated in 1944 when visiting teachers stopped collecting charity funds. Since 1921, ward presidents rather than visiting teachers have been assessing family needs and distributing relief to the needy, under the direction of their respective bishops. Underscoring the high degree of interdependence of the Relief Society president's and the ward bishop's two offices, Elder Harold B. Lee said in 1939, "The bishop is the father of his ward; the Relief Society is the mother" (p. 526). Ward Relief Society presidents also supervise other charitable work, such as caring for the sick, termed "compassionate service" to distinguish it from "welfare service."

President Louise Y. Robison (1928–1939), who led the Relief Society through these institutional changes, made other innovations. She started Mormon Handicraft (1938) in Salt Lake City to help women at home earn money by selling their handiwork on consignment. She also encouraged the formation of stake and ward Relief Society choruses known as Singing Mothers.

During World War II, President Amy Brown Lyman (1940–1945) guided the Relief Society's efforts to limit meetings, simplify activities, and strengthen homes fragmented by the demands of war. In the United States, Canada, Hawaii, New Zealand, and Australia, members sewed projects on workday for the Red Cross as well as for welfare assignments. They gave blood, saved animal fats, refurbished clothing, kept lists of registered nurses, and took nursing and first aid courses. As in World War I, some local ward Relief Societies became Red Cross units. In war-torn Europe, members shared their meager supplies, struggled to do their visiting teaching with makeshift transportation, and comforted each other. Recognizing that some of its curriculum was not relevant outside the United States, the general board began providing alternative lesson materials for the units in other countries.

The Relief Society played an important part in the Church's postwar emergency aid to the Saints in Europe, sending through the Church welfare program clothing, food, and thousands of quilts that had been made and stored by sisters in the United States and Canada. Sisters in Hawaii sent similar help to Japan.

1945–1974.   By the end of 1945, Relief Society membership had reached 102,000. In the years that followed, its membership has kept pace with the accelerating worldwide growth of the Church. The first Relief Societies in Japan were organized in 1949; membership in the Far East increased from 439 in 1950 to 7,400 in 1969. Rapid growth in Mexico and South America led to the printing of the *Relief Society Magazine* in Spanish (1966). By the 1970s, most members were using the same lesson materials and learning to appreciate each other's cultures through monthly cultural refinement lessons.

President Belle S. Spafford traveled widely, both as general president of the Relief Society (1945–1974) and as a two-year president of the U.S. Council of Women (1968–1970). She further professionalized the Relief Society Services Department and directed expansion of its services to include programs for Indian Student Placement Services and youth guidance. The department was housed in Salt Lake City in the Relief Society Building, which had been built in 1956 from contributions from LDS women and matching funds from the Church.

During President Spafford's long administration, the Relief Society moved toward fuller correlation within the larger Church structure. Under the comprehensive Church correlation program, the reporting and financing systems, magazine and lesson materials, and Social Services once managed by the Relief Society became the responsibility of priesthood leaders and professional departments, such as the new LDS SOCIAL SERVICES Department. After September 1971, Relief Society membership automatically included all LDS women and soon exceeded a million.

1974–1990.   As the movement for women's liberation called into question women's traditional work as homemakers and volunteers, the Relief Society increased its support for the vital roles of women in their home and Church responsibilities. The Relief Society Building became a resource center for stake and ward officers, offering ideas, materials, and training for their Relief Society work. President Barbara B. Smith (1974–1984) joined Church officials in opposing passage of the proposed Equal Rights Amendment to the U.S. Constitution, which they were convinced would not help women. The Relief Society promoted scholarly study of women's concerns by helping to establish the Women's Research Center at Brigham Young University (1978) and rallied its members worldwide to contribute to a visible symbol of honor for women, the Monument to Women at Nauvoo, a garden park with thirteen bronze statues portraying the many-faceted contributions of women (1978).

The rapid worldwide growth of Relief Society membership encouraged accommodation for diversity. Stake boards expanded to meet a variety of options for young, single, and working women. The

Church's college sorority, Lambda Delta Sigma, was incorporated into the Relief Society structure. In 1978, under the direction of President Spencer W. Kimball, the first general women's fireside was held. This has become an annual event called the General Women's Meeting and is broadcast worldwide; it has also become a model for women's conferences subsequently held by stake Relief Societies.

CURRENT ADMINISTRATION.   Increased simplification and correlation with priesthood leaders characterized the administration of President Barbara W. Winder (1984–1990). Her first general board had seventeen fewer members than the preceding board. And stake Relief Society boards were released. Ward Relief Society presidencies attended the quarterly (instead of monthly) stake leadership training meetings and carried the training to their own ward boards. The general board maintained contact with stake officers, while members of the general presidency visited stakes on speaking assignments; however, the focal point of Relief Society action subtly shifted to the local level. In the wards and branches, members continued to find the opportunities for service, learning, sisterhood, and spiritual growth.

As President Elaine L. Jack (1990–) moved Relief Society toward a sesquicentennial consideration of its Nauvoo legacy, membership reached 2,784,000. Though the Relief Society's programs have changed substantially over its 150-year history in an effort to meet the changing needs of women and the Church, its basic organizational structure and essential mission have not varied significantly. Emphasis on simplification, diversity, and worldwide sisterhood in the 1970s and 1980s resulted in a basic standard format for Relief Society that affirms common goals and programs for women around the world. Through its changes and growth, Relief Society has exemplified its motto. Sister Jack stated, "It is no minor thing that the motto of the Relief Society is 'Charity Never Faileth'" (p. 74), for "charity is the pure love of Christ, which endureth forever" (Moro. 7:47).

BIBLIOGRAPHY
Cannon, Janath R.; Jill Mulvay Derr; and Maureen Ursenbach Beecher. *Women of Covenant: A History of Relief Society*. Salt Lake City, 1991.
General Board of the Relief Society. *History of Relief Society, 1842–1966*. Salt Lake City, 1966.
Jack, Elaine L. "The Mission of Relief Society." *Ensign* 21 (Jan. 1991):74.
"The Jubilee Celebration." *Woman's Exponent* 20 (March 15, 1892):132–33.

Lee, Harold B. "The Relief Society in the Welfare Plan." *Relief Society Magazine* 26 (Aug. 1939):526–27.

Smith, Barbara B. "A Conversation with Sister Barbara B. Smith, Relief Society General President." *Ensign* 6 (Mar. 1976):7–12.

Smith, Joseph Fielding. "The Relief Society Organized by Revelation." *Relief Society Magazine* 52 (Jan. 1965):4–6.

"Story of the Organization of the Relief Society." *Relief Society Magazine* 6 (Mar. 1919):127–42.

JANATH RUSSELL CANNON
JILL MULVAY DERR

RELIEF SOCIETY MAGAZINE

The *Relief Society Magazine* was the official monthly publication of the women's Relief Society of The Church of Jesus Christ of Latter-day Saints from 1915 to 1970. It preserves the history of the Relief Society for those years, with reports of each annual general Relief Society conference held in the Salt Lake Tabernacle, and with the talks of General Authorities and the Relief Society presidencies given at those conferences. It also contains articles of particular interest to the women of the Church, such as gospel topics, prose and poetry, housekeeping aids, recipes, pictures, and descriptions of Relief Society activities from near and far. Some space each month was devoted to the progress of women worldwide. It also published the Relief Society lessons, which were written by authorities in various fields such as the scriptures, art, architecture, social sciences, economics, the Constitution of the United States, world governments, and literature.

In its first issue, President Joseph F. Smith expressed his hope that the magazine would be "entrenched about by the bulwarks of worthy and capable endeavor and enduring truth." The magazine was owned and operated by the General Board of the Relief Society for all of its fifty-six years. Originally a forty-four-page, black and white publication, it evolved into an eighty-page journal with liberal use of color. Its readers liked its small size, which let it fit neatly into a woman's purse. In 1966 the *Magazine* added a Spanish edition for its 6,000 Spanish-speaking subscribers.

Editors of the *Relief Society Magazine* looked upon their assignments as mission calls to further the work of Relief Society and strengthen the testimonies of its members. Its first editor, Susa Young Gates (1914–1922), was followed by Alice Louise Reynolds (1923–1930), Mary Connelly Kimball (1930–1937), Belle S. Spafford (1937–1945), and Marianne Clark Sharp (1945–1970). Vesta P. Crawford was associate editor (1947–1970).

From 1872 to 1914 Relief Society matters were disseminated in the *Woman's Exponent*, a privately owned and edited women's journal, which ceased publication in 1914 with the announcement of the official Church magazine for women.

The *Relief Society Magazine* had 301,000 subscribers in 1970, when it was incorporated into the *Ensign*, the Church magazine for adults. Relief Society lessons are now published in a manual each year.

[*See also* Ensign; Relief Society; Woman's Exponent.]

BIBLIOGRAPHY

Sharp, Marianne C., and Irene Woodford, eds. *History of Relief Society 1842-1966.* Salt Lake City, 1966.

MARIANNE CLARK SHARP

RELIEF SOCIETY IN NAUVOO

Organized in 1842, the Female Relief Society of Nauvoo differed from other contemporary women's church groups in that it was organized under the priesthood direction of the Prophet Joseph Smith.

The society began as a response to the need for provisions, clothing, and supplies for builders of the Nauvoo Temple. On her own initiative, Sarah M. Granger Kimball invited a group of women to her home on March 4, 1842, to discuss the possibility of organizing a sewing society to aid the workers. Eliza R. Snow drafted possible bylaws and a Constitution for the group and submitted them to Joseph Smith. He told her that there was something better for them than a written constitution and that he would organize the women of the Church as the priesthood was organized. He added that the Church would never be perfectly organized until the women were organized.

Minutes of the charter meeting name twenty women and three men who were present in the upper story of Smith's red-brick store on March 17, 1842. Emma Smith, elected president, chose Sarah M. Cleveland and Elizabeth Ann Whitney as counselors, Eliza R. Snow as secretary, and Elvira A. Cowles as treasurer.

At the first meeting, the Prophet redefined and expanded the object of the society. The women were to look to the needs of the poor, to search after those in need and administer to their wants, and to assist in correcting the morals and strengthening the virtues of the community. He later added the charge to save souls. During a particularly significant address on April 28, 1842, he cited 1 Corinthians 13, from which later members took their motto, "Charity Never Faileth." He then pronounced the much-quoted sentence, "I now turn the key to you in the name of God and this Society shall rejoice and knowledge and intelligence shall flow down from this time" ("Minutes of the Female Relief Society").

The society grew quickly. During its first season, 1,189 women became members. The society received and dispersed money, clothing, provisions, and services to the needy. Its meetings were held first in the upper room and then, for lack of space there, outdoors in "the Grove" until September 28, 1842. When the society reconvened in the following spring, the presidency divided the membership into four WARDS, which then met separately. Each ward had its "necessity committee," forerunner of the present visiting teachers, who canvassed their area in search of people in need (*see* VISITING TEACHING). Meetings again ceased for the winter of 1843–1844, but presumably the charitable works continued.

Beset with differences between its president and Church leaders—differences related to the introduction of plural marriage—the society ceased to function formally after the meetings of March 1844. Aspects of its operation, however, continued through the last days of Nauvoo and the exodus of 1846–1847 in the acts of charity, the sisterly bonding, the gatherings of women in prayer meetings, and the persistence of spiritual manifestations. The leaders of a revived RELIEF SOCIETY in Utah, which President Brigham Young authorized Churchwide beginning in 1867, conscientiously adhered to the patterns established in Nauvoo and resolutely maintained a continuity of operation.

BIBLIOGRAPHY

Kimball, Sarah M. "Early Relief Society Reminiscences." In "The Relief Society Record, 1880–1892." Relief Society General Offices, Salt Lake City.

"Minutes of the Female Relief Society of Nauvoo." LDS Church Historical Department, Salt Lake City.

Sharp, Marianne C., and Irene Woodford, eds. *History of Relief Society, 1842–1966*. Salt Lake City, 1966.

BARBARA W. WINDER

RETRENCHMENT ASSOCIATION

The retrenchment movement, conceived in 1869 by President Brigham Young to encourage LDS women to "spend more time in moral, mental and spiritual cultivation, and less upon fashion and the vanities of the world" (*Woman's Exponent* 11 [Sept. 15, 1882]:59), spawned two similar but distinct organizations. Mary Isabella Horne, appointed by President Young to head the initial movement, established semimonthly women's meetings in Salt Lake City to promote the "reformation." Shortly thereafter, Brigham Young organized his daughters into a Young Ladies Retrenchment Association as a model for similar organizations in each ward of the Church, appointing Emma Young Empey as president (*see* YOUNG WOMEN). Though the young women's retrenchment societies held independent ward meetings, the parent association, calling itself the Senior and Junior Cooperative Retrenchment Association, remained a single, overarching entity that superintended the subsidiary societies while pursuing its own agenda.

Despite its similarity to the RELIEF SOCIETY, the Retrenchment Association was unique among Church organizations. As an ad hoc auxiliary, it was attached to no ecclesiastical unit, had no geographic boundaries (its meetings were open to all LDS women), and functioned under no specific line of ecclesiastical authority. Conducted by President Horne or one of her six counselors, another innovation, the meetings were largely extemporaneous. Members of the congregation (sometimes numbering two hundred) expressed religious sentiments or spoke impromptu on themes suggested by the presiding officers. Timid members were urged to participate, for it was "as essential for the sisters to learn to preach as for the brethren" (Minutes, Feb. 6, 1875).

In its first decade, the Association's principal objectives were reform in "diet and dress" and avoidance of all forms of "worldliness." Affirming LDS distinctiveness from the world became an impassioned and persistent theme. Home industries also fell within the stewardship of the Association. Before the organization of general and stake Relief Society boards, Eliza R. Snow, general head of the Relief Societies, used the Retrenchment Association to coordinate the branches of home industry that Brigham Young had assigned to the ward Relief Societies in 1868. Committees were organized in the retrenchment meetings to implement and supervise silk manufacturing, grain storage, straw braiding, and women's commission stores, all part of President Brigham Young's design to develop a cooperative and self-sustaining economy. Recruiting women to study medicine (*see* MATERNITY AND CHILD HEALTH CARE), urging them to vote (Utah women were enfranchised in 1870), and soliciting contributors and subscribers to the WOMAN'S EXPONENT also found place on the Association's agenda. This initial task orientation brought LDS women firmly into visible kingdom building.

If retrenchment marked the Association's first decade, "circling the wagons" reflected the spirit of its second. Besieged by punitive antipolygamy legislation, women affirmed their commitment to the principle of plural marriage, declared their acceptance of persecution as a refining process, and asserted their belief in God's overruling hand. The Association assuaged the family and religious dislocations imposed by the prolonged federal campaign and provided women an oasis of stability and mutual reassurance during a time of crisis.

In its final years the "ladies semimonthly meetings," as the gatherings were then called, became even more self-consciously faith-promoting. This focus was only briefly interrupted by a revived interest in home industries in response to a national economic slump and the loss of Church properties and funds mandated by the Edmunds-Tucker Act. The aging of first-generation Latter-day Saints prompted redoubled efforts to prepare a second generation of standard bearers. In fervent declarations of faith, affiliated women continued to evoke images of distinctiveness even as many of the elements that made them distinctive gave way to powerful federal and social forces.

This amorphous gathering endured for thirty-five years, mainly through the perseverance of a few devoted women, some of them the "leading sisters," or higher echelon of LDS female leadership. The Retrenchment Association served as an agent of orthodoxy to motivate and inspire and to provide a spiritual bulwark against an encroaching world. As first-generation Latter-day Saints, these women were self-appointed keepers of the faith, who by their own commitment sought to spur commensurate fidelity among all the Saints.

BIBLIOGRAPHY
Minutes of the Junior and Senior Cooperative Retrenchment Association, 1872–1876, LDS Church Archives, Salt Lake City.
Woman's Exponent, 1872–1904, Salt Lake City.

CAROL CORNWALL MADSEN

S

SACRAMENT MEETING

Sacrament meeting is the principal LDS worship service held on the Sabbath and is based on the commandment "Thou shalt go to the house of prayer and offer up thy sacraments upon my holy day" (D&C 59:9). The entire WARD membership, from infants to the elderly, attend the weekly sacrament meeting as families, and partake of the sacrament of the Lord's Supper together.

A sacrament meeting was held on the day the Church was organized, April 6, 1830. It is recorded, "The Holy Ghost was poured out upon us to a very great degree—some prophesied, whilst we all praised the Lord, and rejoiced exceedingly" (*HC* 1:78). In Church annals this primal worship service is called a "time of rejoicing," a time of "great solemnity," and "truly a refreshing season to spirit and body" (*HC* 2:430, 433, 480). At the time of entering the new land of Zion (in Missouri), a revelation was given concerning the Sabbath with the admonition that all should come to this meeting in the spirit of thanksgiving and should offer up "a sacrifice of a broken heart and a contrite spirit" (D&C 59:8). Hence, it is often referred to as a time for the renewing of covenants.

The sacrament meeting is led by the BISHOP of the ward or one of his counselors. To enhance the spirit of worship and fellowship, there are other participants: the organist, music director, and members of the ward preassigned to give talks and the invocation and benediction.

From the earliest days of the Church, music has been essential in the worship of LATTER-DAY SAINTS. In the sacrament meeting, music is manifest in the singing of hymns such as "He Died! The Great Redeemer Died," "While of These Emblems We Partake," "In Memory of the Crucified," and "Reverently and Meekly Now." Each ward is encouraged to maintain a choir to periodically perform hymns and anthems. The orientation of all music is toward the classical tradition.

The two sacrament prayers—one on the bread, one on the water—are offered by priests, usually young men between the ages of sixteen and nineteen. They kneel in the presence of the congregation and ask that all present, by their partaking of the broken bread and the water, witness unto the Father their willingness "to take upon them the name of thy Son," Jesus Christ, to always remember him, to keep his commandments, and to seek his Spirit. These patterns are derived in part from the dramatic introduction of the sacrament in the Book of Mormon, where the Master teaches a multitude of men, women, and children, "And if ye shall always do these things blessed are ye, for ye are built upon my rock" (3 Ne. 18:12). And he promises, "And if ye do always remember me ye shall have my Spirit to be with you" (3 Ne. 18:7, 11).

During the passing of the bread and water to the congregation, silence prevails. The communion aspired to is embodied in statements of modern leaders: Hyrum Smith spoke of the sacramental process as bestowing spiritual sustenance enough to "last a whole week." The ordinance was given, as President Brigham Young taught, "in order that the people may be sanctified" (*JD* 19:91–92). "I am a witness," said Elder Melvin J. Ballard, "that there is a spirit attending the administration of the sacrament that warms the soul from head to foot; you feel the wounds of the spirit being healed" (Hinckley, p. 133).

The typical sacrament meeting is sixty to seventy minutes long and has the following components, with mild variations from week to week:

Organ prelude

Greeting by a member of the bishopric

Opening hymn sung by the congregation

Announcements and ward business

Invocation by a ward member

Sacramental hymn sung by the congregation

Administration and partaking of the sacrament

Musical selection

Speakers

Closing hymn sung by the congregation

Benediction by ward member

Organ postlude

The spoken messages in sacrament meetings are given by different members of the congregation each Sunday, or by visiting officers from the stake organization. All speak with the same purpose: to witness of Jesus Christ, to review gospel principles, to inspire, to uplift, to encourage, and to motivate the congregation to renewed efforts to live a Christlike life. Speakers frequently quote from the scriptures, and members, young and old, are encouraged to bring their own book of scriptures and to follow the cited references. The time is usually shared by several speakers. Sometimes entire families are assigned to develop a gospel topic, and each member contributes to the chosen theme. Youth speakers are likewise regularly invited to give sacrament meeting talks. Sometimes the bishop assigns topics, and sometimes he leaves the choice to the individual or family.

Sacrament meeting is periodically combined with the observance of special events such as Christmas, Easter, Mother's Day, and Father's Day. On such occasions, the meeting follows the usual pattern through the sacrament and then proceeds around the commemoration program.

On one Sunday a month, usually the first, sacrament meeting is a FAST AND TESTIMONY MEETING. After the sacrament, the final portion of the meeting is devoted to extemporaneous testimony bearing by members of the congregation.

BIBLIOGRAPHY

"Church Consolidates Meeting Schedule." *Ensign* 10 (Mar. 1980):73–78.

Hartley, William G. "Mormon Sundays." *Ensign* 8 (Jan. 1978):19–25.

Hinckley, Bryant S. *Melvin J. Ballard . . . Crusader for Righteousness*. Salt Lake City, 1966.

CRAWFORD GATES
GEORGIA GATES

SEALING

[*This entry consists of three articles:*

Sealing Power
Temple Sealings
Cancellation of Sealings

The first article, Sealing Power, *explains the meaning of sealing in the Church and the authority required to perform an ordinance so it will be considered sealed; what is a temple sealing and how it is obtained is presented in the second article,* Temple Sealings; *and the third article,* Cancellation of Sealings, *is a brief statement on who may cancel a sealing.*]

SEALING POWER

Signets and seals have been used from early antiquity to certify AUTHORITY. The word "seal" appears many times in the scriptures. Jesus Christ was "sealed" by God the Father (John 6:27), and Paul reminded ancient Saints that God had anointed and sealed them (2 Cor. 1:21–22) and told others they "were sealed with that Holy Spirit of Promise, which is the earnest [assurance] of our inheritance until the redemption" (Eph. 1:13–14). John spoke of the servants of God being sealed in their foreheads (Rev. 7:3). In the apocryphal Acts of Thomas (verse 131), Thomas prayed that he and his wife and daughter "May receive the seal" and "become servants of the true God." Even today licenses, diplomas, legal documents, and the like bear seals that officially attest to their authenticity.

For Latter-day Saints, the ultimate sealing power is the priesthood power given to authorized servants of the Lord to perform certain acts on earth and have them recognized (sealed) or validated in heaven. They believe it is this authority the Lord Jesus Christ described when he said to Peter, "I will give unto thee the keys of the kingdom of heaven: and whatsoever thou shalt bind on earth shall be bound in heaven: and whatsoever thou shalt loose on earth shall be loosed in heaven" (Matt. 16:19).

The President of the Church holds and exercises the KEYS of sealing on earth. When a man is ordained an APOSTLE and set apart as a member of the QUORUM OF THE TWELVE APOSTLES, sealing is one of the powers bestowed upon him. Other GENERAL AUTHORITIES of the

Church, the presidencies of temples, and a limited number of officiators in each temple receive this sealing power during their tenure. After one is approved by the FIRST PRESIDENCY to receive the sealing power, the President of the Church, one of his counselors, or a member of the Twelve Apostles specifically designated by the President confers the sealing power upon him by the laying on of hands. This is the specific authority to perform the temple sealing ORDINANCES.

This is the authority by which "all covenants, contracts, bonds, obligations, oaths, vows, performances, connections, associations, or expectations" can be "made and entered into and sealed by the Holy Spirit of promise" and receive "efficacy, virtue, or force in and after the resurrection of the dead" (D&C 132:7).

In this dispensation of the fulness of times, the sealing power was restored by Elijah, the last prophet of the Old Testament period to hold it (*TPJS*, pp. 339–40). He bestowed that authority on Joseph Smith and Oliver Cowdery in the Kirtland Temple on April 3, 1836 (D&C 110). As each man who has been President of the Church was ordained an apostle and became a member of the Quorum of the Twelve, he had the sealing power bestowed upon him, and thus it has been transmitted to the present (D&C 110:13–16; 128:11).

What might be called the general sealing power is also vested in the President of the Church. Everyone who receives the PRIESTHOOD obtains this general sealing power to a degree. For example, as Elder Bruce R. McConkie said, "All things that are not sealed by this power have an end when men are dead. Unless a baptism has this enduring seal, it will not admit a person to the celestial kingdom. . . . All things gain enduring force and validity because of the sealing power" (*MD*, pp. 615–16).

BIBLIOGRAPHY
Packer, Boyd K. *The Holy Temple*. Salt Lake City, 1980.
Smith, Joseph Fielding. "Elijah: His Mission and Sealing Power." *DS*, Vol. 2, pp. 115–28. Salt Lake City, 1955.

DAVID H. YARN, JR.

TEMPLE SEALINGS

A "sealing," as a generic term, means the securing, determining, or establishment of a bond of legitimacy. Among members of the Church sealing refers to the marriage of a husband and wife and to the joining together of children and parents in relationships that are to endure forever. This special type of sealing of husband and wife in marriage is referred to as "eternal marriage" or "celestial marriage." It contrasts with civil and church marriages, which are ceremonies recognized only by earthly authority and are only for the duration of mortal life.

The sealing together of husband, wife, and children in eternal family units is the culminating ORDINANCE of the PRIESTHOOD, to which all others are preparatory. It must be performed by one holding the SEALING POWER and today in an LDS TEMPLE dedicated to God. The Savior referred to this sealing power when he gave his apostle Peter the KEYS of the kingdom of heaven, saying that "whatsoever thou shalt bind on earth shall be bound in heaven" (Matt. 16:19). In modern times this sealing authority was restored to the earth in the Kirtland Temple on April 3, 1836, by the prophet Elijah, who was the ancient custodian of this power (D&C 110:13–16).

Both ancient and modern prophets have observed that if families are not sealed together in eternal units—if the hearts of the children and the fathers are not turned to each other (as alluded to in Malachi 4:5–6)—then the ultimate work and glory of God are not attained and the highest purposes of the creation of the earth are not achieved. "For we without them [ancestors or progenitors] cannot be made perfect; neither can they without us be made perfect" (D&C 128:16–18).

To Latter-day Saints, the spirit world is as real as this world. By divine mandate, temple sealings are not only available to living persons, but are extended also to the deceased progenitors of a family through proxy ordinances performed in the temples. This process is known as salvation of the dead. Children born to parents who have been sealed in the temple are born in the covenant and thus are bonded to their parents for eternity without a separate ordinance of sealing.

To receive temple sealing ordinances, Church members must receive a TEMPLE RECOMMEND from a proper Church authority attesting that they are living prescribed Church standards. They then visit a temple and receive initiatory ordinances and the blessing referred to as the temple endowment. This entails the receipt of instruction and being put under covenant to obey eternal laws set forth by God, which, as observed, will ensure a superior standard of morality, marriage, and family life. The sealing ordinances can then be administered, the full benefit of which can be secured only by continued obedience to the divine laws set forth in the gospel of Jesus Christ.

A sealing ceremony is an inspiring and solemn ordinance performed in specially designated and dedicated rooms of a temple. The couple to be married or the family to be sealed kneel at an altar. The officiator is one who has received the sealing power under the highest priesthood authority in the Church (*see* PROPHET, SEER, AND REVELATOR; SEALING POWER).

For members of the Church, sealings endow life with greater purpose and give marriage a sense of divine partnership with spiritual safeguards. Bringing children into the world becomes a divinely inspired stewardship. Sealings can sustain a family in life and console them in death. They establish continuity in life, here and hereafter.

BIBLIOGRAPHY

Derrick, Royden G. In *Temples in the Last Days*, chap. 3. Salt Lake City, 1988.

Smith, Joseph Fielding. *DS* 2:119. Salt Lake City, 1954–1956.

Talmage, James E. *The House of the Lord*, pp. 84–91. Salt Lake City, 1976.

PAUL V. HYER

CANCELLATION OF SEALINGS

The KEYS of the kingdom of heaven, conferred upon Peter by the Lord Jesus Christ (Matt. 16:19) and restored to the earth in recent times (D&C 110) by the prophet Elijah, who was custodian of this power anciently (see Mal. 4:5–6), include the AUTHORITY to "bind and loose" on earth, with corresponding effect in heaven. Currently this power is held and exercised only by the PRESIDENT OF THE CHURCH and others upon whom it is conferred by him or at his direction. Once a sealing ORDINANCE is performed, only the First Presidency can approve a change in sealing status, including the cancellation of a sealing (*General Handbook of Instructions*, 6-5 through 6-7).

The First Presidency may cancel temple sealings when the circumstances of a request for cancellation warrant it.

BIBLIOGRAPHY

General Handbook of Instructions. Salt Lake City, 1989.

RONALD E. POELMAN

SEER

In ancient usage, "seer" is an alternative term for prophet (1 Sam. 9:9). A seer is a person endowed by God with a special gift for seeing spiritually. In the modern Church, members of the FIRST PRESIDENCY and the QUORUM OF THE TWELVE APOSTLES serve as seers. These fifteen apostolic officials are designated PROPHETS, SEERS, AND REVELATORS who direct the Church by means of divine revelation, with the President of the Church being the only one in whom the keys are fully active at any one time. Though all three titles describe revelatory capacity, the terms are not fully synonymous. A "prophet" is one who speaks for God; the office of "seer" extends that divine endowment to a capacity for envisioning future and past. The Book of Mormon teaches that a "seer is greater than a prophet," because a seer is "a revelator and a prophet also"; seers are unique among prophets in that they "can know of things which are past, and also of things which are to come, and by them shall all things be revealed" (Mosiah 8:15–17).

In the Doctrine and Covenants, the Prophet Joseph Smith refers to the spiritual process of seership. He describes "being in the Spirit" along with Sidney Rigdon, and "by the power of the Spirit our eyes were opened and our understandings were enlightened, so as to see and understand the things of God" (76:11–12; cf. JS—H 1:74).

The office of seer is often associated with the use of revelatory instruments, particularly the Urim and Thummim, sometimes called seer stones. The Book of Mormon suggests that "whosoever has these things is called seer, after the manner of old times" (Mosiah 28:16).

Visionary prophets of the Bible, such as Isaiah, Jeremiah, Peter, and John the Revelator, clearly functioned as seers. In the Book of Mormon, Lehi refers to Joseph of Egypt as a seer who foresaw that in modern times God would raise up from among his descendants yet another "choice seer" (2 Ne. 3:6). The ancient calling of seer remains active through modern times. A seer is "one who sees with spiritual eyes. He perceives the meaning of that which seems obscure to others. . . . In short, he is one who sees, who walks in the Lord's light with open eyes" (Widtsoe, p. 205).

BIBLIOGRAPHY

Sperry, Sidney B. *The Voice of Israel's Prophets.* Salt Lake City, 1952.
Widtsoe, John A. *Evidences and Reconciliations*, Vol. 1. Salt Lake City, 1943.

STEVEN C. WALKER

SETTING APART

"Setting apart" is a priesthood ordinance that is performed by the laying on of hands, authorizing a man or woman to serve in a Church CALLING. It occurs after one has been sustained by COMMON CONSENT to perform certain duties and responsibilities in a specific calling in a geographical or organizational part of the Church. It is performed by, or under the direction of, the one in AUTHORITY over that unit. One is "ordained" to priesthood offices, but is "set apart" to preside or serve. In the setting apart, one is given the authority and charged to act; he or she is also counseled, instructed, and blessed. The blessings are conditional upon faithful performance.

The meaning of being set apart to service in the Church is symbolically a setting apart (a separation) from the world to act on a higher plane (Lev. 20:26; Num. 8:14; Ezra 8:24; Rom. 1:1). The act of setting apart is referred to in the Bible in a number of places, though not always using the same terminology. Moses was told to "put some of thine honour" upon Joshua that the Israelites might be obedient to him (Num. 27:20). Seven men of honest report were "set before the apostles," who laid their hands on them to take charge of temporal matters in the early church (Acts 6:6). The early Twelve were told to "separate me Barnabas and Saul for the work whereunto I have called them" (Acts 13:2). The Book of Mormon writers appear to use the terms "consecrate" and "appoint" to describe a setting apart (Mosiah 6:3).

Settings apart concern both the Church unit and the person. When men and women are set apart as presidents of Church organizations, they are given the authority as well as the obligations and responsibilities to act in their offices. The president is always set apart before the counselors, since counselors are set apart as counselors to the specific person serving as president.

In the early days of the Church, the words "ordain" and "set apart" were often used interchangeably for both ordination and setting apart. Therefore, the Doctrine and Covenants speaks of men being ordained high councilors and women being ordained to preside over auxiliaries (D&C 20:67; 25:7). In modern usage, both these would be instances of being set apart.

BIBLIOGRAPHY
Allred, Rex. "Where Does the Church's Practice of Setting Apart Come From?" *Ensign* 13 (Mar. 1983):67–68.

DENNIS L. THOMPSON

SEVENTY

[*This entry contains three articles:*

Overview
First Council of the Seventy
Quorums of Seventy

The first article identifies the office of Seventy in The Church of Jesus Christ of Latter-day Saints. Then it discusses the biblical precedents in Old and New Testament times. It then describes the establishment of the priesthood office of seventy by Joseph Smith in the 1830s and the subsequent development of that office at greater length. The second article discusses the organization of General Authority seventies before the reorganization of 1975, when its functions and officers were incorporated into the current quorums of the Seventy. The third article describes the contemporary constitution and function of seventies in The Church of Jesus Christ of Latter-day Saints. The bibliography for all the articles follows the first entry. See also General Authorities; Melchizedek Priesthood; Organization: Contemporary; Priesthood Quorums.]

OVERVIEW

Seventy is a PRIESTHOOD OFFICE in the Melchizedek Priesthood reserved since 1986 for General Authorities called to assist the FIRST PRESIDENCY and QUORUM OF THE TWELVE APOSTLES in the administration of the Church worldwide. The organization and assignments of seventies have undergone numerous changes as the Church organization has developed.

On February 28, 1835, at Kirtland, Ohio, the organization of the Seventy commenced with individuals selected from among the participants in Zion's Camp. The Prophet Joseph Smith recorded that they were "ordained and blessed at that time, to begin the organization of the first quorum of Seventies, according to the visions and revelations which I have received. The Seventies are to constitute traveling quorums, to go into all the earth, whithersoever the Twelve Apostles shall call them" (*HC* 2:201–202). In a March 1835 revelation the role of the Seventy was further clarified: "The Seventy are also called to preach the gospel, and to be especial witnesses unto the Gentiles and in all the world—thus differing from other officers in the church in the duties of their calling" (D&C 107:25). Further, they are to act in the name of the Lord and under the direction of the Quorum of the Twelve Apostles "in building up the church and regulating all the affairs of the same in all nations, first unto the Gentiles and then to the Jews" (verse 34). Finally, the Seventy are to be "traveling ministers" to Gentiles and Jews (verse 97).

BIBLICAL BACKGROUND.   God instructed Moses to take seventy of the elders of Israel up onto the holy mount, where "they saw God, and did eat and drink" (Ex. 24:1, 9–11). On another occasion, Moses was told to gather seventy men of the elders of Israel to the tabernacle of the congregation. There the Lord put his spirit upon them, empowering them to assist Moses in bearing the burdens of the people (Num. 11:16–17, 24–25). Many Jewish writers have read this as an account of the divine origin of their Sanhedrin, a body of seventy-one or seventy-two elders that regulated many of their affairs, particularly at the time of Jesus Christ.

Luke recorded the Lord's appointment of the seventy whom he sent "two and two before his face into every city and place, whither he himself would come" (Luke 10:1). Of their return he wrote, "And the seventy returned again with joy, saying, Lord, even the devils are subject unto us through thy name" (Luke 10:17). Some regard Luke's statement that "the Lord appointed other seventy also" to be an indication that more than one group of seventies served the Lord during his ministry (Luke 10:1). Latter-day Saints see these seventy as an important part of the organization of the church in New Testament times.

IN THE MODERN CHURCH.   The first quorums of the Seventy in the Restoration were organized in 1835–1836 in Kirtland, Ohio. Their members participated in the momentous events surrounding the dedication of the Kirtland Temple in 1836. On occasions, most notably in the temple dedicatory services, the Prophet referred to members of the Seventy broadly as APOSTLES and special witnesses to the nations in assisting the Twelve (*HC* 2:418). In 1838 the First Quorum of the Seventy organized and led the Kirtland Camp, consisting of 529 people, in their march from Kirtland to Far West and Adam-ondi-Ahman in Missouri.

In Nauvoo the number of seventies rapidly expanded, in part because of a decision that all elders under the age of thirty-five become seventies. To provide leadership for the newly established quorums, the sixty-three members of the First Quorum who were not in its presidency were divided into nine presidencies of seven and assigned to preside over the next nine quorums. The seven presidents who remained in the First Quorum presided over all seventies. These men were designated the First Council of the Seventy and were sustained as General Authorities of the Church. In December 1844 the Seventies' Hall was dedicated in Nauvoo in imposing ceremonies that continued for a week. A famous LDS hymn, "The Seer," written in honor of the recently martyred Prophet, was prepared for these services. The quorums of the Seventy then numbered fifteen. By the time of the exodus from Nauvoo, the number of seventies quorums had increased to thirty-five. These quorums were independent of geographical wards. When one was made a member of a quorum, it was presumed to be for life.

When the Saints arrived in Utah and began to spread throughout the territory, members of a quorum were dispersed geographically, making it impossible for them to meet together as a quorum. Disarray and confusion persisted into the 1880s. Efforts were made to identify and motivate seventies throughout the Church. In 1882 a revelation came to President John Taylor calling on the Twelve to assist the seventies and increase service among the Lamanites (American Indians). This revelation appeared to be a response to the organizational woes of the seventies quorums, but little success resulted from the change. In 1883 the First Presidency prepared instructions on the organization of the Seventy, and President Taylor received a revelation affirming that what they had written "is [God's] will, and is acceptable unto [him]" (Hartley, p. 70). The instructions established the First Quorum of the Seventy, consisting of its seven presidents (the First Council of Seventy) and the senior presidents of the sixty-four oldest quorums. While this action answered the appeal

of many to reorganize the First Quorum, this new quorum never met
or functioned as a body—perhaps because of the increasing pressures from federal antipolygamy legislation.

The headquarters and records of the numbered quorums were
then redistributed throughout the wards and stakes of the Church,
under the direction of the First Council of Seventy, as the numbers
residing in each locality justified. Counsel was given for all seventies in good standing to join the quorum located in their district.
Quorum presidents were released if they did not live in the bound-
ary of their quorum and, where possible, were sustained in new
quorums where they were residing. Some found it difficult to give up
the membership and seniority they enjoyed in their original quorums.
Nevertheless, by April 1884 there were 76 quorums; by 1888 there
were 101.

By October 1904, the number of quorums had reached 146 with
some 10,000 members. President Joseph F. Smith said that their special duty was "to respond to the call of the Apostles to preach the
Gospel, without purse or scrip, to all the nations of the earth. They
are minute men" (*CR*, Oct. 6, 1904, p. 3). Their chief function was
to serve as missionaries for the Church. But, since the quorums were
now geographical, stake and ward officers gradually utilized seventies in the common duties of the Church. For several years the
Seventy had their own course of study, but in 1909 they began to use
the study manuals followed by other Melchizedek Priesthood quorums. In 1912, in Salt Lake City's Granite Stake, the program of stake
missions was initiated with the seventies as the major participants.
This program expanded with occasional adjustments into the 1980s.
Every stake had its "stake mission," largely under supervision of the
seventies.

As the Church expanded, the demands upon its General
Authorities determined much of the future role the seventies would
be given. The presiding offices of the Church established by the revelations consisted only of the quorums of the First Presidency, the
Twelve, and the Seventy. In every revelation, the Seventy are subordinate to, and under the direction of, the other two. Over time, the
First Presidency and the Quorum of the Twelve Apostles have introduced many changes affecting the seventies that have proven to be
appropriate responses to expanding needs of the Church. Decisions

affecting the Seventy in the last three decades have been especially substantial and rapid.

In 1961 the members of the First Council of the Seventy were ordained high priests by the First Presidency. President David O. McKay stated, "The members of the First Council of the Seventy are now given the authority of high priests to set in order all things pertaining to the stake and the wards, under the direction of the Twelve Apostles" (*IE* 65 [Jan. 1962]:42). On January 12, 1964, the seven members of the First Council of Seventy were given the sealing authority. On March 29, 1974, the First Presidency authorized stake presidents to ordain seventies approved by the First Council. On October 3, 1974, all previous seventies units were replaced by quorums in each stake and were designated with the name of the stake, rather than a number.

President Spencer W. Kimball organized the First Quorum of the Seventy on October 3, 1975, and called three new General Authorities as members of that quorum, in addition to the seven presidents. Unlike the stake quorums, members of this quorum would be General Authorities. On October 1, 1976, twenty men previously sustained as ASSISTANTS TO THE TWELVE were added to the First Quorum of the Seventy and the titles First Council of the Seventy and Assistant to the Twelve were dropped. The First Presidency also announced that the seven presidents would not be determined by tenure of service and would be rotated periodically. In the October 1978 general conference, emeritus status was announced for several designated members of the First Quorum of the Seventy whose age and health prevented their full participation. In the April 1984 general conference, six new members of the Seventy were sustained for a period of three to five years—rather than for life, as before. In the general conference held on October 4, 1986, all stake quorums of seventy were discontinued, and all seventies in those quorums were directed to affiliate with the elders quorums in their wards.

In the April 1989 general conference, the Second Quorum of the Seventy was organized, with General Authorities called to temporary service. As additional General Authorities are required to administer the growing worldwide organization, it is assumed that additional quorums of seventy will be formed "until seven times seventy, if the labor in the vineyard of necessity requires it" (D&C 107:95–96). The

First Quorum of Seventy consists of members called for lifetime service or until granted emeritus status. The Presidency of the First Quorum of Seventy presides over both quorums of seventies, as their assignments are not distinguished by quorum.

BIBLIOGRAPHY
Brown, S. Kent. "The Seventy in Scripture." In *By Study and by Faith*, ed. J. Lundquist and S. Ricks, Vol. 1, pp. 25–45. Salt Lake City, 1990.
Hartley, William G. "The Seventies in the 1880s: Revelations and Reorganizing." *Dialogue* 16 (Spring 1983):62–88.
Ivins, Antoine R. "The Seventy and the First Council." *IE* 59 (Nov. 1956):792–93.
Roberts, B. H. *The Seventy's Course in Theology: Outline History of the Seventy and a Survey of the Books of Holy Scripture*, 2nd ed., pp. 3–31. Salt Lake City, 1944.
"Stake Seventies Quorums Discontinued." *Ensign* 16 (Nov. 1986):97–98.
Tuttle, A. Theodore. "The Calling of the Seventy." *IE* 73 (Dec. 1970):84, 86.
Young, Levi Edgar. "The Divine Call of the Seventies." *IE* 56 (Dec. 1953):952, 954.
Young, S. Dilworth. "The Seventies, A Historical Perspective." *Ensign* 6 (July 1976):14–21.

ALAN K. PARRISH

FIRST COUNCIL OF THE SEVENTY

The First Council of the Seventy, comprised of the first seven presidents of the First Quorum of Seventy, was organized on February 28, 1835, at Kirtland, Ohio, by Joseph Smith in response to revelation regarding the organization of priesthood offices. Later, when it was determined that five high priests had been ordained seventies, the First Council was reorganized in April 1837, using only priesthood members who were seventies (*HC* 2:476).

As outlined in Doctrine and Covenants 107:93–98, the Seventy "should have seven presidents to preside over them, chosen out of the number of the seventy." Other seventies could be called as needed, but the first seven presidents (First Council of the Seventy) were to preside over all the additional seventies as well as the First Quorum.

Through the years the role of the First Council of the Seventy and their specific function as General Authorities have been modified in such areas as the Seventy's missionary role, their ability to preside and ordain, and their position as "especial witnesses" (Madsen, pp. 299–300).

By 1936 the various seventies quorums scattered throughout the Church were placed under stake supervision. In 1961 members of the First Council of Seventy were ordained high priests with their primary calling being missionaries, but they also had the authority to act as administrators and direct the affairs of the Church in various parts of the world, under the direction of the First Presidency and the Quorum of the Twelve Apostles. On October 3, 1975, the First Quorum of the Seventy was reconstituted as an entity, and on October 1, 1976, the members of the First Council of the Seventy and the Assistants to the Quorum of the Twelve Apostles were released and added to the First Quorum of the Seventy. A new presidency of the First Quorum of the Seventy was sustained. Additional men were selected to be members of the First Quorum and to act as General Authorities to assist in the expanded functions of Church leadership (*Ensign* 6 [Nov. 1976]:9–10). In 1984 Gordon B. Hinckley, counselor in the First Presidency, announced that in order to infuse "new talent and a much widened opportunity for men of ability and faith to serve" as General Authorities, new members of the First Quorum were to be called to act for a period of three to five years (*CR*, Apr. 1984, p. 4). This policy was redefined on April 1, 1989, when the Second Quorum of Seventy was organized, comprised of men who would be called to serve for a period of five years (*CR*, Apr. 1989, p. 22). President Hinckley later indicated that members of the First Quorum would serve until "factors of age and health" made them candidates for emeritus status (*Ensign* 20 [Jan. 1990]:10). The leaders of the Seventy were identified as the "Presidency of the Seventy."

BIBLIOGRAPHY
Cowan, Richard O. *The Church in the Twentieth Century*. Salt Lake City, 1985.
Madsen, Truman G. *Defender of the Faith: The B. H. Roberts Story*. Salt Lake City, 1980.
Roberts, B. H. *The Seventy's Course in Theology*. Salt Lake City, 1931.

RICHARD C. ROBERTS

QUORUMS OF SEVENTY

The quorums of Seventy consist of general Church officers, ordained to the Melchizedek Priesthood office of seventy, who, under the direction of the FIRST PRESIDENCY and the QUORUM OF THE TWELVE APOSTLES, carry major responsibility for administering the affairs of The Church of Jesus Christ of Latter-day Saints throughout the world. The First Quorum of Seventy constitutes a third presiding quorum over the Church after the First Presidency and the Quorum of the Twelve Apostles (D&C 107:24; see *also* ORGANIZATION: CONTEMPO-RARY). A presidency of seven, all seventies and members of the First Quorum, presides over the quorums of Seventy, conducts quorum meetings, and instructs the members in their specific duties.

Members of the Seventy are called from the membership of the Church by the First Presidency. Generally they are HIGH PRIESTS of considerable experience in Church leadership within their own WARDS and STAKES who have distinguished themselves in their service. Like all LDS leaders, they are not professional clergy but come from many vocations and professions (*see* LAY PARTICIPATION AND LEADERSHIP). Each one is presented to the general membership of the Church for a sustaining vote at a general conference. Then he is ordained a seventy and set apart by the First Presidency of the Church, receiving the authority and powers that pertain to his calling as a GENERAL AUTHORITY. The Seventy have all of the authority necessary to officiate in any capacity assigned to them by the First Presidency and the Quorum of the Twelve Apostles: "The Seventy are to act in the name of the Lord, under the direction of the Twelve . . . in building up the church and regulating all the affairs of the same in all nations" (D&C 107:34).

Some members of the quorums of Seventy are assigned to serve in groups of three as AREA PRESIDENCIES and preside over large geographical subdivisions of the Church. In this capacity, they supervise MISSIONS, stakes, districts, wards, and branches and are responsible for the effective implementation of Church policies and programs in their areas.

For example, as of 1990, the continent of South America included three such areas, continental Europe was designated as another, and the United States and Canada were divided into nine areas. The seventies who preside over these areas administer all the affairs of the Church within their jurisdictions, including MISSIONARY work and all functions designed to enhance the spiritual and temporal welfare of Church members. These seventies make regular visits to missions and stakes within their area to train local leaders in their duties and to counsel and instruct Church members in conference meetings. They also administer the financial affairs of the Church and supervise the construction and maintenance of Church buildings. Those assigned outside North America live within their area and travel to Church headquarters for the general conferences in April and October of each year. Seventies assigned to an area within the United States and Canada generally reside in or near Salt Lake City, close to Church headquarters, and travel at regular intervals to their area. These seventies also administer headquarters departments of the Church, such as operations related to Church history, curriculum, priesthood and auxiliary organizations, temples, family history, missionary work, and correlation. These assignments, as well as those that pertain to area supervision, are made under the direction of the First Presidency and the Quorum of the Twelve Apostles, with recommendations from the presidency of the quorums. All these assignments of the Seventy are rotated periodically. The members of the presidency of the First Quorum of Seventy serve as executive directors of Church headquarters departments.

Members of the quorums of Seventy who are located at Church headquarters meet weekly under the direction of the presidency of the First Quorum of Seventy. These meetings provide instruction for quorum members in Church doctrine and procedure. Seventies who are assigned to international areas meet together regularly as area presidencies within their own assigned territories. Twice a year, during the annual and semiannual general conferences, all the General Authorities meet in Salt Lake City for about two weeks for an intensive review of, and instruction in, Church policies and programs. They report on Church progress and growth in all parts of the world and assess Church programs as they apply to various nationalities and cultures. All who assemble receive spiritual instruction and are given renewed vision and direction by the First Presidency and the Quorum of the Twelve Apostles.

In accordance with the revelation that mandates that the Seventy are to act under the direction of the Twelve, the seven presidents of the First Quorum of Seventy meet regularly with the Twelve to receive instruction and to coordinate the work assigned to them. Such coordination is essential to comply with one of the provisions in the revelation: "And every decision made by either of these quorums must be by the unanimous voice of the same; that is, every member in each quorum must be agreed to its decisions, in order to make their decisions of the same power or validity one with the other" (D&C 107:27).

Because the function of the Seventy in the administrative affairs of the Church remains flexible, future adjustments to accommodate changing situations may be expected.

DEAN L. LARSEN

SICK, BLESSING THE

Latter-day Saints are committed to the reality of healing through faith in Jesus Christ, to a health code (the Word of Wisdom) that is a form of preventive medicine, and to the proper use of modern medical skills.

Latter-day Saints believe that Christ ordained and sent his disciples, in ancient and modern times, with the promise that through faith they might heal. The gift of healing is one of the gifts of the Spirit, a gift that may be present both in the one who administers and the one who receives. The admonition of James is reenacted in LDS practice. "Is any sick among you? let him call for the elders of the church; and let them pray over him, anointing him with oil in the name of the Lord: And the prayer of faith shall save the sick, and the Lord shall raise him up; and if he have committed sins, they shall be forgiven him" (James 5:14–15; cf. D&C 42:43–44).

It is clear from modern revelation that even though not all have this gift of faith, they may still have faith in Christ and the gospel. In many LDS homes there is exercise of the gift of healing through administrations of the father's priesthood. Blessings of the sick are generally given by two MELCHIZEDEK PRIESTHOOD bearers. There are no prescribed prayers for this kind of blessing, but one of the priesthood bearers anoints the head of the sick person with a little consecrated olive oil and says in substance: "In the name of Jesus Christ and by authority of the holy Melchizedek Priesthood, I lay my hands upon your head and anoint you with this consecrated oil, which has been dedicated for the blessing of the sick." Additional words may be said in harmony with, and under the guidance of, the Spirit.

Following this anointing, two or more priesthood bearers lay their hands upon the head of the sick person, and one being spokesman calls the person by name and says in substance, "In the name of Jesus Christ and by the authority of the holy Melchizedek Priesthood, we seal and confirm upon you this anointing with which you have been anointed to the end that . . . " He then voices a prayer of supplication and of blessing as the Spirit directs. The ORDINANCE concludes in the name of Jesus Christ. If two priesthood bearers are not available for the ceremony, one may perform both parts of the blessing.

In the temples of the Church throughout the world, frequent prayers are offered for those who are sick, bereaved, or in need. The names of those afflicted may be placed upon a temple prayer roll by request of family or friends. This practice derives from abundant scriptural counsels regarding unity in prayer—"Be agreed as touching all things ye shall ask" (D&C 27:18)—and the conviction that the modern temple, as anciently, is a house of prayer (D&C 109:8). United prayer and fasting, sometimes by an entire WARD or STAKE and in some historic instances by the full world membership of the Church, is occasionally advocated. This is the fulfillment of a divine admonition: "If ye are not one ye are not mine" (D&C 38:27).

Historically, miraculous healings have followed spiritual administrations to the sick for every kind of affliction, in every generation, and in every part of the Church. The promise is that the blind may receive sight, the deaf hear, the paralytic regain the use of limbs. Illustrative scriptural references are: "He that hath faith in me to be healed, and is not appointed unto death, shall be healed" (D&C 42:48). And those who "have not faith to be healed, but believe, shall be nourished with all tenderness" (verse 43).

Three scriptural cautions apply to the principle of blessing the sick. First, worthiness is to be cultivated by all. At any time, men or women may face the crisis of disease or injury and be asked to exercise faith in behalf of themselves or loved ones. Second, blessings are not to be given as signs for the skeptical, to satisfy curiosity, or to "consume it upon their lusts" (D&C 46:9). Faith in Christ is the prerequisite, not the consequence, of blessing the sick. Third, the resulting relief, healing, and fulfillment are not to be boasted about or heralded, but rather to "be spoken with care, and by constraint of the Spirit" (D&C 63:64; 84:73; 105:24). This is consistent with the plea of the Master in the New Testament after many of his miraculous healings: "See thou tell no man!" (Matt. 8:4; cf. D&C 50:33).

NEPHI K. KEZERIAN

SIGNS OF THE TRUE CHURCH

The New Testament shows that in the meridian of time Jesus Christ established his church with definite doctrines, principles, and ordinances, and specifically ordained officers, giving the church recognizable features by which it could be known. Many of the signs or essential features evident in Christ's New Testament church are also recognizable in the church he restored to the earth through the Prophet Joseph Smith.

FAITH, REPENTANCE, BAPTISM, AND THE HOLY GHOST. One sign of Christ's church is its insistence on the basic principles and ordinances of the gospel. Membership in the New Testament church was obtained by faith in the Lord Jesus Christ, repentance from sin, baptism in water, and the laying on of hands for the gift of the Holy Ghost (Acts 2:37–38). Baptism was by immersion administered by one having authority, just as Jesus was baptized in the Jordan River by John the Baptist (Matt. 3:11–16). Jesus said, "Except a man be born of water and of the Spirit, he cannot enter into the kingdom of God" (John 3:5).

The gift of the Holy Ghost was bestowed through the laying on of hands by one having authority, as exemplified at Samaria when Peter and John encountered some newly baptized persons: "For as yet [the Holy Ghost] was fallen upon none of them: only they were baptized in the name of the Lord Jesus. Then laid they their hands on them, and they received the Holy Ghost" (Acts 8:16–17). The same procedure is demonstrated by Paul at Ephesus (Acts 19:1–6). These same ordinances are required for membership in the Church today (cf. A of F 4).

CHURCH ORGANIZATION. Certain presiding officers, such as APOSTLES and PROPHETS, are characteristic of the church of Jesus Christ. Paul states that Christ "gave some, apostles; and some, prophets; and some, evangelists; and some, pastors and teachers; for the perfecting of the saints, for the work of the ministry, for the edifying of the body [church] of Christ" (Eph. 4:11–12; cf. 2:20). The church of Jesus Christ was restored to the earth in the early nineteenth century through the Prophet Joseph Smith with "the same organization that existed in the Primitive Church, namely, apostles, prophets, pastors, teachers, evangelists, and so forth" (A of F 6; *see also* QUORUM OF THE TWELVE APOSTLES; SEVENTY).

MIRACLES AND GIFTS OF THE SPIRIT. Jesus and the apostles performed miracles by faith and the power of God. Latter-day Saints believe that where there are apostles and prophets the gifts and signs of the Spirit will be present (Matt. 11:5). Where there is true faith, there will be miracles, and God's power will be manifest (Morm. 9:7–25). Bruce R. McConkie, an apostle, wrote, "Miracles wrought by the power of God are the perfect proof of pure religion. They are always . . . without fail, found in the true Church. Their absence is conclusive, absolute, and irrefutable proof of apostasy" (pp. 374–75).

CONTINUED REVELATION. The New Testament church of Jesus Christ experienced frequent revelation, such as the visits of angels (Acts 4:5–19; 10:3; 27:23), visions (Acts 9:3–8), and the workings of the Holy Ghost (cf. John 15:26–27; 16:7–15). Through these means, knowledge was received from heaven. Continued revelation from God is necessary for the leaders of the Church and its members to learn the mind and will of the Lord and how to proceed from day to day. This view of revelation is stated thus in the latter-day church: "We believe all that God has revealed, all that He does now reveal, and we believe that He will yet reveal many great and important things pertaining to the Kingdom of God" (A of F 9).

PERSECUTION. The New Testament shows that true followers of Jesus Christ were inevitably persecuted. Jesus said to his apostles, "If ye were of the world, the world would love his own, . . . but I have chosen you out of the world, therefore the world hateth you" (John 15:19). Paul said that "all that will live godly in Christ Jesus shall suffer persecution" (2 Tim. 3:12). Hence, a sign or characteristic of the true church is rejection and persecution by the wicked (*see* WORLDLINESS).

SEALING POWER. Jesus gave his apostles the power to bind or seal on earth and in heaven. He said, "Verily I say unto you, Whatsoever ye shall bind on earth shall be bound in heaven: and whatsoever ye shall loose on earth shall be loosed in heaven" (Matt. 18:18). This SEALING power is a feature of the latter-day church (D&C 128:8–10).

SALVATION OF THE DEAD. The true church of Jesus Christ promulgates the doctrines and ordinances that provide for salvation of the dead. Evidence thereof is seen in 1 Corinthians 15:29 and 1 Peter 3:18–20 and 4:6. Christ's mission would not be complete without such a provision, because so many persons die without even hearing the name of Jesus Christ, and without either knowledge or understanding of the gospel.

TEMPLES. Jesus called the temple in Jerusalem "my father's house" (John 2:16). A temple is a facility necessary for the total implementation of the laws and ordinances of the church of Jesus Christ; therefore, the latter-day church builds temples for the benefit of the people. From the days of Adam to the present, whenever the Lord has had a people on earth, temples and temple ordinances have been a crowning feature of their worship. In a revelation to the Prophet Joseph Smith regarding temples, endowments, and sacred ordinances, the Lord explained that these have been associated with the people of God in every dispensation (D&C 124:39–40; cf. *MD*, p. 780).

NAME OF THE CHURCH. Christ's church bears his name, and believers in Jesus Christ take upon themselves his name by baptism. When the Nephites asked the Lord what the name of his church should be, Jesus said, "How be it my church save it be called in my name? For if a church be called in Moses' name it be Moses' church; or if it be called in the name of a man then it be the church of a man; but if it be called in my name then it is my church, if it so be that they are built upon my gospel" (3 Ne. 27:8). The name of The Church of Jesus Christ of Latter-day Saints is symbolic of its author and ideal.

MISSIONARY ACTIVITY. Jesus commanded his disciples to go into all the world to teach his gospel and baptize those who believe (Matt. 28:18–20). Extensive missionary activity characterized the New Testament church, as with Paul, Barnabas, Philip, and others. This characteristic is considered urgent by the Church today (D&C 58:64; *see also* MISSIONS).

LOVE.   True faith and obedience bring the fruits of the Spirit, the greatest of which is love. Jesus said, "By this shall all men know that ye are my disciples, if ye have love one to another" (John 13:35; cf. 1 Cor. 13).

BIBLIOGRAPHY
Lee, Harold B. "Signs of the True Church." In *Stand Ye in Holy Places*, pp. 312–15. Salt Lake City, 1974.
McConkie, Bruce R. *Doctrinal New Testament Commentary*, Vol. 2, pp. 374–75. Salt Lake City, 1970.

LEON R. HARTSHORN

SINGLE ADULTS

The Church is generally perceived to be a family church; but for various reasons many Church members become or remain single adults. Thirty percent of North American Latter-day Saint adults are currently widowed, divorced, separated, or have never married (1981 Church Membership Survey). Because of concern for their welfare, the Church has focused attention on the needs of single members and has organized activities and programs targeted to meet these needs.

Results of a demographic study indicated that among LDS single adults, 23 percent were divorced or separated, 13 percent were widowed, and 63 percent had never married. Children were present in 16 percent of single-adult households. Estimates of marital experiences indicate that only 3 percent of LDS men and women between eighteen and thirty in 1981 would never marry by age sixty. Thus while most Latter-day Saints eventually marry, singleness is a relatively common experience for LDS adults. Only 51 percent of women and 64 percent of men between eighteen and thirty in 1981 are expected to be in an intact first marriage by age sixty. The others will have experienced some period of singleness due to having been divorced, widowed, or never married. If these trends continue, one-third of adult Church members will divorce at some time before age sixty (Goodman and Heaton, pp. 92–93, 96).

Poverty is a real threat to LDS single women, especially when children are present. When LDS households have equal numbers of members, those headed by females are 2.5–5.5 times as likely to be living below the poverty level as those headed by a married couple (Goodman and Heaton, p. 101). Church WELFARE SERVICES and the RELIEF SOCIETY seek to address both the immediate needs and the long-term problems of these women and families.

The ratio of single LDS men to single LDS women indicates a high number of women. In 1981, "for every 100 LDS women in the prime marriage ages (20–29 years) there are 89 LDS men" (Goodman and Heaton, p. 90). The ratio of weekly church attenders is even more out of balance: "For all singles over 30 there are 19 active men [who attend church weekly] for every 100 active women" (Goodman and Heaton, p. 91).

Furthermore, single LDS men and women are "mismatched on salient demographic characteristics. Single women over 30 have higher levels of education, occupation, and Church activity than single men. For example, never-married women over 30 are more likely to have four years of college (42 percent compared to 18 percent for never-married men) and professional occupations (70 percent compared to 38 percent)" (Goodman and Heaton, pp. 90–91). Goodman and Heaton conclude that "marriage to an active male is demographically impossible for many active single females over 30. And even when there are available males, they may possess other characteristics that rule them out as potential mates. Obviously, marriage is not a universal solution to singleness if the only acceptable marital option is marriage to an active LDS partner" (p. 91).

For instructional and activity programs, single adults in the Church are divided into two groups: young single adults, aged eighteen through thirty; and single adults, aged thirty-one and above. Wards, stakes, and regions of the Church sponsor a broad range of activities aimed at meeting the needs of these groups. Activities include young single adult Sunday School classes, Family Home Evening groups, service projects, socials, recreational events, and conferences.

For five years (1972–1977), in response to the increasing number of single adults and a concomitant concern with addressing their needs, the Melchizedek Priesthood Mutual Improvement Association developed a uniform organizational program throughout the Church. Its purposes were to identify the needs of singles, to increase awareness of their contribution to the Church, to provide program and activity suggestions, and eventually to incorporate responsibility for the singles into the PRIESTHOOD QUORUMS and Relief Society, which is the situation at present. Each ward now has a committee for single adults that includes one member from the bishopric, the Relief Society presidency, and the elders quorum presidency; a mature married couple to serve as advisers to young single adults; and elders quorum and Relief Society representatives from both the young single adult and single adult groups. Each stake has a similarly composed committee with responsibility for responding to the needs of singles at the stake level. Regional and sometimes multiregional committees are formed on an ad hoc basis to meet the needs of singles by bringing together greater numbers for various social and spiritual activities.

Some stakes have established wards or branches for single adults in areas where there is a high concentration of single members. Single wards have been organized to provide more leadership opportunities for singles and increased social experiences within the Church setting. In general, ward members must reside within the geographic stake boundaries and be a young single adult (ages eighteen to thirty). In areas with significant college student populations, membership may be limited to students. With the exception of the bishop, who is married, positions in the ward are normally staffed by the single adult members.

Church curricula and publications have also addressed the issue of singleness. Numerous articles dealing with challenges encountered by single adults and the place of single adults in the Church have appeared in the official Church magazine, the ENSIGN. In recent years, priesthood and Relief Society lesson manuals have also responded to singles' concerns and have suggested that teachers relate instructional material to single adults in the class.

Latter-day Saints have always placed a high value on marriage and family life. Consequently, the increasing number of single adult members presents a special challenge on how best to blend these single members into the Church community. A 1981 Church Membership Survey provides evidence suggesting that married members of the Church currently have greater opportunities for institutional involvement. Specifically, the survey notes that "singles score higher on the forms of religious involvement that are private, such as prayer and tithing, than on public involvement such as having a calling" (Van Leer). In other words, when leaders consider two equally devout individuals for a Church calling where one is single and one is married, they are more likely to extend the calling to the married individual. In particular, single men traditionally have been excluded from main leadership positions within the wards and stakes of a predominantly married population. Clearly, all of these matters are issues that require special Church attention for the future.

Emphasis on temple marriage and family has grown over time within the Church (Shepherd and Shepherd, p. 76). President Ezra Taft Benson reaffirmed the emphasis placed on marriage in his counsel to LDS single adults (Benson, May and Nov. 1988), reiterating the Church's position concerning temple marriage: To "obtain a fullness of glory and exaltation in the celestial kingdom, one must enter into this holiest of ordinances" (Benson, May 1988). Stressing the importance of marriage, he encouraged singles not to lose sight of the sacred goal of marriage and not to postpone or forego marriage for education and career. He also presented differing models of the responsibility single adults have toward temple marriage, with men having an active responsibility and women placed in a more passive role. In an article addressed to single Latter-day Saint men, President Benson warned single men that they were in danger of losing eternal blessings by failing to marry (Benson, May 1988). On the other hand, he recognized that some women may not have the opportunity for temple marriage in this life. In a later article addressed to single Latter-day Saint women, he noted the Lord's promise that if their lives are "worthy and [they] endure faithfully . . . [they will] be assured of all blessings" (Benson, Nov. 1988, p. 97), if not in this life, then in the eternities.

BIBLIOGRAPHY

Benson, Ezra Taft. "To the Single Adult Brethren of the Church." *Ensign* 18 (May 1988):51–53.

———. "To the Single Adult Sisters of the Church." *Ensign* 18 (Nov. 1988):96–97.

Goodman, Kristen L., and Tim B. Heaton. "LDS Church Members in the U.S. and Canada: A Demographic Profile." *AMCAP* 12, no. 1 (1986):88–107.

Shepherd, Gordon, and Gary Shepherd. *A Kingdom Transformed: Themes in the Development of Mormonism.* Salt Lake City, 1984.

"Single Adult Programs Change, New Guide Issued for Singles Wards." *Ensign* 16 (May 1986):105–106.

Van Leer, Twila. "Singleness Becoming More Common." *Church News*, Nov. 6, 1983, p. 4.

LAWRENCE A. YOUNG

SOCIAL SERVICES

The Church of Jesus Christ of Latter-day Saints calls upon LDS Social Services, a separate corporation, to help meet the social and emotional needs of Church members and others. Services include:

1. Placement of children for adoption with couples who meet legal requirements and the Church's personal worthiness standards.

2. Counseling and support for unwed parents, to help them with issues and decisions pertaining to marriage, adoption, and single parenthood.

3. Placement of children in foster homes that will promote healthy individual development and positive family relationships.

4. Therapy and referrals for members having personal or family problems, to allow them to receive help from resources that are respectful of LDS values.

Members are generally referred for assistance to LDS Social Services by their BISHOPS. The agency staff strives to work in harmony with ecclesiastical leaders and, at moderate fees, to provide services consistent with LDS values, such as individual responsibility, the sanctity of the family and human life, the eternal worth of souls, and the importance of experiences in mortality.

Charitable work among Latter-day Saints dates back to the organization of the Church in 1830. In the nineteenth century, most charitable work was done through the women's RELIEF SOCIETY, whose representatives began regularly calling upon members in their homes to obtain contributions for the poor, assess the needs of families, distribute food or clothing, or perform other compassionate services. Care of the needy is still viewed as a local responsibility, best addressed at the WARD level and provided through local ecclesiastical leaders, mainly the bishop. The bishop regularly involves the Relief Society and, when needed, the local Social Services agency.

To help with the relief effort in World War I, the Church sent Amy Brown Lyman, General Relief Society President, together with another Relief Society delegate, to the National Conference of Charities and Correction in 1917. There these two women learned of charity and relief methods used by the Red Cross and became convinced that adopting these could strengthen their own charity program. Encouraged by Presidents Joseph F. Smith and Heber J. Grant, Sister Lyman founded the Relief Society Social Service Department in 1919. The department provided casework services for LDS families, served as a liaison between the Church and public and private charities, operated an employment bureau for women, and provided social work training for volunteers from local Relief Societies. It also provided adoptive placements and family services, including foster care and counseling for unwed mothers. During the Great Depression of the early 1930s, this department expanded its cooperation with Salt Lake County, providing commodity relief to the poor.

In the 1930s many federally funded public assistance and Social Security programs were established in the United States. Consequently, the Relief Society Social Service Department, like many other private agencies, changed its focus from providing financial relief to offering direct services, or counseling, mostly on child welfare matters.

During the next three decades (1937–1969), the department began hiring trained professionals, mostly social workers. Adoptive placements increased and services to unwed mothers expanded. More children were placed and supervised in foster care. An extensive youth guidance program was developed. The Indian Student Placement Services, a special foster care program for Native Americans, officially began in 1954. It provided Native American children with educational, religious, and cultural experiences in LDS homes. Belle S. Spafford, General Relief Society President, provided direction during those years. In 1962, geographical expansion began, and, by 1969, Social Service agencies had been established in Arizona, Nevada, Idaho, and California.

In October 1969, Church leaders consolidated the Relief Society adoption services, the Indian Student Placement Services, and the Youth Guidance Program under a single department known as Unified Social Services. The change was part of the CORRELATION of all Church programs. Counseling and adoption services continued to increase. Professional employees were encouraged to obtain at least a master's degree in the behavioral sciences, preferably in social work. They began responding to requests from local Church leaders for assistance in counseling members with a variety of social-emotional needs and problems.

In September 1973, Unified Social Services became a separate corporation, renamed LDS Social Services. The new corporation began charging moderate fees for clinical, adoption, and foster care services. Services were expanded with Church growth and with the demand for licensed and clinical services. Agencies were established in the United States, Canada, Australia, New Zealand, and Great Britain. In 1974, there were 16 agencies and 9 suboffices; in 1979, 35 agencies and 13 suboffices; in 1991, 41 agencies with 24 suboffices. Staff size increased to a peak of 280 in 1980, then began decreasing slightly due to reductions in the Indian Student Placement Services and a trend toward emphasizing referral services for personal and family problems.

Shortly before 1990, LDS Social Services began placing greater emphasis on services for adoptive and unwed parents. Outreach efforts were instigated to assist greater numbers of unwed parents. The First Presidency issued letters to local leaders encouraging unwed parents to ensure their children are raised in stable homes with two parents, placing them for adoption through LDS Social Services when marriage is not feasible. At the same time, LDS Social Services changed the focus of its foster care program with a greater emphasis on placing troubled children in the homes of relatives, and on working closer with community agencies to provide services.

Currently, LDS Social Services continues to respond to the requests of Church members for adoption services, counseling for unwed parents, foster care, and referral or therapy for personal or family problems.

BIBLIOGRAPHY

Benson, Ezra T.; Gordon B. Hinckley; and Thomas S. Monson. "Unwed Parents." A letter from the First Presidency to local leaders. Salt Lake City, May 25, 1989.

Derr, Jill M. "A History of Social Services in The Church of Jesus Christ of Latter-day Saints." Unpublished manuscript at Director's office, LDS Social Services, 1988.

C. ROSS CLEMENT

SOCIETIES AND ORGANIZATIONS

The vitality and relevance of The Church of Jesus Christ of Latter-day Saints have spawned the formation of a wide assortment of unofficial organizations serving various Church-related interests and needs. Because the Church encompasses a comprehensive belief system about deity and the purpose of life, some members feel an intense need for outlets that allow them to share their personal insights, question ideas, and apply religious beliefs to daily living.

Unofficial organizations have existed since the early years of the Church (for a discussion of many nineteenth-century organizations, see Heinerman; Jenson). Some eventually became official Church programs, such as the Deseret Sunday School Union in 1849, the Mutual Improvement Association in 1875, and the Primary organization in 1878. Publications by these organizations similarly evolved from unofficial to official Church publications: *Juvenile Instructor* (Sunday School), the *Contributor* and later the *Improvement Era* (Mutual Improvement Association), and *Children's Friend* (Primary).

In recent years, hundreds of unofficial societies and organizations have been created primarily to provide four kinds of activities: They (1) hold regular study groups, usually monthly; (2) meet as professional associations; (3) publish journals and newsletters; or (4) hold annual symposiums or conferences.

The least formal organizations are study groups of neighbors or friends sharing common interests who meet periodically to discuss preselected topics. Although most of these groups have a temporary and unstable life, some have met regularly for many years and have invited scholars or Church leaders to address them. Several professional associations have been formed by members who originally met as special interest groups at professional conferences.

The Society for Early Historic Archaeology (SEHA) was originally chartered with the state of Utah in 1949 as the University Archaeological Society, a nonprofit organization for the purposes of collecting and disseminating information about archaeological research on the scriptures. SEHA distributes a quarterly newsletter, plus papers presented at its annual symposium.

The Mormon History Association was formed in 1965 by both Mormon and non-Mormon historians who wanted an opportunity to share ideas in an atmosphere of openness. The Mormon History Association publishes the *MHA Newsletter* (quarterly) and the *Journal of Mormon History* (annually). The journal contains scholarly articles related to Mormon history that have passed an editorial review board. The association holds a three-day conference annually, usually in historically significant locations, such as Nauvoo, Kirtland, Lamoni, Palmyra, Omaha, England, and Salt Lake City. An annual awards banquet honors distinguished scholars who have written about LDS history from the perspective of their discipline. These conferences have attracted many who are not professional historians plus many non-Mormons. The Mormon History Association has facilitated extensive contacts between Latter-day Saint and Reorganized Latter Day Saint scholars that have contributed to the exchange of historically significant original documents.

Among the organizations that restrict their activities to publishing, one of the best known is *Dialogue: A Journal of Mormon Thought*. The title page of this journal states that it is "an independent national quarterly established to express Mormon culture and examine the relevance of religion to secular life." Started in 1966, it is edited by Latter-day Saints whose intent is to bring their faith into dialogue with human experience as a whole and to foster artistic and scholarly achievement based on their cultural heritage.

Exponent II is a quarterly newspaper founded in 1974 to discuss Mormonism and feminism to help LDS women develop their talents.

The Sunstone Foundation was started in 1975 by a group of graduate students at Berkeley, California, who initially issued a quarterly magazine that was later published bimonthly. The purpose of the magazine is to provide a forum for young scholars to express themselves without being restricted by the professional, literary, and academic standards of established journals or Church publications. In 1979 the first annual Sunstone Symposium was held. Selected presentations from the annual symposium have been published in *Sunstone* and other journals. In addition to full-length articles, *Sunstone* features poetry, fiction, interviews, opinion columns, book reviews, and discussions of contemporary issues, theology, history, art, and drama.

The Association of Mormon Counselors and Psychotherapists (AMCAP) was organized in 1975 to promote fellowship and to enhance personal and professional development of LDS counselors and psychotherapists. AMCAP meets twice annually and publishes a quarterly newsletter and a semiannual journal containing articles on psychotherapy with an LDS emphasis.

The Association of Mormon Letters (AML) was organized in 1976 to promote the writing and study of LDS literature. AML gives awards for outstanding literature and publishes an annual volume of essays on Mormon literature plus a quarterly newsletter.

In 1977, a group of LDS media artists formed an association called ALMA (Associated Latter-day Media Artists), which publishes a bimonthly newsletter and meets monthly to "promote quality media." In 1978, the Society for the Sociological Study of Mormon Life was formed to encourage sociological research on Mormon life.

The Foundation for Ancient Research and Mormon Studies (F.A.R.M.S.), headquartered in Provo, Utah, was organized as a California nonprofit corporation in 1979 to promote, coordinate, finance, and popularly disseminate research on ancient scriptures, particularly the Book of Mormon. F.A.R.M.S. publishes books, an annual review of publications on the Book of Mormon, a bimonthly newsletter, reprints, research reports, tapes, videos, and the writings of Hugh W. Nibley and other Mormon and non-Mormon scholars.

The B. H. Roberts Society was established in 1980 as an association "dedicated to the study of timely issues in Mormonism" and sponsors quarterly meetings in Salt Lake City. Similar societies have been formed in Denver, Los Angeles, and San Francisco.

A group called Affirmation was founded in 1980 to provide a forum and newsletter for discussing homosexuality.

In 1982, a group of medical practitioners formed Collegium Aesculapium for physicians, medical students, and those in the paramedical professions. This professional association publishes the *Journal of Collegium Aesculapium* and holds a semiannual conference. The main purpose of the association is to promote service to society and help to the underprivileged.

The Mormon Women's Forum was founded in 1988 to publish a newsletter and discuss women's issues in monthly meetings in various cities.

Several organizations have been formed by people associated with programs and activities of Brigham Young University. For example, in 1975 the BYU Management Society was organized under the auspices of the School of Management, and in 1988 the J. Reuben Clark Law Society was formed at the Law School to enhance the professional careers of their members through educational and professional opportunities. An International Society was organized in 1989, coordinated by the David M. Kennedy Center for International Studies at BYU. Many other centers and organizations are funded and operated by the university itself.

Unofficial organizations and their publications may serve at least six important functions for Church members and/or the Church.

First, a few serve ecumenical functions, bringing people of different faiths together in an exchange of ideas and understanding. Increased understanding has reduced ignorance, hostility, and intolerance and has led to greater sharing of ideas, historical documents, and research, especially in relationships fostered by the Mormon History Association.

Second, some unofficial organizations provide increased affiliation and social support for members by allowing them to associate with others whose religious beliefs provide a feeling of kinship. Having a common religious heritage provides a social bond that facilitates friendship and the formation of a social support system. Many monthly study groups are attended primarily for the purpose of association.

Third, unofficial publications provide an opportunity to learn and distribute new insights regarding theology, the scriptures, ancient cultures, historical events, and current practices. Dedicated members wanting to combine their religious beliefs with their professional training have made significant scholarly contributions, and unofficial journals provide outlets for publishing them.

Fourth, the creative efforts of those who contribute to these publications add to the collection of Mormon literature by allowing members to write about life and events from a unique LDS perspective. Some literary articles represent personal expressions of faith and testimony in artistic or scholarly ways that most authors would not choose to use in a monthly testimony meeting.

Fifth, certain publications serve as an outlet where individuals with unorthodox beliefs can share their questions, concerns, and doubts in an open forum where they feel adequate acceptance.

And sixth, for members who feel a need to promote change, publications of such organizations provide a forum where they can take an advocacy position. The targets of change have included the elimination of racism and sexism, the acceptance of altered social practices (such as birth control, dress, and grooming standards), and interpretation of the scriptures or historical events.

BIBLIOGRAPHY

Anderson, Edward H. "The Past of Mutual Improvement." *IE* 1 (Nov. 1897):1–10.

Arrington, Leonard J. "Reflections on the Founding and Purpose of the Mormon History Association, 1965–1983." *Journal of Mormon History* 10 (1983):91–103.

Bradford, Mary L., ed. *Personal Voices: A Celebration of Dialogue.* Salt Lake City, 1987.

Heinerman, Joseph. "Early Utah Pioneer Cultural Societies." *Utah Historical Quarterly* 47 (Winter 1979):70–89, discusses the Universal Scientific Society, the Polysophical Society, the Deseret Theological Institution, the Deseret Dramatic Association, and others.

Jenson, Andrew. *Encyclopedic History of the Church of Jesus Christ of Latter-day Saints,* e.g., "Daughters of the Utah Pioneers," "Deseret Agricultural and Manufacturing Society," p. 183, "Deseret Pottery Society," p. 188, and "Utah Silk Association," p. 795. Salt Lake City, 1941.

Warner, Cecelia. "A Guide to the Mormon Network." *Sunstone* 10 (June 1985):42–47.

DAVID J. CHERRINGTON

SOLEMN ASSEMBLIES

In the Old Testament, Israel met in solemn assembly on the seventh day of the Feast of the Passover (Ex. 23:14–17; Deut. 16:8, 16) and the eighth day of the Feast of Tabernacles (Lev. 23:33–36; Neh. 8:18). The dedication of Solomon's Temple occurred during the latter feast (2 Chr. 5:2–3; 7:9–11).

By commandment, the Prophet Joseph Smith convened a solemn assembly on March 27, 1836, in the Kirtland Temple and in a nearby schoolhouse. During the meeting, the Saints sustained Joseph and other Church leaders in their CALLINGS, Joseph offered the dedicatory prayer for the new temple, and Church leaders instructed each other and bore testimony, which led to a rich outpouring of the Spirit of God (D&C 88:70; 108:4; *HC* 2:410–28).

Church leaders have called solemn assemblies for many purposes since then. The foremost is to sustain general Church leaders. Following the death of a PRESIDENT OF THE CHURCH, the Church holds a solemn assembly in the Salt Lake Tabernacle to approve and sustain its new FIRST PRESIDENCY. Church members participate at the

Tabernacle and in other places where the proceedings are broadcast (see, e.g., *CR* [Apr. 1986]:93–95).

A second purpose is to dedicate new or refurbished temples. Worthy Church members attend dedicatory services, which are held in the temples themselves and in other nearby facilities.

A third purpose is to instruct and encourage Church members in their responsibilities. Such solemn assemblies generally take place in temples or STAKE centers. Church members invited to these assemblies are usually PRIESTHOOD leaders. Sometimes in such assemblies the sacrament is served, but traditionally the main function is for those assembled to receive counsel from the presiding Church authorities.

BIBLIOGRAPHY

Norman, Robert J. "I Have a Question." *Ensign* 18 (Dec. 1988):53–54.

Peterson, H. Burke. "A Glimpse of Glory." *Speeches of the Year* [1975], pp. 424–25. Provo, Utah.

Widtsoe, John A. "The Sacred Assembly." *IE* 48 (Nov. 1945):672.

RICHARD E. TURLEY, JR.

STAKE

Stakes are an intermediate unit of organization between Church headquarters and the local WARDS. A stake ordinarily comprises between five and twelve wards, totaling at least 3,000 members. Depending on LDS population density, a stake may cover only a small part of one city or include many towns or cities spread over hundreds of miles. Where there are not sufficient Latter-day Saints to organize functioning wards, members belong to BRANCHES, which are supervised by MISSIONS or stakes. The stake is "a miniature Church to the Saints in a specific geographic area" (Benson, p. 4); the STAKE PRESIDENCY is fully charged and authorized to implement all the programs of the Church within the stake boundaries and directly supervises the BISHOPS of wards. Stake presidents are supervised by AREA presidencies, who report directly to the presiding quorums of the Church. For the sake of administrative convenience, training and support are provided to geographically proximate stakes by REGIONAL REPRESENTATIVES.

THE SCRIPTURAL CONCEPT OF STAKES. When the resurrected Jesus visited the Nephites in the Western Hemisphere, he taught them the words of Isaiah: "Enlarge the place of thy tent, and let them stretch forth the curtains of thy habitations; spare not, lengthen thy cords and strengthen thy stakes . . . and make the desolate cities to be inhabited" (3 Ne. 22:2–5; cf. Isa. 54:2–3). He promised to reveal to them his new covenant of priestly sacrifices and ordinances, including those of the temple (3 Ne. 9:19–20; 10:6–7; *WJS*, pp. 212–13). The rich imagery of Isaiah chapter 54 associates the concept of "stake" with the tent pegs that firmly held the curtains around the tabernacle that Moses built, the central Israelite sanctuary and seat of the Lord. In Doctrine and Covenants 101:43–62, this imagery is expanded: the stakes of Zion are represented as twelve thriving olive trees nurtured in peace (*WJS*, p. 415); in the redemption of Zion, they will never "be removed" (Isa. 33:20).

Stakes are gathering places for the Saints, "the curtains or the strength of Zion" (D&C 101:21). They are established as protected enclaves of spiritual strength and righteousness around the globe, symbolically holding the curtains around God's presence in the Church and among his people, in preparation for the establishment of the New Jerusalem (D&C 115:6; Isa. 4:6) and the rebuilding of the "old" Jerusalem in the Holy Land.

The portable tabernacle of Moses with its sustaining cords and stakes eventually came to rest in Shiloh, and was replaced centuries later with the construction of the temple of Solomon in Jerusalem. In all ages, "the main object" of the gathering of people is to construct a temple, "to build unto the Lord an house whereby he [can] reveal unto his people the ordinances of his house and glories of his kingdom and teach the people the ways of salvation" (*WJS*, p. 212; cf. Benson, p. 4). In the modern Church, stake presidents hold the keys to issue TEMPLE RECOMMENDS, and stake high priests quorums coordinate temple participation to strengthen Zion: "Put on thy beautiful garments, O daughter of Zion; and strengthen thy stakes and enlarge thy borders forever, that thou mayest no more be confounded, that the covenants of the Eternal Father which he hath made unto thee, O house of Israel, may be fulfilled" (Moro. 10:31; cf. Isa. 52:1).

President Ezra Taft Benson listed four purposes that stakes serve in the Church: (1) "to unify and perfect the members . . . by extend-

ing to them the Church programs, the ordinances, and gospel instruction"; (2) to be models or standards of righteousness to the world; (3)
to provide a defense from error, evil, or calamity; and (4) to be "a
refuge from the storm" prophesied to come upon the earth in the last
days (pp. 4–5).

THE ORGANIZATIONAL HISTORY OF STAKES.   For the first several
months following its organization, the Church had no need for a complex organizational structure. In response to increasing membership,
the first stake was organized in Kirtland, Ohio, in 1832. The Kirtland
Stake was presided over by Joseph Smith and his counselors in the
FIRST PRESIDENCY. Most affairs of this original stake that did not fall
under their direct purview were handled by a council of high priests
who operated under the direction of the bishop (Allen and Leonard,
p. 79).

In 1834 the Kirtland HIGH COUNCIL was organized and became
the official judicial body for the stake. The First Presidency continued to function as the presidency of the stake until Kirtland was
abandoned, but as new stakes were organized, these roles changed.
In July 1834, a stake was organized in Clay County, Missouri, with
its own presidency and high council (Allen and Leonard, p. 79).
From that time forward, stakes were presided over by a president
with two counselors, who were assisted by a high council comprised
of twelve high priests residing within the stake's boundaries.

For several decades, stake organization tended to be less emphasized and often quite haphazard in comparison with the ward. While
there was a functioning stake in Salt Lake City following the migration westward, most other areas of the Church had none. Where
stakes existed, they filled two major functions: they held conferences
designed to bring together members of several wards for instruction
and spiritual guidance, and they had responsibility for many disciplinary actions that were brought before the stake high councils.
However, much direction from the top proceeded directly between
general Church authorities and the local ward bishops (Arrington and
Bitton, p. 212).

When President Brigham Young began a major restructuring of
Church organization in 1877, changes were made that significantly
affected the role of the stake (Hartley, p. 3). Earlier, President Young
had declared that the Salt Lake Stake held no authority over other

stakes of the Church, all stakes being equal and autonomous relative to each other (Hartley, p. 5). He also released members of the QUORUM OF THE TWELVE from their callings as stake presidents so that they could assume more fully their general Church leadership assignments. New stake presidencies were called for most of the stakes, and several new stakes were organized by dividing those that had become too large.

As part of the organizational change instituted by Brigham Young, stake presidencies were given responsibility for all Church matters within their stake boundaries. Stake presidencies were instructed to hold quarterly CONFERENCES, which would be visited and presided over by General Authorities. Stake presidencies were also instructed to visit the wards in their stake on a regular basis and to call local priesthood leaders as home missionaries to help them preach in the wards.

Other changes in stake organization were designed to improve administrative efficiency. Stakes were made into more manageable units to give stake presidents more time for their private commitments and to create smaller and more cohesive units with which members could more readily identify (Alexander, pp. 95, 107). During this same period, financial accounting procedures were regularized and Church membership records systematized, and the newly streamlined stakes were given greater oversight responsibility in both areas.

Following these important organizational changes, the stake assumed its role as the major governing unit between the wards and Church headquarters. Stakes were now expected to have responsibility for every person and every program within their boundaries. Decentralization by the transference of more priesthood responsibility to the stakes has continued as Church membership has expanded. Stake presidents and bishops have been clearly identified as the links in the organizational chain between the General Authorities and local Church members.

The historical importance of stakes in the Church is exemplified by the stake-level innovations that have been adopted throughout the Church. Family home evenings and the WELFARE program began as programs of the Granite Stake in Salt Lake City in the early 1900s. The "Home Evening" program was designed to help parents develop closer relationships with their children. The suggested format for these weekly family meetings included prayer, music, scripture reading and gospel instruction, discussion of family concerns, recreational and cultural activities, and refreshments. The Granite Stake welfare plan was designed to promote temporal well-being by stressing home industry and cooperation. Stake committees were appointed to promote gardening, the development of canneries, livestock raising, and the establishment of new industries. This program foreshadowed the work of President Harold B. Lee as president of the Pioneer Stake during the Great Depression, which led to the establishment of a Churchwide welfare program. Other Church programs that originated in stakes include the seminary program for high school students, stake missionary work, systematic stake supervision of temple and genealogical work, and a variety of youth programs.

THE CONTEMPORARY STAKE. The continuing centrality of stakes in the Church's organizational structure is emphasized by additional recent expansions of the responsibilities assigned to stakes. Stake conferences are held semiannually, with stake presidents responsible for presiding when Regional Representatives or General Authorities are not present. Other functions formerly performed by General Authorities but now assigned to stake presidents include issuing temple recommends, setting apart counselors in the stake presidency and missionaries, ordaining bishops and stake patriarchs, and giving special temple recommend clearances.

Stake officers have primary responsibility for training ward priesthood and auxiliary officers. Stake presidencies recommend new bishops to the General Authorities and, with their high councils, train ward bishoprics and quorum leaders. Under the direction of the stake presidency and the high council, stake auxiliary leaders hold regular leadership meetings to train their counterparts at the ward level (see LEADERSHIP TRAINING). Stake presidencies and high councils continue to serve as the major judicial organization of the Church and conduct disciplinary councils for members who have committed serious sins.

New stakes are created when the membership of an existing stake becomes too large or when Church numbers and leadership strength in a mission district where a stake has not previously existed reach a level that justifies its organization (Kimball, p. 11). This process has accelerated greatly since the mid-twentieth century, with stakes being organized in many nations. Before 1840, 11 stakes had been established in Ohio, Missouri, and Illinois. In 1870 there were 12, all located in Utah. By 1882 the number had grown to 27, and by 1940, to 177. The 321 stakes in 1960 included one in Mexico and 19 in English-speaking countries outside the United States. In 1991 there were over 1,800 stakes worldwide, with almost weekly additions.

Stake presidents are called by revelation and set apart by a General Authority under the direction of the Quorum of the Twelve Apostles. They are sustained by the membership of the stake in the stake conference following their call. After a period of service (often about ten years), they are released from their assignment and a replacement is selected in the same manner.

[*See also* Area, Area Presidency; Bishop, History of the Office; Organization: Contemporary; Region, Regional Representative; Ward; Stake President, Stake Presidency.]

BIBLIOGRAPHY

Alexander, Thomas G. *Mormonism in Transition*, pp. 93–115. Urbana, Ill., 1986.

Allen, James, and Glen Leonard. *Story of the Latter-day Saints.* Salt Lake City, 1976.

Arrington, Leonard, and Davis Bitton. *The Mormon Experience.* New York, 1979.

Benson, Ezra Taft. "Strengthen Thy Stakes." *Ensign* 21 (Jan. 1991):2–5.

Coleman, Neil K. "A Study of The Church of Jesus Christ of Latter-day Saints as an Administrative System, Its Structure and Maintenance." Ph.D. diss., New York University, 1967.

Hartley, William G. "The Priesthood Reorganization of 1877: Brigham Young's Last Achievement." *BYU Studies* 20 (Fall 1979):3–36.

Kimball, Spencer W. "The Image of a Stake." Unpublished speech to regional representatives, Salt Lake City, Oct. 4, 1973.

Soltau, Henry W. *The Tabernacle, the Priesthood, and the Offerings*, pp. 135–41. Grand Rapids, Mich., 1972.

STAN L. ALBRECHT

STAKE PRESIDENT, STAKE PRESIDENCY

The Church officer who presides over several WARDS (congregations) that comprise a STAKE is the stake president. A stake president is selected by the General Authority assigned by the Quorum of Twelve

Apostles to preside at that stake's conference. He typically interviews many MELCHIZEDEK PRIESTHOOD leaders in the stake and then seeks inspiration from God to determine whom to call. The General Authority calls the stake president and instructs him to nominate two counselors who are interviewed and called. These three men constitute the stake presidency. They serve voluntarily, receiving no financial remuneration from the Church. Counselors to the stake president advise and assist him in his responsibilities and counsel with him in decision making. As with all officers in the Church, members of the stake presidency must be sustained by the vote of the members over whom they preside (D&C 20:65; see COMMON CONSENT). Each stake president supervises and is responsible for the progress of the Church in his stake, including all Church activities, callings, ORDINANCES performed, and programs.

Members of the stake presidency hold the office of HIGH PRIEST, and they serve as the presidency of the high priests quorum and supervise all Melchizedek Priesthood quorums. This means they hold the proper priesthood authority to act as the Lord's agent in behalf of the members (see KEYS OF THE PRIESTHOOD).

What the stake president performs and authorizes within the scope of his calling is recognized as official and binding by the Church. For example, the stake president authorizes ordinations of worthy men to offices in the Melchizedek Priesthood, such as ELDER and high priest. He submits to the FIRST PRESIDENCY for their approval the names of men to be called as BISHOPS. When the approval is granted, the stake president issues the call and ordains the man a bishop, after he has been sustained by his ward. The stake president calls the presidents of the women's organizations of the stake. He sets them apart after they have been sustained by vote of the stake. Both stake and full-time MISSIONARIES are SET APART and later released by stake presidents. With a few exceptions, stake presidents may delegate to their counselors, or to high councilors, the authority to perform ordinances, issue calls to serve, ordain others to priesthood offices, and give spiritual blessings. Stake presidencies are to draw upon the scriptures and are to seek inspiration through prayer. The stake president is the one ultimately responsible for decisions made, but the stake presidency is to act as a unified quorum when decisions are made and actions taken. The stake presidency is accountable to members of the General Authorities of the Church for the administration of their stake.

During semiannual stake conferences, members of the stake gather to hear instruction and inspirational messages from the stake presidency and other leaders. Stake presidents provide additional spiritual direction through counseling individuals and families and by visiting members' homes.

The stake president also presides over certain council meetings in which the spiritual welfare of Church members is the focus, such as meetings to address the needs of the poor or to prepare for emergencies, or councils that conduct DISCIPLINARY PROCEDURES for Church members who have transgressed fundamental standards of the gospel. Through personal interviews, stake presidencies certify the worthiness of members to enter TEMPLES and to be ordained to Melchizedek Priesthood offices, after they have been recommended to the stake president by their bishop. Bishops are to report their stewardship and the welfare of their congregations to their stake president.

Stake presidents are charged with fiscal responsibility for the stake. CLERKS are called to help with RECORD KEEPING and payments, but the expenditures of all wards, priesthood quorums, and AUXILIARY ORGANIZATIONS within the stake are the responsibility of the stake president. Financial assistance provided to needy individuals is administered by ward bishops, supervised by the stake president. In addition, since most wards meet in Church-owned buildings, the maintenance and operation of all physical facilities in the stake fall under the auspices of the stake president.

The stake president serves until he is released. As is the case with all callings in the Church, he neither campaigns for the position nor chooses the time of his release.

BIBLIOGRAPHY
McConkie, Bruce R. *MD*, p. 763.
Richards, LeGrand. *A Marvelous Work and a Wonder*, chap. 12. Salt Lake City, 1968.

KIM S. CAMERON

STEWARDSHIP

"Stewardship" in LDS vocabulary is responsibility given through the Lord to act in behalf of others. It is based on the understanding that all things ultimately belong to the Lord, whether property, time, talents, families, or capacity for service within the Church organization. An individual acts in a Church CALLING as a trustee for the Lord, not out of personal ownership or privilege. Every position in the Church is received as a calling, a stewardship, from the Lord made through others who are responsible for the supervision of the position. Such stewardships are temporary responsibilities.

Because the stewardship of a lay leader is not a permanent calling, a member of the Church may hold a position of extensive responsibility at one time in life and one of lesser responsibility at another time. Each member given a stewardship is expected to sacrifice time and talent in the service of others, but at the completion of such callings, most report that they have personally grown and benefited. Every calling is important. As members bear one another's burdens, they build a sense of community. When all serve, all may partake of the blessings of service. The ideal attitude toward stewardship suggests that it is not the position held but how well the work is done that counts (*see* MAGNIFYING ONE'S CALLING).

Faithful stewards seek a thorough understanding of their responsibilities and a knowledge of the Lord's will concerning them and their callings. A person with a stewardship reports to an immediate superior in the Church. For example, a ward RELIEF SOCIETY president reports to the BISHOP of her ward. A bishop reports to his STAKE PRESIDENT.

Stewards are accountable to and will be judged by the Lord (Luke 16:2; 19:17). To whom much is given, much is required (cf. Luke 12:48; D&C 82:3). The primary accounting is with the Lord. He knows a person's heart, intentions, and talents. The faithful and wise steward is rewarded; the unjust or slothful steward gains but little, and may even lose what he has (cf. Matt. 25:14–30; D&C 82:3, 11; 78:22).

BIBLIOGRAPHY

Cuthbert, Derek A. "The Spirituality of Service." *Ensign* 20 (May 1990):12–13.

Larsen, Dean L. "Self-Accountability and Human Progress." *Ensign* 10 (May 1980):76–78.

Malan, Jayne B. "The Summer of the Lambs." *Ensign* 19 (Nov. 1989):78–79.
Nelson, Russell M. "The Five A's of Stewardship." *Ensign* 2 (Apr. 1972):24–25.
Pace, Glenn L. "A Thousand Times." *Ensign* 20 (Nov. 1990):8–9.

J. LYNN ENGLAND

SUCCESSION IN THE PRESIDENCY

Upon the death of the President of The Church of Jesus Christ of Latter-day Saints, the senior APOSTLE in the Church's governing quorums (*see* FIRST PRESIDENCY; QUORUM OF THE TWELVE APOSTLES) becomes presiding officer of the Church (*see* PRESIDENT OF THE CHURCH).

The principles underlying the succession process were established at the death of the Prophet Joseph Smith in 1844. Since there was at the time no precedent and no clear procedure providing for succession to the office of president, competing views arose. Brigham Young, then President of the Quorum of the Twelve Apostles, presented the proposition that the Twelve, ordained apostles who held all the KEYS necessary to govern the Church, should be sustained as the authorized leaders in the absence of Joseph Smith. In his favor was the fact that the Twelve in Nauvoo had been carefully tutored by the Prophet in all aspects of Church leadership and had served as his right hand. The Church also understood that this position was in harmony with the 1835 revelation on priesthood (D&C 107). After describing the FIRST PRESIDENCY ("three Presiding High Priests, chosen by the body, appointed and ordained to that office, and upheld by the confidence, faith, and prayer of the church"), that revelation affirmed that the Twelve Apostles "form a quorum, equal in authority and power to the three presidents previously mentioned" (D&C 107:22–24).

Inherent in the Twelve's proposal was the assumption that, although the Quorum of the Twelve Apostles had equal authority and power with the Quorum of the First Presidency, as long as the First Presidency was intact and functioning, they, and not the Twelve, possess the necessary jurisdiction to govern the Church. But the death of the president, thereby disorganizing the presidency and automatically releasing the president's counselors, bestows on the Quorum of the Twelve the required authorization to exercise the keys they already possess and assume full responsibility for governing the Church—including the reorganization of the First Presidency. Representing the Twelve, Brigham Young also reminded the Saints in 1844 of Joseph Smith's "last charge to the Twelve," stipulating that in the event something happened to him, the Twelve were responsible for carrying on the work he had begun (Esplin, pp. 319–20).

Sidney Rigdon, who had been a counselor to Joseph Smith, presented an alternative view. He argued that Joseph Smith's death did not disorganize the presidency or the Church and that, therefore, as first counselor to Joseph Smith, he should be sustained as "guardian" over the Church. This ran directly counter to the Twelve's position that the death of the president automatically dissolves the First Presidency, leaving the counselors without authority over the Church.

Though there were theoretically other possibilities for succession besides these two, the competing claims of Sidney Rigdon and of Brigham Young, representing the Twelve, were the only two practical alternatives at that time. After several private meetings during which leaders reviewed the options, on August 8, 1844, thousands of Church members gathered in the grove near the Nauvoo Temple to decide by a public sustaining vote (*see* COMMON CONSENT) whether Sidney Rigdon or the Twelve would lead the Church. Rigdon, an eloquent speaker, took the stand first and spoke at length of his right and position. Then Brigham Young, with less polish but confident that the Twelve held authority and that they were prepared to "direct all things aright," presented the other view. The result was overwhelming support recognizing the Quorum of the Twelve Apostles as the authorized leaders of the Church, specifically with the keys to act as the First Presidency and with the power to reorganize the First Presidency. Although that decision was clearly sanctioned by the 1835 revelation and was in harmony with the position of the Twelve in Nauvoo, many Latter-day Saints claimed a further deciding factor: when Brigham Young spoke on August 8, his voice and appearance bore a striking resemblance to those of Joseph Smith. Wilford Woodruff, one who was present, later said that if "I had not seen him with my own eyes, there is no one that could have convinced me that it was not Joseph Smith" (*Deseret News*, Mar. 15, 1892; cf. *JD* 15:81).

For the next three years the Church was governed by the Quorum of the Twelve Apostles with Brigham Young as president of the quorum. In December 1847, following the pioneer journey to the Rocky Mountains, the First Presidency was reorganized and Brigham Young was named President of the Church.

Though the right of the Quorum of the Twelve to reconstitute the First Presidency was firmly established, there have been other short periods when the Quorum of the Twelve Apostles governed the Church before a new First Presidency was organized. John Taylor, president of the quorum when Brigham Young died in 1877, did not have the Quorum of the Twelve Apostles formally reorganize the First Presidency until 1880. A similar interim existed after his death in 1887. Wilford Woodruff as President of the Quorum of the Twelve Apostles directed the affairs of the Church on the basis of that position until 1889. Several years later, he instructed Lorenzo Snow, then President of the Twelve Apostles, that it was the will of the Lord that the First Presidency should be organized without delay upon the death of the president (Lorenzo Snow Notes, Dec 3, 1892, Church Archives). Lorenzo Snow, therefore, was named President of the Church in a new First Presidency eleven days after President Woodruff's death, a precedent of reorganizing the presidency without delay that has since been followed.

Since a fundamental doctrine of the Church is the reality of continuing revelation, and since the Twelve Apostles are sustained as PROPHETS, SEERS, AND REVELATORS, there is no apparent reason that the Quorum of the Twelve could not depart from this precedent and select someone other than the senior apostle to lead the Church, if so directed by revelation. Established principles, however, require (1) that a revelation directing any other course of action must come through the senior apostle in the presiding quorum and be approved by unanimous vote of the members of the quorum and (2) that the senior apostle in the presiding quorum by virtue of that position immediately presides over the Church following the death of the president.

The fundamental organizing principle of the Church rests on the reality that it was established by direct commandment from God to Joseph Smith and that those who lead it are specifically called of God to those positions. The existing succession process does not violate that principle, which it would do if succession were decided by a contested election either within the Quorum of the Twelve or by the body of the Church. In keeping with the principle of common consent, the name of each new president is submitted to the body of the Church for its sustaining approval. But this procedure is in no wise an election nor does it affect the legitimacy of the president's divine commission. Rather than empowering the new leader, the vote is an expression by members that they recognize the legitimacy of the calling and that it is binding upon them. To sustain the president is a commitment that no assistance that can aid his success will be withheld and that no barriers that might hinder his efforts will be erected.

BIBLIOGRAPHY

Arrington, Leonard J. *Brigham Young: American Moses*, pp. 113–16. New York, 1985.

Durham, Reed C., Jr., and Steven H. Heath. *Succession in the Church*. Salt Lake City, 1970.

Esplin, Ronald K. "Joseph, Brigham and the Twelve: A Succession of Continuity." *BYU Studies* 21 (Summer 1981):301–341.

MARTIN B. HICKMAN

SUNDAY SCHOOL

Sunday School in The Church of Jesus Christ of Latter-day Saints is held weekly in each local WARD or BRANCH. It lasts about an hour. Each Sunday, ward members assemble at the meetinghouse chapel for prayer and hymn singing, following which those twelve years and older attend age-group classes for religious instruction while younger children attend PRIMARY. The Sunday School courses provide a forum for discussions, socialization, and the integration of gospel principles into everyday life. The adult curriculum includes a gospel doctrine course based on the standard works, a gospel essentials class, and elective alternative classes on family history, teacher development, and family relations. The courses of study between twelve and eighteen are coeducational and focus on gospel principles, teachings of the Savior, Church history, scripture study, and the lives and teachings of the modern prophets. Under the direction of a three-person Sunday School presidency in each ward or branch, members are called to serve as the course teachers, usually for a term of several years.

EARLIEST SUNDAY SCHOOLS. Following the organization of the Church in 1830, most Sunday gatherings were general meetings for all members and visitors. In good weather, large meetings were usually held outdoors. The Prophet Joseph Smith notes, for example, on July 3, 1842, at Nauvoo, Illinois, "This morning I preached at the grove to about 8,000 people" (*HC* 5:56). Smaller groups met in homes or other buildings. Those meetings typically included praying, singing, partaking of the sacrament of the Lord's Supper, and preaching.

Before the exodus from Nauvoo that followed the martyrdom of Joseph and Hyrum Smith in 1844, a few small Sunday School groups met regularly in scattered communities, notably in Nauvoo, Kirtland, and various cities in England. Only after the Saints arrived in the Salt Lake Valley in 1847, however, did Sunday School begin to take on its present form.

In May 1849, Richard BALLANTYNE began plans to start a Sunday School to educate the young people in the principles of the gospel and the scriptures. Some years before, in his native Scotland, he had organized a Sunday School in the Relief Presbyterian Church of which he was then a member. Having no suitable place in his Salt Lake City neighborhood for such a gathering, Ballantyne built a structure to serve both as his home and a place to hold Sunday School. Today, a monument on the northeast corner of 100 West and 300 South streets in Salt Lake City commemorates the location of this first Sunday School. The original building was eighteen feet wide and twenty feet long, furnished with wooden benches, and warmed by a stone fireplace.

On Sunday, December 9, 1849, Ballantyne gathered a group of fifty children into his newly completed home for instruction from the scriptures. Of his purpose Ballantyne wrote, "There is growth in the young. The seed sown in their hearts is more likely to bring forth fruit than when sown in the hearts of those who are more advanced in years" (Sonne, p. 51). Disturbed by observing children at play on the Sabbath day and sensing that their spiritual growth was being neglected, he added, "I wanted to gather them into the school where they could learn not to read and write, but the goodness of God, and the true Gospel of salvation given by Jesus Christ" (Sonne, p. 51).

The following year the Fourteenth Ward, in which Richard Ballantyne was serving as second counselor to Bishop John Murdock, completed its meetinghouse, and the rapidly growing Sunday School was moved from the Ballantyne home to the new building. The expanding Sunday School class was also divided into a number of smaller classes with additional teachers being called into service. Others in the valley soon followed the Ballantyne pattern. Each Sunday School functioned somewhat autonomously, but generally under the direction of a ward bishop.

In 1858 the Sunday School movement was suspended when Johnston's Army entered Salt Lake Valley and many of the Saints moved south to other settlements. When the military climate stabilized in the early 1860s, Sunday Schools and other Sabbath meetings resumed. By 1870, more than 200 Sunday Schools were regularly attended by 15,000 youths and adults.

DESERET SUNDAY SCHOOL UNION. The first Sunday Schools functioned independently, devising their own curricula and administrative guidelines. Seeing the value of a central organization, however, Church leaders interested in the work being done organized a Sunday School Union on November 11, 1867. President Brigham Young and Daniel H. Wells, a counselor in the FIRST PRESIDENCY, attended along with Elders George A. Smith, Wilford Woodruff, George Q. Cannon, of the QUORUM OF THE TWELVE APOSTLES, and Brigham Young, Jr., who became a member of the Quorum in 1868.

At this meeting, first steps were taken toward a permanent organization. Elder Cannon became general superintendent of the Deseret Sunday School Union. A committee of three was appointed to decide on books suitable for Sunday School use. A general secretary and two corresponding secretaries were also appointed. Commencing in June 1872, monthly meetings of the teachers and superintendents were held in Salt Lake City. In 1877, a three-man general board was added, and expanded to six members in 1879.

The organization addressed lesson topics and source materials, punctuality, grading, prizes and rewards, use of hymns and songs composed by members of the Church, recording and increasing the attendance, developing an elementary catechism, and libraries. It also sponsored the publication of administrative guidelines and materials for classroom use, resulting in increased uniformity in Sunday School administration and lesson content.

The Deseret Sunday School Union also sponsored efforts beyond the scope possible for individual schools. The Deseret Sunday School Musical Union was formed and its brass band organized, with Charles J. Thomas serving as director. The Musical Union, though of short duration, was artistically and financially successful. Contributing to its success were many whose compositions left a lasting imprint upon music in the Church, including Evan Stephens, George Careless, and Joseph J. Daynes. Commencing in 1874, annual musical festivals were presented in the Tabernacle at Salt Lake City, with similar festivals being sponsored in many of the larger settlements. A Union Music Book was published, containing hundreds of pieces of original music.

In 1866, before the Deseret Sunday School Union was formed, publication of the JUVENILE INSTRUCTOR commenced privately, with Elder Cannon as editor. Early editions included catechisms on the Bible, Book of Mormon, and Doctrine and Covenants. Its pages also presented a variety of musical compositions, editorial teachings, and other aids to gospel instruction. As the Deseret Sunday School Union grew in stature, the *Juvenile Instructor* became its official voice. In January 1901, the Deseret Sunday School Union purchased the *Juvenile Instructor* from the Cannon family but continued publishing under that name until 1929, when the name was changed to INSTRUCTOR.

As stakes increased in size and number, it became customary to designate a stake Sunday School superintendency to supervise local Sunday Schools operating within the stake boundaries.

SACRAMENT IN SUNDAY SCHOOL.   Following the organization of the Church in 1830, partaking of the sacrament of the Lord's Supper became a customary part of Sabbath meetings held on a community or stake basis and attended principally by adults. Gradually these meetings were replaced by ward sacrament meetings. In early 1877, President Young asked bishops and their counselors to attend Sunday School and administer the sacrament to all children under eight years of age as well as to those over that age who had been baptized and confirmed members of the Church. The practice of administering the sacrament in Sunday School was discontinued in 1980, when the three Sunday meetings were consolidated in a three-hour block.

GROWTH OF SUNDAY SCHOOLS.   Upon the death of Superintendent Cannon on April 12, 1901, he was succeeded by Lorenzo Snow,

President of the Church. But President Snow died within a few months and was succeeded in both callings by President Joseph F. Smith.

In 1884 stake Sunday School superintendencies began holding monthly meetings of Sunday School officers and teachers for instruction and coordination. General meetings of the Deseret Sunday School Union convened twice a year in connection with general conferences of the Church.

In the early 1900s the Sunday School added five new classes for the older children and youth. In 1904, the Sunday Schools in the Weber Stake introduced an adult class. Shortly thereafter, adult classes became an integral part of the Sunday School program.

When President Joseph F. Smith died in 1918, Elder David O. McKay became general superintendent of the Sunday Schools. He was succeeded by George D. Pyper, who served until early 1943. Others serving included Milton Bennion (1943–1949), George R. Hill (1949–1966), and David Lawrence McKay (1966–1971).

SUNDAY SCHOOL CORRELATION. As the Church expanded throughout the world, the Sunday School general board was enlarged and its members traveled extensively to provide support and training for local leaders in diverse lands, languages, and cultures. Growth in the number of Sunday School units and in attendance have matched the growth of the Church.

Over the years, there emerged an effort to draw all Church functions and programs into harmonious coordination under priesthood leadership. The Deseret Sunday School Union, designated an AUXILIARY, had functioned with considerable autonomy under separate organizational leadership, sending correspondence and instructions directly to local leaders. However, in April 1971, Church leadership created an all-Church coordinating council composed of three age-group committees (child, youth, and adult) assigned to correlate the curricula within the priesthood and auxiliary organizations of the Church.

In June 1971, Russell M. Nelson was called as general superintendent, with Joseph B. Wirthlin and Richard L. Warner as assistants. Spurred by the correlation movement, they brought dynamic changes to the Sunday School organization between 1971 and 1979. Reflecting the Sunday School's transition to an integrated part of the worldwide, unified Church organization under priesthood direction, the name was changed from Deseret Sunday School Union to simply

Sunday School. The title of superintendent was changed to president to comport with traditional terminology commonly used in the priesthood and other auxiliary organizations.

Curriculum planning and writing became coordinated and centralized. Separate Sunday School general conferences were discontinued, and communication to Sunday School leaders was directed principally through priesthood channels. The frequency of regional visits by general board members was significantly reduced. Materials and programs were simplified and consolidated. Stake boards and ward Sunday School faculties were reduced in size, and reporting relationships were simplified as accountability of ward Sunday School officers to their ward priesthood leaders, rather than to stake auxiliary leaders, was strengthened.

An eight-year cycle of scripture instruction for the adult gospel doctrine course was instituted. Later reduced to four years, it focused one year of study each on (1) the Old Testament and the Pearl of Great Price, (2) the New Testament, (3) the Book of Mormon, and (4) the Doctrine and Covenants and Church history.

In October 1979, Russell M. Nelson was succeeded as general president by Elder Hugh W. Pinnock, of the Seventy, initiating a pattern of having GENERAL AUTHORITIES serve as the general presidency of the Sunday School, thus completing the organization's full integration as a correlated arm of the priesthood-directed Sunday School efforts throughout the world.

Attendance at Sunday School has continued to increase each year. By 1990 there were 17,676 Sunday Schools in the Church throughout the world, with more than 4.7 million members age eleven and older.

BIBLIOGRAPHY

"Brief Review of the Sunday School Movement." *Juvenile Instructor* 34 (Nov. 1, 1899):666–74.

Hartley, William G. "Mormon Sundays." *Ensign* 8 (Jan. 1978):19–25.

Jubilee History of the Latter-day Saint Sunday Schools, pp. 9–28. Salt Lake City, 1900.

McKay, David O. "Sunday Schools of the Church." *IE* 33 (May 1930):480–81.

Nelson, Russell M. *From Heart to Heart*, pp. 125–140. Salt Lake City, 1979.

Sonne, Conway B. *Knight of the Kingdom: The Story of Richard Ballantyne*. Salt Lake City, 1949.

Sunday School Handbook. Salt Lake City, 1990.

B. LLOYD POELMAN

T

TEACHER, AARONIC PRIESTHOOD

A DEACON in the AARONIC PRIESTHOOD is, when worthy, advanced to the office of "teacher" at age fourteen and serves for a period of two years. Teachers meet together regularly for gospel instruction and other activities. Latter-day scriptures indicate that "the teacher's duty is to watch over the church always." His authority is "to warn, expound, exhort, and teach, and invite all to come unto Christ" (D&C 20:53–59). Teachers can function in all the duties of a deacon. In addition, they are to observe the counsel of the bishopric and teachers quorum president, prepare the sacrament, perform HOME TEACHING, usher or speak in Church MEETINGS, be an example of moral integrity and uprightness, care for the poor, and help maintain the meetinghouse and grounds.

As the organization of the New Testament Church took form, teachers played a primary role (Acts 13:1; Eph. 4:11; 2 Tim. 1:11; James 3:1). The qualities teachers were to exhibit included reverence, temperance, and integrity (Titus 2:1–15). Postapostolic sources indicate that teachers served under prophets and later under bishops and that these higher offices comprehended the teaching function as well.

Teachers are organized into a PRIESTHOOD QUORUM of up to twenty-four members (D&C 107:86). Each quorum is headed by a presidency acting under the direction and supervision of the ward bishopric. To be ordained a teacher, candidates must be carefully interviewed by the bishop for personal worthiness and then approved in sacrament meeting by the members of the ward.

Teachers meet weekly on Sunday for instruction as a quorum and at other times for social activities or service projects, often with the YOUNG WOMEN or other YOUNG MEN. In the United States and other areas, some of these activities are organized around the scouting program designed for young men of this age group.

The Book of Mormon mentions teachers frequently, but—unlike modern teachers—they evidently were adult leaders of their congregations and held the Melchizedek Priesthood with administrative powers (Mosiah 23:17; 25:19; 26:7; Alma 4:7; 15:13).

BIBLIOGRAPHY

Lowrie, Walter. *The Church and Its Organization in Primitive and Catholic Times: An Interpretation of Rudolph Sohm's* Kirchenrecht. New York, 1904.

Palmer, Lee A. *The Aaronic Priesthood Through the Centuries.* Salt Lake City, 1964.

JACK R. CHRISTIANSON

TEACHERS, TEACHER DEVELOPMENT

Latter-day Saints consider Jesus the master teacher who sets the example. He commissioned his disciples to teach, and still admonishes members of his Church to "teach one another the doctrine of the kingdom" (D&C 88:77). In the Church, therefore, lessons are taught regularly in ward and branch programs—PRIESTHOOD, RELIEF SOCIETY, SUNDAY SCHOOL, YOUTH organizations, HOME TEACHING and VISITING TEACHING, MISSIONARY work, seminary classes, and family home evenings. Instruction is intended to help members understand the principles Christ has taught in his life and through the prophets and apply them in their daily lives. This gospel-centered purpose of teaching was characterized by Joseph Smith when he explained concerning Church members: "I teach them correct principles, and they govern themselves" (*MS* 13:339). Teachers are counseled to study, to seek, and to teach with the spirit (D&C 42:14).

Teaching the gospel is a duty implicit in Church membership. Responsibility for teaching, either directly or indirectly, is an element of virtually every Church calling. Each fully staffed ward requires more than thirty people in formal weekly teaching assignments, and so there are now an estimated 400,000 teachers Churchwide. Almost every active member will be called to serve at times as a teacher. Teaching is considered also as an opportunity to strengthen the teacher's own faith and knowledge through study and service to others.

A Teacher Development program designed to help teachers understand the principles of learning and gain confidence in their teaching ability is offered in most local units. This eight-week program advocates the use of learning objectives determined by pre-assessment of student needs and ability, and stresses the divine aspects of a Church teacher's calling.

Scripture-based lesson manuals are provided for each class. These bring a degree of consistency to the curriculum throughout the Church and offer teaching structures for the inexperienced teacher. The manuals suggest supporting resources from other Church publications and from a wide variety of materials produced by the Church Curriculum Department. These materials are generally made available in local meetinghouse or stake libraries. Extensive catalogues of teaching resources are maintained and published regularly to encourage their use in the classroom and the home.

BIBLIOGRAPHY
Chidester, C. Richard. "Christ-Centered Teaching." *Ensign* 19 (Oct. 1989):6–9.
Church of Jesus Christ of Latter-day Saints, The. *Teaching: No Greater Call*. Salt Lake City, 1978.
———. *Teacher Development Basic Course*. Salt Lake City, 1980.
Dunn, Paul H. *You Too Can Teach*. Salt Lake City, 1962.
Packer, Boyd K. *Teach Ye Diligently*. Salt Lake City, 1975.

HARLEY K. ADAMSON

TEMPLE ORDINANCES

The ordinances performed only in the temple are baptisms for the dead, washings and anointings, endowments, and marriages or sealings for eternity. The privilege of entering the House of the Lord, the temple, and participating in its ordinances is a spiritual apex of LDS religious life. Through temple ordinances, one receives a ceremonial overview of and commitment to the Christlike life. Temple ordinances are instruments of spiritual rebirth. In the words of President David O. McKay, they are the "step-by-step ascent into the eternal presence." Through them, and only through them, the powers of godliness are granted to men in the flesh (D&C 84:20–22). Temple ordinances confirm mature discipleship; they are the essence of fervent worship and an enabling and ennobling expression of one's love for God (*see* TEMPLE WORSHIP).

All participants must be baptized and confirmed members of the Church, and must receive a temple recommend. However, children under eight years of age may participate in their own family sealings before being baptized. Members who are twelve years of age or older may serve as proxies in baptisms for the dead. Worthy adults may participate in the temple endowment ceremonies. All men must have been ordained to the Melchizedek Priesthood. Temple ordinances are performed in sequence.

WASHINGS AND ANOINTINGS. Washings and anointings are preparatory or initiatory ordinances in the temple. They signify the cleansing and sanctifying power of Jesus Christ applied to the attributes of the person and to the hallowing of all life. They have biblical precedents (*see* TEMPLES THROUGH THE AGES). Women are set apart to administer the ordinances to women, and men are set apart to administer the ordinances to men. Latter-day Saints look forward to receiving these inspired and inspiring promises with the same fervent anticipation they bring to baptism. They come in the spirit of a scriptural command: "Cleanse your hands and your feet before me" (D&C 88:74; cf. 1 John 2:27). A commemorative garment is given with these ordinances and is worn thereafter by the participant.

TEMPLE ENDOWMENT. The temple endowment is spoken of in scripture as an "endowment," or outpouring, of "power from on high" (D&C 84:20–21; 105:11; 109:22, 26; cf. Luke 24:49). Participants in white temple clothing assemble in ordinance rooms to receive this instruction and participate in the unfolding drama of the plan of salvation. They are taught of premortal life; the spiritual and temporal creation; the advent of Adam and Eve, and their transgression and expulsion into the harsh contrasts of the mortal probation; the laws and ordinances required for reconciliation through the atonement of

Christ; and a return to the presence of God. The endowment is a series of symbols of these vast spiritual realities, to be received only by the committed and spiritual-minded (*TPJS*, p. 237; *see also* TEMPLES: MEANINGS AND FUNCTIONS OF TEMPLES). "All the ordinances," wrote Heber C. Kimball, "are signs of things in the heavens. Everything we see here is typical of what will be hereafter" ("Address to My Children," unpublished). The endowment increases one's spiritual power, based in part "on enlarged knowledge and intelligence— a power from on high, of a quality with God's own power" (Widtsoe, 1921, p. 55; Widtsoe, 1939, p. 335).

During the endowment, solemn covenants are made pertaining to truthfulness, purity, righteous service, and devotion. In this way, the temple is the locus of consecration to the teaching of the law and the prophets and to the ways of God and his Son. One does not assume such covenants lightly. Modern commandments relating to temple building have been addressed to those "who know their hearts are honest, and are broken, and their spirits contrite, and are willing to observe their covenants by sacrifice—yea, every sacrifice which I, the Lord, shall command" (D&C 97:8–9). As with Abraham of old, latter-day revelation says that to obtain "the keys of the kingdom of an endless life" one must be willing to sacrifice all earthly things (*TPJS*, p. 322).

Before taking these solemn vows, new converts prepare for at least a year after baptism. Missionaries typically receive the temple blessings prior to their service. Couples receive them on, shortly before, or sometimes well in advance of the day of their temple marriage (*see* TEMPLES: TEMPLE WORSHIP AND ACTIVITY).

This order of instruction and covenant making culminates in the celestial room, which represents the highest degree of heaven, a return to the presence of God, a place of exquisite beauty and serenity, where one may feel and meditate "in the beauty of holiness" (Ps. 29:2). Communal sensitivity in the presence of like-dedicated and like-experienced loved ones enhances deep fellowship. The temple is "a house of glory" and "a place of thanksgiving for all saints" (D&C 88:119; 97:13).

SEALING OF FAMILIES.   Only after patrons make these unconditional covenants with and through Jesus Christ may they receive "the most glorious ordinances of the temple," the covenants of marriage and family sealing (Widtsoe, 1937, p. 128). Marriage and sealing covenants are performed in temple sealing rooms convenient to the celestial room. Officiators and close family and friends often attend the couple. Kneeling opposite each other at the altar, the bride and groom are placed under mutual covenants to each other, and are married through the sealing power of Jesus Christ; their children will thus be born in the covenant, and the family kingdom will become a nucleus of heaven. If the couple has been previously married under secular authority and now has children, the husband and wife are sealed in the temple under the new and everlasting covenant and their children are then brought to the altar and are sealed to them. All subsequent children born to this family are born in the covenant. By apostolic authority, the blessings of Abraham, Isaac, and Jacob are explicitly invoked upon all marriages and sealings. It is envisioned that eventually further sealings will link all the couple's progenitors and all of their descendants in an unbroken chain (see SEALING: TEMPLE SEALINGS). Thus, divine parenthood is imaged on earth. The saintly life is not in renunciation but in glorification of the family. The quest for happiness and completeness within the marital state is transformed from the banal and temporary toward the divine and eternal.

SEALING OF ADOPTED CHILDREN.   If a couple elects to adopt children, those children are brought to the temple for a ceremony of sealing to their adoptive parents just as children born to them may be sealed.

PROXY ORDINANCES.   All temple ordinances, beginning with baptism, may be performed by proxy for persons who died not having the opportunity to receive them for themselves.

BIBLIOGRAPHY
Madsen, Truman G. *The Highest in Us*, pp. 93–107. Salt Lake City, 1978.
Widtsoe, John A. "Temple Worship." In *Utah Genealogical and Historical Magazine*, 12 (Apr. 1921):55.
———. *A Rational Theology*, pp. 125–29. Salt Lake City, 1937.
———. *Priesthood and Church Government*, pp. 332–47. Salt Lake City, 1939, 1967 printing.

ALLEN CLAIRE ROZSA

TEMPLE PRESIDENT AND MATRON

Temple presidents and their wives, who serve as matrons, are appointed to specific LDS temples by the FIRST PRESIDENCY of The Church of Jesus Christ of Latter-day Saints, usually for three years. Their principal responsibilities are to set the spiritual tone of the temple, to supervise the performance of sacred ceremonies and ordinances therein, and to oversee the physical facility. Although instructions and ORDINANCES are the same in all LDS temples, the size of the temple and the number of patrons using it alter the procedures from temple to temple.

On a typical day in a fully operating temple, the president meets with the male supervisors and ordinance workers and the matron meets with the female supervisors and ordinance workers in prayer meeting before beginning each of the several daily shifts. They may also greet patrons, give preparatory instructions and guidance to those coming for the first time, and coordinate the performance of the ordinances. The president and matron may also answer personal inquiries of patrons and resolve procedural questions, by phone or correspondence, from BISHOPS, STAKE PRESIDENTS, RELIEF SOCIETY presidents, and other Church and community leaders within the temple district. Time is also spent consulting with counselors in the temple presidency, assistants to the president, and supervisors. In addition, the president and matron meet regularly with the temple executive council to resolve matters pertaining to the functioning of the temple.

The work in the temple is conducted prayerfully as befits the "House of the Lord." The phrase "Holiness to the Lord" appears prominently on the outside of each temple and symbolizes the spirit of temple worship (cf. Psalm 93:5). Although the temple ordinances are performed repetitiously, participating in them can be continuously revelatory and inspiring because of their rich symbolism and multiple applications. The temple president and matron are responsible for enhancing this spirit that all may "worship the Lord in the beauty of holiness" (Psalm 29).

DAVID H. YARN, JR.
MARILYN S. YARN

TEMPLE RECOMMEND

Temples have always been revered and reserved as sacred ground. Anciently, the prophet Ezekiel declared, "Thus saith the Lord God; No stranger, uncircumcised in heart, nor uncircumcised in flesh, shall enter into my sanctuary" (Ezek. 44:9). The Prophet Joseph Smith prayed that "[the temple] may be sanctified and consecrated to be holy, and that thy holy presence may be continually in this house" (D&C 109:12), "and that no unclean thing shall be permitted to come into thy house to pollute it" (D&C 109:20).

After construction and before a TEMPLE of The Church of Jesus Christ of Latter-day Saints has been dedicated to the Lord, an open house is held and the general public is invited to enter and view the rooms. But for participation in a TEMPLE DEDICATION and for all ORDINANCES performed in the temple thereafter, only members of the Church who have a current identification card, called a temple recommend, may enter.

Temple recommends are given to members of the Church who have completed the preliminary steps of faith, repentance, baptism, and confirmation. Adult males must also have been ordained to the MELCHIZEDEK PRIESTHOOD. Temple recommends are usually issued by a BISHOP and countersigned by a member of the STAKE PRESIDENCY in interviews conducted in private. The bishop, who is responsible as a "judge in Israel" (D&C 107:72, 74, 76), conducts the initial interview. He seeks to discern personal worthiness and standards of Christlike living and counsels appropriately with those whose lives are in need of any change or repentance. It is considered a serious matter to become prepared to receive the covenants, ordinances, and blessings of the temple. Questions are asked to ascertain one's faith in God the Eternal Father, in his Son Jesus Christ, and in the Holy Ghost; and inquiry is made regarding the person's testimony of the restored gospel and loyalty to the teachings and leaders of the Church. Worthiness requirements include being honest, keeping the commandments, such as chastity—sexual continence before marriage and fidelity within marriage—obeying the laws of TITHING and the Word of Wisdom, fulfilling family responsibilities and avoiding affiliation with dissident groups. The FIRST PRESIDENCY often emphasizes that it is a solemn responsibility for a bishop or stake president to conduct a temple recommend interview. An equal responsibility rests upon the person who is interviewed to respond to questions fully and honestly (*Ensign* 8 [Nov. 1978]:40–43). One practical purpose of the recommend interview is to help the applicant be adequately prepared to commit to the way of life the temple covenants will require.

Currently three different types of recommends are given: (1) for members to receive their own endowment, to be sealed to a spouse, or to be married in the temple for time only; (2) for members who have received their endowment to participate in all temple ordinances for the dead; and (3) for unendowed members to (*a*) be baptized on behalf of the dead, (*b*) be sealed to their parents, or (*c*) witness SEALINGS of their living brothers and sisters to their parents. The same standards of worthiness apply for all recommends.

BIBLIOGRAPHY
Packer, Boyd K. *The Holy Temple*, pp. 11, 26–28, 50–53. Salt Lake City, 1980.

ROBERT A. TUCKER

TEMPLES

[The articles included under this entry are:

Latter-day Saint Temple Worship and Activity
History of LDS Temples from 1831 to 1990
LDS Temple Dedications
Administration of Temples
Meanings and Functions of Temples
Temples Through the Ages

The first four articles pertain to temples in The Church of Jesus Christ of Latter-day Saint tradition. See also Endowment Houses. *The fifth article treats the meanings and functions of temples in world religions generally, and the concluding article discusses ancient temples in particular, including the continuities between ancient Israelite and Latter-day Saint temples.*

See also Prayer Circle; Sealing; *and* Temple Ordinances.]

LATTER-DAY SAINT TEMPLE WORSHIP AND ACTIVITY

Performing ordinances and seeking the will of the Lord in the temple are a sacred and meaningful form of worship in Latter-day Saint religious life. In the temple, holy truths are taught and solemn covenants are made in the name of Jesus Christ, both by the individual members on their own behalf and as proxies on behalf of others who have died (the latter have the choice in the spirit world to accept or reject such vicarious service). Obedience to temple covenants and reverence in doing temple ordinances give peace in this world and the promise of eternal life in the world to come.

There are special areas inside each temple for the various ordinances. A large baptismal font supported on the backs of twelve sculpted oxen (cf. 1 Kgs. 7:25) is used for baptism for the dead. In other areas are cubicles in which individuals are ritually washed and anointed before endowments can be performed. In the older temples, larger rooms are decorated to represent the Creation, the Garden of Eden, this world, and the terrestrial kingdom, and in such endowment rooms, participants watch and hear figurative presentations in which scenes are acted out, depicting by whom and why the earth was created and how one may come to dwell again in God's presence. The participants make covenants and receive promises and blessings. This is known as receiving one's endowment. The Prophet Joseph Smith taught that this endowment was necessary to empower one "to overcome all things" (*TPJS*, p. 91). A veil symbolically divides the terrestrial room from the celestial room, which suggests through furnishings and decor the peace, beauty, and glory of the highest degree of heaven. Also in the temple are smaller SEALING rooms, where temple marriages and sealings are solemnized for the living and vicariously for the dead. A temple may also have an upper room where SOLEMN ASSEMBLIES can be convened.

The first visit to the temple for one's own endowment is a major event in the life of a Latter-day Saint. (Children enter the temple only to be sealed to their parents or, after age twelve, to be baptized for the dead.) Full-time missionaries receive their endowment shortly before they begin to serve; other members generally do so shortly before temple marriage or, if unmarried, at a mature time in life. All Latter-day Saints attending a temple must be worthy, and the men must hold the MELCHIZEDEK PRIESTHOOD.

After receiving his or her personal endowment, a Church member is encouraged to return often to re-experience the same ordinances on behalf of persons who have died without receiving them. The temple goer stands as a proxy for a person of his or her gender on each visit to the temple. This selfless service of "saviours . . . on mount Zion" (cf. Obad. 1:21) is rooted in faith in the literal resurrection and afterlife of all human beings.

After being dedicated, LDS temples are not open to the public but are restricted to Latter-day Saints. Even among themselves, Latter-day Saints do not talk about the details of the temple ceremony outside the temple, because they are sacred. In the temple, worshipers go through several steps that symbolize withdrawal from the world and entrance into the abode of deity. They present their TEMPLE RECOMMEND to enter, change from street clothes to all-white clothing, and communicate only in quiet voices while in the holy building. Temples are not open on Sunday, because the Sabbath day is dedicated to worshiping the Lord in homes and in Church gatherings at MEETINGHOUSES.

For those who enter the house of the Lord with "clean hands, and a pure heart" (Ps. 24:4), with a "broken heart and a contrite spirit" (3 Ne. 9:20; cf. Ps. 51:17), and with no ill feelings toward others (Matt. 5:23–24), the temple is an ideal place to worship through meditation, renewal, prayer, and quiet service. The Lord described his house as "a house of prayer, a house of fasting, a house of faith, a house of learning, a house of glory, a house of order, a house of God" (D&C 88:119). The reverence in the temple is hospitable to the spirit of humble worship and holiness. In the stillness of the Lord's house, those who yearn to hear the word of the Father and to be heard by him pray silently or join in solemn supplications on behalf of the sick and afflicted and those seeking inspiration and guidance (cf. 1 Kgs. 8:30–49; *see also* PRAYER CIRCLES).

Words spoken in the temple endowment give "the answers of eternity" (Hinckley, p. 37) lodged in the perspective of all God's children. The words set forth eternal principles to be used in solving life's dilemmas, and they mark the way to become more Christlike and progressively qualify to live with God. There, the laws of the new and everlasting covenant are taught—laws of obedience, sacrifice, order, love, chastity, and consecration. In the temple, one learns the sacred roles of men and women in the eternal plan of God the Father and toward each other, receives a stable perspective on the repeating pattern of life, and gains a greater love for ancestors and all mankind.

This refuge from the world is part of the fulfillment for Latter-day Saints of the ancient prophecy that "in the last days . . . the Lord's house shall be established . . . and all nations shall flow unto it" (Isa. 2:2). In the house of the Lord, faithful Church members seek to understand whom they worship and how to worship, so that in due time they may come to the Father in Christ's name and receive of the Father's fulness (D&C 93:19).

BIBLIOGRAPHY

Derrick, Royden G. *Temples in the Last Days*. Salt Lake City, 1987.

Edmunds, John K. *Through Temple Doors*. Salt Lake City, 1978.

Hinckley, Gordon B. "Why These Temples?" *Ensign* 4 (Aug. 1974):37–41.

Leone, Mark P. "The New Mormon Temple in Washington, D.C." In *Historical Archaeology and the Importance of Material Things*. Charleston, S.C., 1977.

Madsen, Truman G. "The Temple and the Restoration." In *The Temple in Antiquity*, ed. Truman G. Madsen. Provo, Utah, 1984.

Packer, Boyd K. *The Holy Temple*. Salt Lake City, 1980.

Talmage, James E. *The House of the Lord*. Salt Lake City, 1976.

IMMO LUSCHIN

HISTORY OF LATTER-DAY SAINT TEMPLES FROM 1831 TO 1990

Latter-day Saints are a temple-building people. Theirs is a history of temples projected and built, often under intense opposition. An early revelation declared that "my people are always commanded to build [temples] unto my holy name" (D&C 124:39–40). In the last weeks of his life, the Prophet Joseph Smith affirmed: "We need the temple more than anything else" (Journal History of the Church, May 4, 1844).

The functions of latter-day temples parallel in some aspects those of the ancient Tabernacle and biblical temples, which were dedicated as sacred places where God might reveal himself to his people (Ex. 25:8, 22), and where sacrifices and holy priesthood ORDI-NANCES might be performed (D&C 124:38). Although the Bible does not clarify the precise nature and extent of these rites, it is clear that sacrifice by the shedding of blood anticipated the supreme sacrifice of Jesus Christ.

The New Testament uses two words that are translated as temple:

naos for the sanctuary, and *hieron* for the general grounds and court-yards. Although Jesus vigorously condemned abuses in the temple courts, he nevertheless held the holy sanctuary in highest esteem as "my Father's house" (John 2:16) or as "my house" (Matt. 21:13). His cleansing of the temple and condemnation of abuses (John 2:13–16; Matt. 21:12–13) related to the *hieron* rather than the *naos*.

RESTORATION OF TEMPLE WORSHIP AND ORDINANCES.   Latter-day Saints built their first temple at Kirtland, Ohio. A solemn cornerstone-laying ceremony in 1833 marked the beginning of construction. Over a period of about three years, the saints sacrificed their means, time, and energies to build the House of the Lord (the word "temple" was not generally used at that time). Even though the temple's exterior looked much like a typical New England meeting-house, its interior had some unique features. A revelation specified that the building should include two large rooms, the lower hall being a chapel, while the upper was for educational purposes (D&C 95:8, 13–17). There were no provisions for the sacred ceremonies that were yet to be revealed.

Notable spiritual blessings followed the years of sacrifice. The weeks just preceding the Kirtland Temple dedication witnessed remarkable spiritual manifestations. On January 21, 1836, when Joseph Smith and others met in the nearly completed temple, they received washings and anointings and saw many visions, including a vision of the celestial kingdom. They learned that all who had died without a knowledge of the gospel, but who would have accepted it if given an opportunity, were heirs of that kingdom (D&C 137:7–8). This was the earliest latter-day revelation on the subject of salvation of the dead, a major doctrinal principle related to ordinances in LDS temples.

On Sunday, March 27, 1836, the Kirtland Temple was dedicated. Toward the conclusion of the daylong service, Joseph Smith read the dedicatory prayer that he had previously received by revelation (D&C 109). Following this prayer, the choir sang "The Spirit of God," a hymn written for the occasion by William W. Phelps. After the sacrament was administered and several testimonies were borne, the congregation stood and rendered shouts of "Hosanna, Hosanna; Hosanna, to God and the Lamb!" Formal dedicatory prayers, the singing of this hymn, and the Hosanna Shout have characterized all temple dedications since (*see* HOSANNA SHOUT).

Significant manifestations occurred in the Kirtland Temple on April 3, one week after its dedication. Jesus Christ appeared and accepted the temple. Moses, Elias, and Elijah then appeared and restored specific PRIESTHOOD powers (D&C 110). Through the SEALING keys restored by Elijah, priesthood ordinances performed on earth for the living and the dead could be bound or sealed in heaven, thus helping to turn the hearts of the fathers and children to one another (Mal. 4:5–6).

At the time when Joseph Smith was planning the temple in Kirtland, he was also giving attention to developments in Missouri. In 1831 he had placed a cornerstone for a future temple at Independence in Jackson County, which had been designated as the "center place" of Zion (D&C 57:3). In June 1833 he drew up a plat for the city of Zion, specifying that twenty-four temples or sacred buildings would be built in the heart of the city to serve a variety of priesthood functions. When the Latter-day Saints were forced to flee from Jackson County that fall, plans to build the city of Zion and its temples were postponed.

In 1838 cornerstones were laid for a temple at Far West in northern Missouri. This structure was to be for the gathering together of the Saints for worship (D&C 115:7–8). However, persecution prevented construction.

The Nauvoo Temple, dedicated in 1846, was the first temple designed for the recently restored sacred ordinances for the living and the dead. Vicarious baptisms for the dead were inaugurated in 1840. They were first performed in the Mississippi River until a font was completed in the basement of the temple. In 1842 the Prophet gave the first endowments in the assembly room above his red brick store (*TPJS*, p. 237). Given at this time only to living persons, this ceremony reviewed the history of mankind from the Creation, emphasizing the lofty standards required for returning to God's presence. The first sealings or marriages of couples for eternity were also performed at about this time. Then all such ordinance work was stopped until the temple was completed.

The main outside walls of the temple were only partially completed when Joseph Smith and his brother Hyrum were murdered in

1844. The martyrdom, however, caused only a temporary lull in temple construction. Even though the Saints knew they would soon be forced to leave Nauvoo and lose access to the temple, they were willing to spend approximately one million dollars to fulfill their Prophet's vision of erecting the House of the Lord. By December 1845, the rooms in the temple were sufficiently completed that endowments could be given there. During the next eight weeks 5,500 persons received these blessings even as they were hurriedly preparing for their exodus to the West. Brigham Young and other officiators stayed in the temple day and night. To maintain order, Heber C. Kimball insisted that only those with official invitations be admitted to the temple, which perhaps marked the beginning of issuing temple recommends.

TEMPLES IN THE TOPS OF THE MOUNTAINS.   Temple building remained a high priority for the Mormon pioneers as they made their trek to the Rocky Mountains. Only four days after entering the Salt Lake Valley, Brigham Young selected the site for the temple there. Temporary provisions were made for giving the endowment until this temple could be completed, and an adobe endowment house opened on Temple Square in 1855. President Young explained that not all ordinances could appropriately be performed there, however, so in the mid-1870s he encouraged the Saints to press forward with the construction of other temples in Utah.

The site for the temple at St. George was swampy, but Brigham Young insisted that it be built there because the spot had been dedicated by ancient Book of Mormon prophets (statement by David H. Cannon, Jr., Oct. 14, 1942, quoted in Kirk M. Curtis, "History of the St. George Temple," Master's thesis, Brigham Young University, 1964, pp. 24–25). An old cannon, filled with lead, became an improvised pile driver to pound rocks into the soggy ground. In 1877 the St. George Temple was completed, the first in Utah. Endowments for the dead were inaugurated there in January of that year, enabling the Saints to perform these important rites as proxies on behalf of their forebears.

As the number of endowments for the dead increased, the basic design of temples was modified to accommodate the ordinance. The Logan and Manti temples (dedicated in 1884 and 1888, respectively) contain large upper assembly rooms and a series of smaller lower rooms especially designed for presenting the endowment instructions. Murals on the walls depict different stages in man's eternal progression. Because of outside political hostility in 1888, Church leaders dedicated the Manti Temple first in private ceremonies. At the public dedication a short time later, members of the congregation reported unusual spiritual experiences including hearing heavenly choirs.

Completion of the Salt Lake Temple lifted the Saints' spirits during dark days of persecution. Symbolic stones on the great temple's exterior represent the degrees of eternal glory and other gospel principles. The east center spire is topped by a statue of the angel Moroni, symbolic of John's prophecy of a heavenly herald bringing the gospel to the earth (Rev. 14:6). The interior includes council rooms for the GENERAL AUTHORITIES. On the afternoon prior to its dedication on April 6, 1893, visitors of many faiths were invited to tour the temple. Such prededication open houses have grown in importance and become the norm during the twentieth century.

TWENTIETH-CENTURY TEMPLES.   During the first third of the twentieth century, temples were built more and more distant from Church headquarters, reflecting Church expansion and growth. President Joseph F. Smith spoke of the need to provide temple blessings to scattered Saints without requiring them to travel often thousands of miles to the intermountain West to receive them. The temples built at this time were comparatively small, without towers or large assembly halls.

President Smith, who had served a MISSION to Hawaii as a young man, selected the temple site at Laie on the island of Oahu. Because traditional building materials were scarce on the island, the temple was built of reinforced concrete. It was dedicated in 1919, one year after President Smith's death. Meanwhile, construction had also begun on a temple at Cardston, Alberta, Canada. Following its dedication in 1923, Church members from Oregon and Washington organized annual caravans to attend that temple, the forerunners of temple excursions that became an increasingly important facet of religious activity for members not living close to these sacred structures.

At the 1927 dedication of the Arizona Temple in Mesa, President Heber J. Grant petitioned divine blessings for the American Indians and other modern-day descendants of Book of Mormon peoples. In 1945 the endowment and other temple blessings were presented there in Spanish, the first time these ceremonies were offered in a language other than English. In subsequent decades, members in the southwestern United States, Mexico, and as far away as Central America traveled to attend Spanish temple sessions in Mesa.

President Grant also approved sites for temples in California and Idaho. Although construction of the Idaho Falls Temple began in 1937, shortages of materials during World War II delayed its completion until 1945.

The rapid growth of Church membership in southern California during and following World War II led to the construction of the Los Angeles Temple, the largest in the Church at that time. Dedicated in 1956, it was the first in the twentieth century to include a large upper hall for priesthood leaders to conduct SOLEMN ASSEMBLIES, as well as an angel Moroni statue on its 257-foot tower. Architectural plans called for the angel to face southeast, as did the temple itself. President David O. McKay, however, insisted that the statue be turned to face due east. Most (but not all) LDS temples face east, symbolic of the anticipated second coming of Christ, which Jesus compared to the dawning in the east of a new day (Matt. 24:27). Members in California regarded this temple as the fulfillment of Brigham Young's prophecy that the shores of the Pacific would one day be overlooked from the Lord's house, and that temples would have a central tower and would feature reflecting ponds and have plantings on their roofs.

THE FIRST OVERSEAS TEMPLES.   The decision to build temples abroad signaled a new emphasis. Although for decades Church leaders had counseled the overseas Saints not to gather to America, but to build up the Church where they were, the blessings of the temple were not available in their homelands. The Swiss Temple near Bern in 1955 and the New Zealand and London temples in 1958 partially met this need. The use of film and projectors allowed the endowment ordinance to be presented in one place of instruction rather than in a series of muraled rooms. President McKay had announced that future temples would be smaller, so that more of them could be built around the world. Furthermore, on film, these ceremonies could be presented in several languages with only a small group of attending temple ordinance workers.

Those responsible for locating these temples were convinced that they had divine assistance. Swiss Mission officials experienced prolonged difficulties in acquiring a site they had selected and petitioned the Lord for help. Immediately they found a larger site at half the cost; they soon learned that the original site was rendered useless by the unexpected construction of a highway through one portion of the lot. When the original price asked for the New Zealand temple plot seemed excessive, attorneys representing the owners and the Church reviewed the matter and independently arrived at exactly the same lower figure. Engineers cautioned against building the London Temple on the ground selected by President McKay because it was too swampy, but bedrock was discovered at the proper depth to support the foundations.

MODERN TEMPLES IN NORTH AMERICA. During the decade 1964–1974, four more temples were dedicated in the United States. The Oakland Temple (1964) had been eagerly anticipated by the Saints in northern California. Forty years earlier, Elder George Albert Smith had spoken while in San Francisco of the day when a beautiful temple would surmount the East Bay hills and be a beacon to ships sailing through the Golden Gate. During World War II property became available high in the Oakland Hills. However, two decades passed before Church growth in the area warranted construction of a temple. The Oakland Temple now uses film projection to present the endowment ceremony. Three spacious rooms allow large groups to receive these instructions simultaneously.

Even though early leaders had spoken of future temples in Ogden and Provo, the 1967 announcement of these two Utah temples came as a surprise to many Latter-day Saints. Church leaders explained that the Salt Lake Temple was being used beyond its capacity, so building two new nearby temples would ease the pressure and also reduce travel time for the Saints in Ogden and Provo. When the temples were completed five years later, each featured six endowment rooms, enabling a new group to begin the presentation every twenty minutes for up to sixty sessions daily.

The Washington, D.C., temple not only met the needs of Saints living in the eastern United States and Canada but, located close to the U.S. capital, became a monument to the restored Church. Architects designed it as a modern and easily recognizable adaptation of the familiar six-towered pattern of the Salt Lake Temple. Its 289-foot east central spire is tallest of any LDS temple in the world. The Washington Temple included a complex of six endowment rooms, and it became the second twentieth-century temple to have the large upper-level priesthood assembly room.

During the 1970s, the Arizona Temple and several other temples were remodeled to utilize film projection in presenting the endowment. Because these renovations were extensive, open houses were held for visitors prior to rededication of the temples. During this same decade, construction began on three other large temples in North America: the Seattle Temple (dedicated in 1980), first in the U.S. Pacific Northwest; the Jordan River Temple (1981), second in the Salt Lake Valley; and the Mexico City Temple (1983), which features a Mayan architectural style. While at the dedication of the Mexico City Temple, Elder Ezra Taft Benson was impressed to emphasize the Book of Mormon—a theme that later characterized his administration as President of the Church.

WORLDWIDE EXPANSION.   In 1976 two revelations (now D&C 137 and 138) were added to the standard works. One recorded Joseph Smith's 1836 vision of the celestial kingdom. The other was an account of President Joseph F. Smith's 1918 vision of the Savior's organizing the righteous to preach his gospel in the world of departed spirits. Both contributed to the Saints' comprehension of salvation for the dead, and provided new stimulus for unprecedented temple building.

Plans had already been announced for temples in São Paulo and Tokyo—the first in South America and Asia, respectively. Then, in 1980, a dramatic acceleration came when the FIRST PRESIDENCY announced that seven new temples were to be built. These included the first temple in the southeastern United States, two more temples in South America, and four in the Pacific. The following year, plans for nine more temples were announced—two each in the United States, Europe, and Latin America; plus a temple each in Korea, the Philippines, and South Africa. By 1984, plans to build ten additional temples were announced, including one in the German Democratic Republic. These temples were smaller than most built in earlier decades. Since many were built at the same time, they are of similar design.

Most of these new temples were located where they could make temple blessings available to the living even though they might not contribute large numbers of ordinances for the dead. More than ever before, temples were within the reach of Latter-day Saints living around the world, who greeted the construction of these temples with gratitude and joy. When President Spencer W. Kimball announced the intention to build the São Paulo Temple, for example, there was an audible gasp that swept the huge congregation gathered for the Brazil area conference; tears flowed freely as families throughout the hall embraced one another at the news. Church leaders suggested that rather than sacrificing lifetime earnings to reach a distant temple, members would now need to make a different kind of sacrifice—finding time for regular attendance at their temple.

Latter-day Saints expect that this rapid expansion of temple building will continue. Sacred temple ordinances are to be made available to all. Brigham Young prophesied that during the Millennium there would be thousands of temples dotting the earth. At that time, tens of thousands of the faithful are to enter and perform sacred ordinances around the clock.

TEMPLE BLESSINGS FOR THE DEAD.   When the Saints in Nauvoo performed vicarious baptisms for close relatives, information on them was readily accessible. More difficult genealogical research became necessary, however, as Church members met their responsibility to provide temple blessings for all deceased ancestors as far back as they could trace them. The introduction of endowments for the dead in 1877, which took far more time than baptisms, represented a significant expansion in Church members' temple commitment.

Heretofore the Saints had performed vicarious ordinances only for their own deceased relatives or friends. While directing the unfolding of the vicarious service at the St. George Temple, however, Elder Wilford Woodruff declared that the Lord would allow members to help one another in this important work.

A further innovation came during the early twentieth century when those living in faraway mission fields were allowed to send names of deceased loved ones to the temple where other proxies would perform the ordinances. Church leaders then exhorted members living near a temple to take time to perform this unselfish service. In the Salt Lake Temple, for example, there had been at first only one endowment session per day. By 1921, however, that increased to four, and in 1991 to ten.

With the growing number of temples, the number of endowments performed increased. Beginning in the 1960s, therefore, Church leaders directed Genealogical Society of Utah employees to obtain names from microfilmed vital records and make them available for temple work. By the early 1970s, three-fourths of all names for temple ordinances were being submitted in this manner.

To facilitate the members assuming a greater share in providing names for the temples, in 1969 they were permitted to submit names individually rather than only in family groups. Computers could then assist in determining family relationships. Beginning in 1978, small groups of Church members were called to spend a few hours each week in the name extraction program copying names and data from microfilm records. In this way most names for temple work were supplied by members rather than by professionals at Church headquarters. In 1988 the 100 millionth endowment for the dead was performed; over five million were accomplished that year.

THE HOUSE OF THE LORD.   As did ancient Israel, Latter-day Saints regard temples as sacred places set apart where they can go to draw close to God and receive revelations and blessings from him (D&C 97:15–17; 110:7–8). The physical structure as such is not the source of its holiness. Rather, the character of those who enter and the sacred ordinances and instructions received there nurture the spiritual atmosphere found in the temple. When members enter this holy house and center their thoughts on serving others, their own understandings are clarified and solutions to personal problems are received.

Because of the spiritual nature of temple activity, personal preparation is essential. Latter-day Saints insist that temple ceremonies are sacred. This is consistent with ancient practice when, for example, only specifically qualified persons were admitted into the holiest precincts of the Tabernacle. The function of local Church leaders in issuing temple recommends is not only to establish the individual's worthiness and preparation but also to assure the sanctity of the temple.

BIBLIOGRAPHY

For a scholarly treatise of temples and their ordinances, see James E. Talmage, *The House of the Lord* (Salt Lake City, 1962); Boyd K. Packer in *The Holy Temple* (Salt Lake City, 1980) explains the spirit and importance of temple work; Richard O. Cowan in *Temples to Dot the Earth* (Salt Lake City, 1989) traces the history of LDS temples and temple service. For an in-depth discussion of some of the ancient background, see Hugh Nibley, *Message of the Joseph Smith Papyri: An Egyptian Endowment* (Salt Lake City, 1975); N. B. Lundwall, *Temples of the Most High* (Salt Lake City, 1971) includes dedicatory prayers and descriptive data about individual temples; Royden G. Derrick in *Temples in the Last Days* (Salt Lake City, 1987) has a collection of essays on temple-related topics; and Laurel B. Andrew explains architectural influences in her *Early Temples of the Mormons* (Albany, N.Y., 1989).

RICHARD O. COWAN

LDS TEMPLE DEDICATIONS

A temple dedication is a supremely sacred ceremonial enactment in the Church, which consecrates the building to the Lord before the beginning of temple ordinance work. From the time of the dedication of the Kirtland Temple in 1836 until 1990, forty-six LDS temples have been dedicated.

The dedication of a temple is a time of great rejoicing and spiritual celebration. Men, women, and sometimes children who live within the area to be served by the temple and have temple recommends are invited to sessions held within, or adjacent to, the temple. These ceremonies are repeated several times to accommodate all who can participate. Most come in the spirit of fasting and prayer. The ceremonies include sacred choral anthems, such as Evan Stephens's "Holiness Becometh the House of the Lord," and special addresses from the GENERAL AUTHORITIES. A formal dedicatory prayer is offered under apostolic authority. Historically these prayers encompass the whole sweep of the modern dispensation, invoking divine blessings on all mankind, living and dead. They have often been prophetic of world events (see D&C 109).

At some point in all temple dedications the congregation rises and, while waving white handkerchiefs, unites in the shout "Hosanna, hosanna, hosanna, to God and the Lamb" three times (*see* HOSANNA SHOUT). This solemn expression was introduced by Joseph Smith at Kirtland (see D&C 19:37; 36:3; 39:19). It is reminiscent of the praise of the followers of Jesus as he descended the Mount of Olives (Matt. 21:1–11), and of the outcry of the multitudes in America while surrounding the temple in the land Bountiful:

"Blessed be the name of the Most High God" (3 Ne. 11:17); it also parallels the "praising and thanking the Lord" by voices and instruments at the dedication of Solomon's temple (2 Chr. 5:11–14).

The dedication of a temple is ultimately the dedication of people. In the spirit of sacrifice, they build it, and in the same spirit they perform sacred ordinances within it. The dedication sets the building apart from all other Church edifices. It becomes a consecrated sanctuary not for regular Sabbath worship sessions but for daily performances of temple ordinances.

All the gifts of the Spirit and of the holy priesthood mentioned in scripture have been manifest at one time or another in the spiritual outpourings attending temple dedications, including visions, revelations, healings, discernment, and prophecy; and likewise the fruits of the Spirit—love, joy, peace, long-suffering, gentleness, meekness, faith. For Latter-day Saints on such occasions it is as if the earthly and heavenly temples meet and as if the rejoicing of ancient worthies mingles with that of mortals. These experiences and subsequent service in the temples lead to "the communion and presence of God the Father, and Jesus the mediator of the new covenant" (D&C 107:19). They are earthly demonstrations of celestial unity. President Wilford Woodruff wrote, "The greatest event of the year [1893] was the dedication of the Great Salt Lake Temple. The power of God was manifest . . . and many things revealed" (Journal of Wilford Woodruff, Dec. 31, 1893, *HDC*).

BIBLIOGRAPHY
Woodbury, Lael. "The Origin and Uses of the Sacred Hosanna Shout." *Sperry Lecture Series*. Provo, Utah, 1975.

D. ARTHUR HAYCOCK

ADMINISTRATION OF TEMPLES

The administration and internal working of a temple are designed to reflect the faith of members of The Church of Jesus Christ of Latter-day Saints that each temple is in every way "The House of the Lord." Only in dedicated temples can certain sacred ORDINANCES be performed, certain covenants between man and God be made, and the promise of certain blessings be conveyed. Through them a person may more fully comprehend the purpose of earth life, the ultimate destinies of mankind, and the importance of developing Christlike attributes here in mortality.

ENTERING THE TEMPLE.   All who enter the temple must come as worthy members duly certified by ecclesiastical leaders—the BISHOP and the STAKE PRESIDENT. The individual's temple recommend or certification to enter the temple is presented upon arrival to the recommend desk attendant. The signatures are verified and the expiration date is checked. A recommend is issued annually and is valid for one year.

Everyone in the temple, temple workers and patrons alike, is dressed in white clothing and is free of worldly ornamentation. All are encouraged to speak with soft voices and guard against extraneous thoughts and conversations, which detract from the spiritual tone of the sanctuary.

The temple is not used for Sunday worship but is rather a sacred edifice where ordinances may be performed and covenants may be made in quiet dignity, away from the cares and din of the outside world. The temple is closed on Sunday, the day in which members worship and learn in their ward meetinghouses. The temple is normally closed on Monday as well, for cleaning and maintenance work in preparation for the scheduled days of operation.

GENERAL SUPERVISION.   All temples are administered under the direction of the FIRST PRESIDENCY of the Church and the QUORUM OF THE TWELVE APOSTLES. The Temple Department under the direction of the First Presidency and with the guidance of the Temple and Family History Executive Council is the agency responsible for the supervision of all temples. Special attention is given to the following:

- Proper performance of all ordinances of the temple following scriptural patterns as approved by the First Presidency
- Upkeep, maintenance, and security of temples and grounds
- Technical facilities of all temples, especially audiovisual equipment and computers
- Personnel relationships in all temples
- Budgetary matters
- Monitoring temple clothing inventories
- Operation of laundries and cafeterias in temples

TEMPLE PRESIDENCY AND WORKERS.   The TEMPLE PRESIDENT is selected and called to his position by the First Presidency of the Church. This is a Church CALLING of usually two to three years. Normally the wife of a temple president serves as the matron of the temple. The president is assisted by two counselors, and the matron by two assistants. Each temple has a temple recorder.

THE TEMPLE EXECUTIVE COUNCIL.   The temple president, his counselors, the temple matron, and the recorder constitute the temple executive council. They meet weekly to do all master planning. As needed, other key personnel are invited into this meeting.

VOLUNTEER WORKERS.   Each temple relies heavily on volunteer workers to assist in administering the TEMPLE ORDINANCES. A large temple may have as many as two thousand volunteer workers. These ordinance workers, usually assigned two six-hour shifts each week, assist the patrons as they participate in baptisms, confirmations, the endowment, and temple SEALINGS.

All of these workers are recommended by their local priesthood leaders. Each person recommended is cleared by the First Presidency of the Church, name by name. This procedure emphasizes the importance of those selected to assist in the temple. Each ordinance worker is finally interviewed carefully by the temple president or one of his counselors who, when satisfied as to personal worthiness, attitude, and ability, sets the person apart by the laying on of hands, thus conveying the authority essential to officiate in temple ordinances.

TRAINING TEMPLE WORKERS.   The temple president is anxious that all that transpires in the temple is in complete harmony with the desires and specifications outlined by scripture and the First Presidency of the Church. The temple is a "house of glory," "of order," "of God" (D&C 88:119). Each ordinance worker undergoes an initial training program wherein the actions and words of the ordinances and covenants to be administered are memorized and rehearsed. In addition to the initial instructions, there is a continuation training to make sure all is carried out in an acceptable manner each day. All training is performed in a quiet and gentle manner.

Each shift (forty to eighty workers) begins the day with a prayer meeting that sets a spiritual tone and permits instruction for the work to follow. Usually, a few minutes of each prayer meeting are given to follow-up training. All persons assigned to train others are carefully and prayerfully selected by the temple presidency and the matron.

TEMPLE SEALERS.   A sealer in the temple has authority to seal families for time and for all eternity—husbands and wives to each other and children to parents. The process of sealing families together for time and for eternity is the very essence of temple work, and an important foundation stone of Latter-day Saint theology. Worthy male members of demonstrated faithfulness, ability, and integrity may be called to be sealers in the temple. All such calls and authorization come from the First Presidency of the Church.

THE BAPTISTRY.   The temple baptistry is used for proxy baptisms, living persons being baptized for and in behalf of deceased individuals who have lived through mortality without the opportunity of receiving this sacred ordinance.

The fundamental program encouraged is for members of the Church to perform this work for their deceased ancestors; however, a proven kindred relationship is not essential for the work to be valid. Males are proxies for males; females for females.

Baptisms for the dead often involve young people, ages twelve to seventeen. By appointment, they will spend two to three hours in the temple baptistry area, each person being baptized typically, for a score or more deceased persons. They dress in all-white baptismal clothing, attend a brief worship service, and then participate in the proxy baptisms. Those performing the baptism often include the adult male supervisors traveling with the group.

It is understood that in the spirit world all persons for whom temple work by proxy is performed will have heard of the gospel and its ordinances (*see* TEMPLES: MEANINGS AND FUNCTIONS OF TEMPLES).

BIBLIOGRAPHY
Packer, Boyd K. *The Holy Temple*. Salt Lake City, 1980.
Talmage, James E. *The House of the Lord*. Salt Lake City, 1968.

ROBERT L. SIMPSON

MEANINGS AND FUNCTIONS OF TEMPLES

The temple is the primal central holy place dedicated to the worship of God and the perfecting of his covenant people. In the temple his faithful may enter into covenants with the Lord and call upon his holy name after the manner that he has ordained and in the pure and pristine manner restored and set apart from the world. The temple is built so as to represent the organizing principles of the universe. It is the school where mortals learn about these things. The temple is a model, a presentation in figurative terms, of the pattern and journey of life on earth. It is a stable model, which makes its comparison with other forms and traditions, including the more ancient ones, valid and instructive.

THE COSMIC PLAN.   From earliest times, temples have been built as scale models of the universe. The first known mention of the Latin word *templum* is by Varro (116–27 B.C.), for whom it designated a building specially designed for interpreting signs in the heavens—a sort of observatory where one gets one's bearings on the universe. The root *tem-* in Greek and Latin denotes a "cutting," or intersection of two lines at right angles and hence the place where the four regions of the world come together, ancient temples being carefully oriented to express "the idea of pre-established harmony between a celestial and a terrestrial image" (Jeremias, cited in *CWHN* 4:358). According to Varro, there are three temples: one in heaven, one on earth, and one beneath the earth (*De Lingua Latina* 7.8). In the universal temple concept, these three are identical, one being built exactly over the other, with the earth temple in the middle of everything, representing "the Pole of the heavens, around which all heavenly motions revolve, the knot that ties earth and heaven together, the seat of universal dominion" (Jeremias, cited in *CWHN* 4:358). Here the four cardinal directions meet, and here the three worlds make contact. Whether in the Old World or the New, the idea of the three vertical levels and four horizontal regions dominated the whole economy of such temples and of the societies they formed and guided.

The essentials of Solomon's temple were not of pagan origin but a point of contact with the other world, presenting "rich cosmic symbolism which was largely lost in later Israelite and Jewish tradition" (Albright, cited in *CWHN* 4:361). The twelve oxen (1 Kgs. 7:23–26) represent the circle of the year, and the three stages of the great altar represent the three worlds. According to the Talmud, the temple at Jerusalem, like God's throne and the law itself, existed before the foundations of the world (*Pesahim* 54a–b). Its measurements were all sacred and prescribed, with strict rules about it facing the east.

Its nature as a cosmic center is vividly recalled in many passages of the Old Testament and in medieval representations of the city of Jerusalem and the Holy Sepulcher. These show the temple as the exact center, or navel, of the earth. It was in conscious imitation of both Jewish and Christian ideas that the Muslims conceived of the Kaaba in Mecca as "not only the centre of the earth, [but] the centre of the universe. . . . Every heaven and every earth has its centre marked by a sanctuary as its navel" (von Grunebaum, cited in *CWHN* 4:359). What is bound on earth is bound in heaven. From the temple at Jerusalem went forth ideas and traditions that are found all over the Jewish, Christian, and Muslim worlds.

THE PLACE OF CONTACT. As the ritual center of the universe, the temple was anciently viewed as the one point on earth at which men and women could establish contact with higher spheres. The earliest temples were not, as once supposed, permanent dwelling places of divinity but were places at which humans at specific times attempted to make contact with the powers above. The temple was a building "which the gods transversed to pass from their celestial habitation to their earthly residence. . . . The ziggurat is thus nothing but a support for the edifice on top of it, and the stairway that leads between the upper and lower worlds"; it resembled a mountain, for "the mountain itself was originally a place of contact between this and the upper world" (Parrot, cited in *CWHN* 4:360).

Investigation of the oldest temples represented on prehistoric seals concludes that these structures were also "gigantic altars," built both to attract the attention of the powers above (the burnt offering being a sort of smoke signal) and to provide "the stairways which the God, in answer to prayers, used in order to descend to the earth, . . . bringing a renewal of life in all its forms" (Amiet, cited in *CWHN* 4:360). From the first, it would seem, towers and steps for altars were built in the hope of establishing contact with heaven (Gen. 11:4).

At the same time, the temple is the place of meeting with the lower world and the one point at which passage between the two is possible. In the earliest Christian records, the gates and the keys are closely connected with the temple. Some scholars have noted that the keys of Peter (Matt. 16:19) can only be the keys of the temple, and many studies have demonstrated the identity of tomb, temple, and palace as the place where the powers of the other world are exercised for the eternal benefit of the human race (cf. *CWHN* 4:361). The gates of hell do not prevail against the one who holds these keys, however much the church on earth may suffer. Invariably temple rites are those of the ancestors, and the chief characters are the first parents of the race (see, for example, Huth, cited in *CWHN* 4:361, n. 37).

THE RITUAL DRAMA.   The pristine and original temple rites are dramatic repetitions of the events that marked the beginning of the world. This creation drama was not a simple one, for an indispensable part of the story is the ritual death and resurrection of the king, who represents the founder and first parent of the race, and his ultimate triumph over death as priest and king, followed by some form of *hieros gamos*, or ritual marriage, for the purpose of begetting the race. This now familiar "year-drama" is widely attested—in the Memphite theology of Egypt, in the Babylonian New Year's rites, in the great secular celebration of the Romans, in the *panagyris* and beginnings of Greek drama, in the temple texts of Ras Shamra, and in the Celtic mythological cycles. These rites were performed "because the Divinity—the First Father of the Race—did so once in the beginning, and commanded us to do the same" (Mowinckel, cited in *CWHN* 4:362).

The temple drama is essentially a problem play, featuring a central combat, which may take various mimetic forms—games, races, sham battles, mummings, dances, or plays. The hero is temporarily beaten by the powers of darkness and overcome by death, but calling from the depths upon God, "he rises again and puts the false king, the false Messiah, to death" (Weinsinck, cited in *CWHN* 4:363). This resurrection motif is essential to these rites, whose purpose is ultimate victory over death. These rites are repeated annually because the problem of evil and death persists for the human race.

INITIATION.   The individuals who toiled as pilgrims to reach the waters of life that flowed from the temple were not passive spectators. They came to obtain knowledge and regeneration, the personal attainment of eternal life and glory. This goal the individual attempted to achieve through purification (washing), initiation, and rejuvenation, which symbolize death, rebirth, and resurrection.

In Solomon's temple, a large bronze font was used for ritual washings, and in the Second Temple period, people at Jerusalem spent much of their time in immersions and ablutions. Baptism is one specific ordinance always mentioned in connection with the temple. "When one is baptized one becomes a Christian," writes Cyril, "exactly as in Egypt by the same rite one becomes an Osiris" (*Patrologiae Latinae* 12:1031), that is, by initiation into immortality. The baptism in question is a washing rather than a baptism, since it is not by immersion. According to Cyril, this is followed by an anointing, making every candidate, as it were, a messiah. The anointing of the brow, face, ears, nose, breast, etc., represents "the clothing of the candidate in the protective panoply of the Holy Spirit," which however does not hinder the initiate from receiving a real garment on the occasion (*CWHN* 4:364). Furthermore, according to Cyril, the candidate was reminded that the whole ordinance is "in imitation of the sufferings of Christ," in which "we suffer without pain by mere imitation his receiving of the nails in his hands and feet: the antitype of Christ's sufferings" (*Patrologiae Graecae* 33:1081). The Jews once taught that Michael and Gabriel will lead all the sinners up out of the lower world: "they will wash and anoint them, healing them of their wounds of hell, and clothe them with beautiful pure garments and bring them into the presence of God" (R. Akiba, cited in *CWHN* 4:364).

LOSS OF THE TEMPLE ORDINANCES.   The understanding of the temple and its ancient rites was eventually corrupted and lost for several reasons.

Both Jews and Christians suffered greatly at the hands of their enemies because of the secrecy of their rites, which they steadfastly refused to discuss or divulge because of their sanctity. This caused misunderstanding and opened the door to unbridled fraud: Gnostic sects claimed to have the lost rites and ordinances of the apostles and patriarchs of old. Splinter groups and factions arose. A common cause of schism, among both Jews and Christians, was the claim of a particular group that it alone still possessed the mysteries of God.

The rites became the object of various schools of interpretation. Indeed, mythology is largely an attempt to explain the origin and meaning of rituals that people no longer understand. For example, the Talmud tells of a pious Jew who left Jerusalem in disgust wondering, "What answer will the Israelites give to Elijah when he comes?" since the scholars did not agree on the rites of the temple (*Pesahim* 70b; on the role of Elijah, see A. Wiener, *The Prophet Elijah in the Development of Judaism* [London, 1978], pp. 68–69).

Ritual elements were widely copied and usurped. The early Christian fathers claimed that pagan counterparts had been stolen from older legitimate sources, and virtually every major mythology tells of a great usurper who rules the world.

Comparative studies have discovered a common pattern in all ancient religions and have traced processes of diffusion that spread ideas throughout the world. The task of reconstructing the original prototype from the scattered fragments has been a long and laborious one, and it is far from complete, but an unmistakable pattern emerges (*CWHN* 4:367).

Reconstructions of great gatherings of people at imposing ceremonial complexes for rites dedicated to the renewal of life on earth are surprisingly uniform. First, there is tangible evidence, the scenery and properties of the drama: megaliths; artificial giant mounds or pyramids amounting to artificial mountains; stone and ditch alignments of mathematical sophistication correlating time and space; passage graves and great *tholoi*, or domed tombs; sacred roads; remains of booths, grandstands, processional ways, and gates—these still survive in awesome combination, with all their cosmic symbolism.

Second is the less tangible evidence of customs, legends, folk festivals, and ancient writings, which together conjure up memories of dramatic and choral celebrations of the Creation, culminating in the great Creation Hymn; ritual contests between life and death, good and evil, and light and darkness, followed by the triumphant coronation of the king to rule for the new age, the progenitor of the race by a sacred marriage; covenants; initiations (including washing and clothing); sacrifices and scapegoats to rid the people of a year of guilt and pollution; and various types of divination and oracular consultation for the new life cycle.

OTHER FUNCTIONS OF THE TEMPLE. Many things surrounding the temple were not essential to its form and function, but were the inevitable products of its existence. The words "hotel," "hospital," and "Templar" go back to those charitable organizations that took care of sick and weary pilgrims traveling to the holy places. Banking functions arose at the temple, since pilgrims brought offerings and needed to exchange their money for animals to be sacrificed, and thus the word "money" comes from the temple of Juno Moneta, the holy center of the Roman world. Along with that, lively barter and exchange of goods at the great year rites led to the yearly fair, when all contracts had to be renewed and where merchants, artisans, performers, and mountebanks displayed their wares.

Actors, poets, singers, dancers, and athletes were also part of temple life, the competitive element (the *agonal*) being essential to the struggle with evil and providing the most popular and exciting aspects of the festivals. The temple's main drama, the *actio*, was played by priestly temple actors and royalty. Creation was celebrated with a creation hymn, or *poema*—the word "poem" meaning "creation"—sung by a chorus that, as the Greek word shows, formed a circle and danced as they sang (*CWHN* 4:380).

The temple was also the center of learning, beginning with the heavenly instructions received there. It was the *Museon*, or home of the Muses, representing every branch of study: astronomy, mathematics, architecture, and fine arts. People would travel from shrine to shrine exchanging wisdom with the wise, as Abraham did in Egypt. Since the Garden of Eden, or "golden age" motif, was essential to this ritual paradise, temple grounds contained trees and animals, often collected from distant places. Central to the temple school was the library, containing sacred records, including the "Books of Life," the names of all the living and the dead, as well as liturgical and scientific works.

The temple rites acknowledged the rule of God on earth through his agent and offspring, the king, who represented both the first man and every man as he sat in judgment, making the temple the ultimate seat and sanction of law and government. People met at the holy place for contracts and covenants and to settle disputes.

THE TEMPLE AND CIVILIZATION.   All this indicates that the temple is the source, and not a derivative, of the civilizing process. If there is no temple, there is no true Israel; and where there is no true temple, civilization itself is but an empty shell—a material structure of expediency and tradition alone, bereft of the living organism at its center that once gave it life and made it flourish.

Many secular institutions today occupy structures faithfully copied from ancient temples. The temple economy has been perverted along with the rest: feasts of joy and abundance became orgies; sacred rites of marriage were perverted; teachers of wisdom became haughty and self-righteous, demonstrating that anything can be corrupted in this world, and as Aristotle notes, the better the original, the more vicious the corrupted version.

THE RESTORATION AND THE TEMPLE.   Latter-day Saint temples fully embody the uncorrupted functions and meanings of the temple. Did the Prophet Joseph Smith reinvent all this by reassembling the fragments—Jewish, Orthodox, Masonic, Gnostic, Hindu, Egyptian, and so forth? In fact, few of the fragments were available in his day, and those poor fragments do not come together of themselves to make a whole. Latter-day Saints see in the completeness and perfection of Joseph Smith's teachings regarding the temple a sure indication of divine revelation. This is also seen in the design of the Salt Lake Temple. One can note its three levels; eastward orientation; central location in Zion; brazen sea on the back of twelve oxen holding the waters through which the dead, by proxy, pass to eternal life; rooms appointed for ceremonies rehearsing the creation of the world; and many other symbolic features.

The actual work done within the temple exemplifies the temple idea, with thousands of men and women serving with no ulterior motive. Here time and space come together; barriers vanish between this world and the next, between past, present, and future. Solemn prayers are offered in the name of Jesus Christ to the Almighty. What is bound here is bound beyond, and only here can the gates be opened to release the dead who are awaiting the saving ordinances. Here the whole human family meets in a common enterprise; the records of the race are assembled as far back in time as research has taken them, for a work performed by the present generation to assure that they and their kindred dead shall spend the eternities together in the future. Here, for the first time in many centuries, one may behold a genuine temple, functioning as a temple in the fullest and purest sense of the word.

BIBLIOGRAPHY
Nibley, Hugh W. "Christian Envy of the Temple." In *CWHN* 4:391–434.
———. "What Is a Temple?" In *CWHN* 4:355–87.

————. "The Hierocentric State." *Western Political Quarterly* 4 (June 1951):226–53.

————. *Message of the Joseph Smith Papyri*. Salt Lake City, 1975.

Packer, Boyd K. *The Holy Temple*. Salt Lake City, 1980.

Talmage, James E. *The House of the Lord*. Salt Lake City, 1962.

For a lengthy bibliography on temples, see Donald W. Parry, Stephen D. Ricks, and John W. Welch, *Temple Bibliography*, Lewiston, N.Y., 1991.

HUGH W. NIBLEY

TEMPLES THROUGH THE AGES

The center of the community in ancient Israel and in other parts of the ancient Near East was the temple, an institution of the highest antiquity. Its construction regularly represented the crowning achievement in a king's reign. Thus, it was the central event in the reign of King Solomon, far overshadowing any of his other accomplishments (1 Kgs. 6–8), and it was a crucial event in the establishment of the Nephite monarchy (2 Ne. 5:16–18). The presence of the temple represented stability and cohesiveness in the community, and its rites and ceremonies were viewed as essential to the proper functioning of the society. Conversely, the destruction of a temple and the cessation of its rites presaged and symbolized the dissolution of its community and the withdrawal of God's favor. The fall of Jerusalem and its temple (586 B.C.), along with the rifling of its sacred treasures, symbolized, like no other event, the catastrophe that befell Judah. Following the return of the Jews from exile in Babylon (c. 500 B.C.), the prophets Haggai and Zechariah persistently reminded their people that no other achievement would compensate for their failure to reconstruct a temple. Temples were so important that, when distance or other circumstances made worship at the Jerusalem temple impractical, others were built. Thus, Israelite temples were built at Arad near Beersheba, at Elephantine and Leontopolis in Egypt, and a Nephite temple was erected in the land of Nephi.

Several studies have shown that certain characteristics regularly recur in the temples of the ancient Near East. Among the features that have been identified that distinguish the temple from the meetinghouse type of sacred structure such as synagogue or church are: (1) the temple is built on separate, sacral, set-apart space; (2) the temple and its rituals are enshrouded in secrecy; (3) the temple is oriented toward the four world regions or cardinal directions; (4) the temple expresses architecturally the idea of ascent toward heaven;

(5) the plans for the temple are revealed by God to a king or prophet; and (6) the temple is a place of sacrifice (Lundquist, pp. 57–59).

Latter-day Saints recognize among these features several that are characteristic of ancient Israelite temples as well as their own. For example, the sites of ancient Israelite and modern Latter-day Saint temples are viewed as holy, with access restricted to certain individuals who are expected to have "clean hands and a pure heart" (Ps. 24:3–6; cf. Ps. 15; Isa. 33:14–16; *see* TEMPLE RECOMMENDS). Like the tabernacle and temple in ancient Israel, many Latter-day Saint temples are directionally oriented, with the ceremonial main entrance (indicated by the inscription "HOLINESS TO THE LORD" on modern temples) facing east. Ancient Israelite temples were divided into three sections, each representing a progressively higher stage, reaching from the netherworld to heaven; similar symbolism can be recognized in the LDS temples as well. The plans for the temple of Solomon were revealed to King Solomon. Likewise, plans for many Latter-day Saint temples were received through revelation.

What occurred within temples of antiquity? The temple is a place of sacrifice, a practice that is well attested in ancient Israel. Animal sacrifice is not to be found in temples of the Latter-day Saints because blood sacrifice had its fulfillment in the death of Jesus (3 Ne. 9:19). Still, Latter-day Saints learn in their temples to observe the eternal principles of sacrifice of a broken heart and contrite spirit (3 Ne. 12:19). In addition, inside the temples of the ancient Near East, kings, temple priests, and worshippers received a washing and anointing and were clothed, enthroned, and symbolically initiated into the presence of deity, and thus into eternal life. In ancient Israel—as elsewhere—these details are best seen in the consecration of the priest and the coronation of the king. LDS TEMPLE ORDI-NANCES are performed in a Christian context of eternal kingship, queenship, and priesthood.

The features of temple worship described above are also found among many other cultures from ancient to modern times. Several explanations of this can be offered. According to President Joseph F. Smith, some of these similarities are best understood as having spread by diffusion from a common ancient source:

> Undoubtedly the knowledge of this law [of sacrifice] and of the other rites and ceremonies was carried by the posterity of Adam into all lands,

and continued with them, more or less pure, to the flood, and through Noah, who was a "preacher of righteousness," to those who succeeded him, spreading out into all nations and countries. . . . If the heathen have doctrines and ceremonies resembling . . . those . . . in the Scriptures, it only proves . . . that these are the traditions of the fathers handed down, . . . and that they will cleave to the children to the latest generation, though they may wander into darkness and perversion, until but a slight resemblance to their origin, which was divine, can be seen [*JD* 15:325–26].

When Jesus drove the moneychangers from the temple—which he referred to as "my Father's house" (John 2:16)—it reflected his insistence on holiness for the sanctuaries in ancient Israel. Neither Stephen's nor Paul's statements that "the most High dwelleth not in temples made with hands" (Acts 7:48; 17:24; cf. Isa. 66:1–2) imply a rejection of the temple, but rather an argument against the notion that God can be confined to a structure. Solomon, at the dedication of the temple in Jerusalem, said similarly, "The heaven of heavens cannot contain thee; how much less this house that I have builded?" (1 Kgs. 8:27; 2 Chr. 6:18). As late as the fourth century A.D., Christians were able to point to the spot on the Mount of Olives "where they say the sanctuary of the Lord, that is, the Temple, is to be built, and where it will stand forever . . . when, as they say, the Lord comes with the heavenly Jerusalem at the end of the world" (Nibley, p. 393).

While the idea of the temple was somewhat submerged in the later Jewish–Christian consciousness, it was never completely forgotten. As Hugh Nibley points out, the Christian church sensed that it possessed no adequate substitute for the temple. Jerusalem remained at the center of medieval maps of the world, and the site of the temple was sometimes indicated on such maps as well. When the Crusaders liberated the holy places in Jerusalem, the site of the temple was visited immediately after that of the Holy Sepulcher, even though no temple had been there for over 1,000 years (Nibley, pp. 392, 399–409).

Jews and Christians who take the vision of the reconstruction of the temple in Ezekiel seriously—and literally—anticipate the place in God's plan of rebuilding a future temple, as well as the reconstitution of distinct tribes of Israel (Ricks, pp. 279–80). While Jewish life proceeded without the temple following its destruction by the

Romans in A.D. 70, it retained a significant role in their thought and study. In the modern period, the temple remains important to some Jews, who continue to study their sacred texts relating to it.

BIBLIOGRAPHY

Lundquist, John M. "The Common Temple Ideology in the Ancient Near East." In *The Temple in Antiquity*, ed. T. Madsen, pp. 53–74. Provo, Utah, 1984.

Nibley, Hugh W. "Christian Envy of the Temple." In *CWHN* 4:391–433.

Ricks, Stephen D. "The Prophetic Literality of Tribal Reconstruction." In *Israel's Apostasy and Restoration: Essays in Honor of Roland K. Harrison*, ed. A. Gileadi, pp. 273–81. Grand Rapids, Mich., 1988.

STEPHEN D. RICKS

TESTIMONY BEARING

Testimony bearing among members of The Church of Jesus Christ of Latter-day Saints is a person's verbal expression of what he or she knows to be true concerning the divinity of Jesus Christ, the restoration of the fulness of his gospel in our time, and the blessings that come from living its principles. By divine mandate, bearing testimony is to be done "in my name, in solemnity of heart, in the spirit of meekness, in all things" (D&C 100:7). Latter-day Saints often bear testimony when teaching in Church services, when explaining gospel principles to members of other faiths, and in the FAST AND TESTIMONY MEETING, held monthly in each congregation.

Bearing testimony while teaching the gospel of Jesus Christ is pervasive in the Church and is based on two central beliefs. The first is that the primary responsibility of members is to "teach one another" (D&C 88:118) rather than to depend upon one formal teacher or minister only. The second is that the power that motivates individuals to live as Christ taught is the power of the Holy Ghost, rather than the power of logic or the eloquence of gospel teachers: "For when a man speaketh by the power of the Holy Ghost the power of the Holy Ghost carrieth it unto the hearts of the children of men" (2 Ne. 33:1). Testimony bearing complies with the Lord's instruction through Isaiah: "Ye are my witnesses, saith the Lord, that I am God" (Isa. 43:12).

Latter-day Saints who speak in SACRAMENT MEETING or teach

classes in the organizations of the Church (i.e., SUNDAY SCHOOL, PRI-
MARY, RELIEF SOCIETY, YOUNG WOMEN and YOUNG MEN, and PRIEST-
HOOD) are urged to conclude their presentations by bearing personal
testimony that the things which they have said are true. Hearing
testimony borne under the influence of the Holy Spirit enables those
listening under the Spirit's influence to understand the message
both intellectually and spiritually (1 Cor. 2:11; D&C 50:17–24;
100:6–10).

Latter-day Saint missionaries, in particular, rely on testimony
bearing, rather than on logic or artifice, to reach their listeners. The
impact of this faith and practice is illustrated by Brigham Young's
account of his own conversion to the gospel when an LDS missionary, Eleazar Miller, bore his testimony:

> If all the talent, tact, wisdom and refinement of the world had been sent
> to me with the Book of Mormon, and had declared, in the most exalted
> of earthly eloquence, the truth of it, undertaking to prove it by learning,
> and worldly wisdom, they would have been to me like the smoke which
> arises only to vanish away. But when I saw a man without eloquence, or
> talents for public speaking, who could only say, "I know, by the power of
> the Holy Ghost, that the Book of Mormon is true, that Joseph Smith is a
> prophet of the Lord," the Holy Ghost proceeding from that individual
> illuminated my understanding, and light, glory, and immortality were
> before me. I was encircled by them, filled with them, and I knew for
> myself that the testimony of the man was true [*JD* 1:90].

Fast and testimony meetings, usually held in each congregation of
the Church as part of the sacrament meeting on the first Sunday of
each month, provide all members the opportunity to bear testimony.
In these meetings, no one is assigned in advance to prepare a sermon. Rather, any member who desires may stand before the congregation and testify of the things he or she has learned to be true
through trying to live in the manner Christ has taught. Members typically come to these meetings fasting, abstaining from food and drink
for at least two meals. Opportunities to bear testimony are also given
to young children in Primary, to young people in youth conferences or
family home evenings, to missionaries in various conferences, and to
all members in a wide variety of settings.

Spoken testimony is the foundation of faith and with written testimony becomes the essence of scripture. Faith comes by hearing—as well as by reading—"the word of the Lord." The Doctrine and Covenants says, "Whatsoever they shall speak when moved upon by the Holy Ghost . . . [whether or not it is recorded or written] shall be scripture" and "the power of God unto salvation" (D&C 68:4). Said the Prophet Joseph Smith, "No generation was ever saved or destroyed upon dead testimony neither can be; but by Living" (*WJS*, p. 159). He taught further that the living word of the Lord "has such an influence over the human mind—the logical mind—that it is convincing without other testimony" (*WJS*, p. 159). "Faith cometh by hearing the word of God through the testimonies of the servants of God," he said, and is "always attended by the spirit of prophecy and revelation" (*WJS*, p. 3). These principles are the background of the constancy of the mode of testimony bearing in Church life.

Patterns of testimony bearing in ancient churches closely parallel today's practice. The apostle Paul, for example, said that he was "determined not to know anything among you, save Jesus Christ, and him crucified," and spoke "not with enticing words of man's wisdom, but in demonstration of the Spirit" (1 Cor. 2:2–5). In early Christian sources (e.g., the Didache) one reads of sacrament meetings or feasts where hymn singing was followed by an opportunity for individual testimonies (Davies, pp. 342–43). The Book of Mormon prophet Alma$_2$ concluded that the only way to reclaim his people from selfishness and pride was "in bearing down in pure testimony against them" (Alma 4:19). Amulek testified in a manner similar to Latter-day Saint testimony bearing today: "And now, behold, I will testify unto you of myself that these things are true. Behold, I say unto you, that I do know that Christ shall come among the children of men, to take upon him the transgressions of his people, and that he shall atone for the sins of the world; for the Lord God hath spoken it" (Alma 34:8).

BIBLIOGRAPHY

Davies, J. G., ed. *The Westminster Dictionary of Liturgy and Worship*. Philadelphia, 1986.

Stoker, H. Steven, and Joseph C. Muren, comps. *Into Your Heart Like Fire*. Ogden, Utah, 1975.

CLAYTON CHRISTENSEN

TIMES AND SEASONS

The journalistic voice of The Church of Jesus Christ of Latter-day Saints in Nauvoo, Illinois, the *Times and Seasons*, was published in 135 issues of sixteen pages each between November 1839 and February 1846. It was a monthly from November 1839 to October 1840, then a biweekly, issued, about the first and the fifteenth of each month, until February 15, 1846. It was the fourth major semi-official newspaper published by the Church. During the seven months in 1842 that the Prophet Joseph Smith was the editor, he published several important documents of Mormon history in its pages: the translation and facsimiles of the book of Abraham, the Wentworth Letter, and the early segments of the *History of the Church*.

The *Times and Seasons* was first established and edited by Don Carlos Smith, Joseph Smith's youngest brother, and Ebenezer Robinson for the Saints who had been scattered by the Missouri conflict and were anxious "to learn of the condition and welfare of the Church." They proposed to publish "all general information respecting the Church" (*T&S* 1 [Nov. 1839]:16). This included Church news and history, world news and history, political and literary materials, Nauvoo city news, obituaries, announcements, doctrinal expositions, conference reports, mission reports, letters from missionaries, and notices and trial minutes of excommunications. The *Times and Seasons* also responded to polemic and apologetic treatment of Mormonism by other newspapers in an attempt to establish goodwill and understanding.

In Nauvoo the press offices were first located in a warehouse basement at Water and Bain (Fifth) streets. The operations of the newspaper later moved to the new, brick *Times and Seasons* Printing Office building at Kimball and Main (Seventh) streets, which is now restored in Nauvoo.

John Taylor and Wilford Woodruff, both apostles and later Presidents of the Church, edited the paper from late 1842 until April 1844, and then John Taylor edited it alone until its last issue on February 15, 1846, just before the Saints left Nauvoo on their exodus west.

BIBLIOGRAPHY

Bray, Robert T. "*Times and Seasons*: An Archaeological Perspective on Early Latter Day Saints Printing." *Historical Archaeology* 13 (1979):53–119.

Sorensen, Parry D. "Nauvoo *Times and Seasons*." *Journal of the Illinois State Historical Society* 55 (1962):117–35.

REED C. DURHAM, JR.

TITHING

Tithing is the basic contribution by which Latter-day Saints fund the activities of the Church. By revelation to the Prophet Joseph Smith, the Lord stated that members should pay "one-tenth of all their interest [increase] annually; and this shall be a standing law unto them forever" (D&C 119:4).

The law of tithing has ancient origins. The word "tithe" means "tenth" and connotes a tenth part of something given as a voluntary contribution. Abraham paid tithes to Melchizedek (Gen. 14:18–20; Alma 13:14–15). Jacob also covenanted to pay a tenth of everything the Lord gave him (Gen. 28:20–22). Tithing was a fundamental part of the law of Moses (Lev. 27:30–32; Num. 18:25–28; Deut. 26:12–14) and was used in support of priests, holy edifices, and sanctuaries (Amos 4:4).

The prophet Malachi underscored the seriousness of paying tithes:

Will a man rob God? Yet ye have robbed me . . . in tithes and offerings. Ye are cursed . . . for ye have robbed me. . . . Bring ye all the tithes into the storehouse . . . and prove me . . . if I will not open you the windows of heaven, and pour you out a blessing, that there shall not be room enough to receive it [Mal. 3:8–10].

The collection of tithing is the responsibility of the BISHOP in each ward. Tithes are presented confidentially to him or his counselors. He forwards the tithes collected locally to Church headquarters, where a committee consisting of the FIRST PRESIDENCY, the PRESIDING BISHOPRIC, and the QUORUM OF THE TWELVE APOSTLES supervises the distribution and expenditure of tithing funds (D&C 120). These funds are used for such purposes as the building and maintenance of meetinghouses, temples, and other facilities, as well as for the partial support of the missionary, educational, and welfare programs of the Church.

At the end of each year, ward members meet individually with their bishop in a tithing settlement interview to verify Church records of their individual contributions and to declare confidentially to the bishop whether or not the amount contributed is a "full tithe."

The common mode of tithing payment is by cash. However, when income has been received in some other form, the member may pay accordingly, as was done anciently (Lev. 27:30, 32). In its early years the Church maintained "tithing houses" to receive payments in grain, livestock, vegetables, and fruits.

A 1970 letter from the First Presidency stated that notwithstanding the fact that members should pay one-tenth of their income, "every member of the Church is entitled to make his own decision as to what he thinks he owes the Lord and to make payment accordingly" (Mar. 19, 1970; cf. Doxey, pp. 16, 18). Hence, the exact amount paid is not as important as that each member feels that he or she has paid an honest tenth.

As part of the latter-day restoration of the gospel, the law of tithing was reestablished. Joseph Smith and Oliver Cowdery initiated implementation of the principle in 1834, when they pledged one-tenth of all the Lord should give them as an offering for the poor (*HC* 2:174–75). In 1838 the Prophet inquired about tithing for the Church (*HC* 3:44) and received the law, now published as Section 119 of the Doctrine and Covenants. The term "tithing" had been used in some revelations before 1838 (e.g., D&C 64:23; 85:3; 97:11–12) but connoted all free-will offerings or contributions, whether they were less or more than 10 percent.

Prior to the revelation on tithing, an adaptation of the law of consecration of property was practiced by the Church to care for the poor, to purchase lands, and to build Church facilities (D&C 42:30–39). The declared spiritual object of that law was to "advance the cause" of "the salvation of man" (D&C 78:4–7) by creating equality in both "earthly things" and "heavenly things." This proved too difficult at the time, especially under the disruptive conditions suffered by Church members in Missouri, and the practice was temporarily suspended in 1840 (*HC* 4:93). The law of tithing was given in part to fulfill material needs and to prepare the membership of the Church to live the material aspects of the law of consecration at some future time. Tithing has variously been described as the donation of

(1) a tenth of what people owned when they converted; (2) a tenth of their "increase" or income each year; and (3) one workday in ten of their labor, teams, and tools to public projects. Today, tithe payers pay a tenth of their "increase," or income.

Although many in the early decades of the Church were slow to obey the principle and practice of tithing, leaders continued to affirm the obligatory nature of the commandment. In January 1845 the Quorum of the Twelve Apostles under the direction of President Brigham Young issued an epistle reminding the Saints of their duty to pay tithing (*HC* 7:358). In 1881 obedience to the law of tithing became a requirement for temple attendance (*JD* 22:207–208) for those with an income. In May 1899 a manifestation was given to President Lorenzo Snow that even though the Church was beleaguered by financial difficulties, it was nonetheless bound by the law of tithing, as were its members individually, and all would be blessed materially and spiritually by heeding it (Snow, p. 439).

As with all commandments, there is a correlation between observance of the law of tithing and blessings or punishments. The promises to the obedient are great, but the revelation also warns, "It shall come to pass that all . . . shall observe this law, or they shall not be found worthy to abide among you" (D&C 119:5). President Joseph F. Smith taught that the disobedient "have cut themselves off from the blessings of Zion," but added that the Lord will fulfill his rich promises to the faithful tithe payers of the Church (*GD*, pp. 225–27). "A host of testimonies might be secured of the joy in life that follows obedience to this important law of the Lord" (Widtsoe, Vol. 1, p. 228). President Heber J. Grant counseled the Church that obedience to the law of tithing provides a protective shield (D&C 64:23–24) from economic distress (pp. 59–60).

[*See also* Bishop, History of the Office.]

BIBLIOGRAPHY

Doxey, Roy W. *Tithing: The Lord's Law*. Salt Lake City, 1976.

Grant, Heber J. *Gospel Standards*. Salt Lake City, 1941.

Kimball, Spencer W. "Tithing." In *Faith Precedes the Miracle*, pp. 281–90. Salt Lake City, 1975.

Snow, LeRoi C. "The Lord's Way Out of Bondage." *IE* 41 (July 1938):400–401, 439–42.

Widtsoe, John A. *Evidences and Reconciliations*, 3 vols. Salt Lake City, 1943.

HOWARD D. SWAINSTON

TRUE AND LIVING CHURCH

"The only true and living church upon the face of the whole earth" is a phrase from a revelation given to the Prophet Joseph Smith (D&C 1:30) often used by members of The Church of Jesus Christ of Latter-day Saints when they testify to the truthfulness of the restored gospel in testimony meetings, MISSIONARY presentations, or other settings. The phrase echoes Paul's "the living and true God" (1 Thes. 1:9), which also occurs elsewhere in the scriptures.

Latter-day Saints speak of "the only true and living church" because of their belief that Jesus Christ and his apostles organized the Church during their ministry on the earth. This organization included prophets and apostles at its head, along with various other offices such as bishop, elder, seventy, and so on. The holders of these offices were given authority to preach the gospel, perform ORDI-NANCES, and govern the Church.

However, as Christ and his apostles had prophesied, the "true" church they established was lost from the earth through APOSTASY (JS—M 1:7–9, 22; 2 Thes. 2:3). Therefore there was a need for a restoration. Guided by angelic messengers and by revelation from God, Joseph Smith and his successors have reestablished Christ's church in these "latter days." Members bear testimony that the Church is true because they believe it is the restored church of Christ, with the same authority, teachings, organization, and spirit found in the church that the Savior originally established.

The Church is a "living" church with "living" scripture, not only because it has been restored by a "living God" who continues to reveal his will to his living prophets and people to lead them to life eternal, but also because it is a growing, dynamic organization that plays an important role in the way of life of active members. The Church has a lay ministry; therefore its offices are filled by the general membership. Many young men and women begin early in life to serve in Church positions as teachers and leaders, and continue to serve throughout their lives. Being involved in a significant way in an organization that is directed by continuing revelation and is dramatically growing leads its members to speak of it as a true and living church.

To its members, as President Spencer W. Kimball has stated, the

LDS Church "is not *a* church. [It] is *The* Church of Jesus Christ" (*The Teachings of Spencer W. Kimball*, ed. E. L. Kimball, p. 421, Salt Lake City, 1982).

BIBLIOGRAPHY
Romney, Marion G. "We, The Church of Jesus Christ of Latter-day Saints." *Ensign* 9 (May 1979):50–52.
Stapley, Delbert L. "What Constitutes the True Church." *Ensign* 7 (May 1977):21–23.

SOREN F. COX

U

UTAH GENEALOGICAL AND HISTORICAL MAGAZINE

Printed from 1910 to 1940 by the Genealogical Society of Utah, *Utah Genealogical and Historical Magazine* provided instruction for local Church leaders and members on how to do genealogy and submit names of ancestors for temple ordinances. It often contained material for ward genealogical classes and reports about stake activities in genealogy and temple work. For serious genealogists it contained articles on sources and methodology. It also printed genealogies, biographies, and news about activities of the Genealogical Society of Utah and its library.

In 1940 the role of the Utah Genealogical Society in directing genealogical and temple activities among the Latter-day Saints was changed, and with it, the need for its magazine as a separate publication. Its last issue (October 1940) announced that the First Presidency had assigned responsibility for genealogical and temple activities to local priesthood leaders. From this time on, genealogy columns began to appear as regular features in the *Instructor* and the *Improvement Era*, and later in the *Church News*, which became the new forum for official Church statements about genealogy and temple activities.

RAYMOND S. WRIGHT III

V

VISITING TEACHING

Visiting teaching is an organized means whereby the women of the Church receive regular instructional and compassionate service visits—usually by personal contact in the home—from other female members of the Church. The purpose is to promote sisterhood, present inspirational messages, and note instances of need wherein the temporal and spiritual resources of the Church might be helpful.

In practice, the ward RELIEF SOCIETY president or those assisting her assign pairs of visiting teachers to keep in contact with specific families over a period of several months or even years. More frequent contact is made with women and families exhibiting special needs, such as those new to the Church, the less active, single parents, the divorced, the widowed, the aged, and those faced with illness, death, or other difficulties.

The need for such visitors was recognized soon after the founding of the Relief Society in 1842. At the second meeting of the society on March 24, Emma Smith, wife of the Prophet Joseph Smith, suggested appointing persons to wait upon the poor. On July 28, 1843, a Necessity Committee of sixteen was named "to search out the poor and suffering, to call upon the rich for aid, and thus as far as possible, relieve the wants of all." The original functions of this committee were twofold: "to ascertain the condition of the families

451

visited, and to accept contributions for charitable purposes" (General Board, 1942, pp. 43–44; 1966, p. 68).

In the early years of the Church in Nauvoo, Illinois, visiting teachers reported their visits at the regular Relief Society meeting before all members present, citing specific instances of need. It was also customary for visiting teachers during this period to apportion and distribute to needy families the commodities donated to the society.

In 1921 visiting teachers were relieved of the personal responsibility of both ascertaining and meeting the material needs of families, but since then they have continued to report confidentially (to the ward Relief Society president) any instances of illness or need requiring attention. Upon hearing such reports, the Relief Society president either visits the family herself or designates the visiting teachers or someone else to give aid as a representative of the society. In cases of economic need, the Relief Society president and ward bishop confidentially inquire concerning the family's condition to arrange for any needed assistance from Church resources and for means to remedy the situation causing need. This modification of assignment brought visiting teachers into the more agreeable role of friendly visitors carrying messages from the society to the home, yet still fulfilling the original assignment from the Prophet Joseph Smith to "provoke the brethren to good works in looking after the wants of the poor—searching after objects of charity, and in administering to their wants" (General Board, 1966, p. 18).

An observation of Eliza R. Snow, an early president of the Relief Society organization, encapsulates the spirit of visiting teaching: "Many times a kind expression—a few words of counsel, or even a warm or affectionate shake of the hand—will do more good and be better appreciated than a purse of gold" (General Board, 1966, p. 40).

The importance of visiting teaching has been consistently reemphasized by Church Presidents. Spencer W. Kimball exhorted visiting teachers to do as the priesthood teachers do:

"Watch over the Church always"—not twenty minutes a month but always—"and be with and strengthen them"—not a knock at the door, but to be *with* them, and *lift* them, and strengthen them, and empower them, and fortify them—"and see that there is no iniquity, . . . neither hardness, . . . backbiting, nor evil speaking" (D&C 20:53–54). . . . How glorious is the privilege of two sisters going into a home, soft-pedaling anything that could be detrimental, and instead, building up all the authorities of the Church, the Church itself, its doctrines, its policies, its practices—"And see that [they] meet together often, and . . . do their duty" (D&C 20:55) [*Ensign*, June 1978, p. 24].

Visiting teaching allows every sister to serve in the Church. Whether active or inactive, single or married, newly baptized or a member of long standing, each can serve effectively as a visiting teacher.

Because of their sensitivity to the home and family and their consequent ability to identify needs that might otherwise go unobserved, visiting teachers give complementary support to the bishop and Relief Society president. They can also become a readily organized corps in times of emergency, crisis, or death. Countless recorded stories demonstrate the effectiveness of the visiting teaching program in extending essential service, love, and compassion to members, particularly the sisters of the Church.

[*See also* Compassionate Service.]

BIBLIOGRAPHY
General Board of the Relief Society. *A Centenary of Relief Society*. Salt Lake City, 1942.
———. *History of Relief Society, 1842–1966*. Salt Lake City, 1966.
Relief Society Handbook, pp. 3–4. Salt Lake City, 1988.

MARIAN R. BOYER

VOLUNTEERISM

Latter-day Saint doctrine teaches that basic tenets of a Christ-centered life are charity, love, and joy through service. Volunteerism in the Mormon community strives to implement the principles of service and concern for one's neighbor as taught in the gospel of Jesus Christ. The volunteering of time, energy, talents, and other resources for the betterment of the community and individual lives is a daily occurrence, primarily inside but also often outside a formal ecclesiastical setting. Church members are taught that cultivating the attribute of service is a spiritual obligation. This responsibility is reflected in the motto of the women's RELIEF SOCIETY organization, "Charity Never Faileth," from 1 Corinthians 13:8.

WARD and STAKE organizations are staffed by members with CALLINGS to serve in various capacities in carrying out the programs of the Church (*see* LAY PARTICIPATION AND LEADERSHIP). In this manner MISSIONARIES, TEACHERS, leaders, and many others voluntarily donate their time and talents. A balance exists in Mormon volunteerism between the spontaneous actions of members and organized Church initiatives. Some Church programs have begun at the grassroots level through volunteer-member initiative; however, most Church operations are centrally approved and implemented under the guidance of the GENERAL AUTHORITIES. Members strive to govern themselves and voluntarily find ways to serve within the principles, objectives, and guidelines taught by the Church. While all members are commanded to be "anxiously engaged in a good cause, and do many things of their own free will" (D&C 58:27), it is not customary for members to offer unsolicited advice, to intervene in the responsibilities of others, or to suggest themselves for specific Church callings. Most members accept whatever callings are extended to them, and few request to be released except under difficult circumstances.

In areas with concentrated Latter-day Saint populations, Mormons traditionally organize themselves to help members and, where possible, all others in the community in times of need. Local Church leaders often use PRIESTHOOD QUORUMS, the Relief Society, and Church YOUTH groups as vehicles for volunteer efforts. Latter-day Saints are also encouraged to volunteer their efforts in civic service. Examples of volunteer service extend to the national and international levels, as when members rally together to help in times of crisis. Latter-day Saints in many parts of the world have joined with others in the aftermath of natural disasters, famine, and war to donate and deliver goods and services, to perform clean up, and to rebuild communities.

Many types of volunteer service are seen in LDS congregations and communities. Typical activities include refurbishing homes of the elderly or the cleanup of public parks or buildings. Handicapped individuals are visited by members who assist them with their rehabilitation efforts. Visits to hospitals, nursing centers, or prisons with programs or projects for the patients or inmates are typical services. Groups of members frequently work together to raise money to help ease heavy medical bills for neighborhood families. Food and clothing are donated to charitable organizations, including the Deseret Industries. A call for help in such diverse activities as harvesting crops or moving a family usually generates willing volunteers. Many members spend hours of volunteer service translating materials for the deaf and the blind. Others work to preserve cultural or genealogical records. Returned missionaries offer their language skills when foreign visitors or immigrants are in the community. In addition, other professionally trained members teach the application of home nursing or agricultural technology in cross-cultural settings. Although not all members find themselves in circumstances permitting extensive service both inside and outside the Church, charitable service is highly admired and valued in the Mormon lifestyle.

Whether living in a community having few or many Latter-day Saints, Church members are taught and encouraged to render acts of kindness to their neighbors. Some charitable acts are done as a result of HOME TEACHING, VISITING TEACHING, or COMPASSIONATE SERVICE assignments. These Church callings bring to those who render unselfish service the joy of Christlike love for one's fellow beings. Many other deeds of service occur as the result of a need seen by an individual who is willing to fulfill that need. Hot meals, shoveled winter sidewalks, visits to the sick, the lonely, or the elderly, child care in times of despair, tutoring, painting, yard work, housekeeping, the sharing of musical talents, the remaking of clothing or home furnishings, and donating food from family garden plots are all small acts of volunteer kindness given, sometimes anonymously, to those in need.

BIBLIOGRAPHY
Cuthbert, Derek A. "The Spirituality of Service." *Ensign* 20 (May 1990):12–13.
For numerous references concerning Church counsel on volunteerism and service, or specific stories of individual or group volunteer efforts, see *Index to the Periodicals of The Church of Jesus Christ of Latter-day Saints*, Salt Lake City, 1961–present. Key Words: Volunteers, Service, Compassionate Service, Community Service, and Service Projects.

MARIBETH CHRISTENSEN

W

WARD

The ward is the basic ecclesiastical unit in The Church of Jesus Christ of Latter-day Saints. It is comparable to a Protestant congregation or a Roman Catholic parish. Normally, its membership ranges between 300 and 600 people. A ward is part of a larger unit called a STAKE, which usually includes between five and ten wards. When a ward or stake grows beyond the usual size in membership and in number of active MELCHIZEDEK PRIESTHOOD holders, it is divided, creating a new ward or a new stake, usually determined by geographical boundaries.

The ward is presided over by a BISHOP and his two counselors. Assisted by several CLERKS, these men comprise the BISHOPRIC. All are laymen and serve without monetary compensation. Bishops of wards extend CALLINGS to men and women in the ward so that each may serve in one of numerous offices or teaching positions in the ward.

The first wards were organized early in the history of the Church in the 1840s in Nauvoo, Illinois. By 1844 the city was divided into ten wards, with three more in the surrounding rural neighborhood. The name "ward" was borrowed from the term for political districts of the frontier municipality. Joseph Smith, who was simultaneously mayor of the city and President of the Church, assigned a bishop to preside over each ward. The bishop's chief responsibility to begin with was temporal rather than spiritual leadership. To prevent hunger, he surveyed the physical needs of the members living within his ward boundaries. Second, the bishop organized his members for Church work assignments, particularly to serve one day in ten as laborers on the Nauvoo Temple. This was a form of paying tithing.

Many of the Saints who fled Nauvoo under persecution in 1846 gathered at Winter Quarters, located near present-day Florence, Nebraska. There Brigham Young and other leaders again set up ward organizations. Their function was similar—to look after the temporal welfare of the people.

Soon after the first group of pioneer immigrants arrived in the valley of the Great Salt Lake, Brigham Young divided the area into several wards and called a bishop to preside over each. The temporal well-being of the people was still the bishop's chief concern. Soon bishops were assigned to collect tithes from the members and deliver them to the central tithing office. At this time, most of the tithes were paid in produce and livestock because of a lack of circulating currency.

Initially, worship meetings in the Salt Lake Valley were held in the Bowery, erected in the block now occupied by Temple Square. But soon the population increased until the various wards started building their own meetinghouses and holding separate worship services.

Brigham Young determined quickly to move the immigrants beyond the limits of Salt Lake City. Thus, he established small agricultural settlements throughout the Rocky Mountain valleys in the Great Basin. Through this colonization effort nearly four hundred Mormon villages were founded during his lifetime, built on nearly every available water source. Each village was eventually organized into a ward, and several wards into a stake. The bishop of each village ward was essentially the community leader, serving as the judge and mayor as well as the bishop. In the villages the bishops out of necessity became the temporal as well as ecclesiastical leaders. Each ward also tried to support an elementary school.

Gradually, the activities and programs of several organizations were added to the normal weekly worship meetings. Sunday Schools, priesthood quorums, the Relief Society, and youth groups emerged in the rural areas as well as in the cities. All were nominally guided by the bishopric, but each received some encouragement from stake and central Church leaders.

In 1890 the Manifesto was published, which ended Church support for the performance of plural marriages. The Manifesto was also an important landmark in the separation of the church and state in Utah. Gradually the wards and the villages turned many secular functions over to non-religious leaders. Bishops withdrew from being mayors and judges. Ward schools gave way to public schools. Water companies took over the administration of pioneer irrigation systems. Church-run cooperative stores were gradually replaced by private commercial enterprises. As this separation occurred, the ward became more and more an exclusively ecclesiastical organization rather than both a religious and political-economic one. Nonetheless, the resulting ward was more than just a congregation; it still retained much of the spirit of a close-knit community that it had so long been.

In the nineteenth century, wards and stakes were organized mainly in the intermountain United States, in Alberta, Canada, and in northern Mexico. Most members outside these regions were organized into missions and branches, the name given to small dependent units within the mission. By the outbreak of World War II, a few wards and stakes were organized in states beyond the intermountain region, particularly California and Hawaii. Then following the war, as the Church became established all over the United States, wards and stakes were organized throughout the country. By the 1960s, wards and stakes were organized in Europe and the Pacific. Asian and Latin American wards soon followed. Today wards exist in many parts of the world. This means that these units are essentially able to provide their own leadership. On January 1, 1991, the Church had a total of 18,090 wards and branches in 1,784 stakes, and 497 districts.

Today LDS wards continue many of the community functions of pioneer times. The Sunday meetings are just an outer evidence of the unit. Social life and friendship among members are largely developed within the ward. Youth programs bind teenagers and their parents to the ward. Education of children is supplemented by teachers of the youth and Primary programs. Family education is furthered through training parents in the ward programs. Sports and other activities are promoted in the ward.

Great diversity exists among wards. Many are located in Mormon communities. Others are in areas where Mormons are a distinct minority. Some have an overabundance of leadership and talent. Others suffer from lack of leadership or lack of youth involvement. Some cover a small neighborhood; others, a widespread area. But wherever located, wards have much similarity, following the same curriculum, working under equitable budget allocations, and adhering closely to central authority from Church headquarters. Increasingly, materials such as videotapes or satellite broadcasts from the GENERAL AUTHORITIES in Salt Lake City are received in all wards, promoting uniformity and commitment.

As Latter-day Saints move throughout the world, they typically transfer from one ward to another with ease, finding acceptance, responsibility, and similarity of doctrine and practice everywhere. The ward system is successful partly because wards are kept small and because, ideally, everyone in them is needed and asked to accept a calling. Serving one another, bearing each other's burdens, is the norm. Socializing the young is everywhere a mainstream activity, and the youth also contribute much to the dynamics of the ward.

BIBLIOGRAPHY

Alder, Douglas D. "The Mormon Ward: Congregation or Community?" *Journal of Mormon History* 5 (1978):61–78.

Allen, James B., and Glen M. Leonard. *The Story of the Latter-day Saints*. Salt Lake City, 1976.

Arrington, Leonard J. *From Quaker to Latter-day Saint: Bishop Edwin D. Woolley*. Salt Lake City, 1976.

————; Feramorz Fox; and Dean May. *Building the City of God: Community and Cooperation Among the Mormons*. Salt Lake City, 1976.

Beecher, Dale. "The Office of Bishop." *Dialogue* 15 (Winter 1982):103–115.

Nelson, Lowry. *The Mormon Village: A Pattern and Technique of Land Settlement*. Salt Lake City, 1952.

DOUGLAS D. ALDER

WARD BUDGET

A WARD budget is the fund from which local congregations (wards) finance their activities. Historically, the ward budget was raised through voluntary donations. Since January 1, 1990, ward and stake budgets in the United States and Canada are funded entirely from general tithing without additional local contributions. (Before 1990, bishops and ward members agreed privately on voluntary annual contributions. Wards sometimes organized supplementary fund-raising activities.) Building operation and maintenance costs are reimbursed from Church headquarters. The quarterly allowance for each stake and ward is based on average meeting attendance. Additional fund raising is discouraged, and expenditures are carefully monitored. Donations are not solicited in worship services.

In parts of the world other than the United States and Canada, some local costs are still financed by voluntary contributions, although building rentals, maintenance, and some other expenses are reimbursed from central funds.

The ward budget continues to cover costs of general operations, materials, and activities of the wards and stakes. Each unit of the ward organization prepares annually a detailed estimate of needs, which the BISHOPRIC then uses to develop a ward budget proposal. The BISHOP presents this for a sustaining vote of the ward membership at a special meeting, and then submits the proposal to the stake, from which it goes to Church headquarters.

ROBERT J. SMITH

WARD COUNCIL

The ward council (formerly known as the Ward Correlation Council) is the meeting of local leaders wherein the doctrines of the gospel are turned into plans of action. The shared activities that help turn ward members into a community of Saints are coordinated by the ward council. This council is composed of the ward PRIESTHOOD EXECUTIVE COMMITTEE and the presidents of the ward AUXILIARY ORGANIZATIONS, and the chair of the Activities Committee. These leaders coordinate the efforts of all ward quorums and organizations to support the families of the Church, meet the needs of individuals from all age groups, and provide Christian service. The BISHOP presides in this monthly meeting, where ward programs are reviewed and activities are proposed. The bishop may invite other individuals to participate in the ward council as necessary. Approval of activities is based on such matters as their appropriateness, the ability to conduct them without additional cost to ward members (*see* TITHING), and how well an activity will strengthen ward members. For example, if HOME TEACHERS were to discover that a group of elderly members felt neglected, and if youth leaders reported that they were searching for a service project, an activity could be planned that would place the youth in the service of the elderly.

BIBLIOGRAPHY

Benson, Ezra Taft. "Church Government Through Councils." *Ensign* 9 (May 1979):86–89.

General Handbook of Instructions. Salt Lake City, 1989.

DENNIS L. THOMPSON

WARD ORGANIZATION

A WARD is a geographically defined Church unit organized to provide every member the opportunity to find fellowship with the Saints and give service to others. The ward is led by a BISHOP and two counselors (*see* BISHOPRIC). An executive secretary and ward CLERKS assist the bishopric with the tasks of RECORD KEEPING and management. PRIESTHOOD and AUXILIARY presidencies (a president and two counselors) are assigned to attend to various needs of ward members. Other leaders supervise missionary activities, provide gospel instruction, and help ward members with temporal needs, such as searching for employment. Frequent social and service activities involve adults and youth.

Typically, the administration of the ward is carried out in a weekly bishopric meeting attended by the bishop, his two counselors, and his executive secretary. These same men hold a weekly ward PRIESTHOOD EXECUTIVE COMMITTEE meeting with the HIGH PRIEST group leader, the ELDERS quorum president, the ward mission leader, and the YOUNG MEN president. They consider such matters as ward TEMPLE attendance, family history activity, MISSIONARY work, HOME TEACHING, and member activation. When the female RELIEF SOCIETY president attends this meeting (at least monthly) for a discussion of the temporal needs of ward members, it becomes the ward welfare services committee. The Relief Society president helps the bishop coordinate appropriate assistance and COMPASSIONATE SERVICE to the sick, the aged, the lonely, and the needy. Under her direction, monthly home visits are made to each adult woman in the ward in which brief gospel instruction and encouragement are given (*see* VISITING TEACHING). Once each month this ward welfare services group becomes the WARD COUNCIL when joined by the SUNDAY SCHOOL president, the YOUNG WOMEN president, the PRIMARY president, and the activities committee chairman. The ward council discusses and plans all ward activities and correlates the services and programs of the Church in relation to individuals and families. Historically, youth usually have been given leadership roles in planning their own activities and in helping with events to which all ward members are invited. Since the mid-1970s, youth leadership has been nurtured on a monthly basis by the bishopric in the bishopric youth committee meeting, where youth activities and service projects are planned. Often members of a ward activities committee are called to supervise and carry out special wardwide events as requested by the bishopric.

Since 1980, when the Church adopted the consolidated meeting schedule, each ward holds three general meetings during a three-hour block of time on Sunday. In SACRAMENT MEETING family members worship together, renew covenants through partaking of the sacrament, and listen to talks and sermons based on the scriptures. During a second hour, Sunday School classes are held in age groups from twelve to adult. Each year in the adult classes, one of the standard works of scripture is studied: Old Testament, New Testament, the Book of Mormon, the Doctrine and Covenants, and the Pearl of Great Price. During a third hour Priesthood quorums, Young Women, and Relief Society meet separately, where youth, men, and women are taught how to put gospel principles into action in everyday life. Priesthood quorums and the Relief Society are the service arms of the ward. Their members provide the volunteer help necessary to implement the plans made by the bishopric and auxiliary leaders. Adult holders of the priesthood attend quorum meetings according to whether they are HIGH PRIESTS or ELDERS. Young men (ages twelve to eighteen) meet in AARONIC PRIESTHOOD quorums for DEACONS (ages twelve and thirteen), TEACHERS (ages fourteen and fifteen), and PRIESTS (ages sixteen to eighteen). The Young Women are organized in age groups similar to the Young Men: Beehives (ages twelve and thirteen), Mia Maids (ages fourteen and fifteen), and Laurels (ages sixteen and seventeen). From age eighteen, women are members of the Relief Society, a benevolent society dedicated to caring for the needy and to assisting in spiritual, social, and personal development. Relief Society lessons focus on spiritual living, home and family education, compassionate service, and social relations.

Concurrent with the Sunday School and the men's and women's activities, the PRIMARY organization holds a nursery for children from ages eighteen months to three years, and classes for those three through eleven years of age, where children are taught lessons about Jesus Christ and the scriptures and are involved in singing and speaking.

Special activities (service projects and socials) are held for the women and youth on a day other than Sunday. The Relief Society holds a monthly evening meeting in which the sisters are taught home management techniques and skills.

The bishop is responsible for the finances of the ward, and is assisted in this matter by a financial clerk. Ward activities are either financed locally by individual contributions of ward members, or by a system wherein each ward receives an operating budget from general tithing funds based on the number and level of activity of its members. There are to be no other fund-raising activities.

The ward organization is a tool to help assure that Church activities complement, rather than compete with, family activities; that social activities are inclusive, rather than exclusive; and to nurture those who feel that geographic boundaries are artificial and thus exclude them from Sabbath day association with longtime Church friends.

Ideally, the ward organization becomes the means of creating an intimate religious community where the work of the kingdom of God on earth is carried out by every member in a lay ministry. Through the ward organization members teach the gospel, perform the ordinances, provide fellowship with the saints, and in all ways nurture one another in the faith.

BIBLIOGRAPHY

Alder, Douglas D. "The Mormon Ward: Congregation or Community?" *Journal of Mormon History* 5 (1978):61–78.

Arrington, Leonard J., and Davis Bitton. "The Nineteenth Century Ward." In *The Mormon Experience: A History of the Latter-day Saints*, pp. 206–219. New York, 1979.

L. ROBERT WEBB

WARD WELFARE COMMITTEE

Certain officers of each WARD form the ward welfare committee, headed by the BISHOP. Through his priesthood CALLING, the bishop is entrusted with the sacred responsibility to know the temporal circumstances of his ward members and to ensure that proper care is given to those in need (D&C 84:112).

The bishop is assisted in these efforts by his two counselors, the HIGH PRIESTS quorum group leader, the ELDERS quorum president, the YOUNG MEN president, the RELIEF SOCIETY presidency, the ward executive secretary, the ward CLERK, and others. The bishop convenes the ward welfare committee at least monthly. These leaders report and confidentially discuss any welfare needs in the ward that they have become aware of, either personally or by reports from HOME TEACHERS and VISITING TEACHERS. Where possible, the priesthood quorums and the Relief Society serve as the first Church source of assistance to members who need help beyond what the family can provide (D&C 52:39–40). When these ward resources have been exhausted, the committee may suggest that additional help be sought from the "Lord's storehouse" (D&C 51:13; 83:5–6) or from other people or services.

In addition, the committee may also help ward members in learning to provide for themselves and their families, to live the principle of the monthly fast, and to contribute a generous monetary FAST OFFERING, and in preparing for unexpected adversity, rendering service in return for Church assistance, and preparing for emergencies in the community.

BIBLIOGRAPHY

The Church of Jesus Christ of Latter-day Saints. *Caring for the Needy*, pp. 4–5. Salt Lake City, 1986.

Romney, Marion G. "The Role of Bishops in Welfare Services." *Ensign* 7 (Nov. 1977):79–81.

Welfare Services Resource Handbook, pp. 8–10. Salt Lake City, 1980.

JOHN H. COX

WELFARE

[It is a major concern of The Church of Jesus Christ of Latter-day

Saints to care for the physical, as well as the spiritual, welfare of its own members, and of others as far as possible.

Institutionally, the Church operates an extensive program that delivers food, clothing, and other essentials of life to those in need. See Bishop's Storehouse; Compassionate Service; Elder; Fast Offerings; Hospitals; Relief Society; Social Services; Ward Welfare Committee; Welfare Farms; Welfare Services; *and* Welfare Square.

It encourages and assists members in finding suitable employment. See Social Services.

The Church counsels all its members to store food and commodities in preparation for possible disasters. It also extends aid and assistance to other peoples of the world in times of emergency.]

WELFARE FARMS

The purchase of farmlands by the Church began in the late 1930s. The intent was to give unemployed people an opportunity to work and to produce commodities to help the poor and needy. In the 1940s, stakes and groups of stakes began purchasing farms as approved welfare projects. Sometimes the Church would purchase a farm, and the local unit would repay the Church loan from farm revenues. In the 1970s, farms were purchased on a shared basis, with half of the funds coming from the local unit and half from Church headquarters. All new farmlands are now purchased solely by the Church. In 1990 the Church owned and operated about 160 localized welfare farms, which raised many kinds of produce for its welfare program. In addition, it had extensive farm holdings in its welfare reserve system and investment portfolio.

Produce from the welfare farms is canned in local Church canneries and transferred to the BISHOP'S STOREHOUSES. Surpluses are sold on the open market, and the revenues from these sales are used to help pay for the production overhead of the farm. Under the supervision of a stake president, a stake farm committee from the local priesthood units involved directs the local welfare farm operations, including its finances. Day-to-day business matters are handled by a farm manager, who is usually a full-time employee. Where feasible, donated farm labor from Church members is utilized, which is counted as a contribution to the stake's welfare program. Local ward units organize crews of volunteers who work different shifts at the farms. As modern agricultural work becomes more sophisticated, the welfare farms are relying increasingly on hired farm labor.

Currently, Church farm properties fall into three categories. First, there are about 160 Church welfare farms, which are operated by a farm committee as described above, transferring their products to Church canneries and bishop's storehouses. Second, the Church owns about 250 reserve farms, which are held by the Church primarily for possible future welfare needs. These properties are assigned to the Church-owned Farm Management Corporation. They have been acquired over the years for a variety of reasons and are not always the best-quality agricultural lands. They tend to be concentrated in areas where Church populations are located. Their products are sold on the open market. Third, the Church owns other properties for various purposes, such as investment diversification (*see* FINANCES OF THE CHURCH). These farms are leased to private individuals or companies which operate them as private enterprises.

Church farms are tax-exempt only to the extent that they fill Church welfare needs. Above their welfare function, these farms pay taxes as regular businesses. In 1983 the Church sold more than 200 farms that exceeded its welfare needs.

Farm projects vary according to locale, need, climate, and soil conditions. Welfare farms produce grain, fruit, and vegetables. There are also beef, pork, and poultry projects, as well as such specialized projects as honey production. The first priority of all farm production is to supply the needs of welfare canneries and bishop's storehouses, and to use as much donated labor as possible, giving opportunities for charitable service.

Farms may vary in size from just a few acres to several thousand. Most are located in the United States, primarily in Utah, Arizona, California, and Idaho. The largest reserve farm is in California. A notable investment farm is a 300,000-acre ranch in Florida that raises livestock and citrus fruit and is used as a hunting and forestry reserve.

T. GLENN HAWS

WELFARE SERVICES

The basic philosophy underlying the welfare services system of The Church of Jesus Christ of Latter-day Saints was succinctly stated by the Church's sixth President, Joseph F. Smith: "It has always been a cardinal teaching with the Latter-day Saints, that a religion which has not the power to save the people temporally and make them prosperous and happy here cannot be depended upon to save them spiritually, and exalt them in the life to come" (quoted in L. Arrington, *Great Basin Kingdom*, 1958, p. 425, n. 16).

This Christlike objective of caring for the physical well-being of humans has been pursued throughout the history of the Church, involving a wide variety of activities undertaken in radically different circumstances, but all based on the same set of principles drawn from ancient and modern scripture:

- Self-sufficiency and family support are seen as a spiritual as well as a temporal obligation (1 Tim. 5:8; D&C 42:42). The Church is responsible for teaching principles and providing necessary assistance to enhance self-reliance.

- Those who are economically deprived for reasons either within or beyond their control (Mark 14:7) are to be provided with short-term emergency help, then assisted to a state of self-reliance, if possible, and provided with support if not.

- Assistance provided should exalt, rather than demean, the poor (D&C 104:16).

- The salvation of a person who is not poor depends to a substantial degree upon the care that person gives to the poor (Mosiah 4:16–22; D&C 56:16; 104:18).

- The salvation of the poor depends in part on the spirit in which they receive assistance (Mosiah 4:24–25; D&C 56:17–18).

HISTORY OF WELFARE SERVICES.   During its first century, the modern Church applied these principles primarily by assisting Church members to gather at central locations—Kirtland, Ohio; western Missouri; Nauvoo, Illinois; the Great Basin—and to obtain land on which they could become self-sufficient. But all were not able to support themselves as farmers or in other pursuits, so other employment opportunities were created for the poor. They helped to build temples and other Church buildings and assisted in public works projects, receiving pay out of contributions given by those who had regular incomes. As early as 1896, forty years before the inauguration of a public employment service in America, the Church had an employment bureau, gathering and publishing information on employment opportunities as well as compiling data about those needing employment.

The present-day system for helping the poor had its roots in the Great Depression of the 1930s, which hit urban Church members hardest. Though often struggling in the 1930s, farm-owning Latter-day Saints usually were self-sufficient, while city-dwellers deprived of employment were in the most serious straits. Stake presidents in urban areas contacted nearby farmers who faced prices so low that it was not profitable to harvest their crops. Arrangements were made so that idle urban members could harvest the crops in return for a share thereof. The produce thus obtained was stored in Church-controlled warehouse facilities and distributed according to need. Drawing upon that experience, welfare farms were soon established under Church ownership in areas surrounding Mormon-populated cities. Other Church units undertook processing and manufacturing projects based on the rural produce. BISHOP'S STOREHOUSES were created for storage and distribution, and products were moved from location to location by a Church-sponsored transportation system. A sheltered workshop program, Deseret Industries, was introduced in 1938 to create jobs for the unemployed and the handicapped, refurbishing used clothing, furniture, and household goods for retail sale at low cost.

With the return of prosperity in the United States following World War II, these facilities were expanded to offer short-term emergency work and commodities during recessions, strikes, and natural disasters, as well as employment assistance to the aged, the handicapped, and others with limited ability for self-support. As the complexities of urban life increased and other obstacles such as unemployment and the need for various types of counseling became more evident, a Social Services agency was added. When needs became apparent, other welfare service functions were also added, growing into the system that currently operates, primarily in the

United States and Canada. Meanwhile, the rapid growth of the international membership of the Church, especially in less developed lands, poses new challenges, which the welfare services system is adapting to meet.

WELFARE PRINCIPLES AND PRACTICES. Emphasizing family self-reliance, the Church welfare obligation begins with the teaching of principles of provident living, encouraging the use of appropriate community services, and then filling in with Church assistance when other resources prove to be inadequate.

Individuals and families are expected to live prudently, providing for their own needs and when possible, producing a surplus to use in helping others. Organizations within the Church such as the RELIEF SOCIETY, PRIESTHOOD QUORUMS, the SUNDAY SCHOOL, and youth programs teach the appropriate principles, while the Relief Society and the priesthood, through VISITING TEACHING and HOME TEACHING, encourage self-reliance and identify individual and family needs. Areas of emphasis are literacy and education; career development and counseling; financial and resource management; home production and storage; physical health; and social, emotional, and spiritual support.

Latter-day Saints view education as a spiritual, as well as a temporal, obligation. All members are expected to take advantage of available educational opportunities. Church leaders counsel parents to read to their children, teach them, and encourage them to study the scriptures and other good literature and to communicate well in writing and speaking. Church organizations reinforce these family efforts. Instruction in family relations strengthens the family's ability to meet its challenges. People are given counsel to help them select careers in which their talents and skills can be used in meaningful employment. Adults and youth are expected to become proficient through appropriate training. The Church accepts responsibility for arranging for career counseling, encouraging access to training, providing assistance as necessary, and motivating members to assist each other in finding employment.

Church directives teach members to establish financial goals, pay tithing and fast offerings, avoid excessive debt, pay their obligations, use their resources wisely, and pursue a regular savings program. Keeping property in good repair is also encouraged. LDS families are taught to grow and preserve fruits and vegetables, sew clothing, and make household items. Every family is urged to be prepared for emergencies and to maintain a year's supply of food, clothing, and, if possible, fuel. The Word of Wisdom obliges members to avoid tobacco, alcohol, tea, coffee, and harmful drugs. Church organizations teach principles and skills of nutrition, physical fitness, immunization, sanitation, health, accident prevention, medical care, and the maintenance of a healthy home environment. Members are also advised to carry adequate health and life insurance when feasible and to avoid questionable medical practices.

It is assumed that, barring the unforeseen, most members and their extended families will be self-sufficient and able to give, rather than need to receive, assistance. Nevertheless, the Church stands ready to assist whatever needs exist. The *Welfare Services Handbook* states:

> No true Latter-day Saint, while physically or emotionally able, will voluntarily shift the burden of his own or his family's well-being to someone else. So long as he can, under the inspiration of the Lord and with his own labors, he will work to the extent of his ability to supply himself and his family with the spiritual and temporal necessities of life. As guided by the Spirit of the Lord and through applying these principles, each member of the Church should make his own decisions as to what assistance he accepts, be it from governmental or other sources. In this way, independence, self-respect, dignity and self-reliance will be fostered, and free agency maintained (1980, p. 5).

Latter-day Saints are encouraged to avoid "unearned" public assistance programs insofar as possible. They are also encouraged to take full advantage of all available education and training programs and, as appropriate, to draw upon public insurance programs established for the benefit of employees, such as unemployment insurance and social security pensions.

ADMINISTRATION. While all members of the Church have the duty to "succor those that stand in need" (Mosiah 4:16) and to "bear one another's burdens" (Mosiah 18:8), the institutional responsibility for the welfare of others in the WARDS belongs to BISHOPS, Relief Society presidencies, priesthood quorum leaders, and home and visiting teachers. These Church leaders are admonished to be alert to the condition of each family and to offer assistance when needs exceed family resources and extended families are unable or unwilling to assist. Assignments are made to "succor the weak, lift up the hands which hang down, and strengthen the feeble knees" (D&C 81:5; Heb. 12:12).

Marshaling the resources of the Church on behalf of needy families is then the primary responsibility of the bishop. For this purpose, he can use cash from fast offering funds and direct the personal help of members (*see* VOLUNTEERISM) or can refer members to community resources or give temporary assistance from the storehouse resource system.

Members receiving Church assistance are expected to work to the extent of their ability to compensate for the help received. The local ward leadership has responsibility to provide work opportunities, which may be on a Church welfare project, in Church building maintenance, or in behalf of another needy member. Following short-term emergency assistance, a rehabilitation program is developed to bring the member back to self-sufficiency.

Faithful members of the Church are deemed to have a right to assistance, and the bishop can aid inactive members and non-members at his discretion. Help is to be extended graciously without embarrassment to the recipient and with complete confidentiality.

Within a year of the organization of the Church in 1830, Latter-day Saints in Ohio and Missouri were instructed through revelation to consecrate their surplus properties to the Church for the care of the poor. The bishop allocated properties to the members as STEWARD-SHIPS, through which the people were to become self-supporting. Properties and commodities over and above immediate needs were "kept in [the Lord's] storehouse, to administer to the poor and the needy" (D&C 42:34); such accumulated assets were called "storehouse resources." Today these resources include fast offerings, production projects and commodities, the Church employment system, Deseret Industries, and LDS Social Services.

PRODUCTION. The Church welfare production system, as of 1985, consisted of 199 agricultural production projects, 51 canneries, and 27 large and 36 small grain-storage facilities feeding into 12 central, 69 regional, and 32 branch storehouses. These storehouses are essentially a combination of warehouses and outlet stores. The commodities in them are distributed after Relief Society leaders meet with families to determine their needs and bishops sign written orders for the needed commodities, which the family can pick up or have picked up for them at the storehouses or at Deseret Industries outlet stores. Also available in the storehouses are the products of a meat-packing plant, a milk-processing facility, a bakery, a soap factory, a pasta factory, and a number of Relief Society sewing projects. Items not produced in the Church system can be purchased at the bishop's discretion from outside sources. The bulk of the production occurs in the western United States, with a fleet of trucks moving commodities to the storehouses scattered around the country for distribution. As of the late 1980s, commodities conservatively valued at $30 million were dispersed in response to approximately 350,000 bishops' orders a year. The production system provides service opportunities as well: 872,000 hours of volunteer labor were donated in 1987. Recipients are encouraged to provide as much of this labor as possible, but about half of the volunteer hours are donated by nonrecipients. Longer-term recipients are also given meaningful training through production projects.

EMPLOYMENT SERVICES. The most visible components of the Church employment system are the thirty-six employment centers staffed with full-time professionals and the fifty-one centers operated by Church service volunteers. These are located in the United States in areas of membership concentration, with a few abroad. The volunteer-run centers function as satellites under the direction of the professional centers. However, the bulk of the employment activity occurs at the ward and stake levels. Each ward and stake has an employment specialist who contacts ward officers to identify any employment needs and job openings of which they are aware. Possible matches are made, and unfilled job openings are reported to the stake specialist, who disseminates the information to other wards and to the employment centers. Employment specialists are expected to be familiar with the workings of local labor markets and to counsel jobseekers on improving their job search skills and their employability. Professionals from the employment centers hold periodic seminars to train the stake and ward specialists and provide them on an ongoing basis with lists of current job openings. The specialists are encouraged to refer needy people to an employment center for career counseling, training in job search skills, information on the local and national labor markets, and referral to community job agencies.

DESERET INDUSTRIES. In the western United States there are twenty-one parent and twenty-seven branch Deseret Industries installations. Through periodic donation drives in the wards and stakes, clothing, furniture, appliances, toys, and other items are collected to be refurbished and sold by Deseret Industries' employees in sheltered workshops and stores. In addition, new products are manufactured in a mattress and furniture factory. A homecraft program offers productive opportunities for the homebound. Deseret Industries provides kits, patterns, materials, and supplies for items, which are then manufactured at home and picked up for sale through Deseret Industries retail stores.

WELFARE SERVICES MISSIONS. A welfare services missionary program responds to requests from Church units around the world with special needs that exceed local resources. Primarily young women and older persons with special skills are called to go, at their own expense, to these areas to train people in basic child development, family relations, nutrition, sanitation, health care, social work, counseling, and agricultural or vocational training. In 1990 there were about 280 welfare services missionaries.

Few social phenomena are more challenging to cope with than widespread poverty. Nevertheless, in all geographical areas where the Church program is established, members have some Church resources to assist them. Church welfare projects supply commodities to prevent serious deprivation. Since teaching self-sufficiency and counseling are unending one-on-one tasks, the fellowship of the Church provides a personal and reassuring support system to help members confront the problems of poverty.

The Church now faces the challenge of establishing its program in developing nations. Not since its early years has the Church struggled with situations in which a majority of members in some areas are plagued with poverty in conditions that arise from severe economic and social circumstances. To meet these challenges, programs are beginning, first with the teaching of self-reliance principles and the wise use of fast offerings, then with projects in conjunction with experienced Third World economic development agencies and with the establishment of Church employment centers. What will happen and what patterns or institutions will emerge cannot be foreseen; but that the effort will be made to establish the welfare system of Zion in all parts of the world is inherent in LDS doctrine.

BIBLIOGRAPHY

Arrington, Leonard J., and Wayne K. Hinton. "Origin of the Welfare Plan of the Church of Jesus Christ of Latter-day Saints." *BYU Studies* 5 (1965):67–85.

Barton, Betty L. "Mormon Poor Relief: A Social Welfare Interlude." *BYU Studies* 18 (1977):66–68.

Blumell, Bruce D. "Welfare Before Welfare: Twentieth-Century LDS Church Charity Before the Great Depression." *Journal of Mormon History* 6 (1979):89–106.

Child, Paul C. "Physical Beginnings of the Church Welfare Program." *BYU Studies* 14 (1974):383–85.

GARTH L. MANGUM

WELFARE SQUARE

Welfare Square in Salt Lake City is the largest and most complete facility in the Church welfare system. It produces and delivers food and clothing and provides other services to needy people in the Salt Lake area. It also supplies and coordinates welfare efforts of the Church in other areas.

The first structures built on Welfare Square, in 1938, were a BISHOP'S STOREHOUSE, a root cellar (now used as a storage building), and a cannery. A milk-processing plant and a 300,000-bushel grain elevator were built in 1941. A new milk-processing plant replaced the old one in 1960, and a new cannery replaced the old one in 1963. The original Bishop's Storehouse was replaced with a larger facility in 1976. In 1981 a Deseret Industries plant and its affiliated store were built on Welfare Square, and an office building to house the Social Services Department and employment services was added in 1983. A bakery was added in 1986.

Welfare Square provides regular employment for about fifty people, and volunteer assistance to run its operations and services is provided on a regular basis by about 200 people from fifty surrounding stakes. Financial support for Welfare Square comes largely from the FAST OFFERINGS of local members.

Most of the recipients of food and services at Welfare Square are members of The Church of Jesus Christ of Latter-day Saints, but there is also a transient service center associated with the Bishop's Storehouse that gives temporary assistance to the homeless of all faiths.

Welfare Square became functionally and symbolically important to the Church in the 1930s and 1940s. It was the flagship of the Church welfare program initiated in the Pioneer Stake in Salt Lake City in 1932. Over the years, the pattern established at Welfare Square has been replicated in more than a hundred Bishop's Storehouse facilities. Welfare Square continues to be the central supplier and coordinator for many of these other locations.

Welfare Square stands for all the principles of welfare advocated and practiced by the Church—industry, work, and caring for the poor and needy. A visitors center is located on Welfare Square to distribute information about the Church welfare program and to teach the principles of the gospel of Jesus Christ concerning social and religious obligations toward those in need.

T. GLENN HAWS

WOMAN'S EXPONENT

The *Woman's Exponent* (1872–1914) was the first publication owned and published by Latter-day Saint women. An eight-page, three-column, quarto (10 inch x 13½ inch) newspaper, it was issued bimonthly, or in later years, monthly. During the forty-two years of its publication, Louisa Lula Greene (1872–1877) and Emmeline B. Wells (1877–1914) served as editors. Although not owned by the Church, the *Exponent* had the approval and encouragement of the GENERAL AUTHORITIES of the Church.

First discussed among RELIEF SOCIETY leaders, the idea of a newspaper exclusively for women came to the attention of Edward L. Sloan, editor of the *Salt Lake Herald*. Not only did he agree with the prospect, but he actively promoted it, suggesting twenty-two-year-old Louisa Lula Greene as editor and the Woman's Exponent as a possible name, and offered help in the form of editorial advice and actual printing until the paper could become established. Reluctant to become the editor because of her lack of experience, Greene said she would consent if her great-uncle, President Brigham Young, would call her to the position as a mission. This he did and gave her a blessing as well.

The number of *Exponent* subscribers is uncertain (perhaps reaching to one thousand or more). However, its influence within, and sometimes outside, the Church was greater than its circulation figures would suggest. One writer declared that it wielded more power in state politics "than all the newspapers in Utah put together" (*Tullidge's Quarterly Magazine*, p. 252). If not quite that important, the paper was widely read and much quoted. Without question, it was a forceful voice for women.

Loyal to the Church and its leaders, the *Exponent* often carried editorials defending the practice of polygamy. The paper's independence made its case the more persuasive since, as one outsider observed, the writers were obviously not "under direction" or "prompted by authority" (Bennion, p. 223).

To the editor of a Chicago paper who wrote of her "amiable and liberal spirit," then-editor Greene responded, "Had we treated it in any other spirit than that of womanly frankness and courtesy we should have done discredit to our home education as well as to the religion we profess, and consequent injustice to our own conscience" (*Woman's Exponent* 2 [Aug. 15, 1873]:44). While this reply may have been of some benefit to Chicago readers, such editorials undoubtedly had their greatest value among LDS women who, reading their own feelings articulated with such surety, were fortified in their sometimes difficult roles.

Principally under the direction of Emmeline B. Wells, the paper vigorously supported woman suffrage and often wrote about it, although the women of Utah had initially been granted voting rights two years before the *Woman's Exponent* began publication. The *Exponent* was also a force in the successful effort to have the voting franchise included in the 1896 Utah constitution. Many other items also found their place, but the topic most often discussed was women's roles, with a closely allied subject of education for women: "the brain should also be instructed how to work, and allowed to expand and improve" (*Woman's Exponent* 1 [Oct. 1, 1872]:69).

Woman's Exponent was not a single-cause paper, unless that cause might have been women and their families. The first edition stated: "The aim of this journal will be to discuss every subject interesting and valuable to women" (*Woman's Exponent* 1 [July 15, 1872]:32). A detailed index of items published during its forty-two years in print reveals how remarkably this purpose was followed.

Along with editorials and articles, the paper published original poems, short stories, and essays written by LDS women and others. It carried regular reports of the PRIMARY, RETRENCHMENT/M.I.A., and Relief Society activities throughout the Church, and published a number of the Society's histories, one written by Emmeline Wells.

Just before the turn of the century, the *Exponent* began having financial problems. In 1914, Wells offered the paper to the Relief Society as its official organ, but was turned down, and the *Exponent* ceased publication in February of that year. It had fulfilled its role in "speaking for women," as it promised it would in the first issue. For forty-two years, *Woman's Exponent* was the voice for women in the Church. The *Bulletin*, and subsequently the *Relief Society Magazine* (1915), became the official organ of the Relief Society.

BIBLIOGRAPHY

Bennion, Sherilyn Cox. "The *Woman's Exponent*: Forty-two Years of Speaking for Women." *Utah Historical Quarterly* 44 (Summer 1976):222–39.

"Emmeline B. Wells." *Tullidge's Quarterly Magazine* 1 (Jan. 1881):250–53.

History of Relief Society, 1842–1966, pp. 95–96. Salt Lake City, 1966.

Robinson, Phil. *Sinners and Saints*. Boston, 1883.

SHIRLEY W. THOMAS

Y

YOUNG MEN

The AARONIC PRIESTHOOD is the basic organization for the young men of the Church, ages twelve through eighteen. The Young Men organization is an auxiliary to the PRIESTHOOD and includes scouting and other programs designed to help with the full development of young male members of the Church, including spiritual, social, and physical aspects. Its purpose is to help each young man come to Christ through conversion to the gospel of Jesus Christ, understand the priesthood he holds, learn to give service to others, prepare to advance to the MELCHIZEDEK PRIESTHOOD, and live in such a way that will qualify him to enter the temple and become a worthy husband and father. Through PRIESTHOOD QUORUM instruction and activities, including combined Young Men and YOUNG WOMEN activities, young men learn fundamental principles and have opportunities to apply them in their lives. The Young Men organization serves hundreds of thousands of young men in most parts of the world. Its literature is published in many languages and is adapted for use in various cultures.

The organization is under the direction of the BISHOPRIC or branch presidency in WARDS and BRANCHES, with assistance from a Young Men presidency comprised of adult advisers to the PRIESTS, TEACHERS, and DEACONS quorums or others as the BISHOP may call. Young Men presidencies also function at the stake and general levels. The Young Men general presidency is comprised of members of the quorums of seventy and is assisted by a general board to develop programs and materials.

The Young Men groups are the priesthood groups, determined by age. Twelve- and thirteen-year-olds constitute the deacons quorum (Scouts); fourteen- and fifteen-year-olds, the teachers quorum (Venturers); and sixteen-, seventeen-, and eighteen-year-olds, the priests quorum (Explorers). Each deacons and teachers quorum is presided over by a three-member presidency. The president from the group is selected by the bishop and he then selects his two counselors. The priests quorum is presided over by the bishop, and he selects assistants from the quorum.

Quorums meet individually or collectively, depending on the type of activity and the purpose of their gathering. On Sundays the quorums usually meet separately for lessons on gospel subjects. On one evening during the week, they may meet for activities, such as scouting, sports, service projects, or career education. Occasionally, all three groups meet together to perform service or to enjoy athletic or cultural events, either as participants or spectators. All activities are designed to help the young men become well-rounded and well-prepared individuals with self-confidence, motivation, and a desire to make a significant contribution to their communities.

Once each month, all three age groups meet together with young women from their ward or branch who are organized into similar age-group categories. These joint activities are designed to help young men and young women learn to work together, to respect one another, and to develop social and communication skills that will help them regard one another as individuals. In addition to the traditional activities of dancing and socializing, they solve problems together and overcome stereotypical gender images, while maintaining strong, independent gender identities. Individuality, creativity, teamwork, a sense of belonging, and unity are stressed by adult Young Men and Young Women advisers.

Primarily in the United States, but in several other countries as well, the Young Men organization uses the scouting movement as part of its activity program. Young men register and participate in scouting and embrace its values and principles while adhering to their own religious and moral code. They are encouraged to earn the Eagle

Scout Award (or its international equivalent). In Great Britain and in other Commonwealth countries, many young men participate in the Duke of Edinburgh Award Scheme or its equivalent. The Church also encourages young men to earn the LDS Duty to God and On My Honor awards, which are religious service recognitions.

LDS young men participate in a wide range of competitive and noncompetitive athletics as part of their quorum experience. Most Church buildings in the United States, for example, are equipped with facilities for playing basketball, and many have adjoining softball diamonds. In Europe, South America, and parts of Asia, soccer is a major part of the Young Men athletic program. Tennis, swimming, racquetball, squash, handball, golf, volleyball, and other popular sports are pursued as tournament events in many Young Men organizations.

In addition to athletic participation, young men are encouraged to develop interest in cultural events by participating in or attending theatrical productions or musical programs. Occasionally wards and stakes sponsor "road shows," in which the young men and young women of each ward write, produce, and perform short plays or skits. Young men may also participate in choral groups, comprised either entirely of young men or, more often, combined with young women, or with youth and adults, such as in a ward or stake choir.

In the decades since its founding, the Young Men organization has undergone many changes in structure, format, frequency of meeting, and leadership, but it has, for the most part, maintained its original purpose and direction: to provide for "the establishment in the youth of individual testimony of the truth and magnitude of the great latter-day work; the development of the gifts within them" (*IE* 1 [Nov. 1897]:3).

Associations for the spiritual and cultural growth of the youth began in the early days of the Church. In February 1843 the Prophet Joseph Smith authorized the formation of a Young Gentlemen's and Young Ladies' Relief Society, and in 1854, Elder Lorenzo Snow organized the Polysophical Society. As Church membership increased, various types of youth societies were organized. President Brigham Young, aware that these organizations were individually good but lacked unity and structure, organized the young men into one association, the Young Men's Mutual Improvement Association (YMMIA), in 1875 (*CHC* 5:480). President Young instructed YMMIA leaders to help the young men develop the gifts within them, stand up and speak, and bear testimony.

With the growth of the association, a central committee (later general board) was formed in December 1876 to oversee all ward YMMIAs, conduct missionary work among the young people, receive reports, and issue general instructions. The central committee recommended that an advisory committee be appointed with some General Authority members. In 1880, Church President John Taylor proposed that a general YMMIA superintendency (later presidency) be formed.

From 1876 to 1905, young men were called to serve full-time YMMIA missions to increase membership and assist local superintendencies. Because of rapid Church growth, this program was discontinued in 1905.

In the first YMMIA meetings, before class study was formalized, all of the young men met together, without regard to age, to hear the lesson. In 1900 a preliminary program of prayer, announcements, and singing was added. In 1901 the YMMIA was divided into junior and senior classes, and social and cultural activities were added to theological studies. An athletic committee, formed in 1909, brought outdoor activities into the junior program by fostering athletic meets. As the programs developed and as needs of the youth changed, Church leaders divided the YMMIA into smaller classes.

Until around 1900 the YMMIA met separately from the Young Women's Mutual Improvement Association (YWMIA). Joining the YWMIA with the YMMIA to form the Mutual Improvement Association (MIA) was another step in strengthening youth programs.

In 1911 the Church formed the YMMIA Scouts, patterned after the Boy Scouts of America (BSA), for young men ages twelve through eighteen. The YMMIA Scouts were later invited to be affiliated with BSA and were issued a national charter on May 21, 1913.

By the 1950s the activities of YMMIA, which included sports, dance, drama, music, and public speaking, were often conducted with the YWMIA as well. Athletics had become a major part of the program. From local stake tournaments, winners progressed to all-Church finals held annually in Salt Lake City. The all-Church tournaments were discontinued in the early 1970s.

The young men ages twelve and older were divided into five classes or age groups, including a Special Interest class for those twenty-six and older. The general level organization at this time consisted of a superintendency of five men and a general board of sixty to seventy men. The general level was financed by a general fund (paid by stakes based on YMMIA membership), sale of YMMIA materials, and investments. General board members instructed local YMMIA and YWMIA leaders.

The 1960s brought changes for both the general and local organizations. The responsibility of training local leaders gradually shifted to local priesthood leaders, significantly reducing the size of the general board and simplifying its responsibilities. The general fund was discontinued, and all finances were handled by the Church. Production and sales of materials were also centralized.

Early in the 1970s the YMMIA was divided into separate youth and adult organizations. In November 1972 the Church organized two priesthood-oriented MIAs: the Aaronic Priesthood—MIA for young men ages twelve through seventeen, and the Melchizedek Priesthood—MIA, or Special Interests, for unmarried men ages eighteen and older. At this time, the MIA became part of the priesthood and was no longer an auxiliary. The Aaronic Priesthood—MIA conducted lessons, service projects, and activities centered around the Aaronic Priesthood quorums.

In June 1974 the name Aaronic Priesthood—MIA was shortened to Aaronic Priesthood. For a time, the organization was under the jurisdiction of the Presiding Bishopric and there was no general presidency. However, in May 1977 the name was changed to Young Men and a general presidency was reinstated. In October 1979 the Church announced that the Young Men general presidency would be comprised of three General Authorities from the First Quorum of the Seventy. Since 1989, the small general board has been made up of the deacon, teacher, and priest committees.

BIBLIOGRAPHY

Anderson, Edward H. "The Past of Mutual Improvement." *IE* 1 (Nov. 1897):1–10.

Strong, Leon M. "A History of the Young Men's Mutual Improvement Association 1875–1938." Master's thesis, Brigham Young University, 1939.

Williams, John Kent. "A History of the Young Men's Mutual Improvement Association 1939 to 1974." Master's thesis, Brigham Young University, 1976.

CHARLES E. MITCHENER
MARK E. HURST

YOUNG WOMAN'S JOURNAL

A monthly magazine published in Salt Lake City from 1889 to 1929, *Young Woman's Journal* served the young female members of The Church of Jesus Christ of Latter-day Saints and their leaders. Susa Young Gates conceived the idea of a magazine for girls and was encouraged by the FIRST PRESIDENCY and the YOUNG WOMEN general presidency to publish one.

The first issue appeared in October 1889, with Susa Young Gates as managing editor, business manager, subscription manager, art director, and manager of all the other details. Although the Church encouraged publication, it did not provide financial assistance, and the *Journal* was plagued with financial problems for the first ten years. However, printing the 1899 lessons for the Young Women classes increased the number of subscribers, thus reducing the financial strains. Because the subscription of the magazine was $1 per year, very few young women could actually subscribe; additionally, it was directed mostly to their teachers and leaders. Initially published privately, and only later by the Church, the *Journal* was nonetheless the official organ of the Young Women's Mutual Improvement Association (in 1977 Young Women). Succeeding editors included May B. Talmage (1900–1902), Ann M. Cannon (1902–1907), Mary Connelly Kimball (1907–1923), Clarissa Beesley (1923–1929), and Elsie Talmage Brandley (1929).

The publication featured articles on theology, fashion, literature, marriage, housekeeping, hygiene, gardening, and ethics, and talks by GENERAL AUTHORITIES and Young Women leaders. It also printed recipes and patterns for sewing and handiwork, as well as short stories, poems, and lesson guides.

At the June 1929 conference, the decision was made to combine the *Young Woman's Journal* and the Young Men's IMPROVEMENT ERA into one publication to serve both youth organizations. Elsie Talmage Brandley, the last editor of the *Journal*, became an associate editor of the *Improvement Era*.

BIBLIOGRAPHY

Josephson, Marba C. *A History of YWMIA*, pp. 109–21. Salt Lake City, 1955.

PETREA GILLESPIE KELLY

YOUNG WOMEN

The Young Women program of the Church in 1990 reached an international membership of one million young women between the ages of twelve and eighteen. It sponsored weekly meetings and classes with prepared manuals. It extended a full range of activity programs for young women that relate to their intellectual and spiritual growth, physical fitness, speech, drama, music, dance, vocational and home-making talents, outdoor and camping skills, and leadership development.

The Young Women organization began as the Cooperative RETRENCHMENT ASSOCIATION in November 1869. President Brigham Young organized the society in the Lion House, his official residence in Salt Lake City, with his daughters as charter members. He challenged them to grow spiritually, to resist idleness and gossip, to retrench from the styles of the world in dress and deportment, and thus to be proper examples of Latter-day Saints. They were not to give in to rude or harsh frontier ways. The poet and Relief Society President Eliza R. Snow became the supervisor of the new association, and Ella V. Empey, age twenty-three, was chosen as president.

The leaders designed a retrenchment costume, conservative in comparison to the high fashion of the day (no furbelows, flounces, or ruffles), with skirts to boot tops, pantaloons beneath, and necklines to the base of the throat.

By 1870 each ward in Salt Lake Valley had its own similar young women's organization with its own stated resolutions. The "one central thought" in all resolutions was "electing a greater simplicity of dress and of living; and . . . cultivating the mind rather than ministering to the pleasure of the body" (Gates, pp. 60–61). For example, the Fourteenth Ward resolved: "Feeling that we have worshipped at the shrine of fashion too long [we] do solemnly pledge ourselves to retrench in our dress, and to wear only that which is becoming to women professing to be Saints" (Gates, p. 61). And the Eighth Ward resolved: "Inasmuch as order is the first law of heaven, we will endeavor to learn the law by making ourselves acquainted with the principles of life and salvation. We will study the Bible, Book of Mormon, Doctrine and Covenants, and all works pertaining to our holy religion. . . . We will also study all literature that will qualify us to become ornaments in the kingdom of God, that we may merit the approbation of our brethren and sisters and of God. . . . We will not speak evil of anyone, but will be kind to all, especially the aged and infirm, the widow and orphan. We will endeavor to become acquainted with the laws of nature, that we may become strong, healthy and vigorous" (Gates, pp. 64–65).

In 1871 the leaders renamed the society "YL," short for Young Ladies' Retrenchment Association. They focused on the teenage girls by sponsoring weekly meetings, charitable deeds, instruction in public speaking, and lively discussions of the gospel and current events. A modest exercise program consisted of ball bouncing and throwing, knee bends, and side stretches. Later they introduced croquet.

The program expanded and flourished. Eliza R. Snow and her women companions traveled throughout the territory of Deseret in wagons pulled by oxen, and usually acted as their own teamsters. Fervent prayer, a few candles, baskets of bread and molasses, and personal enthusiasm for the cause kept them going.

Following Ella Empey, the presidents of the organization were as follows: Elmina S. Taylor (1880–1904), Martha Horne Tingey (1905–1929), Ruth May Fox (1929–1937), Lucy Grant Cannon (1937–1948), Bertha S. Reeder (1948–1961), Florence S. Jacobsen (1961–1972), Ruth Hardy Funk (1972–1978), Elaine Anderson Cannon (1978–1984), and Ardeth G. Kapp (1985–).

In 1875 an organization similar to YL was established for young men. It was called The Young Men's Mutual Improvement Association, and the goal was "personal improvement rather than entertainment." The two organizations soon began monthly conjoint meetings. In 1877 the YL name was changed to Young Ladies National Mutual Improvement Association to correlate with the young men's group and to reflect the growth of many units in many places across the nation. The first general conference for the YLN-MIA was held April 4, 1880. Leaders admonished those attending to find new ways to teach girls how to develop every gift and grace of true womanhood.

Supportive efforts were developed. Susa Young Gates had personally published a magazine called *Young Woman's Journal* and now gave one-third of its space to the YL organization. A guide for all YL groups was printed, containing lessons and instructions for the girls and leaders and even ideas for beautifying the meetingplaces with pretty cloths and flowers. Typical lesson outlines included "What is the meaning of the word 'Chastity'?" and "Why have you not the right to take the pin comb out of your sister's drawer?" A favorite couplet became: "One cheerful face in a household will keep everything bright—put envy, selfishness, despondency to shame and flight." Tuesday night became "Mutual" night for both boys and girls. The weekly talent programs, preceding separate lesson sessions for Young Ladies and Young Men, attracted large groups of young people, including many of other faiths.

In 1880 several prominent Utah women attended the first National Suffrage Convention in Washington, D.C. Church President John Taylor sent them with his blessing and the reminder that the Mormon women enjoyed voting and other rights afforded few other women in the country. Both the YL and Relief Society organizations became charter members of the National Council of Women of the United States and of the International Council of Women.

In 1886 and 1887, semi-annual training conferences for YL were held at the time of general conferences of the Church in April and October. In 1888, the first annual June Conference for Young Women and Young Men organizations was held. Leaders provided special training in physical activity, story-telling, and music and class instruction. Four decades later, in 1929, they launched a new camping program for girls. In 1929 they combined *Young Woman's Journal* and *Improvement Era*, to make one magazine for young men and young women. President Heber J. Grant was editor, with Elsie Talmage Brandley as associate editor and Hugh J. Cannon as managing editor. During this period they introduced the hymn "Carry On" as the anthem for LDS youth. Ruth May Fox wrote the words and Alfred M. Durham the music. They adopted the scriptural statement, "The glory of God is intelligence" (D&C 93:36) as the motto for both groups.

The Lion House, birthplace of the Retrenchment Association, became a cultural and social center for many young women. Young women received cultural enrichment through reviews and lessons in charm. Their service projects included wrapping bandages for soldiers and knitting baby clothing and shawls for the Primary Children's Hospital. At the National Council of Women exhibit at the

Century of Progress Fair in Chicago in 1932, LDS Young Women leaders gave a demonstration on the monumental accomplishments of women in the previous one hundred years.

In the 1930s, leaders gave new emphasis to music, dance, and the performing arts. They published a recreational song book, and sociable singing became popular. They sponsored ten-minute musical programs or "road shows" that were locally created and rehearsed and then presented in successive wards in each LDS stake. They sent instructions in music and dance from Church headquarters to all MIA units, many of which then participated in an annual June Conference dance festival, a spectacle of choreography with up to 2,000 participants each year. Social dancing was also featured in the ward and stake houses, and "Gold and Green Balls," featuring the MIA colors, became popular events throughout the Church.

In 1937 Lucy Grant Cannon became president of the YWMIA. She organized the youth according to age and interest, with special manuals, incentive programs, and symbols that fostered development and recreation for all girls twelve years of age and over. She introduced an annual theme to be memorized and recited at every MIA meeting throughout the world. For example, in 1941 the theme was, "I, the Lord, am bound when ye do what I say; but when ye do not what I say, ye have no promise" (D&C 82:10). Manuals were written in Salt Lake City but adapted to the needs and customs of non-English speaking members of the Church. By 1948, during the administration of President Bertha S. Reeder, coordination, translation, and communication with the youth presidencies worldwide were a great challenge and new programs were created. Increasingly general board members were sent on weekend convention tours to present programs in activities, dance, drama, music, athletics, and camping.

In the late 1940s and 1950s, the First Presidency turned over to the YWMIA the girls enrollment incentive program that had been previously administered by the Presiding Bishopric. It was designed to increase attendance at all Church meetings. Individual awards were presented annually to qualifying youth at ward sacrament meetings.

In this period the Young Men and Young Women leaders initiated stake youth conferences that grew into major events. Sometimes they combined youth from multiple stakes for workshops, discussion groups, or meetings with keynote speakers from Church head-quarters. They reinforced dress and dating standards and stressed morality. They generated a series of posters with full-color illustrations called "Be Honest With Yourself." These included such admonitions as "Virtue Is Its Own Reward," "Great Men Pray," and "Temple Marriage Is Forever." They distributed wallet and purse-size reproductions to the Church youth. In 1960 they launched *Era of Youth*, an insert for youth in the monthly *Improvement Era*, with Elaine Cannon and Marion D. Hanks as editors. They prepared and announced musical productions from Church headquarters. In 1960 hundreds of stakes sponsored and produced the musical pageant "Promised Valley" by Crawford Gates, which celebrated the 1847 trek of the Mormon pioneers across the plains and into the Salt Lake Valley.

By the 1960s work for sixty or more women on the general board became a full-time Church assignment. Subcommittees prepared new manuals, programs, leadership training, and special youth confer-ences.

Youth leaders sponsored the restoration and full renovation of the Lion House for the centennial celebration of the organization of the first Young Ladies' group, November 18, 1869. The new Young Women general president, Florence Smith Jacobsen, placed a prayer bell in a niche in the front hall of the Lion House with a brass plaque describing how Brigham Young used it to call his daughters together to form the Retrenchment Association. A historical publication, *A Century of Sisterhood*, was also prepared. New full-color manuals were introduced to lead the girls forward from Beehives, named to symbolize industry and dedication, to Gleaner Girls, whose biblical model was Ruth. Girls sixteen to eighteen had been named Junior Girls, but were soon called Laurels with appropriate symbols, songs, and motto.

An elaborate June Conference was held in 1969, with many for-eign countries represented. An early morning reception on Temple Square was followed by banquets, dance festivals, musicals, dramatic readings, road show presentations, camp training in the nearby mountains, athletic seminars, and testimony meetings. The final general session was held in the Tabernacle on Sunday.

Church President Harold B. Lee in the early 1970s introduced a correlation program designed to integrate many Church programs for youth. The new Young Women president, Ruth H. Funk, and the general presidencies and boards of other Church auxiliary organizations began to meet with priesthood leaders to formulate and initiate the best possible spiritual and social experiences for youth. Coordinated with departments of instructional development, audio-visual materials, library resources, and translation, they subordinated all other activities to the quest for spirituality. From this effort came the personal progress program and the young womanhood achievement awards. June Conference was replaced by regional training meetings under the direction of the priesthood. Under the aegis of Church correlation, a special magazine was introduced: *New Era*, a magazine for youth twelve to eighteen.

Elaine Anderson Cannon, as Young Women president in 1978, called twelve women with daughters between the ages of twelve and eighteen to serve on a governing board. Young women were encouraged to "prepare themselves to perform": to develop a personal testimony of Jesus, study the scriptures, and share the truth. They were to keep personal diaries, gather family histories and genealogy, set educational goals, and strengthen their families.

In 1980, at the Church's sesquicentennial celebration, a Days of '47 parade opened with 1,500 Young Women in white dresses forming a phalanx a full city block long and marching to the beat of 100 young trumpet and drum instrumentalists. Each girl carried her own three-by-five-foot banner mounted on a tall staff. Each banner was embroidered, quilted, appliqued, or painted to depict the girl's personal goals. This activity was repeated by other young women across the world in local celebrations.

During this period Sunday classes for Young Women began to be held at the same time as priesthood meeting for Young Men. This focus on gospel principles was carried into activity programs on weekday evenings. The consolidated schedule of all Sunday meetings required new manuals that featured units of study and in-depth training on principles and practices relevant to a girl's life. Preparation for the temple endowment was stressed for Young

Women. Teachers of Sunday classes applied the manuals to timely local needs. Leadership training was conducted through special prototype discussion groups. "Open house" displays during general conference allowed for one-on-one conversations between stake Young Women leaders and priesthood leaders across the Church. Special helps were given leaders to assist in spiritual presentation of Sunday lessons. General board representatives held area conferences combining many stakes and regions in two-day sessions, and training sessions were given for Young Women and Relief Society leadership.

In this same period the presidency introduced semi-annual General Women's meetings. Under the direction of the First Presidency, these meetings were held shortly before general conference week. Representative women leaders and General Authorities spoke. Women and girls from age ten were invited to attend, and some participated in special choruses. The meetings were held in the Tabernacle in Salt Lake City and were broadcast via satellite.

President Ardeth Kapp introduced the Young Women motto, "We stand for truth and righteousness." She made a presentation to the U.S. Attorney General's program against pornography and continued this effort as a member of a national task force. In the tradition of Brigham Young's challenge, she encouraged girls to become "bell-ringers" or special examples to others in word, conversation, charity, faith, and purity. Her presidency focused on seven values for the Young Women program, each with a symbolic color and definitive direction: Faith, Divine Nature, Individual Worth, Knowledge, Choice and Accountability, Good Works, and Integrity. On the same day and at the same time, a special program sponsored Churchwide the release of helium-filled balloons carrying the testimony and commitment to these ideals of the young women of the Church.

Over the years, whatever the variations in programs and organizational structure, the emphasis among young women on being true daughters of God in appearance, demeanor, and testimony has not changed. Young Women units worldwide welcome nonmembers to participate in the personal progress program, to draw closer to Jesus Christ, and to increase their knowledge of eternal principles and appreciation for the worth and potential of their own souls.

BIBLIOGRAPHY
Evans, Joyce O., et al. *A Century of Sisterhood, 1869–1969*. Salt Lake City, 1970.
Gates, Susa Young. *History of the Young Ladies' Mutual Improvement Associations*. Salt Lake City, 1911.
Josephson, Marba C. *History of YWMIA*. Salt Lake City, 1956.

ELAINE ANDERSON CANNON

YOUTH

The Church defines "youth" as all men and women ages twelve to eighteen. Church policies and programs for youth are designed to help them make the transition from childhood to young adulthood with feelings of confidence and well-being, avoiding the pitfalls of adolescence, gaining more mature testimonies of the gospel of Jesus Christ, and drawing closer to their families and the Church.

The Church expects full participation from youth, who plan and administer many of their own activities, share the gospel with others, serve as examples of LDS teachings to their friends, render Christian service in the Church and community, and participate in baptisms for the dead in the TEMPLE. They also receive leadership and speaking assignments and are taught to be examples to other members of their families and WARDS.

Young people in the Church sometimes are referred to as "youth of the noble birthright," sons and daughters of God, born at this time in the earth's history for a sacred purpose. Although the moral climate and religious values of society seem to be weakening, the youth of the Church are asked to be "standard bearers" and lights to guide others to Jesus Christ. Each individual is considered by the Church to have a purpose for and mission in life, and adolescents are asked to draw near to the Lord to learn how best to fulfill that purpose (*see* PATRIARCHAL BLESSINGS). LDS youth are taught that they can function in and contribute to society without participating in its ills (John 17:15).

Not all LDS youth desire the same level of participation in Church programs, although the level of activity is high as compared to youth in many other religious traditions. Most LDS youth organizations try to understand and accommodate individual differences and competing claims for young people's time. However, if an individual seems to be drifting from the Church or to be involved with undesirable or dangerous activities, Church resource care is made available to aid the family in helping the youth find a healthier and happier path.

Young men and young women of the Church are guided by adult advisers, who also teach the quorums and classes. Each quorum and class has a youth presidency that conducts meetings, involves group members in class experiences, and helps plan and carry out activities. Each group follows a prescribed course of study, and group members are encouraged to build friendships with each other and to encourage and strengthen each other in keeping the standards of the Church.

Church programs for youth are designed to support parents in preparing their children to live responsible adult lives as faithful Christians. Parents and youth often are involved in events and activities together. Youth are encouraged to seek parental counsel, share experiences with parents and siblings, and help strengthen family bonds.

The AARONIC PRIESTHOOD and the YOUNG MEN and YOUNG WOMEN organizations provide the major avenues for Church-sponsored youth activity. The purpose of the Aaronic Priesthood and Young Men organizations is identical: to help each young man come to Christ, become converted to the gospel, respect and fulfill his priesthood callings, give meaningful service, and prepare to receive the Melchizedek Priesthood, serve a full-time mission, and become an honorable husband and father.

The purpose of the Young Women program is similar: Each young woman is to become converted to the gospel, strengthen her testimony of the Heavenly Father and Jesus Christ, recognize her identity as a daughter of God, and be a witness for God by living the Young Women Values: Faith, Divine Nature, Individual Worth, Knowledge, Choice and Accountability, Good Works, and Integrity. Each young woman is encouraged to keep covenants that she made at baptism, prepare spiritually for temple ordinances, and appreciate the importance of service as a wife and mother.

The missions and purposes of the youth programs are mutually supportive. As young men and women meet together to be taught, to share activities, and to give service, they gain leadership experience.

This combined youth program helps young men and women learn to appreciate each other, to understand and value strengths and differences, and to prepare for responsible adulthood. Their shared values help them reinforce the commitment of all to the gospel.

Young Men–Young Women combined activities are regularly planned by the BISHOP or BRANCH PRESIDENT and Ward Youth Council. Youth leaders represent their peers and counsel with their leaders in making the decisions and solving the problems associated with planning and implementing activities. The Church youth programs include a range of wholesome activities in addition to lessons, speakers, discussion groups, and service projects. Sports and physical fitness, camping, Boy Scouts of America, socials, conferences, skills training, and opportunities in drama, dance, and music are encouraged. Sharing such experiences helps youth to meet the social, physical, cultural, and emotional/spiritual needs. Additional study of the scriptures is provided to high school students through the Church Educational System seminary program.

Because the standards of the Church are different from the standards acceptable to much of the world, LDS youth face many significant decisions, expectations, and pressures. They are encouraged to seek all things good and virtuous both inside and outside the Church (see A of F 13) and to decide early in life to build their testimonies and remain faithful to the teachings of Jesus Christ.

BIBLIOGRAPHY

Aaronic Priesthood-Young Men Handbook. Salt Lake City, 1977.
Benson, Ezra T. *To Young Men of the Priesthood*. Salt Lake City, 1986.
New Era 18 (March, 1988):5–67.
Young Women Handbook. Salt Lake City, 1988.

ARDETH GREENE KAPP

APPENDIX 1

This register contains basic biographical information on all persons sustained as General Church Officers in the general Church conferences since the Church was organized on April 6, 1830. The entries are listed alphabetically for ease of reference. For a list of general officers of the Church in the chronology of their being called, *see* Appendix 3, General Church Officers, A Chronology.

Where the information is available, the entry includes general Church calling(s) and date(s); birth and death dates and places; family information such as spouse and number of children; vocation at time of calling; former Church service positions (stake, mission, or temple president; regional representative; or general board office). Although the names of some of the auxiliary organizations have changed through the years, references use only the current names. Because public records for many plural marriages do not exist, it was decided to list only that the man practiced plural marriage when that is known rather than give partial or incomplete marriage information.

ABREA, Angel. Seventy, April 4, 1981; b. Sept. 13, 1933, Buenos Aires, Argentina; married Maria Victoria Chiapparino, three children; certified public accountant; regional representative, temple and mission president.

ALDRICH, Hazen. Seventy, Feb. 28, 1835; released April 6, 1837, having previously been ordained a high priest.

AMADO, Carlos H. (Humberto). Seventy, April 7, 1989; b. Sept. 25, 1944, Guatemala City, Guatemala; m. Mayavel Pineda, six children; Church Educational System area director; regional representative, mission and stake president.

ANDERSEN, H. (Hans) Verlan. Seventy, April 6, 1986–Oct. 5, 1991; b. Nov. 6, 1914, Logan, Utah; m. Shirley Hoyt Anderson, eleven children; emeritus educator; stake president.

ANDERSEN, Lucy Taylor. Second counselor to general president Lucy Grant Cannon, Young Women, July 1944–April 6, 1948; b. Aug. 26, 1900, Salt Lake City, Utah; d. June 18, 1978, Salt Lake City; m. Waldo M. Andersen, one child; homemaker.

ANDERSON, Helen Woodruff. Second counselor to general president Belle S. Spafford, Relief Society, Jan. 1957–Aug. 1958; b. Jan. 1, 1901, Salt Lake City, Utah; d. June 7, 1990, Salt Lake City; m. Alexander P. Anderson, five children; homemaker; Relief Society general board member, stake Relief Society president.

ANDERSON, Joseph. Asst. to the Twelve, April 6, 1970; Seventy, Oct. 1, 1976; Emeritus General Authority, Dec. 31, 1978; b. Nov. 20, 1889, Salt Lake City, Utah; m. Norma Peterson, three children; secretary to the First Presidency.

ANDERSON, May. First counselor to general president Louie B. Felt, Primary, Dec. 29, 1905–Oct. 6, 1925; General president, Oct. 6, 1925–Sept. 11, 1939; b. June 8, 1864, Liverpool, England; d. June 10, 1946, Salt Lake City, Utah; editor, *Children's Friend*, 1902–1940.

ARRINGTON, Leonard J. (James). Church historian, Jan. 14, 1972–June 26, 1980; b. July 2, 1917, Twin Falls, Idaho; m. Grace Fort (d. 1983), three children; m. Harriet Ann Horne; educator.

ASAY, Carlos E. (Egan). Seventy, April 3, 1976; b. June 12, 1926, Sutherland, Utah; m. Colleen Webb, seven children; educator; regional representative, mission president.

ASHTON, Marvin J. (Jeremy). Asst. to the Twelve, Oct. 3, 1969; Apostle, Dec. 2, 1971; b. May 6, 1915, Salt Lake City, Utah; m. Norma Bernston, four children; businessman; Boy Scouts of America national committee member.

ASHTON, Marvin O. (Owen). First counselor to Presiding Bishop LeGrand Richards, April 6, 1938–Oct. 7, 1946; b. April 8, 1883, Salt Lake City, Utah; d. Oct. 7, 1946, Salt Lake City; m. Rae Jeremy, seven children; businessman; stake president.

AYALA, Eduardo. Seventy, Mar. 31, 1990; b. May 3, 1937, Coronel, Chile; m. Blanca Ester Espinoza, three children; business management; regional representative, mission and stake president.

BACKMAN, Robert L. (LeGrand). Second counselor to general president W. Jay Eldredge, Young Men, June 25–Nov. 9, 1972; general president,

Nov. 9, 1972–June 23, 1974; Seventy, April 1, 1978; b. Mar. 22, 1922, Salt Lake City, Utah; m. Virginia Pickett, seven children; attorney and state legislator; regional representative, mission and stake president.

BADGER, Rodney C. (Carlos). Second counselor to general president Junius F. Wells, Young Men, 1876–1880; b. Sept. 8, 1848, Salt Lake City, Utah; d. April 12, 1923, Salt Lake City; m. Harriet Ann Whitaker Taylor; practiced plural marriage, seventeen children on record; businessman.

BAIRD, J. (Joseph) Hugh. Second counselor to general president Richard L. Warner, Sunday School, Aug. 1979–Oct. 1979; b. July 25, 1929, Salt Lake City, Utah; m. Florence Richards, nine children; educator; Sunday School general board member.

BALLARD, M. (Melvin) Russell, Jr. Seventy, April 3, 1976; Apostle, Oct. 10, 1985; b. Oct. 8, 1928; m. Barbara Bowen, seven children; businessman; mission president.

BALLARD, Melvin J. (Joseph). Apostle, Jan. 7, 1919–July 30, 1939; b. Feb. 9, 1873, Logan, Utah; d. July 30, 1939, Salt Lake City; m. Martha Annabelle Jones, eight children; businessman, civic leader; mission president.

BANGERTER, William Grant. Asst. to the Twelve, April 4, 1975; Seventy, Oct. 1, 1976; b. June 8, 1918, Granger, Utah; m. Mildred Schwantes (d. 1952), three children; m. Geraldine Hamblin, seven children; building contractor; regional representative, mission president.

BANKS, Ben B. (Berry). Seventy, April 7, 1989; b. April 4, 1932, Murray, Utah; m. Susan Kearnes, seven children; businessman; mission and stake president.

BARKER, Kate Montgomery. Second counselor to general president Louise Yates Robinson, Relief Society, April 3, 1935–Dec. 1939; b. May 30, 1881, North Ogden, Utah; d. Feb. 13, 1972, Salt Lake City; m. James L. Barker, three children.

BARRATT, Matilda Morehouse W. First counselor to general president Louie B. Felt, Primary, June 19, 1880–Oct. 1888; b. Jan. 17, 1837, Stockport, England; d. April 14, 1902; m. John Barratt, four children.

BEEBE, Clara M. Woodruff. Second counselor to general president Louie B. Felt, Primary, Dec. 29, 1906–Oct. 6, 1925; b. July 23, 1868, Salt Lake City, Utah; d. Dec. 27, 1927; m. Ovando C. Beebe, eight children.

BEESLEY, Clarissa Alice. Second counselor to general president Ruth May Fox, Young Women, Mar. 30, 1929–Oct. 1937; b. Nov. 13, 1878, Salt Lake City, Utah; d. July 7, 1974, Salt Lake City.

BENNETT, Emily Higgs. First counselor to general president Bertha S. Reeder, Young Women, June 13, 1948–Sept. 30, 1961; b. June 27, 1896, Salt Lake City, Utah; d. Mar. 19, 1985, Salt Lake City; m. Harold H. Bennett, eight children; homemaker; Young Women general board member.

BENNETT, John C. (Cook). Assistant President with the First Presidency, April 8, 1841; disfellowshipped, May 25, 1842; excommunicated 1842; b. Aug. 3, 1804, Fair Haven, Massachusetts; d. Aug. 5, 1867, Polk City, Iowa.

BENNETT, William H. (Hunter). Asst. to the Twelve, April 6, 1970; Seventy, Oct. 1, 1976; Emeritus General Authority, Dec. 31, 1978; b. Nov. 5, 1910, Taber, Alberta, Canada; d. July 23, 1980, Bountiful, Utah; m. Patricia June Christiansen, six children; educator; regional representative, stake president.

BENNION, Adam S. (Samuel). Apostle, April 9, 1953–Feb. 11, 1958; b. Dec. 2, 1886, Taylorsville, Utah; d. Feb. 11, 1958, Salt Lake City; m. Minerva Young, five children; educator, general superintendent of Church Schools; Sunday School general board member.

BENNION, Milton. First asst. to general superintendent George D. Pyper, Sunday School, Oct. 1934–May 1943; general superintendent, May 1943–Sept. 1949; b. June 7, 1870, Salt Lake City, Utah; d. April 5, 1953, Salt Lake City; m. Cora Lindsay, eleven children; educator; Sunday School general board member.

BENNION, Samuel O. (Otis). Seventy, April 6, 1933–Mar. 8, 1945; b. June 9, 1874, Taylorsville, Utah; d. Mar. 8, 1945, Salt Lake City; m. Charlotte Trowler, two children; newspaper executive; mission president.

BENSON, Ezra T. (Taft). Apostle, July 16, 1846–Sept. 3, 1869; b. Feb. 22, 1811, Mendon, Massachusetts; d. Sept. 3, 1869, Ogden, Utah; m. Pamelia Andrus; practiced plural marriage, thirty-four children on record; businessman-contractor; mission president.

BENSON, Ezra Taft. Apostle, Oct. 7, 1943; President of the Quorum of the Twelve Apostles, Dec. 30, 1973; President of the Church, Nov. 10, 1985; b. Aug. 4, 1899, Idaho; m. Flora Smith Amussen, six children; farm bureau executive, U.S. Secretary of Agriculture in President Eisenhower's cabinet; mission and stake president.

BENTLEY, Joseph T. (Taylor). General superintendent, Young Men, July 21, 1958–Oct. 6, 1962; b. Mar. 6, 1906, Colonia Juárez, Chihuahua, Mexico; m. Kathleen Bench, six children; certified public accountant, educator; mission president.

BILLINGS, Titus. Second counselor to Presiding Bishop Edward Partridge, Aug. 1, 1837; released at the death of Bishop Partridge, May 27, 1840; b. Mar. 24 or 25, 1793, Greenfield, Massachusetts; d. Feb. 6, 1866, Provo, Utah; m. Diantha Morely; practiced plural marriage, nineteen children on record; carpenter.

BOWEN, Albert E. (Ernest). Apostle, April 8, 1937–July 15, 1953; b. Oct. 31, 1875, Henderson Creek, Idaho; d. July 15, 1953, Salt Lake City, Utah; m. Aletha E. Reeder (d. 1906), two children; m. Emma Lucy Gates; attorney; Young Men general board member.

BOYER, Marian L. Richards. Second counselor to general president Barbara B. Smith, Relief Society, Oct. 3, 1974–Nov. 1978; First counselor, Nov. 1978–April 7, 1984; b. Dec. 31, 1912, Salt Lake City, Utah; m. Harold Boyer, five children; homemaker; Relief Society general board member, stake Relief Society president.

BOYLE, Dessie (Martha Deseret) Grant. Second counselor to general president Adele Cannon Howells, Primary, July 20, 1943–April 14, 1951; b. April 21, 1886, Liverpool, England; d. Sept. 18, 1970, Salt Lake City, Utah; m. Ashby D. Boyle, five children.

BOYNTON, John F. (Farnham). Apostle, Feb. 15, 1835–Sept. 3, 1837; disfellowshipped, Sept. 3, 1837; excommunicated same year; b. Sept. 20, 1811, Bradford, Massachusetts; d. Oct. 20, 1890, Syracuse, New York; m. Susannah (Susan) Lowell (d.), five children; m. Caroline Foster Harriman; businessman.

BRADFORD, William R. (Rawsel). Seventy, Oct. 3, 1975; b. Oct. 25, 1933, Springville, Utah; m. Mary Ann Bird, six children; businessman; mission president.

BREWERTON, Ted E. (Eugene). Seventy, Sept. 30, 1978; b. Mar. 30, 1925, Raymond, Alberta, Canada; m. Dorothy Hall, six children; pharmacist; regional representative, mission and stake president.

BROCKBANK, Bernard P. (Park). Asst. to the Twelve, Oct. 6, 1962; Seventy, Oct. 1, 1976; Emeritus General Authority, Oct. 4, 1980;

b. May 24, 1909, Salt Lake City, Utah; m. Nada Rich (d. 1967), six children; m. Frances Morgan; building contractor; mission president.

BROUGH, Monte J. (James). Seventy, Oct. 1, 1988; b. June 11, 1939, Randolph, Utah; m. Lanette Barker, seven children; businessman; regional representative, mission president.

BROWN, Hugh B. (Brown). Asst. to the Twelve, Oct. 4, 1953; Apostle, April 10, 1958–Dec. 2, 1975; Second counselor to President McKay, Oct. 12, 1961; First counselor, Oct. 4, 1963; released at the death of President McKay, Jan. 18, 1970, and returned to the Quorum of the Twelve; b. Oct. 24, 1883, Granger, Utah; d. Dec. 2, 1975, Salt Lake City; m. Zina Young Card, eight children; attorney, educator; mission and stake president.

BROWN, Victor L. (Lee). Second counselor to Presiding Bishop John H. Vandenberg, Sept. 30, 1961; Presiding Bishop, April 6, 1972; Seventy, April 6, 1985; Emeritus General Authority, Oct. 1, 1989; b. July 31, 1914, Cardston, Alberta, Canada; m. Lois Kjar, five children; business executive; temple president.

BUEHNER, Carl W. (William). Second counselor to Presiding Bishop Joseph L. Wirthlin, April 6, 1952–Sept. 30, 1961; Second assistant to general superintendent Joseph T. Bentley, Young Men, Oct. 25, 1961–Oct. 1967; b. Dec. 27, 1898, Stuttgart, Germany; d. Nov. 18, 1974, Salt Lake City, Utah; m. Lucile Thurman, three children; business executive; regional representative, stake president.

BURTON, Robert T. (Taylor). Second counselor to Presiding Bishop Edward Hunter, Oct. 9, 1874; First counselor to Presiding Bishop William B. Preston, Oct. 5, 1884–Nov. 11, 1907; b. Oct. 25, 1821, Amherstburg, Ontario, Canada; d. Nov. 11, 1907, Salt Lake City, Utah; m. Maria Susan Haven; practiced plural marriage, twenty-seven children on record; sheriff.

BURTON, Theodore M. (Moyle). Asst. to the Twelve, Oct. 8, 1960; Seventy, Oct. 1, 1976; Emeritus General Authority, Oct. 1, 1989; b. Mar. 27, 1907, Salt Lake City, Utah; d. Dec. 22, 1989, Salt Lake City; m. Minnie Susan Preece, one child; educator; mission president.

BUSCHE, F. (Friedrich) Enzio. Seventy, Oct. 1, 1977; b. April 5, 1930, Dortmund, Germany; m. Jutta Baum, four children; business executive; regional representative, temple and mission president.

BUTTERFIELD, Josiah. Seventy, April 6, 1837; excommunicated, Oct. 7, 1844; b. Mar. 13 or 18, 1795, Saco, Maine; d. April 1871, Watsonville, California; m. Polly Mouton, one child.

CALL, Waldo P. (Pratt). Seventy, April 6, 1985–Oct. 6, 1990; b. Feb. 5, 1928, Colonia Juárez, Mexico; m. Beverly Johnson, seven children (d. 1986); m. LaRayne Whetten; farmer; regional representative, stake president.

CALLIS, Charles A. (Albert). Apostle, Oct. 12, 1933–Jan. 21, 1947; b. May 4, 1865, Dublin, Ireland; d. Jan. 21, 1947, Jacksonville, Florida; m. Grace E. Pack, eight children; attorney; mission president.

CAMARGO, Helio R. (da Rocha). Seventy, April 6, 1985–Oct. 6, 1990; b. Feb. 1, 1926, Resende, Brazil; m. Nair Belmira de Gouvea, six children; farmer and ret. Brazilian Army officer; regional representative, stake president.

CANNON, Abraham H. (Hoagland). Seventy, Oct. 8, 1882; Apostle, Oct. 7, 1889–July 19, 1896; b. Mar. 12, 1859, Salt Lake City, Utah; d. July 19, 1896, Salt Lake City; m. Sarah Ann Jenkins; practiced plural marriage, seventeen children on record.

CANNON, Clare Cordelia Moses. Second counselor to general president Louie B. Felt, Primary, June 19, 1880–Oct. 4, 1895; b. April 21, 1839, Westfield, Massachusetts; d. Aug. 21, 1926, Centerville, Utah; m. William H. Mason (d. 1860), two children; m. Angus M. Cannon, three children.

CANNON, Elaine Anderson. General president, Young Women, July 12, 1978–April 7, 1984; b. April 9, 1922, Salt Lake City, Utah; m. D. James Cannon, six children; editor "Era for Youth" in *Improvement Era*.

CANNON, George I. (Ivins). Seventy, April 6, 1986–Oct. 5, 1991; b. Mar. 9, 1920, Salt Lake City, Utah; m. Isabel Hales, seven children; businessman; regional representative, mission and stake president.

CANNON, George Q. (Quayle). Apostle, Aug. 26, 1860; Counselor to President Young, April 8, 1873; Asst. counselor to President Young, May 9, 1874; released at death of President Young, Aug. 29, 1877; First counselor to President John Taylor, Oct. 10, 1880; released at the death of President Taylor, July 25, 1887; First counselor to President Woodruff, April 7, 1889; First counselor to President Snow, Sept. 13, 1898–April 12, 1901; b. Jan. 11, 1827, Liverpool, England; d. April 12, 1901, Monterey, California; m. Elizabeth Hoagland; practiced plural marriage, thirty-four children on record; businessman, editor.

CANNON, Janath Russell. First counselor to general president Barbara B. Smith, Relief Society, Oct. 3, 1974–April 7, 1984; b. Oct. 28, 1918, Ogden, Utah; m. Edwin Q. Cannon, six children; educator and writer; temple matron.

CANNON, John Q. (Quayle). Second counselor to Presiding Bishop William B. Preston, Oct. 5, 1884; excommunicated, Sept. 5, 1886; rebaptized May 6, 1888; b. April 19, 1857, San Francisco, California; d. Jan. 14, 1931, Salt Lake City, Utah; m. Elizabeth Ann Wells; practiced plural marriage, twelve children on record.

CANNON, Joseph J. First asst. to general superintendent George Q. Morris, Young Men, 1937–1945; b. May 22, 1877, Salt Lake City, Utah; d. Nov. 4, 1945, Salt Lake City; m. Ramona Wilcox, five children; newspaper editor; mission president.

CANNON, Lucy Grant. Second counselor to general president Martha Horne Tingey, Young Women, July 15, 1923–Mar. 28, 1929; First counselor to general president Ruth May Fox, Mar. 28, 1929–Oct. 1937; general president, Nov. 1937–April 6, 1948; b. Oct. 22, 1880, Salt Lake City, Utah; d. May 27, 1966, Salt Lake City; m. George J. Cannon, seven children.

CANNON, Sylvester Q. (Quayle). Presiding Bishop, June 4, 1925; Asst. to the Twelve, April 6, 1938; Apostle, April 14, 1938; member of the Twelve, April 6, 1939–May 29, 1943; b. June 10, 1877, Salt Lake City, Utah; d. May 29, 1943, Salt Lake City; m. Winnifred Seville, two children; mission and stake president.

CANNON, Virginia Beesley. First counselor to general president Dwan J. Young, Primary, April 5, 1980–April 2, 1988; b. Feb. 5, 1925, Salt Lake City, Utah; m. H. Stanley Cannon, six children; homemaker; Primary general board member.

CARMACK, John K. (Kay). Seventy, April 7, 1984; b. May 10, 1931, Winslow, Arizona; m. Shirley Fay Allen, five children; attorney; regional representative, mission president.

CARRINGTON, Albert. Apostle, July 3, 1870; Counselor to President Brigham Young, April 8, 1873; Asst. counselor to President Young, May 9, 1874; released, Aug. 29, 1877 at the death of President Young; excommunicated, Nov. 7, 1885; rebaptized, Nov. 1, 1887; b. Jan. 8, 1813, Royalton, Vermont; d. Sept. 19, 1889, Salt Lake City, Utah; m. Rhoda Maria Woods; practiced plural marriage, fifteen children on record; attorney, educator; mission president.

CHILD, Hortense Hogan. First counselor to general president Ruth H. Funk, Young Women, Nov. 9, 1972–July 12, 1978; b. May 6, 1919, Thatcher, Idaho; m. Romel Child, two children; civic worker; Young Women general board member.

CHILD, Julia Alleman. Second counselor to general president Louise Yates Robison, Relief Society, Oct. 7, 1928–Jan. 23, 1935; b. Sept. 8, 1873, Springville, Utah; d. Jan. 23, 1935, Salt Lake City, Utah; m. George N. Child, three children; educator; Relief Society general board member.

CHOULES, Albert, Jr. Seventy, Oct. 1, 1988; b. Feb. 15, 1926, Driggs, Idaho; m. Rosemary Phillips (d. 1984), three children; m. Marilyn Jeppson; businessman; regional representative, mission president.

CHRISTENSEN, Joe J. (Junior). Seventy, April 8, 1989; b. July 21, 1929, Banida, Idaho; m. Barbara Kohler, six children; president of Ricks College, Rexburg, Idaho; regional representative, mission president.

CHRISTIANSEN, ElRay L. (LaVar). Asst. to the Twelve, Oct. 11, 1951–Dec. 1, 1975; b. July 13, 1897, Mayfield, Utah; d. Dec. 1, 1975, Salt Lake City; m. Lewella Rees, three children; educator; temple and stake president.

CLAPP, Benjamin L. (Lynn). Seventy, Dec. 2, 1845; excommunicated, April 7, 1859; b. Aug. 19, 1814, West Huntsville, Alabama; d. 1860, Liberty, California; m. Mary Shultz; practiced plural marriage, twelve children; farmer.

CLARK, J. (Joshua) Reuben, Jr. Second counselor to President Grant, April 6, 1933; First counselor to President Grant, Oct. 6, 1934; Apostle, Oct. 11, 1934; First counselor to President George Albert Smith, May 21, 1945; Second counselor to President David O. McKay, April 9, 1951; First counselor to President McKay, June 12, 1959–Oct. 6, 1961; b. Sept. 1, 1871, Grantsville, Utah; d. Oct. 6, 1961, Salt Lake City; m. Luacine Savage, five children; U.S. ambassador to Mexico, attorney.

CLARKE, J. (John) Richard. Second counselor to Presiding Bishop Victor L. Brown, Oct. 1, 1976; Seventy, Oct. 1, 1988; b. April 4, 1927, Rexburg, Idaho; m. Barbara Jean Reed, eight children; businessman; regional representative, mission and stake president.

CLAWSON, Rudger. Apostle, Oct. 10, 1898–June 21, 1943; Second counselor to President Lorenzo Snow, Oct. 6, 1901; President of the Quorum of the Twelve Apostles, Mar. 17, 1921; b. Mar. 12, 1857, Salt Lake City, Utah; d. June 21, 1943, Salt Lake City; m. Florence Dinwoodey; practiced plural marriage, eleven children on record; businessman; mission and stake president.

CLEVELAND, Sarah Marietta Kingsley. First counselor to general president Emma Hale Smith, Relief Society, Mar. 17, 1842–Mar. 16, 1844; b. Oct. 20, 1788, Berkshire, Massachusetts; m. John Cleveland.

CLYDE, Aileen Hales. Second counselor to general president Elaine L. Jack, Relief Society, Mar. 31, 1990; b. May 18, 1928, Springville, Utah; m. Hal M. Clyde, three children; homemaker, educator; Young Women general board member.

COLTRIN, Zebedee. Seventy, Feb. 28, 1835; released April 6, 1837, having previously been ordained high priest; b. Sept. 7, 1804, Ovid, New York; d. July 20, 1887, Spanish Fork, Utah; m. Julia Ann Jennings; practiced plural marriage, sixteen children on record; farmer.

CONDIE, Spencer J. (Joel). Seventy, April 7, 1989; b. Aug. 27, 1940, Preston, Idaho; m. Bridgitte Dorothea Speth, five children; educator; regional representative, mission and stake president.

COOK, Gene R. (Raymond). Seventy, Oct. 3, 1975; b. Sept. 1, 1941, Lehi, Utah; m. Janelle Schlink, eight children; management; regional representative, mission president.

CORRILL, John. Second counselor to Presiding Bishop Edward Partridge, June 3, 1831; released Aug. 1, 1837; excommunicated Mar. 17, 1839; b. Sept. 17, 1794, Worcester Co., Massachusetts; m. Margaret, five children.

COWDERY, Oliver. Apostle, May–June 1829; Second Elder of the Church, April 6, 1830; Asst. president of the High Priesthood, Dec. 5, 1834; Asst. counselor to President Joseph Smith, Sept. 3, 1837; excommunicated April 11, 1838; rebaptized Nov. 12, 1848; b. Oct. 3, 1806, Wells, Vermont; d. Mar. 3, 1850, Richmond, Missouri; m. Elizabeth Ann Whitmer, six children; attorney, educator.

COWLEY, Matthew. Apostle, Oct. 11, 1945; b. Aug. 2, 1897, Preston, Idaho; d. Dec. 13, 1953, Los Angeles, California; m. Elva Taylor, three children; attorney; mission president.

COWLEY, Matthias F. (Foss). Apostle, Oct. 7, 1897; resigned, Oct. 28, 1905; priesthood suspended, May 11, 1911; restored to full membership, April 3, 1936; b. Aug. 25, 1858, Salt Lake City, Utah; d. June 16, 1940, Salt Lake City; m. Abbie Hyde; practiced plural marriage, thirteen children on record.

CRAVEN, Rulon G. (Gerald). Seventy, Dec. 5, 1990; b. Nov. 11, 1924, Murray, Utah; m. Donna Lunt, six children; secretary to Council of the Twelve; regional representative, Sunday School general board member, mission president.

CRITCHLOW, William J. (James), Jr. Asst. to the Twelve, Oct. 16, 1958–Aug. 29, 1968; b. Aug. 21, 1892, Brigham City, Utah; d. Aug. 29, 1968, Ogden; m. Anna Marie Taylor, three children; business executive; stake president.

CULLIMORE, James A. (Alfred). Asst. to the Twelve, April 6, 1966; Seventy, Oct. 1, 1976; Emeritus General Authority, Sept. 30, 1978; b. Jan. 17, 1906, Lindon, Utah; d. June 14, 1986, Salt Lake City; m. Grace Gardner, three children; businessman; stake president.

CURTIS, Elbert R. (Raine). General superintendent, Young Men, 1948–1958; b. April 24, 1901, Salt Lake City, Utah; m. Luceal Rockwood, three children; mission and stake president.

CURTIS, LeGrand R. (Raine). First counselor to general president Robert L. Backman, Young Men, Nov. 1972–June 23, 1974; Seventy, Mar. 31, 1990; b. May 22, 1924, Salt Lake City, Utah; m. Patricia Glade, eight children; dentist; regional representative, mission and stake president.

CUTHBERT, Derek A. (Alfred). Seventy, April 1, 1978–April 7, 1991; b. Oct. 5, 1926, Nottingham, England; d. April 7, 1991, Salt Lake City, Utah; m. Muriel Olive Mason, ten children; business executive; regional representative, mission and stake president.

CUTLER, Clinton L. (Louis). Seventy, Mar. 31, 1990; b. Dec. 27, 1929, Salt Lake City, Utah; m. Hellie Helena Sharp, six children; retired business management; regional representative, mission and stake president.

DARGER, Arlene Barlow. First counselor to general president Elaine A. Cannon, Young Women, July 12, 1978–April 7, 1984; b. July 14, 1925, Salt Lake City, Utah; m. Stanford P. Darger, five children; Tabernacle Choir member.

DÁVILA PEÑALOZA, Julio E. (Enrique). Seventy, April 6, 1991; b. May 23, 1932, Bucaramanga, Colombia; m. Mary Zapata, two children; education administration; regional representative, stake president.

DE JAGER, Jacob. Seventy, April 3, 1976; b. Jan. 16, 1923, The Hague, Netherlands; m. Bea Lim, two children; business executive; regional representative.

DELLENBACH, Robert K. (Kent). Seventy, Mar. 31, 1990; b. May 10, 1937, Salt Lake City, Utah; m. Mary-Jane Broadbent, three children; scientific education management; regional representative, mission and stake president.

DERRICK, Royden G. (Glade). Seventy, Oct. 1, 1976; Emeritus General Authority, Oct. 1, 1989; b. Sept. 7, 1915, Salt Lake City, Utah; m. Allie Jean Olson, four children; businessman; temple and mission president.

DIDIER, Charles A. (Amand) A. (Andre). Seventy, Oct. 3, 1975; b. Oct. 5, 1935, Ixelles, Belgium; m. Lucie Lodomez, two children; business executive; regional representative, mission president.

DOUGALL, Maria Young. First counselor to general president Elmina Shepherd Taylor, Young Women, 1877–Dec. 6, 1904; b. Dec. 10, 1849, Salt Lake City, Utah; d. April 30, 1935, Salt Lake City; m. William B. Dougall, three children.

DOXEY, Graham W. (Watson). First counselor to general president Neil D. Schaerrer, Young Men, April 7, 1977–Oct. 1979; Seventy, April 6, 1991; b. Mar. 30, 1927, Salt Lake City, Utah; m. Mary Louise Young, twelve children; business executive; mission and stake president.

DOXEY, Joanne Bushman. Second counselor to general president Barbara W. Winder, Relief Society, May 21, 1984–Mar. 31, 1990; b. April 17, 1932, Salt Lake City, Utah; m. David W. Doxey, eight children; Primary general board member.

DOXEY, Leone B. Watson. Second counselor to general president LaVern Watts Parmley, Primary, Sept. 10, 1953–April 6, 1962; First counselor, April 6, 1962–Oct. 23, 1969; b. Sept. 3, 1899, Salt Lake City, Utah; m. Graham H. Doxey, four children; Primary general board member.

DUNN, Loren C. (Charles). Seventy, April 6, 1968; b. June 12, 1930, Tooele, Utah; m. Sharon Longden; five children; business executive; stake and mission president.

DUNN, Paul H. (Harold). Seventy, April 6, 1964; Emeritus General Authority, Oct. 1, 1989; b. April 24, 1924, Provo, Utah; m. Jeanne Alice Cheverton, three children; educator.

DUNYON, O. (Olive) Eileen Robinson. Second counselor to general president LaVern Watts Parmley, Primary, April 6, 1962–June 3, 1963; b. June 3, 1917, Preston, Idaho; m. Joy F. Dunyon, three children; school librarian.

DURHAM, G. (George) Homer. Seventy, April 2, 1977–Jan. 10, 1985; b. Feb. 4, 1911, Parowan, Utah; d. Jan. 10, 1985, Salt Lake City; m. Eudora Widtsoe, three children; former president of Arizona State University, and former Commissioner of Higher Education for State of Utah; regional representative, stake president.

DUSENBERRY, Ida Smoot. Second counselor to general president Bathsheba W. Smith, Relief Society, Nov. 10, 1901–Sept. 20, 1910; b. May 5, 1873, Salt Lake City, Utah; d. April 25, 1955; m. George Albert Dusenberry, two children; educator.

DYER, Alvin R. (Rulon). Asst. to the Twelve, Oct. 11, 1958; Apostle, Oct. 5, 1967–Mar. 6, 1977; Counselor to President David O. McKay, April 6, 1968; released, Jan. 18, 1970, at the death of President McKay; resumed position as Asst. to the Twelve, Jan. 23, 1970; Seventy, Oct. 1, 1976; b. Jan. 1, 1903, Salt Lake City, Utah; d. Mar. 6, 1977, Salt Lake City; m. May Elizabeth Jackson, two children; businessman; mission president.

ELDREDGE, Horace S. (Sunderlin). Seventy, Oct. 7, 1854–Sept. 6, 1888; b. Feb. 6, 1816, Brutus, New York; d. Sept. 6, 1888, Salt Lake City, Utah; m. Sarah Gibbs; practiced plural marriage, twenty-eight children on record; businessman, superintendent of ZCMI; mission president.

ELDREDGE, W. Jay. General superintendent, Young Men, Sept. 17, 1969–June 25, 1972; general president, Young Men, June 25, 1972–Nov. 9, 1972; b. April 27, 1913, Salt Lake City, Utah; m. Marjory Hyde, five children; businessman; mission and stake president.

EVANS, Joy Frewin. First counselor to general president Barbara W. Winder, Relief Society, May 21, 1984–Mar. 31, 1990; b. Jan. 31, 1926, Salt Lake City; m. David C. Evans, ten children; homemaker; Relief Society general board member.

EVANS, Richard L. (Louis). Seventy, Oct. 7, 1938; Apostle, Oct. 8, 1953–Nov. 1, 1971; b. Mar. 23, 1906, Salt Lake City, Utah; d. Nov. 1, 1971, Salt Lake City; m. Alice Ruth Thornley, four children; voice of the "Spoken Word" in weekly Mormon Tabernacle Broadcast, 1930–1971; editor, *Improvement Era.*

EYRING, Henry B. (Bennion). First counselor to Presiding Bishop Robert D. Hales, April 6, 1985; b. May 31, 1933, Princeton, New Jersey; m. Kathleen Johnson, six children; Commissioner of Church Education, former president of Ricks College, Rexburg, Idaho; regional representative, Sunday School general board member.

FARNSWORTH, Burton K. (Kent). Asst. to general superintendent George Q. Morris, Young Men, 1937–1945; b. Mar. 6, 1890, Beaver, Utah; d. Oct. 27, 1945, Seattle, Washington; m. Mabel Pearce, six children; educator; Young Men general board member.

FAUST, James E. (Esdras). Asst. to the Twelve, Oct. 6, 1972; Seventy, Oct. 1, 1976; Apostle, Oct. 1, 1978; b. July 31, 1920, Delta, Utah; m. Ruth Wright, five children; attorney; regional representative, mission and stake president.

FEATHERSTONE, Vaughn J. Second counselor to Presiding Bishop Victor L. Brown, April 6, 1972; Seventy, Oct. 1, 1976; b. Mar. 26, 1931, Stockton, Utah; m. Merlene Miner, seven children; business executive; mission and stake president.

FELT, Louie Bouton. General president, Primary, June 19, 1880–Oct. 6, 1925; b. May 5, 1850, Norwalk, Connecticut; d. Feb. 13, 1928, Salt Lake City, Utah; m. Joseph H. Felt.

FJELSTED, Christian D. (Daniel). Seventy, April 6, 1884–Dec. 23, 1905; b. Feb. 20, 1829, Sundbyvester, (near) Copenhagen, Denmark; d. Dec. 23, 1905, Salt Lake City, Utah; m. Karen Olsen; practiced plural marriage, fifteen children on record; mission president.

FOSTER, James. Seventy, April 6, 1837–Dec. 21, 1841; b. April 1, 1786, Hillsborough County, New Hampshire; d. Dec. 21, 1841, Morgan County, Illinois; m. Abigail Glidden, six children.

FOX, Ruth May. First counselor to general president Martha Horne Tingey, Young Women, April 5, 1905–Mar. 28, 1929; general president, Mar. 28, 1929–Oct. 1937; b. Nov. 16, 1853, Wiltshire, England; d. April 12, 1958; m. Jesse W. Fox, Jr., twelve children.

FREEZE, Lillie Tuckett. First counselor to general president Louie B. Felt, Primary, Dec. 29, 1905–Oct. 6, 1925; b. Mar. 26, 1855, Salt Lake City, Utah; d. Mar. 23, 1937, Salt Lake City; m. James Perry Freeze, four children; Primary and Young Women general board member.

FUNK, Ruth Hardy. General president, Young Women, June 23, 1974–July 12, 1978; b. Feb. 11, 1917, Chicago, Illinois; m. Marcus C. Funk, four children; high school choral director; Young Women general board member.

FYANS, J. (John) Thomas. Asst. to the Twelve, April 6, 1974; Seventy 1976–1985; Emeritus General Authority, Oct. 1, 1989; b. May 17, 1918,

Moreland, Idaho; m. Helen Cook, five children; business executive; regional representative, mission president.

GARFF, Gertrude Ryberg. Second counselor to general president Belle S. Spafford, Relief Society, April 6, 1945–Sept. 30, 1947; b. Nov. 2, 1910, Hyrum, Utah; m. Mark Brimhall Garff; Relief Society general board member.

GATES, Jacob. Seventy, April 6, 1860–April 14, 1892; b. Mar. 9, 1811, Saint Johnsbury, Vermont; d. April 14, 1892, Provo, Utah; m. Mary Minerva Snow; practiced plural marriage, thirteen children on record; farmer.

GAUSE, Jesse. Counselor to President Joseph Smith, Mar. 8, 1832; sent on mission from which he never returned; excommunicated, Dec. 3, 1832; b. about 1784, East Marlborough, Virginia; d. about 1836; m. Martha Cuntry, five children.

GAYLORD, John. Seventy, April 6, 1837; excommunicated, Jan. 13, 1838; rebaptized Oct. 5, 1839; b. July 12, 1797, Pennsylvania; d. July 17, 1878; m. Elvira Edmonds.

GEE, Salmon. Seventy, April 6, 1837; fellowship withdrawn, Mar. 6, 1838; b. Oct. 16, 1792, Lyme, Connecticut; d. Sept. 13, 1845, Ambrosia, Iowa; posthumously reinstated, Sept. 14, 1967; m. Sarah Watson Crane, two children.

GEORGE, Lloyd P. (Preal). Seventy, Oct. 1, 1988; b. Sept. 17, 1920, Kanosh, Utah; m. Leola Stott, three children; real estate broker; regional representative, mission and stake president.

GIBBONS, Francis M. (Marion). Seventy, April 6, 1986–Oct. 5, 1991; secretary to First Presidency for 16 years; b. April 10, 1921, St. Johns, Arizona; m. Helen Bay, four children; attorney; stake president.

GILES, John D. (Davis). First asst. to general superintendent George Q. Morris, Young Men, 1937–1948; b. Aug. 1, 1883, Salt Lake City, Utah; d. Sept. 23, 1955, Salt Lake City; m. Una Pratt, four children; businessman, Boy Scout official.

GOASLIND, Jack H, Jr. Seventy, Sept. 30, 1978; b. April 18, 1928, Salt Lake City, Utah; m. Gwen Caroline Bradford, six children; business executive; Young Men general president, regional representative, mission and stake president.

GODDARD, George. First asst. to general superintendent George Q. Cannon, Sunday School, June 1872–Jan. 1899; b. Dec. 5, 1813, Leicester,

England; d. Jan. 12, 1899, Salt Lake City, Utah; m. Elizabeth Harrison; practiced plural marriage, eighteen children on record.

GODDARD, Verna Wright. Second counselor to general president Lucy Grant Cannon, Young Women, Nov. 1937–July 1944; First counselor, July 1944–April 6, 1948; b. Nov. 24, 1889, Salt Lake City, Utah; d. Nov. 26, 1949; m. J. Percy Goddard, four children.

GOULD, John. Seventy, April 6, 1837–May 9, 1851; b. May 11, 1808, Ontario, Canada; d. May 9, 1851, Cooley's Mill, Iowa; m. Abigail Harrington, two children.

GRANT, Heber J. (Jeddy). Apostle, Oct. 16, 1882; President of the Quorum of the Twelve Apostles, Nov. 23, 1916; President of the Church, Nov. 23, 1918–May 14, 1945; b. Nov. 22, 1856, Salt Lake City, Utah; d. May 14, 1945, Salt Lake City; m. Lucy Stringham; practiced plural marriage, twelve children; businessman.

GRANT, Jedediah M. (Morgan). Seventy, Dec. 2, 1845; Apostle, April 7, 1854; Second counselor to President Brigham Young, April 7, 1854–Dec. 1, 1856; b. Feb. 21, 1816, Windsor, New York; d. Dec. 1, 1856, Salt Lake City, Utah; m. Caroline Van Dyke; practiced plural marriage, eight children (including one adopted child) on record; his seventh wife, Rachel Ridgeway Ivins, was the mother of President Heber J. Grant; farmer, civil servant.

GRASSLI, Michaelene Packer. General president, Primary, April 2, 1988; b. June 19, 1940, Salt Lake City, Utah; m. Leonard M. Grassli, three children; homemaker; stake Primary president.

GROBERG, John H. (Holbrook). Seventy, April 3, 1976; b. June 17, 1934, Idaho Falls, Idaho; m. Jean Sabin, eleven children; business executive; regional representative, mission president.

HAIGHT, David B. (Bruce). Asst. to the Twelve, April 6, 1970; Apostle, Jan. 8, 1976; b. Sept. 2, 1906, Oakley, Idaho; m. Ruby Olsen, three children; business executive; regional representative, mission and stake president.

HALE, Arta Matthews. First counselor to general president LaVern Watts Parmley, Primary, May 16, 1951–April 6, 1962; b. Oct. 24, 1898, Oakley, Idaho; d. July 11, 1990, Salt Lake City, Utah; m. Dewey Hale, two children; Primary general board member.

HALES, Janette Callister. Second counselor to general president Ardeth G. Kapp, Young Women, Mar. 31, 1990; b. June 7, 1933, Springville, Utah;

m. Robert H. Hales, five children; homemaker, legislator; Primary general board member.

HALES, Robert D. (Dean). Asst. to the Twelve, April 4, 1975; Seventy, Oct. 1, 1976; First counselor to general president Hugh W. Pinnock, Sunday School, July 1981–July 1985; Presiding Bishop, April 6, 1985; b. Aug. 24, 1932, New York City, New York; m. Mary Elene Crandall, two children; business executive; regional representative, mission and stake president.

HAMMOND, F. (Frank) Melvin. Seventy, April 7, 1989; b. Dec. 19, 1933, Blackfoot, Idaho; m. Bonnie Sellers, six children; educator, legislator; mission and stake president.

HAN, In Sang. Seventy, June 1, 1991; b. Dec. 9, 1939, Seoul, Korea; m. Lee Hyn In, five children; business management; regional representative and mission president.

HANCOCK, Levi W. (Ward). Seventy, Feb. 28, 1835; released April 6, 1837, having supposedly previously been ordained a high priest; restored to place in First Council of the Seventy, Sept. 3, 1837; b. April 7, 1803, Springfield, Massachusetts; d. June 10, 1882, Washington, Utah; m. Clarissa Reed; practiced plural marriage, nineteen children on record; cabinet maker.

HANKS, Marion D. (Duff). Seventy, Oct. 4, 1953; Asst. to the Twelve, April 6, 1968; b. Oct. 13, 1921, Salt Lake City, Utah; m. Maxine Christensen, five children; educator; temple and mission president.

HANSEN, W. (Warren) Eugene. Seventy, April 8, 1989; b. Aug. 23, 1928, Tremonton, Utah; m. Jeanine Showell, six children; attorney; stake president.

HARBERTSON, Robert B. Seventy, April 7, 1984–Oct. 1, 1989; b. April 19, 1932, Ogden, Utah; m. Norma Creer, five children; business executive; regional representative, mission president.

HARDY, Leonard W. (Wilford). First counselor to Presiding Bishop Edward Hunter, Oct. 6, 1856–Oct. 16, 1883, and to Bishop William B. Preston, April 6, 1884–July 31, 1884; b. Dec. 31, 1805, Bradford, Massachusetts; d. July 31, 1884, Salt Lake City, Utah; m. Elizabeth Harriman Nichols; practiced plural marriage, eighteen children on record; farmer, businessman.

HARDY, M. (Milton) H. First asst. to general superintendent Junius F. Wells, Young Men, 1876–1880; b. Sept. 26, 1844, Groveland,

Massachusetts; d. Aug. 23, 1905, Provo, Utah; m. Elizabeth Smoot, five children.

HARDY, Ralph W. (Williams). Second asst. to general superintendent Elbert R. Curtis, Young Men, 1948–1957; b. May 6, 1916, Salt Lake City, Utah; d. Aug. 6, 1957, Ogden; m. Maren Eccles, four children; radio executive.

HARDY, Rufus K. (Kay). Seventy, Oct. 6, 1934–Mar. 7, 1945; b. May 28, 1878, Salt Lake City, Utah; d. Mar. 7, 1945, Salt Lake City; m. Alelade Underwood Eldredge; business executive; mission president.

HARRIMAN, Henry. Seventy, Feb. 6, 1838–May 17, 1891; b. June 9, 1804, Rowley (Georgetown), Massachusetts; d. May 17, 1891, Huntington, Utah; m. Clarissa Boynton; practiced plural marriage, nine children on record.

HARRIS, Devere. Seventy, April 7, 1984–Oct. 1, 1989; b. May 30, 1916, Portage, Utah; m. Velda Gibbs, five children; businessman; regional representative, temple and stake president.

HART, Charles H. (Henry). Seventy, April 9, 1906–Sept. 29, 1934; b. July 5, 1866, Bloomington, Idaho; d. Sept. 29, 1934, Salt Lake City, Utah; m. Adelia Greenhalgh (d. 1913), ten children; m. LaLene Hendricks.

HATCH, Lorenzo H. (Hill). Second asst. to general superintendent George Q. Morris, Young Men, 1937–1948; b. Feb. 23, 1893, Franklin, Idaho; d. Nov. 27, 1971, Salt Lake City, Utah; m. Ina Porter, four children; stake president.

HIGBEE, Elias. Church historian, April 6, 1838–June 8, 1843; b. Oct. 23, 1795, Galloway, New Jersey; d. June 8, 1843, Nauvoo, Illinois; m. Sarah Elizabeth Ward, eight children; judge.

HILL, George R. (Richard), II. General superintendent, Sept. 1949–Nov. 1966; b. Apr. 10, 1884, Ogden, Utah; m. Elizabeth Odette McKay, three children; research director; Young Men general board member.

HILL, George R. (Richard), III. Seventy, April 4, 1987; b. Nov. 24, 1921, Ogden, Utah; m. Melba Parker, seven children; educator; regional representative.

HILLAM, Harold G. (Gordon). Seventy, Mar. 31, 1990; b. Sept. 1, 1934, Sugar City, Idaho; m. Carol Lois Rasmussen, seven children; orthodontist; regional representative, mission and stake president.

HINCKLEY, Alonzo A. (Arza). Apostle, Oct. 11, 1934–Dec. 22, 1936; b. April 23, 1870, Cove Fort, Utah; d. Dec. 22, 1936, Salt Lake City; m.

Rose May Robison, 14 children; stake president (christened Arza Alonzo Hinckley, but signed his name Alonzo A. Hinckley).

HINCKLEY, Gordon B. (Bitner). Asst. to the Twelve, April 6, 1958; Apostle, Oct. 5, 1961; Counselor to President Spencer W. Kimball, July 23, 1981; Second counselor, Dec. 2, 1982; First counselor to President Ezra Taft Benson, Nov. 10, 1985; b. June 23, 1910, Salt Lake City, Utah; m. Marjorie Pay, five children; business executive; stake president.

HINCKLEY, May Green. General president, Primary, Jan. 1, 1940–May 2, 1943; b. May 1, 1885, Brampton, England; d. May 2, 1943, Salt Lake City, Utah; m. Bryant S. Hinckley; nurse; stake Young Women president.

HOLLAND, Jeffrey R. (Roy). Seventy, April 7, 1989; b. Dec. 3, 1940; m. Patricia Terry, three children; educator, President of BYU and former Commissioner of Church Education; regional representative.

HOLLAND, Patricia Terry. First counselor to general president Ardeth G. Kapp, Young Women, May 11, 1984–April 6, 1986; b. Feb. 16, 1942, St. George, Utah; m. Jeffrey R. Holland, three children; homemaker; Young Women general board member.

HOLT, Dorothy Martha Porter. Second counselor to general president Florence S. Jacobsen, Young Women, Sept. 30, 1961–Nov. 9, 1972; b. Feb. 5, 1912, Salt Lake City, Utah; m. A. Palmer Holt, five children; homemaker.

HOWARD, F. (Fred) Burton. Seventy, Sept. 30, 1978; b. Mar. 24, 1933, Logan, Utah; m. Caroline Heise, five children; attorney; stake president.

HOWELLS, Adele Cannon. First counselor to general president May Green Hinckley, Primary, Jan. 1, 1940–May 2, 1943; general president, July 29, 1943–April 14, 1951; b. Jan. 12, 1886, Salt Lake City, Utah; d. Apr. 14, 1951, Salt Lake City; m. David P. Howells, three children; homemaker, educator.

HOWELLS, Marcia Knowlton. First counselor to general president Amy Brown Lyman, Relief Society, April 1940–April 6, 1945; b. May 28, 1888, Farmington, Utah; d. June 10, 1976, Salt Lake City, Utah; m. Thomas J. Howells, one child; homemaker; Relief Society general board member.

HUNTER, Edward. Presiding Bishop of the Church, April 7, 1851–Oct. 16, 1883; b. June 22, 1793, Newton, Pennsylvania; d. Oct. 16, 1883, Salt Lake City, Utah; m. Ann Standly (Stanley); practiced plural marriage, thirteen children on record; farmer.

HUNTER, Howard W. (William). Apostle, Oct. 15, 1959; Acting President of the Quorum of the Twelve Apostles, Nov. 10, 1985; President of the Quorum of the Twelve Apostles, June 2, 1988; b. Nov. 24, 1907, Boise, Idaho; m. Clara May Jeffs (d. 1983), three children; m. Inis Egan; attorney; stake president.

HUNTER, Milton R. (Reed). Seventy, April 6, 1945–June 27, 1975; b. Oct. 25, 1902, Holden, Utah; d. June 27, 1975, Salt Lake City; m. Ferne Gardner, six children; educator.

HYDE, Annie M. Taylor. First counselor to general president Bathsheba W. Smith, Relief Society, Nov. 10, 1901–Mar. 12, 1909; b. Oct. 20, 1849, Salt Lake City, Utah; d. Mar. 12, 1909; m. Alonzo E. Hyde, eight children.

HYDE, Orson. Apostle, Feb. 15, 1835; dropped from the Quorum, May 4, 1839; restored to the Quorum, June 27, 1839; President of the Quorum of Twelve Apostles, Dec. 27, 1847; seniority adjusted to date of second entry into the Quorum, April 10, 1875; b. Jan. 8, 1805, Oxford, Connecticut; d. Nov. 28, 1878, Spring City, Utah; m. Marinda Nancy Johnson; practiced plural marriage, thirty-two children on record; editor.

ISAACSON, H. (Henry) Thorpe B. (Beal). Second counselor to Presiding Bishop LeGrand Richards, Dec. 12, 1946; First counselor to Presiding Bishop Joseph L. Wirthlin, April 6, 1952; Asst. to the Twelve, Sept. 30, 1961; Counselor to President David O. McKay, Oct. 28, 1965; released at death of President McKay, Jan. 18, 1970; resumed position as Asst. to the Twelve, Jan. 23, 1970–Nov. 9, 1970; b. Sept. 6, 1898, Ephraim, Utah; d. Nov. 9, 1970, Salt Lake City; m. Lula Maughn Jones, two children; businessman.

IVINS, Anthony W. (Woodward). Apostle, Oct. 6, 1907; Second counselor to President Heber J. Grant, Mar. 10, 1921; First counselor to President Grant, May 28, 1925–Sept. 23, 1934; b. Sept. 16, 1852, Toms River, New Jersey; d. Sept. 23, 1934, Salt Lake City, Utah; m. Elizabeth Ashby Snow, nine children; rancher, businessman; Young Men general board member.

IVINS, Antoine R. (Ridgeway). Seventy, Oct. 8, 1931–Oct. 18, 1967; b. May 11, 1881, St. George, Utah; d. Oct. 18, 1967, Salt Lake City; m. Vilate Romney; farm manager; mission president.

JACK, Elaine Low. Second counselor to general president Ardeth G. Kapp, Young Women, April 4, 1987–Mar. 31, 1990; general president, Relief Society, Mar. 31, 1990; b. Mar. 22, 1928, Cardston, Alberta, Canada; m. Joseph E. Jack, four children; homemaker; Relief Society general board member, stake Relief Society president.

JACOBSEN, Florence Smith. General president, Young Women, Sept. 30, 1961–Nov. 9, 1972; b. April 7, 1913, Salt Lake City, Utah; m. Theodore C. Jacobsen, three children; homemaker, businesswoman; Church curator of museums.

JENSEN, Marlin K. (Keith). Seventy, April 7, 1989; b. May 18, 1942, Ogden, Utah; m. Kathleen Bushnell, eight children; attorney; regional representative, stake president.

JEPPSEN, Malcolm S. (Seth). Seventy, April 7, 1989; b. Nov. 1, 1924, Mantua, Utah; m. Marian Davis, five children; physician; regional representative, stake president.

JEPSEN, Betty Jo Nelson. First counselor to general president Michaelene P. Grassli, Primary, April 2, 1988; b. Dec. 3, 1940, Boise, Idaho; m. Glen F. Jepsen, four children; educator, homemaker; Primary general board member, stake Primary president.

JOHNSON, Kenneth. Seventy, May 31, 1990; b. July 5, 1940, Norwich, England; m. Pamela Wilson, one child; business executive; regional representative, stake president.

JOHNSON, Luke S. Apostle, Feb. 15, 1835; excommunicated, April 13, 1838; rebaptized in 1846; b. Nov. 2, 1807, Pomfret, Vermont; d. Dec. 9, 1861, Salt Lake City, Utah; m. Susan Poteet; practiced plural marriage, fifteen children on record; educator, doctor.

JOHNSON, Lyman E. (Eugene). Apostle, Feb. 14, 1835; excommunicated, April 13, 1838; b. Oct. 24, 1811; Pomfret, Vermont; d. Dec. 20, 1856, Prairie du Chien, Wisconsin; m. Sarah Land (Lang, Long), two children; attorney.

JUDD, Margaret Romney Jackson. First counselor to general president Florence S. Jacobsen, Young Women, Sept. 30, 1961–Nov. 9, 1972; b. Sept. 7, 1909, Colonia Juárez, Mexico; m. Junius M. Jackson (d. 1981), five children; m. George E. Judd; homemaker; Young Women general board member.

KAPP, Ardeth Greene. Second counselor to general president Ruth H. Funk, Young Women, Nov. 9, 1972–July 12, 1978; general president, Young Women, April 7, 1984; b. Mar. 19, 1931, Glenwood, Alberta, Canada; m. Heber B. Kapp; educator; Church Correlation Committee member.

KAY, F. (Ferril) Arthur. Seventy, Oct. 6, 1984; Emeritus General Authority, Oct. 1, 1989; b. July 15, 1916, Annabella, Utah; m. Eunice D. Nielsen, six children; dentist; temple president.

KENDRICK, L. (Larry) Lionel. Seventy, April 2, 1988; b. Sept. 19, 1931, Baton Rouge, Louisiana; m. Myrtis Lee Noble, four children; educator; regional representative, mission and stake president.

KIKUCHI, Yoshihiko. Seventy, Oct. 1, 1977; b. July 25, 1941, Horoizumi, Japan; m. Toshiko Koshiya, four children; business executive; mission and stake president.

KIMBALL, Heber C. (Chase). Apostle, Feb. 14, 1835; First counselor to President Brigham Young, Dec. 27, 1847–June 22, 1868; b. June 14, 1801, Sheldon, Vermont; d. June 22, 1868, Salt Lake City, Utah; m. Vilate Murray; practiced plural marriage, sixty-five children on record; potter, businessman.

KIMBALL, J. (Jonathan) Golden. Seventy, April 5, 1892–Sept. 2, 1938; b. June 9, 1853, Salt Lake City, Utah; d. Sept. 2, 1938, Reno, Nevada; m. Jennie Knowlton, six children; Young Men general board member, mission president.

KIMBALL, Spencer W. (Woolley). Apostle, Oct. 7, 1943; President of the Quorum of the Twelve Apostles, 1970; President of the Church, Dec. 30, 1973–Nov. 5, 1985; b. Mar. 28, 1895, Salt Lake City, Utah; d. Nov. 5, 1985, Salt Lake City; m. Camilla Eyring, four children; businessman; stake president.

KING, David S. (Sjodahl). Second asst. to general superintendent Elbert R. Curtis, Young Men, 1948–1958; b. June 20, 1917, Salt Lake City, Utah; m. Rosalie Lehner, three children; former United States Congressman.

KIRKHAM, Oscar A. (Ammon). Seventy, Oct. 5, 1941–Mar. 10, 1958; b. Jan. 22, 1880, Lehi, Utah; d. Mar. 10, 1958, Salt Lake City; m. Ida Murdock, eight children; Young Men general board member, Boy Scouts of America executive.

KNIGHT, Lucy Jane (Jennie) Brimhall. First counselor to general president Clarissa Smith Williams, Relief Society, April 2, 1921–Oct. 7, 1928; b. Dec. 13, 1875, Spanish Fork, Utah; d. Mar. 31, 1957, Provo, Utah; m. Jesse William Knight, two children; executive for Utah County Red Cross.

KOFFORD, Cree-L. Seventy, April 6, 1991; b. July 11, 1933, Santaquin, Utah; m. Ila Macdonald, five children; attorney; regional representative, mission and stake president.

KOMATSU, Adney Y. (Yoshio). Asst. to the Twelve, April 4, 1975; Seventy, Oct. 1, 1976; b. Aug. 2, 1923, Honolulu, Hawaii; m. Judy Nobue

Fujitani, four children; businessman; regional representative, temple and mission president.

LAMBERT, Edith Elizabeth Hunter. Second counselor to general president May Anderson, Primary, Dec. 11, 1933–Dec. 31, 1939; b. Mar. 14, 1878, Salt Lake City, Utah; d. Mar. 3, 1964, Salt Lake City; m. James N. Lambert, three children.

LANE, Florence Reece. Second counselor to general president LaVern Watts Parmley, Primary; Jan. 8, 1970–Oct. 5, 1974; b. Feb. 24, 1915; m. Perry L. Lane, three children; educator; Primary general board member.

LARSEN, Dean L. (LeRoy). Seventy, Feb. 22, 1980; b. May 24, 1927, Hyrum, Utah; m. Geneal Johnson, five children; coach, educator; regional representative, mission president, Young Men general board member.

LASATER, John R. (Roger). Seventy, April 4, 1987; b. Dec. 8, 1931, Farmington, Utah; m. Marilyn Jones, five children; USAF ret.; regional representative, mission and stake president.

LAW, William. Second counselor to President Joseph Smith, Jan. 24, 1841; excommunicated, April 18, 1844; b. Sept. 8, 1809, Tyrone County, North Ireland; d. Jan. 19, 1892, Shullsburg, Wisconsin; m. Jane Silverthorn, eight children; businessman, doctor.

LAWRENCE, W. (William) Mack. Seventy, Dec. 5, 1990; b. Oct. 28, 1926, Salt Lake City, Utah; m. Jacqueline Young, three children; business executive; regional representative.

LEE, George P. (Patrick). Seventy, Oct. 3, 1975; excommunicated, Sept. 1, 1989; b. Mar. 23, 1943, Towaoc, Colorado; m. Katherine Hettich, three children; educator; mission president.

LEE, Harold B. (Bingham). Apostle, April 10, 1941; President of the Quorum of the Twelve Apostles and first counselor to President Joseph Fielding Smith, Jan. 23, 1970; President of the Church, July 7, 1972–Dec. 26, 1973; b. Mar. 28, 1899, Clifton, Idaho; d. Dec. 26, 1973, Salt Lake City, Utah; m. Fern Lucinda Tanner (d. 1962), two children; m. Freda Joan Jensen; educator, civil servant; stake president.

LEMMON, Colleen Bushman. Second counselor to general president Naomi M. Shumway, Primary, Oct. 5, 1974–April 2, 1977; First counselor, April 2, 1977–April 5, 1980; b. July 14, 1927, Salt Lake City, Utah; m. George Van Lemmon, four children; president New Mexico State American Mothers Committee; Primary general board member.

LEWIS, Theodore B. (Belden). Seventy, Oct. 8, 1882; [on Oct. 9, when he was to be set apart, he reported that he was already a high priest, so he was not set apart and did not serve in this position]; b. Nov. 18, 1843, St. Louis, Missouri; d. July 20, 1899; m. Martha J. Coray; practiced plural marriage, sixteen children on record.

LINDSAY, Richard P. (Powell). Seventy, April 7, 1989; b. Mar. 18, 1926; m. Marian Bangerter, six children; managing director Special Affairs/Public Communication Dept. of the Church; stake president.

LONGDEN, John. Asst. to the Twelve, Oct. 6, 1951–Aug. 30, 1969; b. Nov. 4, 1898, Oldham, England; d. Aug. 30, 1969, Salt Lake City, Utah; m. Frances LaRue Carr, three children; businessman; stake president.

LONGDEN, Frances LaRue Carr. Second counselor to Bertha S. Reeder, Young Women, June 13, 1948–Sept. 30, 1961; b. April 2, 1901; d. May 16, 1991, Salt Lake City, Utah; m. John Longden, three children; stake Young Women president.

LUND, Anthon H. (Henrik). Apostle, Oct. 7, 1889; Second counselor to President Joseph F. Smith, Oct. 17, 1901; First counselor, April 7, 1910; First counselor to President Heber J. Grant, Nov. 23, 1918–Mar. 2, 1921; b. May 15, 1844, Älborg, Denmark; d. Mar. 2, 1921, Salt Lake City, Utah; m. Sarah Ann Peterson; nine children on record; Young Men general board member, mission president, president of the Genealogical Society of Utah.

LYBBERT, Merlin R. (Rex). Seventy, April 1, 1989; b. Jan. 31, 1926, Cardston, Alberta, Canada; m. Nola Cahoon, seven children; attorney; regional representative, stake president.

LYMAN, Amasa M. (Mason). Apostle, Aug. 20, 1842; Counselor to President Joseph Smith, Feb. 4, 1843; released at the death of President Joseph Smith, June 27, 1844; returned to Quorum of the Twelve Apostles, Aug. 12, 1844; deprived of apostleship, Oct. 6, 1867; excommunicated, May 12, 1870; b. Mar. 30, 1813, Lyman, New Hampshire; d. Feb. 4, 1877, Fillmore, Utah; blessings restored after death; m. Louisa Maria Tanner; practiced plural marriage, thirty-seven children on record; farmer.

LYMAN, Amy Brown. General president, Relief Society, Jan. 1, 1940–April 6, 1945; b. Feb. 7, 1872, Pleasant Grove, Utah; d. Dec. 5, 1959; m. Richard R. Lyman, two children.

LYMAN, Francis M. (Marion). Apostle, Oct. 27, 1880; President of the Quorum of the Twelve Apostles, Oct. 6, 1903–Nov. 18, 1916; b. Jan. 12,

1840, Good Hope, Illinois; d. Nov. 18, 1916, Salt Lake City, Utah; m. Rhoda Ann Taylor; practiced plural marriage, twenty-two children on record; businessman; mission president.

LYMAN, Richard R. (Roswell). Apostle, April 7, 1918; excommunicated, Nov. 12, 1943; rebaptized Oct. 27, 1954; b. Nov. 23, 1870, Fillmore, Utah; d. Dec. 31, 1963, Salt Lake City, Utah; m. Amy Brown, two children; asst. superintendent in Young Men.

MADSEN, Louise Wallace. Second counselor to general president Belle S. Spafford, Relief Society, Aug. 1958–Oct. 3, 1974; b. April 25, 1909, Salt Lake City, Utah; d. Oct. 4, 1987, Salt Lake City; m. Francis A. Madsen, five children.

MAESER, Karl G. (Gottfried). Second asst. to general superintendent George Q. Cannon, Sunday School, July 1894–Jan. 1899; First asst., Jan. 1899–Feb. 1901; b. Jan. 16, 1828, Meiszen, Saxony, Germany; d. Feb. 15, 1901, Salt Lake City, Utah; m. Anna Meith; practiced plural marriage, nine children on record; educator; mission president.

MALAN, Jayne Broadbent. First counselor to Ardeth G. Kapp, Young Women, April 4, 1987; b. April 18, 1924, Heber City, Utah; m. Terry Malan, two children; professional writer; Relief Society and Young Women general board member.

MARSH, Thomas B. (Baldwin). Apostle, April 26, 1835; President of the Quorum of the Twelve Apostles, May 2, 1835; excommunicated for apostasy, Mar. 17, 1839; rebaptized, July 16, 1857; b. Nov. 1, 1799, Acton, Massachusetts; d. Jan. 1866, Ogden, Utah; m. Elizabeth Godkin; one child on record; educator, physician to the Church.

MARTIN, Douglas J. (James). Seventy, April 4, 1987; b. April 20, 1927, Hastings, New Zealand; m. Amelia Wati Crawford, four children; business executive; regional representative, stake president.

MARTINS, Helvécio. Seventy, Mar. 31, 1990; b. July 27, 1930, Rio de Janeiro, Brazil; m. Ruda Tourinho de Assis, four children; educator, business management; mission president.

MAXWELL, Neal A. (Ash). Asst. to the Twelve, April 6, 1974; Seventy, Oct. 1, 1976; Apostle, July 23, 1981; b. July 6, 1926, Salt Lake City, Utah; m. Colleen Hinckley, four children; educator, Commissioner of Church Education; regional representative, Young Men general board member.

MCCONKIE, Bruce R. (Redd). Seventy, Oct. 6, 1946; Apostle, Oct. 12, 1972–April 19, 1985; b. July 29, 1915, Ann Arbor, Michigan; d. April 19, 1985, Salt Lake City; m. Amelia Smith, eleven children; attorney; mission president.

MCKAY, David Lawrence. Second asst. to general superintendent George R. Hill, Sunday School, Sept. 1949–Oct. 1952; First asst., Oct. 1952–Nov. 1966; general superintendent, Nov. 1966–June 1971; b. Sept. 30, 1901, Ogden, Utah; m. Mildred Dean Calderwood, four children; attorney; mission president.

MCKAY, David O. (Oman). Apostle, April 9, 1906; Second counselor to President Heber J. Grant, Oct. 6, 1934; Second counselor to President George Albert Smith, May 21, 1945; President of the Quorum of the Twelve Apostles, Sept. 30, 1950; President of the Church, April 9, 1951–Jan. 18, 1970; b. Sept. 8, 1873, Huntsville, Utah; d. Jan. 18, 1970, Salt Lake City; m. Emma Ray Riggs, seven children; educator.

MCKAY, Quinn G. (Gunn). Second counselor to general president Neil D. Schaerrer, Young Men, April 7, 1977–Oct. 1979; b. Oct. 30, 1926; m. Shirley Frame, five children; management consultant; mission president.

MCKAY, Thomas E. (Evans). Asst. to the Twelve, April 6, 1941–Jan. 15, 1958; b. Oct. 29, 1875, Huntsville, Utah; d. Jan. 15, 1958, Salt Lake City; m. Faun Brimhall, five children; businessman, educator; mission president.

MCLELLIN, William E. Apostle, Feb. 15, 1835; excommunicated, May 11, 1838; b. Jan. 18, 1806, Smith County, Tennessee; d. April 24, 1883, Independence, Missouri; m. Cynthia Ann; three children; educator.

MCMURRIN, Joseph W. (William). Seventy, Oct. 5, 1897–Oct. 24, 1932; b. Sept. 5, 1858, Tooele, Utah; d. Oct. 24, 1932, Los Angeles, California; m. Mary Ellen Hunter, seven children; teamster, stone cutter; mission president.

MELCHIN, Gerald E. (Eldon). Seventy, Oct. 1, 1988; b. May 24, 1921, Kitchener, Canada; m. Evelyn Knowles, seven children; businessman; regional representative, mission president.

MERRILL, Joseph F. (Francis). Apostle, Oct. 8, 1931–Feb. 3, 1952; b. Aug. 24, 1868, Richmond, Utah; d. Feb. 3, 1952, Salt Lake City; m. Annie Laura Hyde, two children.

MERRILL, Marriner W. (Wood). Apostle, Oct. 1889–Feb. 6, 1906; b. Sept. 25, 1835, Sackville, New Brunswick; d. Feb. 6, 1906, Richmond, Utah; m. Sarah A. Atkinson; practiced plural marriage, forty-five children.

MICKELSEN, Lynn A. (Alvin). Seventy, Mar. 31, 1990; b. July 21, 1935, Idaho Falls, Idaho; m. Jeanine Andersen, nine children; farmer; regional representative, mission and stake president.

MILES, Daniel S. (Sanborn). Seventy, April 6, 1837–Oct. 12, 1845; b. July 23, 1772, Sanbornton, New Hampshire; d. Oct. 12, 1845, Hancock Co., Illinois; m. Electa Chamberlin, one child.

MILLER, George. Sustained in Nauvoo as Second Bishop of the Church, Oct. 7, 1844; dropped prior to 1847; disfellowshipped, Oct. 20, 1848; b. Nov. 25, 1794, Orange County, Virginia; d. 1856, Meringo County, Illinois; m. Mary Catherine Fry; practiced plural marriage, four children on record; carpenter-lumberman, farmer.

MILLER, Orrin Porter. Seventy, Feb. 10, 1884–July 7, 1918; Second counselor to Presiding Bishop Charles W. Nibley, Oct. 24, 1901; First counselor, Dec. 4, 1907–July 7, 1918; b. Sept. 11, 1858, Mill Creek, Utah; d. July 7, 1918, Salt Lake City; m. Elizabeth M. Morgan, nine children; businessman, rancher; stake president.

MONSON, Thomas S. (Spencer). Apostle, Oct. 4, 1963; Second counselor to President Ezra Taft Benson, Nov. 10, 1985; b. Aug. 21, 1927, Salt Lake City, Utah; m. Frances Beverly Johnson, three children; business executive; mission president.

MORGAN, John. Seventy, Oct. 8, 1884–Aug. 14, 1894; b. Aug. 8, 1842, Greensburg, Indiana; d. Aug. 14, 1894, Preston, Idaho; m. Helen M. Groesbeck, eleven children.

MORLEY, Isaac. First counselor to Presiding Bishop Edward Partridge, June 6, 1831; released at death of Bishop Partridge; b. Mar. 11, 1786, Montague, Massachusetts; d. June 24, 1865, Fairview, Utah; m. Lucy Gunn Blakeslee; practiced plural marriage, ten children; civic leader.

MORRIS, George Q. (Quayle). Asst. to the Twelve, Oct. 6, 1951; Apostle, April 8, 1954–April 23, 1962; b. Feb. 20, 1874, Salt Lake City, Utah; d. April 23, 1962, Salt Lake City; m. Emma Ramsey, three children; Young Men general board member, mission president.

MORRISON, Alexander B. (Baillie). Seventy, April 4, 1987; b. Dec. 22, 1930, Edmonton, Alberta, Canada; m. Shirley E. Brooks, eight children; educator; regional representative.

MOYLE, Henry D. (Dinwoodey). Apostle, April 10, 1947; Second counselor to President David O. McKay, June 12, 1959; First counselor, Oct. 12,

1961–Sept. 18, 1963; b. April 22, 1889, Salt Lake City, Utah; d. Sept. 18, 1963, Deer Park, Florida; m. Clara Alberta Wright, six children; attorney, business executive; stake president.

MURDOCK, Dorthea Lou Christiansen. Second counselor to general president Naomi M. Shumway, Primary, April 2, 1977–April 5, 1980; b. May 23, 1929; m. Robert Murdock, five children; homemaker; Primary general board member.

MUREN, Joseph C. (Carl). Seventy, April 6, 1991; b. Feb. 5, 1936, Richmond, California; m. Gladys Smith, six children; Church administration; mission and stake president.

NADAULD, Stephen D. (Douglas). Seventy, June 1, 1991; b. May 31, 1942, Idaho Falls, Idaho; m. Margaret Dyreng, seven children; business management, former president of Weber State College; regional representative.

NELSON, Russell M. (Marion). Apostle, April 12, 1984; b. Sept. 9, 1924, Salt Lake City, Utah; m. Dantzel White, ten children; heart surgeon; Sunday School general president, regional representative, stake president.

NEUENSCHWANDER, Dennis B. (Bramwell). Seventy, April 6, 1991; b. Oct. 6, 1939, Salt Lake City, Utah; m. LeAnn Clement, four children; Church administration; mission president.

NIBLEY, Charles W. (Wilson). Presiding Bishop of the Church, Dec. 4, 1907; Second counselor to President Heber J. Grant, May 28, 1925–Dec. 11, 1931; b. Feb. 5, 1849, Hunterfield, Scotland; d. Dec. 11, 1931, Salt Lake City, Utah; m. Rebecca Neibaur; practiced plural marriage, twenty-four children on record.

NYSTROM, Mae Taylor. Second counselor to general president Martha Horne Tingey, Young Women, April 5, 1905–July 15, 1923; b. Aug. 11, 1891, Salt Lake City, Utah; m. Theodore Nystrom, two children; Young Women general board member.

OAKS, Dallin H. (Harris). Apostle, May 3, 1984; b. Aug. 12, 1932, Provo, Utah; m. June Dixon, six children; Utah Supreme Court Justice, former President of BYU; regional representative.

OKAZAKI, Chieko Nishimura. First counselor to general president Elaine L. Jack, Relief Society, Mar. 31, 1990; b. Oct. 26, 1926, Kohala, Hawaii; m. Edward Yulio Okazaki, two children; homemaker, educator; Primary and Young Women general board member.

ORTON, Roger. Seventy, April 7, 1845, sustained but was never set apart and did not function; dropped from this position, Oct. 6, 1845; m. Clarissa Bicknell.

OSBORN, Spencer H. (Hamlin). Seventy, April 7, 1984–Oct. 1, 1989; b. July 8, 1921, Salt Lake City, Utah; m. Avanelle Richards, seven children; businessman; regional representative, mission and stake president.

OSWALD, William D. (Duncan). Second counselor to general president Russell M. Nelson, Sunday School, May 1978–Aug. 1979; b. Dec. 26, 1935; m. Mavis Morris, six children; attorney; Sunday School general board member.

PACE, Glenn L. (Leroy). Second counselor to Presiding Bishop Robert D. Hales, April 6, 1985; b. Mar. 21, 1940, Provo, Utah; m. Jolene Clayson, six children; certified public accountant; managing director of Welfare Services.

PACK, Sadie Grant. First counselor to general president May Anderson, Primary, Oct. 6, 1925–Sept. 11, 1939; b. Dec. 20, 1877, Bountiful, Utah; d. Aug. 23, 1960, Salt Lake City; m. Frederick J. Pack, four children.

PACKER, Boyd K. (Kenneth). Asst. to the Twelve, Sept. 30, 1961; Apostle, April 9, 1970; b. Sept. 10, 1924, Brigham City, Utah; m. Donna Smith, ten children; educator, assistant administrator of Seminaries and Institutes of Religion; mission president.

PAGE, John E. (Edward). Apostle, Dec. 19, 1838; disfellowshipped, Feb. 9, 1846; excommunicated, June 27, 1846; b. Feb. 25 or 26, 1799, Trenton Township, New York; d. Oct. 14, 1867, near Sycamore, De Kalb Co., Illinois; m. Lorain Stevens; practiced plural marriage, three children on record.

PARAMORE, James M. (Martin). Seventy, April 2, 1977; b. May 6, 1928, Salt Lake City, Utah; m. Helen Heslington, six children; executive secretary to the Quorum of the Twelve Apostles; regional representative, mission president.

PARMLEY, LaVern Watts. Second counselor to general president May Green Hinckley, Primary, May 1942–May 2, 1943; First counselor to general president Adele Cannon Howells, July 20, 1943–April 14, 1951; general president, May 16, 1951–Oct. 5, 1974; b. Jan. 1, 1900, Murray, Utah; d. Jan. 27, 1980; m. Thomas J. Parmley, three children; educator; Primary general board member.

PARTRIDGE, Edward. First Bishop of the Church, Feb. 4, 1831–May 27, 1840; b. Aug. 27, 1793, Pittsfield, Massachusetts; d. May 27, 1840, Nauvoo, Illinois; m. Lydia Clisbee, seven children; businessman.

PATTEN, David W. (Wyman). Apostle, Feb. 15, 1835–Oct. 25, 1838; b. Nov. 14, 1799, Theresa, New York; d. Oct. 25, 1838, at the Battle of Crooked River, Missouri; m. Phoebe Ann Babcock.

PAULSEN, Sara Broadbent. First counselor to general president Naomi M. Shumway, Primary, Oct. 5, 1974–April 2, 1977; b. Sept. 15, 1920, Heber City, Utah; m. Finn B. Paulsen, five children; stake Primary president, Primary general board member, temple matron.

PENROSE, Charles W. (William). Apostle, July 7, 1904; Second counselor to President Joseph F. Smith, Dec. 7, 1911; Second counselor to President Heber J. Grant, Mar. 10, 1921–May 16, 1925; b. Feb. 4, 1832, London, England; d. May 16, 1925, Salt Lake City, Utah; m. Lucetta Stratford, three children; mission president.

PERRY, L. (Lowell) Tom. Asst. to the Twelve, Oct. 6, 1972; Apostle, April 11, 1974; b. Aug. 5, 1922, Logan, Utah; m. Virginia Lee (d. 1974), three children; m. Barbara Dayton; business executive; stake president.

PETERSEN, Mark E. (Edward). Apostle, April 20, 1944–Jan. 11, 1974; b. Nov. 7, 1900, Salt Lake City, Utah; d. Jan. 11, 1974, Salt Lake City; m. Emma Marr McDonald, two children; newspaper editor.

PETERSON, H. (Harold) Burke. First counselor to Presiding Bishop Victor L. Brown, April 6, 1972; Seventy, April 6, 1985; b. Sept. 19, 1923, Salt Lake City, Utah; m. Brookie Cardon, five children; civil engineer; regional representative, temple and stake president.

PINEGAR, Rex D. (Dee). Seventy, Oct. 1, 1976; b. Sept. 18, 1931, Orem, Utah; m. Bonnie Lee Crabb, six children; educator; mission president.

PINNOCK, Hugh W. (Wallace). Seventy, Oct. 1, 1977; b. Jan. 15, 1934, Salt Lake City, Utah; m. Anne Hawkins, six children; business executive; regional representative, mission president.

POELMAN, B. (Byron) Lloyd. First counselor to general president Russell M. Nelson, Sunday School, April 1975–May 1978; b. July 1, 1934, Salt Lake City, Utah; m. Catherine Edwards, eight children; attorney; mission president.

POELMAN, Ronald E. (Eugene). Seventy, April 1, 1978; b. May 10, 1928, Salt Lake City, Utah; m. Claire Howell Stoddard (d. 1979), four children; m. Anne G. Osborn; business executive.

PORTER, L. (Lloyd) Aldin. Seventy, April 4, 1987; b. June 30, 1931, Salt Lake City, Utah; m. Shirley Palmer, six children; business executive; regional representative, mission and stake president.

PRATT, Orson. Apostle, April 26, 1835; excommunicated Aug. 20, 1842; rebaptized and reordained an Apostle, June 20, 1843–Oct. 3, 1881; seniority adjusted to date of second entry into the Quorum; b. Sept. 19, 1811, New York; d. Oct. 3, 1881, Salt Lake City, Utah; m. Sarah Marinda Bates; practiced plural marriage, forty-five children on record.

PRATT, Parley P. (Parker). Apostle, Feb. 21, 1835–May 13, 1857; b. April 12, 1807, Burlington, New York; assassinated, May 13, 1857, near Van Buren, Arkansas; m. Thankful Halsey; practiced plural marriage, thirty-one children on record.

PRATT, Rey L. (Lucero). Seventy, Jan. 29, 1925–April 14, 1931; b. Oct. 11, 1878, Salt Lake City, Utah; d. April 14, 1931, Salt Lake City; m. Mary Stark, 13 children; mission president.

PRESTON, William B. (Bowker). Presiding Bishop, April 6, 1884; released due to ill health, Dec. 4, 1907; b. Nov. 24, 1830, Halifax, Virginia; d. Aug. 2, 1908, Salt Lake City, Utah; m. Harriet A. Thatcher; stake president.

PULSIPHER, Zera. Seventy, Mar. 6, 1838; released, April 12, 1862; b. June 24, 1789, Rockingham, Vermont; d. Jan. 1, 1872, Hebron, Utah; m. Polly Randall (d.); m. Mary Brown; practiced plural marriage, sixteen children on record; farmer; stake patriarch.

PYPER, George D. (Dollinger). Second asst. to general superintendent David O. McKay, Sunday School, Dec. 1918–Oct. 1934; general superintendent, Dec. 1934–Jan. 1943; b. Nov. 21, 1860, Salt Lake City, Utah; d. Jan. 16, 1943, Salt Lake City; m. Emmaretta S. Whitney, two children; manager of Tabernacle Choir.

RANDALL, Naomi H. Ward. First counselor to general president LaVern Watts Parmley, Primary, Oct. 4, 1970–Oct. 5, 1974; b. Oct. 5, 1908, Pleasantville, Utah; m. Earl A. Randall, one child; author; Primary general board member (author of "I Am a Child of God," *Hymns*, no. 301).

READING, Lucile Cardon. Second counselor to general president LaVern Watts Parmley, Primary, July 23, 1963–Jan. 8, 1970; First counselor, Jan. 8, 1970–Aug. 6, 1970; b. Aug. 16, 1909, Logan, Utah; d. Mar. 22, 1982, Centerville; m. Keith E. Reading, two children; editor of the *Friend*.

RECTOR, Hartman, Jr. Seventy, April 6, 1968; b. Aug. 20, 1924, Moberly, Missouri; m. Constance Kirk Daniel, nine children; analyst, U.S. Department of Agriculture.

REEDER, Bertha Stone. General president, Young Women, April 6, 1948–Sept. 30, 1961; b. Oct. 28, 1893; m. William H. Reeder, Jr., three children.

REEVE, Rex C. (Cropper), Sr. Seventy, April 1, 1978; Emeritus General Authority, Oct. 1, 1989; b. Nov. 23, 1914, Hinckley, Utah; m. Phyllis Mae Nielson, seven children; business executive; regional representative, mission president.

REISER, A. (Albert) Hamer. First asst. to general superintendent George R. Hill, Sunday School, May 1943–Sept. 1949; b. Aug. 31, 1897, Salt Lake City, Utah; d. April 25, 1981, Salt Lake City; m. Elizabeth Baxter, seven children; business management; mission and stake president.

REYNOLDS, George. Seventy, April 5, 1890–Aug. 9, 1909; b. Jan. 1, 1842, London, England; d. Aug. 9, 1909, Salt Lake City, Utah; m. Mary Ann Tuddenham; practiced plural marriage, thirty-two children on record.

RICH, Charles C. (Coulsen). Apostle, Feb. 12, 1849–Nov. 17, 1883; b. Aug. 21, 1809, Campbell Co., Kentucky; d. Nov. 17, 1883, Paris, Idaho; m. Sarah DeArmen Pea; practiced plural marriage, fifty-one children on record; legislator.

RICH, Leonard. Seventy, Feb. 28, 1835; released April 6, 1837, having previously been ordained a high priest; m. Keziah.

RICHARDS, Florence Holbrook. Second counselor to general president LaVern Watts Parmley, Primary, May 16, 1951–June 11, 1953; b. July 7, 1905, Logan, Utah; m. Lorin L. Richards, three children; Primary general board member.

RICHARDS, Franklin D. (Dewey). Apostle, Feb. 12, 1849; President of the Quorum of the Twelve Apostles, Sept. 13, 1898–Dec. 9, 1899; b. April 2, 1821, Richmond, Massachusetts; d. Dec. 9, 1899, Ogden, Utah; m. Jane Snyder; practiced plural marriage, twenty-two children on record; judge.

RICHARDS, Franklin D. (Dewey). Asst. to the Twelve, Oct. 8, 1960; Seventy, Oct. 1, 1976–Nov. 13, 1987; b. Nov. 17, 1900, Ogden, Utah; d. Nov. 13, 1987, Salt Lake City; m. Helen Kearnes, four children; temple and mission president.

RICHARDS, George F. (Franklin). Apostle, April 9, 1906; Acting patriarch to the Church, Oct. 8, 1937–Oct. 3, 1942; President of the Quorum of the Twelve Apostles, May 21, 1945–Aug. 8, 1950; b. Feb. 23, 1861, Farmington, Utah; d. Aug. 8, 1950, Salt Lake City; m. Alice A. Robinson, fifteen children; mission president.

RICHARDS, Jane Snyder. First counselor to general president Zina Diantha Young, Relief Society, Oct. 11, 1888–Nov. 10, 1901; b. Jan. 31, 1823, Pamelia, New York; d. Nov. 17, 1912, Ogden, Utah; m. Franklin D. Richards, six children.

RICHARDS, LeGrand. Presiding Bishop, April 6, 1938; Apostle, April 10, 1952–Jan. 11, 1983; b. Feb. 6, 1886, Farmington, Utah; d. Jan. 11, 1983, Salt Lake City; m. Ina Jane Ashton, six children; businessman; mission and stake president.

RICHARDS, Lynn S. (Stephen). Second asst. to general superintendent George R. Hill, Sunday School, Oct. 1952–Nov. 1966; First asst. to general superintendent David Lawrence McKay, Nov. 1966–June 1971; b. Feb. 3, 1901, Salt Lake City, Utah; m. Lucille Janet Covey, four children; attorney.

RICHARDS, Stayner. Asst. to the Twelve, Oct. 6, 1951–May 28, 1953; b. Dec. 20, 1885, Salt Lake City, Utah; d. May 28, 1953, Salt Lake City; m. Jane Foote Taylor, six children; real estate, home construction; mission and stake president.

RICHARDS, Stephen L. Apostle, Jan. 18, 1917; First counselor to President David O. McKay, April 9, 1951–May 19, 1959; b. June 18, 1879, Mendon, Utah; d. May 19, 1959, Salt Lake City; m. Irene Merrill, nine children; attorney; Sunday School general board member.

RICHARDS, Willard. Apostle, April 14, 1840; Second counselor to President Brigham Young, Dec. 27, 1847–Mar. 11, 1854; b. June 24, 1804, Hopkinton, Massachusetts; d. Mar. 11, 1854, Salt Lake City, Utah; m. Jennetta Richards; practiced plural marriage, twenty children on record; physician, editor, historian.

RIGDON, Sidney. First counselor to President Joseph Smith, Mar. 18, 1833; excommunicated, Sept. 8, 1844; b. Feb. 19, 1793, Saint Clair Township, Pennsylvania; m. Phebe Brook, eleven children; d. July 14, 1876, Friendship, New York; preacher.

RINGGER, Hans B. (Benjamin). Seventy, April 6, 1985; b. Nov. 2, 1925, Zurich, Switzerland; m. Helene Suzy Zimmer, four children; architect, industrial designer; regional representative, stake president.

ROBERTS, B. (Brigham) H. (Henry). Seventy, Oct. 7, 1888–Sept. 27, 1933; b. Mar. 13, 1857, Warrington, England; d. Sept. 27, 1933, Salt Lake City, Utah; m. Sarah Louise Smith; practiced plural marriage, eight children on record; mission president.

ROBINSON, George W. Church historian, 1837–1840; b. May 14, 1814, Pawlet, Vermont; d. 1878, Friendship, New York; m. Athalia Rigdon.

ROBISON, Louise Yates. General president, Relief Society, Oct. 7, 1928–Dec. 1939; b. May 27, 1866, Scipio, Utah; d. Mar. 30, 1946, San Francisco, California; m. Joseph Lyman Robison, six children.

ROCKWOOD, Albert P. (Perry). Seventy, Dec. 2, 1845–Nov. 25, 1879; b. June 5, 1805, Holliston, Massachusetts; d. Nov. 25, 1879; m. Nancy Haven; practiced plural marriage, twenty-two children on record.

ROJAS ORNELAS, Jorge A. (Alfonso). Seventy, April 6, 1991; b. Sept. 27, 1940, Delicias, Mexico; m. Marcela Burgos, five children; businessman; regional representative, mission and stake president.

ROMNEY, Marion G. (George). Asst. to the Twelve, April 6, 1941; Apostle, Oct. 11, 1951; Second counselor to President Harold B. Lee, July 7, 1972; Second counselor to President Spencer W. Kimball, Dec. 30, 1973; First counselor to President Kimball, Dec. 2, 1982; President of the Quorum of the Twelve Apostles, Nov. 10, 1985–May 20, 1988; b. Sept. 19, 1897, Colonia Juárez, Mexico; d. May 20, 1988, Salt Lake City, Utah; m. Ida Jensen, two children; attorney; stake president, managing director of the Church Welfare Program.

ROSS, Isabelle Salmon. Second counselor to general president May Anderson, Primary, Oct. 6, 1925–Sept. 11, 1929; First counselor, Sept. 11, 1929–Dec. 31, 1939; b. Nov. 1, 1867, Percy, Utah; d. Dec. 28, 1947, Salt Lake City; m. Charles James Ross, three children; educator; Primary general board member.

RUDD, Glen L. (Larkin). Seventy, April 4, 1987; b. May 18, 1918, Salt Lake City, Utah; m. Marva Sperry, eight children; director of Welfare Square; regional representative, temple and mission president.

RUSSELL, Gardner H. (Hale). Seventy, April 6, 1986–Oct. 5, 1991; b. Aug. 12, 1920, Salt Lake City, Utah; m. Dorothy Richardson, four children; businessman; regional representative, mission president.

SACKLEY, Robert E. (Edward). Seventy, April 2, 1988; b. Dec. 17, 1922, Lismore, New South Wales, Australia; m. Marjorie Orth, five children; educator; mission president.

SCHAERRER, Neil D. (Dean). General president, Young Men, April 7, 1977–Oct. 1979; b. Apr. 12, 1930, Payson, Utah; d. Jan. 18, 1985, Salt Lake City; m. June Coon, four children; attorney; mission president.

SCOTT, Richard G. (Gordon). Seventy, April 2, 1977; Apostle, Oct. 6, 1988; b. Nov. 7, 1928, Pocatello, Idaho; m. Jeanene Watkins, seven children; nuclear engineer; regional representative, mission president.

SCOTT, Verl F. (Franklin). Second asst. to general superintendent G. Carlos Smith, Young Men, June 9, 1961–Oct. 4, 1961; b. July 8, 1919, Hinckley, Utah; d. April 17, 1989, Salt Lake City; m. Arline Martindale, seven children; *Improvement Era* business manager; stake president, Young Men general board member.

SHARP, Marianne Clark. First counselor to general president Belle S. Spafford, Relief Society, April 6, 1945–Oct. 3, 1974; b. Oct. 28, 1901, Grantsville, Utah; d. Jan. 2, 1990, Salt Lake City; m. Ivor Sharp, three children; editor of *Relief Society Magazine*.

SHERMAN, Lyman R. (Royal). Seventy, Feb. 28, 1835; released, April 6, 1837, having previously been ordained a high priest; b. May 22, 1804, Salem, Massachusetts; d. Jan. 27, 1839, Far West, Missouri; m. Delcena Didamia Johnson, six children.

SHIMABUKURO, Sam K. (Koyei). Seventy, July 5, 1991; b. June 7, 1925, Waipahu, Hawaii; m. Amy Michiko Hirose, one child; retired state employee; mission and stake president.

SHUMWAY, Naomi Maxfield. General president, Primary, Oct. 5, 1974–April 5, 1980; b. Oct. 3, 1922, Provo, Utah; m. Roden Grant Shumway, three children; stake Primary president, Primary general board member.

SILL, Sterling W. (Welling). Asst. to the Twelve, April 6, 1954; Seventy, Oct. 1, 1976; Emeritus General Authority, Sept. 30, 1978; b. Mar. 31, 1903, Layton, Utah; m. Doris Mary Thornley, three children; business executive.

SIMONSEN, Velma Nebeker. Second counselor to general president Belle S. Spafford, Relief Society, Oct. 3, 1947–Dec. 17, 1956; b. July 15, 1896; m. John O. Simonsen, four children; Relief Society general board member.

SIMPSON, Robert L. (Leatham). First counselor to Presiding Bishop John H. Vandenberg, Sept. 30, 1961; Asst. to the Twelve, April 6, 1972; Seventy, Oct. 1, 1976; Emeritus General Authority, Oct. 1, 1989; b. Aug. 8, 1915,

Salt Lake City, Utah; m. Jelaire Chandler, four children; business executive; mission president.

SLOAN, James. Church historian, 1841–1843; b. Oct. 28, 1792, Donaghmore, Ireland; d. Salt Lake City, Utah; m. Mary Magill.

SMITH, Barbara Bradshaw. General president, Relief Society, Oct. 3, 1974–April 7, 1984; b. Jan. 22, 1922, Salt Lake City, Utah; m. Douglas H. Smith, seven children; Relief Society general board member.

SMITH, Bathsheba Wilson. Second counselor to general president Zina Diantha Young, Relief Society, Oct. 11, 1888–Nov. 10, 1901; general president, Nov. 10, 1901–Sept. 20, 1910; b. May 3, 1822, Shinnston, West Virginia; d. Sept. 20, 1910, Salt Lake City, Utah; m. George A. Smith, three children.

SMITH, David A. (Asael). Second counselor to Presiding Bishop Charles W. Nibley, Dec. 4, 1907; First counselor, July 18, 1918; First counselor to Presiding Bishop Sylvester Q. Cannon, June 4, 1925; released April 6, 1938, when Bishop Sylvester Q. Cannon was ordained an apostle; b. May 24, 1879, Salt Lake City, Utah; d. April 6, 1952, Salt Lake City; m. Emily Jenkins, nine children.

SMITH, Douglas H. (Hill). Seventy, April 4, 1987; b. May 11, 1921, Salt Lake City, Utah; m. Barbara Jean Bradshaw, seven children; business executive; regional representative, stake president.

SMITH, Eldred G. (Gee). Patriarch to the Church, April 10, 1947; Emeritus General Authority, Oct. 4, 1980; b. Jan. 9, 1907, Lehi, Utah; m. Jeanne Ness (d. 1977), five children; m. Hortense Child.

SMITH, Emma Hale. First general president of the Relief Society, May 17, 1842–Mar. 16, 1844; b. July 10, 1804, Harmony, Pennsylvania; d. April 30, 1879, Nauvoo, Illinois; m. Joseph Smith, Jr. (d. 1844), eleven children; m. Lewis Crum Bidamon.

SMITH, G. (George) Carlos, Jr. General superintendent, Young Men, 1963–1969; b. Aug. 23, 1910, Salt Lake City, Utah; d. Mar. 29, 1987, Salt Lake City; m. La Von Petersen, five children; regional representative, mission and stake president.

SMITH, George A. (Albert). Apostle, April 26, 1839; First counselor to President Brigham Young, Oct. 7, 1868–Sept. 1, 1875; b. June 26, 1817, Potsdam, New York; d. Sept. 1, 1875, Salt Lake City, Utah; m. Bathsheba

Wilson Bigler; practiced plural marriage, thirty children on record; farmer, legislator; Church historian and recorder.

SMITH, George Albert. Apostle, Oct. 8, 1903; President of the Quorum of the Twelve Apostles, July 1, 1943; President of the Church, May 21, 1945–April 4, 1951; b. April 4, 1870, Salt Lake City, Utah; d. April 4, 1951, Salt Lake City; m. Lucy Emily Woodruff, three children; businessman; mission president.

SMITH, Hyrum. Second counselor to the First Presidency, Sept. 3, 1837; Second counselor to President Joseph Smith, Nov. 7, 1837; given all priesthood offices that had been originally held by Oliver Cowdery, including Apostle; Patriarch to the Church and Assistant President of the Church, Jan. 24, 1841–June 27, 1844; b. Feb. 9, 1800, Tunbridge, Vermont; martyred June 27, 1844, at Carthage Jail, Carthage, Illinois; m. Jerusha Barden (d. 1836), six children; m. Mary Fielding, two children; practiced plural marriage, no other children on record; farmer.

SMITH, Hyrum Gibbs. Patriarch to the Church, May 9, 1912–Feb. 4, 1932; b. July 8, 1879, South Jordan, Utah; d. Feb. 4, 1932, Salt Lake City; m. Martha Gee, six children; dentist.

SMITH, Hyrum Mack. Apostle, Oct. 24, 1901–Jan. 23, 1918; b. Mar. 21, 1872, Salt Lake City, Utah; d. Jan. 23, 1918, Salt Lake City; m. Ida Bowman, five children; business executive; mission president.

SMITH, John. Asst. counselor in the First Presidency, Sept. 3, 1837; released at death of Joseph Smith, June 27, 1844; Patriarch to the Church, Jan. 1, 1849–May 23, 1854; b. July 16, 1781, Derryfield, New Hampshire; d. May 23, 1854, Salt Lake City, Utah; m. Clarissa Lyman; practiced plural marriage, four children on record; stake president.

SMITH, John (son of Hyrum Smith). Patriarch to the Church, Feb. 18, 1855–Nov. 5, 1911; b. Sept. 22, 1832, Kirtland, Ohio; d. Nov. 5, 1911, Salt Lake City, Utah; m. Helen Maria Fisher, nine children.

SMITH, John Henry. Apostle, Oct. 27, 1880; Second counselor to President Joseph F. Smith, April 7, 1910–Oct. 13, 1911; b. Sept. 18, 1848, Carbunca (now Council Bluffs), Iowa; d. Oct. 13, 1911, Salt Lake City, Utah; m. Sarah Farr; practiced plural marriage, nineteen children on record; railroad businessman, legislator; mission president.

SMITH, Joseph, Jr. Apostle, May–June 1829, ordained by Peter, James, and John; First Elder and President of the Church, April 6, 1830–June 27, 1844; President of the high priesthood, Jan. 25, 1832; b. Dec. 23, 1805,

Sharon, Vermont; martyred June 27, 1844, at Carthage Jail, Carthage, Illinois; m. Emma Hale, eleven children (including two adopted); practiced plural marriage, no other children on record; farmer.

SMITH, Joseph F. (Fielding). Apostle and counselor to President Brigham Young, July 1, 1866; released at the death of President Young, Aug. 29, 1877; Second counselor to President John Taylor, Oct. 10, 1880; released at President Taylor's death, July 25, 1887; Second counselor to President Wilford Woodruff, April 7, 1889; Second counselor to President Lorenzo Snow, Sept. 13, 1898; First counselor to President Snow, Oct. 6, 1901; President of the Church, Oct. 17, 1901–Nov. 19, 1918; b. Nov. 13, 1838, Far West, Missouri; d. Nov. 19, 1918, Salt Lake City, Utah; m. Levira Annett Clark; practiced plural marriage, forty-eight children on record; farmer, civic official.

SMITH, Joseph F. (Fielding). Patriarch to the Church, Sept. 17, 1942–Oct. 6, 1946; b. Salt Lake City, Utah, Jan. 30, 1899; d. Salt Lake City, Aug. 29, 1964; married Ruth Pingree, seven children; educator; Young Men's General Board.

SMITH, Joseph Fielding. Apostle, April 7, 1910; Acting president of the Quorum of the Twelve Apostles, Sept. 30, 1950; President of the Quorum of the Twelve Apostles, April 9, 1951; Counselor in the First Presidency, Oct. 29, 1965; President of the Church, Jan. 23, 1970–July 2, 1972; b. July 19, 1876, Salt Lake City, Utah; d. July 2, 1972, Salt Lake City, Utah; m. Louie E. Shurtliff (d. 1908), two children; m. Ethel G. Reynolds (d. 1937), nine children; m. Jessie Ella Evans; historian.

SMITH, Joseph, Sr. Patriarch to the Church, Dec. 18, 1833; Asst. counselor to the First Presidency, Sept. 3, 1837–Sept. 14, 1840; b. July 12, 1771, Topsfield, Massachusetts; d. Sept. 14, 1840, Nauvoo, Illinois; m. Lucy Mack, ten children; farmer.

SMITH, Julina Lambson. Second counselor to general president Emmeline B. Wells, Relief Society, Oct. 3, 1910–April 2, 1921; b. June 18, 1849, Salt Lake City, Utah; d. Jan. 10, 1936, Salt Lake City; m. Joseph F. Smith, eleven children; homemaker.

SMITH, Nicholas G. (Groesbeck). Asst. to the Twelve, April 6, 1941–Oct. 27, 1945; b. June 20, 1881, Salt Lake City, Utah; d. Oct. 27, 1945, Salt Lake City; m. Florence Gay, four children; business executive, mission president.

SMITH, Norma Broadbent. Second counselor to general president Elaine A. Cannon, Young Women, July 12, 1978–April 7, 1984; b. May 24, 1923,

Heber City, Utah; m. Lowell D. Smith, eight children; Primary general board member.

SMITH, Sylvester. Seventy, Feb. 28, 1835; released April 6, 1837, having previously been ordained a high priest; b. approximately 1805; left the Church by 1838; m. Elizabeth.

SMITH, William. Apostle, Feb. 15, 1835; dropped from the Quorum, May 4, 1839; restored to the Quorum, May 25, 1839; dropped from the Quorum, Oct. 6, 1845; excommunicated, Oct. 19, 1845; b. Mar. 13, 1811, Royalton, Vermont; d. Nov. 13, 1894, Osterdock, Iowa; m. Caroline Amanda Grant; practiced plural marriage, seven children on record.

SMOOT, Reed. Apostle, April 8, 1900–Feb. 9, 1941; b. Jan. 10, 1862, Salt Lake City, Utah; d. Feb. 9, 1941, St. Petersburg, Florida; m. Alpha M. Eldredge, six children; business executive, U.S. Senator 1903–1932.

SNOW, Eliza R. (Roxcy, most often spelled Roxey). General president, Relief Society, 1866–Dec. 5, 1887; b. Jan. 21, 1804, Becket, Massachusetts; d. Dec. 5, 1887, Salt Lake City, Utah; m. Joseph Smith, Jr. (d. 1844); m. Brigham Young; writer, poet.

SNOW, Erastus. Apostle, Feb. 12, 1849–May 27, 1888; b. Nov. 9, 1818, Saint Johnsbury, Vermont; d. May 27, 1888, Salt Lake City, Utah; m. Artimesia Beaman; practiced plural marriage, thirty-six children on record; mission president.

SNOW, Lorenzo. Apostle, Feb. 12, 1849; Counselor to President Brigham Young, April 8, 1873; Asst. counselor, May 9, 1874; President of the Quorum of the Twelve Apostles, April 7, 1889; President of the Church, Sept. 13, 1898–Oct. 10, 1901; b. April 3, 1814, Mantua, Ohio; d. Oct. 10, 1901, Salt Lake City, Utah; m. Mary Adaline Goddard; practiced plural marriage, forty-two children on record; educator.

SONNE, Alma. Asst. to the Twelve, April 6, 1941; Seventy, Oct. 1, 1976–Nov. 27, 1977; b. Mar. 5, 1884, Logan, Utah; d. Nov. 27, 1977, Logan; m. Geneva Ballantyne (d. 1941), five children; m. Leona Ballantyne Woolley; businessman; mission and stake president.

SONNENBERG, John. Seventy, Oct. 6, 1985–Oct. 1, 1989; b. April 11, 1922, Schneidemuhle, Germany; m. Joyce C. Dalton, seven children; dentist; regional representative, stake president.

SONNTAG, Philip T. (Tadje). Seventy, April 7, 1984; Second counselor to general president Robert L. Simpson, Sunday School, Aug. 1987–Aug.

1988; b. July 13, 1921; m. Voloy Andreasen, three children; jeweler; regional representative, director of Temple Square.

SORENSEN, Donna Durrant. Second counselor to general president Amy Brown Lyman, Relief Society, April 1940–Oct. 12, 1942; b. Dec. 24, 1904, Spanish Fork, Utah; d. June 4, 1990, Salt Lake City; m. Wesley A. Sorensen, three children.

SORENSEN, Lynn A. (Andrew). Seventy, April 4, 1987; b. Sept. 25, 1919, Salt Lake City, Utah; m. Janet Elaine Weech, nine children; management; mission president.

SPAFFORD, Belle Smith. General president, Relief Society, April 6, 1945–Oct. 3, 1974; b. Oct. 8, 1895, Salt Lake City, Utah; d. Feb. 2, 1982, Salt Lake City; m. Willis Earl Spafford, two children; writer.

STAPLEY, Delbert L. (Leon). Apostle, Oct. 5, 1950–Aug. 19, 1978; b. Dec. 11, 1896, Mesa, Arizona; d. Aug. 19, 1978, Salt Lake City, Utah; m. Ethel Davis, three children; business executive; stake president.

STEVENSON, A. (Alfred) Walter. First asst. to general superintendent Elbert R. Curtis, Young Men, 1948–1958; b. Oct. 6, 1900, Ogden, Utah; d. Nov. 27, 1974; m. Effie Peck, four children.

STEVENSON, Edward. Seventy, Oct. 7, 1894–Jan. 27, 1897; b. May 1, 1820, Gibraltar, Spain; d. Jan. 27, 1897, Salt Lake City, Utah; m. Nancy Arede Porter; practiced plural marriage, twenty-four children on record; tinsmith.

STONE, O. (Oscar) Leslie. Asst. to the Twelve, Oct. 6, 1972; Seventy, Oct. 1, 1976; Emeritus General Authority, Oct. 4, 1980; b. May 28, 1903, Chapin, Idaho; d. April 26, 1986, Salt Lake City, Utah; m. Dorothy Cobbley, four children; business executive; regional representative, temple and stake president.

TALMAGE, James E. (Edward). Apostle, Dec. 8, 1911–July 27, 1933; b. Sept. 21, 1862, Hungerford, England; d. July 27, 1933, Salt Lake City, Utah; m. Mary May Booth, eight children; writer, former president of the University of Utah.

TANNER, Joseph Marion. Second asst. to general superintendent Lorenzo Snow, Sunday School, May 1901–Oct. 1901; Second asst. to general superintendent Joseph F. Smith, Sunday School, Nov. 1901–April 1906; b. Mar. 26, 1859, Payson, Utah; d. Aug. 19, 1927, Lethbridge, Alberta, Canada; m. Josephine Snow; practiced plural marriage, seventeen children on record; former president of Utah Agricultural College (now Utah State University).

TANNER, N. (Nathan) Eldon. Asst. to the Twelve, Oct. 8, 1960; Apostle, Oct. 11, 1962; Second counselor to President David O. McKay, Oct. 4, 1963; Second counselor to President Joseph Fielding Smith, Jan. 23, 1970; First counselor to President Harold B. Lee, July 7, 1972; First counselor to President Spencer W. Kimball, Dec. 30, 1973–Nov. 27, 1982; b. May 9, 1898, Salt Lake City, Utah; d. Nov. 27, 1982, Salt Lake City; m. Sara Isabelle Merrill, five children; businessman and educator.

TAYLOR, Anstis Elmina Shepherd. General president, Young Women, June 19, 1880–Dec. 6, 1904; b. Sept. 12, 1830, Middlefield, New York; d. Dec. 6, 1904, Salt Lake City, Utah; m. George Hamilton Taylor.

TAYLOR, Henry D. (Dixon). Asst. to the Twelve, April 6, 1958; Seventy, Oct. 1, 1976; Emeritus General Authority, Sept. 30, 1978; b. Nov. 22, 1903, Provo, Utah; d. Feb. 24, 1987, Salt Lake City; m. Alta Hansen (d. 1967), four children; m. Ethelyn Peterson; business executive; mission and stake president.

TAYLOR, John. Apostle, Dec. 19, 1838; President of the Quorum of the Twelve Apostles, Oct. 6, 1877; President of the Church, Oct. 10, 1880–July 25, 1887; b. Nov. 1, 1808, Milnthrope, England; d. July 25, 1887, Kaysville, Utah; m. Leonora Cannon; practiced plural marriage, thirty-five children on record; farmer.

TAYLOR, John H. (Harris). Seventy, Oct. 6, 1933–May 28, 1946; b. June 28, 1875, Salt Lake City, Utah; d. May 28, 1946, Salt Lake City; m. Susan Rachel Grant, two children; dentist; mission president.

TAYLOR, John W. (Whittaker). Apostle, April 9, 1884; resigned, Oct. 28, 1905; excommunicated for polygamy, Mar. 28, 1911; b. May 15, 1858, Provo, Utah; d. Oct. 10, 1916, Salt Lake City; m. May Leona Rich; practiced plural marriage, twenty-nine children on record.

TAYLOR, Margaret Young. First counselor to general president Elmina Shepherd Taylor, Young Women, June 19, 1880–1887; b. April 24, 1837, Westport, Connecticut; d. May 3, 1919, Salt Lake City, Utah; m. John Taylor, nine children.

TAYLOR, Russell C. (Carl). Seventy, April 7, 1984–Oct. 1, 1989; b. Nov. 25, 1925, Red Mesa, Colorado; m. Joyce Elaine Mortensen, six children; business executive; regional representative, mission and stake president.

TAYLOR, William W. (Whittaker). Seventy, April 7, 1880–Aug. 1, 1884; b. Sept. 11, 1853, Salt Lake City, Utah; d. Aug. 1, 1884, Salt Lake City;

m. Sarah Taylor Hoagland; practiced plural marriage, eight children on record.

TEASDALE, George. Apostle, Oct. 16, 1882–June 9, 1907; b. Dec. 8, 1831, London, England; d. June 9, 1907, Salt Lake City, Utah; m. Emily Emma Brown; mission president.

TENORIO, Horacio A. (Antonio). Seventy, April 1, 1989; b. Mar. 6, 1935, Mexico, D.F., Mexico; m. Maria Teresa de Tenorio, three children; businessman; regional representative, mission and stake president.

THATCHER, Moses. Apostle, April 9, 1879; dropped from the Quorum, April 6, 1896; b. Feb. 2, 1842, Springfield, Illinois; d. Aug. 21, 1909, Logan, Utah; m. Celestia Ann Farr; practiced plural marriage, eleven children on record; businessman; mission president.

THOMAS, Edna Harker. Second counselor to general president May Anderson, Primary, Sept. 11, 1929–Dec. 11, 1933; b. Apr. 11, 1881, Taylorsville, Utah; d. Apr. 29, 1942, Washington, D.C.; m. Elbert D. Thomas, three children.

THOMAS, Shirley Wilkes. Second counselor to general president Barbara B. Smith, Relief Society, Nov. 28, 1978–April 7, 1984; b. Feb. 26, 1925, Englewood, California; m. Robert K. Thomas, three children; Relief Society general board member, stake Relief Society president.

THOMPSON, Robert B. (B[l]ashel). Church historian, 1840–1841; b. Oct. 1, 1811, Great Driffield, England; d. Aug. 27, 1841, Nauvoo, Illinois; m. Mercy Rachel Fielding, one child.

THOMPSON, Janet Lennox Murdock. Second counselor to general president May Green Hinckley, Primary, Jan. 1, 1940–May 2, 1943; b. Aug. 8, 1884, Salt Lake City, Utah; d. April 24, 1953, Salt Lake City; m. Jerrold E. Thompson.

TINGEY, Earl C. (Carr). Seventy, Dec. 5, 1990; b. June 11, 1934, Bountiful, Utah; m. Joanne Wells, four children; attorney; regional representative, mission president.

TINGEY, Martha Jane Horne. General president, Young Women, April 5, 1905–Mar. 28, 1929; b. Oct. 15, 1857, Salt Lake City, Utah; d. Mar. 11, 1938, Salt Lake City; m. Joseph S. Tingey, seven children.

TURLEY, Maurine Johnson. Second counselor to general president Ardeth G. Kapp, Young Women, May 11, 1984–April 6, 1986; First counselor, April 6, 1986–April 4, 1987; b. May 2, 1931; m. Robert S. Turley, Jr., five children; educator.

TUTTLE, A. (Albert) Theodore. Seventy, Oct. 1, 1976–Nov. 28, 1986; b. Mar. 2, 1919, Manti, Utah; d. Nov. 28, 1986, Salt Lake City; m. Marné Whitaker, seven children; educator; mission and temple president.

VAN COTT, John. Seventy, Oct. 8, 1862–Feb. 18, 1883; b. Sept. 7, 1814, Canaan, New York; d. Feb. 18, 1883, Salt Lake City, Utah; m. Lucy Sackett; practiced plural marriage, twenty-eight children on record; businessman, legislator, farmer.

VANDENBERG, John H. (Henry). Presiding Bishop, Sept. 30, 1961; Asst. to the Twelve, April 6, 1972; Emeritus General Authority, Sept. 30, 1978; b. Dec. 18, 1904, Ogden, Utah; m. Ariena Stok, two children; rancher, businessman; mission president.

WARNER, Richard L. (Longstroth). Second counselor to general president Russell M. Nelson, Sunday School, June 1971–April 1975; m. Marian Nelson, nine children; businessman; regional representative, stake president.

WASHBURN, J Ballard. Seventy, Mar. 31, 1990; b. Jan. 18, 1929, Blanding, Utah; m. Barbara Harries, ten children; physician; regional representative, mission and stake president.

WELLS, Daniel H. (Hanmer). Second counselor to President Brigham Young, Jan. 4, 1857; released at the death of President Young, Aug. 29, 1877; Counselor to the Twelve, Oct. 6, 1877–Mar. 24, 1891; b. Oct. 27, 1814, Trenton, New Jersey; d. Mar. 24, 1891, Salt Lake City, Utah; m. Eliza Rebecca Robinson; practiced plural marriage, thirty-five children on record; public servant, educator, farmer; mission president.

WELLS, Emmeline B. (Blanche) Woodward. General president, Relief Society, Oct. 3, 1910–April 2, 1921; b. Feb. 29, 1828, Petersham, Massachusetts; d. April 25, 1921, Salt Lake City, Utah; m. James Harvey Harris (d. 1845), two children; m. Newel K. Whitney (d. 1850), two children, m. Daniel H. Wells, three children; writer and editor.

WELLS, John. Second counselor to Presiding Bishop Charles W. Nibley, July 18, 1918; Second counselor to Presiding Bishop Sylvester Q. Cannon, June 4, 1925; released, April 6, 1938, when Bishop Cannon was ordained an apostle; b. Sept. 16, 1864, Carlton, England; d. April 18, 1941, Salt Lake City, Utah; m. Almena Thorpe, seven children; hospital administrator.

WELLS, Junius F. (Free). Seventy, Oct. 1875–Mar. 24, 1891; general superintendent, Young Men, 1876–1880; b. June 1, 1854, Salt Lake City, Utah; d. April 15, 1930, Salt Lake City; m. Helena Middleton Fobes, two children; asst. Church historian.

WELLS, Robert E. (Earl). Seventy, Oct. 1, 1978; b. Dec. 28, 1927, Las Vegas, Nevada; m. Meryl Leavitt (d. 1960); m. Helen Walser, seven children; banking executive; regional representative, mission and stake president; father of Sharlene Wells Hawkes, Miss America, 1985.

WELLS, Rulon S. (Seymour). Seventy, April 5, 1893–May 7, 1941; b. July 7, 1854, Salt Lake City, Utah; d. May 7, 1941, Salt Lake City; m. Josephine E. Beatie, seven children; businessman; Young Men general board member, mission president.

WEST, Franklin L. (Lorenzo). Second asst. to general superintendent Albert E. Bowen, Young Men, 1935–1937; b. Feb. 1, 1885, Ogden, Utah; d. Oct. 21, 1966, Salt Lake City; m. Violet Madsen, six children; educator; Commissioner of Church Education.

WEST, Josephine Richards. Second counselor to general president Louie B. Felt, Primary, Dec. 15, 1896–Nov. 24, 1905; b. May 25, 1853, Salt Lake City, Utah; d. April 23, 1933, Logan; m. Joseph A. West, six children; stake Primary president.

WHITMER, John. Church historian, 1831–1835; excommunicated, Mar. 10, 1838; b. Aug. 27, 1802; d. July 11, 1878, Far West, Missouri; m. Sarah Jackson, five children; farmer.

WHITNEY, Elizabeth Ann Smith. Second counselor to general president Emma Hale Smith, Relief Society, May 17, 1842–Mar. 16, 1844; Second counselor to general president Eliza R. Snow, Relief Society, June 19, 1880–Feb. 15, 1882; b. Dec. 26, 1800, Derby, Connecticut; d. Feb. 15, 1883, Salt Lake City, Utah; m. Newel K. Whitney, eleven children.

WHITNEY, Newel K. (Kimball). First Bishop of Kirtland, Oct. 7, 1844; Presiding Bishop, April 6, 1847–Sept. 23, 1850; b. Feb. 5, 1795, Marlborough, Vermont; d. Sept. 23, 1850, Salt Lake City, Utah; m. Elizabeth Ann Smith; practiced plural marriage, fourteen children on record; merchant.

WHITNEY, Orson F. (Ferguson). Apostle, April 9, 1906–May 16, 1931; b. July 1, 1855, Salt Lake City, Utah; d. May 16, 1931, Salt Lake City; m. Zina Beal Smoot; practiced plural marriage, twelve children on record.

WIDTSOE, John A. (Andreas). Apostle, Mar. 17, 1921–Nov. 29, 1952; b. Jan. 31, 1872, Dalöe, Island of Fröyen, Norway; d. Nov. 29, 1952, Salt Lake City, Utah; m. Leah Eudora Dunford, seven children; educator, former president of Utah State Agricultural College and of the University of Utah; Young Men general board member.

WIGHT, Lyman. Apostle, April 8, 1841; excommunicated, Dec. 3, 1848; b. May 9, 1796, Fairfield, New York; d. Mar. 31, 1858, Dexter, Texas; m. Harriet Benton, six children.

WILCOX, Keith W. (Wilson). Seventy, Oct. 6, 1984–Oct. 1, 1989; b. May 15, 1921, Hyrum, Utah; m. Viva May Gammell, six children; architect; regional representative, temple, mission, and stake president. (Architect of the Washington, D.C. Temple.)

WILLIAMS, Clarissa Smith. First counselor to general president Emmeline B. Wells, Relief Society, Oct. 3, 1910–April 2, 1921; general president, Relief Society, April 2, 1921–Oct. 7, 1928; b. April 21, 1859, Salt Lake City, Utah; d. Mar. 8, 1930; m. William N. Williams, eleven children.

WILLIAMS, Frederick G. (Granger). Second counselor to President Joseph Smith, Mar. 18, 1833; rejected, Nov. 7, 1837; excommunicated, Mar. 17, 1839; restored to fellowship, April 8, 1840; b. Oct. 28, 1787, Suffield, Connecticut; d. Oct. 25, 1842, Quincy, Illinois; m. Rebecca Swain, four children; businessman.

WILLIAMS, Helen Spencer. First counselor to general president Lucy Grant Cannon, Young Women, Nov. 1937–May 17, 1944; b. Nov. 29, 1896, Salt Lake City, Utah; d. Aug. 10, 1965, Salt Lake City; m. Rex W. Williams, three children.

WINDER, Barbara Woodhead. General president, Relief Society, April 7, 1984–Mar. 31, 1990; b. May 9, 1931, Midvale, Utah; m. Richard W. Winder, four children; homemaker; Relief Society general board member.

WINDER, John R. (Rex). Second counselor to Presiding Bishop William B. Preston, April 8, 1887; First counselor to President Joseph F. Smith, Oct. 17, 1901–Mar. 27, 1910; b. Dec. 11, 1821, Biddenham, England; d. Mar. 27, 1910, Salt Lake City, Utah; m. Ellen Walters Winder (d. 1892), ten children; m. Maria Burnham; business executive.

WIRTHLIN, Joseph B. (Bitner). First counselor to general president Russell M. Nelson, Sunday School, June 1971–April 1975; Asst. to the Twelve, April 4, 1975; Seventy, Oct. 1, 1976; Apostle, Oct. 9, 1986; b. June 11, 1917, Salt Lake City, Utah; m. Elisa Young Rogers, eight children; businessman.

WIRTHLIN, Joseph L. (Leopold). Second counselor to Presiding Bishop LeGrand Richards, April 6, 1938; First counselor, Dec. 12, 1946; Presiding Bishop, April 6, 1952–Sept. 30 1961; b. Aug 14, 1893, Salt Lake City,

Utah; d. Jan. 25, 1963, Salt Lake City; m. Madeline Bitner, five children; businessman; stake president.

WOODRUFF, Abraham O. (Owens). Apostle, Oct. 7, 1897–June 20, 1904; b. Nov. 23, 1872, Salt Lake City, Utah; d. June 20, 1904, El Paso, Texas; m. Helen May Winters.

WOODRUFF, Wilford. Apostle, April 26, 1839; President of the Quorum of the Twelve Apostles, Oct. 10, 1880; President of the Church, April 7, 1889–Sept. 2, 1898; b. Mar. 1, 1807, Avon (now Farmington), Connecticut; d. Sept. 2, 1898, San Francisco, California; m. Phoebe Whittemore Carter; practiced plural marriage, thirty-three children on record; miller.

WOOLSEY, Durrel A. (Arden). Seventy, Mar. 31, 1990; b. June 12, 1926, Stockton, California; m. LaRae Wood, three children; businessman; mission and stake president.

WRIGHT, Ruth Broadbent. Second counselor to general president Michaelene P. Grassli, Primary, April 2, 1988; b. Bingham, Utah; m. Gary E. Wright, five children; educator; stake Primary president, stake Young Women president.

YOUNG, Brigham. Apostle, Feb. 14, 1835; President of the Quorum of the Twelve Apostles, April 14, 1840; President of the Church, Dec. 27, 1847–Aug. 29, 1877; b. June 1, 1801, Whitingham, Vermont; d. Aug. 29, 1877, Salt Lake City, Utah; m. Miriam Words (d. 1824), two children; m. Mary Ann Angell; practiced plural marriage, sixty-one children on record (including four adopted children); carpenter-glazier.

YOUNG, Brigham, Jr. Apostle, Feb. 4, 1864; Member of the Quorum of the Twelve Apostles, Oct. 9, 1868; Counselor to President Young, April 8, 1873; Asst. counselor to President Young, May 9, 1874; released, Aug. 29, 1877, at the death of President Young; President of the Quorum of Twelve Apostles, Oct. 17, 1901–April 11, 1903; b. Dec. 18, 1836, Kirtland, Ohio; d. April 11, 1903, Salt Lake City, Utah; m. Catherine Curtis Spencer; practiced plural marriage, eighteen children on record; mission president.

YOUNG, Clifford E. (Earle). Asst. to the Twelve, April 6, 1941–Aug. 21, 1958; b. Dec. 7, 1883, Salt Lake City, Utah; d. Aug. 21, 1958, Salt Lake City; m. Edith Grant, four children; businessman, civic leader; stake president.

YOUNG, Dwan Jacobsen. General president, Primary, April 5, 1980–April 2, 1988; b. May 1, 1931, Salt Lake City, Utah; m. Thomas Young, Jr., five children; homemaker; Primary general board member.

YOUNG, John W. (Willard). Counselor to President Brigham Young, April 8, 1873; Asst. counselor, May 9, 1874; First counselor, Oct. 7, 1876; released at death of President Young; Counselor to the Twelve, Oct. 6, 1877–Oct. 6, 1891; b. Oct. 1, 1844, Nauvoo, Illinois; d. Feb. 11, 1924, New York City, New York; m. Lucy Maria Canfield; practiced plural marriage, ten children on record; builder of Utah railroads.

YOUNG, Joseph. Seventy, Feb. 28, 1835–July 16, 1881; b. April 7, 1797, Hopkinton, Massachusetts; d. July 16, 1881, Salt Lake City, Utah; m. Jane A. Bicknell; practiced plural marriage, twenty children on record.

YOUNG, Joseph Angell. Apostle, Feb. 4, 1864–Aug. 5, 1875; never served in Quorum of the Twelve; b. Oct. 14, 1834, Kirtland, Ohio; d. Aug. 5, 1875, Manti, Utah; m. Clara Federata Stenhouse; practiced plural marriage, eleven children on record.

YOUNG, Levi Edgar. Seventy, Oct. 6, 1909–Dec. 13, 1963; b. Feb. 2, 1874, Salt Lake City, Utah; d. Dec. 13, 1963, Salt Lake City; m. Valeria Brinton, three children; mission president.

YOUNG, Seymour B. (Bicknell). Seventy, Oct. 14, 1882–Dec. 15, 1924; b. Oct. 3, 1837, Kirtland, Ohio; d. Dec. 15, 1924, Salt Lake City, Utah; m. Ann Elizabeth Riter; practiced plural marriage, thirteen children on record; physician.

YOUNG, S. (Seymour) Dilworth. Seventy, April 6, 1945–July 9, 1981; Emeritus General Authority, Sept. 30, 1978; b. Sept. 7, 1897, Salt Lake City, Utah; d. July 9, 1981, Salt Lake City; m. Gladys Pratt (d. 1964), two children; m. Huldah Parker; Boy Scouts of America official; mission president.

YOUNG, Zina Diantha Huntington. First counselor to general president Eliza R. Snow, Relief Society, June 19, 1880–April 1888; general president, Relief Society, April 8, 1888–Aug. 28, 1901; b. Jan. 31, 1821, Watertown, New York; d. Aug. 28, 1901, Salt Lake City, Utah; m. Henry B. Jacobs (div. 1841), m. Joseph Smith, Jr. (d. 1844); m. Brigham Young, four children.

APPENDIX 2
CHURCH PERIODICALS

YEAR	TITLE	FIRST EDITOR OR ORGANIZATION	PLACE
1832–1834	*Evening and the Morning Star, the*	W. W. Phelps	Independence, Missouri
1832–1834 [1835–1836]	*Evening and the Morning Star, the*	Oliver Cowdery	Kirtland, Ohio
1834–1837	*Latter Day Saints' Messenger and Advocate*	Oliver Cowdery	Kirtland, Ohio
1837–1838	*Elders' Journal*	Joseph Smith, Jr.	Kirtland, Ohio and Far West, Missouri
1839–1846	*Times and Seasons*	E. Robinson and Don Carlos Smith	Commerce (Nauvoo), Illinois
1840–1970	*Millennial Star, the*	European Mission	Manchester, Liverpool, and London, England
1841	*Gospel Reflector, the*	Benjamin Winchester	Philadelphia, Pennsylvania

1845–1865	*Prophetic Almanac*	Orson Pratt	New York City, New York
1853–1856	*Zion's Watchman*, the	Agustus A. Farnham	Sydney, Australia
1853–1854	*Seer*, the	Orson Pratt	Washington, D.C., and Liverpool, England
1854–1886	*Journal of Discourses*	George D. Watt	Liverpool, England
1854	*LDS Millennial Star and Monthly Visitor*, the	Richard Ballantyne	Madras, India
1866–1970	*Juvenile Instructor* (Changed to the *Instructor* 1929)	George Q. Cannon Sunday School	Salt Lake City, Utah
1872–1914	*Woman's Exponent*	Louisa Lula Green Relief Society	Salt Lake City, Utah
1879–1896	*Contributor*, the	Junius F. Wells	Salt Lake City, Utah
1886–1890	*Historical Record*	Andrew Jenson	Salt Lake City, Utah
1889–1929	*Young Woman's Journal*, the	Susa Young Gates	Salt Lake City, Utah
1897–1970	*Improvement Era*, the	YMMIA	Salt Lake City, Utah
1898–1900	*Southern Star*	Southern States Mission	Chattanooga, Tennessee
1899–1901	*Truth's Reflex*	Southwestern States Mission	St. Johns, Kansas
1902–1970	*Children's Friend*, the	Primary	Salt Lake City, Utah
1903–1907	*Elder's Journal*, the	Southern States Mission	Atlanta, Georgia, and Chattanooga, Tennessee
1907–1945	*Liahona*, the (Changed to *Liahona the Elders' Journal* 1907)	B. F. Cummings	Independence, Missouri

YEAR	TITLE	FIRST EDITOR OR ORGANIZATION	PLACE
1907–1913	Elder's Messenger (Changed to Messenger 1908)	New Zealand Mission	Auckland, New Zealand
1917–1956	Truth	Northern States Mission	Chicago, Illinois
1910–1940	Utah Genealogical and Historical Magazine	Genealogical Society of Utah	Salt Lake City, Utah
1912–1975	Messenger to the Sightless (Braille) (Changed to New Messenger 1953)		Provo, Utah Louisville, Kentucky
1914–1970	Relief Society Magazine	Susa Young Gates	Salt Lake City, Utah
1924–1947	Genealogical and Historical Magazine of Arizona Temple District	Arizona Temple District	Mesa, Arizona
1925–1937, 1959–	BYU Studies	BYU	Provo, Utah
1927–1970	Cumorah Monthly Bulletin (Changed to Cumorah's Southern Cross 1929; Cumorah's Southern Messenger 1933)	South African Mission	Mowbray, South Africa
1965–	Priesthood Bulletin (Changed to Bulletin)		Salt Lake City, Utah
1963–1971	Liahona, the (for American Indians)	Indian Committee	Salt Lake City, Utah
1971–	Ensign of The Church of Jesus Christ of Latter-day Saints, the	The Church of Jesus Christ of Latter-day Saints	Salt Lake City, Utah

1971–	New Era	The Church of Jesus Christ of Latter-day Saints	Salt Lake City, Utah
1971–	Friend, the	The Church of Jesus Christ of Latter-day Saints	Salt Lake City, Utah
1976–	Ensign Talking Book		Salt Lake City, Utah
1977–	Tambuli	International Magazines	Manila and Makati, Philippines

International Magazines

YEAR	TITLE	FIRST EDITOR OR ORGANIZATION	PLACE
	CHINESE		
1959–	Sheng te jr sheng (Changed to Shentao che sheng 1986; changed to Sheng tu chih sheng 1988; Unified 1967)	Southern Far East Mission	Hong Kong
			Taiwan
	CZECH		
1929–1939	Hvezdika	Czechoslovakian Mission	Prague, Czechoslovakia
1945–1949	Novy Hlas	Czechoslovakian Mission	Prague, Czechoslovakia

YEAR	TITLE	FIRST EDITOR OR ORGANIZATION	PLACE
		DANISH	
1851–1984	*Skandinaviens Stjerne* (Changed to *Den Danske*	Scandinavian Mission	Copenhagen, Denmark
1985–	*Stjerne* 1957; changed to *Stjernen* 1985) (Unified 1967)		Frankfurt, Germany
1880–1887	*Ungdommens Raadgiver*	N. Wilhelmse	Copenhagen, Denmark
1882–1885	*Morgenstjernen*	Andrew Jenson	Salt Lake City, Utah
		DUTCH	
1896–	*De Ster* (Unified 1967)	Netherlands Mission	Rotterdam and The Hague, Holland Frankfurt, Germany
		FINNISH	
1950–	*Valkeus* (Unified 1967)	Finnish Mission	Helsinki, Finland Frankfurt, Germany
		FRENCH	
1851–1852	*Etoile Du Deseret*	John Taylor	Paris, France
1853	*Le Reflecteur*	T. B. H. Stenhouse	Geneva, Switzerland
1928–	*L'Etoile* (Changed to *La Nouvelle Etoile* 1963; changed to *L'Etoile* 1967) (Unified 1967)	French Mission	Geneva, Switzerland Liege, Belgium, and Lyon, France Frankfurt, Germany

GERMAN

1851–1852	*Zion's Panier*	German Mission	Hamburg, Germany
1855–1861	*Der Darsteller der Heiligen der Letzten Tage*	German Mission	Geneva and Zurich, Switzerland
1862–1863	*Die Reform der Heiligen der Letzten Tage*	John L. Smith	Geneva, Switzerland
1869–	*Der Stern* (Unified 1967)	German Mission	Zurich, Bern, and Basel, Switzerland Frankfurt, Germany
1927–1936	*Der Wegweiser*	Swiss-German and German-Austrian Mission	Basel, Switzerland

HAWAIIAN

1908–1911	*Ka Elele Oiaio*	Hawaiian Mission	Honolulu, Hawaii

ITALIAN

1967–	*La Stella* (Unified)	Italian Mission	Florence, Italy, and Frankfurt, Germany

JAPANESE

1967–	*Seito No Michi* (Unified 1968)	Northern Far East Mission	Tokyo, Japan

KOREAN

1965–	*Songdo Wi Bot* (Changed to *Songdo ui pot*, 1988; Unified 1967)	Korean Mission	Seoul, South Korea

YEAR	TITLE	FIRST EDITOR OR ORGANIZATION	PLACE
		MAORI	
1907–1955	*Te Karere*	New Zealand Mission	Auckland, New Zealand
		NORWEGIAN	
1922–1925	*Morgenstjernen*	Norwegian Mission	Oslo, Norway
1937–	*Lys Over Norge* (Unified 1967)	Norwegian Mission	Oslo, Norway, and Lynge, Denmark Frankfurt, Germany
		PORTUGUESE	
1948–	*A Gaivota* (Changed to *A Liahona* 1951) (Unified 1968)	Brazilian Mission	São Paulo, Brazil
		SAMOAN	
1968–	*O Le Liahona* (Unified)	Samoan Mission	Auckland, New Zealand
		SPANISH	
1927–1930	*Evangelio Restaurado*	Mexican Mission	El Paso, Texas
1937–	*El Atalaya* (Changed to *In Yaotlapiyoui* 1937; changed to *Atalaya* 1944; changed to *Liahona* 1945; Unified 1967)	Mexican Mission	Los Angeles, California Mexico City, Mexico
1937–1955	*El Mensajero* (Changed to *El Mensajero Deseret* 1941)	Argentine Mission	Buenos Aires, Argentina

Years	Title	Mission	Location
1951–1961	*El Candil*	Uruguayan Mission	Montevideo, Uruguay
1954–1955	*El Deseret Oriental*	Uruguayan Mission	Montevideo, Uruguay
SWEDISH			
1877–	*Nordstjernan* (Changed to *Nordstjärnan* 1894) (Unified 1967)		Copenhagen, Denmark, and Stockholm, Sweden Frankfurt, Germany
TAHITIAN			
1907–1961	*Te Heheuraa Api*	Tahitian Mission	Papeete, Tahiti
1968–1970	*Te Tiarama* (Unified 1968)	French-Polynesian Mission	Auckland, New Zealand
THAI			
1984–	*Khaawaansidthichon*	International Magazines	Bangkok, Thailand
TONGAN			
1954–	*Ko E Tuhulu* (Changed to *Tuhulu* 1980; Unified 1968)	Tongan Mission	Auckland, New Zealand
WELSH			
1846–1858	*Prophwyd y Jubili* (Changed to *Udgorn Seion* 1849)	Dan Jones and John Davis	Merthyr Tydfil, Caerfyrddin, and Abertawy, Wales

Church Newspapers

DATE	TITLE	FIRST EDITOR	PLACE
1832–1833	Upper Missouri Advertiser, the	W. W. Phelps	Independence, Missouri
1835–1836	Northern Times, the	Frederick G. Williams	Kirtland, Ohio
1842–1843	Wasp, the	William Smith	Nauvoo, Illinois
1843–1845	Nauvoo Neighbor, the	John Taylor	Nauvoo, Illinois
1844–1845	Prophet, the	William Smith	New York City, New York
1845	New York Messenger, the	Parley P. Pratt	New York City, New York
1847–1848	California Star, the	E. P. Jones	Yerba Buena (San Francisco), California
1849–1852	Frontier Guardian, the	Orson Hyde	Kanesville, Iowa
1850–	Deseret News	Willard Richards	Salt Lake City, Utah
1852	Western Bugle	Almon W. Babbitt	Kanesville, Iowa
1854–1855	Saint Louis Luminary, the	Erastus Snow	St. Louis, Missouri
1855–1857	Mormon, the	John Taylor	New York City, New York
1856–1857	Western Standard, the	George Q. Cannon	San Francisco, California
1931–	"Church Section" in Deseret News (Changed to Church News 1943)		Salt Lake City, Utah
1944–1948	Church News, LDS Servicemen's Edition		Salt Lake City, Utah

Foreign Language Newspapers Published in Salt Lake City, Utah

DANISH

1876–1935	*Bikuben*	Local Danish-Norwegian groups
1873–1874	*Utah Posten*	Local Danish-Norwegian groups
1874–1877	*Utah Skandinav*	Local Danish groups

DUTCH

1914–1935	*De Utah Nederlander*	Local Dutch groups

GERMAN

1890–1935	*Salt Lake City, Beobacher*	Local German groups

SWEDISH

1885–1892	*Svenska Hardden*	Local Swedish groups
1900–1935	*Utah-Posten*	Local Swedish groups

APPENDIX 3
GENERAL CHURCH OFFICERS, A CHRONOLOGY

Presidents of the Church

Joseph Smith (April 1830–June 1844)

Brigham Young (Dec. 1847–Aug. 1877)

John Taylor (Oct. 1880–July 1887)

Wilford Woodruff (April 1889–Sept. 1898)

Lorenzo Snow (Sept. 1898–Oct. 1901)

Joseph F. Smith (Oct. 1901–Nov. 1918)

Heber J. Grant (Nov. 1918–May 1945)

George Albert Smith (May 1945–April 1951)

David O. McKay (April 1951–Jan. 1970)

Joseph Fielding Smith (Jan. 1970–July 1972)

Harold B. Lee (July 1972–Dec. 1973)

Spencer W. Kimball (Dec. 1973–Nov. 1985)

Ezra Taft Benson (Nov. 1985–)

Assistant Presidents of the Church

Oliver Cowdery (1834–1837)

Hyrum Smith (1841–1844)

First Counselors in the First Presidency

Sidney Rigdon (1833–1844)

Heber C. Kimball (1847–1868)

George A. Smith (1868–1875)

John W. Young (1876–1877)

George Q. Cannon (1880–1887; 1889–1901)

Joseph F. Smith (1901–1901)

John R. Winder (1901–1910)

Anthon H. Lund (1910–1921)

Charles W. Penrose (1921–1925)

Anthony W. Ivins (1925–1934)

J. Reuben Clark, Jr. (1934–1951; 1959–1961)

Stephen L Richards (1951–1959)

Henry D. Moyle (1961–1963)

Hugh B. Brown (1963–1970)

Harold B. Lee (1970–1972)

N. Eldon Tanner (1972–1982)

Marion G. Romney (1982–1985)

Gordon B. Hinckley (1985–)

Second Counselors in the First Presidency

Frederick G. Williams (1833–1837)

Hyrum Smith (1837–1841)

William Law (1841–1844)

Willard Richards (1847–1854)

Jedediah M. Grant (1854–1856)

Daniel H. Wells (1857–1877)

Joseph F. Smith (1880–1887;
1889–1901)
Rudger Clawson (1901)
Anthon H. Lund (1901–1910)
John Henry Smith (1910–1911)
Charles W. Penrose (1911–1921)
Anthony W. Ivins (1921–1925)
Charles W. Nibley (1925–1931)
J. Reuben Clark, Jr. (1933–1934;
1951–1959)
David O. McKay (1934–1951)
Henry D. Moyle (1959–1961)
Hugh B. Brown (1961–1963)
N. Eldon Tanner (1963–1972)
Marion G. Romney (1972–1982)
Gordon B. Hinckley (1982–1985)
Thomas S. Monson (1985–)

*Other Counselors in the First
Presidency*

Jesse Gause (1832)
John C. Bennett (1841–1842)
Amasa M. Lyman (1843–1844)
Joseph F. Smith (1866–1877)
Lorenzo Snow (1873–1874)
Brigham Young, Jr. (1873–1874)
Albert Carrington (1873–1874)
John W. Young (1873–1874)
George Q. Cannon (1873–1874)
Hugh B. Brown (1961)
Joseph Fielding Smith
(1965–1970)
H. Thorpe B. Isaacson
(1965–1970)
Alvin R. Dyer (1968–1970)
Gordon B. Hinckley (1981–1982)

*Assistant Counselors in the First
Presidency*

Oliver Cowdery (1837–1838)
Joseph Smith, Sr. (1837–1840)
Hyrum Smith (1837)

John Smith (1837–1844)
Lorenzo Snow (1874–1877)
Brigham Young, Jr. (1874–1877)
Albert Carrington (1874–1877)
John W. Young (1874–1876)
George Q. Cannon (1874–1877)

*Apostles in the Quorum of the
Twelve*

Thomas B. Marsh (1835–1839)
David W. Patten (1835–1838)
Brigham Young (1835–1847)
Heber C. Kimball (1835–1847)
Orson Hyde (1835–1839;
1839–1878)
William E. McLellin
(1835–1838)
Parley P. Pratt (1835–1857)
Luke S. Johnson (1835–1838)
William Smith (1835–1839;
1839–1845)
Orson Pratt (1835–1842;
1843–1881)
John F. Boynton (1835–1837)
Lyman E. Johnson (1835–1838)
John E. Page (1838–1846)
John Taylor (1838–1880)
Wilford Woodruff (1839–1889)
George Albert Smith
(1839–1868)
Willard Richards (1840–1847)
Lyman Wight (1841–1848)
Amasa M. Lyman (1842–1843;
1844–1867)
Ezra T. Benson (1846–1869)
Charles C. Rich (1849–1883)
Lorenzo Snow (1849–1898)
Erastus Snow (1849–1888)
Franklin D. Richards
(1849–1899)
George Q. Cannon (1860–1880)
Brigham Young, Jr. (1868–1903)

Joseph F. Smith (1867–1880)
Albert Carrington (1870–1885)
Moses Thatcher (1879–1896)
Francis M. Lyman (1880–1916)
John Henry Smith (1880–1910)
George Teasdale (1882–1907)
Heber J. Grant (1882–1918)
John W. Taylor (1884–1905)
Marriner W. Merrill (1889–1906)
Anthon H. Lund (1889–1901)
Abraham H. Cannon
    (1889–1896)
Matthias F. Cowley (1897–1905)
Abraham O. Woodruff
    (1897–1904)
Rudger Clawson (1898–1943)
Reed Smoot (1900–1941)
Hyrum Mack Smith (1901–1918)
George Albert Smith
    (1903–1945)
Charles W. Penrose (1904–1911)
George F. Richards (1906–1950)
Orson F. Whitney (1906–1931)
David O. McKay (1906–1934)
Anthony W. Ivins (1907–1921)
Joseph Fielding Smith
    (1910–1970)
James E. Talmage (1911–1933)
Stephen L Richards (1917–1951)
Richard R. Lyman (1918–1943)
Melvin J. Ballard (1919–1939)
John A. Widtsoe (1921–1952)
Joseph F. Merrill (1931–1952)
Charles A. Callis (1933–1947)
Alonzo A. Hinckley (1934–1936)
Albert E. Bowen (1937–1953)
Sylvester Q. Cannon
    (1938–1943)
Harold B. Lee (1941–1970)
Spencer W. Kimball
    (1943–1973)
Ezra Taft Benson (1943–1985)

Mark E. Petersen (1944–1984)
Matthew Cowley (1945–1953)
Henry D. Moyle (1947–1959)
Delbert L. Stapley (1950–1978)
Marion G. Romney (1951–1972;
    1985–1988)
LeGrand Richards (1952–1983)
Adam S. Bennion (1953–1958)
Richard L. Evans (1953–1971)
George Q. Morris (1954–1962)
Hugh B. Brown (1958–1961;
    1970–1975)
Howard W. Hunter (1959–)
Gordon B. Hinckley (1961–1981)
N. Eldon Tanner (1962–1963)
Thomas S. Monson (1963–1985)
Boyd K. Packer (1970–)
Marvin J. Ashton (1971–)
Bruce R. McConkie (1972–1985)
L. Tom Perry (1974–)
David B. Haight (1976–)
James E. Faust (1978–)
Neal A. Maxwell (1981–)
Russell M. Nelson (1984–)
Dallin H. Oaks (1984–)
M. Russell Ballard, Jr. (1985–)
Joseph B. Wirthlin (1986–)
Richard G. Scott (1988–)

Patriarchs to the Church

Joseph Smith, Sr. (1833–1840)
Hyrum Smith (1841–1844)
William Smith (1845–1845)
John Smith (1849–1854)
John Smith (1855–1911)
Hyrum Gibbs Smith (1912–1932)
George F. Richards (1937–1942)
    (Acting Patriarch)
Joseph Fielding Smith
    (1942–1946)
Eldred G. Smith (1947–1979)

Assistants to the Twelve

Marion G. Romney (1941–1951)
Thomas E. McKay (1941–1958)
Clifford E. Young (1941–1958)
Alma Sonne (1941–1976)
Nicholas G. Smith (1941–1945)
George Q. Morris (1951–1954)
Stayner Richards (1951–1953)
ElRay L. Christiansen
   (1951–1975)
John Longden (1951–1969)
Hugh B. Brown (1953–1958)
Sterling W. Sill (1954–1976)
Gordon B. Hinckley (1958–1961)
Henry D. Taylor (1958–1976)
William J. Critchlow, Jr.
   (1958–1968)
Alvin R. Dyer (1958–1967;
   1970–1976)
N. Eldon Tanner (1960–1962)
Franklin D. Richards
   (1960–1976)
Theodore M. Burton (1960–1976)
H. Thorpe B. Isaacson
   (1961–1965; 1970)
Boyd K. Packer (1961–1970)
Bernard P. Brockbank
   (1962–1976)
James A. Cullimore (1966–1976)
Marion D. Hanks (1968–1976)
Marvin J. Ashton (1969–1971)
Joseph Anderson (1970–1976)
David B. Haight (1970–1976)
William H. Bennett (1970–1976)
John H. Vandenberg
   (1972–1976)
Robert L. Simpson (1972–1976)
O. Leslie Stone (1972–1976)
James E. Faust (1972–1976)
L. Tom Perry (1972–1974)
J. Thomas Fyans (1974–1976)

Neal A. Maxwell (1974–1976)
William Grant Bangerter
   (1975–1976)
Robert D. Hales (1975–1976)
Adney Y. Komatsu (1975–1976)
Joseph B. Wirthlin (1975–1976)

Seventies

First Council of the Seventy

Hazen Aldrich (1835–1837)
Joseph Young (1835–1881)
Levi W. Hancock (1835–1882)
Leonard Rich (1835–1837)
Zebedee Coltrin (1835–1837)
Lyman R. Sherman (1835–1837)
Sylvester Smith (1835–1837)
John Gould (1837–1837)
James Foster (1837–1841)
Daniel S. Miles (1837–1845)
Josiah Butterfield (1837–1844)
Salmon Gee (1837–1838)
John Gaylord (1837–1838)
Henry Harriman (1838–1891)
Zera Pulsipher (1838–1862)
Roger Orton (1845–1845)
Albert P. Rockwood (1845–1879)
Benjamin L. Clapp (1845–1859)
Jedediah M. Grant (1845–1854)
Horace S. Eldredge (1854–1888)
Jacob Gates (1860–1892)
John Van Cott (1862–1883)
William W. Taylor (1880–1884)
Abraham H. Cannon
   (1882–1889)
Theodore B. Lewis (1882–1882)
   (sustained but never set apart)
Seymour B. Young (1882–1924)
Christian D. Fjelsted
   (1884–1905)
John Morgan (1884–1894)
B. H. Roberts (1888–1933)
George Reynolds (1890–1909)

J. Golden Kimball (1892–1938)
Rulon S. Wells (1893–1941)
Edward Stevenson (1894–1897)
Joseph W. McMurrin (1897–1932)
Charles H. Hart (1906–1934)
Levi E. Young (1909–1963)
Rey L. Pratt (1925–1931)
Antoine R. Ivins (1931–1967)
Samuel O. Bennion (1933–1945)
John H. Taylor (1933–1946)
Rufus K. Hardy (1934–1945)
Richard L. Evans (1938–1953)
Oscar A. Kirkham (1941–1958)
S. Dilworth Young (1945–1975)
Milton R. Hunter (1945–1975)
Bruce R. McConkie (1946–1972)
Marion D. Hanks (1953–1968)
A. Theodore Tuttle (1958–1975)
Paul H. Dunn (1964–1975)
Hartman Rector, Jr. (1968–1975)
Loren C. Dunn (1968–1975)
Rex D. Pinegar (1972–1975)
Gene R. Cook (1975–1975)

First and Second Quorums of the
Seventy (1976–1991)

Angel Abrea (1981–)
Carlos H. Amado (1989–)
H. Verlan Andersen (1986–1991)
Joseph Anderson (1976–1978)
Carlos E. Asay (1976–)
Eduardo Ayala (1990–)
Robert L. Backman (1978–)
M. Russell Ballard, Jr.
  (1976–1985)
William Grant Bangerter
  (1976–1989)
Ben B. Banks (1989–)
William H. Bennett (1976–1978)
William R. Bradford (1975–)
Ted E. Brewerton (1978–)

Bernard P. Brockbank
  (1976–1980)
Monte J. Brough (1988–)
Victor L. Brown (1985–1989)
Theodore M. Burton (1976–1989)
F. Enzio Busche (1977–)
Waldo P. Call (1985–1990)
Helio R. Camargo (1985–1990)
George I. Cannon (1986–1991)
John K. Carmack (1984–)
Albert Choules, Jr. (1988–)
Joe J. Christensen (1989–)
J. Richard Clarke (1985–)
Spencer J. Condie (1989–)
Gene R. Cook (1975–)
Rulon G. Craven (1990–)
James A. Cullimore (1976–1978)
LeGrand R. Curtis (1990–)
Derek A. Cuthbert (1978–1991)
Clinton L. Cutler (1990–)
Julio E. Dávila (1991–)
Jacob de Jager (1976–)
Robert K. Dellenbach (1990–)
Royden G. Derrick (1976–1989)
Charles A. Didier (1975–)
Graham W. Doxey (1991–)
Loren C. Dunn (1975–)
Paul H. Dunn (1975–1989)
G. Homer Durham (1977–1985)
Alvin R. Dyer (1976–1977)
James E. Faust (1976–1978)
Vaughn J. Featherstone (1976–)
J. Thomas Fyans (1976–1989)
Lloyd P. George, Jr. (1988–)
Francis M. Gibbons (1986–1991)
Jack H. Goaslind, Jr. (1978–)
John H Groberg (1976–)
Robert D. Hales (1976–1985)
F. Melvin Hammond (1989–)
In Sang Han (1991–)
Marion D. Hanks (1976–)
W. Eugene Hansen (1989–)

Robert B. Harbertson
(1984–1989)
Devere Harris (1984–1989)
George R. Hill, III (1987–)
Harold G. Hillam (1990–)
Jeffrey R. Holland (1989–)
F. Burton Howard (1978–)
Marlin K. Jensen (1989–)
Malcolm S. Jeppsen (1989–)
Kenneth Johnson (1990–)
F. Arthur Kay (1984–1989)
L. Lionel Kendrick (1988–)
Yoshihiko Kikuchi (1977–)
Cree-L Kofford (1991–)
Adney Y. Komatsu (1976–)
Dean L. Larsen (1976–)
John R. Lasater (1987–)
W. Mack Lawrence (1990–)
George P. Lee (1975–1989)
Richard P. Lindsay (1989–)
Merlin R. Lybbert (1989–)
Douglas J. Martin (1987–)
Helvécio Martins (1990–)
Neal A. Maxwell (1976–1981)
Gerald E. Melchin (1988–)
Lynn A. Mickelsen (1990–)
Alexander B. Morrison (1987–)
Joseph C. Muren (1991–)
Stephen D. Nadauld (1991–)
Dennis B. Neuenschwander
(1991–)
Spencer H. Osborn (1984–1989)
James M. Paramore (1977–)
H. Burke Peterson (1985–)
Rex D. Pinegar (1975–)
Hugh W. Pinnock (1977–)
Ronald E. Poelman (1978–)
L. Aldin Porter (1987–)
Hartman Rector, Jr. (1975–)
Rex C. Reeve, Sr. (1978–1989)
Franklin D. Richards
(1976–1987)

Hans B. Ringger (1985–)
Jorge A. Rojas (1991–)
Glen L. Rudd (1987–)
Gardner H. Russell (1986–1991)
Robert E. Sackley (1988–)
Richard G. Scott (1977–1988)
Sam K. Shimabukuro (1991–)
Sterling W. Sill (1976–1978)
Robert L. Simpson (1976–1989)
Douglas H. Smith (1987–)
Alma Sonne (1976–1977)
John Sonnenberg (1984–1989)
Philip T. Sonntag (1984–1989)
Lynn A. Sorensen (1987–)
O. Leslie Stone (1976–1980)
Henry D. Taylor (1976–1978)
Russell C. Taylor (1984–1989)
Horacio A. Tenorio (1989–)
Earl C. Tingey (1990–)
A. Theodore Tuttle (1975–1986)
John H. Vandenberg
(1976–1978)
J Ballard Washburn (1990–)
Robert E. Wells (1976–)
Keith W. Wilcox (1984–1989)
Joseph B. Wirthlin (1976–1986)
Durrel A. Woolsey (1990–)
S. Dilworth Young (1975–1978)

Presiding Bishops of the Church

Edward Partridge (1831–1840)
Newel K. Whitney (1847–1850)
Edward Hunter (1851–1883)
William B. Preston (1884–1907)
Charles W. Nibley (1907–1925)
Sylvester Q. Cannon
(1925–1938)
LeGrand Richards (1938–1952)
Joseph L. Wirthlin (1952–1961)
John H. Vandenberg
(1961–1972)
Victor L. Brown (1972–1985)

Robert D. Hales (1985–)

First Counselors in the Presiding Bishopric

Isaac Morley (1831–1840)
Leonard W. Hardy (1856–1884)
Robert T. Burton (1884–1907)
Orrin P. Miller (1907–1918)
David A. Smith (1918–1938)
Marvin O. Ashton (1938–1946)
Joseph L. Wirthlin (1946–1952)
H. Thorpe B. Isaacson (1952–1961)
Robert L. Simpson (1961–1972)
H. Burke Peterson (1972–1985)
Henry B. Eyring (1985–)

Second Counselors in the Presiding Bishopric

John Corrill (1831–1837)
Titus Billings (1837–1840)
Jesse C. Little (1856–1874)
Robert T. Burton (1874–1884)
John Q. Cannon (1884–1886)
John R. Winder (1887–1901)
Orrin P. Miller (1901–1907)
David A. Smith (1907–1918)
John Wells (1918–1938)
Joseph L. Wirthlin (1938–1946)
H. Thorpe B. Isaacson (1946–1952)
Carl W. Buehner (1952–1961)
Victor L. Brown (1961–1972)
Vaughn J. Featherstone (1972–1976)
J. Richard Clarke (1976–1985)
Glenn L. Pace (1985–)

Church Historians

Oliver Cowdery (1830–1831; 1835–1837)
John Whitmer (1831–1835)

George W. Robinson (1837–1840)
John Corrill (1838–1839)
Elias Higbee (1838–1843)
Robert B. Thompson (1840–1841) (General Clerk)
James Sloan (1841–1843) (General Clerk)
Willard Richards (1842–1854)
George A. Smith (1854–1870)
Albert Carrington (1870–1874)
Orson Pratt (1874–1881)
Wilford Woodruff (1883–1889)
Franklin D. Richards (1889–1899)
Anthon H. Lund (1900–1921)
Joseph Fielding Smith (1921–1970)
Howard W. Hunter (1970–1972)
Leonard J. Arrington (1972–1980)
Alvin R. Dyer (1972–1975) (Managing Director)
Joseph Anderson (1975–1977) (Managing Director)
G. Homer Durham (1977–1985) (Managing Director and Historian)
Dean L. Larsen (1985–1989) (Executive Director and Historian)
John K. Carmack (1989–1991) (Executive Director and Historian)
Loren C. Dunn (1991–) (Executive Director and Historian)

Sunday School General Superintendencies and Presidencies

George Q. Cannon, Superintendent (1867–1901)

First Assistants
George Goddard (1872–1899)
Karl G. Maeser (1899–1901)
Second Assistants
John Morgan (1883–1894)
Karl G. Maeser (1894–1899)
George Reynolds
(1899–1901)
Lorenzo Snow, Superintendent
(1901–1901)
First Assistant
George Reynolds
(1901–1901)
Second Assistant
J. M. Tanner (1901–1901)
Joseph F. Smith, Superintendent
(1901–1918)
First Assistants
George Reynolds
(1901–1909)
David O. McKay
(1909–1918)
Second Assistants
J. M. Tanner (1901–1906)
David O. McKay (1907–
1909)
Stephen L Richards (1909–
1918)
David O. McKay, Superintendent
(1918–1934)
First Assistant
Stephen L Richards (1918–
1934)
Second Assistant
George D. Pyper (1918–
1934)
George D. Pyper, Superintendent
(1934–1943)
First Assistant
Milton Bennion (1934–1943)
Second Assistant
George R. Hill (1934–1943)

Milton Bennion, Superintendent
(1943–1949)
First Assistant
George R. Hill (1943–1949)
Second Assistant
A. Hamer Reiser
(1943–1949)
George R. Hill, Superintendent
(1949–1966)
First Assistants
A. Hamer Reiser
(1949–1952)
David Lawrence McKay
(1952–1966)
Second Assistants
David Lawrence McKay
(1949–1952)
Lynn S. Richards
(1952–1966)
David Lawrence McKay,
Superintendent (1966–1971)
First Assistant
Lynn S. Richards (1966–1971)
Second Assistant
Royden G. Derrick (1966–
1971)
Russell M. Nelson,
Superintendent (1971–1972)
First Assistant
Joseph B. Wirthlin (1971–
1972)
Second Assistant
Richard L. Warner (1971–
1972)
Russell M. Nelson, President
(1972–1979)
First Counselors
Joseph B. Wirthlin (1972–
1975)
B. Lloyd Poelman (1975–1978)
Joe J. Christensen (1978–
1979)

William D. Oswald (1979–
1979)
Second Counselors
Richard L. Warner (1972–
1975)
Joe J. Christensen (1975–
1978)
William D. Oswald (1978–
1979)
J. Hugh Baird (1979–1979)
Hugh W. Pinnock, President
(1979–1986)
First Counselors
Ronald E. Poelman (1979–
1981)
Robert D. Hales (1981–1985)
Adney Y. Komatsu (1985–
1986)
Second Counselors
Jack H Goaslind, Jr.
(1979–1981)
James M. Paramore
(1981–1983)
Loren C. Dunn (1983–1985)
Ronald E. Poelman
(1985–1986)
Robert L. Simpson, President
(1986–1989)
First Counselors
Adney Y. Komatsu
(1986–1987)
Devere Harris (1987–1989)
Second Counselors
A. Theodore Tuttle
(1986–1986)
Devere Harris (1987–1987)
Philip T. Sonntag
(1987–1988)
Derek A. Cuthbert
(1988–1989)
Hugh W. Pinnock, President
(1989–)

First Counselors
Derek A. Cuthbert
(1989–1991)
H. Verlan Andersen
(1990–1991)
Hartman Rector, Jr. (1991–)
Second Counselors
Ted E. Brewerton
(1989–1990)
H. Verlan Andersen
(1990–1991)
Rulon G. Craven
(1991–1991)
Clinton L. Cutler (1991–)

*Young Men General
Superintendencies and Presidencies*

Junius F. Wells, Superintendent
(1876–1880)
First Counselor
M. H. Hardy
Second Counselor
Rodney C. Badger
Wilford Woodruff,
Superintendent (1880–1898)
First Assistant
Joseph F. Smith
Second Assistant
Moses Thatcher
Lorenzo Snow, Superintendent
(1898–1901)
First Assistant
Joseph F. Smith
Second Assistant
Heber J. Grant
Assistant
B. H. Roberts
Joseph F. Smith, Superintendent
(1901–1918)
First Assistant
Heber J. Grant

Second Assistant
B. H. Roberts
Anthony W. Ivins,
Superintendent (1918–1921)
First Assistant
B. H. Roberts
Second Assistant
Richard R. Lyman
George Albert Smith,
Superintendent (1921–1935)
First Assistant
B. H. Roberts
Second Assistants
Richard R. Lyman
Melvin J. Ballard
Albert E. Bowen, Superintendent
(1935–1937)
First Assistant
George Q. Morris
Second Assistant
Franklin West
George Q. Morris,
Superintendent (1937–1948)
First Assistants
Joseph J. Cannon
John D. Giles
Second Assistants
Burton K. Farnsworth
Lorenzo H. Hatch
Elbert R. Curtis, Superintendent
(1948–1958)
First Assistant
A. Walter Stevenson
Second Assistants
Ralph W. Hardy
David S. King
Joseph T. Bentley,
Superintendent (1958–1962)
First Assistants
Alvin R. Dyer (1958–1958)
G. Carlos Smith (1958–1961)

Marvin J. Ashton
(1961–1962)
Second Assistants
Marvin J. Ashton
(1958–1961)
Verl F. Scott (1961–1961)
Carl W. Buehner
(1961–1962)
G. Carlos Smith, Superintendent
(1962–1969)
First Assistant
Marvin J. Ashton
(1962–1969)
Second Assistants
Carl W. Buehner
(1962–1967)
George R. Hill (1967–1969)
W. Jay Eldredge, Superintendent
(1969–1972)
First Assistant
George R. Hill (1969–1972)
Second Assistant
George I. Cannon
(1969–1972)
W. Jay Eldredge, President
(1972–1972)
First Counselor
George I. Cannon
(1972–1972)
Second Counselor
Robert L. Backman
(1972–1972)
Robert L. Backman, President
(1972–1974)
First Counselor
LeGrand R. Curtis
(1972–1974)
Second Counselor
Jack H Goaslind, Jr.
(1972–1974)
Neil D. Schaerrer, President
(1977–1979)

First Counselor
  Graham W. Doxey
  (1977–1979)
Second Counselor
  Quinn G. McKay
  (1977–1979)
Robert L. Backman, President
  (1979–1985)
First Counselor
  Vaughn J. Featherstone
  (1979–1985)
Second Counselor
  Rex D. Pinegar (1979–1985)
Vaughn J. Featherstone,
  President (1985–1990)
First Counselors
  Rex D. Pinegar (1985–1989)
  Jeffrey R. Holland
  (1989–1990)
Second Counselors
  Robert L. Simpson
  (1985–1986)
  Hartman Rector, Jr.
  (1986–1988)
  Robert B. Harbertson
  (1988–1989)
  Monte J. Brough (1989–1990)
Jack H Goaslind, Jr., President
  (1990–)
First Counselors
  LeGrand R. Curtis
  (1990–1991)
  Robert K. Dellenbach (1991–)
Second Counselors
  Robert K. Dellenbach
  (1990–1991)
  Stephen D. Nadauld (1991–)

Primary General Presidencies

Louie Bouton Felt, President
  (1880–1925)
First Counselors

Matilda W. Barrett
  (1880–1888)
Lillie T. Freeze (1888–1905)
May Anderson (1905–1925)
Second Counselors
  Clare C. M. Cannon
  (1880–1895)
  Josephine R. West
  (1896–1905)
  Clara W. Beebe (1905–1925)
May Anderson, President
  (1925–1939)
First Counselors
  Sadie Grant Pack
  (1925–1929)
  Isabelle Salmon Ross
  (1929–1939)
Second Counselors
  Isabelle Salmon Ross
  (1925–1929)
  Edna Harker Thomas
  (1929–1933)
  Edith Hunter Lambert
  (1933–1939)
May Green Hinckley, President
  (1940–1943)
First Counselor
  Adele Cannon Howells
  (1940–1943)
Second Counselors
  Janet Murdock Thompson
  (1940–1942)
  LaVern Watts Parmley
  (1942–1943)
Adele Cannon Howells,
  President (1943–1951)
First Counselor
  LaVern Watts Parmley
  (1943–1951)
Second Counselor
  Dessie Grant Boyle
  (1943–1951)

LaVern Watts Parmley, President
(1951–1974)
First Counselors
Arta M. Hale (1951–1962)
Leone W. Doxey
(1962–1969)
Lucile C. Reading
(1970–1970)
Naomi W. Randall
(1970–1974)
Second Counselors
Florence H. Richards
(1951–1953)
Leone W. Doxey
(1953–1962)
Eileen R. Dunyon
(1962–1963)
Lucile C. Reading
(1963–1970)
Florence R. Lane
(1970–1974)
Naomi M. Shumway, President
(1974–1980)
First Counselors
Sara B. Paulsen (1974–1977)
Colleen B. Lemmon
(1977–1980)
Second Counselors
Colleen B. Lemmon
(1974–1977)
Dorthea C. Murdock
(1977–1980)
Dwan J. Young, President
(1980–1988)
First Counselor
Virginia B. Cannon
(1980–1988)
Second Counselor
Michaelene P. Grassli
(1980–1988)
Michaelene P. Grassli, President
(1988–)

First Counselor
Betty Jo Jepsen (1988–)
Second Counselor
Ruth B. Wright (1988–)

Young Women General Presidencies

Elmina Shepard Taylor,
President (1880–1904)
First Counselors
Margaret Young Taylor
(1880–1887)
Maria Young Dougall
(1887–1904)
Second Counselor
Martha Horne Tingey
(1880–1904)
Martha Horne Tingey, President
(1905–1929)
First Counselor
Ruth May Fox (1905–1929)
Second Counselors
Mae Taylor Nystrom
(1905–1923)
Lucy Grant Cannon
(1923–1929)
Ruth May Fox, President
(1929–1937)
First Counselor
Lucy Grant Cannon
(1929–1937)
Second Counselor
Clarissa A. Beesley
(1929–1937)
Lucy Grant Cannon, President
(1937–1948)
First Counselors
Helen S. Williams
(1937–1944)
Verna W. Goddard
(1944–1948)
Second Counselors
Verna W. Goddard

(1937–1944)
Lucy T. Anderson
(1944–1948)
Bertha S. Reeder, President
(1948–1961)
First Counselor
Emily H. Bennett
(1948–1961)
Second Counselor
LaRue C. Longden
(1948–1961)
Florence S. Jacobsen, President
(1961–1972)
First Counselor
Margaret R. Jackson
(1961–1972)
Second Counselor
Dorothy P. Holt (1961–1972)
Ruth H. Funk, President
(1972–1978)
First Counselor
Hortense H. Child
(1972–1978)
Second Counselor
Ardeth G. Kapp (1972–1978)
Elaine A. Cannon, President
(1978–1984)
First Counselor
Arlene B. Darger
(1978–1984)
Second Counselor
Norma B. Smith (1978–1984)
Ardeth G. Kapp, President (1984–)
First Counselors
Patricia T. Holland
(1984–1986)
Maurine J. Turley
(1986–1987)
Jayne B. Malan (1987–)
Second Counselors
Maurine J. Turley
(1984–1986)

Jayne B. Malan (1986–1987)
Elaine L. Jack (1987–1990)
Janette C. Hales (1990–)

Relief Society General Presidencies

Emma Hale Smith, President
(1842–1844)
First Counselor
Sarah M. Cleveland
(1842–1844)
Second Counselor
Elizabeth Ann Whitney
(1842–1844)
Eliza Roxcy Snow, President
(1866–1887)
First Counselor
Zina Diantha Young
(1880–1888)
Second Counselor
Elizabeth Ann Whitney
(1880–1882)
Zina Diantha Young, President
(1888–1901)
First Counselor
Jane S. Richards
(1888–1901)
Second Counselor
Bathsheba W. Smith
(1888–1901)
Bathsheba W. Smith, President
(1901–1910)
First Counselor
Annie Taylor Hyde
(1901–1909)
Second Counselor
Ida Smoot Dusenberry
(1901–1910)
Emmeline B. Wells, President
(1910–1921)
First Counselor
Clarissa Smith Williams
(1910–1921)

Second Counselor
Julina L. Smith (1910–1921)
Clarissa Smith Williams,
President (1921–1928)
First Counselor
Jennie Brimhall Knight
(1921–1928)
Second Counselor
Louise Yates Robison
(1921–1928)
Louise Yates Robison, President
(1928–1939)
First Counselor
Amy Brown Lyman
(1928–1939)
Second Counselors
Julia A. Child (1928–1935)
Kate M. Barker (1935–1939)
Amy Brown Lyman, President
(1940–1945)
First Counselor
Marcia K. Howells
(1940–1945)
Second Counselors
Donna D. Sorensen
(1940–1942)
Belle S. Spafford
(1942–1945)
Belle S. Spafford, President
(1945–1974)
First Counselor
Marianne C. Sharp
(1945–1974)
Second Counselors

Gertrude R. Garff
(1945–1947)
Velma Simonsen
(1947–1956)
Helen W. Anderson
(1957–1958)
Louise W. Madsen
(1958–1974)
Barbara B. Smith, President
(1974–1984)
First Counselors
Janath R. Cannon
(1974–1978)
Marian R. Boyer
(1978–1984)
Second Counselors
Marian R. Boyer
(1974–1978)
Shirley W. Thomas
(1978–1984)
Ann S. Reese (1983–1984)
Barbara W. Winder, President
(1984–1990)
First Counselor
Joy F. Evans (1984–1990)
Second Counselor
Joanne B. Doxey
(1984–1990)
Elaine L. Jack, President (1990–)
First Counselor
Chieko N. Okazaki (1990–)
Second Counselor
Aileen H. Clyde (1990–)

APPENDIX 4

The following letters of the First Presidency of The Church of Jesus Christ of Latter-day Saints were selected to illustrate some of the many interests of the Presidency in the leadership of the Church. Letters included here are of a regulatory and directive nature and represent only one facet of a wide range of responsibilities and activities.

Examples of other types of documents emanating from the First Presidency are contained in an additional Appendix titled Temple Dedicatory Prayers. Members of the First Presidency also deliver formal messages at general conferences and other conferences, and publish an annual Christmas message and statements on other occasions when needed.

Letters from the First Presidency carry the official letterhead:

The Church of Jesus Christ of Latter-day Saints
OFFICE OF THE FIRST PRESIDENCY
Salt Lake City, Utah

To conserve space in this Appendix the letterhead does not appear with the individual selections. A brief notation indicates the general subject matter of each letter.

Cub Scout Program Encouraged

December 19, 1960

To the Priesthood, Primary Workers, and Cub Scout Leaders

It is the desire of the First Presidency that Latter-day Saint boys have the full advantage of the Scouting program, including Cub Scouting, Boy Scouting, and Exploring. It is also the desire of the First Presidency that Latter-day Saint boys have this experience in units sponsored by the Church, under the direction of Church leaders, and according to

Church policies and standards. When we do not accept this responsibility but leave it to the school, the community, or another church, we do two things: we place our boys in a situation where their activities may not be conducted according to Church standards; we may be sowing the seeds of Church inactivity at a most impressionable age.

The Cub Scout program was adopted by the Church in 1953. That year 114 Packs were organized. At the close of 1960 there were about 1,075 Packs and 28,000 Cub Scouts.

The Latter-day Saint belief in the eternal nature of the family places special emphasis on the value of this home-centered program. Cub Scouting is a potent and effective part of the youth program of the Church and must have the enthusiastic support of the priesthood and Primary workers.

We extend congratulations and commendation for the outstanding success of this program to date, and pray that the blessings of the Lord will ever be with you as you continue willingly to give of yourselves for the protection and guidance of our youth.

Sincerely yours,

THE FIRST PRESIDENCY
David O. McKay
J. Reuben Clark, Jr.
Henry D. Moyle

For the Strength of Youth

June 2, 1965

Preface "For the Strength of Youth"

The general officers of the Young Men's and Young Women's Mutual Improvement Associations, together with the Brigham Young University and the Church School System and a large group of representative youth of the Church, have prepared an excellent treatise on Latter-day Saint standards and entitled it "For the Strength of Youth," with sub-titles on Dress, Manners, Dating, Dancing, and Clean Living.

We wish to endorse what has been here written, commend all responsible for their efforts, and express the hope that all members of the Church, not only the youth, will familiarize themselves with the suggestions herein contained and conform to the regulations set forth.

All rules and regulations, in fact all laws, especially the laws of

God, are made for the benefit of the people. It is, of course, of the utmost importance that we become familiar therewith and conform thereto that we may have the blessings which were intended.

Let us never lose sight of the eternal principle enunciated by the Master that while free agency will not be trammeled by our Heavenly Father, conformity to established rules of conduct is a necessary prerequisite to the blessings promised to those who obey and keep his commandments.

THE FIRST PRESIDENCY
David O. McKay
Hugh B. Brown
N. Eldon Tanner

National Family Week

May 3, 1967

Presidents of Stakes and Bishops of Wards in the United States

Dear Brethren:

The Family Service Association of America has recommended the observance of Family Week, May 7–14. The Church of Jesus Christ of Latter-day Saints is pleased to join with all other religious and with civic organizations in the observance of this occasion.

We urge that the true spirit of the home be emphasized in church meetings, in bulletins, by the family home teachers as they visit the homes of the people, and by the families in their home evening gatherings. We cannot emphasize too strongly the need for a concerted effort to strengthen the relationship between husband and wife and parents and children, and the respect that should be maintained for moral, ethical and spiritual values.

Sincerely yours,

THE FIRST PRESIDENCY
David O. McKay
Hugh B. Brown
N. Eldon Tanner
Joseph Fielding Smith

Home Beautification Encouraged

September 20, 1974

To Stake and Mission Presidents, Bishops, Branch Presidents, and District Presidents

Dear Brethren:

Attached is a statement regarding a cleanup and beautification effort which we ask you to implement immediately.

We suggest that you organize these and other methods of implementation which you feel will be effective:

1. Ask home teachers to stress in their messages to families the need to clean up and beautify their homes and surroundings. . . .

2. Assign elders quorums . . . to clean up and beautify our meetinghouse buildings and grounds. Also, make arrangements for the upkeep of our meetinghouses and grounds so that they are always neat and attractive. Aaronic Priesthood quorum members may be asked to assist in this effort where desired.

3. Encourage Young Adult and Special Interest groups to organize themselves to assist the elderly, the fatherless, and the needy in improving the appearance of their homes and surroundings and in properly maintaining them. . . .

4. Request that Sunday School and Primary teachers, in the course of their lesson presentations, instruct class members in orderliness, in respecting buildings and property generally, in taking care of their belongings, and in keeping them in their proper places.

5. Encourage the leadership of the Relief Society to provide "how to" suggestions to women in keeping with the spirit of this effort. . . .

May the Lord bless you in this and your other leadership responsibilities in building the kingdom of God on earth.

Sincerely yours,

THE FIRST PRESIDENCY
Spencer W. Kimball
N. Eldon Tanner
Marion G. Romney

American Woman's Movement

October 7, 1974

To Stake Presidents, Stake Relief Society Presidents

Dear Brethren and Sisters:

We are enclosing a pamphlet containing a copy of the talk given by President Belle S. Spafford at the Lochinvar Club in New York on the subject "The American Woman's Movement."

This talk is an excellent presentation of the history of the women's movement in the United States and the world. It also emphasizes the efforts of the Church to give status to women and to enhance the role of motherhood.

We hope you will take the opportunity in future talks to share with the membership in your stake the pertinent information contained in this pamphlet.

Sincerely,

THE FIRST PRESIDENCY
Spencer W. Kimball
N. Eldon Tanner
Marion G. Romney

Support for Boy Scout Programs

June 20, 1975

To all Regional Representatives, Stake and Mission Presidents, Bishops, District and Branch Presidents in the United States

Dear Brethren:

For the past 62 years the Church has enjoyed a rewarding relationship with the Boy Scouts of America. The ideals of Scouting fostering citizenship training, physical fitness, and moral integrity, based upon a firm belief in God, are in harmony with the objectives of the Church.

We are pleased to support Scouting in the Church. The attached letter from the Presiding Bishopric is included to give you information regarding a policy change concerning the Church's relationship with the Venturing and Exploring programs. We urge the support of local priesthood leaders in the Scouting program as explained in the letter from the Presiding Bishopric.

We encourage priesthood leaders to do all possible in strengthening the young men of the Church through the Aaronic Priesthood and the use of the Scouting program.

Sincerely yours,

THE FIRST PRESIDENCY
Spencer W. Kimball
N. Eldon Tanner
Marion G. Romney

National Bible Week

November 1, 1975

To all Stake and Mission Presidents in the United States

Dear Brethren:

As we approach National Bible Week, November 23–30, we suggest that you ask all bishops and branch presidents under your leadership to read at sacrament meeting the following statement on this observance:

"America continues to be shaken by rising crime, widespread permissiveness, and the breakdown of far too many marriages and homes.

"One positive way to combat these destructive forces is to lead our youth into a new appreciation of the scriptures.

"In them they will find ways to build greater strengths in the home and in the individual. Also in the scriptures are time-tested keys to a personal happiness which endures.

"We therefore urge Latter-day Saints to fully support National Bible Week, November 23–30.

"Read the scriptures together as a family. Ponder them as individuals. Enjoy the scriptures at Family Home Evenings and otherwise.

"What a treasure of wisdom, inspiration, and practical suggestions for more abundant living are found in our Standard

Works: the Bible, Book of Mormon, Doctrine and Covenants, and Pearl of Great Price!

"'For my soul delighteth in the scriptures . . .' wrote Nephi. (2 Nephi 4:15)

"Teach your family, beginning with yourself, to love the scriptures, to delight in them, and to realize that in them are the answers to most of the problems besetting this great nation today."

Encourage our people to turn more to the Lord's words. All of us so much need them to meet the daily challenges of today's world.

Sincerely yours,

THE FIRST PRESIDENCY
Spencer W. Kimball
N. Eldon Tanner
Marion G. Romney

Proper Conversion to the Gospel

January 3, 1977

To all Mission Presidents

Dear Brethren:

We are pleased with the great number of stable and sound converts who are coming into the Church, and we extend our highest commendation to you, your missionaries, and all who labor with you. Your devotion, sacrifice, and achievements are deeply appreciated. We hope and pray that through your continued labors, additional worthy and honest truth seekers will receive the blessings of the gospel.

As we begin this new year of missionary efforts, we might review the revealed requirements that our Heavenly Father's children should attain to qualify for baptism:

> All those who humble themselves before God, and desire to be baptized, and come forth with broken hearts and contrite spirits, and witness before the Church that they have truly repented of all their sins, and are willing to take upon them the name of Jesus Christ, having a determination to serve him to the end, and truly manifest by their works that they have received of the Spirit

of Christ unto the remission of their sins, shall be received by baptism into His Church. (D&C 20:37)

As part of the necessary preparation for baptism, investigators should come to a knowledge of Christ and the first principles of the gospel; they should have attended Church meetings and should feel a unity and oneness with Church members; and they should desire to love and serve God with all their hearts.

New members should be carefully fellowshipped and involved in suitable activity and service in Church programs to encourage their continued growth and understanding of the gospel.

We pray that the Lord will continue to bless and prosper you, your missionaries, and all those who labor with you, that the great harvest now underway will continue, all to the honor and glory of His name.

Sincerely,

THE FIRST PRESIDENCY
Spencer W. Kimball
N. Eldon Tanner
Marion G. Romney

Fast Day and Donation to the Needy of Africa

January 11, 1985

To General Authorities, Regional Representatives, Stake Presidents, Bishops and Branch Presidents in the United States and Canada

Dear Brethren:

People throughout the world have been touched by the portrayal in the media of the plight of many thousands of starving people in Africa. There are others in similar circumstances in other areas. We have sent funds to assist those in need. We now feel that our people would like to participate more extensively in the great humanitarian effort to assist those in Ethiopia, other areas of Africa, and perhaps in other parts of the world.

The First Presidency and the Council of the Twelve have accordingly determined that Sunday, January 27, should be designated as a special fast day when our people will be invited to refrain from partaking of two meals and contribute the equivalent value, or more, to the Church to assist those in need. All fast offering funds contributed on this day will be dedicated for the use of the victims of famine and other causes resulting in hunger and privation among people of Africa, and possibly in some other areas. They will be placed through agencies of unquestioned integrity.

The regular February fast day will be held on the first Sunday of the month as usual and funds contributed on that day will be used in the customary way to assist those in need in the Church. We repeat, however, that all funds contributed on January 27 will be earmarked particularly to assist the hungry and needy in distressed areas regardless of Church membership.

We shall appreciate your advising the people of your wards and stakes accordingly. This letter may be read in the Sacrament meetings of all wards and branches. We are confident that there will be a great outpouring from this effort.

Sincerely, your brethren,

THE FIRST PRESIDENCY
Spencer W. Kimball
Marion G. Romney
Gordon B. Hinckley

National Day of Fasting To Be Observed

November 15, 1985

To Area Presidencies in the United States

Dear Brethren:

Attached is a letter to priesthood leaders outlining the First Presidency's desire to have Church members participate in a National Day of Fasting and prayer for hunger relief on Sunday, November 24, 1985, as declared by Congress and the President of the United States. This letter will be sent from Church headquarters today. . . .

Priesthood leaders should be advised that—

1. Sunday, November 24, has been designated as a National Day of Fasting and prayer for hunger relief.

2. The First Presidency is encouraging Church members to join in this special day by fasting two meals on November 24 and contributing the equivalent value, or more, to hunger relief. It will be administered to the needy regardless of their church membership.

3. Instructions for forwarding contributions to Church headquarters are in the mail and will be received by priesthood leaders on November 18 or 19.

Thank you for your assistance in this very special undertaking.

Sincerely your brethren,

THE FIRST PRESIDENCY
Ezra Taft Benson
Gordon B. Hinckley
Thomas S. Monson

An Invitation to Come Back

December 23, 1985

To: All Stake Presidents

Dear Brethren:

There are members of the Church who have become inactive, or who have been disciplined, or who otherwise have become alienated from the Church. At this time of the year it is important that we reach out to all such persons to encourage them to return to full activity and thereby to enjoy all the blessings the Church affords.

You will find the enclosed statement from the First Presidency which was published in the December 22 issue of the Church News which elaborates on this theme. We request that you make copies of this statement available to all bishops and that you ask them to read the statement at a sacrament meeting. At that time the bishops should also encourage the members of the Church in attendance to reach out and to endeavor to reactivate those who may have become alienated.

Sincerely your brethren,

THE FIRST PRESIDENCY
Ezra Taft Benson
Gordon B. Hinckley
Thomas S. Monson

December 25, 1985

AN INVITATION

FROM THE FIRST PRESIDENCY OF THE CHURCH OF JESUS CHRIST OF LATTER-DAY SAINTS

Come back, Come back and

feast at the table of the Lord, and taste again

the sweet and satisfying fruits of

fellowship with the Saints.

We rejoice in the blessings that come of membership and activity in this Church whose head is the Son of God, the Lord Jesus Christ. In deep sincerity we express our love and gratitude for our brethren and sisters everywhere.

We are aware of some who are less active, of others who have become critical and are prone to find fault, and of those who have been disfellowshipped or excommunicated because of serious transgressions.

To all such we reach out in love. The Lord said: "I, the Lord, will forgive whom I will forgive, but of you it is required to forgive all men." (D&C 64:10)

We encourage members to forgive those who may have wronged them. To those who have ceased activity and to those who have become critical, we say, "Come back. Come back and feast at the table of the Lord, and taste again the sweet and satisfying fruits of fellowship with the saints."

We are confident that many have longed to return, but have felt awkward about doing so. We assure you that you will find open arms to receive you and willing hands to assist you.

We know there are many who carry heavy burdens of guilt and

bitterness. To such we say, "Set them aside and give heed to the words of the Savior, who gave His life for the sins of all. 'Come unto me, all ye that are heavy laden, and I will give you rest.

"'Take my yoke upon you, and learn of me; for I am meek and lowly in heart; and ye shall find rest unto your souls.

"'For my yoke is easy, and my burden is light.'" (Matt. 11:28–30)

We plead with you. We pray for you. We invite and welcome you with love and appreciation.

Sincerely your brethren,

Ezra Taft Benson
Gordon B. Hinckley
Thomas S. Monson

Political Neutrality and Non-Use of Church Buildings

June 9, 1988

To General Authorities and the following priesthood leaders in the United States: Regional Representatives; Stake, Mission and District Presidents; Bishops; and Branch Presidents

Dear Brethren:

Political Neutrality (To be read in sacrament meeting.)

In this election year, we reiterate the long-standing policy of the Church of strict political neutrality, of not endorsing political candidates or parties in elections, and of not using Church facilities for political purposes, including voter registration.

The Church of Jesus Christ of Latter-day Saints does not favor one political party over another. We have no candidates for political office and we do not undertake to tell people how to vote.

We do urge all voters to involve themselves in the political process and to study carefully and prayerfully candidates' positions on issues and to vote for those who will most nearly carry out their views of government and its role.

The use of branch, ward, or stake premises, chapels or other Church facilities or equipment in any way for voter registration or political campaign purpose is contrary to our counsel and advice. This stricture applies to speech-making, class discussion, fund-raising, or preparation or distribution of campaign literature. Church directories or mailing lists should not be made available for any purpose to candidates for distribution of campaign literature or fund solicitation or to those involved in voter registration.

Those who attempt to use Church meetings or facilities or equipment to further their own or another's political ambitions injure their own cause and do the Church a disservice. We appeal, therefore, to all candidates for public office to take notice of this instruction and to conduct their campaigns in strict compliance with this requirement pertaining to use of Church facilities, equipment, meetings and membership lists.

We also call on all political candidates who are members of The Church of Jesus Christ of Latter-day Saints neither to state nor imply the endorsement of their candidacy by the Church or its leaders.

Sincerely your brethren,

THE FIRST PRESIDENCY
Ezra Taft Benson
Gordon B. Hinckley
Thomas S. Monson

APPENDIX 5

LETTERS OF THE PRESIDING BISHOPRIC

The role and duties of the Presiding Bishopric of The Church of Jesus Christ of Latter-day Saints change as the Church grows and needs dictate. The following excerpts were selected from many available documents to illustrate a few of the responsibilities of the Presiding Bishopric.

Consecration of Property, 1832

Following is an excerpt from a formal document labeled a "Lease of inheritance in Jackson Co. and loan of property there." It is dated October 12, 1832, and signed by Edward Partridge, Bishop. A printed form was used; words in brackets indicate the handwritten parts. Spelling and punctuation are preserved as in the original.

BE IT KNOWN, THAT I, [Edward Partridge—]
Of Jackson county, and state of Missouri, bishop of the church of Christ, organized according to law, and established by the revelations of the Lord, on the 6th day of April, 1830, have leased, and by these presents do lease unto [Joseph Knight Junr] of Jackson county, and state of Missouri, a member of said church, the following described parcel of land, being a part of section No. [thirty three] township No. [forty nine] range No. [thirty three] situated in Jackson county, and state of Missouri, and is bounded as follows, viz:—
[Beginning forty two rods E. from the N. W. corner of S*d*. Sec. thence E. on the N. line of the S*d*. Sec ten rods, thence S. 5½" W. thirty rods twenty one L. thence W. six rods to land leased to N. Knight, thence N. thirty six rods to the place of beginning, containing one acre and eighty one hundredths be the same more or less.]

And also have loaned the following described property, viz:—[Sundry articles of crockery, tinware, knives, forks and spoons valued nine

dollars forty three cents,— Sundry articles of iron ware and household furniture valued twelve dollars ninety two cents,—one bed and
bedding, valued nineteen dollars,—Sundry articles of clothing valued twenty two dollars thirteen cents,—grain valued seven dollars,—
Sundry articles of joiner tools valued twenty dollars forty four
cents,—one cow valued twelve dollars.

TO HAVE AND TO HOLD the above described property by him
the said [Joseph Knight Junr.—] to be used and occupied as to him
shall seem meet and proper. And as a consideration for the use of the
above described property unto the said [Edward Partridge—] bishop
of said church, or his successor in office, of myself and family. . . .

Spiritual Welfare of Young Men Ages 18 and Over

August 31, 1973

To all Stake Presidents, Mission and District Presidents, Bishops and
Branch Presidents

Dear Brethren:

The October 1972 *Priesthood Bulletin* (item No. 1) contained the
following policy statement:

> At the age of eighteen, Aaronic Priesthood bearers may be
> ordained to the office of an Elder in the Melchizedek Priesthood
> or transferred to the prospective elders program. If, in the judg-
> ment of the bishop, such qualifying circumstances as date of
> graduation from high school, individual maturation, or peer
> group association seem to indicate a need for a postponement, a
> young man may remain in the priests quorum until such cir-
> cumstances change, or until the young man becomes nineteen.

This policy should be applied in the new correlated reporting
system when determining the organization that is responsible for
reporting the activities of eighteen-year-old men. If the eighteen-
year-old is not ordained to the office of an elder, or transferred to the
prospective elders program, he continues to be the responsibility of
the priests quorum and is listed on the Priests Quorum roll. As soon
as he reaches nineteen, he should either be ordained an elder, if worthy, or transferred to the prospective elders program. . . .

The prime concern of all leaders must be the welfare, spirituality and improvement of the individual.

Sincerely,

THE PRESIDING BISHOPRIC
Victor L. Brown
H. Burke Peterson
Vaughn J. Featherstone

Utah Flood Disaster Aid

14 June 1983

To Executive Administrators, Regional Representatives, Stake Presidents and Bishops in Utah

Dear Brethren:

As a result of the flood disaster in Utah each stake president and bishop should carefully apply the concepts outlined in the First Presidency's letter of 10 June 1983 entitled "Rebuilding and Giving Service Following Disasters." Give particular attention to:

"The responsibility for each member's spiritual, social, emotional, physical or economic well-being rests first with the member, second upon the family, and third, upon the Church."

When disaster assistance is requested by members, the bishop and stake president should handle these requests using normal procedures for obtaining and handling fast-offering funds as outlined in the *Church Financial Records* booklet. . . .

We trust this will help priesthood leaders administer fast-offering assistance where required and needed.

Sincerely your brethren,

THE PRESIDING BISHOPRIC
Victor L. Brown
H. Burke Peterson
J. Richard Clarke

Implementing the Budget Allowance Program; Sacred Nature of Tithing Funds

5 December 1989

To General Authorities, Regional Representatives, and Stake Presidents in the United States and Canada

Dear Brethren:

Local Unit Budget Allowance Program

On 15 November 1989 the First Presidency announced a new method of providing financial support for wards and stakes in the United States and Canada. This plan provides a budget allowance for stakes and wards from general Church funds and eliminates the need for local units to receive or to seek budget contributions from their members.

The announcement letter indicated additional instructions concerning the plan would be forthcoming. Attached are the materials priesthood leaders will need in order to implement the budget allowance program. . . .

Any questions concerning the program should first be directed to the stake president. In the event a question remains, stake presidents may make inquiry at Church headquarters. . . .

Church members should be reminded of the blessings associated with the payment of an honest tithe. They should also be encouraged to care for the poor by being generous in their fast offering contributions and should feel their responsibility to financially support missionary activities.

Tithing funds, by their very nature, are sacred. Priesthood and auxiliary leaders must be wise stewards over the budget allowance given them to ensure sacred funds are used to bless people and further gospel purposes. . . .

As this new program is implemented, all priesthood leaders are asked to be sensitive to the broad interests of the entire Church rather than the provincial concerns of a local unit.

May our Father in Heaven's blessings be with you as you implement this important new program and apply the principles associated with it.

Sincerely your brethren,
THE PRESIDING BISHOPRIC
Robert D. Hales
Henry B. Eyring
Glenn L. Pace

Guidelines for New Meetinghouse Projects

1 February 1991

To General Authorities, Regional Representatives, Stake and District Presidents, Bishops and Branch Presidents

Dear Brethren:

Approval has been given to new guidelines for local units to qualify for a meetinghouse project. These new guidelines are attached and are effective with the receipt of this letter.

Because of budget limitations, it is possible some requests for projects which fully meet the guidelines may not be undertaken when requested. Area Presidencies will give priority to projects within approved budgets. In some areas, Area Presidencies may also use additional requirements to assist in establishing priorities. . . .

These guidelines are designed to encourage priesthood leaders to use meetinghouse facilities more fully in meeting the Church's ever-expanding needs.

Sincerely your brethren,
THE PRESIDING BISHOPRIC
Robert D. Hales
Henry B. Eyring
Glenn L. Pace

APPENDIX 6

LINES OF PRIESTHOOD AUTHORITY

This compilation shows the line of highest priesthood authority and date of ordination for those persons who have served as PRESIDENTS OF THE CHURCH, Counselors in the First Presidency, and members of The QUORUM OF THE TWELVE APOSTLES. Everyone in the Church today holding the holy priesthood will be able to trace his line of authority to one or more of these persons.

The Three Witnesses to the Book of Mormon—Oliver Cowdery, David Whitmer, and Martin Harris—were appointed by revelation to choose the Twelve Apostles (D&C 18:37). The Three Witnesses were set apart for this purpose by the First Presidency—Joseph Smith, Sidney Rigdon, and Frederick G. Williams—on February 14, 1835 (*HC* 2:187).

Oliver Cowdery was with the Prophet Joseph Smith in 1829, when Peter, James, and John conferred the Melchizedek Priesthood upon them and ordained them apostles. An 1829 revelation verifies that Oliver Cowdery and David Whitmer both held the apostolic office (D&C 18:9). Martin Harris was ordained to the High Priesthood on June 3, 1831, by Lyman Wight, who had been ordained to the High Priesthood that same day by Joseph the Prophet. President Rigdon was ordained to the High Priesthood by Lyman Wight, and President Williams by Joseph Smith and Oliver Cowdery.

Peter, James, and John had been ordained apostles by Jesus Christ (John 15:16).

The Three Witnesses were subsequently set apart by the First Presidency to ordain the Twelve. After the Three Witnesses had ordained the Twelve "to the apostleship," the First Presidency then laid their hands on the Twelve and confirmed the blessings and ordinations (from Heber C. Kimball's journal, published in *T&S*, vol. 6, #7, April 15, 1845, p. 868).

Tracing the Line of Authority. The person named in bold print identifies the person ordained. Regular type identifies the person who performed the ordination on the date indicated. Code: (A) = Apostle; (HP) = High Priest

Ashton, Marvin Jeremy (A)
Harold B. Lee, December 2, 1971

Ballard, Melvin Joseph (A)
Heber J. Grant, January 7, 1919

Ballard, Melvin Russell, Jr. (A)
Gordon B. Hinckley, October 10, 1985

Bennett, John Cook
Presented as assistant president with the First Presidency, April 8, 1841

Bennion, Adam Samuel (A)
David O. McKay, April 9, 1953

Benson, Ezra T. (A)
Brigham Young, July 16, 1846

Benson, Ezra Taft (A)
Heber J. Grant, October 7, 1943

Bowen, Albert Ernest (A)
Heber J. Grant, April 8, 1937

Boynton, John Farnham (A)
The Three Witnesses, February 15, 1835

Brown, Hugh Brown (A)
David O. McKay, April 10, 1958

Callis, Charles Albert (A)
Heber J. Grant, October 12, 1933

Cannon, Abraham Hoagland (A)
Joseph F. Smith, October 7, 1889

Cannon, George Quayle (A)
Brigham Young, August 26, 1860

Cannon, Sylvester Quayle (A)
Heber J. Grant, April 14, 1938

Carrington, Albert (A)
Brigham Young, July 3, 1870

Clark, Joshua Reuben, Jr. (HP) (A)
Called to First Presidency April 6, 1933, ordained High Priest by Heber J. Grant, April 13, 1933, ordained Apostle by Heber J. Grant, October 11, 1934

Clawson, Rudger (A)
Lorenzo Snow, October 10, 1898

Cowdery, Oliver (A)
Peter, James, and John, May–June 1829

Cowley, Matthew (A)
George Albert Smith, October 11, 1945

Cowley, Matthias Foss (A)
George Q. Cannon, October 7, 1897

Dyer, Alvin Rulon (A)
David O. McKay, October 5, 1967 (Never served in the Quorum of the Twelve)

Evans, Richard Louis (A)
David O. McKay, October 8, 1953

Faust, James Esdras (A)
Spencer W. Kimball, October 1, 1978

Gause, Jesse
Ordained a counselor in the Presidency of the High

Priesthood by Joseph Smith,
March 8, 1832

Grant, Heber Jeddy (A)
George Q. Cannon, October 16,
1882

Grant, Jedediah Morgan (A)
Brigham Young, April 7, 1854
(Never served in Quorum of the
Twelve)

Haight, David Bruce (A)
Spencer W. Kimball, January 8,
1976

Hinckley, Alonzo Arza (A)
Heber J. Grant, October 11,
1934

Hinckley, Gordon Bitner (A)
David O. McKay, October 5,
1961

Hunter, Howard William (A)
David O. McKay, October 15,
1959

Hyde, Orson (A)
The Three Witnesses,
February 15, 1835

Isaacson, Henry Thorpe Beal (HP)
Charles A. Callis, October 1,
1941

Ivins, Anthony Woodward (A)
Joseph F. Smith, October 6,
1907

Johnson, Luke S. (A)
The Three Witnesses,
February 15, 1835

Johnson, Lyman Eugene (A)
The Three Witnesses,
February 14, 1835

Kimball, Heber Chase (A)
The Three Witnesses,
February 14, 1835

Kimball, Spencer Woolley (A)
Heber J. Grant, October 7, 1943

Law, William
Set apart as second counselor
to President Joseph Smith,
January 24, 1841

Lee, Harold Bingham (A)
Heber J. Grant, April 10, 1941

Lund, Anthon Henrik (A)
George Q. Cannon, October 7,
1889

Lyman, Amasa Mason (A)
Brigham Young, August 20,
1842

Lyman, Francis Marion (A)
John Taylor, October 27, 1880

Lyman, Richard Roswell (A)
Joseph F. Smith, April 7, 1918

Marsh, Thomas Baldwin (A)
The Three Witnesses, April 26,
1835

Maxwell, Neal Ash (A)
Nathan Eldon Tanner, July 23,
1981

McConkie, Bruce Redd (A)
Harold B. Lee, October 12, 1972

McKay, David Oman (A)
Joseph F. Smith, April 9, 1906

McLellin, William E. (A)
Oliver Cowdery and David
Whitmer, February 15, 1835

Merrill, Joseph Francis (A)
Heber J. Grant, October 8, 1931

Merrill, Marriner Wood (A)
Wilford Woodruff, October 7,
1889

Monson, Thomas Spencer (A)
Joseph Fielding Smith,
October 10, 1963

Morris, George Quayle (A)
David O. McKay, April 8, 1954

Moyle, Henry Dinwoodey (A)
George Albert Smith, April 10, 1947

Nelson, Russell Marion (A)
Gordon B. Hinckley, April 12, 1984

Nibley, Charles Wilson (HP)
Joseph F. Smith, June 9, 1901

Oaks, Dallin Harris (A)
Gordon B. Hinckley, May 3, 1984

Packer, Boyd Kenneth (A)
Joseph Fielding Smith, April 9, 1970

Page, John Edward (Edmonds?) (A)
Brigham Young and Heber C. Kimball, December 19, 1838

Patten, David Wyman (A)
The Three Witnesses, February 15, 1835

Penrose, Charles William (A)
Joseph F. Smith, July 7, 1904

Perry, Lowell Tom (A)
Spencer W. Kimball, April 11, 1974

Petersen, Mark Edward (A)
Heber J. Grant, April 20, 1944

Pratt, Orson (A)
The Three Witnesses, April 26, 1835

Pratt, Parley Parker (A)
Joseph Smith, Oliver Cowdery, and David Whitmer, February 21, 1835

Rich, Charles Coulsen (A)
Brigham Young, February 12, 1849

Richards, Franklin Dewey (A)
Heber C. Kimball, February 12, 1849

Richards, George Franklin (A)
Joseph F. Smith, April 9, 1906

Richards, LeGrand (A)
David O. McKay, April 10, 1952

Richards, Stephen L (A)
Joseph F. Smith, January 18, 1917

Richards, Willard (A)
Brigham Young, April 14, 1840

Rigdon, Sidney (HP)
Lyman Wight, June 3, 1831

Romney, Marion George (A)
David O. McKay, October 11, 1951

Scott, Richard Gordon (A)
Thomas S. Monson, October 6, 1988

Smith, George A. (A)
Heber C. Kimball, April 26, 1839

Smith, George Albert (A)
Joseph F. Smith, October 8, 1903

Smith, Hyrum (HP) (A)
Ordained HP by Joseph Smith, June 3, 1831; given all priesthood callings formerly held by Oliver Cowdery, by Joseph Smith, about January 19, 1841 (D&C 124:94–95)

Smith, Hyrum Mack (A)
Joseph F. Smith, October 24, 1901

Smith, John (HP)
Sidney Rigdon, June 6, 1833

Smith, John Henry (A)
Wilford Woodruff, October 27, 1880

Smith, Joseph (A)
Peter, James, and John,
May-June 1829

Smith, Joseph, Sr. (HP)
Lyman Wight, June 3, 1831

Smith, Joseph F. (A)
Brigham Young, July 1, 1866,
sustained to Quorum of the
Twelve October 8, 1867

Smith, Joseph Fielding (A)
Joseph F. Smith, April 7, 1910

Smith, William (A)
The Three Witnesses,
February 15, 1835

Smoot, Reed (A)
Lorenzo Snow, April 8, 1900

Snow, Erastus (A)
Brigham Young, February 12,
1849

Snow, Lorenzo (A)
Heber C. Kimball, February 12,
1849

Stapley, Delbert Leon (A)
George Albert Smith, October 5,
1950

Talmage, James Edward (A)
Joseph F. Smith, December 8,
1911

Tanner, Nathan Eldon (A)
David O. McKay, October 11,
1962

Taylor, John (A)
Brigham Young and Heber C.
Kimball, December 19, 1838

Taylor, John Whittaker (A)
John Taylor, April 9, 1884

Teasdale, George (A)
John Taylor, October 16, 1882

Thatcher, Moses (A)
John Taylor, April 9, 1879

Wells, Daniel Hanmer (A)
Brigham Young, January 4,
1857 (Never served in Quorum of
the Twelve)

Whitney, Orson Ferguson (A)
Joseph F. Smith, April 9, 1906

Widtsoe, John Andreas (A)
Heber J. Grant, March 17, 1921

Wight, Lyman (A)
Joseph Smith, April 8, 1841

Williams, Frederick Granger (HP)
Oliver Cowdery, October 25,
1831

Winder, John Rex (HP)
Edward Hunter, March 4, 1872

Wirthlin, Joseph Bitner (A)
Thomas S. Monson, October 9,
1986

Woodruff, Abraham Owen (A)
Wilford Woodruff, October 7,
1897

Woodruff, Wilford (A)
Brigham Young, April 26, 1839

Young, Brigham (A)
The Three Witnesses,
February 14, 1835

Young, Brigham, Jr. (A)
Brigham Young, February 4,
1864, sustained to Quorum of the
Twelve October 9, 1868

Young, John Willard (A)
Brigham Young, February 4,
1864 (Never served in Quorum of
the Twelve)

Young, Joseph Angell (A)
Brigham Young, February 4,
1864 (Never served in Quorum of
the Twelve)

APPENDIX 7

TEMPLE DEDICATORY PRAYERS
(EXCERPTS)

The dedicatory prayers of the temples are inspired statements and supplications. The following selections illustrate important points of LDS doctrine, especially related to the nature and importance of temples. The first LDS temple in Kirtland, Ohio, was dedicated by the Prophet Joseph Smith, and because the entire text is given as Doctrine and Covenants section 109, it is not included in this appendix. Spelling and punctuation of the printed sources are preserved.

St. George Temple (First Temple in Utah)

Dedicatory prayer by President Daniel H. Wells, April 6, 1877

We thank Thee, O Lord, that Thy people . . . have been enabled to gather together the materials of which this building is composed; to put together and erect the same, even a Temple, which we dedicate and now consecrate to Thee that it may be holy unto Thee the Lord our God, for sacred and holy purposes and that the blessing, even life for evermore, may be commanded here from heaven, even from Thy presence, and may flow through the ordinances which appertain unto Thy holy place, unto us Thy children. We pray that the blessings pertaining to our eternal salvation and to the establishing of Thy Kingdom upon this, Thine earth, may be poured out upon Thy holy Priesthood and Thy people, who shall worship and officiate in this Thy Holy House. . . .

We pray that Thy blessing may attend those of Thy servants who administer and who may officiate in the ordinances that may be performed therein in behalf of Thy people, and in behalf of those our progenitors, our relatives and friends, who have gone before us to the spirit world, so far as we may be enabled and permitted to officiate for them. We dedicate also to Thee the rooms of this building . . . for the purposes for which they may be used, by the Priesthood, for prayer, for worship, for councils or meetings, or for administering the Holy Ordinances of Thy House, that they may be holy unto Thee, the Lord Our God. . . .

Accept, O God, of this tribute of our hearts, and let Thy peace and blessing dwell and abide here in this Holy Temple, which we now, with uplifted hearts and hands, present and consecrate and dedicate entire as a sacred offering unto Thee for Thine acceptance. May it stand as a monument of purity and holiness as long as the earth shall remain, commemorative of Thy great goodness toward us, Thy People, and Thy name shall have the honor, the praise and glory, for we ask all in Jesus' name, and unto Thee and our blessed Lord and Savior, and to the Holy Spirit be all power, might and dominion worlds without end. Amen. [N. B. Lundwall, *Temples of the Most High*, pp. 79–83, Salt Lake City, 1947.]

Salt Lake Temple

Dedicated by President Wilford Woodruff, April 6, 1893

We thank Thee, O Thou Great Eloheim, that Thou didst raise up Thy servant, Joseph Smith through the loins of Abraham, Isaac and Jacob, and made him a Prophet, Seer, and Revelator, and through the assistance and administrations of angels from heaven Thou didst enable him to bring forth the Book of Mormon, the stick of Joseph, in the hand of Ephraim, in fulfillment of the prophecies of Isaiah and other prophets, which record has been translated and published in many languages. We also thank Thee, our Father in heaven, that Thou didst inspire Thy servant and give him power on the earth to organize Thy Church in this goodly land in all its fullness, power and glory, with Apostles, Prophets, Pastors and Teachers with all the gifts and graces belonging thereto and all this by the power of the Aaronic and Melchizedek Priesthood, which Thou didst bestow upon him by the administration of holy angels, who held that Priesthood in the days of the Savior. We thank Thee, our God, that Thou didst enable Thy servant Joseph to build two Temples, in which ordinances were administered for the living and the dead; that he also lived to send the Gospel to the nations of the earth and to the islands of the sea, and labored exceedingly until he was martyred for the word of God and the testimony of Jesus Christ.

We also thank Thee, O our Father in Heaven, that Thou didst raise up Thy servant Brigham Young, who held the keys of the Priesthood on the earth for many years, and who led Thy people to these valleys of the mountains, and laid the corner-stone of this great Temple. . . .

O Lord, we regard with intense and indescribable feelings the completion of this sacred house. Deign to accept this the fourth Temple which Thy covenant children have been assisted by Thee in erecting in these mountains. In past ages Thou didst inspire with Thy Holy Spirit Thy servants, the prophets, to speak of the time in the latter days when the mountain of the Lord's house should be established in the tops of the mountains, and should be exalted above the hills. We thank Thee that we have had the glorious opportunity of contributing to the fulfillment of these visions of Thine ancient Seers, and that Thou hast condescended to permit us to take part in the great work. And as this portion of Thy servants' words has thus so marvelously been brought to pass, we pray Thee, with increased faith and renewed hope, that all their words with regard to Thy great work in gathering Thine Israel and building up Thy kingdom on earth in the last days may be as amply fulfilled, and that, O Lord, speedily. . . .

And today we dedicate the whole [temple] unto Thee, with all that pertains unto it, that it may be holy in Thy sight; that it may be a house of prayer, a house of praise and of worship; that Thy glory may rest upon it; that Thy holy presence may be continually in it; that it may be the abode of Thy Well-Beloved Son, our Savior; that the angels who stand before Thy face may be the hallowed messengers who shall visit it, bearing to us Thy wishes and Thy will, that it may be sanctified and consecrated in all its parts holy unto Thee, the God of Israel, the Almighty Ruler of Mankind. And we pray Thee that all people who may enter upon the threshold of this, Thine House, may feel Thy power and be constrained to acknowledge that Thou hast sanctified it, that it is Thy House, a place of Thy holiness. . . .

O Thou God of our fathers Abraham, Isaac, and Jacob, whose God Thou delightest to be called, we thank Thee with all the fervor of overflowing gratitude that Thou hast revealed the powers by which the hearts of the children are being turned to their fathers, and the hearts of the fathers to the children, that the sons of men, in all their generations can be made partakers of the glories and joys of the kingdom of heaven. Confirm upon us the spirit of Elijah, we pray Thee, that we may thus redeem our dead and also connect ourselves with our fathers who have passed behind the veil, and furthermore seal up our dead to come forth in the first resurrection, that we who dwell on the earth may be bound to those who dwell in heaven. We thank Thee for their sake who have finished their work in mortality, as well as for our own, that the prison doors have been opened, that deliverance has been proclaimed to the captive, and the bonds have been loosened from those who were bound. We praise Thee that our fathers from last to first, from now, back to the beginning, can be united with us in indissoluble links, welded by the Holy Priesthood and that as one great family united in Thee and cemented by Thy power, we shall together stand before Thee, and by the power of the atoning blood of Thy Son be delivered from all evil, be saved and sanctified, exalted and glorified. Wilt Thou also permit holy messengers to visit us within these sacred walls and make known unto us with regard to the work we should perform in behalf of our dead. And, as Thou has inclined the hearts of many who have not yet entered into covenant with Thee to search out their progenitors, and in so doing they have traced the ancestry of many of Thy Saints, we pray Thee that Thou wilt increase this desire in their bosoms, that they may in this way aid in the accomplishment of Thy work. Bless them, we pray Thee, in their labors, that they may not fall into errors in preparing their genealogies; and furthermore, we ask Thee to open before them new avenues of information and place in their hands the records of the past, that their work may not only be correct but complete also. . . .

And now, our Father, we bless Thee, we praise Thee, we glorify Thee, we worship Thee, day by day we magnify Thee, and give Thee thanks for Thy great goodness towards us, Thy children, and we pray Thee, in the name of Thy Son Jesus Christ, our Savior, to hear these our humble petitions, and answer us from heaven, Thy holy dwelling place where Thou sittest enthroned in glory, might, majesty, and dominion, and with an infinitude of power which we, Thy mortal creatures, cannot imagine, much less comprehend. Amen and Amen. [Lundwall, *Temples of the Most High*, pp. 126–36, Salt Lake City, 1947.]

Hawaii Temple (First Outside of North America)

Dedicated by President Heber J. Grant, November 27, 1919

We thank Thee, O God, the Eternal Father, that Thou and Thy Son, Jesus Christ, didst visit the boy, Joseph Smith, Jr., and that he was instructed by Thee and Thy beloved Son.

We thank Thee that Thou didst send Thy servant, John the Baptist, and that he did lay his hands upon Joseph Smith and Oliver Cowdery and ordain them to the Aaronic, or Lesser, Priesthood.

We thank Thee for sending Thy servants Peter, James and John, Apostles of the Lord Jesus Christ who ministered with the Savior in the flesh and after His crucifixion, and that they did ordain Thy servants Joseph Smith and Oliver Cowdery apostles of the Lord Jesus Christ, and bestowed upon them the Holy Melchizedek Priesthood, by which Authority and Apostleship we do dedicate unto Thee, this day, this holy edifice.

We thank Thee for the integrity and devotion of Thy servants, the Prophet and the Patriarch, Joseph Smith and Hyrum Smith. We thank Thee that they labored all the days of their lives, from the time of the restitution of the Gospel of Jesus Christ until the day of their martyrdom, and that they sealed their testimony with their blood. . . .

We thank Thee that the plates containing the Book of Mormon were preserved so that they could be translated, and that Thy words to the Prophet Joseph Smith might be fulfilled; namely, That the Lamanites might come to the knowledge of their fathers, and that they might know the promises of the Lord, and that they may believe the Gospel and rely upon the merits of Jesus Christ, and be glorified through faith in His name, and that through their repentance, they might be saved.

We thank Thee, that thousands and tens of thousands of the descendants of Lehi, in this favored land, have come to a knowledge of the gospel, many of whom have endured faithfully to the end of their lives. We thank Thee, our Father and our God, that those who are living and who have embraced the gospel are now to have the privilege of entering into this holy house and laboring for the salvation of the souls of their ancestors. . . .

We also thank Thee for sending Thy servants, Moses, and Elias, and Elijah, to the Kirtland temple, and delivering to Thy servants, Joseph and Oliver the keys of every dispensation of the gospel of

Jesus Christ from the days of Father Adam down to the present dispensation, which is the dispensation of the fulness of times.

We thank Thee, that Elijah has appeared and that the prophecy of Thy servant Malachi, that the hearts of the fathers should be turned to the children, and the hearts of the children to the fathers, lest the earth be smitten with a curse, has been fulfilled in our day, and that our hearts in very deed, go out to our fathers; and we rejoice beyond our ability to express that we can, through the ordinances of the gospel of Jesus Christ, become saviors of our ancestors. . . .

. . . We have dedicated this House unto Thee, by virtue of the Priesthood of the Living God which we hold, and we most earnestly pray that this sacred building may be a place in which Thou shalt delight to pour out Thy Holy Spirit in great abundance, and in which Thy Son may see fit to manifest Himself and to instruct Thy servants. In the name of Jesus Christ, our Redeemer. Amen and Amen. [Lundwall, *Temples of the Most High*, pp. 151–59, Salt Lake City, 1947.]

Swiss Temple (First Temple in Europe)

Dedicated by President David O. McKay, September 11, 1955

O Father, we sense that the crying need of the world today is acceptance of Jesus Christ and his Gospel to counteract false teachings that now disturb the peace of honest men and women, and which undermine the faith of millions whose belief in Thee has been faltering and unstable, because they have not yet had presented unto them the eternal Plan of Salvation.

Guide us, O God, in our efforts to hasten the day when humanity will renounce contention and strife, when nation shall not lift up sword against nation, neither shall they learn war any more.

To this end bless the leaders of nations that their hearts may be cleared of prejudices, suspicion, and avarice, and filled with a desire for peace and righteousness.

As one means of uniting the children in the bond of peace and love, this Temple and other Holy Houses of the Lord are erected in thy Name.

Help Thy people to realize that only by Obedience to the eternal principles and ordinances of the Gospel may loved ones who died without baptism be permitted the glorious privilege of entrance into the Kingdom of God. Increase our desire, O Father, to put forth even greater effort toward the consummation of Thy purpose to bring to pass the immortality and eternal life of all thy children. This edifice is one more means to aid in bringing about this divine consummation. . . .

May this building ever be held sacred, that all who enter may feel a peaceful and hallowed influence, and may those who pass the grounds whether members or non-members of the Church feel a hallowed influence and substitute for a doubt or possible sneer in their minds, a prayer in their hearts.

Now, O God, Our Heavenly Eternal Father, the faithful membership of thy Church, through love for Thee and thy children, have erected to Thee by tithes and offerings this Holy House in which shall be performed ordinances and ceremonies pertaining to the happiness and salvation of thy children living in mortality and in the Spirit World.

Accept of our offering, hallow it by Thy Holy Spirit and protect it from destructive elements and the bitterness of ignorance and wickedness of bigoted hearts until its divine purposes shall have been consummated; and Thine be the glory, honor, and praise forever, through Jesus Christ, our Lord and Savior, Amen and Amen! [*Church News*, p. 4, September 17, 1955.]

New Zealand Temple (First Temple in South Pacific)

Dedicated by President David O. McKay, April 20, 1958

We express gratitude that to these fertile islands Thou didst guide descendants of Father Lehi, and hast enabled them to prosper, to develop, and to become associated in history with leading and influential nations among mankind. [*Church News*, pp. 2, 6, May 10, 1958.]

London Temple

Dedicated by President David O. McKay, September 7, 1958

O God, our Heavenly Father, Thou who hast created all things, whose Plans Infinite and Progressive, ever serve to foster closer relationship between Thee and the human family. We, Thy children assemble before Thee this day in gratitude and praise. Thou hast said that Thy work and Thy Glory is "to bring to pass the immortality and eternal life of man."

Therefore, human beings are engaged in life's highest activity when they cooperate with Thee in bringing about this consummation. . . . Temples are but one means of man's cooperation with Thee in accomplishing this divine purpose. . . .

When in the Middle Ages the Church departed from Christ's teachings, Thou didst inspire honest, upright men here in Great Britain to raise their voices against corrupt practices. Mingling with the denunciatory messages of Luther and Melanchthon in Germany, and Zwingli in Switzerland, were the voices of George Wishart, and later John Knox of Scotland. We thank Thee that before the scorching flames silenced his tongue and reduced his body to ashes Thou didst permit George Wishart to glimpse that: "This Realm shall be illuminated with the light of Christ's Evangel as clearly as ever was any Realm since the days of the Apostles. The house of God shall be builded in it; yea, it shall not lack the very capstone."

Much clearer was the inspiration given President Wilford Woodruff, and President Joseph F. Smith, and other more recent Apostles, who stated prophetically that: "Temples of God . . . will be erected in the divers countries of the earth," and that "Temples will appear all over the land of Joseph—North and South America—and also in Europe and elsewhere; and all the descendants of Shem, Ham, and Japheth, who received not the Gospel in the flesh, must be officiated for in the temples of God, before the Savior can present the kingdom to the Father, saying, "It is finished." [*Church News*, p. 3, September 13, 1958.]

Provo Utah Temple

Dedicated by President Harold B. Lee, February 9, 1972

O God, the Eternal Father, the Creator of heaven and earth and all things that in them are; Thou Man of Holiness who hast created us, Thy children in Thine own image and likeness, and endowed us with power and agency to follow Thee; Thou who knowest all things and hast all power, all might, and all dominion; Thou who created the universe and ruleth with justice and equity and mercy over all the works of Thy hands—hallowed be Thy great and holy name! . . .

O our Father, we seek to be like Thee; we seek to pattern our lives after the life of Thy Son; we desire righteousness, for ourselves and our children and our children's children; we turn our faces to this holy house; and we plead with Thee to make us worthy to inherit the fulness of those blessings found only in Thy holy temples—even those blessings which grow out of the continuation of the family unit forever.

Thou knowest, O Father, that we seek these blessings, not only for ourselves and our descendants, but also for our forebears; for Thou hast said that we, as saviors on Mount Zion, have power to save and redeem our worthy dead; we seek so to do, and we plead for Thy guidance and directing light as we go forward in this work—one of the greatest ever revealed to the children of men in any age of the earth. . . .

We thank Thee, O our God, that Thou didst ordain and establish the Constitution of the United States "by the hands of wise men whom" Thou didst raise up unto this very purpose. We thank Thee for the freedoms and "rights and privileges" which are guaranteed to us in this sacred document and pray that they may be established forever. . . .

Let that great temple of learning, The Brigham Young University, and all that is associated with it, and all other church schools, institutes, and seminaries—be prospered to the full. . . .

May those who teach and study in all academic fields have their souls enlightened with spiritual knowledge, so they will turn to Thy house for blessings and knowledge and learning that surpass all that may be found elsewhere.

. . . acting in the authority of that priesthood which is after the order of Thy Son and in His Holy Name, we dedicate this Temple unto Thee, the Lord.

We dedicate it as a house of baptism, a house of endowment, a house of marriage, and a house of righteousness, for the living and the dead. . . .

O Lord God of our fathers, who sitteth upon Thy throne, and who liveth, and reigneth over all things—blessed be Thy Holy Name, both now and forever.

In the name of the Lord Jesus Christ, Thine Only Son, even so, amen and amen. [*Church News*, pp. 4–5, February 12, 1972.]

Washington [D.C.] Temple

Dedicated by President Spencer W. Kimball, November 19, 1974

Father, we are concerned with the political world of today, and that nations seem to need only the lighting of a match to bring war and desolation and destruction. Bless, we pray Thee, the leaders of nations, that they may rule wisely and righteously, and give Thy people freedom to worship Thee in truth and righteousness. Stay the powers, our Father, that would bring us to the brink of annihilation. . . .

Our Gracious Father, there are national gates which seemingly need to be unlocked and doors that need to be opened, and hearts of kings, presidents, emperors, and ministers, which need to be softened, that they may permit the gospel to be taken to their people.

Our Father, bless the countless millions in the world, that they may receive Thy truth, and bless the missionaries on whom the sun never sets, that nothing will prevail against them in their faithful presentation of Thy gospel to the world, and bless especially, our Father, the children of Thy people in overseas countries, that they may devote their sons to this holy work. Wherein we have failed, help us to see our duties; wherein we have been prevented, open the doors, we pray, and swing the gates wide open and let Thy servants cover the earth with their testimonies. [*Church News*, p. 5, November 23, 1974.]

Mexico City Temple

Dedicated by President Gordon B. Hinckley, December 2, 1983

Bless thy saints in this great land and those from other lands who will use this temple. Most have in their veins the blood of Father Lehi. Thou hast kept thine ancient promise. Many thousands "that walked in darkness have seen a great light." (Isaiah 9:2) May the harvest that we have witnessed here foreshadow greater things to come as Thy work rolls on in power and majesty in this, the dispensation of the fulness of times. [*Church News*, pp. 4–5, December 11, 1983.]

Freiberg Germany Temple (First in Eastern Europe)

Dedicated by President Gordon B. Hinckley, June 29, 1985

We are met here today as people of various nations bound by a common love for thee our Father and thy Son, the Redeemer of all mankind. We thank Thee for the peace which makes this possible and for the hospitality of this nation in permitting us to join together in this house of sacred worship. Our hearts are touched by the bond of fellowship we feel one with another. Strengthen that bond, and may we reach out in a spirit of love and appreciation and respect for one another. This gospel, which so deeply touches our lives, is the gospel of peace. May we grow in knowledge and understanding of thine everlasting plan for thy children, thy sons and daughters of all nations. . . .

Father, we thank thee for the measure of peace to be found in the world, and pray that it may continue and grow that men and women everywhere may use their time, their talents, and their means for good. May understanding and respect increase between the nations of the earth. [*Church News*, p. 5, June 30, 1985.]

Johannesburg South Africa Temple

Dedicated by President Gordon B. Hinckley, August 24, 1985

We thank thee for the dimensions of thy Church in this nation of South Africa. We thank thee for men and women of great strength who constitute its membership, for the goodness of their lives, for the manner in which thou hast enlightened their minds and quickened their understanding of thy ways and thy purposes. Many of them, dear Father, sacrificed much in years past to travel afar to partake of those blessings which are available only in the Lord's House. . . .

Wilt thou whisper peace to thy people by the power of thy Spirit when they come here with burdened hearts to seek direction in their perplexities. Wilt thou comfort and sustain them when they come in times of sorrow. Wilt thou give them courage, direction, and faith, when they gather, as to a refuge, from the turmoil of the world. Wilt thou reassure them of thy reality and divinity, and of the reality and divinity of thy resurrected Son. Wilt Thou endow them with love in their hearts for their ancestors who have gone before and with a great desire to labor in behalf of these their forebears.

Almighty God, wilt thou overrule for the blessing and safety of thy faithful saints. We pray for peace in this troubled land. Bless this nation which has befriended thy servants. May those who rule in the offices of government be inspired to find a basis for reconciliation among those who now are in conflict one with another. May the presence of thy house on the soil of this land bring blessings to the entire nation. [*Church News*, p. 5, 1 September 1985.]

INDEX

Aaron: John the Baptist descendant
of, 2, 6; priests were
descendants of, 2, 134, 274;
priesthood authority of, 26;
Levitical Priesthood and,
161–62, 284–85. *See also*
Aaronic Priesthood
Aaronic Priesthood: powers and
offices, 1–5, 62–63, 292;
restoration of, 5–7, 27, 153,
278; bishop presides over, 33,
35; reform movement, 41–42;
deacons, 89–90; youth leaders
in, 160; Levitical Priesthood is,
161–62, 284–85; meeting, 175;
magazine for, 216–17; and
ordinances, 224; ordination to,
225–26; Presiding Bishopric
presides over, 269–70; priests,
273–75; history of, 279;
quorums, 294–95; teachers,
405–6; and Young Men
program, 478–82; and youth,
492; letter about young men
over eighteen, 582–83. *See also*
Bishop, history of the office;
Priesthood; Young Men
Abinadi, 25
Abortion, 259
Abraham: given keys, 153, 409;
Melchizedek blesses, 177–78,
283; and the Melchizedek

Priesthood, 186; priesthood
covenant of, 220; as patriarch,
252, 255–56; patriarchal order
and, 257; as patriarch, 283;
keeps records, 331; book of,
444; pays tithes, 445
Abram, 179. *See also* Abraham
Abuse and cruelty, 259
Acquired Immune Deficiency
Syndrome (AIDS), 260
"Acting teachers," 135
Activities, youth, 493. *See also*
Young Men; Young Women
Activities Committee, 460, 462
Activity in the Church, 7–10. *See
also* Apostate; Callings
Adam: as high priest, 134; given
keys, 153; and the Melchizedek
Priesthood, 186; ordination of,
224; as patriarch, 252, 255,
283; patriarchal order and, 257;
keeps records, 331; temple
endowment and, 408
Administrative history of the
Church. *See* Organization
Adopted children, sealing of, 410
Adults, single, 29, 74, 375–78
Affirmation, 384
Africa, 574–75, 603–4
African Temple, 603–4
Alberta Canada Temple, 420
Allegory of Zenos, 13

Pratt, Parley P.: as editor, 195; as missionary, 208; on family life, 257; as author, 318–19; as apostle, 324

Pratt, Romania, 167

Prayer circle, 262–64, 415. *See also* Temple ordinances; Temples

Prayers, 353. *See also* Prayer circle; Temple Dedicatory Prayers (Excerpts) (Appendix 7)

Presidency, concept of, 238–39, 264–65

President of the Church, 265–69; is senior apostle, 18; presides over Church, 63; and Council of the First Presidency, 86; and the First Presidency, 116–19; following the, 119–20; is presiding high priest, 133, 272; holds all keys, 152, 184; setting apart of the, 226; as prophet, seer, and revelator, 314, 359; sealing power of the, 356; succession to, 396–99. *See also* First Presidency; Prophets

President of the High Priesthood, 268

Presiding Bishopric, 269–72; first, 38, 208; early responsibilities of, 38–40; First Presidency meets with the, 118; as General Authorities, 125; organization of the, 229; responsibilities of the, 236; contemporary organization of the, 243–44; supervises tithes, 445; Letters of the, (Appendix 5), 581–85. *See also* Bishop, history of the office; Letters of the Presiding Bishopric (Appendix 5)

Presiding high priest, 227, 272–73, 293

Press and publications, 273. *See also* Magazines; Newspapers, LDS

Preston, William B., 270

Priest, Aaronic Priesthood, 63, 273–75, 292, 294, 479. *See also* Aaronic Priesthood; Priesthood

Priesthood, 275; lines of authority, 26, 62–63; 587–91; reform movement, 41–42; keys of the, 152–54; available to all races, 210; oath and covenant of the, 219–20; ordinances, 221–24, 371, 416; ordination to the, 224–26; correlation, 233; Executive Council, 241–42; source of priesthood power, 275; definitions, 275–77; history, orders, and offices of the, 277–80; and the family, 280–81; the power of God unto exaltation, 281–82; publications for, 320; sealing power of the, 355–56. *See also* Aaronic Priesthood; Melchizedek Priesthood; Priesthood offices; Priesthood quorums

Priesthood Authority, Lines of, (Appendix 6), 587–91. *See also* Appendices

Priesthood blessings, 170, 253–54, 286–88

Priesthood Bulletin, 52, 582

Priesthood councils, 238–39, 288–89

Priesthood executive committee, stake and ward, 235, 290, 460–61

Priesthood in biblical times, 282–86